WHO *IS* DAVID?
Anointed King - Servant of God

Angeline Leito

Volume One

Mazo Publishers

WHO *IS* DAVID?
Anointed King - Servant of God

by Angeline Leito
Email: leito.amt@gmail.com

ISBN: 978-1-94612465-4
Copyright © 2019

Mazo Publishers
www.mazopublishers.com

Cover design and artwork by
ER Studios

54321-1910
All rights reserved.
No part of this publication may be translated, reproduced, stored in a retrieval system, or transmitted in any form or by any means, electronic, mechanical, photocopying, recording or otherwise, without prior permission in writing from the publisher.

To my husband and children

CONTENTS

The Author	8
Introduction – The Green Olive Tree	9

Part I
David, God's Servant – 11

David's Roots	12
David's Parents	22
Intermezzo: Jephthah, Son Of Another Mother	
David's Sling	47
Intermezzo: Chronology – Saul, David, Solomon	
David's Anointer	62
Intermezzo: Prophets	
David and Jonathan: Covenant of Friendship	82
Intermezzo: New Moon Feast	
David and Saul: Father and Son, Loved and Reconciled	103
Intermezzo 1: Adonai-nissi	
Intermezzo 2: David and Achish	
David and Joab: Wisdom, Patience and Justice	133
Intermezzo: David's Heroes	
David and Absalom: Rebellion, Grieving and Victory	153
Intermezzo: Foreigners	

Part II
David's Shield – 179

Essence	180
Intermezzo: Idols	
Presence	194
Intermezzo: Food	
Creator	201
Intermezzo: The Fallen	
Warrior	221
Intermezzo: Rules of Engagement	

Forgiving Father	233
Intermezzo: Discipline	
King of Kings	252
Intermezzo: The Division	
Judge of Creation	283
Intermezzo: The Rejection	

Part III
David's Queen – 317

Michal, David's Princess	319
Intermezzo: Circumcision	
Abigail, David's Guardian Angel	331
Intermezzo: Widows and Orphans	
Ahinoam, David's Courage and Grief	343
Intermezzo: Unlawful Relations and Murder	
Bathsheba, David's Sin and Repentance	354
Intermezzo: Adultery and Murder	
Abishag, David's Companion	367
Intermezzo: A Father's Wife	
The Lioness, David's Queen	376
Intermezzo: The Lion's Pride	

Part IV
David's Zion, The Apple of God's Eye – 395

The Land	396
Going Up	404
The Promise	414
Contempt	425
The Fall of Israel, Samaria	446
Intermezzo: Foreigners	
The Reconciliation	477
Intermezzo: Chronology	
The Return to Zion	504
Intermezzo: One People	

Time Tables
- History of Israel: Prophets, Judges and Kings 531
- Aliyah – Immigration to Israel 547
- Establishment of the Modern-Day State of Israel 554

Bibliography 559

Ought you not to know that HaShem, the God of Israel, gave the kingdom over Israel to David for ever, to him and <u>to his sons</u> by a <u>covenant of salt</u>?

2 Chronicles 13:5

Thus says HaShem of hosts: therefore love the truth and peace (shalom).

Zechariah 8:19

THE AUTHOR

Angeline Leito has been studying and writing about topics related to the Bible for many years. In this book, she focuses on the biblical personality, David, from his youth through the time that he becomes a servant of God and is anointed King of Israel. She explores the royal family and the effects of their lives on Israelite society in the pre-First Temple era. Backed by the biblical texts, she also delves into David's connection to yet to be fulfilled biblical prophecies.

Motivated by the writings throughout the Bible, Angeline Leito and her family travelled to Israel in 2010 and again in 2014 to seek out the historical remnants that could have influenced David, as well as providing her the unique perspective to be qualified to author this book.

Born in Curacao, Angeline Leito currently lives in the Netherlands with her two daughters and husband.

INTRODUCTION

The Green Olive Tree

I am like a leafy (green) olive-tree in the House of God; I trust in the mercy of God for ever and ever.
Psalm 52:10

The olive tree is known for the freshness of its evergreen leaves, the strength of its roots, its longevity and its resilience. It's drought tolerant, its roots can even penetrate rocks, it lives longer than other fruit trees, and it can endure an environment with salty ground water.

Through the ages the olive became a symbol for pureness, peace and wisdom, power and glory, fertility and long life, and for hope.

And he stayed yet another seven days; and again he sent forth the dove out of the ark. And the dove came in to him at eventide; and in her mouth there was an <u>olive-leaf</u> freshly plucked; so Noah knew that the waters had abated from off the earth.
Genesis 8:10-11

Of all the kind of trees in the Land of Israel, David who always put his trust in God, chose to be as an olive tree, a tree that provides for both life and light! Its fruit is one of the seven spices of the Land of Israel together with wheat, barley, grapes, pomegranates, figs and dates. The Lord provided for a good land flowing with milk and (date) honey for the Children of Israel.

Since ancient times, olives were used as fruit, for cooking and for sacrificial offerings. Olive oil has also been used as fuel for light, for ointment and as an important ingredient by God's command in anointment for priestly and royal office. The Lord also commanded the use of olive oil in its purist form as fuel for His lampstand, the Menorah, in the Tabernacle. He ordained the Levite priests as the ones responsible to keep the Menorah's light burning at all times.

And the angel that spoke with me returned ... And he said to me: What do you see?
And I said: I have seen, and behold a candlestick all of gold,

> with a bowl upon the top of it, and its seven lamps on it; there are seven pipes, yes, seven, to the lamps, which are upon the top thereof; and <u>two olive-trees</u> by it, one upon the right side of the bowl, and the other upon the left side thereof.
>
> What are these <u>two</u> <u>olive-trees</u> upon the right side of the candlestick and upon the left side thereof?
>
> What are these <u>two</u> <u>olive branches</u>, which are beside the two golden spouts, that empty the <u>golden oil</u> out of themselves?
>
> And he answered me and said: You do not know what these are?
>
> And I said: No, my lord.
>
> Then he said: These are the two anointed ones, that stand by the Lord of the whole earth.
>
> Zechariah 4

The Menorah itself represents God's light, which He shines through His nation of Israel. The olive trees symbolize the ones the Lord anointed to serve Him on earth. The king of His choice with the High Priest, Kohen Gadol, by his side.

Was David's choice to be as an olive tree, besides his personal preference on how he viewed himself, also prophetic? The only people with whom the Lord made a Covenant of Salt regarding their task and that of their descendants were Aaron and David. Aaron, whom the Lord had chosen to be His High Priest became the forefather of the High Priests and priests in His service. David, the one the Lord had chosen to give the kingship over the Kingdom of Israel, became father of kings. By God's choice and grace, both will endure for ever.

> Blessed is the man who trusts in HaShem, and whose trust HaShem is. For he shall be as a tree planted by the waters, and that spreads out its roots by the river, and shall not see when heat comes, but its foliage shall be luxuriant; and shall not be anxious in the year of drought, neither shall cease from yielding fruit.
>
> Jeremiah 17:7-8

Endnotes

Deuteronomy 8:8 fruits of Israel / Exodus 3:8 milk and (date-) honey Leviticus 24: 1-4 olive oil, lights of the Menorah / Exodus 25:31-40, Exodus 36:1 the Menorah / Zechariah 4 God's appointed priest and king / Psalm 92:13-16 tree planted by the water.

Part I

DAVID, GOD'S SERVANT

HaShem will certainly make my lord a sure house (lasting dynasty), because, my lord fights the battles of HaShem; and evil is not found in you all your days.

1 Samuel 25:28

DAVID'S ROOTS

David's origin dates back to the days of old. The day his ancestor Abram, seventy-five years of age, took his wife Sarai, his nephew Lot and all their possessions with him out of Haran to a land appointed by the Lord God. They arrived first in Shechem, a place in the land where the Canaanites lived.

> *Now HaShem said unto Abram: Get you out of your country, and from your kindred, and from your father's house, unto the land that I will show you.*
>
> *And I will make of you a great nation, and I will bless you, and make your name great; and be thou a blessing.*
>
> *And I will bless them that bless you, and him that cursed you will I curse; and in you shall all the families of the earth be blessed.*
>
> *And Abram passed through the land unto the place of Shechem.*
>
> *And HaShem appeared unto Abram, and said: Unto your seed will I give this Land; and he built there an altar unto HaShem, who appeared unto him.*
>
> Genesis 12:1-9

Abraham, his son Isaac and his grandson Jacob all resided and dwelled as foreigners in Canaan, the Land promised to them and their descendants by the Lord God, and they were buried there in Hebron.

Israel

In Canaan the people saw an impressive great gathering of people with their chariots and horsemen passing by as they made their way through the dirt of the road. As they could see, these people were on a long journey from Egypt through Canaan. They saw all the dignitaries of Pharaoh's court and the dignitaries of Egypt, all wearing garments for this occasion.

As they arrived at the threshing floor of Atad near the Jordan River, they were lamenting loudly and bitterly. They mourned for seven days, and the Canaanites watching this solemn ceremony said that the Egyptians were in mourning. This was the funeral of Israel (Jacob). The Egyptian dignitaries were accompanying the Hebrews to his funeral. Israel's sons under Joseph's leadership did as he had commanded them. They carried him to the field of Machpelah near Mamre. There they buried him in the cave his grandfather Abraham bought years ago from Ephron the Hittite, to serve as a burial place for his family.

Who was this Israel? He was known as Jacob, son of Isaac and a grandson of Abraham. The Lord God changed his name to Israel. He was married to Leah and Rachel. He had twelve sons and one daughter, Dinah. Jacob lived seventeen years in Egypt. He died when he was one hundred and forty-seven-years-old.

Joseph, Israel's eldest son with Rachel, had promised his father that he would bury him in the family's burial place, as a proof of his love and faithfulness to him. After the funeral, Joseph and his brothers with their household all returned to Egypt. There, the Children of Israel would live for more than four centuries.

The Children of Israel

The Children of Israel lived on, about four hundred years, as strangers in Egypt. Initially in prosperity, owning land in Goshen and being in charge of Pharaoh's livestock. But about nearly two centuries later, their good fortune changed. The Children of Israel went from being a free people to becoming slaves doing hard labour. Working in the fields, making building blocks for the Egyptians, doing building work on the Egyptian cities Pithom and Ramesses, which served as supply and storage cities for the Pharaoh.

How could this happen? The Egyptians, who depended on the Hebrew people for their economic system, came to fear the descendants of Israel because they became more numerous than they were. Afraid that they would continue to increase in numbers, join their enemies, fight against them and leave Egypt, the Pharaoh who did not know Joseph, took drastic measures. He made them slaves and had his slave drivers keep them at work. But the more they oppressed them, the more their number increased.

In an attempt to bring the number of Hebrew people down, Pharaoh ordered the two Hebrew midwives to kill all the Hebrew newborn baby boys. But, the midwives feared God and didn't kill the babies. Pharaoh, noticing his plan didn't work out, summoned them to report about their work. Their explanation was that the Hebrew women were, unlike the Egyptian women, strong and had already had born their babies by the time they had arrived. The Lord blessed these midwives with children of their own. Pharaoh ordered every Egyptian to throw the Hebrew baby boys into the River Nile. Meanwhile, the Lord had seen the oppression, the affliction and suffering of His people.

> *I am the God of your father, the God of Abraham, the God of Isaac, and the God of Jacob. And HaShem said: I have surely seen the affliction of My people that are in Egypt, and have heard their cry by reason of their taskmasters; for I know their pains; and I have come down to deliver them out of the hand of the Egyptians, and to bring them up out of that land into a good and large land, to a land flowing with milk and honey.*
>
> Exodus 3:6-8

Pulled out of the water

Jochebed, of a Levite family, tried to protect the life of her son and put her baby boy in a basket on the River Nile. Miriam stood at some distance while she watched over her little brother. Pharaoh's daughter found him. He was a fine, beautiful three-month-old baby boy. He was crying and she saw that he was a Hebrew baby. He was already circumcised as the Lord commanded Abraham to do this for all generations at the age of eight days. Miriam fetched their mother to serve as a wet nurse to care for and breastfeed the baby. Pharaoh's daughter, unknowing the woman was the baby's mother, agreed to pay her. Later when she had weaned her son, she took him to Pharaoh's daughter.

Was the child the same age as Samuel was when his mother Hannah brought him to the priest Eli after she weaned him?

The boy most likely knew about his people, the Hebrews. He became the adoptive son of Pharaoh's daughter and as such an Egyptian prince, a member of Pharaoh's royal family, who raised and educated him. She named her son Moses, meaning 'pulled out of the water'.

One day Moses, now a grown man who knew about his heritage, went to watch his people doing hard labour. He saw an Egyptian man beating up a Hebrew man. Moses killed this Egyptian man and buried his body. But word of this incident came out, and Pharaoh sought to kill Moses. So, he fled to Midian where he married Zipporah and became a shepherd for Jethro, his father-in-law.

After many years, when the Pharaoh who wanted to kill Moses had already died, the Lord called upon Moses to return to Egypt to free His people, the Children of Israel. One day He spoke to Moses from a burning bush, that wasn't being consumed by the fire, at Mount Horeb. Moses, standing there on his bare feet on holy ground, listened to God's voice. The Lord told him His name and gave him a mission of extreme importance. He told this eighty-year-old man to return to Egypt, to speak with the leaders of His people and to ask the king of Egypt to let His people go into the wilderness to worship Him for three days. To convince Moses that he was the right person for this task, He gave him a spokesman and three signs for him to perform. His staff could turn into a snake, his hand could get a skin disease and be cured, and he could turn water of the Nile into blood.

Moses took his leave of his father-in-law Jethro, put his wife and two sons on a donkey, took the staff of God, and set out to journey through the wilderness to Egypt. Along the way at a lodging place, Zipporah herself circumcised their eldest son Gershom to help her husband. In the meantime the Lord instructed Moses' brother Aaron to go and meet Moses in the wilderness. There at the mountain of the Lord, Aaron met with him as the Lord told Moses he would. Glad to see him, Aaron kissed him, and Moses told him everything about what the Lord asked him to do. On their arrival in Egypt they gathered the elders, told them about God's concern for His people, about His plans for them and Moses performed the signs. They believed and bowed down in worship to the Lord, the God of Abraham, Isaac and Jacob.

And you shall say to Pharaoh: Thus says HaShem: Israel is My son, My firstborn. And I have said unto you: Let My son go, that he may serve Me.

Exodus 4:22-23a

God's eldest son

God sent Moses in His stead to Pharaoh, and his brother Aaron was to be his prophet. But, Pharaoh didn't know the God of the Hebrews. So, he wasn't compelled to listen to Moses and Aaron. Moreover, Pharaoh didn't want them to keep the Hebrews from their hard labour. Moses, performing the sign of the staff becoming a snake, didn't help either. Although the snake ate all the snakes of Pharaoh's magicians, among them Balaam's sons Jannes and Jambres, used secret crafts to imitate Moses, imitation which would soon end by the time the Lord brought the third plague of the gnats, mosquitoes over the Egyptians. Pharaoh made the Hebrews' hard labour even harder, having them gather their own straw to make the same amount of bricks daily. The Hebrew overseers complained with Pharaoh, who accused the

Hebrews of laziness. They became angry with Moses who turned to the Lord in prayer.

From then on, the Lord brought harsh plagues over Egypt and its people, during which He did make a distinction between the Children of Israel and the Egyptians by keeping His people safe from the plagues. The Lord was determined to show His power to the king of Egypt and in fact to the whole world. At the same time He would punish all the gods of Egypt. Each time Moses, who was still in esteem with some of the Egyptian leaders, confronted Pharaoh and he refused to comply, a plague would come over the Egyptians, their animals and their fields. Some of Pharaoh's officials did realise they should listen to Moses. When the plague of hail came over Egypt, some of them listened to Moses' warning and kept their slaves and animals inside, for the hail would strike people, animals, plants, trees and crops. They also told Pharaoh, at the time of the locusts plague, that Egypt was in ruin and that he should let the Hebrew people go to serve their God. Even his magicians told him that the plague of the gnats, mosquitoes, was the finger of God. Still, he did not listen to them either.

> *Thus says HaShem, the God of the Hebrews: Let My people go, that they may serve Me. For I will this time send all My plagues upon your person, and upon your servants, and upon your people; that you may know that there is none like Me in all the earth. Surely now I have put forth My Hand, and smite you and your people with pestilence, and you have been cut off from the earth. But in very deed for this cause have I made you to stand, to show you My power, and that My Name may be declared throughout all the earth.*
>
> Exodus 9:13-16

Moses and Aaron confronted Pharaoh. They spoke, performed signs and prayed. The Lord sheltered His people, and sent His plagues.

He turned the water of the Nile into blood; He filled the Nile with frogs right up into the Egyptian houses; He made mosquitoes out of the dust of the earth to cover people and animals; He poured dense swarms of flies into the houses and over the land; He had all the Egyptian livestock die; He made fine dust out of furnace soot bring festering boils on the Egyptians and their animals; He rained and thundered hail down, with flashing lightning to the ground on the Egyptian fields; He blew with an east wind a swarm of locusts into Egypt that devoured what was left after the hail; He covered the places the Egyptians lived with darkness they could feel for three days; Pharaoh's heart was hardened even more.

Moses and Aaron, trusting their God, remained steadfast. Pharaoh tried changing their plans. He told them, flies were swarming, bring your offering within Egypt; God's servants said they would be stoned by the Egyptians. He told them, locusts were coming, go without your women and children; God's servants said everybody has to be present at the festival for the Lord. He told them, darkness falling, go without livestock; God's servants said livestock was needed for the sacrifices. Pharaoh asked Moses for prayers, for forgiveness of sins. Pharaoh's heart was hardened even more.

Moses and Aaron stopped confronting Pharaoh. The Lord sent an angel of death. He struck all Egypt's firstborn of both men and animals.

Grieving, Pharaoh summoned them; he gave them his permission to leave Egypt. The Egyptians hurried them out with all their livestock, with their neighbours', and given gold and silver.

The Lord sheltered His people, and sent His column of cloud, of fire. He blew His wind all night. He gave them rest to walk on dry land through the Sea of Reeds. Pharaoh, with his best soldiers, chariots and horses, perished in the sea.

The Lord brought the Children of Israel out of Egypt with His Mighty Hand and Outstretched Arm; He led them with care through the wilderness into the Promised Land.

You are My servant, Israel, in whom I will be glorified.
Isaiah 43:3

At the last confrontation God's servants were told to leave Pharaoh's presence, and not return for surely they would be killed. Moses replied that they would not. After the last plague Pharaoh himself summoned them and they were finally given permission to leave. After more than eight decades of slavery, the Children of Israel, joined by a large group of foreigners, set out to journey to the Promised Land. By God's might they left the grieving Egyptians behind with a weakened nation that lost their best soldiers with their chariots and their horses, all their firstborn sons, their health, their livestock, their crops, their possessions and their good drinking water.

In that day HaShem made a covenant with Abram, saying: Unto your seed have I given this Land, from the river of

> *Egypt unto the great river, the Euphrates River; The Kenite, and the Kenizzite, and the Kadmonite, and the Hittite, and the Perizzite, and the Rephaim, and the Amorite, and the Canaanite, and the Girgashite, and the Jebusite.*
>
> Genesis 15:18-21

> *Every place that the sole of your foot shall tread upon, to you have I given it, as I spoke unto Moses. From the wilderness, and this Lebanon, even unto the great river, the Euphrates River, all the land of the Hittites, and unto the Great Sea toward the going down of the sun, shall be your border.*
>
> Joshua 1:3-4

The Promised Land

The Lord brought the Children of Israel through the desert to Mount Sinai where they received God's Laws, the Ten Commandments and regulations. They stayed there three months and built the Tabernacle in accordance to the Lord's instructions given to Moses who would lead them to God's good Land.

> *For HaShem your God brings you into a good land, a land of brooks of water, of fountains and depths, springing forth in valleys and hills; a land of wheat and barley, and vines and fig-trees and pomegranates; a land of olive-trees and honey; a land wherein you shall eat bread without scarceness, you shall not lack anything in it; a land whose stones are iron, and out of whose hills you may dig brass. And you shall eat and be satisfied, and bless HaShem your God for the good land which He has given you.*
>
> Deuteronomy 8:7-10

After two years they arrived at Canaan. But, because of their reluctance to conquer Canaan, they would wander a total of forty years in the wilderness. Of all the adults of that generation that came out of Egypt, only two of them would enter the Promised Land with the grown-up children of those who left Egypt. These two were the ones who put their trust in the Lord concerning conquering the Land. From Judah, Caleb son of Jephunneh and from Joseph the Ephraimite, Hoshea son of Nun, whom Moses renamed Yehoshua (Joshua). Under Joshua's leadership with Caleb's support, the Children of Israel, a free people as their forefathers were, crossed the Jordan River on dry ground and took possession of the Land promised to them through their ancestors Abraham, Isaac and Israel.

> *And I will take you to Me for a people, and I will be to you a God; and you shall know that I am HaShem your God, who brought you out from under the burdens of the Egyptians. And I will bring you into the Land, concerning which I lifted up My hand to give it to Abraham, to Isaac, and to Jacob; and I will give it you for a heritage: I am HaShem.*
>
> Exodus 6:7-8

Once they arrived in the Land, Joshua renewed God's covenant with all the Children of Israel. As descendants of Abraham, Isaac and Jacob they were the only people to whom the Lord gave His covenants, apart from the covenant the Lord made with Noah on behalf of humanity. Foreigners who supported them entered with them and resided as well among them in the Land.

Once Abraham listened to God's calling and he went up. After him hundreds of thousands of Israel's children would follow again and again through the ages. The Lord Himself gathers them to the Land of Israel. Did the Lord bring the Children of Israel to the Promised Land merely to offer them refuge?

> *Now therefore, if you will hearken unto My Voice indeed, and keep My covenant, then you shall be My own treasure from among all people; for all the earth is Mine; and you shall be unto Me a kingdom of priests, and a holy nation.*
>
> Exodus 19:5-6

> *And I will dwell among the Children of Israel, and will be their God. And they shall know that I am HaShem their God, that brought them forth out of the land of Egypt, that I may dwell among them. I am HaShem their God.*
>
> Exodus 29:45-46

Once in the Land, although the Children of Israel showed unfaithfulness to the Lord after Joshua's death, He continued to lead them by appointing Judges. Centuries later at the time of the last Judge Samuel, He provided for kings starting with the Benjaminite king, Saul. After him He had chosen King David. With David, the City of David, and David's scion!

> *Since the day that I brought forth My people Israel out of Egypt, I chose no city out of all the tribes of Israel to build a house, that My name might be there; but I chose David to be over My people Israel. ... Now it was in the heart of David my*

> father to build a house for the name of HaShem, the God of Israel. ... Whereas it was in your heart to build a house for My name, you did well that it was in your heart.
>
> 1 Kings 8:16-18
>
> *As the Host of heaven cannot be numbered, neither the sand of the sea measured; so will I multiply the seed of David My servant, and the Levites that minister unto Me.*
>
> Jeremiah 33:22

Endnotes

The Book of Jasher (Sefer HaYashar) is one of the thirteen history books mentioned in Biblical scripture. Joshua 10:13 and 2 Samuel 1:18 mentions it. Thus scripture recommends this history book as reading material next to Biblical scripture.

Exodus 6:4 Foreigners in Canaan
Genesis 49:29-50:14 Israel's death and funeral
Genesis 32:29, 35:10, 50:2, 1 Kings 18:31,1 Kings 31 Jacob is Israel, twelve sons, twelve stones
Genesis 47:13-31 Famine in Egypt, Joseph's work, Egyptians lose their land to Pharaoh
Genesis 47:11 The Hebrews owned land in Goshen
Genesis 47:5-6 The Hebrews were in charge of the Pharaoh's livestock
Genesis 47:4-6,11 Slaves, hard labour, cities of Pithom and Ramesses
Genesis 15:13 Israelites four hundred years as strangers in Egypt
Jasher 81:3-4 Two hundred and ten years of slavery in Egypt
Exodus 1:5-8 Pharaoh didn't know Joseph
Exodus 1:7 Israelites numerous, lived mainly in Goshen, also other places in Egypt
Exodus 1:8-10 Pharaoh didn't want the Hebrews to leave
Exodus 5:5 The Hebrews were already more numerous than the Egyptians
Exodus 6:20, Numbers 26:59 Moses' parents Amram and Jochebed
Genesis 17:11-12 Circumcision, eight-day-old baby boy
Exodus 2:1-10, 11-25 Moses, birth and flight to Midian
1 Samuel 1:20-28 Moses, same age as Samuel after he was weaned?
Exodus 3:7-10 God knew about the suffering of His people, the Children of Israel
Exodus 7:7 Moses, eighty years old when he returned
Exodus 4:20 Moses took his wife and sons with him
Exodus 2:21-22, 4:24-26 Moses' wife Zipporah circumcised their eldest son
Exodus 4: 1-9 The three signs given to Moses
Jasher 79:27,38 Jannes and Jambres

Exodus 7-10, Psalm 105:29-36 all ten plagues
Exodus 10:7 Officials told Pharaoh that Egypt was ruined
Exodus 10:12 East wind grasshoppers
Exodus 10:23 Darkness, moonlight Israelites
Exodus 9:18-19, 11:1-10 God distinguishes between the Israelites and the Egyptians
Exodus 12:23 The angel of death
Exodus 7:5, 9:14-16, 29 God shows His power to all
Exodus 4:22, Deuteronomy 32:18 God's eldest son
Exodus 19:5-6 Most important possession
Exodus 12:12 All Egypt's gods punished
Exodus 12:38, Jasher 81:1-2 A large group of foreigners joined the Israelites
Exodus 14:23 Egyptian soldiers perished, (Pharaoh not mentioned)
Exodus 12:23 The Israelites give thanks
Exodus 23:5 The Land of milk and honey (date honey)
Exodus 19, 24 The Israelites at Mount Sinai
Exodus 25:1-9 He would live amongst them
Numbers 13:16 Hoshea renamed Joshua
Exodus 3:8 The people that lived in the Promised Land
Genesis 32:32-33 The Children of Israel
Deuteronomy 9:4-7 Israelite righteousness does not give them rights on the Land
Joshua 8:33-35 Joshua renewed the covenant

DAVID'S PARENTS

For though my father and my mother have forsaken me, HaShem will take me up. HaShem is my light and my salvation; whom shall I fear?

Psalm 27:10

HaShem is the stronghold of my life; of whom shall I be afraid?

Psalm 27:1

On the run from King Saul, David went to the cave of Adullam. His father's entire household joined him there. Afterwards he went to Moab. Moab was the territory that the Lord God had given to the descendants of Lot, and which wasn't to be conquered by the Israelites. During David's reign as king of the Kingdom of Israel, they did pay tribute to him after he defeated them. Why did David want to go to Moab? To see the king of Moab.

David therefore departed thence, and escaped to the cave of Adullam ... And David went to Mizpeh of Moab.

1 Samuel 22:1-3a

The connection with Moab's king could have been through his Moabite family still living in Moab. David's father, Jesse, was the grandson of Boaz and Ruth, who was a Moabite woman. She was once married for ten years to Naomi's son Mahlon, who was a relative of Boaz. Some thought this was a forbidden marriage because she wasn't an Israelite. They didn't have children. After Naomi's two sons had died, she returned to her hometown of Bethlehem. One of her daughters-in-law, Ruth, who had chosen to worship no other god than the God of Israel, went with her. It was there that Boaz and Ruth met.

Boaz was a man of standing in Bethlehem. Being Naomi's relative, he married Ruth, the Lord blessed them with a son, Obed, Jesse's father. As Ruth herself had already chosen the God of Israel, she became a convert to Judaism. So their marriage wasn't considered a forbidden marriage as Ruth's first marriage was. Under Naomi's guidance, Obed was raised as an Israelite in accordance with the laws and regulations of the Israelites.

David's father Jesse, an Ephrathite, lived in Bethlehem, in the territory of Judah. He was, as was his grandfather Boaz, from a family of standing. Jesse had seven (eight) sons and two daughters. Jesse's sons were Eliab, Abinadab, Shimea, Nethanel, Raddai, Ozem and David the seventh. They had two sisters, Zeruiah and Abigail. Zeruiah was the mother of Abishai, Joab, and Asahel. Abigail was the mother of Amasa. The three eldest sons of Jesse had joined King Saul's army. In the days of King Saul, Jesse was already very old. One name in Jesse's household isn't mentioned in biblical scripture. The name of David's mother. Her family isn't mentioned either. Why? It could be she was the second wife or a concubine of Jesse. Or that she was a widow whom Jesse married. But, maybe she was Jesse's only wife, and she had done something that brought about contempt to herself and their youngest son David.

> *My enemies speak evil of me: <u>When shall he die, and his name perish</u>?... All that hate me whisper together against me, against me do they devise my hurt: An evil thing (disease) cleaves fast to him; and now that he lies (down), he shall rise up no more. Yea, my own familiar friend, in whom I trusted, who did eat of my bread, has lifted up his heel against me.*
>
> Psalm 41

One thing is sure, David wasn't well liked by people in his community, nor by his family. He was treated as a lesser person, as a reject. Sometimes people who hated David, wished him death. Like the time when he was ill. Even a friend who was close to him was against him. David's brothers weren't friendly either. Amidst all this, David didn't feel sheltered by his father. On the contrary, he felt abandoned, as he clearly mentioned in one of his poems. But, he believed and experienced already at a young age that the Lord God was the only one Who would take him up and be a stronghold to his life. So, David counted on Him for everything and in any situation that might arise. As for David's brothers, their contempt towards him was clear.

For instance, at the battle ground, where King Saul and the Israelites gathered to fight against the Philistines. There, the giant Goliath taunted the Israelites daily. David who went there to bring food for his brothers, seeking some information, spoke with Saul's soldiers.

David's eldest brother Eliab heard him and spoke angrily to him, saying, *'Why have you come down? And with whom have you left those few sheep in the wilderness? <u>I know your presumptuousness</u>, <u>and the naughtiness of your heart</u>; for you have come down so that you might* *see the battle'.**¹ David then said to Eliab, *'What have I now done? Was it not but a word'?**²

Then David, who obviously didn't trust his brothers to ask them anything, continued to talk to the other soldiers asking them questions regarding King Saul's reward for the person who would dare to face the giant.

Was Eliab's attitude towards David like this because David was anointed to be king of Israel? Or because as happened after that, he already was at the king's court playing the harp for Saul? Maybe both gave David's brothers a reason to be jealous of him and to resent him. Jealousy towards David could explain their attitude towards their youngest brother. Similar to Jacob's sons, except for Benjamin, jealousy towards their younger brother Joseph. Contrary to David, Joseph did have his father to protect him. But despite this, his brothers betrayed both him and their father.

Or did the way David's brothers behaved towards him suggest that he was the son from another mother? Did Jesse have another wife? A second wife, or a concubine. In that case, his first wife may have been regarded as being superior to her. So her sons would think, that because of that they would have more rights than David, as was the case in the past with the judge and warrior Jephthah.

And what about Jesse's own behaviour, when Samuel came to anoint one of his sons? Samuel invited Jesse and his sons to the feast of the offering. He didn't specify who should come. But, Jesse took all his sons, except David, to the feast. At the moment of anointing one of Jesse's sons to be king, Jesse still didn't call David to join them. He presented them to Samuel in order of their birth starting with his firstborn son. Maybe he was convinced that one of them would be anointed, so David didn't have to come. Still, in that case David would have been present at the feast to witness this. Samuel had to ask Jesse specifically whether he had anymore sons. Then Jesse called David, who was tending the sheep, to come forward. This suggests that David was regarded by the Lord in the same way as Jesse's other sons.

What did David himself have to say about his mother and family? Could it be he referred to the situation with his family in his prayers, poems and songs? For instance, could the following verse be an indication for how David's brothers initially might have acted towards him? *'Reproach has broken my heart; and I am sore sick; and I looked for some to show compassion, but there was none; and for comforters, but I found none. Yea, they put poison into my food; and in my thirst they gave me vinegar to drink'.**³

Though David also suggests they were all from the same mother, as he said: '*I have become a stranger to my brethren, and an alien to my mother's children*'.*4

So his brothers weren't referred to as half brothers.

Did David also speak about his mother in his artistic work? For instance, when he said, '*O turn to me, and be gracious to me; give Your strength to Your servant, and save the son of Your handmaid*'.*5

If so, here he mentions his mother as being God's servant, His handmaid. The following could be about the circumstances surrounding the conception of David. '*Upon You I have been cast from my birth*'.*6 And, '*Behold, I was brought forth in iniquity, and in sin did my mother conceive me*'.*7

This may refer to the time when his mother got pregnant. That she was living in sin, and that later on Jesse accepted her as his wife. His sister Abigail, also Zeruiah's sister, is mentioned as being the daughter of Nahash. Maybe David's mother was married to Nahash before her marriage to Jesse. So, did Jesse have two wives, and the second, being David's mother, had a lesser position within Jesse's household? If so, was his first wife dead? Because her name isn't mentioned either. But, there is no other woman mentioned as Jesse's wife or concubine in biblical scripture. Maybe Jesse had only one wife. And, it was something she did that caused contempt towards her and her youngest son. There is no conclusive answer within biblical scripture.

Could it be that the reason David wasn't accepted as an equal by his family and was shunned by them and the community was because of something his mother had done? Something that she kept a secret. Something she did not tell her husband. The Talmud*a identifies David's mother as Nitzevet or Natzbath. According the story in the Talmud, her husband Jesse wanted to be sure of the purity of his lineage, his ancestry. With the years came doubt in his mind because his ancestor Ruth was a Moabite. According to the Law of Moses, an Israelite shouldn't marry a Moabite or an Ammonite. Because of the cruel way they treated the Israelites when they were on their way to the Promised Land. For some reason, it seems that Jesse didn't know that this law only applied to Moabite men. Israelites were allowed to marry a converted Moabite*a2 woman, who would raise their children in accordance with Judaism. Because of his doubts, Jesse decided he should marry a Canaanite woman. He perceived this as being less of a problem. But his Canaanite maidservant had pity with Nitzevet, so she told her, her masters intention. They agreed that Nitzevet would sleep with Jesse for one last time instead of with the Canaanite on

25

the wedding night. But, they didn't tell Jesse. In a similar way as happened to Rebbeca and Leah, they switched places. Nitzevet got pregnant, but because she never told her husband about the switch, he thought that her child was from someone else. Thus illegitimate. Jesse had compassion regarding his wife. His sons were not to bother her, nor her son David. All this resulted in Nitzevet being treated as an immoral woman and her youngest son became an outcast, a despised servant, within his own family. This story could be an explanation to all David had to endure. But, there are no references to this story in biblical scripture.

So, according to this story, it's Jesse's perception of his connection to the people of Moab that caused trouble for him and eventually for both his wife and his son David. Though there is no record of the name of David's mother in biblical scripture, it is mentioned that he brought them to safety during the time he was a fugitive from King Saul. He took his parents together, as man and wife, to Moab. He brought them to the king of Moab, whom he asked to let them stay there for a while. This shows that David cared for both his father and mother. So, regardless of whatever may have happened between his parents, and whichever way his parents and brothers treated him, David was kind to both his parents.

> *And he said to the king of Moab: Let my father and my mother, I pray you, come forth, and be with you, until I know what God will do for me. And he brought them before the king of Moab; and they dwelt with him all the while that David was in the stronghold.*
> 1 Samuel 22:3b-4

Intermezzo

Jephthah, Son Of Another Mother

> *And God spoke all these words, saying: I am HaShem your God, who brought you out of the land of Egypt, out of the house of bondage. <u>You shall have no other gods before Me</u>.*
> Exodus 20:1-3

Another man whose mother's name isn't mentioned in biblical scripture is that of Jephthah, son of Gilead. He was a great warrior who became one of the judges of the Israelites at the time that Israel was a tribal nation. He lived in Gilead situated to the east of the Jordan River in the territory of the tribe Gad*[a] or Manasseh*[a]. Just like David,

Jephthah had to endure contempt from his family and his community. But it's mentioned, unlike with David's mother, that Jephthah's mother was a prostitute.

In David's case there were doubts about who his father was, but with Jephthah it was clear that Gilead was his father. Still, after his father's death, his brothers from his father's wife forced him out of the house. They hated him and told him, *'You shall not inherit in our father's house; for you are the son of another woman'*.*[1]

Though he was entitled to inherit from his father, just as for instance all Abraham's sons were, Jephthah left and went to live in the territory of Tob where, similar to David, some men who had problems of their own, gathered to him.

In the case of Abraham's sons, they all received gifts from him. Because Abraham knew that they were not to inherit with his son Isaac, who was the son of his wife Sarah. He arranged that all of them received their portion as a gift from him, after which he sent them away. Only Isaac received his portion, which was all of Abraham's inheritance, after Abraham's death. Isaac was the only son of Abraham who received that which the Eternal God had promised Abraham. The Land promised to him by the Lord God. As Sarah said to her husband, *'Cast out this bondwoman and her son; for the son of this bondwoman shall not be heir with my son, even with Isaac'*.*[2]

And the Lord God told Abraham, *'Let it not be grievous in your sight because of the lad (Ishmael), and because of your bondwoman (Hagar); in all that Sarah says to you, listen to her voice; for in Isaac shall seed be called to you. And also of the son of the bondwoman will I make a nation, because he is your seed'*.*[3]

This part of Abraham's inheritance was only meant for Isaac. So, he listened to his wife and to what the Lord God had told him. Abraham's son Isaac inherited everything the Lord God had promised, while Abraham gave his other sons, including Ishmael, gifts, knowing that the Lord would bless his son Ishmael to be a nation. Jephthah's father could have followed Abraham's example, but for whatever reason he did not, leaving Jephthah at the mercy of his bothers.

Some time after Jephthah had left his father's home, war broke out with the Ammonites. The leaders of Gilead knowing that Jephthah was a brave warrior, went to speak with Jephthah. They asked him to lead the people of Gilead into battle. At first he was reluctant because of the way they, the leaders, had treated him. This implies that these leaders were in agreement with the way Jephthah's brothers had treated him. Maybe his brothers were also part of Gilead's group of leaders.

Jephthah spoke to the leaders about their hate towards him and how they forced him out of his father's house. But, regardless of all this, they agreed with him that if he would do as they requested, he would become their ruler. Did this mean that he could trust these leaders? And, what about his brothers? In David's case, he did not trust his brothers. That's the reason he chose not to seek their advice, nor to depend on them. For instance when he asked for information about the king's reward to fight Goliath. He chose to ask other soldiers at the battlefield for information, instead of asking his brothers.

During the period of war against the Ammonites, Jephthah made a vow to the Lord God. He said, *'If You will indeed deliver the children of Ammon into my hand, then it shall be, that <u>what</u>soever comes forth of the doors of my house to meet me, when I return in peace from the children of Ammon, it shall be HaShem's, and I will offer it up for a burnt-offering'.**4

The Lord granted Jephthah victory over the Ammonites. But when he returned home, the first one to come out of his house to greet him was his own daughter. She was dancing and playing the tambourine. He tore his clothes as soon as he saw her, and he said, *'Alas, my daughter! You have brought me very low, and you have become my troubler; for I have opened my mouth to HaShem, and <u>I cannot go back</u>'.**5

Later on when he told her about his vow, she told him that he would have to keep his vow to God. She asked for two months to grieve, after which she died as Jephthah had vowed.

> *The fathers shall not be put to death for the children, neither shall the children be put to death for the fathers; every man shall be put to death for his own sin.*
>
> Deuteronomy 24:16

Did Jephthah's family, the priestly family and the other leaders within their community think that Jephthah's daughter deserved to die because of the sins of her parents or grandparents? But, the death penalty was only given in the case of someone's own sins. Maybe they thought she lived a sinful life herself. But, there is no mention in biblical scripture that this was the case. And scripture clearly states, that she was a young girl who had never been involved in a sexual relationship with a man. After her death, she was missed and mourned by the young girls of the community.

Wasn't there anything that could have been done to save Jephthah's daughter's life? She was Jephthah's only child. This was something that could have also been taken into consideration. Granting Jephthah some protection for his offspring. Similar to the regulations given for this purpose. She was the only one through whom, just as with Zelophehad through his daughters, Jephthah's family line could have continued. So, couldn't Jephthah's vow be broken or his daughter be redeemed?

> *Notwithstanding, no devoted thing, that a man may devote to HaShem of all that he has, whether of man or beast, or of the field of his possession, shall be sold or redeemed; every devoted thing is most holy to HaShem.*
>
> Leviticus 27:28

Jephthah wasn't the first Israelite who made a vow concerning a person with God. Only in his case, he did this unwittingly of what his daughter had planned to do for him when he returned home. And afterwards, it seems that he was unaware of the Lord's regulations regarding vowing a person to Him. Samuel's mother Hannah for instance, once made a vow of persons to the Lord which she kept when she gave Samuel into the care of the High Priest Eli. Eli said to Hannah and her husband Elkanah, '*HaShem gives you seed of this woman for the loan which was lent to HaShem*'.*[6]

Then the Lord God blessed her with having more children. She had five more children, three sons and two daughters. But in Hannah's case, there wasn't a matter of dispute or someone's actual life at stake. The Lord always considers whatever or whoever is devoted to Him as being holy.

In the case of Jephthah's daughter, she should have been considered as such by the priests if they would have held Jephthah to his vow. Though she had accidentally taken the place of what Jephthah had devoted. Because he had initially devoted something, *whatsoever*[*4], not someone. So, this could have been considered a matter of dispute that had to be resolved.

> *And in a controversy they (the priests) shall stand to judge; according to My ordinances shall they judge it; and they shall keep My laws and My statutes.*
>
> Ezekiel 44:24

But, what if someone doesn't want to or couldn't keep a vow to the Lord for whichever reason? The Lord God told Moses to speak to the Children of Israel concerning this. He told them, *'When a man shall clearly utter <u>a vow of persons</u> to HaShem, according to <u>your evaluation</u>, then your valuation shall be for the male from twenty years old even to sixty years old, even your valuation shall be fifty shekels of silver, after the shekel of the sanctuary. And if it be a female, then your valuation shall be thirty shekels. And if it be from five years old even to twenty years old, then your valuation shall be for the male twenty shekels, and for the female ten shekels'.**7

So, the priests could make a valuation for a payment in shekels, Israelite currency, to redeem the one who was devoted. And, if someone would be too poor to pay according to this valuation, what would then happen? *Then he shall be set before the priest, and the priest shall value him; <u>according to the means of him that vowed</u> shall the priest value him.* *8

So, in the case the priests would have upheld Jephthah to his vow to God, they should have considered his daughter as most holy to Him, and they should have made a valuation to settle this matter. In doing so, they would have saved her life. Did Jephthah know all this? If he did, wouldn't he have chosen to do this? The same goes for his daughter. Jephthah and his daughter needed the priest's guidance and for them to do as the Lord commanded them through His regulations.

> *<u>Everything that opens the womb</u>, of all flesh which they offer to HaShem, <u>both of man and beast</u>, shall be yours; howbeit <u>the firstborn of man shall you surely redeem</u> ... And their redemption-money ... shall be, according to your valuation.*
> Numbers 18:14-18

> *All the <u>heave-offerings of the holy things</u>, which the children of Israel offer to HaShem, have I given you (Aaron), and your sons and your daughters with you, as a due for ever; it is an everlasting <u>covenant of salt</u> before HaShem to you and to your seed with you.*
> Numbers 18:19

The Lord made a covenant of salt with Aaron and through him with the priesthood an everlasting covenant of salt. This entitled the priesthood to receive or be in charge of everything and everyone that had been vowed to the Lord God. The Lord also gave an inheritance to Aaron's tribe, the Tribe of Levi. As is written, 'And to the children of Levi, behold, I have given all the tithe in Israel for an inheritance'. *8

Why? The Lord said to Aaron, '*In return for their service which they serve, even the service of the tent of meeting*'. *[10]

So, He gave the priests and Levites a great responsibility in this regard. If all this was possible in order to save Jephthah's daughter's life, why didn't this happen? Did Jephthah's brothers withhold information concerning these laws from him? And, what about the priests? They were the ones who had the responsibility regarding all that which is vowed to the Lord. They had at least two months to solve this matter. Besides, they must have known from the story of Abraham with his son Isaac, that the Lord God doesn't want people to vow or offer another human being as a sacrifice to God. This is something very different than when someone chooses by himself to sacrifice his own life for others. As for instance happens during wartime. The Lord does want people's faithfulness.

> *But the priests the Levites, the sons of Zadok, that kept the charge of My sanctuary when the children of Israel went astray from Me ... and they shall come near to My table, to minister to Me, and they shall keep My charge.*
>
> Ezekiel 44:15-16

Shouldn't the priests have approached Jephthah to give him guidance? Or, was there at that time corruption within the priesthood? As for instance happened during the time of the kings of Judah when King Josiah brought reforms and a renewal of the Covenant with the Lord. And before then, at the time of Judge Samuel. High Priest Eli's two sons were involved in corrupt practices. Corruption which would have far-reaching consequences for Eli, his sons, their descendants and even for the nation of Israel. Unlike them, the sons of Zadok, a priestly family that remained faithful to the Lord, would continue to come near the Lord's table to minister to Him.

> *The Lord God's eyes are open upon all the ways of the sons of men, to give every one according to <u>his ways</u>, and according to <u>the fruit of his doings.</u>*
>
> Jeremiah 32:19

Due to their corruption, the Lord Himself imposed a punishment on this priestly family. According to prophesies, an end would come to Eli's priestly house regarding performing priestly duties at the Lord's Tabernacle and later on the Lord's Temple. This came to pass when King Solomon removed Eli's descendant Abiathar from the office of

High Priest, and installed Zadok the priest as Kohen Gadol. It was also prophesied by a prophet who came to see Eli and later on also by Samuel, that all the young men in Eli's family and clan would be killed or die at a young age, because of the corruption within his priestly family. After these prophesies were given to Eli, war came to Israel. A war against the Philistines during which the Ark of the Covenant was captured by them. This war also brought about the death of Eli and his two sons.

> *None devoted, that may be devoted of men, shall be ransomed; he shall surely be put to death.*
>
> Leviticus 27:29

The case of Jephthah was not like that of Ahab, one of the kings of Israel. He allowed Benhadad, who was king of Aram, to live and he made a treaty with him. The Lord Himself had already made it clear to Ahab that Benhadad as an enemy of the Israelites, was meant for destruction. When Ahab failed to be obedient to the Lord's command, a prophet of the Lord told Ahab, '*Thus says HaShem: Because you have let go out of your hand the man whom <u>I had devoted to destruction</u>, therefore your life shall go for his life, and your people for his people*'.*[11]

There were others that the Lord God Himself meant for destruction. As happened to some people, when the Israelites were in the wilderness on their way to the Promised Land. Korah and his followers who opposed Moses, fell together with their families into a rift, after a sudden earthquake, and they died. Others died by fire. Or at the time of King Saul.

Israel's enemy, Agag the king of the Amalekites, had to die during the war as the Lord had commanded Saul. Instead, because of Saul's failure to comply with God's command, Agag died at the hands of Samuel. And Saul lost the kingship over the Kingdom of Israel. The same way, the Lord can put a whole town or city up for destruction, as happened to Sodom and Gomorrah. But, these are not about giving sacrifices of human beings to God, nor about someone's personal vow to God. These people were not vowed to God by someone else. But the Lord Himself devoted them to destruction, for the sake of His people, and therefore they couldn't be ransomed.

> *He (God) reveals the deep and secret things; He knows what is in the darkness, and the light dwells with Him.*
>
> Daniel 2:22

Were the priests of Jephthah's time righteous? Didn't they tell him anything about the regulations by which he could have prevented his daughter's death? Jephthah was convinced that he couldn't go back on his vow to God. They should have told him about what he had to pay to free himself from his vow and obligation to the Lord. That way he could have redeemed, ransomed, his daughter which would have saved her life. What went wrong?

Were the priests at that time reluctant to help Jephthah and his daughter? And his brothers, who unjustly threw him out of the house after their father's death, because he had another mother. What about them? In case Jephthah would have known about the regulations but wasn't able to pay the valuation of the priests, they could have come to his aid financially. If not, even then, the priests could have done a new valuation while taking his financial means into account. So they all could have saved his daughter's life.

> *Thus says HaShem of hosts, the God of Israel: Behold, <u>I will bring evil upon this place</u> ... because they have forsaken Me ... and have filled this place with the <u>blood of innocents</u>; and have built the high places of Baal, <u>to burn their sons in the fire for burnt-offerings</u> to Baal; which I commanded <u>not</u>, <u>nor spoke it</u>, <u>neither came it into My mind</u>.*
>
> Jeremiah 19:3-5

Instead, the priests rejected her and let her die. So, neither this priestly family nor Jephthah's brothers were trustworthy. As for the leaders of Gilead, who were in agreement of Jephthah's expulsion from his father's house, none of them came to his, nor his daughter's aid. But, why allow something as horrific as this to happen? Wasn't it because it was a convenient way for Jephthah's family on the father's side to get rid of possible claims to their father's inheritance, by her and by Jephthah's descendants through her? An inheritance to which he, and therefore his daughter, was legally entitled to, since his father didn't give him anything of his inheritance when he was alive as Abraham once gave gifts to his other sons. Jephthah's daughter would otherwise have the right to inherit his father's portion, as the daughters of Zelophehad once did. Jephthah's brothers, who hated him, could have even arranged with the priests to withhold information from Jephthah. It was convenient for them, if she was eliminated. Even more if this was done by her own father, so he would damage his own reputation within the community even more. In this manner these people could put all the blame for her death on Jephthah, resulting in much more contempt for him. So no one helped him, despite the fact that he was the one saving them from their enemies, the Ammonites.

What happened after her death? Similar to what happened at the time of the corrupt priests of the priestly family of Eli. War broke out. This time, a civil war with the Ephraimites, which resulted in the death of forty-two thousand Ephraimites.

> *For I have no pleasure in the death of him that dies, says the Lord God; wherefore turn yourselves, and live.*
>
> Ezekiel 32:19

Those, especially the priestly family in Gilead, who knew the Lord's laws and regulations had even more responsibility to uphold them. They allowed something that had always been completely against the Lord's Will to happen. Her death was *no* sacrifice to the Eternal God, but was rather, on behalf of Jephthah's brothers and the priests who ministered to them and could have prevented this from happening, their own sacrifice to a false god.

> *But the <u>Levites</u> that went far from Me, when Israel went astray, that went astray from Me after their idols, they shall bear their iniquity; ... Because they <u>ministered to them before their idols</u>, and became a stumbling block of iniquity to the House of Israel; therefore have I lifted up My hand against them, says the Lord God, and they shall bear their iniquity. <u>And they shall not come near to Me</u>.*
>
> Ezekiel 44:10-14

For Jephthah's brothers to choose this path, was it because they themselves were people who already participated in idol worship? The priests, in any case, through deceit for their own convenience in solving what they viewed as a problem, a money and family prestige issue, set an excuse to put Jephthah's daughter up for destruction in this manner. They allowed this to happen, while ignoring the Lord God's regulations given to solve these matters. Priests who engaged in actions like this were banned from the presence of the Lord. Banned from serving Him in His holy sanctuary.

So, who is to be blamed? The abuse and betrayal of both Jephthah's brothers and the priestly family in Gilead, by withholding his inheritance and proper priestly guidance from him, led to the death of his daughter, and to an extent to the civil war with the Ephraimites.

Because, him being broken by the grief for the loss of his only child, made it difficult for Jephthah to handle the problematic situation with the Ephraimites in a good manner.

Despite all this, Jephthah would rule six years. After he died, he was buried in Gilead, his hometown. He is mentioned in biblical scripture as one of God's faithful servants that fought against Israel's enemies.

> *You shall have no other gods before Me. They (the priests, the sons of Aaron) shall be holy to their God, and <u>not profane the name of their God</u>.*
>
> Exodus 20:1-3 / Leviticus 21:6a

David's Mother

> *For You are He that took me out of the womb; <u>You made me trust</u> when I was upon my mother's breasts. <u>Upon You I have been cast</u> from my birth; <u>You are my God</u> from my mother's womb.*
>
> Psalm 22:10-11

David's mother, was she a woman of faith? In one of David's prayers where he asked the Lord for strength and a sign on his behalf, he said, *'O turn to me, and be gracious to me; give Your strength to Your servant, and save the son of Your handmaid'*.*[8]

In this prayer he referred to his mother as being a handmaid to God. Thus a servant of His. This suggests that his mother was as a maiden servant to God, a woman of faith. She had to raise and give guidance to her son in an environment that hated him. Though David did feel abandoned by her, as he also felt he was by his father, something he mentioned in one of his poems. He could have been very lonely. But, he did have someone to hold on to. David's complete and deep trust was with the Eternal God Himself, the One he considered to be his shelter. So, David grew up to be a man of faith himself, with a deeply rooted desire to live close to God.

> *<u>One thing</u> have I asked of HaShem, that will I will seek after: that <u>I may dwell in the House of HaShem all the days of my life</u>, to behold the graciousness of HaShem, and to visit early in His Temple. – I will sing ... <u>I will sing praises to HaShem</u>.*
>
> Psalm 27:4 / Psalm 27:6$_c$

To David the Eternal God is *the true God*⁹, the living God*¹⁰* and *the former of all things*¹¹* He was the One who formed him, the One Who has been his God from the start. His *God*¹²* from his *mother's womb.*¹²*

> *For You have made my reins; You have knit me together in my mother's womb. I will give thanks to You, for I am fearfully and wonderfully made; wonderful are Your works; and that my soul knows right well. My frame was not hidden from You, when I was made in secret, and curiously wrought in the lowest parts of the earth. Your eyes did see my unformed substance, and in Your book they were all written – even the days that were fashioned, when as yet there was none of them.*
> Psalm 139:13-16

The One he could always trust. Someone Who would always keep His word.

> *And now, O Lord God, You alone are God, and Your words are truth, and You have promised this good thing to Your servant. – The words of HaShem are pure words, as silver tried in a crucible on the earth, refined seven times. You will keep them, O HaShem.*
> 2 Samuel 7:28 / Psalm 12:7-8a

He was the One, Who in his time of need would always come through for him, who considered himself as a poor man and for whom there would be no inheritance from his father. David didn't count on that, judging by his own experience regarding how things were between him and his family.

> *I am a <u>poor</u> man, and <u>lightly esteemed</u>?*
> 1 Samuel 18:23

> *But, as for me, that <u>I am poor and needy</u>, the Lord will account it to me; You are my help and my deliverer; O my God, tarry (tardy) not.*
> Psalm 40:18

Before David was anointed by Samuel, he already was a man of faith who kept the Lord's Laws and regulations. A man, determined to live by the Lord's Will, in order to be close to Him. Someone who as soon as he would realise that he had sinned against Him would repent, as he did in the case of Bathsheba, the wife of Uriah. He was God's servant who, in obedience to Him, would fight all His battles.

To David, as long as he could remember, the Eternal God has been the One he worshipped. Is this the reason why the Lord had chosen him? David's inner soul was known by the Lord.

David put his faith in the Lord God. Faith that he needed to get through his day-to-day life during which he had to endure so much contempt from his family and community. Also, faith that he needed to protect his father's flock of sheep, with which he was entrusted, against wild animals.

> *HaShem who delivered me out of the paw of the lion, and out of the paw of the bear.*
>
> 1 Samuel 17:37

Once David asked the Eternal God for a sign in his favour, saying in his prayers, '*<u>Work in my behalf a sign for good</u>; that they that hate me may see it, and be put to shame, because You, HaShem, have helped me, and comforted me*'. *[13]

Why did David ask the Lord for this sign? Only because of the contempt he had to endure? Or, maybe because he was also afraid of what his brothers might do to him after their father's death. Similar to what was done to Jephthah. The difference with him was that they did not consider David to be a son of their father. Whereas Jephthah did have a right to their father's inheritance, but his half brothers did not honour it. Maybe even his mother wouldn't be spared more contempt and shame. But, the Lord God heard David's prayer and He gave him all the support he needed.

> *He will cover you with His pinions (pine tree), and under His wings shall you take refuge; His truth is a shield and a buckler (armour).*
>
> Psalm 91:4

The Lord did give him a sign, which would indeed be seen by all, and as David wished, also by those who hated him. One that could not be ignored and that in the long run granted David a good future. In which he would never have to depend on his father's household, nor an inheritance from him to sustain himself. So, in case his brothers would cause trouble for him regarding the matter of his mother, he wouldn't need anything from them. And, they wouldn't have the opportunity to trick him and bring ruin to his life, as Jephthah's half brothers and the priests did to him regarding his daughter. On the contrary, as it

Who Is David?

happened, they had to depend on him for their safety when it came to King Saul's intentions.

So, what was the sign? This, David would one day be called, 'the son of Jesse'. The Lord was the first to refer to David as a son of Jesse.

> *And HaShem said to Samuel: How long will you mourn for Saul, seeing I have rejected him from being king over Israel? Fill your horn with oil, and go, I will send you to <u>Jesse</u> the Bethlehemite; for I have provided Me a king among <u>his sons</u>.*
> 1 Samuel 16:1

Affirming David's true ancestry. Afterwards it was King Saul's servant and more importantly, King Saul himself who referred to David by calling him *'son of Jesse'*.*[b] Who was there to deny David his family name? Now, how did the Lord God make this possible?

> *The stone which the builders rejected has become the <u>chief cornerstone</u>. This is HaShem's doing; it is marvellous in our eyes.*
> Psalm 118:22-23

By choosing the one that was rejected among his own family and community to be His king to rule over the nation of Israel.

The Lord, Who *looks on the heart**[14] and not on outward appearances, had chosen David, the one that no one had expected to be chosen. And He made him His cornerstone for the foundation that He was going to lay in Zion.

David, as a servant of King Saul, introduced him, a good musician, a brave man and a man of war, good looking and an able speaker, and, a *son of Jesse**[b] from Bethlehem. He added, that the Lord was with David. The Lord made David, who said to the Lord God: *'HaShem, my heart is not haughty, nor mine eyes lofty; neither do I exercise myself in things too great, or in things too wonderful for me'.**[15] He is king over His inheritance, the people of Israel.

Against all odds, regardless of the way his family treated him, the fact that the name of his mother wasn't mentioned, or whatever had occurred in the past which had caused contempt towards him and his mother, David would keep his family name. He would always be called, the son of Jesse, while he would be and remain financially, and regarding his position within society, completely independent from his family. The Lord God insured that David wouldn't remain poor and needy. So, David would regardless, always keep the family line of his father Jesse which connected him with Boaz and Ruth, with Perez the son of Judah, Jacob's son, and therefore with the Tribe of Judah. The one tribe that would time and again choose to remain loyal to David throughout his life.

> *Surely I have <u>stilled and quieted my soul</u>; like a weaned child with his mother; my soul is with me like a weaned child.*
> Psalm 131:2

There is something else the Lord had given David, which also supported him through the soul pain he experienced due to the contempt of his family towards him, and through all he had to endure later on in his life. Artistic talents of writing, playing music, singing and dancing. All which he combined with his prayers and worship to the Lord, helping him cope in times of trouble. These, in connection with his trust in the Eternal God, brought deep *shalom* to his inner soul. A profound stillness and quietness.

> *Go your way, eat your bread with joy, and drink your wine with a merry heart; for God has already accepted your works. Let your garments be always white; and let your head lack no oil. Enjoy life with the wife whom you love all the days of the life of your vanity, which He has given you under the sun, all the days of your vanity; for that is your portion in life, and in your labour where in you labour under the sun.*
> Ecclesiastes 9:7-9

Artistic talents that didn't only serve David himself, but also others during his lifetime. As for instance the first king of Israel, King Saul, when he played the harp for him, bringing him relief for his soul. David also used these when he made the arrangements for and with the musicians and singers to perform at the Tent of Meeting. Arrangements, which later on were adopted by other kings of Israel for the Temple of the Lord. For instance by King Hezekiah. Even his joyful dancing when he brought the Ark of the Covenant to Jerusalem. His artistic work has been through ages and up to modern times an inspiration, a source of joy, comfort and hope for people of faith around the world. Especially to those who combine them with prayer, understanding and trust, giving them deep stillness within their heart and soul.

These, and other artistic talents that God the Creator also gives to people in general, shows God's mercy towards humanity as a whole.

Because these, besides being an encouragement to live a joyous life, also enables people to have a way of handling their day-to-day burdens and troubles throughout their lives.

> *Behold, You desire <u>truth</u> in the inward parts; <u>make me</u>, therefore, <u>to know wisdom in my inmost heart</u>.*
>
> Psalm 51:8

David himself, as Israel's king, had many children with several wives and concubines. He would one day be succeeded by one of his sons. God promised David, He Himself would *build a house**16 for him. For David who walked with God in truth and with an upright heart. A royal house, so his descendants would reign after him. A house for which David prayed and asked the Lord God to bless, as he said, 'Now therefore <u>let it please You to bless the house of Your servant</u>, that it may continue for ever before You; for You, O Lord God, have spoken it; and through Your blessing let the house of Your servant be blessed for ever'.*17

The Lord determined that David's son, Solomon was the one to be his successor as king. The Lord Himself showed David great kindness by granting him to have one of his sons to sit on his throne after him, to reign over the nation of Israel. As Solomon himself once prayed.

> *You have shown to Your servant David my father great kindness, according <u>as he walked before You in truth</u>, and <u>in righteousness</u>, and <u>in uprightness of heart with You</u>; and You have kept for him this great kindness, that You have given him a son to sit on his throne, as it is this day.*
>
> 1 Kings 3:6

Solomon's mother Bathsheba had only two sons. The first one died as a baby. Her second son was Solomon. As one who lived by the Lord God's Laws and regulations, David himself also sought God's wisdom. He advised his son Solomon*c to seek wisdom.

> *For <u>I was a son to my father</u>, tender and <u>an only one in the sight of my mother</u>.*
> *And he taught me, and said to me: Let your heart hold fast My words, keep My commandments, and live; <u>Get wisdom</u>, <u>get understanding</u>; forget not, neither decline from the words of my mouth; Forsake her not, and she will preserve you; love her, and she will keep you. <u>The beginning of wisdom is</u>: <u>Get</u>*

> *wisdom; yea, with all your getting get understanding. Extol her, and she will exalt you; she will bring you to honour, when you do embrace her. She will give to your head a chaplet of grace; a crown of glory will she bestow on you.*
>
> Proverbs 4

Solomon did listen to his father, David, and he asked the Lord God, Who appeared to him in a dream, to give him understanding. The Eternal God granted him wisdom, which Solomon needed to govern the nation of Israel. The Lord also made it clear to him that he should keep His Law and regulations. He also had to follow his father David's example. The Lord God put David as the blueprint, the example to follow for all kings of Israel, including Solomon.

> *Give Your servant therefore an understanding heart to judge Your people, that I may discern (distinguish) between good and evil; for who is able to judge this Your great people? ... behold, I have done according to your word: look, I have given you a wise and understanding heart; ... And if you will walk in My ways, to keep My statutes and My commandments, as your father David did walk, then I will lengthen your days.*
>
> 2 Kings 3:9-15

Long after David's lifetime, the Lord God affirmed through his prophets the House of Judah's role concerning the cornerstone that Judah would bring forth.

> *Therefore thus says the Lord God: Behold, I lay in Zion for a foundation a stone, a tried stone, a costly cornerstone of sure foundation; he that believes shall not make haste ... for HaShem of hosts has remembered His flock the House of Judah, and makes them as His majestic horse in the battle. Out of them shall come forth the cornerstone, out of them the stake, out of them the battle bow, out of them every master together.*
>
> Isaiah 28:16 / Zechariah 10:3b-4

David was chosen by the Lord God to be a cornerstone. Fulfilling this task had implications not only for David's lifetime, but also for that of his successors. As the Lord swore to David regarding them, that he would put them on his throne.

> *HaShem swore to David in truth; He will not turn back from it: <u>Of the fruit of your body will I set on your throne</u>. If your children keep My covenant and My testimony that I shall teach them, their children also for ever shall sit upon your throne.*
>
> Psalm 132:12-13

What would the Lord God's attitude be towards David's descendants if they would forsake his laws and regulations?

> *<u>His (David's) seed also will I make to endure for ever</u>, and his throne as the days of heaven. If his children forsake My law, and walk not in My ordinances; If they profane My statutes, and keep not My commandments, then I <u>will visit their transgression with the rod</u>, and <u>their iniquity with strokes</u>. <u>But My mercy will I not break off from him, nor will I be false to My faithfulness</u>.*
>
> Psalm 89

As for the distant future of the people of Israel, the Lord God had also spoken of Jesse. Prophets long after Jesse's and David's lifetime spoke about one particular descendant of David's father Jesse, and of David himself.

> *And there shall come forth <u>a shoot out of the stock of Jesse</u>, and a twig shall grow forth out of his roots. And the Spirit of HaShem shall rest upon him, the Spirit of wisdom and understanding, the Spirit of counsel and might, the Spirit of knowledge and of the fear of HaShem. And his delight shall be in the fear of HaShem; and he shall not judge after the sight of his eyes, neither decide after the hearing of his ears; ... the <u>root of Jesse</u>, that stands for an ensign of the people, to him shall the nations seek; and his resting place shall be glorious. ... And He will set up an ensign for the nations, and <u>will assemble the dispersed of Israel</u>, <u>and gather together the scattered of Judah</u> from the four corners of the earth.*
>
> Isaiah 11

> *There (Zion) will I make <u>a horn to shoot up to David</u>, there have <u>I ordered a lamp for My anointed</u>. His enemies will I clothe with shame; but <u>upon himself shall his crown shine</u>.*
>
> Psalm 132:17-18

Also, this root or shoot, has been spoken of before. Ever since the days of old, when the Israelites were wandering in the wilderness on their way to the Land the Lord God had promised their forefathers, Abraham, Isaac and Jacob. Abraham whose descendant the Eternal God would make into a nation that He would bless. A nation that in turn would be a blessing to the nations of the world, as the Lord said about Abraham, 'Shall I hide from Abraham that which I am doing; seeing that <u>Abraham shall surely</u> <u>become a great and mighty nation</u>, and <u>all the nations of the earth shall be blessed in him</u>'?*[18]

Why would the Lord choose Abraham and his wife Sarah, to form such a nation with their descendants? Out of love for Abraham.

He, Who showed the Israelites, so they would know, that He '*is God; there is none else beside Him*',*[19] made it possible for them to hear His voice so they could receive His instructions, His teachings, and live by them. As is written, '<u>Out of heaven He made you to hear His voice</u>, *that He might <u>instruct you</u>; and upon earth He made you to see His great fire; and you <u>did hear His words</u> out of the midst of the fire. And <u>because He loved your fathers</u>, and <u>chose their seed after them</u>, and brought you out with His presence, with His great power, out of Egypt*'.*[20]

Getting them out of Egypt for which purpose? '*To drive out nations from before you greater and mightier than you, to bring you in, to give you their <u>land for an inheritance</u>, as it is this day; know this day, and lay it to your heart, that HaShem, <u>He is God in heaven above and upon the earth beneath</u>; <u>there is none else</u>'.* *[21]

As for David, the Lord didn't want him to die and for *his name to perish*,*[22] so people would forget him, as his enemies wished. And for future things to come, the Almighty God still wants people to listen to Him and not harden their hearts. Because, there are still prophesies to be fulfilled, and His commandments and regulations are still valid.

> *For He is our God, and we are the people of His pasture, and the flock of His hand. Today, <u>if you would but hearken (listen) to His voice</u>! Harden not your heart.*
>
> Psalm 95:7-8

All these prophesies concerning the root or shoot of Jesse, and other prophesies of the Lord, have been referring to the Messiah, who as a descendant of Abraham, his grandson Jacob, and of David son of Jesse, would rule over God's inheritance millennia after King David's reign. Since the days of old, long before David's time, the root or shoot of Jesse was referred to as, 'a star out of Jacob'.

Who Is David?

> *I see him, but not now; I behold him, but not near; there shall step forth <u>a star out of Jacob</u>, and <u>a scepter shall rise out of Israel</u> ... And out of Jacob shall one have dominion.*
>
> Numbers 24:17-24

Endnotes

*[1] 1 Samuel 17:28$_c$, *[2] 1 Samuel 17:29$_b$, *[3] Psalm 69:21-22, *[4] Psalm 69:9, *[5] Psalm 86:16, *[6] Psalm 22:11$_a$, *[7] Psalm 51:7, *[8] Psalm 86:16, *[9] Jeremiah 10:10$_a$, *[10] Jeremiah 10:10$_a$, *[11] Jeremiah 16, *[12] Psalm 22:10-11, *[13] Psalm 86:17, *[14] 1 Samuel 16:7 *[15] Psalm 131:1, *[16] 2 Samuel 7:11-27 and 1 Chronicles 17:10-11, 25 *[17] 2 Samuel 7:29, *[18] Genesis 18:17-18, *[19] Deuteronomy 4:35, *[20] Deuteronomy 4:36-37, *[21] Deuteronomy 4:38-39, *[22] Psalm 41:5

*[a1] According to the Talmud, Midrashim, David's mother was Nitzevet or Natzbath. The Talmud is the primary source of Jewish theology and halakha, that is religious law, in Rabbinic Judaism. It was, for some still is, a guide for daily Jewish life. Components: the Mishnah (ca 200 CE), a written collection of Rabbinic Judaism's Oral Torah. Gemara (ca 500 CE), a clarification of the Mishnah and the Torah.

Talmud: Wikipedia, https://en.wikipedia.org/wiki/Talmud
Nitzevet: Chabad, https://www.chabad.org/theJewishWoman/article_cdo/aid/280331/jewish/Nitzevet-Mother-of-David.html
Geni, https://www.geni.com/people/Natzbath/6000000000792926156
Got questions, https://www.gotquestions.org/David-mother.html
Wikipedia, https://en.wikipedia.org/wiki/Nitzevet

*[a2] Marriage with a Moabite woman. The Stone Edition Tanach, Artscroll Series: notes Nehemiah 13:1-3, pg 1868. Moabite women exempt from the Law of Moses, Deuteronomy 23:3-5, that Israelites shouldn't marry Moabites. They may convert just as Ruth who married Boaz did. Solomon also had a Moabite wife, 1 Kings 11:1

*[b] David son of Jesse. 1 Samuel 16:1, 1 Samuel 20:27, 20:30-31, 22:7-8,13 King Saul called him David son of Jesse. 1 Samuel 16:18, 22:9, 1 Kings 12:16, 1 Chronicles 12:18, 29:26, 2 Chronicles 10:16, Psalm 72:20, others called him David son of Jesse

*[c] Proverbs 4:3-9. If King Solomon was the man who wrote the Book of Proverbs, as Proverbs 1:1, 10:1, 25:1 says, then it was his father, King David, who gave him this advice

1 Samuel 16:1-13 David's father Jesse

1 Samuel 16:1, 17:12, 58 Jesse was an Ephrathite from Bethlehem, he was very old in Saul's time

1 Samuel 17:12-20, 17:13-14, 28, 1 Chronicles 2:11-17 Jesse's sons, daughters, grandchildren

David's Parents

1 Samuel 16:10, 1 Samuel 17:12 Jesse had seven sons excluding David, thus eight sons
1 Chronicles 2:13-15 Jesse had seven sons including David
1 Samuel 16:11 David youngest son attended the sheep
1 Chronicles 2:13-16, 2 Samuel 17:25 Abigail, Zeruiah's sister, daughter of Nahash not Jesse
1 Samuel 11:1 Nahash, an Ammonite king
2 Samuel 17:25 Abigail was Amasa's mother
1 Samuel 17:10-12 Jesse's three eldest sons in Saul's army
Ruth 1:16, 4:10 Ruth chose God, she was the widow of Naomi's son Mahlon
1 Samuel 16:5 Jesse and his sons invited to the feast
1 Samuel 17:12-16, 1 Samuel 16:1-13 Jesse's sons before Samuel
1 Samuel 16:11 Samuel asked Jesse about more sons
1 Samuel 16:3 Samuel anointed David, the son the Lord indicated
1 Samuel 17:28 Eliab, eldest brother, angry with David
Psalm 69:8, Psalm 22:9, Psalm 139:14 David about his birth, his relation with his family
Deuteronomy 2:9, 2 Samuel 8:2 Moab's land, Moab paid tribute to David
Deuteronomy 23:3-5, Nehemia 13:1-3, Ezra 9, 10 laws about marrying Moabites, Amonites
Deuteronomy 2:9, 2 Samuel 8:2 Moabite land, Moab paid tribute to David
Genesis 38:28-30, 46:12, Ruth 4:12,18, Perez son of Judah, lineage David and Jesse
Psalm 118:22
Isaiah 11:1
1 Samuel 16:12 David's skills and looks, Saul's servant introduced David
1 Samuel 16:21-23 David played the harp for Saul
2 Samuel 6:4-5, 1 Chronicles 15 and 16 David brings the Ark of the Covenant to Jerusalem, music
1 Chronicles 15:16-28, 16:7-36, 1 Chronicles 25:1-31 David's instructions to musicians and singers
2 Chronicles 29:25-30 King Hezekiah adopted David's instructions
2 Samuel 6:14-16, 21, 1 Chronicles 15:29 David's dancing
Jeremiah 5:25, Isaiah 50:20, 59:2 sin blocks communication with God
2 Samuel 7:11-17, 27-29, 1 Chronicles 17:10-15, 24-27 God promised David a royal house
1 Samuel 13:14, 16:12, Psalm 89:20
Deuteronomy 4:36$_a$, Psalm 95:7-8, Hebrew 3:7-8 listen to the Lord's voice

Intermezzo Endnotes

[*1]Judges 11:2, [*2]Genesis 21:10, [*3]Genesis 21:12-13, [*4]Judges 11:30$_b$-31, [*5]Judges 11$_b$:35, [*6]1 Samuel 2:20$_b$, [*7]Leviticus 27:2-5, [*8]Leviticus 27:8, [*9]Numbers 18:21$_a$, [*10]Numbers 18:21$_a$, [*11]1 Kings 20:42
[*a]Map of the twelve tribes of Israel.

Who Is David?

Jewish Virtual Library, The Twelve Tribes,
https://www.jewishvirtuallibrary.org/the-twelve-tribes-of-israel
Also, Moses gave Gilead to the Makirites, descendants of Joseph's son Manasseh, Numbers 26:29-30, 32:39-40
Judges 10:6 Judges 11:7, Jephthah
Judges 11:1 Jephthah's mother was a prostitute
Genesis 25:5, 25:6 Abraham's son Isaac inherits, gifts for other sons
Judges 11:4-7 the leaders of Gilead ask Jephthah to lead them in the war against the Ammonites
Judges 11:30-31 Jephthah's vow
Numbers 6:21, 36:1-13, Deuteronomy 23:22-24 vows to God
Number 27:1-11, Numbers 36 daughters of Zelophehad
Leviticus 27:1-8 redeem/ransom people and things promised to God
Numbers 16:24-34 Moses' opponents meant for destruction
1 Samuel 15:8-35 Agag king of the Amalekites meant for destruction
1 Kings 20, 20:34-43, 42 war Ahab and Benhadad, Benhadad meant for destruction by God
Genesis 22:1-19, Jeremiah 7:31 Abraham and Isaac, God does not ask people to give human sacrifices
1 Samuel 2:22-26, 3:11-21, 4:1-22, 1 Kings 2:26-27, 35 Eli, sons and descendants
2 Kings 23 King Josiah's reforms and renewal of the Covenant with the Lord
2 Kings 23:10 Valley of Ben Hinnom, place sacrifice of sons and daughters in fire to Molech
1 Kings 1:39, 45, Ezekiel 44:15-16 Zadok anointed Solomon king
Judges 11:38-39 Jephthah's daughter was a virgin
Deuteronomy 25:11-12, 25:5-10 regulations for protection of offspring
Deuteronomy 24:16, Jeremiah 32:18, Ezekiel 18 death sentence only for own sins, punishment of sins and repentance

DAVID'S SLING

The souls of your enemies, <u>them shall he sling out</u>, as from the hollow of a sling.

1 Samuel 25:29b

An army gathered in the town of Socoh preparing for battle. They set up camp at Ephes Dammim, between the town and Azekah. Their enemy gathered to their king and set up their army camp in the Valley of Elah. Both armies ready for battle lined up each on one hill having the valley between them. Though ready, they did not engage in battle. What were they waiting for? A mighty warrior came forth out of one of the camps to challenge their opponent. With him a soldier that carried his shield. This warrior was very tall, about three meters. He wore a heavy bronze armour to protect his body and his legs, and a bronze helmet.

He stood there with a spear in his hand and shouted to the opposing army, *'Why do you come out to set your battle in array? Am I not a Philistine, and you servants to Saul? Choose a man and let him come down to me. <u>If he is able to fight with me, and kill me, then we will be your servants</u>; but if I prevail against him, and kill him, then shall you be our servants, and serve us'. And the Philistine said: 'I do taunt the armies of Israel this day; give me a man, that we may fight together'.*[*1]

Who was this warrior that taunted Israel's king and the Israelite's army? The Philistine Goliath, from Gath. The Israelites, though ready for battle, didn't send anyone to fight him, for they were terrified of this giant.[*2] Neither King Saul, a tall man himself, but no giant. Nor his soldiers dared to fight him.

But, who was King Saul?

Saul, a young handsome tall Israelite, was the son of Kish, an influential and wealthy man within his community, who belonged to the Israelite tribe of Benjamin. Saul was chosen by the Eternal God to be the king of His people, after the Israelites requested to have a king like all the surrounding people had. They didn't trust the two sons of Samuel, Joel and Abijah, who made a poor job as judges of the city of Beersheba, which was entrusted to them by their father. In fact they were dishonest judges who took bribes from the people. Though it was sinful for the Israelites to ask for a king, because this meant they put the Eternal God who was their king aside, Samuel got permission from God to give them what they wanted.

Samuel anointed Saul to be king the first time he met him. One day Saul and one of the servants were searching for some donkeys, belonging to his father, that wandered off. They went through the territory of Ephraim and afterwards that of Benjamin, but they couldn't find the donkeys. Saul wanted to go back home because otherwise his father would start to worry about them. But, his servant suggested they go to see a highly respected holy man in a town nearby in the region of Zuph where they were. The servant assured Saul that this man could help them, because everything he says comes true. But, Saul wanted to be able to pay the holy man. Saul didn't seem to know that it wasn't common in Israel to pay a seer or prophet of the Eternal God. They didn't have any food or a gift to give him. But the servant had a silver coin, and they agreed that they would give it to the seer.

Once they arrived at the town, they asked the young women that went out to draw water about the seer. They told them they would find him in town. He was there to bless the sacrifice that the people were offering to the Lord, after which they would all sit down for a festive meal. On their way into the town, Saul and the servant saw the seer walking towards them on his way to meet the people at the place of worship. Saul met with Samuel near the gate. He asked him where the seer lived. Samuel told him that he was the seer. What Saul didn't know was that the Lord already informed Samuel of His intentions concerning Saul, the day before.

The Lord God spoke to Samuel telling him that He would send the ruler of His people to him the next day. He would free the Israelites from the Philistines. The reason why the Lord sent the Israelites a ruler wasn't only because they asked for a king, but also because He had seen their suffering at the hands of the Philistines and He had heard them cry for help. The Lord also spoke to Samuel as soon as he saw Saul, telling him that he was the man He spoke to him about. After Samuel told him who he was, he sent him and the servant to the place of worship while inviting both for the meal. He also told them he would answer all their questions the next day and that the donkeys that were lost, had already been found. Then, Samuel answering his own rhetorical question about who the Israelites want, said Saul and his father's family. Saul asked him why he was talking like that to him. Because his tribe, Benjamin, was the smallest tribe and his family wasn't important in the tribe. When they came at the place of worship, Samuel led them to the table and gave them a seat at the head of the table. Then he told the cook to bring the piece of meat he had given him to put aside, and he placed it for Saul to eat. Samuel told him that he kept it especially for him to eat at the festive meal with his guests. After the meal Samuel took Saul into town, there he arranged for a bed to be set up on the roof – houses had flat roofs at the time and sometimes people slept there – where Saul went to sleep.

The next day, early in the morning, Samuel called to Saul to wake him up. Saul wanted to send him and his servant off. They left the house and walked towards the edge of the town, where Samuel told Saul to send his servant up ahead. After he left, Samuel told Saul that he was about to tell him the Lord's message for him. Samuel took his jar of olive oil to anoint Saul, and he poured the oil over his head. He kissed him and told him, *'Is it not that HaShem has anointed you to be prince over His inheritance'?*[*3]

Then Samuel told Saul about three things that would happen to him on his way home. First, he would meet two men when he reaches the border of Benjamin's territory, near Rachel's Tomb, which was along the way to Bethlehem Ephrathah who would tell him that the donkeys had been found and that his father had begun to worry about his whereabouts. Afterwards, on the plain of Tabor, he would meet three men on their way to Bethel to worship before the Lord God and offer sacrifices. One would be carrying three kids – young goats – the other three loaves of bread and the third one, leather skin containing wine. One of the men would offer him two loaves of bread, which he should accept. Third, on his way to the Hill of God, Kiriath Jearim, where the Ark of the Covenant was placed, he would meet, when he enters the town, with a group of prophets coming down from the Hill of the Lord. And Samuel told him that *'the Spirit of HaShem will come mightily upon you, and you shall prophesy with them, and shall be turned into another man'.*[*4]

Samuel told him that after these signs, he should prepare himself for the kingship as best as he could and that God would be with him. The last thing Samuel told Saul was that he had to go to Gilgal and wait seven days before he would come to meet him. Saul left. *'And it was so, that when he had turned his back to go from Samuel, God gave him another heart'.*[*5]

After Saul met the two groups of men as Samuel had told him, he met with the prophets. *'And when they came here to the hill, behold, a band of prophets met him; and the spirit of God came mightily upon him, and he prophesied among them'.*[*6]

People were wondering, asking, what happened to the son of Kish, and whether he had joined the group of prophets. So, all the three signs given to Saul by Samuel came to pass that day. When Saul stopped prophesying, he reached the High Place of worship. His uncle saw him there, and asked him where he had been. He answered him that he was looking for the donkeys, when he couldn't find them he went to see Samuel, and that he told him that the donkeys were already found. But, Saul said absolutely nothing about what Samuel said regarding his kingship.

Samuel went to Mizpah, where he gathered the people to attend his meeting. There he spoke about how God brought them out of Egypt, rescued them from all the people that oppressed them, saved them from their troubles and misfortunes, and also about their wish to have a king. In order to point out the man to be king over the Children of Israel, Samuel told the people to gather in accordance to their tribe. Then he asked the tribe of Benjamin to come forward according to their families.

The family of Saul's father Kish was singled out and from this family, Kish's son Saul. But Saul was nowhere to be found. When Samuel inquired of the Lord about the whereabouts of Saul, He replied that Saul was hidden among the baggage of supplies. When they looked for him there, they found him and brought him forward in the midst of the people. He was the tallest man present. Samuel then said to the people of Israel, *'See him whom HaShem has chosen, that there is none like him among all the people'*?*[7] And all those present shouted, and they all said, *'Long live the king'*.*[7]

Samuel explained to the Israelite people the protocol of the kingship, the rights and duties of a king, which he wrote down in a book that he placed before the Lord at a holy place. Then Samuel sent everyone home. Saul himself went back to Gibeah accompanied with men whose heart had been inspired and was touched by the Lord God. Could Abner, the son of Saul's uncle Ner, and the future commander of Saul's army, be one of these men? But, there were some other men who questioned whether Saul could save the Israelites. They did not accept him. Therefore they ridiculed and despised Saul, and didn't honour him by giving him gifts. Saul ignored them. Could it be that the sons of Samuel, the eldest being Joel and the youngest Abijah, were among these people who despised Saul?

Sometime later, the king of Ammon, Nahash, marched his army against Jabesh. He besieged this town in the territory of Gilead. The elders of the town requested a treaty with Nahash. He was willing to give them one, but under one condition. He would have had everyone's right eye put out, which would have been a disgrace to the Israelites.

Also, when Joshua entered Canaan, the Tabernacle with the Ark of the Covenant, was in Gilead. Therefore the people of Israel considered Gilead a sacred place. The men of Gilead agreed with Nahash that they would have seven days to decide. In the meantime they sent messengers all over Israel asking for help. They arrived where Saul lived in Gibeah. Saul, who didn't take up his role as king yet, but returned to his civilian life probably because of the opposition of some men, was just coming in from the field with his oxen. He found the people very sad and weeping. He asked what was going on. The messengers told him about what happened in Jabesh. *'And the Spirit of God came mightily upon Saul when he heard those words, and his anger was kindled greatly'.*[*8] Saul sent messengers throughout Israel with the message, *'Whosoever comes not forth after Saul and after Samuel, so shall it be done unto his oxen'.*[*9]

The fear of the Lord fell on the people. What would happen to the oxen of those who didn't come to follow him and Samuel to battle? Their oxen would be cut to pieces, just as his own oxen. Saul had cut them into pieces and he gave the parts to the messengers to take with them to show the people.

The people fearing the Lord, gathered to Saul and Samuel. Three hundred and thirty thousand Israelites, of which thirty thousand were from Judah, gathered for battle at Bezek. The messengers of Jabesh returned with a message for their people, that they would be saved the next day before noon. The people of Jabesh were very happy to hear this, and they sent a message to Nahash telling him that they would surrender to him the next day. At dawn, Saul attacked the Ammonite's military camp with three groups of warriors. They defeated the Ammonites, leaving the survivors scattered while running away each man by himself. After this victory, the people of Israel wanted Samuel to hand over the men who didn't accept Saul as king, to kill them. But Saul prevented this from happening as he said, *'There shall not a man be put to death this day; for today HaShem has wrought deliverance in Israel'.* [*10]

As Samuel requested, the people went to Gilgal, proclaimed Saul king of Israel, and brought offerings to the Lord. There they celebrated both Saul's kingship and the victory over the Ammonites. There, Samuel spoke to the people and encouraged them and the king to live in obedience to the Eternal God of Israel and to serve Him. Samuel prayed for rain, which the Lord God sent. God forgave the Israelites for their sin of asking for a king. The Israelites asked Samuel, *'Pray for your servants unto HaShem your God, that we die not; for we have* *added unto all our sins this evil, to ask us a king'.*[*11]

Samuel replied saying, *'Fear not; you have indeed done all this evil; yet turn not aside from following HaShem, but serve HaShem with all your heart; and turn you not aside; for then should you go after vain things which cannot profit nor deliver, for they are vain'.*[*12]

Samuel also told the Israelites he would do both – continue to pray for them before the Lord, and to instruct them about His ways, because it would be sinful not to do this. Saul reigned forty years, during which he fought fiercely against the enemies of Israel. He defeated the army of Amalek. As long as he was king, he and his sons fought against the Philistines. With their first king, the Israelite's tribal society transitioned to become a state.

> *For <u>HaShem will not forsake His people for His great name's sake</u>; because it has pleased HaShem to make you a people unto Himself ... Only fear HaShem, and serve Him in truth with all your heart; for consider how great things He has done for you.*
>
> 1 Samuel 12:22-24

So King Saul and his army were so terrified that no warrior came forward to fight Goliath. Who would save the nation of Israel from this giant, from the Philistine army and from this daily humiliation? Unexpectedly, a young man who didn't seem to be a warrior at all, volunteered for the fight. His name was David.

Who was this David? He was the son of Jesse of the tribe of Judah. He lived with his family in Bethlehem. Jesse had eight sons, of which David was the youngest. His father always sent him out to tend his herd of sheep. Samuel met for the first time with David at his father's house. Besides a shepherd, David was a musician and a writer of poems. On King Saul's request, David came regularly to his court to play music on the harp for him. But on this day David was at the military camp of the Israelites, though he wasn't enlisted as a soldier. If not as a soldier, why did David go to the camp of the Israelites? Jesse's three eldest sons, Eliab, Abinadab and Shammah, left home and followed King Saul to war against the Philistines. While David's brothers stayed with Saul's army, David, being a shepherd, was back home in Bethlehem taking care of his father's flock. Jesse was worried about his sons at the front line, so he sent David to bring them and the officer over a thousand soldiers food and to inquire about the course of the war.

Early in the morning David, after making sure someone was there to attend the flock, left to the front line. His father gave him ten loaves of bread and about ten kilograms of roasted grain for his brothers. He also gave him ten cheeses for the commanding officer. Jesse told his son where the army was encamped. David set out to do as his father asked and arrived at the Israelite camp just in time to witness the confrontation between the two armies. The Israelites were readying themselves, shouting the battle cry, going to the hill at their side of the valley to take their position facing their enemy standing on the other hill. Immediately David sought the officer who was in charge of the army's supplies and left his heavy baggage of food with him. He then ran to find his brothers at the front line and asked them how they were doing. Just then, Goliath came out and began his now daily routine.

David heard Goliath, who had been challenging and taunting the Israelites for forty days. Every morning and evening he would stand there in the middle of the valley of Elah between the two armies standing in position for battle, forming a battle line each one on a hill facing each other. And every single day the Israelites at the sight of Goliath, they would run away in terror, leaving no one to challenge him. Not the king, not a brave warrior, no volunteer of any sorts. Until today. The first volunteer appeared ready to take Goliath on.

David heard the men around him talking, saying how strong Goliath was, and that the king would reward the warrior who would take him on. Saul would also marry his daughter to him and exempt the father of the warrior from paying taxes. David asked the soldiers standing near him about this matter. He wanted to know how King Saul would reward the person that would take up the challenge successfully. That is, the warrior who would kill Goliath who was challenging the army of the Living God, and in doing so free Israel from disgrace.

As David said, *'What shall be done to the man that kills this Philistine, and takes away the taunt from Israel? For who is this uncircumcised Philistine, that he should have taunted the armies of the living God'?**[13]

David's elder brother Eliab became angry when he heard David speak to the men and asked him what he was doing there. He asked him whether he left the flock of sheep unattended. He had assumed David came just to watch the fight. David replied by asking him what he had done wrong now, and whether he couldn't even ask a question. Then he immediately turned to someone else, asking him about the king's reward. He received the same answer as before. A few men that heard David talking, told Saul about him. Who was this man, who showed no fear for Goliath? The king sent for David.

Intermezzo

Chronology – Saul, David, Solomon

David belonged to the tribe of Judah. David, King Saul's son-in-law, was the first king of the Kingdom of Judah and the second king of the twelve tribes, unified Kingdom of Israel. David ruled over the Kingdom of Judah from Hebron, and later on from Jerusalem over the Kingdom of Israel. He was thirty years old when he became king of Judah. He reigned forty years, seven and a half years over the Kingdom of Judah, and thirty-three years over the unified Kingdom of Israel. By God's grace he established the dynasty of the House of David.

David was the man destined to always fight the Lord's battles. As the prophetess Abigail once said to David ... *'for HaShem will certainly make my lord a sure house, because <u>my lord fights the battles of HaShem</u>'.*[*1]

Which battle was David's first? The one with Goliath. He himself said to Goliath, *'<u>for the battle is HaShem's</u>, and He will give you into our hand'.*[*2]

David was the son of Jesse, who lived in Bethlehem. Jesse had eight sons. When David went to live in Hebron, he took his second and third wife, Ahinoam and Abigail, with him. Living in Hebron, he had six wives. His first six sons were born there. His eldest son was Amnon son of Ahinoam, second was Chileab son of Abigail, who was the widow of Nabal from Carmel. His third son was Absalom whose mother was Maacah. Adonijah was his fourth son, whose mother was Haggith. Followed by Shepathiah and Ithream whose mother was Abital and Eglah. Absalom had a sister, Tamar. His first wife Michal, Saul's daughter, became later on part of David's household, when Ishboshet, Saul's son who became king of the eleven-tribe Kingdom of Israel after him, brought her back to David. Michal didn't have children of her own. In Jerusalem David had more wives and concubines with whom he had more sons and daughters, including Solomon whose mother was Bathsheba. One day Absalom would kill David's eldest son Amnon because of what he had done to his sister Tamar. And two of David's sons, Absalom and Adonijah, would try to sit on his throne. These events would bring much grief to David, and even war to Jerusalem.

Solomon would succeed David as king. He would rule forty years over the unified Kingdom of Israel from Jerusalem. Solomon had seven hundred wives and three hundred concubines. Soon after Solomon's death the unified Kingdom of Israel split up into the Northern Kingdom of Israel, with ten tribes, and the Southern Kingdom of Judah with two tribes. The tribe of Judah and Benjamin. Solomon's son Rehoboam, succeeded him as king over the Kingdom of Judah, including the tribe of Benjamin, and he reigned seventeen years, while the Ephraimite Jeroboam became king of the Northern Kingdom of Israel and he ruled twenty-two years. The descendants of David, the House of David, would continue to reign over the Kingdom of Judah.

King David was preceded by King Saul. Saul was the first king of the twelve tribes, unified Kingdom of Israel. He was the first king of the Israelites. He reigned forty years. With their first king the Israelites transitioned from a tribal society to becoming a nation state in the region. The period of the Judges ended with Judge Samuel, and the time of the monarchy began with King Saul. Saul and his family belonged to the tribe of Benjamin. Unlike David, Saul had one wife. Her name was Ahinoam, the daughter of Ahimaaz, with whom he had four sons and two daughters. His sons were Jonathan, Ishvi, Malchishua and Ishboshet or Ishbaal. His eldest daughter was Merab and Michal was the youngest. Saul's father Kish and his uncle Ner were sons of Abiel. Ner's son, Abner became the commander of Israel's army. One day Abner would, after King Saul and his other sons were killed in battle, make Saul's son Ishboshet king over the Kingdom of Israel, including the tribe of Benjamin but Judah excluded.

Judah remained loyal to David their king. Ishboshet was forty years old when he became king. He would rule just two years. He was murdered in his sleep. Saul also had two daughters. His daughter Michal didn't have children. His daughter Merab had five sons with her husband Adriel, Barzillai's son. Saul also had one concubine, Rizpah, who was the daughter of Aiah. With her he had two sons named Armoni and Mephiboshet.

But, years after Saul's death, his descendants were killed by the people of Gibeon. Saul's two sons with Rizpah and his five grandsons, Merab's sons, were killed. What happened to the descendants of Jonathan with whom David had a covenant of friendship?

> *And Jonathan said to David: but also you shall not cut off your kindness from my house for ever ... And Jonathan caused David to swear again.*
>
> 1 Samuel 20:12-17

Jonathan's son and grandson Mephiboshet, who was crippled on both feet, and his son Micah, were spared, because both of them, Jonathan's son and grandson, were placed under King David's personal protection. In total, seven descendants of Saul were killed by the Gibeonites.

When did these people live? When did these events take place? The kingdom of King Saul, King David and King Solomon date back to the late 11th and 10th century before current era (BCE). Traditionally Saul's reign is placed in the late 11th century BCE. While according to historians in the Middle East, David probably lived during 1000 BCE. And Solomon's reign was around 970 to 931 BCE.

There is a late 9th, early 8th century inscription discovered that may point to the House of David. The Tel Dan Stele. A king of Damascus commemorated his victory on this inscribed stone. His enemies whom he defeated were two kings. There is a phrase on this stele referring to 'house' and to 'David'. The translation of most scholars is, 'House of David' or 'Dynasty of David'. There is still debate among historians and archaeologists about the degree to which the Israelite society was developed. Several archaeological findings in modern day Israel regarding the period these kingdoms were established, and have been providing more and more information in this regard. But, there are still many questions among historians regarding King David as a historical figure and the Israelite kingdoms.

Goliath

When Saul's soldiers brought David before the king, he told him that no one should be afraid of this Philistine. David also told the king that he would fight Goliath. But Saul was certain that David couldn't fight Goliath, the giant that had been taunting them for forty straight days. So, he told David he couldn't defeat Goliath. The reason why? David was a young man and not a warrior, while Goliath had been a warrior all his life ever since his youth. Another matter was, whether Saul would have tried to stop David from fighting if he knew at that time that David was the man anointed by Samuel to become king of Israel.

But David was not persuaded by Saul. He just wasn't afraid of Goliath. He was sure that he could take this warrior on though he himself wasn't one yet. What fuelled his confidence? Previous experiences with impressive opponents. He had fought a lion and a bear to protect the sheep of his father, and he lived to tell the story. As David told Saul, *'Your servant kept his father's sheep; and when there came a lion, or a bear, and took a lamb out of the flock, I went out after it, and smote it (struck it down), and delivered it out of his mouth; and when it arose against me, I caught it by its beard, and smote it, and slew (killed) it. Your servant smote both the lion and the bear; and this uncircumcised Philistine shall be as one of them, seeing he has taunted the armies of the living God'.**14

David continued saying that *'HaShem that delivered me out of the paw of the lion, and out of the paw of the bear, He will deliver me out of the hand of this Philistine'.**14

Once Saul heard this, he understood why David was so confident that he could take on Goliath's challenge and be victorious. So, Saul gave David permission to fight, and said to him, *'Go, and HaShem shall be with you'.**15

Then Saul gave David what he believed he needed to fight Goliath – his armour and weapons. Saul himself put his helmet on David's head, and helped him put on his armour coat. Then David strapped the sword that Saul handed to him over the armour. But David who wasn't used to wearing all these, couldn't walk. Realizing he couldn't possibly fight while wearing this armour, he took all of it off, and he told Saul he couldn't fight wearing it. So David took his shepherd stick and went on his way to the valley where Goliath was taunting the Israelites. After he left, Saul asked his commander Abner about David's father. But Abner really didn't know who he was. In fact, Saul himself had met with David before. At his own court where he played the harp for him. But for some reason he didn't recognise him. If he did recognise him, would he have allowed David to take up Goliath's challenge? One thing was for sure. If David was successful in defeating this Philistine, the king would be interested in having him in his army. Because Saul always enlisted men who were brave and strong. The king asked Abner to make some inquiries about him.

> *Yea, though I walk through the valley of the shadow of death, I will fear no evil, for You are with me; Your rod and Your staff, they comfort me.*
>
> Psalm 23:4

Who Is David?

While David walked along the stream of the brook, he armed himself with five smooth stones that he picked up out of the water. He put these in his knapsack and his shepherd's bag. He kept his slingshot ready in his hand while approaching Goliath. Goliath stood there in the valley with his shield bearer in front of him. When he saw David approaching him, he walked towards him. He noticed David's youthfulness and that he was fair of appearance. Goliath was full of contempt for David, whom he realised wasn't a warrior at all, but just a handsome young man confronting him with a shepherd's stick and a sling in his hand.

He said to David, *'Am I a dog, that you come to me with sticks'*?

Goliath cursed David by his idol gods, and said, *'Come to me, and I will give your flesh to the fowls of the air, and to the beasts of the field'.*[*16]

David, without any sign of discouragement or terror replied, *'You come to me with a sword, and with a spear, and with a javelin; but I come to you in the name of HaShem of hosts, <u>the God of the armies of Israel</u>, whom you have taunted. This day will HaShem deliver you into my hand; and I will strike you down, and take your head from off you; and I will give the carcasses of the host of the Philistines this day unto the fowls (birds) of the air, and to the wild beasts of the earth; that <u>all the earth may know that there is a God in Israel</u>; and that all this assembly may know that HaShem saves not with sword and spear; <u>for the battle is HaShem's</u>, and He will give you into our hand'.*[*17]

Then Goliath came closer and closer to David to fight with him. David quickly start running to him, while he reached into his shepherd's bag, grabbed one of the stones, put it into his sling and slung it to the Philistine. The stone hit and penetrated Goliath's forehead, and he fell on the ground face down. It took one sling shot to topple him, but David wasn't done yet. He ran toward the giant's body, took his large sword out of its sheath and he cut off the Philistine's head from its body. Just as he told Goliath he would do to him. The Philistine army saw their champion dead, the soldiers panicked and ran away with the army of Israel and Judah in pursuit. All along the Shaarim road all the way to Gath and Ekron, the bodies of Israel's enemy fell. When the Israelite army returned, they looted the Philistine camp.

Abner took David to see Saul. David came holding Goliath's head by the hair. Saul asked him about his father and family. He told him his father was Jesse from Bethlehem. After Saul's conversation with David, Saul's eldest son, Jonathan met with David. This would lead to a mutual lifesaving close friendship. When King Saul and his men returned home, the women all over Israel came out to meet the king in celebration, playing music, dancing and singing, *'Saul has slain his thousands, and David his ten thousands'.*[18]

Saul enlisted David in his army, which pleased all his officers. Eventually he made him one of his officers. David became a successful warrior and officer.

As for Goliath's remains and weaponry? Eventually David took Goliath's head to Jerusalem, and he left his weapons in his tent. Later on Goliath's sword would be stored in the Sanctuary at Nob. One day David would use it again.

> *HaShem is my rock, and my fortress, and my deliverer; my God, my rock, in Him I take refuge; my shield, and my horn of salvation, my high tower. Praised, I cry, is HaShem, and I am saved from my enemies.*
>
> Psalm 18:3-4

Endnotes

[1] 1 Samuel 17:8-10, [2] Genesis 6:4, Deuteronomy 2:10-23, 3:1-11 giants, [3] 1 Samuel 10:1, [4] 1 Samuel 10:6, [5] 1 Samuel 10:9a, [6] 1 Samuel 10:10, [7] 1 Samuel 10:24, [8] 1 Samuel 11:6, [9] 1 Samuel 11:7b, [10] 1 Samuel 11:13, [11] 1 Samuel 12:19, [12] 1 Samuel 12:20-21, [13] 1 Samuel 17:26, [14] 1 Samuel 17:34-36, [15] 1 Samuel 17:37, [16] 1 Samuel 17:44, [17] 1 Samuel 17:45-47, [18] 1 Samuel 18:7b

The Green Olive Tree, www.thegreenolivetree.nl
King David, by Angeline Leito
http://www.thegreenolivetree.nl/index.php/14-articles/king-david/36-king-david
National Geographic Magazine December 2010
Kings of Controversy, by Robert Draper
https://www.nationalgeographic.com/magazine/2010/12/david-and-solomon/

Wikipedia: David
https://en.wikipedia.org/wiki/David
Wikipedia: Saul
https://en.wikipedia.org/wiki/Saul
Wikipedia: Solomon
https://en.wikipedia.org/wiki/Solomon
Joshua 4:19 the Ark of the Covenant in Gilead
1 Samuel 6:20-7:2 Ark of the Covenant at Kiriath Jearim, 20 years

Who Is David?

1 Samuel 8:1-21, 8:22, 12:17-22 Israelites ask for a king, God told Samuel to do this, God's forgiveness
1 Samuel 8:1-3 Samuel's sons
1 Samuel 9:2 Saul's looks
1 Samuel 9:17, 12:3 Saul chosen by the Lord to be king
1 Samuel 9:16-17 God's choice for Saul
1 Samuel 9:6-8 Saul's mistake wanting to pay Samuel
1 Samuel 9:18-19 first meeting Samuel and Saul
1 Samuel 9:1-10:8 Saul anointed secretly to be king
1 Samuel 10:1, 15 Saul anointed to be king
1 Samuel 10:19-21 tribe of Benjamin chosen by drawing of lots
1 Samuel 10:2, 10:3-4, 10:5-6, 10:9 Samuel gave Saul three signs, all happened in one day
1 Samuel 9: 3, 10:7, 10:8 Samuel told Saul when they would meet again
1 Samuel 10:9, 10:10-13 God's Spirit over Saul, he becomes another man
1 Samuel 10:5-6, 10-13 Saul first time among the prophets
1 Samuel 19:19-24 later on Saul second time among the prophets
1 Samuel 9:1-10:27, 10 :20-21 Saul made king
1 Samuel 10:25 Samuel spoke of and wrote down the law for the kingship
1 Samuel 10:24, 11:15 people's gathering Saul king
1 Samuel 10:26 brave men went with Saul
1 Samuel 11, 11:14-15 Saul's first battle victory, Saul's kingship renewed
1 Samuel 14:47-48, 52, Saul, king for forty years, saved Israel from its enemies
1 Samuel 13:1 Saul only two years God's backing
1 Samuel 12:1-25 Samuel spoke, speech to the Israelites
1 Samuel 13:1-22 Saul's battle, in conflict with Samuel
1 Samuel 13:23-14:46 Saul's Jonathan, he fights the Philistines
1 Samuel 14:47-52, 2 Samuel 4:1-4, 21:8a Saul's kingship, family, one wife, one concubine
1 Samuel 14:52 Saul enlists brave men to the army
1 Samuel 15:1-35, 15:28 Saul's disobedience, lost kingship over Israel
1 Samuel 16:1-17 David anointed to be king
1 Samuel 16:14-23, 1 Samuel 18:10 evil spirit influences Saul, David at Saul's court
1 Samuel 16:21-22, 17:15 David at Saul's court, went back and forth to his father, father's flock of sheep
1 Samuel 17:11 Saul and all Israelites afraid of Goliath
1 Samuel 17 David fought Goliath
1 Samuel 17:44, 1 Samuel 21:10 Goliath's sword
1 Samuel 18:2 David Saul's servant and not allowed to return home to his father

Intermezzo Endnotes

*[1] 1 Samuel 25:28, *[2] 1 Samuel 17:47
1 Samuel 16:14-21 David at Saul's court
1 Samuel 16:6-11, 18, 17:12-15, 17:58, 22:1 David's family, David's looks
1 Samuel 22:3-4 David's parents
2 Samuel 2:2 David took his wives with him to Hebron
2 Samuel 3:2-5 David's wives and sons
1 Chronicles 3:1-9 David's household
1 Samuel 18:17-29, 2 Samuel 3:13-15, 2 Samuel 6:23 David's first wife Michal, did not have children
2 Samuel 5:13-16, 13:1-2, 1 Chronicles 14:4 David's other sons, daughters, and his daughter Tamar
1 Chronicles 3:9 Tamar
1 Kings 2:10-12 David king 40 years, followed by Solomon
2 Samuel 5:4-5 David 30 years old, king 7 1/2 years Judah, 33 years Israel, total 40 years king
1 Samuel 14:49-51, 2 Samuel 3:8 Saul's family, Saul had brothers, Saul reigned forty years
1 Samuel 14:50 Saul's wife Ahinoam daughter of Ahimaaz
2 Samuel 3:7 Saul's concubine Rizpah
1 Chronicles 8: 1,33, 1 Chronicles 9:35,39 Saul's genealogy
1 Samuel 8:1-3,8, 1 Chronicles 8:33 four sons, Ishbaal or Ishboshet,
1 Chronicles 8:33 Merribaal or Mephiboshet Saul's son or grandson? Son of Jonathan?
1 Chronicles 8:33 Saul and his four sons
1 Chronicles 8:34-40 Saul's son Jonathan and his descendants
1 Samuel 9:1-2 Saul's father Kish
1 Samuel 17:55, 2 Samuel 2:8-10a Abner made Ishboshet king, ruled 2 years
2 Samuel 4:2, 5-7 Ishboshet murdered
2 Samuel 21:1-14 Saul's family killed
1 Samuel 18:19, 2 Samuel 6:23 Merab married to Adriel, Michal didn't have children
2 Samuel 9:1-13, 9:6, 19:25-31 Jonathan's descendants, one of his sons Mephiboshet
2 Samuel 4:4, 9:3,13 Mephiboshet was crippled, both feet
2 Samuel 9:12, 1 Chronicles 8:34-40 Mephiboshet's son Micah
1 Kings 11:3 Solomon's wives and concubines
1 Kings 11:41-43 Solomon king 40 years
1 Kings 14:21 Solomon's son Rehoboam, king 17 years of Judah and Benjamin
1 Kings 14:19-20 Jeroboam, king 22 years of ten-tribe Israel
1 Chronicles 3:10-24 Solomon's descendants

DAVID'S ANOINTER

And shall have appointed you <u>prince over Israel</u>
1 Samuel 25:30

One day, God spoke to Samuel telling him that he had to go to Bethlehem to see a man called Jesse. Because He had found a king for Himself among his sons. The Lord told him to take the horn of olive oil with him. But Samuel was in fear of his life, and he asked God how he could possibly do what He requested. He had just given bad news to King Saul about God's decision concerning his kingship. After that conversation with Saul, Samuel would never again speak to him. Now Samuel expected that Saul would kill him, if he knew about what he was going to do. Saul being the king, he was the one with the highest authority in the Land of Israel. Even more, what would Saul do to the son of Jesse that Samuel was about to anoint? So, the Lord God Himself devised a plan for Samuel to save both his life and that of Jesse's son. He told him to take a heifer, a type of calf, with him to Bethlehem where Jesse lived. He had to tell the people of the town that he was there to bring an offering to the Lord, and he had to invite Jesse and his sons to come to the feast. Then, the Lord Himself would tell him what to do, and whom he had to anoint for Him. Samuel did as the Lord had told him to do.

Why did the Lord ask this man, Samuel, to go out and anoint someone to be king of Israel? At the time, Samuel was the seer and prophet of the Children of Israel. He was also the leader of the Israelites before Saul became king. Samuel's parents were Elkanah and Hannah. He was an Ephraimite who lived in Ramah, in the territory of the tribe of Ephraim. Both Hannah and Peninnah were Elkanah's wives. Peninnah had children, while Hannah was childless. Not having children brought deep sadness to Hannah's soul. Elkanah always brought offerings and sacrifice at the House of the Lord in Shiloh where the Ark of the Covenant was. Elkanah would always take his family with him when he went up to the House of the Lord. Each time at the meal, he would give a portion of meat to Peninnah and to each of her children. And, because he loved Hannah very much, he always gave a nice double portion to her for herself. On these occasions Hannah was very sad. Her husband once said to her, ... 'Hannah, why do you weep? And why don't you eat? And why is your *heart grieved? Am I not better to you than ten sons'?**¹ This wasn't the only reason for Hannah's sadness. Peninnah humiliated Hannah, because she didn't have children, each time they went up to the House of the Lord. She was always trying to provoke Hannah. This made the festive meal year after year, instead of a joyous moment, a deeply painful one for Hannah. So much so, that Hannah was so upset that she sometimes cried and refused to eat. But, despite all this, Hannah went each time with her husband, the whole family, to Shiloh.

On one occasion, after they had finished their meal, Hannah was very upset. She left the table and went to the Lord's Sanctuary. There she stood and prayed a long time to the Lord, while crying continuously, asking Him to give her a son. She solemnly promised the Lord that she would dedicate her son to Him and his hair would never be cut. Meanwhile, someone was observing her, but could not hear her supplications. Because she prayed by her heart pouring her soul out to the Lord God, while only her lips moved. Hannah didn't notice the man sitting on a chair near the door of the Lord's Sanctuary. He watched her lips move, but couldn't hear anything she said, so he thought she was drunk. He spoke to her, telling her that she was drunk. Hannah replied that she had not drunk wine nor strong drink, but that she was praying to the Lord, because she was deeply sad and angry. Then Eli said to her, '*Go in peace, and the God of Israel grant your petition that you have asked of Him*'.*²

Eli was the High Priest, the Kohen Gadol, and his sons Hophni and Phinehas served there as priests. Hannah was no longer sad or angry, and she said to him, '*Let your servant find favour in your sight*'.*³ Afterwards, she left and went to eat some food. The next day, Elkanah and his household got up early in the morning. They worshipped the Lord and then they returned home to Ramah.

Just as God once blessed Sarah whose seed, her child Isaac, He had specifically chosen for Abraham's inheritance, blessed Rebecca whose husband asked Him to bless her with children, and Rachel who was blessed on her own request, God would bless Hannah also on her own request. Some days later, Hannah became pregnant and months later she gave birth to a son, whom she called Samuel. She gave him this name, as she said, '*because I have asked him of HaShem*'.*⁴ When it was time for Elkanah to go to Shiloh to bring offerings to the Lord, as always he took his household with him. But this time, for the first time, Hannah didn't go with him. She told her husband that as long as she nurses their child, she would not go. But, as soon as she had weaned him they would go with him and bring Samuel to the High

Priest Eli so Samuel would remain at the House of the Lord to serve Him. Her husband agreed with her, told her to do what she thought was best, and that may God fulfil His promise.

Sometime later on, Hannah had weaned Samuel, and when her husband went to Shiloh, she and their young son Samuel also went with him. Elkanah also took flour, wine and three bulls with him to bring as offerings and sacrifice at the place of worship in Shiloh. Once there, they brought the offerings. Afterwards, Hannah approached Eli, asking him whether he remembered her and told him about the last time she was there. She showed him Samuel and told him she had promised the Lord she would bring him there to serve the Lord for the rest of his life at the House of the Lord. She dedicated him to the Lord, and Samuel knelt for the Lord at His Sanctuary. This time Hannah's heart was full of joy and praise as she prayed a prophetic prayer to the Lord saying, *'My heart exults in HaShem, my horn is exalted in HaShem; my mouth is enlarged over my enemies; because I rejoice in Your salvation. There is none holy as HaShem, for there is none beside You; neither is there any rock like our God ... for <u>HaShem is a God of knowledge</u>, and <u>by Him actions are weighed</u>. He will keep the feet of His holy ones, but the wicked shall be put to silence in darkness; for <u>not by strength shall man prevail</u>. They that strive with HaShem shall be broken to pieces; against them will He thunder in heaven; HaShem will judge the ends of the earth; and <u>He will give strength unto His king</u>, and <u>exalt the horn of His anointed'</u>.**5

Was part of Hannah's prayer a prophecy referring to future things to come. For at that time, Israel did not have a king yet, like the surrounding people did. The Lord God Himself was the king of the Israelites. But the king of his choosing, He would bless, support and give His strength. After the family worshipped there, they returned home.

This wasn't the last time Hannah and her husband saw Samuel. Each year Hannah made a nice robe for Samuel, that she took with her when Elkanah took his family to Shiloh to bring offerings and to worship the Lord. Each time they met Samuel who lived there and served the Lord, the High Priest Eli blessed Elkanah and Hannah, saying, *'HaShem gives you <u>seed of this woman</u> for the loan which was lent to HaShem'*.*6

The Lord remembered Hannah and He blessed her. She and her husband had five more children, three sons and two daughters.

Samuel grew up while serving the Lord under Eli's supervision. This was a time when the word of the Lord and visions from Him were very scarce. Eli was an old man now and nearly blind. He slept in a separate room, while Samuel slept in the Sanctuary, which was the room where the Ark of the Covenant stood. One day, before the lamp of the Lord went out, Samuel was sleeping in the Sanctuary. Suddenly he stood up and ran to Eli, and said to him that he called him. But Eli told him he did not call him, and sent him back to lie down. This happened three times. The third time Eli understood what was going on. It was not Eli that called Samuel. It was the Lord. But Samuel didn't realise this because the Lord had never spoken to him before that day. So Eli told Samuel when he came to him for the third time, that he should go back and lie down. He also told him that if he was called again, he should answer.*7

The Lord God appeared to Samuel in a vision and called him for the fourth time by his name. Samuel answered as Eli told him to, and the Lord spoke to him about future things to come concerning Eli and his sons. It wasn't good news for Eli and his household. Next morning Samuel got up, and opened the doors to the sanctuary. He remembered all that happened the day before, including the message that the Lord gave him in the vision. He was afraid to tell Eli the message which concerned his whole household and his descendants for years to come. But Eli told Samuel to tell him what the Lord had told him. He insisted that Samuel would tell him everything, and Samuel did.

> *And you shall <u>not</u> profane My holy name – If one man sins against another, God shall judge him; but if a man sins against HaShem, who shall plead for him?*
> Leviticus 22:32a-1 Samuel 2:25

All that the Lord told Samuel about Eli and his family came to pass. What did He tell Samuel? What the Lord told him was a confirmation of what He had already spoken by a prophet who visited Eli sometime before. Eli was already old when this prophet spoke to him about him and his family's future. He told Eli he honoured his sons more than God. The Lord Himself would choose to honour those who honour Him, and He would treat those who treat Him with contempt in such a manner. He would not allow the young men in Eli's family and clan to live long lives and grow old. They would not share in the Lord's blessings given to the people of Israel. All his other descendants would die in a violent way. He would choose someone else for His priestly service. Whoever of Eli's family that would survive what was about to happen to them, would have to go to that priest, and depend on him for some money and food. Samuel told Eli that the Lord would carry out all He had said that He would do against him and his family, as He already had told him before. He also said that Eli knew about the sins of his sons but he did not stop them. No offering or sacrifice would be able to undo the consequences of their sins.

Why did the Lord God punish Eli and his descendants so severely? Eli's sons did not serve the Lord in accordance to all the laws and regulations given to them by Moses. They were lawless in their service at the Lord's Sanctuary in Shiloh. They demanded from the people larger portions of the offerings and sacrifices that were not meant for them. They didn't keep to the appropriation given to them by the Torah. If people refused these priests, they would use intimidation or appropriated the portions by force. They would also do this, before the meat was ready. They were even sleeping with the women that did some work at the entrance of the Tent of the Lord. Their sinful behaviour was known to all. Though Eli said to his sons that they should not sin against the Lord, for who would plead for them when they did? Eli himself, who was High Priest for forty years, didn't listen to the wise words he spoke to his sons. He didn't stop them. Thus, he was also part of their sinful way of life.

All the prophecies concerning Eli and his descendants would happen. Eli's sons, the priests Hophni and Phinehas, were killed, with thirty thousand Israelite soldiers, by the Philistines. They would also capture the Ark of the Covenant that the priests took with them to the military camp. When the ninety-eight-year-old Eli, now heavy and almost blind, sitting on his seat at his usual place near the gate, heard the news of his sons' death and that the Ark of God had been stolen, he fell backwards and broke his neck. Years later at the time of King Saul's descendants of Eli, including the High Priest Ahimelech with his relative, were killed. Eighty-five priests would die by the sword on one day. Ahimelech's relatives also served in Nob. A killing also took place at the Kohanim's priestly city of Nob. Men, women, children, even sucklings, and the cattle were all killed. Ahimelech's son Abiathar would survive the killing, and serve David for years. But, he didn't show the same loyalty he had for King David to King Solomon. So, Solomon would dismiss him from the priestly service, though he remained a priest. He would have to depend on the High Priest that Solomon had chosen, Zadok, for food and money.

As for Samuel, the Lord continued to give revelations to Samuel at His Sanctuary in Shiloh. The Lord was with Samuel, and He insured that all He told him came true. All the people in Israel knew that

Samuel was the Lord's prophet. When he spoke everyone listened. Samuel grew up to became a leader to the Israelites, the last Judge of Israel, at a time when there were no kings in the Land of Israel and everyone did as they pleased.

> *And Samuel grew, and HaShem was with him, and did let none of his words fall to the ground. And all Israel ... knew that Samuel was established to be a prophet of HaShem. ... for HaShem revealed Himself to Samuel in Shiloh by the word of HaShem.*
>
> 1 Samuel 3:19-21

Intermezzo

Prophets

> *"Speak with us, and we will hear; but let not God speak with us, lest we die."*
>
> Exodus 20:15-18

Who said these words? To whom? The Lord brought the Israelites under the leadership of the brothers Moses and Aaron, and their sister Miriam out of Egypt. '*For I brought you up out of the land of Egypt, and redeemed you out of the house of bondage, and I sent before you Moses, Aaron, and Miriam*'.*[1] He took the Israelites out of Egypt, for them to be a kingdom of priests to Him. As the Lord said, '*And I gave them My statutes, and taught them My ordinances, which if a man do, he shall live by them. Moreover, also I gave them My Sabbaths, to be a sign between Me and them, that they might know that I am HaShem that sanctifies them*'.*[2] The Eternal God Himself created, formed Israel, as He said, '*Remember these things, O Jacob, and Israel, for you are My servant; I have formed you, you are My own servant; O Israel, you should not forget Me. I have blotted out, as a thick cloud, your transgressions, and, as a cloud, your sins; return to Me, for I have redeemed you*'.*[3] He brought their descendants to Canaan, for them to establish the future Kingdom of Israel, and the Lord God Himself was to be their King.

> *For HaShem will not forsake His people for His great name's sake; because it has pleased HaShem to make you a people unto Himself.*
>
> 1 Samuel 12:22

One day, on their way to Canaan, the Lord gave instructions to Moses to gather the people at Mount Sinai, but they were not to approach nor touch the foot of the mountain on penalty of death. Moses was to set barriers so they would know where to stand, and to prevent them from approaching. But, they were allowed to approach when they hear the long sound of the horn. The Israelites had two days to prepare themselves for this meeting. As the Lord instructed Moses, saying, *'Go to the people, and sanctify them today and tomorrow, and let them wash their garments, and be ready against the third day; for the third day HaShem will come down in the sight of all the people upon Mount Sinai'*.*4

God appeared on Mount Sinai. There was loud thunder, lightning and smoke. At a certain moment they also heard the long tone of the horn. That's when they were allowed to approach. They trembled with fear and didn't dare to go further near the mountain, despite Moses' reassuring words. Instead they told Moses to approach and speak with God on their behalf, and whatever he would tell them, they would do. So, it was the gathering of the Israelites at Mount Sinai who spoke these words to Moses. Thus, the Israelites themselves asked for a prophet who would listen to God's words, who was actually their King, and convey His message to them. Moses went up, as the Lord had instructed him.

> *As for God, His way is perfect; <u>the Word of HaShem is tried</u> (proven/tested); So shall My Word be that goes forth out of My mouth: it shall not return unto Me void, except <u>it will accomplish that which I please</u>, and <u>make the thing where to I sent it prosper</u>.*
>
> Psalm 18:31 / Isaiah 55:11

Ever since the Lord had given the Children of Israel prophets and seers, both men and women, to whom He would speak giving them His Word, to guide them. But, Moses wasn't the very first prophet. Their Patriarch Abraham was also a prophet, as the Lord Himself told Abimelech, the king that took Sarah at his court, when He told him to give Sarah back to Abraham. As He said, *'Now therefore restore the man's wife; for <u>he is a prophet</u>, and he shall pray for you, and you shall live'*.*5

The Lord God would give the Israelites prophets from among themselves. They said, *'Let me not hear again the voice of HaShem my God, neither let me see this great fire anymore, that I die not'*.*6

The Lord answered to Moses ... 'They have said that which they have spoken. I will raise them up a prophet from among their brethren, like to you; and I will put My words in his mouth, and he shall speak to them all that I shall command him'.[7]

The Lord also told Moses that the prophet would speak His words in His name to the Israelites, and that they should listen to the prophet. The proof that this person was a genuine prophet would be that all he said would come true. It is the Lord God Himself who established a true prophet. Like he did, for instance, with Samuel. But, He also gave a warning regarding false prophets ... *'But the prophet that shall speak a word presumptuously in assuming My name, which I have not commanded him to speak, or that shall speak in the name of other gods, that same prophet shall die'.*[8]

Prophets were also called seers. *Before time in Israel, when a man went to inquire of God, thus he said: 'Come and let us go to the seer', for he that is now called a prophet was before time called a seer.*[9] Samuel and Gad, for instance, were also called seers.

The Word of HaShem came unto Jeremiah ... saying: Call unto Me, and I will answer you, and (I) will tell you great things, and hidden, which you know not.

Jeremiah 33:1-3

The Lord God gives revelations by prophets, through the words He spoke to them. But also, by His written Word, visions and dreams, the Urim as well as with the Tummim which the High Priest used while consulting God. God Himself gives His prophets and seers an insight into His future plans and actions. Sometimes also concerning the history of mankind that is far beyond what people can see or comprehend at the time of the revelations.

For instance, He gave to the prophets Moses and Samuel His words, when He spoke to them. Visions and dreams with the understanding of these, He once gave to Joseph and Daniel. The Lord also sent His faithful angels to His servants. An example of this is the angel Gabriel that went out to Daniel and spoke to him regarding future historic events for Israel and the nations in the region. Revelations that predicted the rise and fall of the Greek and the Roman Empires years later.

The Lord God sometimes chooses people to be prophets for a specific purpose. As He did with Jacob's son Joseph. But also with Moses, Miriam, Deborah, Samuel, Elijah, Elisha, Jeremiah son of

Who Is David?

a priest, the priest Ezekiel, Daniel, Hosea and others. There is also someone who on the Lord's request, volunteered to be a prophet. The prophet Isaiah. Sometimes God gives prophetic words to people whom during their life, until then, weren't seen as being prophets. He could give revelations to a king himself. As he did to David, making him a prophet who spoke of the insight the Lord gave him regarding the future of his descendants regarding his throne, and the Israelites. The Lord Himself establishes His prophets. As He said by Isaiah, *'That confirms the word of His servant, and performs the counsel of His messengers'*.*[10]

Sometimes prophets take up the role of mediator. Prophets then mediated between God and the Israelites. Moses did this during the Israelites' journey through the desert. Others who also played a role as mediator, but aren't considered as prophets, were Noah and Enoch. With Noah and his family, the Lord saved humankind through the flood. Enoch received a somewhat different task. He stood between the Lord God and the angels that fell from grace because of their sinful acts regarding humankind and their own personal choice to abandon the abode given to them by the Lord God.

Through the life of the Lord's servants, including that of prophets one can see that they lived, and lived close to Him. The Lord gave and gives them revelations also for their personal life. They are attuned to Him for their daily life and for whichever task He gives them. Their closeness to God makes it possible for Him to reach them. Therefore, they had to live holy lives, as the Lord stipulated. Whatever happened, they remained faithful and loyal to the Lord. As for instance Daniel did when he refused to forsake the Lord God at the time the king, Darius, issued a law of Medes and Persians – a law that was not to be changed – regarding to whom should anything be requested but to the king. Despite being thrown in a lions pit by Darius, for his requests, prayers, to the Lord, he remained faithful to God. His written Word available to them in their time, and as nowadays can be read in scripture, had always been a lamp to them on their pad in life. As is written, *'Your word is a lamp to my feet, and a light to my path'*.*[11] At the same time while being in this relationship with Him, prophets express and speak of God's wishes, will, love, righteousness, holiness and also His might through miracles. Sometimes miracles that were apparent even after their death. As happened to Elisha, whose buried body brought a dead person to life.

> *I have also spoken unto the prophets, and I have multiplied visions; and have used comparisons by means of the prophets.*
> Hosea 12:11

Those who serve the Lord as prophets weren't only men, but also women. For instance Sarah, Miriam, Deborah, Hannah, Abigail, Huldah, Esther. Sarah foresaw and told her husband Abraham, that his other sons wouldn't inherit with their son Isaac. The Lord told Abraham that his wife was right and that he should listen to her. Deborah was a prophet and Judge. She prophesied to Barak about the victory that the Lord was about to give the Israelites over their enemy. Abigail prophesied to David about what God had in store for his future. The prophet Huldah, who lived at the time of King Josiah, who became king of Judah when he was eight years old, prophesied about things to come for him and the nation. The Book of Law was found in the Temple of the Lord during Josiah's 18th year of reign. After he read the book, he was very sad and tore his robes. He realised that they were not living completely in accordance to God's Law, which would lead to punishment. He sent the Kohen Gadol, High Priest, Hilkiah with his other officials to the prophet Huldah, who was married to Shallum the son of Tikvah, to inquire of the Lord for him and Judah's people about this matter. Huldah's answer? That the people of Judah would be severely punished. But because of his reaction, an act of guilt and repentance, the punishment would happen after his death, so he wouldn't have to see it. Josiah, who reigned thirty-one years, issued many reforms in accordance to God's Law through the nation of Judah. What she said came to pass.

> *And it shall come to pass, that him that escapes from the sword ... shall Elisha slay.*
> 1 Kings 19:17

Sometimes the Lord gives prophets the power over life and death, to protect the Children of Israel and their nation. Once King Saul allowed an enemy king, Agag of the Amalekites whom he had captured after a battle, to live. In doing so he disobeyed the Lord's instructions. Samuel did follow God's instructions. He killed the Amalekite king by the sword. But, being allowed to remove Israel's enemies in such a way, didn't mean that this was to be done at all times. At one time, the entire enemy army went out to find and kill Elisha. He is the only prophet mentioned in scripture that was anointed by another prophet, Elijah, to be his successor as a prophet. Once gathered together at a town, and in front of Elisha, the army didn't recognise him. He gave instructions to the Israelites to feed these men and to let them go, instead of fighting them.

> *Thus says HaShem concerning the <u>prophets that make my people to err (stray away)</u>; ... Therefore it shall be night to you, that you shall have no vision; and it shall be dark to you, that you shall not divine; and the sun shall go down upon the prophets, and the day shall be black over them. And the seers shall be put to shame, and the diviners confounded; ... for <u>there shall be no answer of God</u>.*
>
> Micah 3:5-7

If prophets would live a sinful life, God would rebuke the prophets for this. Israel's leaders and priests should also live by God's Law. In case they would refuse to change their ways, He would be silent to them. Therefore, true prophets of the Lord, live holy lives to serve Him. As those who truly serve the Lord show through their life. Prophets have a household, like Isaiah did. Others with a group of prophets, as for example Elisha lived. While some were like Elijah, who lived his life mostly by himself. Some also have a servant to assist them. Jeremiah had Baruch the son of Neriah.

All God's servants are bound to truthfulness, including His prophets. They should live by the Lord's commandments, and they should seek God's truth at all times. To live by it, speak of it and teach it.

> *Guide me in Your truth and teach me; for You are the God of my salvation; for You do I wait all the day. – And take not the word of truth utterly out of my mouth; for I hope in Your ordinances;*
>
> *HaShem is near to all them that call upon Him, to all that call upon Him in truth.*
>
> Psalm 25:5 / Psalm 119:43 /Psalm 145:18

Something prophets of God would also never do, is to take bribes, payment for prophecies or miracles done by the Lord God. This act would eventually lead to His silence. The Lord Himself doesn't take bribes, He doesn't show partiality. He asks this from His servants, as Moses once said to the Israelites 'And you shall take no gift; for a gift blinds them that have sight, and perverts the words of the righteous'.*[12]

Taking bribes pervert justice, brings ruin to people's households and causes social, political and economic instability within a nation. Moses, Samuel, Elisha, Daniel, and others, are all examples of those who didn't accept payment or gifts from the Israelites or anyone else. Moses and Samuel, not from the Israelites. Elisha not from Naam that was cured from a skin illness, and Daniel not from Belshazzar who succeeded his father Nebuchadnezzar as king. Balaam was someone who initially wanted to accept payment from Balak, the king of Moab. But, the Lord prevented this, and gave him blessings for the Israelites instead of the curse that Balak wanted. But, in the case that prophets, and others, do accept bribes, it's written "*The heads (leaders) thereof judge for reward, and the priests thereof teach for hire, and the prophets thereof divine for money; yet will they lean upon HaShem, and say: 'Is not HaShem in the midst of us? No evil shall come upon us? Therefore shall Zion for your sake be plowed as a field, and Jerusalem shall become heaps, and the mountain of the house as the high places of a forest'.*"*[13]

Those who do these acts are not serving God, but their own ambitions.

> *The prophets prophesy lies in My name; I did not send them, neither have I commanded them, neither have I spoken to them; they prophesy to you a lying vision, and divination, and a thing of nothing, and the deceit of their own heart.*
>
> Jeremiah 14:14-16

Those who earn their living by telling lies and taking bribes for prophesies, are not God's servants.

False prophets, those that the Lord certainly didn't send in His name, these people sadly do much harm when people take them, and not God's warnings, seriously. These people rather hold on to their own belief system for as long as it works for them to achieve their personal goals. Either financially or otherwise, to fulfil their ambitions regardless of the consequences. They *'love evil more than good; falsehood rather than speaking righteousness'.*[14]

As far as the Lord God is concerned, regarding these people, He *'frustrates the tokens of the impostors, and makes diviners mad; that turns wise men backward, and makes their knowledge foolish'.*[15]

The Lord rewards those prophets who remain faithful to Him.

> *He that walks righteously and speaks uprightly; he that despises the gain of oppressions, that shakes his hands from*

> *holding of bribes, that stops his ears from hearing of blood, and shuts his eyes from looking upon evil; He shall dwell on high; his place of defence shall be the munitions of rocks; his bread shall be given, his waters shall be sure. Their eyes shall see the king in his beauty; they shall behold a land stretching afar.*
>
> Isaiah 33:15-17

At the time of the prophet Jeremiah, the false prophet Hananiah was spreading false hope to the people of Israel, by having them believe that everything was going to be all right. While Jeremiah was prophesying about the disaster that was about to come over Jerusalem and Judah. All the people that had chosen to believe the lies and had reassured themselves of peaceful times, didn't have the chance to prepare themselves for what was really going to happen. They held on to their way of life and all they possessed, instead of leaving everything behind and flee to safety when they still had time. The false prophets themselves, having all they gained through their falsehood, they all perished. Later on, after seventy years of the Babylonian exile, when a group of Jews returned to Jerusalem and Judah under Nehemiah's leadership, the false prophet Noadiah tried to intimidate Nehemiah. She and a group of false prophets wanted to prevent Nehemiah and those with him from rebuilding the walls of Jerusalem. Walls that were needed to protect the inhabitants of the city.

> *For the Lord God will do nothing, but He reveals His counsel unto His servants the prophets. The lion has roared, who will not fear? The <u>Lord God has spoken</u>, <u>who can but prophesy</u>?*
>
> Amos 3:7-8

Prophets were to give God's message, including His warnings, regardless of whether the Israelites would want to listen. Often in fear for their own life they had to do as the Lord commanded. Samuel feared King Saul when the Lord gave him the task of anointing David to be king of Israel. Still he did as the Lord asked him to. For instance, Elijah fled to the wilderness where he went into hiding for King Ahab and his wife Jezebel, who wanted him dead. Still, when the Lord told him to leave the wilderness so he could perform a task that He had for him, he did this despite the risks. Jeremiah was incarcerated and thrown into a pit because he warned about war, famine and Judah's coming exile. Though the Lord did give His protection to Elijah and

Jeremiah. A prophet couldn't allow himself to be guided by fear. Prophets remain faithful to the Lord despite persecution.

Israelite kings sometimes chose to ignore the prophets, and sometimes even murdered them. Like when Ahab king of the Northern Kingdom of Israel, ignored the warnings given to him and King Jehoshaphat of Judah, concerning the war against the Syrians. Ahab was the king that together with his wife Jezebel had God's prophets murdered and wanted also Elijah dead. King Zedekiah of Judah ignored Jeremiah, when he spoke about the period of war and exile that was about to come for Jerusalem and Judah.

> *A prophet will HaShem your God raise up unto you, from your midst, of your brethren, like me; to him you shall listen.*
> Deuteronomy 18:15

Shouldn't people listen to and believe everything spoken by God's servants the prophets?! The Lord's prophets are not entertainers for hire. They and the prophecies they spoke of are to be taken seriously. To be able to know and understand the course of humankind's past history and future. If not, faithfulness dies. The Lord God Himself is the origin of true prophecy, so one should pay attention at all times. For God-given prophecy is like the bright light of a lamp shining in a dark place, guiding the way in life. To reconnect with prophecies of the past, also shows the way, the right direction to go today, to live a purposeful, meaningful life close to God the Father.

> *Have faith in the Lord your God and you will be upheld; have faith in his prophets and you will be successful.*
> 2 Chronicles 20:20

A New King

> *Behold, to obey is better than sacrifice, and to listen than the fat of rams. For rebellion is as the sin of witchcraft, and stubbornness is as idolatry and teraphim.*
> 1 Samuel 15:22-23

When the time came that the nation of Israel wanted a king and asked Samuel for one, he followed God's instructions and anointed Saul to be king of Israel. After some time, the Lord wanted Samuel to anoint someone else to be king of the nation of Israel. Why did the Lord want Samuel to anoint someone else to be king? Wasn't Saul

Who Is David?

already king of Israel? Even more, King Saul had sons, his eldest Jonathan, who could succeed him on his throne. Yet, the Lord did not give the throne of Israel to the House of Saul. He preferred someone else to be Israel's king. Because King Saul made two sinful mistakes, by which he showed his disobedience and lack of faith towards God. On two occasions Saul did not carry out His orders regarding battles that he and his army had to fight to keep the Children of Israel secure within Israel.

> *You have anointed my head with oil.*
> Psalm 23

> *The Spirit of HaShem came mightily upon David from that day forward.*
> 1 Samuel 16:13

Samuel arrived in the town of Bethlehem. The elders hurried to meet the seer who came unexpectedly to their town. They were a bit nervous about his visit. One of them asked Samuel whether he came in peace. Samuel told them that he came in peace to bring an offering to the Lord. He invited them and Jesse with his sons to the feast. He told them to prepare themselves. Jesse arrived at the feast, with his sons. As soon as Samuel saw Jesse's eldest son Eliab, he thought that he must be the anointed one in God's eyes. But, this was not the case. The Lord told Samuel, *'Look not on his appearance or on the height of his stature; because I have rejected him; for it is not as man sees: for man looks on the outward appearance, but <u>HaShem looks on the heart</u>'.*[8]

Jesse called his sons one by one to meet with Samuel. After Eliab, he called Abinadab, then Shammah, until all his seven sons were brought to Samuel. But, each time, the Lord told Samuel that He hadn't chosen one of them. Samuel told this to Jesse, and asked him whether he had more sons. He replied he had just one more, the youngest who was tending the sheep. Samuel told him to send for him, because they would not sit at the feast table to eat before he came. Jesse sent someone to fetch him. David came ... *he was ruddy, and withal of beautiful eyes, and goodly to look upon.* And the Lord said to Samuel, *'Arise, anoint him; for this is he (him)'.* *[9] Then Samuel anointed David, there among his brothers, with the olive oil in the horn that he brought with him. As soon as David was anointed, the Spirit of God came over him. Then Samuel left and returned to Ramah.

> *<u>HaShem is my strength</u> and <u>my shield</u>, in Him has my heart*

trusted, and I am helped; therefore my heart greatly rejoices, and with my song will I praise Him. HaShem is a strength to them; and He is a stronghold of salvation to His anointed.
Psalm 28:7-8

David, the youngest son of Jesse, was a shepherd who took care of his father's flock of sheep at the time he was anointed to be king. He was the one responsible to take them to places of good pasture, and water so they would have enough to eat and drink. He had to count them each day at night when he gathered them, to make sure none of the sheep were lost, either by an attack of a wild animal, or losing its way. He had to protect them, and his only means to do that was a staff and a sling. Whenever a wild animal grabbed a lamb and carried it off, David would go after it and attack it, to save the lamb and bring it back to the flock. If a lion or bear were to attack him, he would strike it down, grab it by its throat and beat it to death. To David, it's the Lord that saves him from these animals. To him, the Lord God Himself is his shield, his means of protection. So, by his faith in God and his courage, he cared for and protected his father's sheep. Wouldn't he do the same for the kingdom over which he would rule for his God? Hence, David was the man destined to always fight the Lord's battles, as the prophet Abigail would tell him one day. While out in the field with the flock David spent plenty of time by himself while working as a shepherd. This also gave him more than enough time to write poems, songs and to play music. Though David had plenty of inspiration for his artistic work, while walking those valleys and hills in the wilderness of Judah with his father's sheep, he never lost sight of the flock which was his responsibility to protect. It's David's talent as a musician, that would one day bring him to King Saul's court.

And David came to Saul, and stood before him; and he loved him greatly; and he became his armour-bearer.
1 Samuel 16:21

After David was anointed to be king of the Children of Israel, the Spirit of God departed from King Saul. He became tormented by an evil spirit of melancholy. He was very sad, sombre and at times aggressive. Saul's servants who were with him, saw his sadness. They told him that a spirit from God was tormenting him. But, that it would go away if someone would play the harp for him. They asked him to let them search for a man that can play the harp well to come to his court and play for him so he would be all right. Saul agreed, and told them to go and seek a man that could do just that. One of Saul's young servants spoke of Jesse's son, who was a good musician, brave and handsome. He also said that the Lord was with him. Saul sent a messenger to Bethlehem, to Jesse with a request, saying, *'Send me David your son, who is with the sheep'.*[10]

Jesse immediately prepared gifts for Saul. A jug full of wine, and some bread which he all loaded on one of his donkeys, and a young goat. He then sent David with the gifts to Saul. From the moment that David stood before Saul when they met, Saul liked David. He decided that David should, besides playing the harp for him, become his armour-bearer. Would the latter mean that David would start military training so he could one day become a warrior and enlist in Saul's army? So, Saul sent a new message to Jesse, saying, *'Let David, I pray you, stand before me; for he has found favour in my sight'.*[11]

From then on, David became a musician at Saul's court and his armour-bearer. Whenever the evil spirit saddened Saul, David would come and pickup the harp and play for him so he would find relief and feel better. The evil spirit would depart from him, and he would be all right.

Did Saul know, when he met David the first time, that David was the one Samuel told him about? Before Samuel even knew David, he said to Saul that God had chosen another man to be appointed as king to rule over His people. If Saul did know, he probably would not have allowed him to come to his court. Samuel, who anointed two men, Saul and David, to be God's servants and rule over the Children of Israel, certainly did not tell him. Because after their last conversation they never met each other again.

The Eternal God established the kingship of Israel by the seer and prophet Samuel, initiating a transition from a tribal nation to a state nation. Because of God's friendship with Abraham, his descendants through Isaac and Jacob, became the nation of the Children of Israel by God's grace. And, by His grace, there's a House of David because of David's love for God and his faithfulness to Him. David who loved God and would fight His battles one day, would ascend to be king of the children of Israel one day.

> *HaShem has sought him <u>a man after His own heart</u>, and HaShem has appointed him to be prince over His people.*
> 1 Samuel 13:14

Endnotes

*[1] 1 Samuel 1:8, *[2] 1 Samuel 1:17, *[3] 1 Samuel 1:18, *[4] 1 Samuel 1:20, *[5] 1 Samuel 2:1-10, *[6] 1 Samuel 2:20b, *[7] 1 Samuel 3:10, *[8] 1 Samuel 16:7, *[9] 1 Samuel 16:12, *[10] 1 Samuel 16:19b, *[11] 1 Samuel 17:22b

David's Shield, not the "star of David"!, by Angeline Leito
http://www.thegreenolivetree.nl/index.php/14-articles/king-david/115-king-davids-shield
1 Samuel 1:1-8 Samuel's parents
1 Samuel 1:9-18 Hannah's prayer, meets Eli the High Priest
Genesis 17:16,19 the Lord tells Abraham that he will have a son with Sarah
Genesis 25:21-21 Isaac prayed to the Lord for Rebecca to have children.
Genesis 30:1-2,22-24, 35:18 God answered Rachel's prayers
1 Samuel 1:19-28 Samuel's birth, brought to the Eli
1 Samuel 1:20-21 Samuel's brothers and sisters
1 Samuel 3, Judges 21:25 the Lord calls Samuel, Samuel became a prophet and a Judge
Leviticus 22:32-33 God is holy, don't bring disgrace over His name
1 Samuel 2:12-17, 2:22-26, 3:11-14, 4:1-22 Eli and his sons sinful acts
1 Samuel 2:22a, 3:2 Eli old and almost blind
1 Samuel 2:27-36 a prophet tells Eli a prophecy against him and his descendants
1 Samuel 3:11-14, 4:1-22 God gives Samuel a prophecy against Eli, Samuel told Eli
1 Samuel 14:3,22, 22:20-23 Eli, Eli's sons and his descendants' death, Ahimelech's death
1 Samuel 22:11-19 Ahimelech, descendant of Eli, summoned to the king
1 Samuel 22:18 Ahimelech killed by Doeg before the king on his orders
1 Samuel 22:18-19 eighty-five priests killed
1 Samuel 22:19 priestly families killed in Kohanim's priestly city of Nob
1 Samuel 22:20-23 priest Abiathar, Ahimelech's son, escapes to David
1 Samuel 23:6, 9 Abiathar took the Ephod with him
1 Samuel 1:25-28, Abiathar family of High Priest Eli who brought up Samuel
1 Kings 1:25, 2:26-27, 35, 4:2 Eli's descendant, Abiathar son of Ahimelech lost priestly service
1 Samuel 16:1-13 David anointed king
1 Samuel 16:6-10, 17:28 David's seven brothers, Eliab eldest brother
1 Samuel 16:19-23 David at Saul's court, musician and armour-bearer
1 Samuel 8:1-22 Israelites wanted a king
1 Samuel 20-25 Israelites forgiven for wanting a king other than the Lord God Himself
1 Samuel 13:7-15, 1 Samuel 15:10-31, 34-35 Saul's two mistakes
1 Samuel 9:6 Samuel in high regard with the prophets
1 Samuel 11:7 the Israelites followed King Saul and Samuel to battle

Who Is David?

1 Samuel 8:1-3 Samuel's sons took bribes
1 Samuel 18:11, 19:9-10, 33 Saul throws a spear on two occasions to David, and once to Jonathan
1 Samuel 11:6 Spirit of God over Saul
Judges 3:10, 6:34, 11:29, 13:25 Spirit of God over other Judges
1 Samuel 12:3-4, 1 Samuel 12:22-23 Samuel's character, type of leadership
Deuteronomy 18:15 God's prophet is to be obeyed
Deuteronomy 29:28, Amos 3:7 the Lord tells prophets His plans
1 Chronicles 10:1-13 Saul's unfaithfulness to God and his death
1 Samuel 15:22, Hosea 6:6 trustfulness and love for the Lord
1 Samuel 12:18-22 forgiveness for asking for a king
Jeremiah 33:2-3 the Lord will reveal things you don't know
1 Samuel 3:21 God appeared to Samuel
1 Samuel 12:13-25 Israelites and their king should be obedient to the Eternal God

Intermezzo Endnotes

*[1]Micah 6:4, *[2] Ezekiel 20:11-12, *[3]Isaiah 44:21-22, *[4]Exodus 19:9-13, *[5]Genesis 20:7, *[6]Deuteronomy 18:156b, *[7]Deuteronomy 18:17-18, *[8]Deuteronomy 18:20, *[9]1 Samuel 9:9, *[10] Isaiah 44:26a, *[11]Psalm 119:105, *[12]Exodus 23:8, *[13]Micah 3:9-12, *[14]Psalm 52:2-6, *[15] Isaiah 44:25

Tanach The Stone Edition, Artscroll Series, pg 2038: list of prophets men and women
Isaiah 56:6, 58:13-14, Ezekiel 20:12 Sabbath sign of covenant
Deuteronomy 29:28, 2 Samuel 23:2-3, Amos 3:7-8, Isaiah 42:9, Hosea 12:11, 14 God and prophets
1 Samuel 9:9 seer
Genesis 20:7, 26:24 Abraham a prophet, he always served the Lord
Exodus 15:20, Micah 6:4 Miriam, Aaron's sister a prophet
Judges 4:4 Deborah prophet and Judge
2 Kings 22, 2 Chronicles 34 prophet Huldah and King Josiah
Genesis 21:10-12 Abraham had to listen to Sarah concerning their son Isaac
Genesis 37:1-11 Joseph's own dreams
Exodus 3 God called Moses
2 Kings 13:14, 13:20-21 Elisha ill, died and buried
Isaiah 6 Isaiah volunteered to be a prophet
Jeremiah 1:1-19, 1:18-19 Jeremiah called to be prophet, God's protection
Jeremiah 33:1-3, Lamentations 3:52-63 Jeremiah incarcerated, to a pit
Jeremiah 37, 38 King Zedekiah
Ezekiel 1:26-28-3:21 God calls Ezekiel
The book of Daniel, Isaiah 56:3b-5, Daniel 5:12 Daniel
The Antiquities of the Jews by Flavius Josephus: 10.10.1 pg 333-334, Daniel
Daniel 6 Darius put Daniel in the lions pit

Genesis 5:21-24 and the Book of Enoch, Genesis 6-10 Noah, faithfulness Enoch

Psalm 15:2, God's truth, God the origin of true prophecy

1 Samuel 28:6 the Lord speaks through dreams, Urim and Tummim, prophets

Psalm 52:2-5 evil, lies

Jeremiah 32:12 Baruch, Jeremiah's assistant

Deuteronomy 10:17 God, no bribes, no partiality

Proverbs 15:27, 17:23, 29:4, Micah 7:3 bribes pervert justice, nation's instability, ruins households

Numbers 16:15, 1 Samuel 12:3-4, 2 Kings 5:16, Daniel 5:17 Moses, Samuel, Elisha, Daniel took no bribes, gifts, payments

Jeremiah 23:9-15 prophecy against sinful prophets and priests

1 Samuel 3:19-21, 9:9 Samuel prophet and seer

2 Kings 17:13, Jeremiah 28:8-9, warnings through prophets and seers

Deuteronomy 13:3-5, 18:9-12, Jeremiah 7:29-8:3 no occult practices

2 Chronicles 36:15-16, Jeremiah 8:25-28 faithfulness and people die when they ignore prophets

Nehemiah 6:10-14 false prophets tried to intimidate Nehemiah

2 Samuel 24:11, 1 Chronicles 21:9, 29:29 Gad seer and Nathan prophet

1 Samuel 3:20, 9:13, 18-19 Samuel a prophet and seer

Micah 3 God's rebukes Israel's leaders and prophets because of their sinfulness

1 Samuel 15:32-33 Samuel killed Agag

1 Kings 19:16 Elisha anointed to succeed Elijah

1 Kings 19:17 Elisha allowed to kill Israel's enemies

Micah 2:7d 3:5-7, 3:8 God's prophets

Genesis 14:22-23, 2 Kings 5:15-16, 26-27, Abraham, Elisha, didn't take bribes

1 Kings 22:1-28 Ahab ignored prophet Micaiah

Ezekiel 33:30-33 prophecy not entertainment

Ezekiel 13 and 14 prophecies against false prophets

Jeremiah 28 Jeremiah and the false prophet Hananiah

Nehemiah 6:14 Noadiah, false prophet tried to intimidate Nehemiah

Numbers 22:7, Balaam a false prophet

2 Chronicles 20:20, believe all that the prophets have spoken

DAVID AND JONATHAN
Covenant of Friendship

Though a man may rise up to pursue you, and to seek your soul, yet <u>the soul of my lord shall be bound in the bundle of life with HaShem your God</u>; ...

1 Samuel 25:29a

On that day, when David defeated Goliath, all could see his bravery, as well as his faith and trust in the Almighty God. The Eternal God, Who chose the descendants of Abraham, Isaac and Jacob to be His people. His children gave him victory over the Philistines. King Saul decided that same day, that David would remain for good in his service. So David wasn't allowed to return home to his father's household. He was to join King Saul's army.

After Saul's conversation with David, Jonathan met with him. Jonathan was the king's eldest son, the first in line to his throne. Was this the first time that Jonathan met David? When David spoke with Saul about fighting Goliath, Saul's sons weren't mentioned as taking part in that conversation. So it's possible this is the first time Jonathan met David.

What happened during this first conversation between Jonathan and David and what did they actually speak about? *'And it came to pass ... that the soul of Jonathan was knit with the soul of David, and Jonathan loved him as his own soul'.*[1] And *'then <u>Jonathan made a covenant with David</u> because <u>he loved him as his own soul</u>'.*[2]

And as a token of his friendship with David *'Jonathan stripped himself of the robe that was upon him and gave it to David, and his apparel, even to his sword, and to his bow, and to his girdle'.*[3]

Jonathan, being a warrior himself, and also a man of faith, must have seen David as a person that would become a great soldier one day. Surely he wanted to have him as his closest friend. But, did Jonathan know he made a covenant of friendship with the man chosen by the Lord, and anointed by the prophet Samuel to be king? And, did he realise that David was someone who deeply loved God and would always seek to be close to Him? So much so, that he would live by all His commandments, be faithful and loyal to Him above all, as he again and again expressed in his poems written throughout his life.

David and Jonathan

Also when he was a fugitive living hidden in the desert of Judah.

> *And he (David) said: I love you, O HaShem, my strength.*
> Psalm 18:2

> *For Your loving kindness is better than life.*
> Psalm 63:3

> *One thing have I asked of HaShem, that I may dwell in the House of HaShem all the days of my life, to behold the graciousness of HaShem, and to visit early in His Temple.*
> Psalm 27:4

Sometime before Jonathan met David, he showed his bravery and faith during the war against the Philistines. The Philistines mobilized thirty thousand war chariots, six thousand horsemen and thousands of soldiers and encamped at Michmash. They sent soldiers to guard the pass of Michmash. Three thousand men joined Saul to battle. He kept two thousand with him at Gilgal, and sent a thousand with Jonathan to Gibeah. Earlier Jonathan had already killed the commander of the Philistines. The Hebrew army didn't have efficient weaponry for its soldiers because the Philistines saw to it that there were no blacksmiths in Israel. The Children of Israel had to go the Philistines to have their farming equipment sharpened. They were not allowed to make swords and spears.

On this day of battle only Saul and Jonathan had a proper sword and spear. The rest of the army did not. The Philistines went out with groups to raid the Israelite towns and cities. They brought a great blow to the Hebrews, who were outnumbered. So much so that the people fled into hiding, in caves, behind rocks, in towers, in pits and some even crossed into the Jordan River to escape to Gilead and Gad.

To make matters worse, the people with Saul at Gilgal began to desert him. Saul then made the mistake of not waiting for the seer, the prophet Samuel to bring offerings to the Lord God before they went to battle. Samuel had told him that he had to wait seven days for him. Then he would come to bring the offerings for the Lord God, after which the men would go to battle. But, after seven days, Samuel didn't arrive yet, and afraid that more men would desert him, Saul decided to bring the offerings to the Lord God Himself. His act seemed justified. But as king and servant to the Lord God, he should have been strong enough to resist the opinion of the people, to obey the Lord's word as the prophet Samuel conveyed to him. Just after Saul brought the offerings, Samuel arrived. Saul went to meet him. Samuel gave him

Who Is David?

a reprimand, telling him he should have waited for him, and that because of this act of disobedience to the Lord, his descendants would not rule over Israel. Then Samuel left. Saul counted six hundred men who were still with him. He camped with them and Jonathan at Geba.

One day, Jonathan wanted to go over to the camp of the Philistines. His intention? To attack the Philistines, while hoping that the Lord who can bring victory through many or a few, would help them. He took the young man that carried his weapons with him. He did not tell his father about his plan. Saul was encamped, together with six hundred men, near Gibeah under a pomegranate tree in Migron. Neither did Jonathan's men know where he was. To get to the Philistine's camp, Jonathan had to go through the pass at Michmash where a group of Philistine soldiers were stationed. The pass was flanked by two rocky precipices at both sides, one facing Michmash and the other Geba. Jonathan told his armour-bearer his plan, who told him to do what was in his heart and agreed to go with him. They were to go across to the pass, and let the Philistines see them. If the Philistines would tell them to stop and wait for them, then they would do just that. But, if the Philistines would tell them to go up to them, they would. Why? Because that was the sign of the Lord God that He would give Israel victory over the Philistines that day.

Jonathan and his armour-bearer walked to the pass. The Philistines saw them coming, and commented among themselves that some Hebrews came out of the holes where they were hiding. The Philistines called to Jonathan, telling them to come up because they had something to tell them. Jonathan encouraged by this, told his armour-bearer that the Lord had given the Philistines in the hand of Israel. Jonathan started to climb up along the rocky precipice on his hands and feet, and behind him his armour-bearer also climbed up. Once they reached the first Philistine men, Jonathan began to fight them and killed those upfront, while his armour-bearer fought and killed those behind them. Together they killed twenty Philistines. Meanwhile, there was a great God-inspired fear among the Philistines, at their camp and in the field. Both soldiers and raiders were terrified, as well as the people gathered there, while the ground under their feet shook.

Saul and his men heard and saw the great confusion and tumult among the Philistines, with them running away in all directions including towards them and at the same time fighting each other. At first Saul gave an order to check which of his men were missing in his own camp. They found out it was Jonathan and his armour-bearer.

Saul wanted to join the battle Jonathan initiated and go in pursuit of the Philistines to finish them off. He asked the priest to bring the Ark of the Covenant so they could inquire of the Lord. But, realizing there was no time to do this, Saul decided to immediately lead his men into battle. Other Israelites joined the fight, those who were hiding in the hills. But also, those who days earlier, had sided with the Philistines. These men may have done this out of fear. They were forced to join the Philistine's army, and were therefore among them at their camp. Now they saw their chance to break free from the Philistines.

The Israelites defeated the Philistines that day. But, something happened that could cost Jonathan his life. Saul had ordered, under threat of a curse, that no one should eat before Israel's victory over the Philistines. The reason for this could have been to prevent the men from being distracted from the battle. Jonathan, unknowing of Saul's orders, ate some honey while they went through the forest in pursuit of the Philistines. On his way Jonathan dipped a stick he carried with him in a honeycomb, ate the honey and as soon as he had done that, he felt much better. Though the men were very hungry, no one else ate from the honey, which they could find everywhere in the forest. One of the men told Jonathan about Saul's order. Jonathan didn't agree with his father's decision. He figured that if the men ate from the honey, they would have been stronger and more capable to fight many more Philistines.

Once the Israelites defeated the Philistines, they rushed to get themselves something to eat from the spoils they had from the Philistines. They slaughtered sheep and cattle to eat, but did not do this completely in accordance to the laws of Moses. When word came to Saul about this, he ordered a stone to be rolled and put in place where the men could slaughter the cattle accordingly, to prepare their food the proper way. They were not to eat the meat with blood still in it. The men listened and did as Saul told them. Saul built his first altar to the Lord there. Once all this was done, Saul told his men they should go after the Philistines to fight all of them. He inquired of the Lord whether they should do this. But, the Lord didn't answer him. Saul wanted to know why? Did anyone sin that day causing this silence? Saul promised that whoever was responsible for this, he would be put to death. Eventually it became clear that the person he didn't suspect, his own son Jonathan, was the one because he ate during the battle. But the people interceded for Jonathan, saying that the Lord helped them fight the Philistines that day. Jonathan wasn't put to death, and

Who Is David?

after this the Israelites didn't continue to pursue the Philistines.

David joined Saul's army, became his most successful officer and married his youngest daughter, Michal, who fell in love with David. The Lord was with David, who became well known in Israel, having an outstanding reputation. Meanwhile Saul became more and more jealous of David, a jealousy that had started the day David killed Goliath.

One time Saul told Jonathan and all his officials about his intention to kill David. Did Saul want to do this only out of jealousy, or did he already know that David was the one anointed to be king after him? If he already knew this, he did not mention it. But, Jonathan who still was very fond of David, warned David and told him to go into hiding. Then Jonathan went and talked to Saul, telling him that he should not kill an innocent man. There was no reason at all to do this. Saul was convinced by Jonathan, and in the Lord's name he vowed not to kill David. Jonathan went to see David and told him everything about his conversation with Saul. He brought David back to Saul's court and David continued to serve King Saul. When war with the Philistines broke out again, David was, as before, successful at defeating them.

Being a warrior and an officer in Saul's army didn't keep David from playing the harp for Saul. One day Saul was tormented by an evil spirit, while he was sitting at home. Ever since the Lord God abandoned Saul, because of his disobedience, an evil spirit tormented him from time to time. Saul sent for David, and he played the harp for him, so the evil spirit would leave and Saul would feel better again. But this time it was different. Saul was sitting there holding a lance in his hand. While David was playing the harp, suddenly Saul threw the lance towards David in an attempt to pin him on the wall and thus kill him. But David was fast in dodging the lance and instead of harming David, it lodged into the wall.

This wasn't the first time that Saul tried to kill David with his lance. The day after he defeated Goliath and Israel's victory over the Philistines, Saul was raving incoherently like a madman in his house. The evil spirit was tormenting him. David, now an officer in Saul's army, was there playing the harp as he usually did every day. Saul, who already was jealous of David, was holding a spear in his hand. He threw his spear twice at David with the intention of pinning him on the wall with it. David dodged the spear both times. Saul became afraid of David and he realised that God was with David, and not with him anymore. Saul put him in command of a thousand soldiers.

Now this time David wasn't sent away. Thinking his life was in danger, he immediately ran away. He managed to escape from the king's court. He went to his home where his wife Michal helped him escape Saul's soldiers, who were sent to the house to arrest him. Then he went to Samuel, and he told him everything that happened. Samuel took David to Naioth in Ramah where they stayed. Saul's men were still after him and he had to leave again. David left Naioth and went to see his friend Jonathan. He asked him why his father wanted to kill him. Jonathan said he didn't believe his father really wanted to do this. Besides, his father would tell him about everything and he didn't hide anything from him. David told Jonathan that he wasn't going to the king's New Moon feast. He asked Jonathan to excuse him at the dinner table of the king, by telling Saul that he had to go to Bethlehem to see his family and go to the feast there. If Saul said it's all right then David would know he is safe. However, if he got angry, then he would know for sure that Saul wanted to kill him. In that case, David told Jonathan that he himself has to kill him, instead of bringing him to Saul to be killed. To Jonathan it was unthinkable that David had to die, as he told him. Then they went out to the field for a walk. Jonathan told his friend that he would certainly question his father on this matter. If it's good news, he would send him word. If Saul wanted to harm him, he would bring him the news.

Jonathan also said to David, *'And you shall not only while yet I live show me the kindness of HaShem, that I die not; but also you shall not cut off your kindness from my house for ever; no, not when HaShem has cut off the enemies of David everyone from the face of the earth'*.

So J<u>onathan made a covenant with the House of David:</u> *'Then HaShem even required it at the hand of David's enemies'.**4

And again, Jonathan wanted David to make a promise to him, *'to swear again, for the love that he had to him; for he loved him as he loved his own soul'.**5 Jonathan would bring the news as he had agreed with David. Regarding the covenant they made, the promise they made, Jonathan said, *'Behold, HaShem is between me and you for ever'.**6

On the New Moon festival, the next day, David's absence would be noticed at the king's festive meal. Even more so at the meal on the second festive day of the festival. So, David had to hide. They agreed that David would hide at the same place as before when he fled from Saul the first time, behind a pile of rocks in the fields. After the New Moon feast, which was two days from then, he would let him know

Who Is David?

whether he is safe or not, by shooting three arrows. He would then tell his servant to fetch the arrows, and depending on which side he had to do this, was the signal for David to know whether Saul was out to kill him or not. If he was in danger, he would have to leave immediately. After Jonathan left, David hid in the field.

> *Blow the horn at the New Moon ... for our feast-day. For it is a statute for Israel, an ordinance of the God of Jacob.*
> Psalm 81:4-5

The following day was the first day of the New Moon feast days. Saul held a festive meal at his court with his guests. He sat at his usual seat by the wall, at the table. Saul, his son Jonathan, his son-in-law David and Abner sat close together. Usually David sat next to Saul. But that day, David was absent, so his seat was empty. Abner, the commander of Saul's army, joined them, and sat beside Saul. Of course Saul noticed that David was absent. But he didn't say anything, thinking that something might have happened to him and that for that reason he wasn't ritually pure. The next day, the second day of the month, David's seat was empty again. Saul asked Jonathan why the son of Jesse, David, didn't come to the festive meal on both days. Jonathan replied that David asked his permission to go to see his relatives and brothers in Bethlehem because his brother summoned him to come to the family feast-offering. So, he gave David leave to go.

Saul became furious with his son and said, '*You, son of perverse rebellion, do not I know that you have chosen the son of Jesse to your own shame, and unto the shame of your mother's nakedness? For as long as the <u>son of Jesse lives</u> upon the earth, <u>you shall not be established</u>, <u>nor your kingdom</u>. Wherefore now send and fetch him unto me, for he deserves to die*'.*[7]

To Saul, Jonathan remained the next in line to his throne. But, Jonathan had chosen to be loyal to David instead of Saul. To Jonathan, David's kingship wasn't reason enough to kill him. Jonathan immediately questioned his father's words by saying, '*Wherefore should he be put to death? What has he done*'?*[8]

At hearing this, Saul became enraged, and he threw his lance to Jonathan in an attempt to strike him, just as he tried to do to David twice before. Jonathan, realizing that his father really wanted to kill David, became furious and left. He didn't eat anything on that festive day. He was deeply worried and saddened over what was about to happen to David, and because of the way his father had humiliated him.

This was the first time Saul spoke openly with Jonathan about his friendship with David. But when did Saul find out about his son's covenant of friendship with David? No one told Saul about Jonathan's loyalty to David.

Saul once said, '<u>All of you have conspired against me, and there was none that disclosed it to me when my son made a league with the son of Jesse</u>, and there is none of you that is sorry for me, or discloses to me that my son has stirred up my servant against me'.*⁹

Saul also spoke about Jonathan's kingship, which would not be realised if David would stay alive. But, what Saul didn't realise, was that Jonathan already saw himself as second to or next to David, as he himself would later on tell David.

Intermezzo

New Moon Feast

Who (God) appointed the moon for seasons.
Psalm 104:19a

Ever since creation, the moon has been given, besides as light for the night, specifically to mark the seasons and therefore the feasts. The Moon feast, *Rosh Chodesh* which means "head of the month", is one of those feasts. It is the night of the new moon, when the crescent of the moon appears after the moon has been absent. That is, not visible in the sky to those on earth. The moon is at that moment closest to the sun which shines its light on it, which the moon in turn reflects to light up the night sky of the earth. This feast has to do with the lunar cycle itself and with the way the Jewish people determine their calendar, which is of great importance to all the festive occasions, especially those given to them by the Lord God Himself.

What are the differences regarding the celebration of this feast during the Temple period and modern day? How did the people of Israel determine their calendar? And how did they point out which night was that of the new moon in Israel and elsewhere, both in the past and the present day?

> *And in your new moons you shall present a burnt-offering unto HaShem ... This is the burnt-offering of every New Moon throughout the months of the year.*
>
> Deuteronomy 28:11-15

Rosh Chodesh is a minor festival day to the Jewish people, compared to the other Jewish feasts and festivals. It's celebrated one or two days, depending on when the moon crescent would appear and which month it is. In the days of the Tabernacle and later on the Temple of the Lord, it was celebrated by bringing offerings and with a festive meal, like King Saul arranged every month. In modern times, without the Temple of the Lord, the way the Jewish people celebrate this day has changed. They celebrate in the synagogue with prayers, psalms and a festive meal at home. For Jewish women it is also a day that they do less household work at home.

> *In the beginning God created the heaven and the earth. Now the earth was unformed and void, and darkness was upon the face of the deep; and the Spirit of God hovered over the face of the waters. And God said: <u>Let there be light. And there was light</u>. And God saw the light, that it was good; and <u>God divided the light from the darkness</u>. And <u>God called the light day</u>, and <u>the darkness He called night</u>. And there was evening and there was morning, <u>one day</u>.*
>
> Genesis 1:1-5

Before the Eternal God created the sun and the moon, there was already light, a division between day and night. There was already the passing of time. So, the Eternal God did not create the sun, the moon and the stars only to light up the sky for earth, to divide, illuminate day and night. But also for signs, and to mark the periods of time.

> *And God said: Let there be <u>lights in the firmament of the heaven</u> to divide the day from the night; and <u>let them be for signs</u>, <u>and for seasons</u>, <u>and for days and years</u>; and let them be for lights in the firmament of the heaven <u>to give light upon the earth</u>. ... and God saw that it was good. And there was evening and there was morning, a <u>fourth day</u>.*
>
> Genesis 1:14-19

But the sun, the moon and the stars were not given to be revered as god-like entities. As is written, '*lest you lift up your eyes to heaven, and when you see the sun and the moon and the stars, even all the host of heaven, you be drawn away and worship them, and serve them'.*[1]

They were and still are of utmost importance to determine the different calendars in use in the world. For instance, the general calendar, which is a solar calendar, follows the sun cycle that is according to the position of the sun in relation to the stars. This calendar is based on the solar cycle of 365.25 days. Generally it is adjusted to 365 days a year and every four years 366 days to compensate for the yearly 0.25 day. Another calendar is the Islamic one, which is strictly a lunar calender that follows only the lunar cycle. That is the position of the moon in relation to the earth. In this calendar they keep counting the cycles without any adjustments. How do the Jewish people determine their calendar? By observing, first the movement of the moon, and then make a minor adjustment based on the sun cycle.

> *And HaShem spoke to Moses and Aaron in the land of Egypt, saying: This month shall be the beginning of months (the head of the months) ... the first month of the year to you.*
>   Exodus 12:1-2

The Jewish people regard this commandment as the first given to them as a nation. They were to create a calendar for their people based on the lunar cycle, with the month Nissan, during which they left Egypt, as the first month of the year. The Jewish lunar calendar is based on the cycle of the moon in relation to the earth, but it also has an adjustment to the solar calendar.

The Jewish lunar calendar itself has a 19-year cycle with regular years, about 354 days, and leap years. In the leap years a full thirty-day month is added to the year. The Jewish lunar calendar is adjusted to the sun calendar to insure that the festival of Passover, that is Pesach and the Festival of Unleavened Bread, is celebrated during the first month Nissan, during the period March-April, in springtime as the Torah requires. Ultimately, all the commandments for God's feasts – for instance Pesach, Festival of Unleavened Bread, the Festival of Weeks and the Festival of Tabernacles – and those on which their calendar is based, evens out.

What is the lunar cycle? This is the time that the moon needs to rotate, to complete its revolution around the earth. It takes about 29 and 1/2 days, that is 29 days and twelve hours. During this time the visible moon in the sky changes from a thin crescent to a full moon and then wanes until it disappears all together from the people on earth's view, after which it's seen again as a thin crescent in the night sky. The full moon is visible in the middle of the month. This process of waxing and waning of the moon sets the rhythm of both individual and social life for the Jewish people, for whom the day begins in the evening. But a month, which is important to the Torah's schedule of God's feasts, needs to have full days. So the Jewish calendar has months, which begins with each renewal of the moon, with thirty and with twenty-nine days. The calendar has about 354 days while the calendar based on the solar cycle has 365.25 days. The eleven days difference are used to align the lunar calendar to the solar, which results in the Jewish lunar-solar calender having 12 months and sometimes 13 months. So the Jewish calendar uses both the moon and the sun, and thus their calendar is more in relation to natural phenomena.

Which days of the Jewish calendar is the New Moon? And which visible form of the moon, is the New Moon? The last day of the thirty days month and the first day of the next month is Rosh Chodesh. For the months with twenty nine days, it's the next day. Not the full moon, but, the very first visible crescent of the moon that appears in the sky and is visible from earth is the new moon.

How did, and still do the Jewish people determine the day of the new moon?

And HaShem spoke … saying: 'This month shall be to you…[*2] *this shall be to you'*, was said by the Lord God to Moses and Aaron, who were the leaders of the Hebrew people at the time. So, the leadership of the Hebrew people, the Israelites, took upon themselves the responsibility to determine the new moon day, and with that, the months of the whole year. The new moon was always on the 30th or the 31st day. But at the time, they could not calculate this in advance. So they were not using a fixed calendar. Each time the new moon had to be sighted by at least two people. Though the members of the Sanhedrin were well thought in astronomy and knew when the new moon should appear, the moon had to be seen by at least two people. They questioned the two witnesses and if their story, given separately, was collaborated, they would accept it as evidence. Then, they declared which night was the beginning of the new month, after which they publicized this by means of lighting up huge bonfires on designated hills or mountain tops that night. Those who saw these lit up their own fire so the message could reach Jewish communities in faraway places, such as, for instance, all the way to Damascus. Eventually, centuries later, instead of using the bonfires they sent messengers to the places outside Israel. Ultimately all these methods were discontinued, and replaced by a new method.

Rabbi Hillel, a sage of the Talmud, not to be confused with Hillel the Elder, held the office of Nasi. As such, he was the leader of the Jewish Sanhedrin between 320 to 385 current era. The Sanhedrin was an assembly or council of rabbis that were appointed as judges to sit as a tribunal. The Great Sanhedrin, which functioned similar to a supreme court, consisted of seventy-one judges. Besides the Nasi, there was a chief of the court and sixty-nine general members. Beside this one Great Sanhedrin court, there were several Lesser Sanhedrin courts. These were appointed each to one city. These courts consisted of twenty-three judges. Hillel created and together with his court introduced the Jewish modern perpetual or fixed calendar in 358 current era. This binding decision of the judges at the court of the Great Sanhedrin was to be the last one concerning a general matter to the Jewish communities. After the disbandment of the Sanhedrin in 425 current era, due to the persecutions by the Byzantine Empire or Eastern Roman Empire, this new fixed calender continued to be used. So, the Eternal One gave the New Moon feast to the Israelites, which for centuries has been part of determining the rhythm of life for the Jewish people. Sabbath and New Moon will remain as feasts in the future.

> *And it shall come to pass, that from one New Moon to another, and from one Shabbat to another, shall all flesh come to worship before Me, says HaShem.*
>
> Isaiah 66:23

All God's feasts are connected to both events on earth as those in heaven, to the timing of harvests on earth and signs in heaven for centuries and millennia. These feasts have meaning for the past, present and future of the Jewish people, and with them of the entire world. The Eternal God's timing for His plan of restoration of His people, the heavens and earth is connected to and concealed within these feasts, although the exact dates and instances of events regarding His plan are only known to the Almighty God Himself. On earth, the City of Jerusalem with the City of Bethlehem, the Town of David, both in the Land of Israel form the epicentre of events on earth.

Is it for this reason that the prophet Joel spoke about Judah and Jerusalem?

> But <u>Judah</u> shall be <u>inhabited for ever</u>, and <u>Jerusalem</u> from <u>generation to generation</u>.
> ... and <u>she (Jerusalem)</u> shall be lifted up, and inhabited <u>in her place</u> ...
>
> Joel 4:20 / Zechariah 14:10

David's Trust

> And Jonathan said to him (David): Tomorrow is the <u>New Moon</u>; and you will be missed, <u>your seat will be empty</u>.
>
> 1 Samuel 20:18

David would not be seen at Saul's table that night, where he usually sits during the New Moon feast. Just as the moon disappears from the sky for those who see it from earth signalling the end of each Jewish month, and it reappears as a moon crescent at every beginning of a Jewish month, so would David.

The moon diminishes from a full moon visible in the middle of the month, to become invisible towards the end to the human eye watching from the earth's surface, to start anew at the beginning of the month, when a cycle of renewal begins. While the moon is not visible in its lunar cycle, it's the closest to the sun, which is the source of light that shines on it.

> <u>HaShem is my light</u> and my salvation; whom shall I fear?
> HaShem is the stronghold of my life; of whom shall I be afraid?
>
> Psalm 27:1

To Saul and his kingdom, David diminishes from being one of his military officers, to becoming invisible. Meanwhile, just like the moon David is still there, but closer to his source of light, strength and protection, the Eternal God, Who cares for him and guides him.

David was a man that trusted the God of Israel above all, so much so that David sought to walk in God's truth, and to for ever be a member of His household.

> For Your mercy is before my eyes; and <u>I have walked in Your truth</u>.
> ... <u>HaShem, I love the habitation of Your House, and the place where Your glory dwells</u>.
>
> Psalm 26

> *Surely goodness and mercy shall follow me all the days of my life; and <u>I shall dwell in the House of HaShem for ever</u>.*
>
> Psalm 23

For as the prophet Samuel once said to Saul concerning the man who would reign after him, that the Lord '*has sought him a man after His own heart*'.*[10] And so, by God's grace, David would go through a process of renewal during the time that he was a fugitive, to reappear as the king of Judah and Israel, a position given to him by the Lord God, so he would fight God's battles, as the prophetess Abigail said, and care for the people of Israel. David trusted in the unfailing love and mercy of the God of Israel, the Eternal God.

> *But as for me, I am like a <u>leafy (green) olive tree</u> <u>in the house of God</u>; <u>I trust in the mercy of God for ever and ever</u>. I will give You thanks for ever, because You have done it; and I will wait for Your name, for it is good, in the presence of Your saints.*
>
> Psalm 52:10-11

The next morning, after the second day of the New Moon feast, that is on the third day of the month, Jonathan returned to the field where David was hiding. He took a young boy with him to fetch the arrows that he had thrown. As he had agreed with David, he told the boy with a loud voice where to find the arrows. The signal was clear to David. He was in danger and he had to leave. Jonathan gave his weapons to the boy and sent him home. David came out. Both, saddened by the situation, were crying. David realizing he was in mortal danger and that his daily life was about to change completely, cried even more. Before they went their separate ways, Jonathan said to David, '*Go in peace, for as much as we have sworn both of us in the name of HaShem, saying: <u>HaShem shall be between me and you</u>, <u>and between my seed and your seed</u>, <u>for ever</u>*'.*[11] Afterwards Jonathan returned to town, while David left and went to see someone else hoping for his help.

> *HaShem is my shepherd; I shall not want.*
>
> Psalm 23

After David left Jonathan, he went to see the High Priest Ahimelech, but he did not tell him anything about what happened. David received some help from him, and he immediately left. Still on the run, he went to Achish, left there and went to a cave near the town Abdullam, near the city of Gath. He stayed there, where his family, including his brothers, and some men joined him. Eventually, after he and his men fought and delivered the city of Keilah from the Philistines, he arrived at Horesh in the hill country near Ziph. David knew that Saul was still searching for him. So he and his men hid themselves near Ziph, in the wilderness of the hill country. There they remained out of sight for Saul and his soldiers. It was here that Jonathan came to speak to David. Somehow Jonathan knew where David was. This would be the last time they met. He wanted to encourage David with God's words, and when he met him, he spoke with David about David's kingship, about his own position, that his father now knew this, and that Saul wouldn't be able to prevent David from becoming king. Again they made a covenant before God. Jonathan went home while David and his warriors remained there, hidden in the forest. Saul was still searching for him.

> *And the two of them <u>made a covenant before HaShem.</u>*
> 1 Samuel 23:18a

Was this covenant concerning, besides their friendship, also about what they discussed, David's kingship? This was the first time that Jonathan spoke openly with David about David's kingship, and about David's position in relation to his own. This happened after Jonathan heard from his father about David becoming king. It's not mentioned that David himself spoke to Jonathan about this matter. It could be David kept this from him. Jonathan and David made a covenant on three occasions. First the covenant of friendship they made, on Jonathan's request, after David killed Goliath. Then Jonathan made a covenant with David and David's House, when they were in the fields, on the day before the New Moon festival. This was also of importance to Jonathan, to insure the safety of his own descendants. The third time, was when Jonathan met David for the last time. This is when Jonathan asserted David's kingship, and also spoke about his position next or second to him. Jonathan, who was the next in line to King Saul, initiated all this.

But when did Jonathan find out about David's kingship? Was it when his father spoke about it during the New Moon festive meal? It's the only time Saul mentioned it publically. Saul knew that someone else would be anointed to become king after him, as the prophet Samuel told him on two occasions. The first time Samuel told Saul his descendants would not rule after him. The second time, that the Lord had take away the kingdom from him. After the day that Samuel gave that last message to Saul, Samuel never again met with Saul, though Saul did grieve over him. It is after this meeting that the Lord told Samuel about the son of Jesse, that happened to be David. So Saul did not hear about David's kingship from Samuel. But Jonathan did hear about this matter from Saul at the second festive meal of the New Moon festival, on the second day of the month. Perhaps, Saul thought David would be chosen to become king, because of how successful he was in all he did. Maybe this was just as a result of his jealousy towards David or a combination of both reasons. He figured it out by himself. As he once said about him, *'They have ascribed to David ten thousands, and to me they have ascribed but thousands; and <u>all he lacks is the kingdom</u>'!**[12] Saul would one day speak to David about the kingship granted to David by God.

After Jonathan's last meeting with David, he remained a fugitive on the run from his father-in-law, King Saul. But David wasn't alone. His family, including his brothers and some hundred men who were in distress themselves joined him. There were also people who helped David along the way. Some lost their lives over this at the hand of King Saul. This went on for years.

David was still a young man, now married to Michal. At the time that he killed Goliath, he was a shepherd, not a soldier. Due to his age he couldn't have signed up to become a soldier. To join the king's army, he had to be at least twenty years old. Jonathan who was already a soldier, thus older then twenty, was older than David. So when Saul enlisted David into his army, David was younger than twenty years old, thus a teenager. It was at this point when Saul's jealousy began. Jonathan believed, and said to David, that he would become king one day. Eventually David would become king of first only the tribe of Judah, the Kingdom of Judah, and ultimately after seven years, of the whole Kingdom of Israel. He was thirty years old when he became king. So David was a fugitive for about ten years. As for Jonathan, he would die together with his brothers and father in a battle against the Philistines. Would David stay loyal to the covenants between him and Jonathan? Did he care for Jonathan's family and therefore for his descendants?

> *And Jonathan said to David: but also you shall not cut off your kindness from my house for ever … And Jonathan caused David to swear again.*
>
> 1 Samuel 20:12-17

Jonathan had a son, Mephiboshet. He was five years old when Jonathan died. He was crippled on both feet or legs. When his nursemaid heard the news about Saul and Jonathan's death, she fled in a hurry. She picked up the boy to take him with her. In her hastiness she dropped him on her way out. He got injured and became crippled. Years later he went to King David's court on David's request. David wanted to show kindness to Jonathan's descendants and asked whether there were still family members of Saul alive. A servant of Saul's family, named Ziba, came to see David. David said to him, *'Is there not yet any of the house of Saul, that I may show the kindness of God to him'?* *[13]

Ziba told David about Mephiboshet, and he sent for him. He lived in Lodebar, in Ammiel's house. He was a son of Makir. David sent for him, and when he arrived he deeply bowed down for the king. David said to Mephiboshet, *'Fear not; for I will surely show you kindness <u>for Jonathan your father's sake</u>, and will restore you all the land of Saul your father; and you shall eat bread at my table continually'.* *[14]

Afterward, David called Ziba and said to him, *'All that pertained (belonged) to Saul and to all his house have I given to your master's son. And you shall till (farm) the land for him, you, and your sons, and your servants; and you shall bring in the fruits, that your master's son may have bread to eat; but Mephiboshet your master's son shall eat bread continually at my table'.* *[15]

Ziba answered that he would do as the king commanded. Ziba had a large family of fifteen sons, and he had twenty servants. They all became Mephiboshet's servants. Mephiboshet, who had a son called Micah, lived in Jerusalem and he was the king's personal guest at the table, just as David's sons were. David kept his word, and more than seven years after his Jonathan's death, he cared for his descendants. He took them under his personal protection and insured they would receive Jonathan's inheritance.

> *Go in peace, for as much as we have sworn both of us in the name of HaShem, saying: <u>HaShem shall be between me and you</u>, <u>and between my (Jonathan's) seed and your (David's) seed</u>, <u>for ever.</u>*
>
> 1 Samuel 20:42

More than seven years after the death of Jonathan, in the days that David ruled over the whole of Israel, there was a great famine in Israel. Year after year, there was a lack of provisions for the Children of Israel. David inquired of the Lord about what caused this famine that went on for three years. His answer was that Saul and his family had killed some of the people of Gibeon. The Gibeonites were a small group of Amorites, who were under the protection of the Israelites, which was granted by Joshua at the time the Israelites conquered Canaan. Ever since, they had been servants to the Israelites. But Saul tried to kill these people because of his zeal for the Children of Israel and Judah. This was a serious matter that had to be resolved. David summoned the people of Gibeon to his court. They were clear about the way they wanted to settle what was done to them. They wanted to punish those responsible. But Saul and his sons were dead. So they agreed with David that they would punish seven male family members of Saul, by hanging at Saul's town of Gibeah. David had to decide who he would hand over to them. They were the two son's of Saul's concubine and the five sons of Saul's eldest daughter Merab. They were all hanged in Gibeah. Eventually David was able to bury all these people. David spared Jonathan's son Mephiboshet and his son Micah from the people of Gibeon. In doing so, he secured the survival of Jonathan's descendants for generations to come. Jonathan's grandson Micah had four sons and all of them had children and descendants. They remained part of the tribe of Benjamin. Some of them became very good archers and soldiers.

> *Fear not; for <u>the hand of Saul my father shall not find you</u>; and <u>you shall be king over Israel</u>, and I shall be next to you; and that also Saul my father knows.*
> 1 Samuel 23:17b

Endnotes

[1] 1 Samuel 18:1, [2] 1 Samuel 18:3, [3] 1 Samuel 18:4, [4] 1 Samuel 20:14-16, [5] 1 Samuel 20:17, [6] 1 Samuel 20:23, [7] 1 Samuel 20:30b-31, [8] 1 Samuel 20:32, [9] 1 Samuel 22:8, [10] 1 Samuel 13:14, [11] 1 Samuel 20:41, [12] 1 Samuel 18:8, [13] 2 Samuel 9:3, [14] 2 Samuel 9:7, [15] 2 Samuel 9:9-10

The Green Olive Tree, www.thegreenolivetree.nl
David and Jonathan: astounding friendship!, by Angeline Leito
http://www.thegreenolivetree.nl/index.php/14-articles/king-david/95-astounding-friendshipjonathan-and-david
Psalm 23:6, 26:8 David's love for God
1 Samuel 18:3-4 Jonathan and David covenant of friendship

Who Is David?

1 Samuel 20:16-17 Jonathan covenant with David and his House
1 Samuel 23:18 Jonathan covenant with David, asserting David's kingship
1 Samuel 20:30, 1 Samuel 22:8 Saul found out about David and Jonathan's covenant
1 Samuel 16:14-23, 18:10-11, 19:9 Saul tormented by an evil spirit, David played the harp
Numbers 1:3,22, 26:2 twenty-year-old men sign up for the army
1 Chronicles 23:24,27, Ezra 3:8 men who serve in the Temple at least twenty years old
1 Chronicles 27:23 reason why twenty years of age
1 Samuel 18:5, 13,16 David officer, commander over 1000 men, successful leader
2 Samuel 4:4, 9, 16:1-4 Mephiboshet, Jonathan's son, David took care of Jonathan's descendants
1 Samuel 13:13-14, 15:26-27 told Saul twice about kingship
1 Kings 18:10 David played the harp for Saul every day
1 Kings 12:20 Judah remained loyal to David's House
1 Samuel 20 Jonathan and David, New Moon feast
1 Samuel 13, 14 Philistines at war with the Israelites
1 Samuel 13:3 Jonathan killed the commander of the Philistines
1 Samuel 13:19-23 no blacksmiths, no spears and swords
1 Samuel 13:5 Philistines had horsemen, chariots and weapons
1 Samuel 13:7-15 Saul's first mistake, disobedience, Samuel's reprimand
1 Kings 15:3 David's heart fully committed to God
1 Samuel 25:28 David fought the Lord's battles
1 Samuel 13:14, David a man after God's heart, whom will do everything God wants
Genesis 9:3-4, Deuteronomy 12:16, 23 do not eat meat with blood in it
Psalm 23:6, 26:8, 84:10 David's love for God
1 Samuel 19:1-3, 20:19 David hid himself twice at the same place
1 Samuel 19:11-17 Michal
1 Samuel 19:18-24 to Samuel, with him to Naioth in Ramah
1 Samuel 20:1-42 from Naioth to Jonathan
1 Samuel 21:1-9 to the High Priest Ahimelech
1 Samuel 21:10-15 to Achish
1 Samuel 22:1 to cave near the town Abdullam, near the city of Gath
1 Samuel 23:1-13 went with his men to the city of Keilah
1 Samuel 23:14-16 to the hill country, at Horesh near Ziph
1 Samuel 23: 16-18 Jonathan went to see David at Horesh, last meeting
1 Samuel 20:14-15 David's arrangement for his family with Jonathan
1 Samuel 22:1 David's brothers and family joint him in the cave of Adullam
1 Samuel 22:3-4 David brought his parents to the king of Moab
1 Samuel 18:23 David considered himself a poor man
1 Samuel 18:1-4, 20:8, 22:8, 23:18, 2 Samuel 21:7 covenant of friendship of Jonathan and David

- 1 Samuel 20:14-16, 42 covenant of friendship between the House of David and that of Jonathan
- 1 Samuel 22:8 Saul did not know about covenant of friendship between Jonathan and David
- 1 Samuel 13:1-14:46 Israelite's war against the Philistines
- 1 Samuel 13:19-22 only Saul and Jonathan had a sword, no blacksmiths in Israel, Philistines did
- 1 Samuel 13:19-14:46 Jonathan's heroic attack on the Philistines
- 1 Samuel 14:24-46 battle continued
- 1 Samuel 14:24-32 soldiers not allowed to eat, honey
- 1 Samuel 14:31-34 soldiers eat meat that wasn't properly slaughtered, Saul made arrangement for proper meat
- 1 Samuel 14:35 Saul built an altar, his first
- 1 Samuel 14:37 Saul inquired of the Lord but didn't receive an answer
- 1 Samuel 14:38-46 inquiry under Saul's men, Jonathan's life spared
- 1 Samuel 15:10-29 the Lord rejects Saul's kingship
- 1 Samuel 19:1, 20:2 Saul trusted his son Jonathan
- 1 Samuel 19:17-30 David married Saul's daughter Michal
- 1 Samuel 19:1, 20:2 Saul told Jonathan of his plan to kill David
- 1 Samuel 19:2-7 Jonathan interceded on David's behalf, he returned David to Saul's court
- 1 Samuel 19:6 Saul vowed not to kill David
- 1 Samuel 19:8 war against the Philistines, David also on war campaign
- 1 Samuel 19:9-10 Saul in a bad mood, throws his lance for the second time at David
- 1 Samuel 19:10-17 David fled to his house, Michal helped him escape
- 1 Samuel 19:18-20:1 David went to Samuel
- 1 Samuel 20:1-24 David went to Jonathan
- 1 Samuel 20:24 David hides in the field
- 1 Samuel 20:25-34 New Moon feast, argument between Saul and Jonathan
- 1 Samuel 20:32 Jonathan interceded again for David
- 1 Samuel 20:30-31 Saul mentions kingship during argument with Jonathan
- 1 Samuel 20:33, 34 Saul throws his lance on Jonathan
- 1 Samuel 20:34 Jonathan sad about his father's plan
- 1 Samuel 20:35-21:1 Jonathan met David in the field, throwing of the arrow
- 1 Samuel 23:15-18 Jonathan met with David for the last time, in the desert of Ziph
- 2 Samuel 4:4 Mephiboshet was 5 years old when Jonathan died.
- 2 Samuel 9:1 Jonathan's descendants, Ziba servant of Saul's family
- 2 Samuel 9:1-13, 9:6, 19:25-31, 2 Samuel 4:4 Mephiboshet crippled
- 2 Samuel 21:1 famine in Israel
- 2 Samuel 21:1 Saul and his family murdered Gebionites
- 2 Samuel 21:2, Joshua 9:3-15 Gebionites were Amorites under Israelite protection

2 Samuel 21:1-9 Saul's family killed in Gibeon
2 Samuel 21:7, 9:12 David spared Mephiboshet and Micah from the people of Gibeon
1 Chronicles 8:34-40 Jonathan's grandson Micah, his four sons and descendants

Intermezzo Endnotes

*[1]Deuteronomy 4:16-19, *[2]Exodus 12:1-2

Numbers 10:10, 28:11-15, 1 Chronicles 23:31, 2 Chronicles 2:4, 8:13, 31:3, Colossians 2:16 offerings, celebration Shabbat, New Moon feasts and festivals

Ezekiel 45:16-17, Ezekiel 46:4-6 provisions for appointed feasts and festivals duty of Israel's prince, king

Ezekiel 46:1-3 gate to inner courtyard Temple complex open on Shabbat and New Moon day

Deuteronomy 17:3, Jeremiah 8:2, do not worship sun, moon, stars etc.

Chabad.org

Rosh Chodesh: The New Moon
https://www.chabad.org/library/article_cdo/aid/2100138/jewish/Rosh-Chodesh-The-New-Moon.htm

What Is Rosh Chodesh? The Jewish New Moon by Menachem Posner
https://www.chabad.org/library/article_cdo/aid/1928828/jewish/What-Is-Rosh-Chodesh.htm

The Jewish Month: How is it calculated?
https://www.chabad.org/library/article_cdo/aid/2100146/jewish/The-Jewish-Month.htm

The 29th Day
https://www.chabad.org/parshah/article_cdo/aid/2764/jewish/The-29th-Day.htm

Why is Rosh Chodesh sometimes one day and sometimes two? By Naftali Silberberg https://www.chabad.org/library/article_cdo/aid/526942/jewish/Why-is-Rosh-Chodesh-sometimes-one-day-and-sometimes-two.htm

The Laws of Rosh Chodesh by Eliezer Wenger https://www.chabad.org/library/article_cdo/aid/2100147/jewish/The-Laws-of-Rosh-Chodesh.htm

Wikipedia: Hillel, https://en.wikipedia.org/wiki/Hillel_II
Wikipedia: Sanhedrin, https://en.wikipedia.org/wiki/Sanhedrin

DAVID AND SAUL

Father and Son, Loved And Reconciled

> *... and evil is not found in you all your days*
> 1 Samuel 25:28c

At the walled town of Keilah the people of Israel brought in the new harvest of corn. Soon after, they came under attack from the Philistines, who were stealing the corn. When David heard of this, he inquired of the Lord whether he should attack the Philistines to save Keilah from them. The Lord said that he should. David told his men about the situation and that they had to head out to Keilah to save the town. But, they didn't want to attack the Philistines. They said that they already had to fear Saul, and that they shouldn't make more enemies by attacking the Philistines. David inquired of the Lord God again, and He said to him, *'Arise, go down to Keilah; for I will deliver the Philistines into your hand'*. *[1]

David convinced his men, and they left the forest of Hareth and went to Keilah where they attacked the Philistines. They killed many of them, saved the town, and they took their livestock. When they were in Keilah, the priest Abiathar, son of the High Priest Ahimelech, fled from Saul to David in Keilah. He had taken the ephod – an apron-like garment of the High Priest – with him.

When Saul heard that David and his men were in Keilah, he thought David would be trapped there. Because he was in a walled town with gates that were fortified he decided to take his army to Keilah to besiege David and his men there. But David knowing that Saul was planning to attack him there, consulted with the Lord God. He told Abiathar to bring the ephod. Then David said to the Lord, *'O HaShem, the God of Israel, Your servant has surely heard that Saul seeks to come to Keilah, to destroy the city for my sake. Will the men of Keilah deliver me up into his hand? Will Saul come down, as Your servant has heard? O HaShem, the God of Israel, I beseech You, tell Your servant'*.*[2]

The Lord answered and said, *'He will come down'*.*[3]

David continued, *'Will the men of Keilah deliver me up and my men into the hand of Saul'*?*[4]

And the Lord said to him, *'They will deliver you up'*.*[5] So David decided to leave Keilah immediately with his men, now six hundred

Who Is David?

in total. When Saul was told that they had left, he abandoned his plan. David remained in the hill country, where he dwelt in strongholds or in the mountains of the wilderness nearby Ziph. When he was at Horesh Jonathan came to see him there, to give him some encouragement with God's words. After Jonathan left, David stayed at Horesh.

One day, while Saul was in Gibeah, he received visitors from Ziph, who knew Saul really wanted to catch David. They had news about David's whereabouts, and they told the king that David was in the area of the southern part of Judah's wilderness, in the territory of Horesh, hiding on Mount Hachilah. They offered to help him catch David, and asked Saul to come to their territory. Saul blessed them because they were so kind to him. He told them to go back to Ziph to find out exactly where David was, who had seen him, and to bring him a precise report. Then, if David was still there, he would go with them, search for David and hunt him down. He told them he heard that David was very cunning. The men went back to Ziph. In the meantime Saul and his men made preparations to go to the wilderness of Judah, and they set out to search for David.

David heard that Saul and his men were looking for him. He and his men went to the wilderness of Maon, a rocky hill where they stayed. But, Saul heard about this and he went in pursuit of David. Now both of them were on the hill. Each of them with their men on another side of this hill. Saul and his men were about to capture David, getting closer and closer to them.

While David and his men were hurrying to escape from Saul, Saul received urgent news from a messenger; the Philistines were attacking Israel. Immediately Saul and his men stopped pursuing David, and they left to fight the Philistines. David and his men went into hiding near En Gedi.

You have anointed my head with oil; my cup runs over.
Psalm 23:5b

David lived the life of a fugitive, for no other reason than that he was the one anointed to be king after King Saul. Despite Saul's initial love for David, he was now out to kill him at all costs, even if it meant killing those who in his view were conspiring with David against him. The reason Saul was in pursuit of David was that he was convinced because of all that had already taken place, that David and not his son Jonathan would be king after him. Maybe he was even afraid that if David remained alive, he would become stronger and try to overthrow him to get his throne. Why was Saul so convinced that his descendants wouldn't rule after him, that he wouldn't have a dynasty? Was it only because of his own jealousy towards David?

Saul already knew that his household would lose the kingdom, that his son Jonathan would not become the next king of Israel. Samuel told him this. But, what was the Lord's reason to do this? Perhaps it was Saul's own disobedience towards the Lord that he showed on two occasions before David was anointed to be king of Israel and before he fought Goliath. The first time was when Saul didn't wait for Samuel to do the burnt offerings before the battle against the Philistines at Michmash. The second time was because Saul did not completely carry out God's instructions for the battle against the Amalekites at the city of Amalek.

Michmash was the place where the Philistine soldiers gathered to fight the Israelites, after they heard that Jonathan, with one thousand warriors, had fought the Philistines at Geba and had killed their commander. The Philistines gathered with an impressive army of thirty thousand war chariots, six thousand horsemen and it seemed they also were with thousands of soldiers. Their attack against the Israelites was so strong that people fled and went in hiding in holes or caves in the hills, in wells and pits, and among rocks. Some even crossed the Jordan River to go to the territory of Gilead and Gad. The Israelites were in a dire, very desperate situation. The people with Saul were very much afraid, while Saul waited seven days for the prophet Samuel to arrive to bring the burnt offerings to the Lord God. When Saul saw that the people started to abandon him, he brought the burnt offerings himself instead of Samuel. Just when Saul was finishing doing the burnt offerings, Samuel arrived. Saul welcomed him, but Samuel asked him, '*What have you done*'?*[6]

Saul then told him, that when he saw the people were deserting him while the Philistines could attack him there in Gilgal, he didn't want to have to fight them without asking the Lord's favour. But, this was no excuse for Saul for what he did. Samuel reprimanded Saul and said to the king, '*You have done foolishly; you have not kept the commandment of HaShem your God, which He commanded you; for now would HaShem have established your kingdom upon Israel for ever. But now your kingdom shall not continue; HaShem has sought him a man after His own heart, and HaShem has appointed him to be prince over His people, because you have not kept that which HaShem commanded you*'.*[7]

So, Saul's descendants would not rule. After their conversation

Samuel left, the Israelites followed Saul into battle. But first, Jonathan and his armour-bearer attacked the soldiers of a Philistine post. Then the Lord brought confusion over the Philistines. The Hebrews who were fighting for the Philistines, changed sides and fought against them. On that day, the Israelites fought the Philistines and despite Saul's action, the Lord saved Israel.

Sometime later on, Samuel went to Saul with a message from the Lord God concerning the punishment of the Amalekites because they had not treated the Israelites' ancestors well when they came from Egypt. Samuel said to King Saul, *'Now go and smite Amalek, and utterly destroy all that they have, and spare them not; but slay both man and woman, infant and suckling, ox and sheep, camel and ass'.**8

But, why did the Lord want to destroy the Amalekites? Samuel told Saul the reason, before he gave him the Lord's order to attack the Amalekites, by saying, *"Thus says HaShem of hosts: 'I remember that which Amalek did to Israel, how he set himself against him in the way, when he came up out of Egypt'."**9

The Amalekites had made themselves enemies of the Israelites in the past, when they came out of Egypt, and in the present time when Israelites had established their nation of Israel, though they would also be in the future.

Intermezzo 1

Adonai-nissi

> *And Moses built an altar and called the name of it Adonai-nissi**
>
> Exodus 17:15

The Amalekites made themselves the enemies of the Hebrews in the past when they came up from Egypt and were on their way to Canaan to establish their nation of Israel there. But, where did the Amalekites actually come from? Who was their forefather? And how exactly did the Amalekites oppose the Israelites at the time of Moses?

The Amalekites were descendants of Amalek, one of the grandsons of Jacob's brother Esau from one of his Canaanite wives. The Amalekites lived in the southern territory of Canaan. When the Israelites came out of Egypt on their way to Canaan, the Amalekites attacked them at Rephidim. Initially this wasn't a battle between soldiers. The Amalekites attacked the Israelites from the rear, where there were people who fell behind because they were exhausted from the journey. They killed all these people who at that moment were very weak.

Moses commanded Joshua son of Nun to gather men among the Israelites to fight the Amalekites the next day. Joshua was one of the twelve men who scouted Canaan when they arrived the first time at Canaan's borders and he would be, as the future successor of Moses, the first Judge of the Israelites in the Land of Israel. Moses himself would stand on top of the hill and hold up the stick that God had given him to carry in his hand. Joshua and his men attacked the Amalekites, and while they were fighting, Moses was standing on the hill together with his brother the High Priest Aaron and Hur of the tribe of Judah. Hur's grandson Bezalel, son of Uri, was the one that God granted the knowledge and wisdom to make the items for His Tabernacle and the Ark of the Covenant. Caleb, who was also among the twelve who scouted Canaan, also had a son called Hur, who was his eldest son with his wife Ephrath. Hur's second son Salma founded Bethlehem. Is the man, Hur, from these two stories, one and the same?

On the hill, Moses held up his arms, holding up the stick. As long as he did this, the Israelites were on the winning side. But, the Amalekites started to win as soon as Moses put his arms down, because his arms started to get tired. Aaron and Hur trying to help him, brought him a stone that he could sit on. Then they stood each at one side of Moses and they held his arm up and kept them steady until sun down. Joshua and his men remained on the winning side and defeated the Amalekites. Afterwards, the Lord told Moses to make an account of the events of that day and He gave Moses a word for Joshua. He was to tell Joshua that He would always fight the Amalekites and that He would destroy them. As written, *And HaShem said to Moses: 'Write this for a memorial in the book, and rehearse it in the ears of Joshua: for I will utterly blot out the remembrance of Amalek from under heaven'. And <u>Moses built an altar</u>, and <u>called the name of it Adonai-nissi</u>*¹. And he said: 'The hand upon the throne of HaShem: HaShem will have war with Amalek from generation to generation'.**²

So, Moses told the Joshua and the Israelites not to forget what happened and he gave them the order to always fight the Amalekites. Balaam once prophesied, when the Israelites on their way to Canaan had reached Moab, that Israel's king would be greater than Agag, the king of the Amalekites.

Not only Joshua and King Saul, but also David fought the

Amalekites after they attacked his town. And in the future from Saul and David's time on, the Amalekites would continue to be enemies of the Israelites, like during the reign of King Hezekiah of Judah, and much later on during the period of the exile of Judah's people to Babylonia by Nebuchadnezzar. During the Babylonian exile, at the time of the Jewish Queen Esther, the wife of Ahasuerus or Xerxes, who was king over Babylonia, Queen Esther's uncle, Mordechai, refused to kneel for the king's servant Haman. He was a descendant of Agag, the Amalekite king that Samuel had slain. Mordechai must have known the history of Haman's people regarding his own. Haman would devise a plan against Mordechai and all his people in the nation of the king. By God's grace, through Queen Esther's intervention, Haman would fail miserably in his attempt to exterminate the Jewish people.

Ultimately, the Israelites would overthrow seven nations with their kings, in Canaan. Including the Amalekites and Philistine? No, these nations would be destroyed much later. During Judah's King Hezekiah's reign, the nation of the Amalekites was destroyed by the tribe of Simon, and they took over their land. Something that Moses had ordered to be done centuries before. But despite this, there would still be Amalekite people living elsewhere, in other nations among other people. As for the Philistines, against whom King Saul fought many battles, King Hezekiah would one day defeat their nation. During his reign as king of Judah, he would raid all the Philistine territory, including Gaza. So, the Israelites overthrew seven nations when they came to Canaan, and in time they also overthrew the nation of the Amalekites and the Philistines.

The Amalekites

King Saul gathered his men to fight the Amalekites. From Israel two hundred thousand soldiers and from Judah ten thousand soldiers gathered at Telem where he inspected them. Then they marched to the city of Amalek to ambush the Amalekites. In the meantime Saul sent messengers warning the neighbouring Kenites who had been kind to the Israelites' ancestors, to leave the Amalekites so they wouldn't be harmed during battle. Saul and his army defeated the Amalekites, and they killed everyone, except their king. They also kept the best of their cattle and herd, they only destroyed what was worthless. Afterwards, Saul went to the town of Carmel where he built up a place for an altar.

Saul didn't fight the Amalekites like Joshua did at the time of Moses. This would have consequences for the reign of the king's family, as well as for his own personal life.

Meanwhile, the word of the Lord God came to Samuel, saying, *'It repents Me that I have set up Saul to be king; for he has turned back from following Me, and has not performed My commandments'*.*[10]

This caused a lot of grief to Samuel, who stayed up all night long in prayer and he cried out to the Lord. Early in the morning the next day, Samuel went to see Saul. When he arrived, Saul's people told him that Saul had gone to Carmel and Gilgal. Samuel went to speak to him. He greeted Samuel while telling him that he had done as the Lord had commanded. But, Samuel asked him about the animals that he heard. The bleating of the sheep and the mooing of the cattle. Saul told him about what they kept, saying they were also meant for offerings to Samuel's God. But Samuel said, *'Has HaShem as great a delight in burnt-offerings and sacrifices as in <u>hearkening (listening) to the voice of HaShem</u>? Behold, <u>to obey is better than sacrifice</u>, and <u>to hearken (listen) than the fat of rams</u>'*.*[11]

And Samuel continued by saying, *'For <u>rebellion is as the sin of witchcraft</u>, and <u>stubbornness is as idolatry and teraphim</u> (images). Because you have rejected the word of HaShem, He has also rejected you from being king'*.*[12]

Then King Saul said to Samuel, *'I have sinned; for I have transgressed the commandment of HaShem, and your words; because I feared the people, and hearkened (listened) to their voice'*.*[13]

Saul begged Samuel to forgive him, that he had not obeyed the Lord's command nor Saul's instructions, and to come with him so that he could worship the Lord. But, Samuel told him he would not go back with him, and he also said, *'For you have rejected the word of HaShem, and HaShem has rejected you from being king over Israel'*.*[14]

When Samuel turned to leave, Saul got hold of his cloak and it tore. Samuel then said to Saul, *'That HaShem has rent (tore) the kingdom of Israel from you this day, and has given it to a neighbour of yours, that is better than you. And also the Glory of Israel will not lie nor repent; for He is not a man, that He should repent'*.*[15]

With the latter Samuel made it clear to Saul that he shouldn't expect that the Lord God would change His mind concerning this decision. But Saul insisted, by saying to Samuel that he should come back with him. At least to show some respect in front of the leaders

Who Is David?

and all the people of Israel, and so he could worship Samuel's God. Samuel returned with Saul and in front of all those present, the king worshipped the Lord. So, Saul's second act of disobedience, was that he had not utterly destroyed the Amalekites, including their king, with all that which belonged to them.

Afterwards, Samuel ordered that Agag, the Amalekite king, should be brought to him. They brought the prisoner to him, and Samuel said to Agag, 'As your sword has made women childless, so shall your mother be childless among women'.*16 Then he slew, executed, Agag on the spot. Afterwards Samuel returned to Ramah, while Saul went to his home in Gibeah in the territory of Benjamin. Though Samuel mourned Saul because of what happened, he never saw Saul again. Despite all of this, King Saul ruled a total of forty years.

> *The God Who is my rock, in Him I take refuge; my shield, and my horn of salvation, my high tower, and my refuge; my Saviour, You save me from violence.*
>
> 2 Samuel 22:3

Throughout Saul's reign he persecuted David for some years. Since he made it clear at the New Moon festival that he wanted to kill him, David had been on the run. How much of Saul's initial love for David did he still have? Considering the change in his attitude towards David. Love that he had since David came to play the harp for him. 'And David came to Saul, and stood before him; and <u>he loved him greatly</u>'.*17

Saul already had adult children and even grandchildren, by the time David fought Goliath. For instance, Jonathan's son Mephiboshet. Saul's jealousy towards David began from the moment David fought Goliath. But what Saul did not know yet, because neither Samuel nor David's family had told him, was that at the time David fought Goliath, Samuel had already anointed David to be the next king of Israel.

> *He makes me to lie down in green pastures; He leads me beside the still waters. He restores my soul; He guides me in straight paths for His name's sake.*
>
> Psalm 23:2-3

Again King Saul set out with his army to fight the Philistines. When he returned from battle, there were some people who told him about the whereabouts of David and his men. They were in the wilderness hiding in the strongholds of En Gedi, which provided plenty of shelter.

This place was situated a long and hilly distance away from the town of Keilah, in the wilderness of Judah near the western shore of the Dead Sea, which is a salty lake known to be the lowest body of salt water below sea level on earth. But, there was also some food and fresh drinking water in this area of Judah's wilderness. Unlike the Dead Sea, En Gedi was an oasis, having springs and streams with their waterfalls and water pools, that also formed a haven for the animals in the wilderness.

Saul set out to find David and his men. He took with him three thousand soldiers that he had chosen and went to the rocks of the wild goats. Along the road they came to a sheep enclosure. There, Saul entered a cave to relieve himself. What he didn't know was that David and his men were hiding at the far end of that cave. When they saw Saul there all by himself, David's men told him that the Lord had delivered his enemy into his hands and that he may do as he pleased to him. Then David crept over to Saul and without him noticing, he cut off a piece of Saul's robe. Afterwards, he returned to his men who were still at the back of the cave.

The act of damaging the king's garment started to trouble David's conscience. Trying to prevent them from attacking Saul, David said to his warriors, *'That HaShem forbids me, that I should do this thing unto my lord, HaShem's anointed, to put forth my hand against him, seeing he is HaShem's anointed'*.*[18] David convinced them not to attack Saul while he was still in the cave.

When Saul got up and left the cave to continue his search, David followed him. He called to the king and when Saul turned around, he bowed down before him. He asked the king why he listened to people who told him that he was trying to harm him. David also told him about what just happened when they were in the cave, while showing him the piece of his robe that he had cut. David said, *I will not put forth my hand against my lord; for he is HaShem's anointed'*.*[19]

Furthermore David, who felt sorry for Saul, tried to convince Saul that he wasn't out to rebel against him or to harm him. He said, *'Moreover, <u>my father</u>, see the skirt of your robe in my hand; for I cut off the skirt of your robe, and killed you not, know you and see that there is neither evil nor transgression in my hand, and I have not sinned against you, though you lay in wait for my soul to take it. HaShem will judge between me and you, and HaShem will avenge me of you; but my hand shall not be upon you'.* *[20]

After he spoke of the ancient proverb that wickedness was done by the wicked, David compared himself to a dog or flea that the king was chasing, and he said, *'HaShem therefore be the judge, and give sentence between me and you, and see, and plead my cause, and deliver me out of your hand'.*[21]

Saul replied and said, *'Is this your voice, <u>my son David</u>'?*[22] Then King Saul wept. He said then to his son-in-law, *'<u>You are more righteous than I</u>; for you have rendered to me good, whereas I have rendered to you evil. And you have declared this day how that you have dealt well with me; for as much as when HaShem had delivered me up into your hand, you did not kill me. For if a man finds his enemy, will he let him go well away? Wherefore HaShem rewards you good for that which you have done to me this day'.*[23]

This was the first time that Saul and David spoke face to face about the kingship of the Kingdom of Israel. Saul told David, *'And now, behold, <u>I know that you shall surely be king</u>, and that the kingdom of Israel shall be established in your hand'.*[24]

When did Saul find out about David's kingship? Samuel didn't tell him who would become king after him. But Saul was from the beginning, since David killed Goliath, jealous and suspicious of him. Back then he already thought that the people might make David king one day. Saul wanting to insure the safety of his family, said to David, *'Swear now therefore to me by HaShem, that you will not cut off my seed after me, and that you will not destroy my name out of my father's house'.*[25]

Did Saul at this point also realise that David was the one God had chosen to fight his battles, and that He Himself with His army would march with David's in these battles? David swore to Saul that he would do as Saul asked of him. Did this father and son conversation mean that Saul would genuinely stop a future attempt to find and kill David? Afterwards, David and his men returned to the place they were hiding, and Saul went home.

> *And when HaShem shall have dealt well with my lord, then remember your handmaid (servant).*
>
> 1 Samuel 25:31

After David and Samuel met, the prophet and Judge Samuel, to whom God appeared since his youth, died and all of Israel mourned for him and buried him at his home town of Ramah. David and his men, went to the wilderness of Paran. There, they protected the flock of sheep of Nabal, whom was of the clan of Caleb from the town of

Maon, while it was in the fields with Nabal's shepherds. When David sent messengers to Nabal requesting some provisions from him for the coming feast day, Nabal refused. Maybe he had already heard stories about David and his men, because of what happened some days earlier. That Saul was in pursuit of David in the wilderness of Maon, and he didn't trust him. But, no. Nabal had never heard of David, as he told David's men, '*Who is David? and who is the son of Jesse? There are many servants nowadays that break away every man from his master*'.*[26]

And he added, '*shall I then take my bread, and my water, and my flesh (meat) that I have killed for my shearers, and give it unto men of whom I know not whence they are*'?*[27]

That's the message David's men brought back for him from their visit to Nabal. Nabal's wife Abigail heard from one of Nabal's servants what had happened. He also assured her that David and his men were kind to them when they were out in the wilderness. Realizing they were in danger, she set out to meet David and she took provisions for David and his men.

> *You prepare a table before me in the presence of my enemies.*
> Psalm 23:5a

When she saw David she quickly dismounted the donkey and she threw herself at his feet on the ground. Abigail and David spoke about Nabal, the gifts she brought with her, and she also prophesied to David. Abigail spoke of God's protection for him. This process of God's protection for David, that Abigail spoke about had already begun. And as Abigail's prophecy over David made clear, this would continue throughout his life. She also told him that when the Lord makes him king, he wouldn't have regrets concerning Nabal, as she said, '*that this shall be no stumbling-block to you, nor offense of heart to my lord, either that you have shed blood without cause, or that my lord has found redress for himself*'.*[27]

David was grateful to Abigail for preventing him from seeking his own revenge and blessed her. As David said to her, '*Blessed be HaShem, the God of Israel, who sent you this day to meet me; and blessed be your discretion, and <u>blessed be you</u>, <u>that has kept me this day from blood-guiltiness,</u> and from finding redress for myself with my own hand. For indeed, as HaShem, the God of Israel, lives, <u>Who has withheld me from hurting you</u>, except you had made haste and come to meet me, surely there had not been left to Nabal by the morning light* *so much as one male'.**28

Abigail had one last request for David. To remember her when the Lord fulfils His promise to him. David accepted what Abigail had brought for him. He told her to go back home and that he would do as she requested. She was not to be worried. Sometime later, after Nabal died, David married Abigail. She became David's third wife. Now, he was married to Saul's daughter Michal, Ahinoam from Jezreel and Abigail. But, while David was on the run, Saul gave Michal to Palti, who was the son of Laish, and lived in the town of Gallim.

David wasn't the only one of his family that married a widow. David's great grandfather Boaz married the Moabite widow Ruth. To whom Boaz said on one occasion, *'HaShem recompense your work, and be your reward complete from HaShem, the God of Israel, under whose wings you have come to take refuge'.**29 And, on another occasion Boaz blessed her saying, *'Blessed be you of HaShem ... you have shown more kindness in the end than at the beginning ... all the men in the gate of my people do know that you are a virtuous (good/impeccable) woman'.**30

In Moab, Ruth was married ten years to one of Naomi's sons. They didn't have children. But ... *'Boaz took Ruth, and she became his wife; and he went in to her, and HaShem gave her conception, and she bore a son'.**31 To her mother-in-law Naomi, whose two sons had died and whom didn't have grandchildren, the women said ... *'Blessed be HaShem, who has not left you this day without a near kinsman, and let his name be famous in Israel. And he shall be to you a restorer of life, and a nourisher of your old age; for your daughter-in-law, who loves you, who is better to you than seven sons, has born him'.**32 Thus Ruth became the great-grandmother of David.

Some Zephites went to Gibeah to see Saul. They informed him of David's whereabouts on Mount Hachilah situated at the border of the Judean wilderness. Immediately Saul gathered three thousand of his best soldiers to join him in his search for David. They set out to hunt him down and kill him. The commander of Saul's army, Abner son of Ner, was also with him. When they arrived at Mount Hachilah in the wilderness of Ziph, they encamped by the road.

When David heard that Saul was again searching for him, he sent scouts out to investigate. They located Saul's camp and they found out the exact place where Saul and Abner slept within the camp, surrounded by the camps of the king's men.

David wanted to go into Saul's camp. Why? To speak with Saul? Or to kill him? But he didn't want to go there alone. So he asked

Ahimelech the Hittite and Joab's brother Abishai, which one of them would want to go to the camp with him. At nightfall Abishai went with David to Saul's camp. They went to the place where Saul and Abner slept. Saul was asleep at the center of the camp, and near his head, his spear was stuck into the ground. Neither Saul nor Abner, who was asleep near Saul, noticed David's and Abishai's presence there. In fact none of the soldiers did. They were all in a deep sleep, which the Lord brought over them. Abishai told David that the Lord gave his enemy into his hand. He offered to kill Saul in one blow with his own spear. But, he didn't allow this. David said to him, '*Destroy him not; for who can put forth his hand against HaShem's anointed (chosen), and be guiltless*'?*33

And that, '*As HaShem lives, nay, but HaShem shall smite him; or his day shall come to die; or he shall go down into battle, and be swept away. HaShem forbid it me, that I should put forth my hand against HaShem's anointed*'.*34 Instead, David told him, they should take the lance and the jar of water, both near Saul, and leave. David took both and they left.

> *You have also given me Your shield of salvation, and Your right hand has held me up; and Your condescension (lordliness) has made me great.*
> Psalm 18:36 (2 Samuel 22:36)

They went to the hill at the other side of the valley, while keeping enough distance between them and Saul's camp. From there David shouted to Abner, who being Saul's commander should protect him at all time. Abner woke up while asking who was shouting and waking up their king. David answered Abner with a rhetorical question regarding him being the greatest man in Israel. And asking him why he didn't protect the king that night. David shouted that he deserved to die because he had failed in his duty to the king. He didn't protect him that night. David then held up Saul's spear and the water jar, while asking where the spear and the water jar that was near the king's head had gone.

Saul recognised David's voice, and he said, '*Is this your voice, my son David*'?

David answered: '*It is my voice, my lord, O king*'.*35 He then added, '*Wherefore does my lord pursue after his servant? For what have I done? Or what evil is in my hand? Now therefore, I pray you, let my lord the king hear the words of his servant. If it be HaShem that has stirred you up against me, let Him accept an offering; but if* it be the children of men, cursed be they before HaShem; for they have driven me out this day that I should not cleave unto the inheritance of HaShem, saying: Go, serve other gods. Now therefore, let not my blood fall to the earth away from the presence of HaShem; for the king of Israel has come out to seek a single flea, as when one does hunt a partridge in the mountains'.*36

Saul's response to David's words, 'I have sinned; return, <u>my son David</u>; for <u>I will no more do you harm</u>, because my life was precious in your eyes this day; behold, I have played the fool and erred exceedingly'.*37

Then David said to the king that he should let someone come to fetch the spear and the water jar. He added, 'And HaShem will render to every man his righteousness and his faithfulness; for as much as HaShem delivered you into my hand today, and I would not put forth my hand against HaShem's anointed. And, behold, as your life was much set by this day in mine eyes, so let my life be much set by in the eyes of HaShem, and let Him deliver me out of all tribulation'.*38

Then the king replied to David: '<u>Blessed be you</u>, <u>my son David</u>; you shall both do mightily, and <u>shall surely prevail</u>'.*39

So, David returned to his place of hiding, and Saul left with his men. But David was not convinced that Saul wouldn't try to kill him anyway, despite his reassuring words and blessing. After all, Saul had thrown his spear twice to him. Also once to his own son Jonathan. He went in pursuit of him again and again, and he had people killed because he believed they conspired against him in David's favour. So David decided for a second time, to escape from Saul by going to one of the Philistine kings. To Achish. David hoped that once he would be in Philistine territory, Saul would stop searching for him.

> How long, O HaShem, will You forget me for ever? How long will You hide Your face from me? How long shall I take counsel in my soul, having sorrow in my heart by day? How long shall my enemy be exalted over me? Behold You, and answer me, O HaShem my God; lighten my eyes, lest I sleep the sleep of death; Lest my enemy say: I have prevailed against him, lest my adversaries rejoice when I am moved.
>
> Psalm 13:1-5

Intermezzo 2

David and Achish

Is not this David, the king of the land?
1 Samuel 21:12

After the last time he spoke to Saul, David went to the city of Gath, where the Philistine Achish son of Maoch was king. But, this wasn't the first time that he fled to this city. The first time was after he went to see the High Priest Ahimelech. Just before, Jonathan, who just had a row with Saul at his festive meal during the Moon festival, had told him Saul wanted to kill him.

As soon as David arrived in Nob, where Israel's new communal altar was located after the Tabernacle in Shiloh was destroyed by the Philistines, he went to see Ahimelech. He came out to meet David and asked him why he was there all by himself. David didn't want Ahimelech to know what was going on. Maybe because he realised this could put Ahimelech's life in danger? Or to protect himself from him should he inform Saul about his whereabouts? So he told him that the king sent him on a secret mission and that he would rendezvous with his men at a certain place. Then he asked him for provisions. Five loaves of bread or whatever he had. The priest told him he only had fresh sacred bread that were for replacing that day, and that he could have these, providing that his men had kept themselves from women. David assured him that this was the case and he gave him the bread.

Ahimelech also inquired of the Lord for David as he had done many times before. David noticed that a servant of Saul, a man called Doeg from Edom, was there to fulfil a religious obligation. He then asked Ahimelech whether he had a spear or sword for him. David's excuse was that he had to leave in a hurry because of the king's orders and hadn't had time to take his own weapons with him. The only weapon Ahimelech had there was Goliath's sword. He told David to take it from behind the ephod. David said that there was no better sword like it anywhere. David took the sword and left.

Then, with Goliath's sword in hand, David went alone to Goliath's hometown of Gath. Achish was the Philistine king of that city. The king's servants saw David there. Who is this man? They said to him, '*Is not this David*'?*[1]

But, who is this David?

They continued by saying, '*the king of the land? Did they not sing one to another of him in dances, saying: Saul has slain his thousands, and David his ten thousands'?*[*2]

David's reputation went before him. David took what they said to heart. He was so afraid of Achish, that he changed his behaviour. Whenever Achish's servants were around, David would pretend to be insane and they would try to restrain him. As a madman he would scribble on the city's doors, and dribble his saliva down on his beard. When Achish had enough of this he said to his servants, *'When you see a man that is mad, why do you bring him to me? Do I lack madmen, that you have brought this fellow to play the madman in my presence? Shall this fellow come into my house'?*[*3]

Eventually David fled from the city and went into hiding in a cave near Adullam. When his family, including his parents and brothers, heard he was there, they joined him. About four hundred men also joined him there and he became their leader. These men themselves were embittered because of their own problems and debts. But with David they would become warriors and later on military leaders themselves. David took his father and mother to the king of Moab, who allowed them to stay there in safety for some time. They remained in Moab as long as David was in the cave of Adullam. Then the prophet Gad came to see David in Adullam, and he told him to leave at once and go to the forest of Hereth. David did as the prophet told him. After some time he and his men left the forest to go to the walled town of Keilah that was under attack from the Philistines. There, Abiathar the son of the High Priest Ahimelech joined David. Abiathar had taken the apron-like garment of the High Priest, called the ephod, with him. Like David, he was also in fear of his life. Abiathar told David what happened after he left Ahimelech.

Sometime later King Saul had summoned Ahimelech and all his relatives. The reason? Information that one of his servants had given him. Saul was in Gibeah, in the territory of Benjamin, sitting under a tamarisk tree talking to his servants including Doeg, while holding his spear in his hand. He spoke to them about the situation concerning David. He told them that Jesse's son wouldn't be the one to give them positions in his army, nor would he reward them with vineyards and fields. That no one had told him about his son Jonathan's alliance, covenant, with David. Furthermore, that none of them were in the least concerned about his safety, while his servant David encouraged by his own son Jonathan is looking to kill him. At this moment there was no doubt in Saul's mind that David was out to kill him. And he was even more concerned with the covenant between Jonathan and David, which he perceived to be a deadly conspiracy against him. Then his servant Doeg the Edomite, told Saul that David went to see Ahimelech, who gave him provisions and Goliath's sword, and that he inquired of the Lord for him.

Saul questioned Ahimelech as soon as he and his relatives, the Kohanim of Nob, arrived. Saul asked him why he was plotting with David against him. Also, why he gave David food, a sword and inquired of the Lord for him. He told Ahimelech that David turned against him, and that he was waiting for an opportunity to kill him. Ahimelech was shocked by the accusation of the king, and replied, *'Who among all your servants is so trusted as David, who is the king's son-in-law, and gives heed (attention) to your bidding (command), and is honourable in your house'?*[*4] He added, that he himself and his family had no knowledge of the conflict between him and David, and that he should not accuse them of this matter. The king, probably believing he was dealing with a conspiracy against him, and therefore had the beginnings of a rebellion on his hands, told Ahimelech that he and all his relatives had to die. Because they had conspired with David and did not tell him that he had fled.

Saul showed no concern that these priests were servants of the Lord God. Immediately he gave the order to his guards who were standing there next to him, to kill the Lord's priests. The guards refused to execute the order. Then Saul told Doeg to kill them. On that day, he killed eighty-five priests. Saul also ordered to kill all the inhabitants of the city of Nob, where the priests lived with their families. Levites and priests living among the Israelites in other towns and cities were not killed. They were all put to death by the sword. Men, women, children and babies, and their donkeys, sheep and cattle. Abiathar lost all his relatives. As long as Saul was king, no one inquired about the Ark of the Covenant. As David once said after Saul's death, *'and let us bring back the Ark of our God to us; for we sought not to it in the days of Saul'.*[*5]

After Abiathar's story, David told him he had seen Doeg when he went to talk to his father, and he was sure that he would tell Saul about his visit. He felt responsible for the killing that took place, but that he should stay, because he would be safe with him.

Abiathar stayed and continued some of his priestly duties with David and he remained loyal to David. When David heard Saul was coming to Keilah, he and his now six hundred men left for the wilderness near Ziph, and afterwards for the wilderness of Maon, where Saul was in pursuit of them. All of this occurred before the first time that David spared Saul's life. After that, David went to the wilderness of Paran where he met the woman that would become his third wife, Abigail.

> When a man's ways pleases HaShem, He makes even his enemies to be at peace with him.
>
> Proverbs 16:7

One day Saul went to look for David with an army of three thousand men. He was in hiding on Mount Machilah. David spared Saul's life. Now, after this second time that David spared his father-in-law's life, he went to Achish for a second time. But this time, he was not alone. He took his family, and the six hundred men with him, did the same. Also the king knew this time around that David was a wanted man, persecuted by King Saul.

David himself told Achish that there was no need for him to stay in Gath, the city where the king lived. They settled in a town in the countryside called Ziklag, which Achish had given to him. Making this town the property of Judah's kings. Achish thought David was so hated by his own people in Israel, that he had to serve him for the rest of his life. He trusted David, so much so that he would later on make him his permanent bodyguard. David and his men with their families remained in Philistine territory for sixteen months, during which they attacked and raided the Geshurites, Gizrites, Amalekites, taking all their cattle, sheep, camels and donkeys, and clothing. Leaving no one alive, to tell anyone especially not Achish about who raided them. These were people that were to be driven from Canaan when the Israelites arrived there. They were actually enemies of the people of Israel. When Achish asked David where he had been, he told him he raided Israelite families in the Land of Judah. Achish believed him. When the five Philistine kings were mobilizing their troops against the Israelites, Achish told David that he had to fight for him. David assured him that he was his servant, and that he would show him what he can do. Did David really have the intention to be loyal to Achish, and fight against his own people? Until then, David wasn't loyal to Achish and he didn't fight the Israelites. But, Achish believed whatever David told him. He appointed David his personal bodyguard.

The Philistine kings marched together to Aphek where they set up their army camp. David and his men marched with King Achish in the rear. In the meantime, Saul was also gathering his army at the spring in the Valley of Jezreel. The Philistine officers, princes, who saw David and his men, asked what those Hebrews were doing there. Achish answered, '*Is not this David, the servant of Saul the king of Israel, who has been with me these days or these years, and I have found no fault in him since he fell away to me to this day*'?*[6]

They were angry with Achish, because unlike him they didn't trust David at all. They told Achish to send David back. Because David might turn against them and fight them in an attempt to win back the trust of his master, the king of Israel, so he could reconcile himself with him. Sometime earlier during the battle at Michmash, the Hebrews who fought with the Philistines did change sides, and instead fought with King Saul and Jonathan against them. They also said to Achish, '*Is not this David, of whom they sang one to another in dances, saying: Saul has slain his thousands, and David his ten thousands*'?*[7]

Achish called David and told him that the other kings didn't approve of him going on military campaigns with them to fight the Israelites. Though he himself didn't find any fault in him. He told him to return home and that he shouldn't do anything to displease the kings. David insisted in going with Achish to fight his enemies. Achish told him that he considered him loyal as an angel. But, that he couldn't go with him, because the other kings didn't want this. He told David to leave as soon as it was light. The next morning the Philistine army continued its march to Jezreel, while David and his men returned to Ziklag.

Ziklag

> *Though I walk through the valley of the shadow of death, I will fear no evil, for <u>You are with me</u>; Your rod and Your staff, they comfort me.*
>
> Psalm 23:4

David and his men returned to find Ziklag burned down and empty. There were no wives, sons nor daughters. But there were no deaths either. Where was everyone? And who did this? The place was raided and all the people were carried away, including David's wives Ahinoam and Abigail. These people also took all the flocks and herds with them. With no warriors present when they came, there was no resistance and therefore no fatalities. David and the men were all so sad, they started crying until they were exhausted. This situation created great trouble for David. Because the men were sad and angry at him for losing their children. Their bitterness was so great, that they could stone David to death. But David drew courage and strength from the Lord God. Abiatar the priest brought the ephod to David as he requested. David sought God's counsel, by asking the Lord whether he should go after the raiders. Also, whether he would catch them if he did. The Lord told him to go after the raiders, and that he would catch them. So, David and his men set out to find them.

David left Ziklag with all six hundred men, but he crossed the brook of Besor with four hundred men. The two hundred men he left behind were too tired and weak to cross the brook and continue the journey. Some of David's warriors found an Egyptian man in the countryside and brought him to David. They gave him some water and something to eat. When he regained his strength, he answered David's questions. He told him who he was, who his master was and what had happened. He was an Egyptian slave of an Amalekite, who left him behind to die because he was ill, three full days earlier. They had raided the Cherethite's territory in Judah's southern region, the territory of Caleb's clan and Ziklag, which they burned down. So it was the Amalekites that had raided his town, and had captured their families. David and his men still wanted to save their families, so David asked the Egyptian whether he wanted to lead them to the Amalekites. He would do so on two conditions. If David swore not to hand him over to his Amalekite master, and if he would let him live.

The Egyptian man led them to the Amalekites, who were scattered all over the area where they found them. They were all celebrating, having a great amount of spoils gathered from the Land of Judah and the Philistines. Enjoying themselves drinking and eating, they were off guard. The next day at dawn, David and his men attacked them and they fought until the evening. Only four hundred Amalekite men escaped by taking their camels. David and his men rescued all their families, their possessions and all the livestock. No one and nothing was missing. They took all the loot that the Amalekites had gathered with them. David's men drove all the livestock up front while they were shouting along the way that all of it belonged to David.

David returned to the two hundred men he left at the brook of Besor, and he greeted the men warmly. He didn't only return their families to them, but they were allowed to share in the loot. Some of his men didn't agreed with this. David made a rule that would become the practice in Israel, that those who stayed behind with the supplies would always share in the loot, just as those who went to battle. David told them that it was the Lord God who gave them victory over their enemies. And when they returned to Ziklag, David also sent part of the loot to his friends and to Judah's leaders with the message that it was part of the loot that they had taken from the Lord's enemies. He also sent gifts to the people of the places where he and his men had lingered while on the run from King Saul.

Meanwhile, the Philistine troops set up their camp near the town Shunem. Saul, confronted with the gathered army of the Philistines, was terrified when he saw their camp and he needed advice. But God's prophet Samuel had died. So he couldn't ask him for counsel on what God would want him to do. And the Urim and Tummim? The priestly device placed on the breastplate on which the twelve precious stones symbolizing the twelve tribes were, which the High Priest wore over his ephod. The High Priest used this device to determine God's will for the king, the Sanhedrin – the Israelite court – or someone serving the nation. Saul had the High Priest and his relatives killed, and Abiathar took the ephod with him. So there was no answer from the Urim and the Tummim either. Nor did the Lord answer Saul by prophets or dreams. God kept silent, and Saul remained without God's much needed advice. He understood that God had abandoned him. Saul decided to go to a medium. He ordered his officials to find him one.

The Lord God gave His people a clear prohibition concerning idolatry in His Ten Commandments. As written, '*You shall have no other gods before Me. You shall not make to yourself a graven image, nor any manner of likeness, of anything that is in heaven above, or that is in the earth beneath, or that is in the water under the earth; you shall not bow down to them, nor serve them.*'*[40] And ... *They that make them (idols) shall be like unto them; yea, everyone that trusts in them. O Israel, trust you in HaShem! He is their help and their shield*'!*[41]

Neither were the Israelites to engage into pagan practices such as child sacrifice, divination, the use of spells or charms, nor should they look for occult omens. Also, the Israelites were not to seek advice from false prophets, false interpreters of dreams, nor of people who consult with spirits of the dead. The Israelites should not engage in any of these or other pagan practices. As is written, '*There shall not be found among you anyone that makes his son or his daughter to pass through the fire, one that uses divination, a soothsayer, or an enchanter, or a sorcerer, or a charmer, or one that consults a ghost or* *a familiar spirit, or a necromancer (occultist)'.*[*42]

And the Lord's prophets would always continue to warn against such practices, as did Zechariah. *'For the teraphim (images) have spoken vanity, and the diviners have seen a lie, and the dreams speak falsely, they comfort in vain; therefore they go their way like sheep, they are afflicted, because there is no shepherd'.*[*43] The use of teraphim for pagan practices, like house idols either small ones as Rachel had taken from her father, or large ones as Saul's daughter Michal had at her home, was forbidden by the Lord. Concerning all these, King Saul had followed the Lord's instructions by banning all those who provided for pagan services from the Land of Israel.

Instead he and the people of Israel took counsel from the Lord God, given by His prophets or by the High Priest and priests, who used the Urim and Tummim for these purposes. The Lord God Himself made sure that the prophets' words came to pass. He Himself also gave an insight in matters through personal words, dreams, visions and signs, and the understanding of these.

The Patriarchs, the prophets as for instance Joseph, Deborah, Elijah, Daniel, David and many others received God's guidance in this way. The Lord God is holy, and He gives power and knowledge to His people through His forces of holiness. Therefore, they should avoid the forces of evil. The people of Israel formed a holy nation to the Lord God, Who Himself is Holy.

Though there were no mediums in the whole of Israel, Saul's servants knew of a woman who lived in Endor. Despite God's prohibition, of which he was well aware, Saul went that night in disguise with two of his men to see this woman. The woman recognised the king and he had to promise her that he wouldn't have her killed.

The result of this visit? Saul heard that God had taken the kingdom from him and had in fact given it to David because of his disobedience. This was something Saul already knew, and he had already told David the first time he met him after he spared his life in the cave, that he knew that he would one day become king. He also heard that he and his sons would die the next day. He became terrified. His men persuaded him to eat some food that the woman had prepared for him. Saul was weak because he didn't eat the whole day and night. He ate and then they left the same night. Believing what he was told, still King Saul continued to prepare for war against the Philistines. Their impending death didn't stop him from going to battle against the Philistines.

The Israelites encamped at the spring in the Valley of Jezreel, while the Philistines set up their camp at Aphek. The battle took take place on Mount Gilboa. The Israelites were defeated that day. Many Israelite soldiers died on Mount Gilboa. King Saul, his sons and many Israelite soldiers fled. But the Philistines went in pursuit, caught up with them, fought them and killed them. Saul and three of his sons, Jonathan, Abinadab and Malchishua died that day. Saul was badly wounded by enemy arrows. Then Saul said to his armour-bearer, "*Draw your sword, and thrust me through with it; lest these uncircumcised come and thrust me through, and make a mock of me.*"*[44] The young man who was too terrified refused. So Saul took his own sword or spear and he tried to kill himself by throwing himself on it. When the armour-bearer saw what happened, he killed himself. An Amalekite who lived in Israel and was by chance on Mount Gilboa, would later on tell David how Saul actually died. The Amalekite had escaped from the Israelite army camp when they fled from the battle. He had found Saul dying while thrusted on his spear. Saul looked behind him and when he saw the young man, he called him and asked him, '*Who are you*'?*[45] He told him that he was an Amalekite. Then Saul said to him, '*Stand, I pray you, beside me, and slay me, for the agony has taken hold of me; because my life is just yet in me*'.*[46] The king gave this man permission to kill him.

The Amalekite did as Saul had requested. He killed him, because he knew Saul was about to die at the hand of the Philistines anyway. He saw that their army of horsemen and chariots were overtaking him and his army. The Amalekite did what Saul's armour-bearer didn't dare do. Similar to Doeg the Edomite, who killed the Lord's priests on Saul's orders, while his other servants dared not. So, Saul died at the hand of an Amalekite. Was it God's mercy that he didn't undergo in life what he feared at the time of his death? The Philistines mocking him.

When the Israelites living on the other side of the Jezreel Valley and to the east of Jordan River, heard about Saul and his sons' fate, they all fled, abandoning their town to the Philistines that occupied them. The day after, when the Philistines went to plunder the dead on Mount Gilboa, they found the bodies of Saul and his three sons. They stripped Saul of his armour and they cut Saul's head off. They sent messengers around with these, and they put Saul's armour in the temple of one of their idols. When the people of the town Jabesh in Gilead heard what had happened, they marched all night to get to the place where their bodies were. They recovered the bodies from the wall where the Philistines hanged them, brought them to Jabesh, burned them and buried the bones under the tamarisk tree in the town. They all fasted and mourned them for seven days. When word of Saul's and Jonathan's death reached David, he also grieved for them.

> But as for me, in <u>Your mercy do I trust</u>; my heart shall rejoice in <u>Your salvation</u>. I will sing to HaShem, because He has dealt <u>bountifully</u> with me.
>
> Psalm 13:6-9

David was a fugitive for a lengthy period of time. David, his household, his family and the men who joined him lived together in hiding in the wilderness of Judah. While on the run, David often inquired of the Lord God about what he should do. During this time, David and his men dwelt in many places.

When David fled, he went to his house where he lived with his wife Michal, Saul's daughter. Afterwards he went to Ramah to see Saul. Then to Naioth in Ramah where he spoke to Jonathan. After the New Moon feast, he had a conversation with Jonathan in the field. After which he went to Nob to speak with the High Priest Ahimelech. Then he went to Gath, where Achish a Philistine king ruled. Soon he left there and he went to the stronghold near Adullam, where four hundred men joined him. On the word brought by the prophet Gad, they left there and went to the Land of Judah to the forest of Hereth. They remained in the Land of Judah, and went to Keilah to save the town. After Keilah, David and his men, now six hundred, went to Horesh in the wilderness of Ziph and stayed on the Mount Hachilah. Then they went to the wilderness of Maon, and afterwards to En Gedi where David did not kill Saul when he had the chance. On this occasion, Saul wept and he called his son David a man more righteous than himself for sparing his life. He also told David that he knew that one day he would surely become king of Israel, and he asked David to promise he wouldn't destroy his name out of his father's house.

After En Gedi, they left to the wilderness of Paran where David met Abigail. Afterwards, they went to Mount Hachilah, where David spared Saul's life for a second time. This time, Saul told his son David that he would not try to harm him again, that David would surely prevail. And King Saul blessed David. After this, David and his men went to the territory of the Philistines, to Gath, where Achish gave him the town of Ziklag. They lived there with their families sixteen months. Saul and David never met again, but the last time they spoke, brought reconciliation between them. After Saul's death, David and his men went to Hebron in Judah. It's there where the people of the tribe of Judah, who remained loyal to David, made him king. David ruled from Hebron over this first Kingdom of Judah for seven and a half years.

> *HaShem is my shepherd; I shall not want. ... Surely goodness and mercy shall follow me all the days of my life; and I shall dwell in the house of HaShem for ever.*
>
> Psalm 23:6

Endnotes

*[1]Samuel 23:4, *[2]1 Samuel 23:10-11, *[3]1 Samuel 23:11*[4], 1 Samuel 23:12, *[5]1 Samuel 23:12, *[6]1 Samuel 13:11, *[7]1 Samuel 13:13-14, *[8]1 Samuel 15:3, *[9]1 Samuel 15:2, *[10]1 Samuel 15:11, *[11]1 Samuel 15:22, *[12]1 Samuel 15:23, *[13]1 Samuel 15:24, *[14]1 Samuel 15:26, *[15]1 Samuel 15:28-29, *[16]1 Samuel 15:33, *[17]1 Samuel 16:21, *[18]1 Samuel 24:7, *[19]1 Samuel 24:11, *[20]1 Samuel 24:12-13, *[21]1 Samuel 24:16, *[22]1 Samuel 24:17$_a$, *[23]1 Samuel 24:18-20, *[24]1 Samuel 24:21, *[25]1 Samuel 24:21-22, *[26]1 Samuel 25:10, *[27]1 Samuel 25:11, *[27]1 Samuel 25:31, *[28]1 Samuel 25:32-34, *[29]Ruth 2:10-12, *[30]Ruth 3:10-12, *[31]Ruth 4:13, *[32]Ruth 4:14-15, *[33]1 Samuel 26:9, *[34]1 Samuel 26:10-11, *[35]1 Samuel 26:17, *[36]1 Samuel 26:18-20, *[37] 1 Samuel 26:21, *[38]1 Samuel 26:23-24, *[39]1 Samuel 26:25, *[40]Exodus 20:3-5$_a$, *[41]Psalm 115:4-14, *[42]Deuteronomy 18:9-13, *[43]Zechariah 10:2, *[44]1 Samuel 31:4, *[45]2 Samuel 1:8, *[46]2 Samuel 1:9

David and Saul: father and son reconciliation, by Angeline Leito
http://www.thegreenolivetree.nl/index.php/14-articles/king-david/108-david-and-saul-father-and-sons-reconciliation
Jewish Virtual Library, https://www.jewishvirtuallibrary.org
En Gedi, https://www.jewishvirtuallibrary.org/vie-ein-gedi
1 Samuel 23:29, 24:1-2, Ezekiel 47:8-10 En Gedi
Israel Tourism The Bible Comes To Life – En Gedi
https://www.youtube.com/watch?v=1YfIyZJFvrQ
David sought God's counsel:
1 Samuel 22:10 priest Ahimelech inquires for David
1 Samuel 23:2-12, 4, 6 attack Philistines, go to Keilah, leave Keilah, priest Abiathar
1 Samuel 30:8 pursue raiding party
2 Samuel 2:1 take control of Hebron in Judah
2 Samuel 5:19, 1 Chronicles 14:10 attack Philistines
1 Samuel 13:5, 7-15, 15:10-31, 34-35 Saul's first mistake, Saul's second act of disobedience

Who Is David?

1 Samuel 13:14, 15:23-29, 28:17 because of Saul's disobedience, God gave the kingdom to David
1 Chronicles 10:1-13 Saul's unfaithfulness to God and his death
1 Samuel 16:1-13 David anointed king
1 Samuel 13:14 David a man that does God's will, a man to God's heart
2 Samuel 5:24 God's army marches with David's
1 Samuel 14:20-23 Hebrews changed sides and fought with the Israelites
1 Samuel 15:32-33 Agag's death by Samuel, Saul reigned forty years
1 Samuel 19:1, 20:2 Saul trusted his son Jonathan
1 Samuel 18:6-9, 11,15 Saul jealous of David, and afraid of him
1 Samuel 18:11, 19:9-10, 33 Saul throws a spear on two occasions to David, and once to Jonathan
2 Samuel 4:4, 16:1-4, 21:1-14, 21:8, 1 Samuel 20:15, 2 Samuel 9:3,6 Saul's family, Jonathan's son
1 Samuel 3:21, Deuteronomy 18:14-22 Samuel God's prophet
1 Samuel 12:13-25 Samuel about Israelites king and obedience to God
Ruth 4:17-22 David's great grandfather married the widow Ruth
1 Samuel 18:8-9, 12 Saul jealous and suspicious of David
1 Samuel 16:21-22, 18:22 Saul loved David, David Saul's son-in-law
1 Samuel 18:11, 19:9-10, 33 Saul threw a spear twice to David, once to Jonathan
Psalm 18:1,50 deliverance David from Saul
Psalm 59:1, 1 Samuel 19:10-17 Saul's men watches Michal's house to kill David
Psalm 54:1 Ziphites told Saul that David was among them
Psalm 57:1 David hides in a cave
1 Samuel 16:14-21, 17:12-15, 17:58 David's family, David's looks
1 Samuel 20:14-15 David's arrangement for his family with Jonathan
1 Samuel 22:1 David's brothers and family joint him in the cave of Adullam
1 Samuel 22:3-4 David brought his parents to the king of Moab
1 Samuel 18:23 David considered himself a poor man
1 Samuel 16:1-13 Samuel anointed David to be king
1 Samuel 16:14-23 David at Saul's court, musician, evil spirit on Saul
1 Samuel 17 David and Goliath
1 Samuel 18:11 first time Saul throws his lance twice on David, he evades it twice
1 Samuel 18:12, 28-29, 20:30-31, 22:8 Saul afraid of David
1 Samuel 22:8 Saul did not know about covenant of friendship between Jonathan and David
1 Samuel 18: 16 the people loved David
1 Samuel 17:17-30 David married Saul's daughter Michal
1 Samuel 19:1-8 Saul planned to kill David, Jonathan warned David, Jonathan spoke with Saul, Saul changed his mind, David returned to Saul's court

David and Saul

- 1 Samuel 19:9-10 Saul throws his lance 2nd time to David, David flees to Michal's house
- 1 Samuel 19:11-17 escaped from the soldiers at Michal's house
- 1 Samuel 19:18, 1 Samuel 20:1a David went to Samuel
- 1 Samuel 19:19-24 Saul also went to Samuel
- 1 Samuel 20:1a David left Samuel
- 1 Samuel 20:1b-23 David went to Jonathan, Jonathan's plan
- 1 Samuel 20:24 David hid in the field
- 1 Samuel 20: 18-34 new moon feast
- 1 Samuel 20:24-26, 27-34 1st day new moon feast, 2nd day new moon feast
- 1 Samuel 19:1, 20:31, 20:27-33 Saul says David had to die, argument Saul and Jonathan
- 1 Samuel 30:33 Saul threw his spear at Jonathan
- 1 Samuel 20:35-21:1 David met Jonathan in the field, David leaves
- 1 Samuel 21:2-10, 21:8 David went to the priest Ahimelech, weapons and food, the Edomite Doeg
- 1 Samuel 21:11-16 David fled to Achish the king of Gath
- 1 Samuel 22:1-5 David went to the cave of Adullam, commander of 400 men who gathered there
- 1 Samuel 22:3-4 David brought parents to the king of Moab
- 1 Samuel 22:1, 24:1 Adullam, En Gedi
- 1 Samuel 22:5 prophet Gad's message, David went to Judah, forest of Hereth
- 1 Samuel 22:6-23, 22:7-8 Saul with his men in Gibeah, Saul's speech to his men
- 1 Samuel 20:31a, 22:8 Saul thought David wanted to kill him
- 1 Samuel 23:1-5 David went to Keilah to fight the Philistines, freed inhabitants of Keilah
- 1 Samuel 23:10-12 David inquired of the Lord what to do, left Keilah
- 1 Samuel 23:13 David left Keilah, with 600 men he travelled around without a place to live
- 1 Samuel 23:14a, 30:27-31 strongholds in the wilderness/desert, several places where David went
- 1 Samuel 23:14-15 David went to the stronghold of Ziph
- 1 Samuel 23:14 Saul's daily persecution of David
- 1 Samuel 23:16-18 Jonathan visited David, covenant of friendship
- 1 Samuel 23:19-24 some inhabitants of Ziph betrayed David to Saul, plan to capture David
- 1 Samuel 23:25 David on the Rock in the desert of Maon
- 1 Samuel 23:25-28 Saul in pursuit of David, Saul had to leave to fight Philistines
- 1 Samuel 24:1 David went to the stronghold of En Gedi
- 1 Samuel 24:1-23, 24:10-11 David spared Saul's life, David felt sorry for Saul
- 1 Samuel 24:12, 24:17 father and son conversation

Who Is David?

1 Samuel 25:1, 28:3 Samuel died
1 Samuel 25:1 David in Paran desert
1 Samuel 25:2-44, 1-3 David meets Abigail, her husband was Nabal lived in Maon
1 Samuel 26:1 second time some inhabitants of Ziph betrayed David to Saul
1 Samuel 26:2 Saul changed his mind, with 3000 men persecuted David
1 Samuel 26:1-25 second time David saved Saul's life, reconciliation
1 Samuel 27:1 David still afraid Saul would kill him
1 Samuel 28:3-4, 5-6 Samuel died, Saul had banned mediums
1 Samuel 28:5-6 Saul sought the Lord's advice, He remained silent
1 Samuel 28:7-25 Saul asked for a medium, and went to her
Leviticus 19:31, Deuteronomy 13:1-18, 18:9-13 no pagan practices
Genesis 31:34, 1 Samuel 19:13,16 Rachel, Michal had teraphim
1 Samuel 28:6, Exodus 28:30 Urim and Tummim
1 Samuel 31, 1 Chronicles 10:2 Philistines killed Saul's sons Jonathan, Abinadab and Malki-Shua
1 Samuel 31:4, 2 Samuel 1:5-10 Saul thrusted himself on his sword, killed by an Amalekite
2 Samuel 1:1-16 David hears about Saul's and Jonathan's death

Intermezzo 1 Endnotes

*¹*Adonai-nissi*, in other translations, such as: Tanach, Artscroll: "Hashem is my Miracle"
*²Exodus 14:14-16
Genesis 36:16 Amalek grandchild of Esau
Numbers 13:29 territory where the Amalekites and other people lived in Canaan
Deuteronomy 25:17-19 Israel should fight the Amalekites
Exodus 17:10-12, 24:14, 31:1-3, 35:30-31, 38:22 Hur
1 Chronicles 2:42, 50-51 Hur son of Caleb, Salma founded Bethlehem
Exodus 14:39-45 without God's support Israelites can't defeat Amalekites
Numbers 24:7 Balaam's prophecy: Israel's king would be greater than Agag
Deuteronomy 25:17-19, 1 Samuel 15:2, Exodus 17:8-13 God's reason to destroy the Amalekites
Exodus 17:8-16 Joshua fought the Amalekites on Moses' orders
2 Samuel 1:6-10 an Amalekite killed King Saul
1 Samuel 15 Saul fights the Amalekites, Agag killed by Samuel
1 Samuel 30 David defeats the Amalekites
Esther 3:1 Haman a descendant of Agag, Amalekite kind, tried to eradicate Jews in Babylonia
Esther 3:2-4, 5-6 Mordechai didn't bow down for Haman, Haman planned to eradicate the Jews
Deuteronomy 7: 1, Joshua 3:10, Israelites overthrew seven nations in Canaan
Deuteronomy 25:19,1 Chronicles 4:41-43 Amalekite nation overthrown, destroyed by Simon's tribe

2 Kings 18:5-8 King Hezekiah defeated the Philistine nation

Intermezzo 2 Endnotes

*¹1 Samuel 21:12, *²1 Samuel 21:12, *³1 Samuel 21:15-16, *⁴1 Samuel 22:14, *⁵1 Chronicles 13:3, *⁶1 Samuel 29:3, *⁷1 Samuel 29:5

Holy Land Uncovered | i24news / Routes Uncovered: Tel Tzafit, Ancient City of Gath
https://www.youtube.com/watch?v=ZpLQut1Q1L8
Holy Land Uncovered | i24news
Routes Uncovered: King Saul & King David
https://www.youtube.com/watch?v=bu1vIk94ayQ
Jewish Virtual Library, Ancient Jewish History: The Urim & Tummim
https://www.jewishvirtuallibrary.org/the-urim-and-Tummim
1 Samuel 17:4, 21:10 Goliath was from Gath, David takes Goliath's sword
1 Samuel 21:1-2 David escapes to Achish, first time
1 Samuel 14:3, 22:9-11, 23:20 Ahimelech or Ahijah, Ahitub's son, Phinehas' son, Eli's son
1 Samuel 1:25-28, Abiathar family of High Priest Eli who brought up Samuel
1 Samuel 22:20, 1 Kings 1:25, 2:26-27, 35 ultimately Eli's descendant, Abiathar son of High Priest Ahimelech lost service as High Priest
1 Samuel 1:27-36, 4:1-22, 14:3,22, 22:20-23 prophecy against Eli and his descendants, their death
1 Kings 1:25, 2:26-27, 35 Abiathar would lose the priesthood
1 Samuel 22:6-23 King Saul against the Lord's priests
Psalm 52:1 Edomite told Saul that David met with the High Priest Ahimelech
1 Samuel 22:9-10 Doeg's told Saul about Ahimelech and David
1 Samuel 22:18-19 Ahimelech killed eighty-five priests by Doeg before the king on the king's orders
1 Samuel 22:18 Ahimelech killed by Doeg before the King Saul on his orders
1 Samuel 22:18-19 eighty-five priests killed
1 Samuel 22:19 priestly families killed in Kohanim's priestly city of Nob
1 Samuel 23:6 Abiathar son of Ahimelech fled to David in Keilah
1 Samuel 23:6, 9 Abiathar took the Ephod with him
Exodus 28:15-30, Leviticus 8:8I, Numbers 27:21, 1 Samuel 28:6, I Samuel 14:3,18 Urim and Tummim
1 Samuel 22:1, 5, 1 Samuel 23:5 David in stronghold Adullam, then forest Hereth, then Keilah in the wilderness near Ziph, then Maon
1 Samuel 22:2, 1 Chronicles 12: 1 the men who joined David in Adullam
1 Samuel 25:43-44 David's first three wives, Michal, Ahinoam and Abigail
1 Samuel 27:1-12, 28:1-2, 29:1-11 David second time with Achish, the Philistines
1 Samuel 30 David fights against the Amalakites
1 Samuel 22:2, 23:13 400 men, later 600 men with David
1 Samuel 27:6 town of Ziklag David's and the kings of Judah's possession

Who Is David?

1 Samuel 27:2, 27:5-6 David with 600 men goes to Achish son of Maoch king of Gath
1 Samuel 27:4-6 Achish gives Ziklag to David
1 Samuel 27:3 David's wives Ahinoam and Abigail with him, men also their household with them
1 Samuel 27:7 David stays one year and four month in Philistine territory
1 Samuel 27:4 Saul stopped his persecution of David
1 Samuel 28 Saul goes to a medium
1 Samuel 29:1-11 Philistines mistrust David and sent him and his men away
1 Samuel 13:5-7, 14:20-21 Hebrews changed sides and fought instead with King Saul and Jonathan
1 Samuel 30:1 after three days David and his men arrived in Ziklag
1 Samuel 30 Ziklag was raided, David and his men rescued their families, they divided the spoils
1 Samuel 27:8-12 David attacked the Geshurites, Gizrites, Amalakites
Deuteronomy 20:16-18, people to be driven out of Canaan
1 Samuel 29:2 five Philistine kings

DAVID AND JOAB
Wisdom, Patience and Justice

Unto David, and unto his seed, and unto his house, and unto his throne, shall there be peace for ever from HaShem.

1 Kings 2:33b

David and his men returned to Ziklag with their families after their victory over the Amalekites. On the third day that they were in town, David received a visitor. It was a young man, who had earth on his head and whose clothes were torn. He bowed to the ground in front of David. David asked him where he came from, and he replied that he came from the Israelite military camp. On David's question about what had happened, he told him that the Israelites fled during the battle against the Philistines, and that many men were killed including King Saul and his son Jonathan. Then David asked him how he could be so sure that both Saul and Jonathan had died. He told him that he was the person that had ultimately killed Saul on his own request. And he showed David the crown and Saul's arm bracelet that he brought for him. David tore his garments, and all his men and the people with him did this as well. They fasted and wept all day long until the evening. They were in mourning for Saul, Jonathan, the many men that had fallen by the sword that day with them and for the nation of Israel. David asked the young man who brought him the news, where he was from. He said that he was an Amalekite that lived in Israel. David said to him, '*How were you not afraid to put forth your hand to destroy HaShem's anointed*'?*[1] Saul was chosen by the Lord God and he was anointed to be king of Israel. He was not to be harmed. So, David didn't consider what happened to him and his sons as being good news. David's own conscience troubled him once at the thought of he himself harming Saul, when he had the chance to kill him. Instead he said to Abishai, who was one of his men, that Saul might one day die of natural causes or in battle. David punished this man who in his view murdered Saul, by ordering one of his men to kill him. And David said, '*Your blood be upon your head; for your mouth has testified against you, saying: I have slain HaShem's anointed*'.*[2] Afterwards David spoke fondly of Jonathan while lamenting over him and King Saul.

Who Is David?

Now that the king had died, David could leave Ziklag and safely return to the Land of Israel. But, he had to decide where to go. He consulted with the Lord by asking Him whether he should go up to one of Judah's cities. The Lord made it clear to him that he should go up to the city of Hebron. Then David took his wives, Ahinoam from Jezreel and Abigail from Carmel, with him to Hebron. And so did his men with their families. They all went to Hebron and settled in the towns around the city.

Would Judah still be loyal to David? Whether they were or not became apparent when the men, the leaders of Judah, came to Hebron to see David. There, Judah's tribe anointed him to be their king. As king over the House of Judah, he therefore was king of Judah, but not of all Israel. David, the first king of the first Kingdom of Judah would rule from Hebron for seven and a half years. So, instead of someone from the tribe of Joseph, the Lord had chosen David of Judah's tribe to rule over His people. David was the one destined by the Eternal God to rule over the whole of Israel skilfully and with integrity.

> *Moreover, He abhorred the tent of Joseph, and chose not the tribe of Ephraim; but <u>chose the tribe of Judah</u>, the mount Zion which He loved.*
>
> *And He built His sanctuary like the heights, like the earth which He has founded for ever. <u>He chose David also His servant</u>, and took him from the sheepfolds.*
>
> *From following the ewes that give suck He brought him, <u>to be shepherd over Jacob His people, and Israel His inheritance</u>.*
>
> *So he shepherded them according to <u>the integrity of his heart</u>; and lead them by <u>the skilfulness of his hands</u>.*
>
> Psalm 78:67-72

These men also knew about the burial of Saul and his sons. They were the ones who spoke to him about this matter, by telling him that the men of Jabesh from Gilead had buried the remains of Saul and his sons in their town. When David heard this, he sent messengers to Gilead with a message saying, *'Blessed be you of HaShem, that you have shown this kindness to your lord, even to Saul, and have buried him. And now HaShem shows kindness and truth to you; and I also will requite you this kindness, because you have done this thing. Now therefore let your hands be strong, and be valiant (courageous); for Saul your lord is dead, and also the House of Judah have anointed me king over them'*.*[3]

Years later David would take their remains to another burial site.

Meanwhile, someone else was made king over the rest of the territory of Israel, including over Gilead. Saul and Jonathan died, but Saul's army commander Abner son of Ner survived the battle. He fled with Saul's son Ishboshet to Mahanaim. A place across the Jordan River. There he made the forty-year-old Ishboshet king over Gilead, Ephraim, Benjamin, Jezreel, Asher and over all the territories of Israel. But, he would rule only two years over the Kingdom of Israel. As for David, his own tribe, Judah, remained loyal to him. He stayed in Hebron where his first six sons were born. From there he ruled seven and a half years over the first Kingdom of Judah. Afterwards he would become king of all Israel. Thus Israel would at one point be without a king for about five and a half years. But why was Ishboshet's reign so short? Abner was loyal to the House of Saul, until his fallout with Ishboshet. Did he end the king's reign? And how did David become king over all Israel?

After King Saul's death, the forces of the Kingdom of Judah and the Kingdom of Israel were at war. The House of David grew stronger, while the House of Saul became weaker by the day. Joab son of Zeruiah, whose brothers were Abishai and Asahel, was at that time one of the senior officers of David, while Abner son of Ner was the army commander of Israel. His influence among the followers of Saul increased. During this period there was an accusation towards Abner. It came from the king himself. Ishboshet found fault in Abner concerning a woman. He was sleeping with Saul's concubine, Rizpah daughter of Aiah. When he accused him of this, Abner became furious. He said to him, '*Am I a dog's head that belongs to Judah? This day do I show kindness to the House of Saul your father, to his brethren, and to his friends, and (I) have not delivered you into the hand of David, and yet you charge me this day with a fault concerning this woman*'.*[4] And Abner made Ishboshet a promise by saying, '*God do so to Abner, and more also, if, <u>as HaShem has sworn to David</u>, I do not even so to him; <u>to transfer the kingdom from the House of Saul, and to set up the throne of David over Israel and over Judah</u>, from Dan even to Beersheba*'.*[5]

Ishboshet couldn't say a word, because of his fear of Abner. So, within two years of Saul's death Abner would seek to ally himself with King David. Was this just out of revenge on Ishboshet? Or was this Abner's own wish for the nation of Israel, while the accusation concerning his affair with Rizpah was just a pretext?

Who Is David?

> *Judah, you shall your brothers praise; your hand shall be on the neck of your enemies; your father's sons shall bow down before you.*
>
> Genesis 49:8

Immediately Abner sent messengers to speak with King David, who was at Hebron. His message, *'Whose is the land'*? And also saying, *'Make your league with me, and, behold, my hand shall be with you, to bring over all Israel to you'*.*[6] David's response? That he would make an agreement with him, on the condition that he would bring David's wife Michal, Saul's daughter, with him when he came to see him. And David also sent a message to Ishboshet regarding Michal, saying, *'Deliver me my wife Michal, whom I betrothed to me for a hundred foreskins of the Philistines'*.*[7]

Meanwhile, Abner was having talks with the leaders of Israel, the king excluded. He said to Israel's elders, *'In times past you sought for David to be king over you'*.*[8] It seemed, that these leaders themselves had one time the wish to have David as their king. He continued, saying, *'Now then do it; for <u>HaShem has spoken of David</u>, saying: <u>By the hand of My servant David I will save My people Israel out of the hand of the Philistines, and out of the hand of all their enemies</u>'*.*[9]

Abner also held talks with Saul's tribe, that of Benjamin. After this he went to see King David to tell him the decision of the leaders of Israel and of the tribe of Benjamin. He took twenty men and Michal with him. David received them with a feast. Afterwards, David sent Abner and his men on their way in peace. Before he left, Abner said to David, *'I will arise and go, and will gather all Israel to my lord the king, that they may make a covenant with you, and that you may reign over all that your soul desires'*.*[10]

Abner left just before Joab and some of David's men arrived from a raid, from which they brought many spoils with them. Abner and his men had already left Hebron in peace as David had arranged with him. Someone informed Joab about Abner's visit and that he had already left. He went to see David to speak with him about this matter. Joab said to David, *'What have you done? Behold, Abner came to you; why is it that you have sent him away, and he is quite gone'?*[11]

He continued by saying, *'You know Abner the son of Ner, that he came to deceive you, and to know your going out and your coming in, and to know all that you do'*.*[12] Joab clearly did not trust Abner and he did not agree with David's decision. Was he really concerned for David's safety? For the nation? Or did he have some other reason to disapprove? Joab sent messengers after Abner. By this time Abner and his men had already reached the well of Sirah. Joab's messengers reached him there, and they brought him back to Hebron. But, when he arrived he didn't get the chance to meet with David, who wasn't informed about Joab's action. Did Abishai know about his brother Joab's intention? It was Joab who received Abner at the gate, where he greeted him friendly and wanted to talk to him in private. But, when he took Abner aside, instead of having a friendly talk with him, he took his life by stabbing him in his belly. Abner's men could not have prevented this. Abner died at the hand of Joab, who at this point was acting alone. This would not be the last time that Joab would assassinate a man, under the pretence of war while there was peace. Joab didn't confess, and there were no witnesses to his crime, making it difficult for King David to take legal action against him. It was wise at that moment not to pursue it.

When David heard that Israel's army commander Abner was assassinated, he said, '*I and my kingdom are guiltless before HaShem for ever from the blood of Abner the son of Ner; let it fall upon the head of Joab, and upon all his father's house*'.*[13] He also said a curse, some dreadful punishments that the Lord God should inflict on Joab and his household. Then David gave instructions for Abner's burial. He ordered Joab and all the men that were with him, to tear their clothes. They were to wear sackcloth, while mourning over Abner. When Abner's bier was taken to the place of burial at Hebron, King David himself walked behind it. At Abner's grave David wept aloud, and with him all the people. He lamented a dirge, a song for Abner saying, '*Should Abner die as a churl died? Your hands were not bound, nor your feet put into fetters; as a man falls before the children of iniquity, so did you fall*'.*[14]

The people who were at the burial wept again over Abner. To David, Abner's death was the result of a crime, not of warfare, because, he as king had sent him on his way in peace, something Joab was well aware of. The rest of the day David didn't eat anything, though people encouraged him to. Everything King David did that day regarding Abner's burial pleased the people. Everyone in Judah and all Israel understood that he had nothing to do with Abner's death.

David spoke to his servants about Abner, asking them whether they realised that he was a great Israelite leader. He said, '*Don't you know that a prince and a great man fell this day in Israel*'?*[15]

Why did Joab kill Abner? What was his true reason to commit such

Who Is David?

an act? But, first, who was Joab? He was one of David's warriors, and he was a relative of David.

David's father, Jesse, had seven (eight) sons, of which David was the youngest. He also had two daughters, Zeruiah and Abigail. Abigail's son was Amasa, who would one day become commander of Israel's army. Appointed by both Absalom and David. Her eldest sister Zeruiah had three sons, Abishai, Joab and Asahel. So, they were David's nephews. They were probably part of the group of men that had gathered to David at the cave near Adullam. The reason for Joab's act? It had to do with what happened to one of his brothers during a battle that took place at Gibeon some time before. The Kingdom of Judah and the Kingdom of Israel were at war, and both Joab and Abner went with a group of soldiers to Gibeon where each of them gathered with their group at the opposite side of the pool there. Abner came up with the idea of letting some of the young men of each group fight in an armed contest. Joab agreed. Twelve of David's men fought with twelve Benjaminite men representing Ishboshet. But, the contest got out of hand, and became a battle of life and death, ending with the death of all those who fought in the contest. They all grabbed their opponents by the head and killed each other with their swords. This led to a fierce battle resulting in a victory for David's men. Abner lost three hundred and sixty men, while twenty of David's men were killed. But, one of the fallen warriors was Asahel, while his two brothers, Joab and Abishai, remained unharmed.

How did Asahel die? When the battle started, Asahel who could run very fast, started chasing Abner straight away. While running, Abner looked behind him and asked whether it was Asahel chasing him. When he answered yes, Abner told him to run after one of the soldiers and take whatever he had. Was Abner, knowing that Asahel was no match for him, trying to spare his life? But Asahel, determined to get him, didn't listen. Abner told him again to stop chasing him because in doing so he would force him to kill him. If that would happen, how could he possibly face his brother Joab. But again, Asahel didn't listen. Then suddenly Abner struck Asahel with his spear that went through his belly and came out at his back. Asahel fell down and died on the spot. All those who came along there, stopped and looked at him, except for his brothers. They went after Abner. At sunset they came on the road leading to Gibeon's wilderness. There on the hill the men of Benjamin gathered. They stood around Abner, and he called out to Joab and David's men. He said, *'Shall the sword devour for ever? Know you not (don't you know) that it will be bitterness in the end? How long shall it be then, before you bid the people return from following their brethren'*?*[16]* Joab said to him, that if he wouldn't have spoken, his men would have continued chasing him until morning light. Then Joab blew the horn for the men to stop their pursuit and the fight ended.

Abner and his men returned to Mahanaim. They marched all night through the Jordan Valley and crossed the Jordan River to get there. Abner and David's men gathered, they took Asahel's body and went to Bethlehem. There they buried him in the family tomb. Afterwards they marched all night and reached Hebron at dawn. While Asahel was killed in battle in time of war, Joab committed a criminal act by murdering Abner in times of peace.

Did David do anything against Joab because of the crime that he had committed? No. Though there were no witnesses to this crime nor a confession from Joab, David must have realised that it was Joab who murdered Abner, because his men would have told him about what had happened to Asahel when he was killed by Abner in battle. But, David left the punishment to the Lord God, as he said concerning the sons of Zeruiah, '*And I am this day weak, and just anointed king; and these men the sons of Zeruiah are too hard for me; HaShem reward the evildoer according to his wickedness*'.*[17]* David considered both Joab and his brother Abishai as being hard, difficult, for him. Did David also consider Joab to be a danger to others and himself? Though Abishai, who seemed to be and remained loyal to his brother, did not partake in the actual murder of Abner. Abishai did in the past request David to let him kill Saul with Saul's own lance, and in the future he would ask David to let him kill a civilian, a man called Shimei. David would be patient for a long time before speaking out his mind regarding Joab's crime and the right punishment for him. So, justice would be done another day. For as is written, '*God has spoken once, twice have I heard this: that strength belongs to God; Also to You, O Lord, belongs mercy; for You render to every man according to his work*'.*[18]* Until then, both Joab and his brother Abishai would remain in King David's service, and they would prove themselves to be useful to the nation during military campaigns against Israel's enemies. With Abishai becoming one of David's famous soldiers.

The news of Abner's death was alarming to the people of Israel. Ishboshet, instead of feeling relieved because of their earlier fallout, became afraid when he heard about what happened to Abner in

Who Is David?

Hebron. Was this because he now had to do without the protection of Israel's army commander who had played an important role in making him king?

Two of Ishboshet's captains of raiding parties, the brothers Baanah and Rechab from Beeroth in the territory of Benjamin, came to his house one day. They arrived at noon. Pretending to be wheat bearers they got access to the house. Once inside, they started to look for Ishboshet. They found him in his room where he was sound asleep on his bed, having his daily afternoon rest. They then killed the king by the sword, cutting his head off. They escaped. They travelled all night to Hebron, where they presented Ishboshet's head to King David. They thought they were bringing good tidings for him. Instead of rewarding them, David told them what happened to the man that brought him news of Saul's death. He had the Amalakite put to death. David then said to the brothers, '*How much more, when wicked men have slain a righteous person in his own house upon his bed, shall I not now require his blood of your hand, and take you away from the earth*'?*[18]

David gave an order to his men, and they killed both brothers. They cut off their hands and feet and in the vicinity of Hebron's pool, they hung them up. The head of Ishboshet? They buried it there in Hebron, in Abner's tomb. With Jonathan's son Mephiboshet being lame, the House of Saul didn't have an heir to sit on Saul's throne. So, after all this, a pressing matter was at hand – the kingship over all Israel.

> *Judah is a lion's whelp ... The sceptre shall not depart from Judah, nor the ruler's staff from between his feet, as long as men come to Shiloh; and to him shall the obedience of the people be.*
>
> Genesis 49:9-10

Sometime later on, all the leaders of Israel's tribes came to Hebron to see King David. They said to him, '*Behold, we are your bone and your flesh. In times past, when Saul was king over us, it was you that did lead out and bring in Israel; and HaShem said to you: You shall feed My people Israel, and you shall be prince over Israel*'.*[19] There, before the Lord God, King David made a covenant, an agreement, with them. And they anointed him to be their king – the king over all Israel. David was the only king of Israel who was anointed three times to be king. First by the prophet and Judge Samuel, years later by the people of Judah, and now by the people of Israel. David reigned with the Eternal God's divine approval.

Which city was to be the Kingdom of Israel's capital city? Until then the Israelites didn't choose a city to be the capital city in the Land of Israel. They had made the transition from a tribal society to a state nation with Saul as their king, but they still didn't have a capital city for their nation. Which city would David choose? Hebron? That's the city from where he reigned over the Kingdom of Judah.

No, David chose Jerusalem. A walled city where Jebusites and Benjaminites lived. At the time the Israelites were conquering Canaan, led by Joshua, they fought against the Jebusites, and Jerusalem was allocated to the tribe of Benjamin's people as part of their inheritance. But they never completely conquered the city because they weren't able to remove the Jebusites entirely. So they lived with them in the city. Following David's instructions, Joab and David's men entered Jerusalem, fought the Jebusites, and defeated them. As a reward, Joab who led the attack became the commander of Israel's army.

David conquered Jerusalem, made it the City of David and the capital city of the Kingdom of Israel, to which he brought the Tabernacle with the Ark of the Covenant. David ruled thirty-three years from Jerusalem.

> *Nevertheless <u>David took the stronghold of Zion</u>; the same is the city of David. ... And David dwelt in the stronghold, and called it the <u>City of David</u>.*
> 2 Samuel 5:7-9

Intermezzo

David's Heroes

> *My Lord fights the battles of HaShem.*
> 1 Samuel 25:28

One of the reasons scripture mentions that David was chosen to be Israel's king was that he fought the battles of the Lord God. When it came to fighting Israel's enemies, he started at a young age when he fought the giant Goliath. Afterwards he was enlisted in King Saul's army. Later on when he fled from Saul, he continued to fight against the enemies of the Israelites. A group of thirty men, *The Thirty*, and within that group a smaller group of three men, *The Three*, distinguished themselves as David's heroes. Beside these men there were other brave men who became his warriors, as were also experienced soldiers who joined his troops.

Who Is David?

The Three's leader was Josheb Basshebeth from Tachemon, or Jashobeam of the Hachmon's clan. He fought eight hundred men in one battle and killed them all with his spear. Eleazar, Dodo's son, of the Ahoh's clan, was the second who was also part of these famous three. He fought with David against the Philistines at Pas Dammim. He and his men didn't join the Israelites that fell back from the battle. Instead, they took a stand in a barley field. Standing his ground, he fought until he couldn't let go of his sword because his hand became stiff. The Lord granted them a great victory that day.

After the battle, the Israelites who fled came back to strip the armour from those who died. Shammah was the third warrior of The Three. He was the son of Agee, who was from Harar. At Lehi, near a field of peas, the Philistines gathered for battle. During battle, some Israelites fled. Not Shammah, who stood his ground defending the field of peas. That day, the Lord gave them a great victory.

Around harvest time, three of the thirty leading soldiers, The Thirty, went to David, who was staying on a fortified hill near the cave of Adullam. A group of Philistines were encamped in Rephaim's valley, while David's hometown of Bethlehem was occupied by a band of Philistines. Meanwhile on the hill, David got so homesick that he longed for water from the well near Bethlehem's gate.

David said, *'Oh that one would give me water to drink of the well of Bethlehem, which is by the gate'*![1] Three warriors heard David's words and they planned to fulfil his wish and bring him water from that well. David was unaware of this. These three warriors risked their lives by going down to Bethlehem, forcing themselves through the Philistine camp all the way to the well, where they drew some water from it. Then they returned to David to whom they gave the water. But David, realizing the danger they put themselves in, said to the Lord that he couldn't possibly drink the water, because it would be like drinking the blood of those who risked their lives to get it.

As David said to the Lord, *'Be it far from me, O HaShem, that I should do this; shall I drink the blood of the men that went in jeopardy of their lives'*?[2] So, as an offering to God, David poured the water out.

Abishai, Joab's brother, became the leader of The Thirty famous soldiers. After he fought three hundred men with his spear and killed them, he became the most famous of that group of warriors, though he wasn't as famous as The Three. Joab's brother, Asahel, was also part of this group. Another warrior who was part of The Thirty was

Benaiah, Jehoiada's son, from Kabzeel. He did many brave military deeds. He killed two great Moabite warriors.

Once, on a snowy day, he killed a lion when he went down into a pit. He also fought and killed a two-meters-tall Egyptian. Armed with a club, he attacked the Egyptian while snatching his weapon, a large spear, out of his hand and he killed him with his own spear. Benaiah wasn't as famous as The Three, though David gave him a position in charge of his bodyguards. Besides the group of The Thirty, including The Three, there were many other warriors loyal to David, that did brave military deeds. Who were these warriors?

After David had fled from King Saul for the second time, he eventually ended up at the cave near Adullam, where he stayed for some time. His friend Jonathan had warned him that King Saul was determined to kill him. As Saul himself told his son during the feast of the New Moon, Rosh Chodesh, a feast about which the following is written. *'And it shall come to pass, that from one New Moon to another, and from one Sabbath to another, shall all flesh come to worship before Me'*, says HaShem.*[3]

There his family, including his parents whom he later on brought to the king of Moab for their safety, gathered to him. But also some of these men came to David when he was on the run. They were part of the first group of four hundred men who came under David's leadership. They were ... *everyone that was in distress, and everyone that was in debt, and everyone that was discontented, gathered themselves to him*.*[4] These people were in trouble themselves, being in distress, having debts, and being discontent with the situation they personally had found themselves in, they gathered at the cave near Adullam, and they accepted David to be their leader. These men grew under David's leadership and became the heroes he would count on during the years he was a fugitive from Saul and even during his future reign over all Israel. From people having no hope or future, into warriors positioned in David's troops and therefore having a livelihood. Later on they became captains in his army. After them, others kept joining David's forces, including trained and experienced soldiers, while he was staying at different places in the Land.

When David was living at Ziklag in Philistine territory, experienced warriors from Benjamin, Saul's tribe, joined him. Their weapons were arrow and bow, and sling. They could use these with both the right and the left hand. Warriors from the tribe of Gad, who were experienced soldiers skilful with spears and shields, joined David when he and his

Who Is David?

men were staying at a stronghold in the wilderness. Some of these men were senior and junior officers in command of a thousand and a hundred men. At one time they crossed the Jordan River even though it had overflowed.

Once David went out to meet a group of men from both the tribes of Judah and Benjamin who was looking for him. These men would later become officers in his army. But the day when they met, David wasn't sure he could trust them. So David said to these men, *'If you have come peaceably to me to help me, my heart shall be knit unto you; but if you have come to betray me to my adversaries, seeing there is no wrong in my hands, the God of our fathers looks on that and gives judgment'.*[*5]

Then Amasai, the captains' leader, became clothed with God's Spirit and he said to David, *'We are yours David, and on your side, you son of Jesse; peace (shalom), peace (shalom) be to you, and peace (shalom) be to your helpers; for your God helps you'.*[*6] Then David accepted them and made them captains of his troops. A group of Menasseh's warriors also joined David, at the time that David and his men went out with Achish, a Philistine king, to fight the Israelites. David, who always fought the enemies of Israel, had no intention of fighting Israelites on behalf of the Philistines now.

Did he have a plan of action when the time came to fight for the Philistines that day? In fact, the Philistine kings didn't trust him. So Achish sent him and his men back to Ziklag. On their way back, the men from Menasseh joined David. Later on they too would become officers in David's army. All the years that David was on the run from King Saul, the Lord provided for him and those with him, while he fought the enemies of the Israelites. He always inquired of the Lord God about what he should or should not do. So, He stood by him in battle and guided his choices and decisions, and He saved David out of his troubles.

> *Because he has set his love upon Me, therefore will I deliver him; I will set him on high, because he has known My name. He shall call upon Me, and I will answer him; I will be with him in trouble; I will rescue him, and bring him to honour. With long life will I satisfy him, and make Him to behold My salvation.*
>
> Psalm 91

Soldiers kept joining David's troops almost on a daily basis, and his troops grew into a big army. This continued when David became King of Judah. During that period of seven and a half years, the Lord added more warriors, including trained and experienced soldiers and officers to David's forces.

At the time David became King of Judah, thousands of soldiers from all the tribes of Israel went to Hebron to pledge their allegiance to him. They wanted him as king over all the Kingdom of Israel, and they were determined to make this happen. They spent three days at Hebron while having a feast. Other Israelites had prepared the food, which they brought to Hebron loaded on mules, oxen, and camels. They also brought sheep, cattle, and enough to drink.

All David's men were loyal to him, including the foreigners that later on became part of David's forces. As were the six hundred men from Gath, led by Ittai. During his reign over all Israel, when David had to leave Jerusalem to prevent its destruction by the war declared on him by his son Absalom, Ittai with his men wanted to leave with David, who was urging him to stay in Jerusalem where he and his men would be better off. But Ittai said to David, *'As HaShem lives, and as my lord the king lives, surely in what place my lord the king shall be, whether for death or for life, even there also will your servant be'.*[7] So, staying behind was no option to him. He and his men remained loyal to David.

During David's reign over the Kingdom of Israel, they fought many battles against the Philistines, including against the giants that were part of their troops. Giants or Nephilim were children of the fallen angels with human women. The women were literally pregnant with evil, sin. As written, *'They conceive mischief, and bring forth iniquity, and their belly prepares deceit'.*[8] Only their male offspring is mentioned. Were there ever any female offspring? At one time during one of these battles, David became tired during the battle and a giant tried to take him out. The giant, Ishbibenob, carried a very heavy spear and a new sword. He wanted to kill David by using these. But one of David's warriors, Abishai son of Zerujah, Joab's brother, came to help David. He attacked Ishbibenob, fought with him and killed him. It's after this battle that David's men made him promise, that when they go out for a fight, he would never again go with them. They said, *'You shall go no more out with us to battle, that you quench not the lamp of Israel'.*[9]

Later on, David and his men also fought the Philistines at Gob, or Gezer, and Gath. At Gob, a giant named Saph was killed in battle by Sibbecal from Hushah. One of the giants killed by David's men was Lahmi, the brother* of Goliath from Gath. This happened during another battle at Gob. He was killed in battle by a warrior from Bethlehem, Elhanan son of Jaareoregim. Another giant from Gath, defied the Israelites in battle. He had six toes on each of his feet, and six fingers on each of his hands. Jonathan, son of Shammah or Shimeah who was Jesse's third son, thus a brother of David, killed him during battle. Shammah's son being part of David's troops, suggests that his brothers also were. They, with the rest of David's family, did join him in the cave at Adullam. In addition to Goliath, whom David killed in battle, four giants were killed by David's heroes.

> *These were the chiefs of David's mighty warriors – they, together with all Israel, gave his kingship strong support to extend it over the whole Land, as the Lord had promised.*
> 1 Chronicles 11

And Joab? He was not mentioned on the list as being one of David's heroes. Joab's assassination of two commanders, Abner and Amasa, was probably the reason why he wasn't mentioned. Despite Joab's actions, his brothers Abishai and Asahel were mentioned as being part of the group of The Thirty famous warriors. Which confirms that Abishai didn't have anything to do with Joab's crimes. Naharai, Joab's armour-bearer, was also mentioned. All those who were mentioned, were loyal servants of David. David's famous military heroes did brave deeds under David's leadership defeating Israel's enemies, such as the Philistines, the Arameans and the Ammonites. To David it was the Eternal God that fought together with him that granted him these victories. He honoured Him in his song of victory.

> *For You are my lamp, O HaShem; and HaShem does lighten my darkness.*
> *For by You I run upon a troop; by my God do I scale a wall.*
> *As for God, His way is perfect; <u>the word of HaShem is tried</u>; He is a shield to all (of) them that take refuge in Him.*
> *For who is God, save HaShem? And who is a Rock, save our God?*
> *The God who is my strong fortress, and who lets my way go forth straight;*

> *HaShem lives and blessed be my Rock; and exalted be the God, my Rock of salvation;*
>
> *Therefore I will give thanks to You, O HaShem, among the nations, and (I) will sing praises to Your Name.*
>
> 2 Samuel 22

Famine

> *If you say: Behold, we knew not this, doesn't He that weighs the hearts consider it? And He that keeps your soul, doesn't He know it? And shall not <u>He render to every man according to his works</u>?*
>
> Proverbs 24:12

During King David's reign over the unified Kingdom of Israel, there was a period of severe famine in the Land of Israel that lasted three years. What caused it? David inquired of the Lord about this long period of drought. He answered, *'It is for Saul, and for his bloody house, because he put to death the Gibeonites'*.*[20] Then David summoned the Gibeonites to resolve this matter, which resulted in the death of seven of Saul's male descendants, including two sons of Saul's concubine Rizpah. They were put to death by hanging in late spring. Rizpah in mourning for her sons, stayed where they died. She made a shelter for herself from sackcloth, which was needed because she stayed there from the day of their deaths until early autumn when the rain season would start. She protected the bodies from birds during the day, and from wild animals during the night. When David heard about all this, he took the bones of Saul and Jonathan out of Gilead, and together with the bones that he had gathered of the seven hanged men, he buried them. Saul and Jonathan's bones were buried in the grave of Kish, Saul's father, which was in Zela in Benjamin's territory. After all this, the Lord answered their prayers regarding rain for the nation. All of this happened at the time when David came back to Jerusalem.

Why did David leave the city and from where did he have to return? He had left Jerusalem because of the troubles caused by his third son Absalom, who conspired with David's most trusted adviser Achithophel. King David returned to Jerusalem from across the Jordan River. This was expedited by his decision to make Amasa, son of Jether, commander of the army of the Kingdom of Israel instead of keeping Joab in that position. Who was Amasa? He was the son of Jether who was an Ishmaelite. His mother was Abigail, a sister of Zeruiah who was the mother of Joab. So Amasa and Joab were cousins. Amasa was once appointed commander of Israel's army by Absalom. When David wanted to return to Jerusalem he had sent messengers to Amasa telling him he would make him the commander of Judah's army for life. David and all those with him, people of both Judah and the rest of Israel, crossed the Jordan River, and they went on their way to Jerusalem. On David's way home, a Benjaminite Sheba son of Bikri, called out a rebellion at Gilgal, causing the people of Israel to leave David. But, the men of Judah remained loyal to David and they brought him, his family and his servants all the way to Jerusalem. In the meantime, Sheba's rebellion was getting momentum among the Israelites.

Once in Jerusalem, King David gave the army commander Amasa an order to gather the men of Judah and to return with them to him the day after the next day. David wanted to fight those who rebelled before they could cause more trouble. When Amasa wasn't back at David's planned time, David told Abishai, Joab's brother, to go in pursuit of Sheba and the men that joined him in an attempt to prevent him from reaching a fortified city. He set out taking David's guard, all the men in Jerusalem and Joab's men with him. When they reached Gibeon, Amasa and the men of Judah met with them. Joab, dressed for the battle, approached Amasa, calling him his brother, taking hold of his beard with his right hand to kiss him, but with his left hand he struck Amasa with his sword, which had fallen out of its sheath on the ground as he approached him, into his belly, and he died instantly with his entrails spilled out on the road. Unfortunately for Amasa, he wasn't on his guard for Joab's sword. Afterwards Joab and Abishai continued their pursuit of Sheba leaving one of Joab's young men standing at Amasa's body. He called out to everyone saying that all who were for Joab and David, should follow Joab. But, Amasa's lifeless body covered in blood was in the middle of the road, so everyone stopped there. The young man removed the body from the road, laying it in the field and he covered it with a blanket. After the body was removed, everyone continued the chase of Sheba and his men after Joab and Abishai, and after a long pursuit they caught up and dealt with them.

What was Joab's reason for murder this time? A grudge against Amasa, for losing his position as commander to him? Moses once said, *'You shall not take vengeance, nor bear any grudge against the children of your people, but you shall love your neighbour as yourself:*

I am HaShem'.*²¹ For some reason, either personal or political, David would choose to leave it up to his successor to do justice regarding Abner and Amasa. He would one day say of both Abner and Amasa, that they were ... *two men more righteous and better than he (Joab)*.*²²*

Did this assassination confirm David's earlier assessment of the situation concerning Joab when he had killed Abner? And was David's decision not to punish him because he himself felt that Joab could still be dangerous? Joab was successful in putting down the rebellion, and because of this was popular. So, David decided to reinstate Joab as commander of Israel's army. As for justice concerning this murder, and that of Abner, it would come after David's reign at the hand of the king that would succeed him.

Years later, when it was time for David to appoint a successor to his throne, and to make the necessary arrangements for him, he did this for Solomon. He was his son with Bathsheba. The Lord God had made it clear to David that Solomon should be the next king of Israel. David gave advice to Solomon regarding either punishment or reward for some people. One of them was Joab. He was, except for the crimes he had committed, loyal to David in nearly everything else. He played a key role in conquering Jerusalem, he intervened between David and his son Absalom to bring him home, he fought the battles of the Lord with David and he was a good commander for the army. But the blood he had shed remained. There must have been no doubt in David's mind that the assassination of both Abner and Amasa was a crime. As David would say years later to his son Solomon, '*So shall their blood return upon the head of Joab, and upon the head of his seed for ever*'.*²³ Why? Maybe because David was well aware of the consequences of Joab's crimes for the Land of Israel. The blood that Joab had shed by murdering these two men made the Land unclean.

As the Lord God once said to Moses, '*So you shall not pollute the land wherein you are; <u>for blood, it pollutes the land</u>; and <u>no expiation (atonement) can be made for the land</u> for the blood that is shed therein (in it), <u>but by the blood of him that shed it</u>*'.*²⁴ This meant, that Joab had to die. In addition, to David, what Joab had done to Abner and Amasa, he had done to him personally, as he said to Solomon, '*Moreover you know also what <u>Joab</u> the son of Zeruiah <u>did to me</u>, even what he did to the two captains of the hosts of Israel, to Abner the son of Ner and to Amasa the son of Jether, whom he slew, and <u>shed the blood of war in peace</u>, and put the blood of war upon his girdle that was about his loins, and in his shoes that were on his feet*'.*²⁵ Therefore, after waiting patiently all those years, King David's advice to his son King Solomon was, *'Do therefore according to your wisdom, and <u>let not his hoar (gray) head go down to the grave in peace</u>'.**26

Thus, one day after David's death, but still relevant to the atonement of the Land, Solomon would follow his father's advice. Joab, who was loyal to David, would not be to Solomon. This would lead to Joab's third crime, that of treason, for which he would also be punished. He would be dealt with on King Solomon's orders.

> And David waxed greater and greater; for HaShem, the God of hosts, was with him ... And David perceived that <u>HaShem had established him king over Israel</u>, and that <u>He had exalted his kingdom for His people Israel's sake</u>.
>
> 2 Samuel 5:10-12

Endnotes

*1 2 Samuel 1:14, *2 2 Samuel 1:16, *3 2 Samuel $2:5_b$-7, *4 2 Samuel 3:8, *5 2 Samuel 3:9-10, *6 2 Samuel 12_b, *7 2 Samuel $3:14_b$, *8 2 Samuel $3:17_b$, *9 2 Samuel $3:17_b$-18, *10 2 Samuel 3:21, *11 2 Samuel $3:24_a$, *12 2 Samuel 3:25, *13 2 Samuel $3:28_b$-29 *14 2 Samuel $3:33_b$-34, *15 2 Samuel $3:38_b$, *16 2 Samuel $2:26_b$, *17 2 Samuel 3:39, *18 Psalm 62:12-13, *19 2 Samuel 4:11, *19 2 Samuel 5:1-2 , *20 2 Samuel $21:1_b$, *21 Leviticus 19:18, *22 1 Kings 2:32, *23 1 Kings $2:33_a$, *24 Numbers 35:33, *25 1 Kings 2:5, *26 1 Kings 2:6

The Green Olive Tree, www.thegreenolivetree.nl
David and Joab: wisdom and justice, by Angeline Leito
http://www.thegreenolivetree.nl/index.php/14-articles/
    king-david/113-david-and-joab-wisdom-and-justice
1 Samuel 31:8-13, 2 Samuel 21:13-14 Saul and Jonathan's remains
2 Samuel 1:1-16, 4:10 news of Saul's and Jonathan's death
1 Samuel 24:5 David's conscience troubled
1 Samuel 26:9-11 Saul a natural death or die in battle
2 Samuel 1:17-27 David's lament over Saul and Jonathan
2 Samuel 2:10-11 David reigned seven and a half years over Judah
2 Samuel 2:10 Ishboshet king of Israel two years
2 Samuel 3:7, 21:8, 21:10-11 Rizpah, Saul's concubine
2 Samuel 3:2-5 David's eldest six sons born in Hebron
2 Samuel 2:12-32, 3:1, 3:6 war between Judah and Israel's army, David's army became stronger
2 Samuel 3:6-11, 12-21 Abner's fallout with Ishboshet, allied with David
2 Samuel 3:22-39 Abner murdered and buried
1 Chronicles 2:13-16 Joab son of Zeruiah, was David's nephew

David and Joab

2 Samuel 2:17-23 Joab's brother killed
2 Samuel 3:33-34 David's lament for Abner
1 Samuel 26:8, 2 Samuel 19:9 Abishai's requests to David
2 Samuel 4:1-12 Ishboshet murdered and buried
1 Kings 2:5 Joab killed Abner and Amasa
2 Samuel 5:3, Genesis 49:8,10 Jacob's sons would bow for Judah
Judges 1:8 the men of Judah had conquered Jerusalem, set it on fire
Judges 1:21 Benjaminites didn't drive away the Jebusites
Joshua 15:63 first Judah lived in Jerusalem with the Jebusites, they couldn't drive them out
Joshua 18:28 Jerusalem part of Benjaminites inheritance
2 Samuel 5:1-4, 5 David king of Israel, ruled from Jerusalem 33 years
2 Samuel 5:4-5 David 30 years when he became king, ruled 7 1/2 years over Judah, 33 years over Israel
2 Samuel 5:8-9, 1 Chronicles 11:1-9 David conquers Jerusalem, Joab becomes commander
2 Samuel 6:1-23, 1 Chronicles 13:1-14, 15:25-16:6, 43 Ark from Abinadab to Obed Edom to Jerusalem
1 Chronicles 2:17 Amasa son of Jether, Joab's nephew, mother Abigail sister of Zeruiah
2 Samuel 17:25 Amasa's father was an Ishmaelite
2 Samuel 17:25 Amasa commander Israel's army instead of Joab, appointed by Absalom
2 Samuel 19:13, 1 Kings 2:32 Amasa appointed commander of Judah's army for life instead of Joab
2 Samuel 20:9, 1 Kings 2:5 Amasa killed by Joab
1 Kings 2:5 David's advice to Solomon concerning Joab
1 Kings 2:32 Abner and Amasa better men than Joab

Intermezzo Endnotes

*[1]2 Samuel 23:15, *[2]2 Samuel 23:17, *[3]Isaiah 66:23-24, *[4]1 Samuel 22:2$_a$, *[5]1 Chronicles 12:18, *[6]1 Chronicles 12:19, *[7]2 Samuel 15:21$_b$, *[8]Job 15:35, *[9]2 Samuel 21:17

* 2 Samuel 21:19, 1 Chronicles 20:5 Goliath's brother
1 Samuel 22:2, 1 Samuel 23:13, 27:2, 30:9 four hundred men joined David at Adullam, later on six hundred is mentioned
1 Samuel 22:3 David brought his parents to Moab
1 Chronicles 11:2 David considered leader of Israel, military leader
1 Chronicles 12:1 the people who joined David at Ziklag
2 Samuel 23:15-16, 1 Chronicles 11:17-18 water for David
1 Samuel 22:2 at Adullam, four hundred men
2 Samuel 23:13, 1 Chronicles 11:15 at Adullam the thirty heroes including the three joined David
1 Samuel 23:13 at Keilah, six hundred men

Who Is David?

2 Samuel 23:8-39, 1 Chronicles 11:10-14 the three heroes of the thirty heroes, famous soldiers
2 Samuel 23:18, 13-17 Joab's brother Abishai, commander of the three heroes, part of the thirty heroes
1 Chronicles 11:15 at Adullam the three heroes joined David
2 Samuel 23:37, 1 Chronicles 11:29 Joab's armour-bearer Naharai
2 Samuel 23:24, 1 Chronicles 11:26 Joab's brother Asahel, member of the thirty heroes
1 Chronicles 11:22-25 Benaiah, commander David's bodyguard
2 Samuel 23:8-39, 1 Chronicles 11:10-47, 12:1-40 (41) David's heroes, famous soldiers
1 Kings 1:8-10 remained loyal to David
1 Chronicles 12:1-7(8) at Ziklag, men from Benjamin's tribe, arrows and slings, trained soldiers
1 Chronicles 12: 8(9)-15(16) at the desert stronghold, from Gad's tribe, shields and spears, experienced
1 Chronicles 12:16(17)-18(19) at stronghold, from Benjamin and Judah, they became officers
1 Chronicles 12:19(20)-21(22) at Ziklag, from Menasseh's tribe, officers over David's troops
1 Chronicles 12:22 (23) men joined David daily
1 Chronicles 12:23(24)-37(38) at Hebron, trained soldiers of all the tribes, to make David king
1 Chronicles 12:38(39)-40(41) at Hebron, they brought food and olive oil, feast three days
2 Samuel 15:18-22 Ittai with six hundred men, foreigners joined David
1 Chronicles 12:4, 18(19) one of the thirty, Amasai commander of the thirty
1 Chronicles 11:16-19 David offered water / 1 Chronicles 11:20-21 three and thirty heroes
2 Samuel 23:15-16, 1 Chronicles 11:16(17)-19 David homesick refused water brought by three heroes
2 Samuel 23:8-39, 1 Chronicles 11 David's famous soldiers, military victories
2 Samuel 5:17-25, 1 Chronicles 14:8-17 King David's victory over Philistines
2 Samuel 10:1-19, 1 Chronicles 19:1-19 King David's defeats Arameans and Ammonites
2 Samuel 18:1-18 David's son Absalom defeated
1 Samuel 17, 2 Samuel 21:15-22, 1 Chronicles 20:4-8 David and his men fought Philistine giants
1 Samuel 16:9, 17:13, 2 Samuel 21:21, 1 Chronicles 2:13, 20:7 Jonathan, son of David's brother Shimeah or Shammah
Genesis 6:4, Deuteronomy 2:10-12, 2:20-22, 3:11-14, Numbers 13:33 Nephilim, giants
2 Samuel 22 David's song of victory
Deuteronomy 23:9 when encamped against enemy, prevent uncleanness

DAVID AND ABSALOM
Rebellion, Grieving and Victory

*HaShem will certainly make my lord a sure house,
because my lord fights the battles of HaShem.*

1 Samuel 25:28b

King David ruled from the City of David. After he had conquered Jerusalem, he brought the Tabernacle to the city. There at his court, he received those who sought his favour. One day a poor widow came to speak with David. She asked him for his help in saving the life of her son. She told him that her two sons fought with each other while in the field. There, there was no one to separate them. One of them killed the other. She only has one son now to carry the name of her late husband, and to provide for her. But, her relatives demanded from her that she hand over her son so they could kill him because he had murdered his brother. To her, if her relative would kill her only son she had left, it would be an even greater crime than that of her son.

The widow asked for protection for her son. She said to David that whatever he decides, she and her family would be the ones to take the blame. Then David promised her that her son would not be harmed. She told him that she came to speak with him because the people were threatening her. To her, the king's promise would insure safety for her and her son. After David's assurance, she also spoke with him about his son in exile, telling him that he had wronged God's people by not allowing his own son to come out of exile. Also, that he had just condemned himself by the words he had just said to her. She was talking about David's son Absalom. She concluded her request by saying, '*Let, I pray you, the word of my lord the king be for my comfort; for as <u>an angel of God</u>, so is my lord the king to discern good and bad; and HaShem your God be with you*',*[1] making it clear that David knew everything that was going on, or that he would find out about it. Before she could leave, David told her that he was going to ask her one question, and that she had to tell him the whole truth. She told him to ask her anything. He asked her whether Joab, David's military commander, had put her up to speak with him like this. She answered truthfully that it was Joab who had told her to come, and that he had also told her what she should do and what she should say. He did this to help him out with this matter, and she added, *'My lord is wise, according to the wisdom of an angel of God, to know all things that are in the earth'*.*² Later David would speak with Joab about Absalom.

What was the reason for Joab to send this woman to speak with David? To help Absalom return to Jerusalem out of exile.

Who was Absalom? He was one of David's first six sons. They were all born at Hebron. His first six sons grew up to adulthood and he had more sons and daughters in Jerusalem. The education of David's sons was in the hands of his Uncle Jonathan and of Jehiel who was a scholar. During his reign, David experienced much grief because of the troubles that his sons, especially Absalom, caused him.

Absalom's mother was Maacah daughter of Talmai who was king of Geshur. Absalom had a sister, Tamar. Absalom was well known in Israel for his good looks. He had long, very thick hair. As a nazarite, he would not have been allowed to cut his hair regularly. He only did this once a year, so his hair would not become too heavy. Absalom had children of his own. Three sons and one daughter, Tamar. She grew up to become a beautiful woman.

Why did Joab want to do this? Joab cared for David, but he cared more for his revenge. As future events, regarding the military commander Amasa and Adonijah's ambition to be king would show, Joab also cared more for his military position than for David.

Joab knew about David's grief and that he truly missed his son Absalom. Joab cared for David. This was the same Joab that had killed Abner years earlier. In that case he didn't care much for what his action would mean to David and the nation of Israel. At that time David was the king of Judah having his seat of power in Hebron, the city where the Patriarchs and Matriarchs where buried at Machpela, the place believed to be the burial place of Adam and Eve.

Absalom had been away a few years. Joab decided to help him return to Jerusalem. Why did Absalom need Joab's help to return to Jerusalem? Why wasn't he at David's court? Absalom fled Jerusalem, or rather Hebron. He wasn't allowed to go to Jerusalem. King David exiled him. What were the grounds for such exile? A crime he had committed. Absalom had murdered his brother Amnon, David's eldest son with his second wife Ahinoam. Why? Because Amnon brought disgrace for Absalom's sister princess Tamar[a], David's daughter, two years earlier. He forced her to sleep with him, and after he raped his half sister he cast her off as being unwanted. David was furious about this. Absalom hated his brother so much that he didn't talk to him anymore. Jonadab, David's brother Shammah's son, told David that Absalom had already made up his mind to kill Amnon, since he had raped his sister. Losing Amnon brought much grief to David. Absalom sought refuge with his grandfather Talmai, who was the king in Geshur. He stayed there for three years.

The people of Geshur and Maacah were not driven out of the Land. They lived within their territory among the Israelites. At the time David was on the run for King Saul and lived at Ziklag, in Philistine territory, he and his men raided the Geshurites and other non-Israelite people such as the Amalekites and the Girzites. He told Achish, one of the Philistine kings, that he raided the Israelites which he believed. Did David take Absalom's mother Maacah, who was a princess, as a captive of war and marry her in accordance to the Israelite law?

So, Joab did all this in an attempt to bring about a reconciliation between father and son. In fact Joab put his request to David to allow Absalom to return from exile, by sending a widow to speak with him. David spoke to Joab later on, and told him that he granted him his request. He was to bring the young man to Jerusalem. Joab went to Geshur and he took Absalom back with him. But, David gave specific orders concerning where he should live and his court visits. He was not to live in the palace, and David did not want to see him. So Absalom did not go to David's court, and he lived in a house he owned. He was back out of exile, but there was no reconciliation between him and David yet.

Two years later, Absalom wanted to see the king. Was it because he wanted a reconciliation between them? Or did Absalom have ambitions of his own, and therefore needed to be at the king's court? In order to do this he needed Joab to get him a meeting with the king. Twice he sent a message to Joab for him to come to see him. But he refused both times. So Absalom told his servants to go and set Joab's field, which was next to his own, on fire. Immediately Joab went to see Absalom at his house. He demanded to know why Absalom's servants set his field on fire. He told him it was because he didn't want to come to see him. Now that he was there, he told him to arrange a meeting for him with the king. If according to the king he was guilty, then it would be up to him to sentence him to death. So, Joab went to see David. He spoke to him about Absalom's request and about what he had said. David then

Who Is David?

sent for Absalom. When he met with the king, he bowed down to the floor. David welcomed his son Absalom with a kiss. The two were reconciled. But certain future events would show that this would turn out to be a cold reconciliation as far as Absalom was concerned.

After that meeting, Absalom made arrangements, and imposed on himself a daily routine. He provided himself with an escort of fifty men, and as a means of transportation, a chariot with horses, with which he went to the city gate every day early in the morning. There he stood by the road and he called everyone who came by for a talk. The Israelites he spoke with were those who wanted the king to settle some dispute. Absalom would ask those who approached him from which tribe they were and he would tell them that although the law was on their side, that there was no representative of the king to hear them out and render them justice. He also told them that he wished that he was a judge so they would come with their claim, or matter of dispute to him. Then he would render them justice. When they wanted to bow down before him, he would reach out and greet them with a kiss. This was Absalom's way to win the loyalty of the people.

After four or forty*b years of plotting against his father, Absalom brought the final phase of his plan for his coup d'etat into practice. One day, Absalom went to see King David. He asked him permission to visit Hebron to worship the Lord there. He told David that he made a promise to the Lord when he was living at Geshur in Aram. If He would bring him back to Jerusalem, he would worship Him in Hebron. David told him to go in peace, and he left for Hebron. He sent messengers to all Israel's tribes with the message, that their people should all shout when they heard the sound of the trumpets. Saying what? That Absalom became king in Hebron. Meanwhile the two hundred guests he invited left Jerusalem with him to attend his feast at Hebron. Not knowing about Absalom's plot, they went with him in good faith. There was one person who wasn't invited yet. So, Absalom sent messengers to the town of Gilo with an invitation for Ahitophel, for him to be Absalom's guest. Who was Ahitophel? He was David's most trusted adviser. His advice was regarded in those days as though it came from God. The number of Absalom's supporters grew and there were more Israelites pledging their loyalty to him.

David's son couldn't have done all this alone. Who helped him? One of his guests. Ahitophel. But, why would Ahitophel become disloyal to David? Could this have anything to do with how David treated Bathsheba*c, Solomon's mother? She was Achithophel's grand daughter. The daughter of his son Eliam. But Eliam*ᵈ himself remained loyal to David as one of The Thirty famous heroes of David. Ahitophel was locked in a conspiracy with Absalom for a coup d'etat against his father King David.

Meanwhile, David received messengers who brought him news about what was happening in Hebron. They also told him that there were Israelites who were pledging their loyalty to his son Absalom. As soon as David heard this, realizing this was a coup d'etat, he decided it was time to leave Jerusalem before Absalom's return. They had to escape before Absalom and his followers would come and kill all of them. He spoke to all his servants and officials, and told them to hurry. They remained loyal to him, and said they would do whatever he said. David's family, his entire household, and his servants went with him, except for the people he left behind at the palace. They were ten concubines whom remained in charge of his palace. David and all his men stopped at a last or faraway house as they were leaving Jerusalem. While he stood there, his servants and officials passed him. Among them was Ittai the Gittite with six hundred warriors. They were foreigners that also chose to go with David. King David and all those with him passed the Kidron brook.

Intermezzo

Foreigners

And a <u>stranger</u> (foreigner) shall you not wrong, neither shall you oppress him; for you were strangers in the land of Egypt. And a stranger shall you not oppress; for you know the heart of a stranger, seeing you were strangers in the land of Egypt.
Exodus 22:20-Exodus 23:9

The <u>stranger</u> that sojourns with you shall be to you as the home-born among you, and you shall love him as yourself; for you were strangers in the land of Egypt: I am HaShem your God.
Leviticus 19:34

Absalom and his followers would certainly go to Jerusalem to depose King David. So, as soon as David heard the news about Absalom's rebellion against him, he decided to leave the city. He left Jerusalem in a hurry together with his family, his servants and warriors. David and his men stopped at a last or faraway house. There the people going with him came and passed before him as they were leaving Jerusalem. Ittai and his six hundred men also wanted to go with him. They were foreigners, exiles that came with him from Gath. They all passed before David. But David didn't want them to come with him. It would be safer for them if they stayed in Jerusalem.

David asked him, *'Are you also going with us? Return, and abide with the king (Absalom), for <u>you are a foreigner</u>, and also an exile from your own place. Whereas you came but yesterday, should I this day make you go up and down with us, seeing I go whither I may? Return you, and take back your brethren with you in kindness and truth'.*[1]

But Ittai replied, *'As HaShem lives, and as my lord the king lives, surely in what place my lord the king shall be, whether for death or for life, even there also will your servant be'.*[2] Then David allowed him and his men to come with him. Ittai and all his men passed the Kidron brook together with all those who were with them. David who knew the Laws and regulations of the Lord, treated Ittai and his men well. When he told him to stay in Jerusalem, it was for their own well being.

> *Thus says HaShem, your Redeemer, and He that <u>formed you from the womb</u>: I am HaShem, that makes all things; that stretched forth the heavens alone; that spread abroad the earth by Myself.*
>
> Isaiah 44:24

The Lord God Who loves the people of Israel and redeemed Jacob gave the Israelites specific instructions on how to deal with strangers, foreigners living within their territory, while making a distinction between them and the enemies of Israel in the Land of Israel. He even made it clear that the commandments and regulations He had given them would also apply to the foreigners.

> *As for the congregation, there shall be one statute both for you, and for the stranger that sojourns with you, a statute for ever throughout your generations; as you are, so shall the <u>stranger</u> be before HaShem. One law and one ordinance shall be both for you, and for the stranger that sojourns with you.*
>
> Numbers 15:14-16

This also applied to God's feasts, for instance the feast of Tabernacles or Sukkot, which He had given to the descendants of Jacob, to all the Israelites.

> *And you shall rejoice before HaShem your God, you, and your son, and your daughter, and your man-servant, and your maid-servant, and the Levite that is within your gates, and the <u>stranger</u>, and the fatherless, and the widow, that are in the midst of you, in the place which HaShem your God shall choose to cause His name to dwell there. ... You shall keep the feast of Tabernacles seven days, after that you hast gathered in from your threshing-floor and from your wine press. And you shall rejoice in your feast, you, and your son, and your daughter, and your man-servant, and your maid-servant, and the Levite, and the <u>stranger</u>, and the fatherless, and the widow, that are within your gates.*
> Deuteronomy 16:10-14

The strangers may even have an inheritance within the Land of Israel. As for instance the non-Jewish woman Rahab, who helped the Israelite spies in Jericho, with her family and Ruth. They had chosen the God of Israel and they remained in Israel.

> *And it shall come to pass, that you shall divide it by lot for an inheritance to you and to the <u>strangers</u> that sojourn among you, who shall have children among you; and they shall be to you as the <u>home-born among the children of Israel</u>; <u>they shall have inheritance with you</u> among the tribes of Israel. And it shall come to pass, that in what tribe the stranger sojourns, there shall you give him his inheritance, says the Lord God.*
> Ezekiel 47:21-23

But, the Israelites were not to take up customs from the foreigner that were contrary to God's commands and regulations. As for the enemies of the people of Israel within the Land that seeks their destruction, they were not to make treaties with them.

> *When HaShem your God shall bring you into the land whither you go to possess it, and shall cast out many nations before you, ... you shall make no covenant with them.*
> Deuteronomy 7:1-5

The Hivites living in Gibeon were the only people within the Land of Israel with whom the Israelites, Joshua, made a peace treaty. But, why did the Lord God give the Israelites this regulation?

> *For <u>you are a holy people to HaShem your God</u>: HaShem your <u>God has chosen you to be His own treasure</u>, out of all people that are upon the face of the earth. HaShem did not set His love upon you, nor choose you, because you were more in number than any people – for you were the fewest of all people – but <u>because HaShem loved you</u>, and because <u>He would keep the oath which He swore to your fathers</u>, has HaShem brought you out with a mighty hand, and <u>redeemed you out of the house of bondage</u>, from the hand of Pharaoh king of Egypt. Know therefore that <u>HaShem your God</u>, <u>He is God; the faithful God, who keeps covenant and mercy with them that love Him and keep His commandments to a thousand generations.</u>*
>
> Deuteronomy 7;6-9

> *For <u>HaShem has redeemed Jacob</u>, and <u>does glorify Himself in Israel</u>.*
>
> Isaiah 44:23

The Lord God had already said to Abraham that those who would bless him would also be blessed. King Solomon also requested the Lord God to bless all foreigners who would come to His House of Worship, the Temple of the Lord. The Lord gave a promise of joyfulness regarding especially the foreigners who had joined Him. Those who would come themselves and those He Himself would bring to His House of Worship, which *shall be called a House of Prayer for all people.*[*3]

> *Thus says HaShem: Keep you justice, and do righteousness; for My salvation is near to come, and My favour to be revealed. Happy is the man that does this, and the son of man that holds fast by it: that keeps the Sabbath from profaning it, and keeps his hand from doing any evil. ... Also the <u>foreigners</u> that <u>join themselves to HaShem</u>, to minister to Him, and <u>to love the name of HaShem</u>, to be His servants, <u>every one that keeps the Sabbath</u> from profaning it, and holds fast by My covenant: <u>Even them will I bring to My Holy Mountain</u>, and <u>make them joyful</u> in My House of Prayer; their burnt-offerings and their sacrifices shall be acceptable upon My altar; for My House shall be called a House of Prayer for all people. Says the Lord God who gathers the dispersed of Israel: <u>yet I will gather others to him</u>, beside those of him that are gathered.*
>
> Isaiah 56:1-8

The Ark of the Covenant

As all the people passed the brook, they were all weeping out loud going on their way to the road in the wilderness. The High Priest Zadok was also there, with the Levites carrying the Ark of the Covenant of God. They put down the Ark. The priest Abiathar went up until everybody that left the city had passed. Then the Levites picked up the Ark, ready to leave with David. But he didn't want them to come with him. David said to Zadok, to carry it back into Jerusalem and that "*if I shall find favour in the eyes of HaShem, He will bring me back, and show me both it, and His habitation; but if He say thus: I have no delight in you; behold, here am I, let Him do to me as seems good to Him.*"*3 Zadok and Abiathar returned to the city with the Ark.

David, his household and all those with him were on foot, walking from the city of Jerusalem, through the Kidron Valley to the Mount of Olives. They climbed the mount to continue their journey to the Jordan River. While going up the Mount of Olives, David was very sad. He was weeping, walking barefoot and with his head covered. All those who followed him were also weeping and just like him they covered their head as a sign of grieving. While on their way, someone told David that Ahitophel was part of Absalom's conspiracy against him. Then David prayed saying, "*O HaShem, I pray You, turn the counsel of Ahitophel into foolishness.*"*4 When David reached the top of the Mount of Olives, he went to a place of worship there. David's friend Hushai the Archite met him there. His clothes were torn and his head was covered with earth. After they talked, David told him to return to Jerusalem. So he did, and he arrived just about the time that Absalom and his followers did.

David had just passed the top of the mount and he was suddenly met by King Saul's servant Ziba. His master Mephiboshet, a son of Jonathan and therefore King Saul's grandson, wasn't with him. Ziba had with him a couple of donkeys loaded with food. A leather bag full of wine, bunches of two hundred loaves of breath, a hundred bunches of fresh fruit, and a hundred bunches of raisins. David asked Ziba what he was going to do with all that. He told David that everything he had with him was meant for him and those with him. The donkeys were for his family so they can ride them. The food and the wine for his men to eat and to drink during their journey through the wilderness. David then asked him where Mephiboshet was. Ziba told him that he stayed in Jerusalem, because he was convinced that Absalom would give him the kingdom of his grandfather Saul. Was this a truthful answer? The king said to Ziba, that everything that belonged to Mephiboshet now belonged to him. Ziba told David that he would remain his servant.

Leaving the Mount of Olives behind them, King David and those with him arrived at a place along the road to the Jordan Valley, the town of Bahurim. Someone came out of the town to meet him. It was Shimei son of Gera, who was one of King Saul's relatives. He did not come to greet David, but to curse him. He started to throw stones at David and as well as at his servants, even though David was surrounded by his people and soldiers. He called David a criminal who took Saul's kingdom and a murderer of Saul's family. He also said that he was being punished by God who gave the kingdom to his son Absalom. Joab's brother Abishai, who was one of David's heroes, told David that he should not accept what Shimei was doing to him. He asked David to let him go and cut off Shimei's head. But David said to him, *'What have I to do with you, you sons of Zeruiah? So let him curse, because HaShem has said to him: Curse David; who then shall say: Wherefore have you done so'*?*[5]

He also said, *'Behold, my son, who came forth of my body, seeks my life; how much more this Benjaminite now? Let him alone, and let him curse; for HaShem has told him'*.*[6]

David then said a prayer, *'It may be that HaShem will look on my eye (my misery), and that HaShem will requite me good for his cursing of me this day'*.*[7]

David didn't allow anyone to stop Shimei from doing what he did. Shimei continued to curse David as he went some distance along the way with them. David and all those with him were very tired as they reached a place in the wilderness at a crossing of the Jordan River where they could rest.

King David, his household and all his followers walked out of Jerusalem in a hurry. It was a very sad day.

> *He chose David also His servant, and took him from the sheep folds; ... So he shepherded them according to the integrity of his heart; and led them by the skilfulness of his hands.*
>
> Psalm 78:70-72

David walked out of Jerusalem, barefoot, grieving and having a long journey ahead. But, amid all this, David had a plan. Which, he had already set in motion on his way out. It involved the support of those who remained loyal to him. People that he trusted. People he himself told to stay in Jerusalem, and to keep him informed about Absalom's actions and plans. Who were these people? And when did David have the chance to tell him about his plan? The High Priest Zadok was the first person David told to stay in Jerusalem when he spoke to him on his way out of Jerusalem. He didn't only tell him to take the Ark of the Covenant back to Jerusalem, but also with whom he should send news for him and where they could reach him. He told him to let his son Ahimaaz and Jonathan, Abiathar's son, be the messengers. They would find him in the wilderness at the river crossing, where he would wait for them. Then there was his trusted friend Hushai. David told him too to stay in Jerusalem and to pledge his loyalty to Absalom, by telling him that he would be his faithful servant as he was to his father King David. In the meantime he was to oppose Ahitophel's advice and in doing so thwart Absalom's plans. David also told him about the priests Zadok and Abiathar and their sons. He was to tell all he hears in the royal palace to the priests, who then would give the information to their sons to bring for him.

Meanwhile Absalom arrived at Jerusalem. He entered the city with the men of Israel, that is the leaders including Ahitophel, and the Israelites that supported him. When Hushai met with the Absalom, he said to him, *'Long live the king, long live the king'*.*[8]* Absalom asked him why he didn't leave with his friend, David.

Hushai answered, *'Who HaShem, and this people, and all the men of Israel have chosen, his will I be, and with him will I abide. And again, whom should I serve? Should I not serve in the presence of his son? As I have served in your father's presence, so will I be in your presence'*.*[9]*

Then Absalom, who was anointed king at Hebron by the Israelites, turned to Ahitophel to seek his advice. He asked him what they should do now that he was in Jerusalem. He told him to sleep with David's concubines who were left to take care of the palace. This would make him an enemy of his father, which would encourage his followers, who would then be sure that he wasn't going to reconcile himself with him as he had done once before when he returned to Jerusalem. So, they wouldn't be left as traitors of King David. Did Ahitophel have another motive for this advice to Absalom? It is possible he aspired to be king himself. The Law of Moses punished those who slept with their father's wife with death. If this would have happened, Ahitophel himself could have tried to become king. But because of certain future events, it would never come to that. Absalom followed Ahitophel's advice. He did this in plain sight for everyone to see, in a tent they set up for him on the palace roof terrace.

Sometime earlier the prophet Nathan did prophesy to David about what would happen to his concubines. But, he didn't mention them specifically. This was at the time David sinned, by having Uriah positioned to die in battle and his relationship with Bathsheba, Uriah's wife, with which the Lord God didn't agree, as is written, *'The thing that David had done displeased HaShem'*.*[10]

As a result of this, two things would happen to David. He would be punished through his own household, as Nathan prophesied God's words to David, *'Behold, I will raise up evil against you out of your own house, and I will take your wives before your eyes, and give them unto your neighbour, and he shall lie with your wives in the sight of this sun. For you did it secretly; but I will do this thing before all Israel, and before the sun'*.*[11]

When David heard this he sincerely confessed to have sinned against the Lord God. In doing so he showed repentance for what he had done. Then the prophet gave another message to him. He said to him that, *'HaShem also has also put away your sin; you shall not die'*.*[12]

So, God spared David's life, but his first child with Bathsheba, their newborn son, would die. And the last thing that the prophet Nathan told David about the matter of his punishment was, *'However, because by this deed you have greatly blasphemed the enemies*[e] of HaShem, the child also that is born to you shall surely die'*.*[13] His son died after an illness on the seventh day, which meant that the child wasn't circumcised. As the Law given to Moses concerning this matter states *'in the eighth day the flesh of his foreskin shall be circumcised'*.*[14]

Both Absalom and his brother Amnon slept with women that they shouldn't have slept with. Even though Absalom had a political motive to do so, what they both did was sinful. The difference between them and their father David, who slept with Bathsheba, then the wife of Uriah, was that David asked forgiveness from the Lord God for this sin against Him. He forgave David, as He would others, out of His own goodness. As is written, *'I, even I, am He that blots out your transgressions for My own sake; and your sins I will not remember'*.*[15]

Even though God punishes children for the sins of their fathers, ... *visiting the iniquity of the fathers upon the children,**[16] each and every person remains responsible for their own sinful actions. As is written,

'Behold, all souls are Mine; as the soul of the father, so also the soul of the son is Mine; the soul that sins, it shall die'.[17]

And, *'Therefore I will judge you, O house of Israel, every one according to his ways, says the Lord God. Return you, and turn yourselves from all your transgressions; so shall they not be a stumbling block of iniquity to you. Cast away from you all your transgressions, wherein you have transgressed; and make you a new heart and a new spirit; for why will you die, O house of Israel? For <u>I have no pleasure in the death of him that dies</u>, says the Lord God; wherefore <u>turn yourselves</u>, <u>and live'</u>.*[18]

The Lord always wants to settle the matter of wrongdoings and sinfulness. As is written, *'Come now, and let us reason together, says HaShem; though your sins be as scarlet, they shall be as white as snow; though they be red like crimson, they shall be as wool'.*[19]

What would the Lord would want the people to do? As is written, *'Wash you, make you clean, put away the evil of your doings from before My eyes, cease to do evil; Learn to do well; seek justice, relieve the oppressed, judge the fatherless (give justice to orphans), plead for the widow'.*[20]

Not long afterwards, Ahitophel provided Absalom with more advice, this time regarding David who had fled Jerusalem. He told Absalom to let him choose twelve thousand men to go after David that night. He would attack David and his men when they were tired, disheartened and frightened. He would then kill only David, since that was the only person Absalom wanted to kill. Then he would return with all David's men and people safely to him in Jerusalem. The Israelite leaders, elders, and Absalom thought this to be good advice. Nevertheless, they wanted to hear what Hushai had to say. Absalom called for Hushai, and when he arrived, he told him Ahitophel's plan. He asked him his opinion about this, and encouraged him to tell him what to do if Ahitophel's plan wasn't good enough. Immediately Hushai contradicted Ahitophel's advice, saying that this time his advice was not good. The reason? Because both David and his men had a reputation, well known by everyone, of them being skilful, brave and mighty warriors. David being an experienced warrior and commander would not stay with his men, but he would hide somewhere in a cave. As soon as David would attack Ahitophel with his men, people would say that they were defeated by David and his men. Then everyone would become afraid. Hushai proposed a different plan, which would involve gathering all the men nationwide to fight David, led by

Who Is David?

Absalom himself. Neither David nor his men would then survive this battle. Absalom and the Israelite elders thought that this plan was the better one of the two, though this meant it would take far more time to gather all the men they wanted for this campaign. So, the Lord had decided that they wouldn't follow Ahitophel's good advice. What did Ahitophel do?

After this decision was taken, Hushai left and met with the priests Zadok and Abiathar. He told them about what had just happened. They had to send a message to David, telling him that he and his men should not stay in the wilderness at the river crossing. They had to cross the river immediately, or they could all get killed. They spoke to their sons, Jonathan and Ahimaaz who had been going back and forth to David bringing him news about Jerusalem. They were to go to David to warn him. So, Hushai gathered intelligence, gave it to the priests, and they in turn gave it to their sons. Then they would serve as messengers to report news to David.

Where were these men hiding? Outside of Jerusalem at the spring of Enrogel. They didn't want to be seen going into the city. So, they remained safely there and were not bothered by anyone. But then, how did they receive the messages meant for David? One of the servants would go out to tell them, when she went out to fetch water. She spoke to them about what was happening in Jerusalem. As soon as the men heard what she had to say, they left Enrogel and went to the wilderness where King David was staying with his people. But one day, they suddenly left quickly to go to the town of Bahurim. As it happened, a boy saw them, he went to Jerusalem and told Absalom. Absalom sent his men out to look for them. In the meantime Jonathan and Ahimaaz went into hiding at the house of a man in the town. Instead of staying in his house, they climbed down into the well that he had near his house. Then his wife spread a covering over the opening of the well. To avoid anyone noticing the well she also scattered grain over the covering. Absalom's men were looking for them at the outskirts of Jerusalem including Enrogel and Bahurim. When they arrive at the house where the men were hiding, they found the woman at home and they asked her about the two men. She answered that they had crossed the river. They kept searching for them, but they couldn't find them. Ultimately they returned empty-handed to the city.

After Absalom's men left, Jonathan and Ahimaaz climbed out of the well and they went on their way to meet with David. When they arrived, they spoke with him telling him all about Ahitophel's plan. David had to cross the river to prevent a confrontation. So, immediately David and all the people with him began to cross the river. By morning light, they had all crossed the Jordan River. Not one person was left behind. They went on their way to the city of Mahanaim, where they could rest for a while. When they arrived there, David was met by three men. Shobi son of Nahash from Rabbah in the territory of Ammon, Ammiel's son Machir from Lodebar, and from the territory of Gilead came Barzillai from Rogelim. These men knew that David and those with him would be exhausted, thirsty and hungry after their journey through the wilderness. So, they brought for David and his people a variety of provisions and bedding.

Meanwhile in Jerusalem, Absalom himself marched out with Israelite soldiers in pursuit of King David. Absalom had appointed Amasa son of Jether the Ishmaelite*[f] or Ithra the Israelite, the commander of the army to replace Joab who remained loyal to King David. Ahitophel whose advice wasn't followed, wasn't so sure that Absalom would be able to succeed in his attempt to kill David. He left Jerusalem on his donkey and returned to his home city. Once there, he put all his affairs in good order. Afterwards he hanged himself and he was buried in his father's grave. So, convinced that David would regain power and have him executed for being a traitor, Ahitophel chose to take his own life.

David and his people remained in the walled city of Mahanaim. While there, he gathered all his men and he divided them into units of a thousand and a hundred men. He placed each of his officers, Joab, Abishai and Ittai, who was from Gath, in command of a third of the men. Then David said to them that he himself would go with them. But his officers didn't want him to go with them. Their reason? As they told David, '*You shall not go forth; for if we flee away, they will not care for us; neither if half of us die, will they care for us; but you are worth ten thousand of us. Therefore now it is better that you be ready to help us out of the city*'.*[21]

David then told them that he would do what they thought was best. Then he stood at the city gate while all his men marched out, all in accordance with their units. David gave one last order, which all the troops could hear, to his officers. He said, '*Deal gently for my sake with the young man, even with Absalom*'.*[22]

The battle took place in the forests of Ephraim and spread out across the land. David's army defeated the Israelite army. Twenty thousand men lost their lives that day, either by the sword or by the dangers within the forest. Absalom was riding a mule when all of a sudden he met with some of David's men. In a hurry he rode away, finding his way through the forest which had large trees with thick branches. Suddenly, he found himself hanging from an oak tree with his head caught in the branches. One of David's men reported to Joab that he saw Absalom hanging in the tree. Joab asked him why he didn't kill him. He would have given him a belt and ten pieces of silver. He told Joab that he wouldn't lift a finger to harm the king's son, not for a thousand silver pieces. They all heard the order that King David had given him, Abishai and Ittai. David hears about everything, and in this case Joab wouldn't defend him against the king. Joab told him he wouldn't waste more time with him and went to kill Absalom himself. He took three spears and threw them into his chest. Then, while Absalom was still alive hanging in the tree, men who were loyal to Joab closed in on Absalom and finished killing him. Afterwards, Joab gave the order to blow the shofar, which was the sign to the troops to stop fighting. Then David's troops stopped pursuing the Israelites who fled to their own homes. As for Absalom's dead body, Joab's men left it in a deep pit in the forest where they threw him and covered him with a big pile of stones. So Absalom who rebelled against his father King David died in the Battle of Ephraim's Wood. A monument remained in Absalom's memory. One that he himself had built during his life, because he didn't have children to carry his name. His sons must have died at an early age, or in any case a while before he was killed in battle.

Two messengers brought the good news to David about his troops' victory. First Ahimaaz and afterwards an Ethiopian slave. But only the Ethiopian man told him that Absalom had died in battle. David was full of grief over the death of his son Absalom. As he went up to the room over the gateway he wept and he said, *'O my son Absalom, my son, my son Absalom! Would I had died for you, O Absalom, my son, my son'*! *23

Joab was told that the king was crying and mourning for his son. David's men all came back from battle. But instead of going into the city cheerful shouting victory, they went quietly as if they were ashamed they had just fled from the battle ground. David continued to mourn his son, covering his face while he wept loudly saying, *'O my son Absalom, O Absalom, my son, my son'*! *24

Joab went to speak with David. Not to comfort him, but to remind him of his men who supported him. He told him he was humiliating those who put their lives on the line to save him and his household. Joab said to David, *'You have shamed this day the faces of all your servants, who this day have saved your life, and the lives of your sons and of your daughters, and the lives of your wives, and the lives of your concubines; in that you love them that hate you, and hate them that love you. For you have declared this day, that princes and servants are nought to you; for this day I perceive, that if Absalom had lived, and all of us had died this day, then it had pleased you well. Now therefore arise, go forth, and speak to the heart of your servants; for I swear by HaShem, if you go not forth, there will not tarry a man with you this night; and that will be worse to you than all the evil that had befallen you from your youth until now'.*[*25]

David listened to Joab. He then went out of the chamber to go and sit at the city gate. When the people heard that their king was there, they gathered before him.

Meanwhile the Israelite soldiers had all fled to their own homes. The people of Israel started to quarrel while trying to determine among themselves, who was to be their king now that Absalom, whom they had anointed king, was killed in battle. David, who saved them from the Philistines, had left the country. Their question was whether someone would try to bring David back to Jerusalem to be their king once again. While David was still in Mahanaim the news about the Israelites' quarrels reached him. When he heard about what they were saying, he sent messengers to the priests Zadok and Abiathar in Jerusalem, telling them to speak to the elders, the leaders of Judah. They were to ask them why they should be the last to bring him back to his house in Jerusalem. That they were relatives and therefore should not be the last to return him to Jerusalem. The messengers also had a message for Amasa, who was Absalom's military commander, telling him that David made him commander of Israel's army instead of Joab, whom he had dismissed. Did David make Amasa son of Jether the commander of Israel's army only because he wanted to facilitate his return to Jerusalem? Or, maybe, to some extent also because Joab had just killed his son Absalom in battle? David's messages which showed that he sought reconciliation instead of retribution won the complete loyalty of all Judah's leaders and men. They sent a message to David, that he should return with his household and all his servants. David and all those with him left the city and went to the crossing of the Jordan River. There he met with the men of Judah who had come to Gilgal, situated at the other side of the river, to escort him across the

Who Is David?

Jordan into Judah.

On his way back to Jerusalem, David would meet with both friends and enemies along the way. Shimei, Ziba and Mephiboshet came to the river crossing. Shimei, who hurried to the river crossing taking a thousand men from the tribe of Benjamin with him, met with David when he was getting ready to cross the river. Shimei threw himself on the ground before David asking him forgiveness for his sin of cursing him while he was leaving Jerusalem. He told David that this was the reason, that he was the first one of the northern tribes, so not of the tribe of Judah, that set out to meet him. Abishai said that Shimei should be put to death for what he had done. But, David gave Shimei his word that he wouldn't die that day. He asked Abishai and Joab whether they were going to cause trouble for him. Then he told them that he was the king of Israel now, and that no one would be put to death on that day.

Saul's grandson Mephiboshet came from Jerusalem to speak with King David. From the time David had fled Jerusalem, he had not washed his feet, cut his beard nor washed his clothes. David asked him why he didn't come with him when he left Jerusalem. He told him that because he was crippled, he asked his servant to saddle his donkey for him, so he could ride along with the king, but he did not. Instead he deceived him and lied to the king about him. This was a different story than what Ziba had told David. So, which one was telling the truth, Ziba or Mephiboshet? Then Mephiboshet told David, whom he said was *as an angel of God**[26], to do with him as he thought was best. For, though all his family deserved death, the king had given him a place at his royal table. He said to the king that he had no right to ask him, David, for any favours. David told him that he and Ziba should share his grandfather Saul's property. David changed his earlier decision to let Ziba have the whole property. Mephiboshet said that Ziba may have it all, and that it was enough for him that the king was returning to Jerusalem. Did he say this just to be polite, while in reality he would share Saul's property with Ziba for the rest of his life?

Barzillai from Gilead, an eighty-year-old man, came as well to the river crossing. He was a very rich man who during David's stay at the city of Mahanaim, supplied him with food. Now he took his fifteen sons and twenty servants with him, and they arrived at the river before David. They crossed the Jordan to help David and his household to cross, and to help him with whatever else he needed. David invited him to go with him to Jerusalem, where he would take good care of him. He told him he preferred to stay because he was already so old that he would be a burden to him. Besides, to him he didn't deserve such a great reward. He told David he should take his son Chimham with him to serve him. David accepted and told him that he would do for Chimham and for him, Barzillai, whatever he wanted. When David and all his men had crossed the Jordan, Chimham went with him, while Barzillai went with David just a little way beyond the river. David then gave him his blessing, kissed him goodbye and Barzillai returned home. So, escorted by the leaders and men of Judah, with the Israelites who joined them, David went on his way to Jerusalem.

On their way back to the capital city, they went to Gilgal. Once there, the leader of the Israelites, the ten tribes, came to speak to King David. They asked him why the men of Judah thought they had the right to escort him, his household and his men across the Jordan River. The men of Judah themselves answered them by saying that David was one of them, that's why they escorted him. The men of Judah also said that David didn't pay them anything nor paid for their food supplies, while asking them why they were so angry. They replied they had ten times as many claims on King David even if he is from Judah. They said they shouldn't look down on them, and that it was their idea in the first place to bring the king back. There at Gilgal was a Benjaminite, Sheba son of Bikri, who began a rebellion against David. He blew the horn and said to the Israelites, *"We have no portion in David, neither have we inheritance in the son of Jesse; every man to his tents, O Israel."*[*27] The Israelites at Gilgal followed Sheba and they left Gilgal. But Judah's men remained loyal to David, and they escorted him to Jerusalem.

Once there he put the ten concubines whom he left behind to take care of the palace under guard. He provided for their needs, but for the rest of their lives they were kept confined and they lived as widows. He didn't sleep with them. Though David returned victorious to Jerusalem, he had Sheba's rebellion to deal with. He gave orders to Amasa, the commander of Israel's army, and to Joab to deal with Sheba. While Amasa gathered the troops, Joab and his men went in pursuit of Sheba. When Joab met up with Amasa along the way, he treacherously killed him. Afterwards Joab continued in pursuit of Sheba. Sheba and his men went through all the territory of Israel. All Sheba's clan members, of the Bikri clan, gathered to him. All of them followed Sheba into the walled city of Abel Beth Maacah. There is where Joab and his men caught up with him. They besieged the city

Who Is David?

by building ramps of earth against the city's outer wall and digging under its wall so it would fall down. A wise woman within the city shouted asking to speak with Joab. She told him that the city of Abel was a peaceful city that was one of the most loyal cities in Israel. Then she asked him why he was trying to destroy the city, to ruin what belonged to the Lord. Joab made it clear to her that he would never destroy nor ruin the city. He told her the city should hand over Sheba son of Bikri, who began a rebellion against King David, to him and he would withdraw from the city. She told him that they would throw his head over the wall. Afterwards she went to the city's inhabitants and told them about what she planned to do. They agreed. They found out who Sheba was, they cut off his head and they threw it over the wall to Joab. He blew the shofar, which was the sign for his men to lift the siege. They all went home, and Joab returned to Jerusalem. After Amasa's death, Joab was once again the commander of Israel's army. But, Joab would one day be punished for the crime of killing Amasa after David's death, by King David's successor.

Even in his old age, David did God's will. He made sure that his son Solomon became king after him. King David told his son to be faithful to God's commands, and to *'have joy of the wife of your youth'*.*g *[28]

David also advised him on Joab, Shimei and Barzillai. Solomon was to be kind for the sons of Barzillai from Gilead, and to take care of them. He told him not to leave Joab and Shimei unpunished. So, Solomon would be the one to punish Joab, Shimei and even the priest Abiathar. Joab because of the murder of Abner and Amasa. Abiathar because of his treason when he allied himself with David's son Adonijah. He attempted in a similar way as Absalom, but also by trying to marry David's youngest wife Abishag, to become king after David. As for Shimei, after David's death Solomon sent for him and told him to build a house in Jerusalem where he could live. He was not to leave the city. If he would go beyond the brook of Kidron he would certainly be put to death. Shimei agreed to this arrangement. Three years later he went to Achish, the king of Gath, to find his runaway slaves, and he brought them back with him to Jerusalem. Solomon summoned Shimei and spoke to him. He also spoke to him about his wrongdoings regarding his father, King David. Then after he left, Solomon ordered Benaiah to kill Shimei, which he did.

David was a man to God's heart and the king that fought the Lord's battles. Chosen by the Eternal God to be the shepherd of His inheritance, the people of Jacob. He conquered Jerusalem, and brought the Tent of Meeting, the Tabernacle, to Jerusalem. Initially it stood for years in Shiloh in the Ephraim hills. That was the first location where it stood in the Land of Israel, where Joshua cast lots in God's presence to divide the Land of Israel among the tribes of Israel. King David made Jerusalem his seat of power.

Through David, the Lord God established the House of David. The House of David would continue to reign for centuries after him, from the capital city Jerusalem. David's kingdom, initially the Kingdom of Judah and later on the Kingdom of Israel, would evolve through time when it comes to its territory, borders and influence, transcending from a tribal state, into a national state governed by a monarchy, and eventually into a modern democratic nation. Its history would cover millennia from its beginning in ancient times, through periods of the rise and fall of world empires that ruled over its territory, such as that of the Assyrians, Babylonians, Persians, Greeks, Romans to modern day times.

> *A tower of salvation is He to His king; and shows mercy to His anointed, to David and to his seed, for evermore.*
>
> 2 Samuel 22:51

Endnotes

*[1]2 Samuel 14:17, *[2]2 Samuel 14:20, *[3]2 Samuel 15:25$_b$-26, *[4]2 Samuel 15:31$_b$, *[5] 2 Samuel 16:10, *[6] 2 Samuel 16:11, *[7]2 Samuel 16:12, *[8]2 Samuel 16:16$_b$, *[9]2 Samuel 16:18-19, *[10]2 Samuel 11:27$_b$, *[11] 2 Samuel 12:11-12, *[12]2 Samuel 12:13$_b$, *[13]2 Samuel 12:14, *[14]Leviticus 12:1-3, *[15]Isaiah 43:25, *[16]Exodus 37:7, *[17]Ezekiel 18:1-4, *[18]Ezekiel 18:30-32, *[19]Isaiah 1:16-18, *[20]Isaiah 1:16-17, *[21]2 Samuel 18:3, *[22] 2 Samuel 18:5$_b$,*[23]2 Samuel 19:1$_c$ (18:33), *[24]2 Samuel 19:5$_c$, *[25]2 Samuel 19:6$_b$-8, *[26] 2 Samuel 19:28$_b$, *[27]2 Samuel 20:1$_b$, *[28]Proverbs 5:15-20

*[a] Artscroll Tanach, The Stone Edition, notes: 2 Samuel 13:1 and 13, page 752-753

Tamar and Amnon could have married, because they were technically not considered siblings according to the Sages. Her mother was a converted captive of war and Tamar was born before her conversion. By the Law of Moses Amnon had to pay a bride price, whether he would marry her or not as Exodus 22:16-17 says.

*[b] Artscroll Tanach, The Stone Edition, notes: 2 Samuel 15:7, page 759

According to the Talmud, it was forty years, not four years. Forty years since the kingship of Israel, with King Saul, was instituted. Being the thirty-seventh year of David's reign.

*c1 Artscroll Tanach, The Stone Edition, notes: 2 Samuel 11:4, page 746. According to the Talmud, Bathsheba was technically divorced when David met her. She received a conditional divorce from her husband. David's troops did this to allow their wives to be able to remarry if they went missing in action. And David recognised Bathsheba as his Divinely intended mate, according to the Talmud. But, David did repent from his act, Psalm 51:5.

*c2 Divinely mate or Beshert

- Article: 40 Days – Divinely Intended Mates, by Moshe Ben-Chaim, http://www.mesora.org/40days.html
- Article: Beshert, November 14th 2009, by Emuna Braverman, https://www.aish.com/d/w/69266117.html

*d Eliam son of Ahitophel

According to 1 Chronicles 3:5, 11:36 the names were different. Ahitophel and Bathsheba might not have been related.

*e Artscroll Tanach, The Stone Edition, notes: 2 Samuel 12:14, page 750-751. A euphemism for blaspheming the Lord God Himself.

*f Artscroll Tanach, The Stone Edition, notes: 2 Samuel 17:25, page 767

1 Chronicles 2:17: Itra the Israelite, because he was a Jew living in Ishmaelite territory. Amasa and Joab were first cousins. And they were nephews of David. Zeruiah and Abigail were David's sisters.

*g Proverbs 5:15-20 If King Solomon was the man who wrote the Book of Proverbs, as Proverbs 1:1, 10:1, 25:1 says, then it was his father, King David, who gave him this advice.

The Green Olive Tree, www.thegreenolivetree.nl

David and Absalom: from betrayal to victory by grace, by Angeline Leito http://www.thegreenolivetree.nl/index.php/14-articles/king-david/126-david-and-absalom-from-betrayal-to-victory

Queen Esther, Feast of Purim, https://www.aish.com/h/pur/mm/Purim_Animated.html?s=rab

Purim Animated, March 3rd 2012, by aish.com https://www.aish.com/h/pur/mm/84336062.html?s=rab

Lego Purim, A unique retelling of the story of Purim, February 14th 2010, by aish.com and Moshe Schlussel

2 Samuel 2:13 Joab son of Zeruiah, David's half sister

2 Samuel 3:2-5 David's first sons, Ahinoam's son Amnon was the eldest, Abigail's son the second

2 Samuel 5:13, 13:1, 1 Chronicles 14:3 David's daughters, Tamar was Absalom's sister

2 Chronicles 27:32 David's uncle Jonathan and Jehiel took care of David's sons' education

2 Samuel 6:23 Michal, David's first wife didn't have own children

David and Absalom

2 Samuel 3:3 Maacah daughter of Talmai king of Geshur, Absalom's mother
Deuteronomy 21:10-14 law to marry a captive of war
Deuteronomy 3:14 territory Maacathites and Geshurites not conquered by Jair, of Menasseh
Joshua 13:13 people of Geshur and Maacah not driven out by the Israelites, they lived among them
Joshua 13:2, 11, 13, 1 Samuel 27:8 David at Ziklag raided the Amalekites, Girzites and Geshurites
2 Samuel 14:13 Absalom in exile, David did not allow him to return
2 Samuel 14:25-26 Absalom's good looks
2 Samuel 14:27, 2 Samuel 18:18 Absalom had one daughter and three sons,
2 Samuel 14:27 Absalom's monument, he had no sons when he died
2 Samuel 13 Amnon abused Tamar and Absalom's revenge
2 Samuel 13:37 Absalom fled to his grandfather the king of Geshur, Talmai the son of Ammihud
2 Samuel 13:38 Absalom stayed three years in Geshur
2 Samuel 13:37-38 David mourned Amnon, longed for Absalom
2 Samuel 14:1-24 Absalom's return to Jerusalem, with Joab's help
2 Samuel 14:25-33 Absalom and David reconciled
2 Samuel 15:1-12 Absalom's plan
2 Samuel 15:10, 19:10 Israelites anointed Absalom king at Hebron
2 Samuel 15:12 plot against David grew
2 Samuel 15:12 Absalom invites Ahitophel from Gilo, David's adviser to his feast in Hebron
2 Samuel 15:13-37 David leaves Jerusalem
2 Samuel 9:1-4, 9:9-13, Ziba had 15 sons and 20 servants, servant Saul's grandson Mephiboshet
2 Samuel 16:1-4, 19:29 Ziba meets David while he was leaving, Ziba inherits Saul's property
2 Samuel 19: 17-18 Ziba with his sons meet David on his way back
2 Samuel 16:5-14 Shimei son of Gera meets, cursed him, David on his way out of Jerusalem
2 Samuel 16:15-23 Absalom slept with David's concubines in Jerusalem on Ahitophel's advice
Exodus 22:16-17, Leviticus 18:18, 20:11 sleeping with a father's wife punishable by death
2 Samuel 12:18 Bathsheba's first child died the 7th day
Genesis 9:5, Leviticus 24:17 punishment for killing a person is death
2 Samuel 16:23, 1 Chronicles 27:33 Ahitophel David's adviser, advice as from the Lord
2 Samuel 16:20-22, 23, 17:1-4 Ahitophel gave Absalom advice on David's concubines and pursuit
2 Samuel 11:3, 2 Samuel 23:34 Uriah's wife Bathsheba was the daughter of Eliam who was Ahitophel's son

Who Is David?

2 Samuel 17:5-14 Hushai's advice on pursuit of David accepted
2 Samuel 16:23 Ahitophel's advice regarded as from God
2 Samuel 17:23 Ahitophel's death
1 Chronicles 27:34 after Ahitophel's death Abiathar and Jehoiada, Benaiah's son, become advisers
2 Samuel 23:34 Eliam son of Ahitophel from Gilo was one of The Thirty famous heroes of David
2 Samuel 15:27-29 priests Zadok and Abiathar, their sons Ahimaaz and Jonathan stay and sent news
2 Samuel 15:37, 1 Chronicles 27:33 Hushai the Archite, David's friend, confidant and counsellor
2 Samuel 15:32-37 Hushai stay in Jerusalem, gather information, give to the priests
2 Samuel 16:16-19 Hushai was David's spy
2 Samuel 17:7-14, 15-29 Hushai sent a warning to David, he escapes by crossing the Jordan River
2 Samuel 17:24-29 David reached Mahanaim, and Shobi, Machir and Barzillai meet him with provisions and bedding
2 Samuel 18:1-18 Absalom's defeat and death
2 Samuel 18:19-33 David receives the news of Absalom's death
2 Samuel 19:1-8, 1 Chronicles 27:34 David reprimanded by Joab, commander of the army
2 Samuel 19:8-18 David escorted on his way back
2 Samuel 19:16-17 Shimei with 1000 Benjaminites meets David on his way back
2 Samuel 19:18-23 David prevents Shimei's death
1 Kings 2:36-46 Shimei's death, son of Gera from Bahurim
2 Samuel 19:24-30 David was kind to Mephiboshet and Ziba
2 Samuel 19:31-39 David was kind to Barzillai, a rich man who supplied David with food
2 Samuel 19:40-43 Judah and Israel argued about David's return
2 Samuel 20, 20:14-22 Sheba rebelled, Sheba defeated
Joshua 18:1, 8-10 Shiloh, location of the Tabernacle, Joshua cast lots to divide the Land
Ezekiel 18 responsibility for own actions
Psalm 78:70-72 David, shepherd over God's inheritance
2 Samuel 9:1-13 Ziba tells David about Mephiboshet, Saul's grandson
Isaiah 43:25
1 Kings 2:1-4 David's advice to Solomon to be faithful to the Lord
1 Kings 2:5-9 David's last instructions concerning Joab, Shimei and Barzillai

Intermezzo Endnotes

*¹ 2 Samuel 15:19-20, *² 2 Samuel 15:21, *³ Isaiah 56:7
Numbers 15:14-16 God's rules regarding foreigners
Exodus 22:20, 23:9 treat foreigners well
Leviticus 19:34 love foreigners as themselves
Joshua 2:1-24, 6:22-25 Rahab remained with her family in Israel
Deuteronomy 16:10-14 foreigners also welcome to God's festivals and dwelling place
Deuteronomy 30:9-13 God's blessings to those who keep his commands, which aren't too hard
Deuteronomy 29:9-15 God's covenant with Israel
Isaiah 44:23-24 the Lord the redeemer of Jacob
Isaiah 56:1-8 God's reward for non-Jews who keep God's covenant
Deuteronomy 33:26-29 God drives out the enemies of Israel
Exodus 34:12-15, Deuteronomy 7:2,23:6 no treaties with enemies within the Land of Israel
Joshua 11:19 peace treaty with the Hivites of Gibeon
Genesis 12:3 others blessed by blessing Abraham
1 Kings 8:41-43 Solomon's prayer regarding foreigners that came to the Temple of the Lord
Isaiah 56:1-2,6-8

Part II
DAVID'S SHIELD

I am HaShem your God, ...
You shall have no other gods before Me.

Exodus 20:2-3

Hear, O Israel: The Lord our God, the Lord is one.
Love the Lord your God with all your heart
and with all your soul and with all your strength.

Deuteronomy 6:4-5

See now that I, even I, am He, and there is no god with Me.

Deuteronomy 32:39a

Is there a God beside Me?
Yea, there is no Rock; I know not any.

Isaiah 44:8c

For I am God, and not a man, the Holy One among you.

Hosea 11:9b

Thus says HaShem, the King of Israel, and his Redeemer HaShem of hosts: I am the first, and I am the last, and beside Me there is no God.

Isaiah 44:6

He is the former of all things, and Israel is the tribe of His inheritance; HaShem of hosts is His name.

Jeremiah 10:16b

He chose David also His servant ... to be shepherd over Jacob His people, and Israel His inheritance. So he shepherded them according to the integrity of his heart; and led them by the skilfulness of his hands.

Psalm 78:70-72

ESSENCE

See now that I myself am He! There is no god besides Me. I put to death and I bring to life, I have wounded and I will heal, and no one can deliver out of My hand.

Deuteronomy 32:38-40

There aren't enough words to capture the essence of God Almighty, the Creator of heaven and earth, the only One who says, *'There is no god besides Me'*.

All others who refer to themselves or who are idolized as gods and goddesses, gather or accept others beside them.

Who is this God?

This God, the only One, the first and the last, the Creator of heaven and earth, identifies Himself and is identified by others through many names. The king and priest of Jerusalem, Melchizedek, called Him, 'God the Most High', when he blessed Abraham. When God appeared to Abraham and told him to walk before Him faithfully and blameless, He called Himself 'God Almighty'. Later when He spoke to Isaac He identified Himself as 'the God of his father Abraham', and in the vision God gave Jacob when he was in Luz, named Bethel by Him, about a stairway resting on the ground but reaching to heaven, He called Himself 'the God of Abraham and of Isaac'.

Besides these names, God has many more. 'God of the Hebrews', 'Eternal God', 'God of Israel', 'God of all the earth', 'the Living God', 'God of heavens', 'God the Father', 'the Holy One', 'the Lord', 'the Lord God', 'the Holy One of Israel', 'God the Great King', 'Redeemer', 'God the Saviour', 'the Rock' and others.

Once Moses asked God what he should say to the Israelites when they ask him about God's name. He answered, *'I Am Who I Am'*, and told him to tell them that *'I Am'* sent him.

God also added that he should say that the God of their fathers, *'the God of Abraham, Isaac and Jacob'* sent him. Furthermore, He told Moses that the name, *'the God of Abraham, Isaac and Jacob'*, would be His name for ever, from generation to generation.

Where did God speak with Moses to tell him these?

He spoke with Moses, aged 80 years, in the desert where he was attending the flock of his father-in-law Jethro, the priest of Midian. Moses lived in Midian after spending the first part of his life, about

Essence

forty years, in Egypt where he was born and later raised by his stepmother, the Pharaoh's daughter. He left Egypt after the Pharaoh tried to kill him, because he had killed an Egyptian that he then buried in the sand.

The reason for his action? He saw the slavemaster beat a Hebrew while he was doing hard labour.

Now Moses came to the mountain of God, Mount Horeb, where God would make His covenant with him and the Israelites later after they left Egypt. There Moses saw a bush on fire, and noticing the bush wasn't burning up, he decided to have a look, not realizing this strange sight was caused by an angel of God that appeared as burning fire within the bush.

While approaching the fiery bush, Moses heard a voice calling him by his name, and he replied "Here I am." Then God told him not to come any closer and to take off his sandals because he was on holy ground. Once Moses complied with God's request, He identified Himself to Moses as the God of his fathers, the God of Abraham, the God of Isaac and the God of Jacob.

In his conversation with Moses, God made clear that He was sending him back to Egypt to tell Pharaoh to let His people go for three days into the desert to worship Him, and to become the leader of the Israelites with his brother Aaron at his side as his spokesman. Moses followed God's instructions.

God is not human, that He should lie, not a human being.
Numbers 23:19

This God is a spiritual being or entity, He is Spirit. This was clear from the beginning when He, His Spirit was hovering over the waters of the earth when it was formless and empty. But, He isn't just any spirit. He is the only one with the capacity to create the visible out of the unseen. He is also able to sustain all and everyone He created in heaven and earth. He is the only one with full control over life and death. There is only one of Him, He is the only God. He is One, which also means he is undivided.

God wraps himself in light as if it were a garment, because He is light and the source of light. There is no darkness within him. He brings light where there is darkness, and reveals that which is in darkness. He makes His light shine on people whenever He chooses. To walk by His light, is also to walk by His word.

The Menorah, lamp stand, he had Moses make is a symbol and sign of His light. God is pure, holy and free of sin, which started within the fallen angels and spread to human beings through Adam and Eve by the choices they made. God is unlike any other being, although He did create angels and human beings to His likeness or image, which means they resemble Him. But, He isn't one of them, nor does He present Himself as one of them. Not as an angel nor as a man, a human being.

Because God is more awesome than all those who surround Him in the council of the Holy Ones, regardless of how powerful God created them to be, He is the One greatly feared. He rules by His wisdom and righteousness. He needs no one's council, and He shares His glory with no one. Neither does He want to share those He loves. Not with gods nor idols. He is a jealous God, a consuming fire.

Didn't He give people their spirit that they should return to God? He is always faithful to those who are faithful to Him, not that His faithfulness depends on theirs. Who has ever given God anything for Him to be in debt to anyone? He created all! He may refer though to a human being as being a god to others in the sense of him being someone else's inspiration as He did with Moses in relation to Aaron. In turn he would be Moses' prophet because he would speak for Him to the Pharaoh of Egypt. He did this for the purpose of His plans.

There are human beings who present themselves as self-proclaimed idols and gods. These 'want to be gods', whose source of inspiration is evil, are not creators within themselves, nor do they possess the all-knowing insight as the true God has.

> *For the Lord is the great God, the great King above all gods.*
> Psalm 95:3

At one time during their journey through the desert, Moses asked the Israelites whether they saw God's form when He made His presence known to them on Mount Sinai. Their answer was no. Does this mean that God being Spirit doesn't have a form? He does, as God revealed to Moses and the prophet Ezekiel.

To Moses, He was revealed when God's glory passed him by. He told Moses that he could stand on a rock next to Him. But when God passed by, He put Moses in a cleft of the rock and shielded him with His hand. After God passed by, He removed His hand so Moses could see His back. The reason? Moses wasn't allowed to see His face, because he would die. In this way God revealed himself to Moses in a way unlike the first time he spoke to him through the burning bush that didn't get burned up by the fire.

To the prophet Ezekiel, God revealed Himself in two of the visions He gave him. One was about God leaving the first Temple built by Solomon, which was destroyed by the Babylonians. In the other vision he saw God returning to the new to be built future Temple. God, who is good, asks all to seek goodness not wickedness. If not, He also declared He wouldn't leave the guilty unpunished. So, to resist evil at all times is not futile. Those who do would receive forgiveness of sins, and they would one day be pure of heart. Those who are pure of heart, have clean hands, who don't trust in idols or false gods may ascend the Lord's mountain, stand in His holy place and receive His blessing. He gives good and perfect gifts from above to those who love Him.

Intermezzo

Idols

> *You saw no form of any kind the day the Lord spoke to you at Horeb out of the fire. Therefore watch yourselves very carefully, so that you do not become corrupt and make for yourselves an idol, an image of any shape, whether formed like a man or a woman, or like any animal on earth or any bird that flies in the air, or like any creature that moves along the ground or any fish in the waters below.*

God didn't want His people to make idols, images of any form to represent Him. They should know whom to worship, but not through these. He wanted them to serve Him. Neither did God want any idols symbolizing the celestial bodies, which some would carry with them and worship as a star-god in the desert, to be made as He warned the Israelites through Moses.

> *And when you look up to the sky and see the sun, the moon and the stars – all the heavenly array – do not be enticed into bowing down to them and worshipping things the Lord your God has apportioned to all the nations under heaven.*
>
> Deuteronomy 4:11-19

To worship handmade idols is futile. Because they have no breath in them, they can't hear, see, speak or do anything. They are made of earthly materials, the same materials that are used for different purposes. From the same wood used to carve and fashion an idol, the rest of the wood is used as fuel for cooking or heating. Idols that know or understand nothing, can't teach a thing. It is all an idea in the mind of those who create them for numerous reasons.

Shouldn't someone know to whom he worships? Once the prophet Isaiah spoke of these. No one stops to think, no one has the knowledge or understanding to say,

> *Half of it I used for fuel; I even baked bread over its coals. I roasted meat and I ate. Shall I make a detestable thing from what is left? Shall I bow down to a block of wood?*
>
> Isaiah 44:16-17

Such a person feeds on ashes; a deluded heart misleads him; he cannot save himself, or say, *'Is not this thing in my right hand a lie'*?

The worshippers of idols, whether handmade or otherwise, would ultimately come to shame because they can't redeem or save them.

There was a brief period, just before the prophet Samuel started his service for God as Judge of Israel, that the ark of God wasn't in the possession of the Israelites. It was captured by the Philistines after they won a battle against the Israelites.

Initially the Philistines were terrified when they heard that the Israelites brought the ark to their camp. They feared the God of the Israelites, because they were well informed about God's actions when He took the Israelites out of Egypt. Still they fought the Israelites, won, and took the ark to Ashdod where they placed it in the temple of their idol, beside a large statue of their idol. The next day early in the morning when the people of Ashdod went to the temple, they found the statue of their idol face down on the ground before the ark of the Lord. They lifted it up and set it back in place. The next morning, there was their idol again, on the ground before the ark of the Lord. But this time, only its body remained. Its head and hands had been broken off and they were lying on the threshold, where since that day no one ever wanted to step on.

Didn't God say that He wouldn't tolerate any god, idol beside him? From that day on, God's hand was heavy on the people of Ashdod, causing illness with tumours and devastation. The people of Ashdod, realizing that the hand of the God of Israel was heavy on them and their idol, decided to move the ark of the Lord elsewhere after their meeting with their Philistine rulers. But, to wherever the Philistines moved the ark, God was against that city and the people became ill and terrified. Ultimately the Philistine rulers decided to give the ark back to the Israelites.

The use and worshipping of idols by the Israelites gives God much grief and arouses His anger. So much so, that He destroys the idols and their temples, and all the witchcraft that comes with it. As He ultimately would do to his own people in Israel and Judah, the Temple in which they would bring and worship idols, and make the Land of Israel desolate until the fulfilment of His prophecies concerning the restoration of His people and the Land of Israel.

> *Who among the gods is like you, Lord? Who is like you – majestic in holiness, awesome in glory, working wonders?*
> Exodus 15:11

God's message not to have gods or idols beside him doesn't say instead of Him. So this is, first of all, a message to those who believe faithfully in the Almighty God. Those He chose and formed to be the people of His inheritance, as well as His servants, and all believers with them. At the same time this message means He actually is the only one true God. Ignoring God's explicit wish and command not to have or serve gods and idols beside him, does have serious consequences. He would bring punishment on those who disregard His wishes and warnings.

Joshua told the Israelites that if they forsake the Lord and serve foreign gods, He will turn and bring disaster on them and make an end of them, after He has been good to them. He told them to decide whom they want to serve, and made it clear to them that he and his household would serve the Lord. He is the Living God, not an idol made of earthly materials and energy, which He created in the first place. He is self-conscious, expressing feelings of joy, anger, regret, and so on. Sometimes He shows His sense of humour, which is also visible in His creation, in His interactions with people. As He did for example with Abraham by telling him to call his son with his wife Sarah, Isaac, which means "he who laughs", referring to both Abraham and Sarah laughing when they heard that they would have a son despite their old age. He makes His own plans and has a plan with mankind, from which He doesn't deviate despite evil and sin. God is the Holy One of Israel, in the midst of the Israelites. Those who live a holy life will see God. It is His holiness that makes others and even places, the ground, a city, a mountain holy. The first time God revealed himself to Moses,

He told him to take off his sandals because he was standing on holy ground, which was where the burning bush that didn't burn up stood. God asked from the Israelites and with them believers to live a holy life because He is holy. He wants to teach believers His ways, what is best for them, which direction to go, so they may know him and learn to live holy lives.

God told Moses to tell his people, *'You must observe My Sabbaths. This will be a sign between Me and you for the generations to come, so you may know that I am the Lord, who makes you holy'.*

God calls Jerusalem the city of the Great King and His Holy City which in time will also be His Faithful City. Mount Zion where He installed His king, He calls His Holy Mountain. God's Promised Land is also called the Holy Land.

Hannah, the mother of the prophet Samuel once prayed, *'There is no one holy like the Lord; there is no one besides You; there is no Rock like our God'.*

As the Creator of heaven and earth, God has therefore power over life and death. Life, for He has given life to all, and as He has sometimes done by bringing people who died back to life by miracles performed through His servants. Death by His wisdom and righteousness when He has to act often to prevent worse from happening. His wisdom is pure, unlike human wisdom which is earthly and non-spiritual, based on selfish ambition and envy, leading to disorder and evil practices.

God's wisdom is peace-loving, impartial, sincere, gentle, free of prejudice and hypocrisy, full of mercy resulting in good deeds. God's actions can be deadly especially when it concerns His faithful servants while executing His plans. Didn't He give David, through battles, rest from all his enemies? On a few occasions when the Israelites were on their journey to the Promised Land some of His decisions were deadly to the Israelites. An example was God's decision concerning the descendants of the Israelites, their next generation with their leaders Joshua and Caleb being the ones who would live in the Promised Land.

In doing so God insured Himself of a more willing group of people to conquer the land, instead of their ancestors who regrettably declined to do so when the twelve spies returned from their reconnaissance mission to the land. Of them, only two, Caleb and Joshua, were willing to do God's will. It would take all together forty years in contrast with the two years it initially took them to reach Canaan; years in which God provided them with all they needed. His protection, water, food, while their clothes and sandals didn't wear out.

Another occasion was when Moses himself met with opposition within the group of leaders.

What actually happened?

Korah, one of the descendants of Levi, attempted to obtain the priesthood. Being part of the tribe of Levi that God brought closer to Him to minister in the Tabernacle and the people obviously wasn't enough for him. He and three men of the tribe of Ruben, including two sons of Eliab, with two hundred and fifty Israelite council members who were well-known leaders in the community, opposed Moses and Aaron. As a group they claimed that Moses and Aaron were placing themselves above the Lord's assembly while ignoring that the whole community was holy and that the Lord was with them.

With their actions, these men were defying the Lord God Himself. Moses told Korah and his followers to come to the entrance of the tent of meeting the next morning. Each one should take their censer to put burning coals and incense in them for the Lord. Aaron also had to be present in the Lord's presence. The Lord would choose who is holy, and have that man come near him. The next day they came.

When Korah and his followers, except the sons of Eliab, who didn't want to come when Moses summoned them, while saying that Moses brought them to the desert to die instead of bringing them to the Promised Land of milk and honey, stood opposite to Moses and Aaron at the entrance of the tent of meeting, the glory of the Lord appeared to the whole assembly. He told Moses and Aaron to separate themselves from the assembly so that He could put an end to them at once. But Moses and Aaron fell face down to the ground and cried to the Lord asking Him whether He was angry with the whole assembly because of the sins of one man. Then God told them to tell the assembly to move away from the tents of Korah and the sons of Eliab.

Moses, followed by the elders, went to their tents and warned everybody to stay away so they wouldn't be part of God's punishment, because of their sins. The assembly did. As soon as Moses finished saying what the Lord would do because of these men, all three of them, standing at the entrance of their own tent with their family, who treated the Lord with contempt, the ground under them split apart and they with Korah's associates with their families and all they owned fell into the opening of the ground. Then the ground closed again. After which the Lord sent fire down, which consumed the two hundred and fifty men who were offering the incense.

Moses did pray asking God not to accept their incense offering, not knowing He would respond like this. That day God made it clear, and had a sign of remembrance made with their censers, that no one except a descendant of Aaron should come and burn incense before the Lord.

If Moses' opponents had their way, would the Israelites have ever reached the Promised Land?

God's might isn't shown only through His creation, but also by His insight in all which enables Him to practice His power, to handle His whole creation by His wisdom and righteousness. God, being the Creator, has an insight in people, angels, both holy and fallen, and in all of creation. Even darkness can't hide anything from Him. He can reveal anything that's hidden, just as He did with David concerning the case of Uriah the Hittite, for which David received punishment during his life.

God probes, tests and searches minds and hearts. David, who knew and had experienced this, tried to pass this on to his son saying: *'And you, my son Solomon, acknowledge the God of your father, and serve Him with wholehearted devotion and with a willing mind, for the Lord searches every heart and understands every desire and every thought. If you seek Him, He will be found by you; but if you forsake Him, He will reject you for ever'.*

The prophet Jeremiah, when confronted with deceit while leaving vengeance to God, acknowledged God's ability to acquire all the insight in human nature He needs to judge each one in accordance to their conduct. He doesn't leave any good deed unrewarded or any bad act unpunished, whether visible or hidden deeds. God's insight enables Him to be right in everything He does, not needing anyone's counsel.

Knowing God is necessary for people to gain insight in matters of life, and in God's plans, which aren't always understood.

The reason?

His thoughts, plans and ways are higher than that of human beings. He has therefore unsearchable ways, though He does give messages through within His word. The words He speaks accomplishes His wishes, and purpose just as they did when He created all things. By His verbal command, the entire visible universe was formed out of the unseen. He always has time on His side because He is eternal. To him a year is like a day or as a watch in the night. His insight in all, His higher thoughts and plans, His eternal timelessness enables Him to oversee centuries of everything and everyone in His creation, both in heaven and on earth.

On earth, He has at any given time awareness of generations of billions and billions of people living in their numerous societies in the past, present and future. He sustains the weight, the lives of all people on the whole planet. Not being able to understand this spiritual being, God, who is so much higher in everything in comparison to people and other beings, of course doesn't give people a right to question or defy Him about His decisions.

Clay just doesn't question the potter while being moulded into pottery, either for common or special use. Pottery is more easily smashed as clay is moulded.

God does reveal himself, His plans, great things to come to His servants, the prophets whom He does ask to put their questions to him.

What does God have to say about himself?

Centuries ago, a few days ago to Him, He proclaimed to Moses whom He spoke to face to face, not through dreams, visions nor riddles, as He passed in front of him.

The Lord, the Lord, the compassionate and gracious God, slow to anger, abounding in love and faithfulness, maintaining love to thousands, and forgiving wickedness, rebellion and sin. Yet He does not leave the guilty unpunished.

Exodus 34:7

God, who doesn't tell lies, declares Himself as being righteous. His righteousness has to do with His rules and commandments, God's Laws. He loves righteousness that, together with justice, are the foundations of His throne, and by which He judges the people with equity. The Spirit of the Lord rules over land and people in righteousness. He asks of His servants, believers to serve Him in the way He requires them to do. That is, to serve Him faithfully, while seeking His righteousness, living by His will, commands and laws, which includes His feasts.

Besides Moses, many more have served Him faithfully, including Noah, Abraham, and David who were righteous in God's eyes.

Faithfulness springs forth from the earth, and righteousness looks down from heaven.

Psalm 85:11

David was the one man God called 'a man after His own heart', through His prophet Samuel. David, who serving God, while living by the sword God entrusted him with as a warrior and king, escaped the edge of the sword when he died. But, people who are righteous in God's eyes are not exempt of experiencing difficulty and sorrows during their life, as in the case of Job. David's own life, on his way to become king of Israel, also testifies to that.

> *Your heavens above, rain down my righteousness; let the clouds shower it down. Let the earth open wide, let salvation spring up, let righteousness flourish with it; I, the Lord, have created it.*
>
> Isaiah 45:8

God is love, and His love endures for ever. He asks His servants to love one another as oneself, and also others even if they were foreigners or enemies. God is eternal, and He is the only one that can give true eternal life. Because, unlike the cosmos, God is infinite! All these merely reflect some of the essence, being of God.

Where does this God reside?

His residence is in heaven where He has His throne, while the earth is His footstool. The city of Jerusalem in the Land of Israel is the place He has chosen to be worshipped on His footstool.

> *King David rose to his feet and said: Listen to me, my fellow Israelites, my people. I had it in my heart to build a house as a place of rest for the ark of the covenant of the Lord, for the footstool of our God, and I made plans to build it.*
>
> 1 Chronicles 28:2

Who was God to David His faithful servant?

The first time David spoke of his faith in God was on the battlefield, when he spoke to the Israeli soldiers and King Saul. While confronting the giant Goliath, David continued to speak of his God. He called him *'the Living God'* and *'Lord Almighty'*.

David considered the armies of Israel to be the armies of the Living God, a name for God used prior to David by Joshua, Moses' successor who led the Israelites into the Promised Land. He rendered his God as being powerful and expected His protection as well as victory from Him, who rescued him from the paw of lion and bear. How? Not by him being passive, but through action. David, through whom God also spoke concerning his kingship and legacy, had to fight to get the sheep they took back.

David's God, in his own words:

You, Lord, are my lamp;
The Lord turns my darkness into light.

With your help I can advance against a troop;
With my God I can scale a wall.

As for God, His way is perfect:
The Lord's word is flawless;
He shields all who take refuge in Him.

For who is God besides the Lord?
And who is the Rock except our God?

It is God who arms me with strength
And keeps my way secure.

He makes my feet like the feet of a deer;
He causes me to stand on the heights.

He trains my hands for battle;
My arms can bend a bow of bronze.

You make your saving help my shield;
Your help has made me great.

You provide a broad path for my feet,
So that my ankles do not give way.

2 Samuel 22

Endnotes

Genesis 1 and 2, Numbers 16:22, Psalm 104, Psalm 24:1-2, 36:10, Isaiah 45:12 God

Genesis 14: 18-20,17:1, 21:33, Deuteronomy 5:25-27, Joshua 3:10, 1 Samuel 17:26

2 Chronicles 36:23, Daniel 2:18-20, Isaiah 48:2, 54:5, Amos 5:14, Psalm 89:19-29

Psalm 24:5, 2 Samuel 22:47, Exodus 15:18, Psalm 95:3, 145:1, Exodus 5:3, Isaiah 40 God's names

Exodus 3:14-45 I Am Who I Am
Genesis 26:23-25 God appeared to Isaac
Genesis 28:12-14 God in a vision to Jacob
Exodus 3, 7:7 Moses calling, age
Exodus 4:14-17, 7:1-2 Moses like a god
Genesis 31:42, 32:9 God of Abraham and Isaac
Genesis 1:2 God is Spirit
Genesis 1:26-28, Psalms 8:6-9   Human beings created in His image, resembling Him
Proverbs 8 Wisdom
Isaiah 48:11 Doesn't share His glory
Exodus 34:14, Joshua 24:19b, Deuteronomy 4:24, 6:15, 32:16, Psalm 78:58, 79:5 Jealous God
Song of Songs 8:6, Ecclesiastes 12:7, Isaiah 42:5 People's spirit belongs to God
Isaiah 48:12 The first and the last
Psalm 89:6-9 God is awesome
Isaiah 45:22-23 The only God, everybody kneels for Him
Isaiah 44:6-8, 24 God needs no one's help, counsel
Deuteronomy 6:4, 2 Samuel 22:32 Only God, is One
Genesis 8:21-22 God thinks by Himself
Genesis 6:5-8 God expresses His feelings
Genesis 17:17-19 God's sense of humour
Exodus 33, 34:5-7 God's proclamation to Moses

Intermezzo Endnotes

Joshua 24:14-15 Joshua's choice
Joshua 24:20, Isaiah 44, 57:3-13, Jeremiah 8:19, 10:1-16, 44:15-23, Idols
1 Samuel 4:5-11, 5:1-5 Micah 1:7, 5:12 The Ark captured, idols destroyed
Psalm 97:7, Amos 5:26 Servants of idols, star-god, know whom to worship
Psalm 18:28, 104:2, 118:27, 119:105, Isaiah 2:5, 60:19, Daniel 2:22 God is light
Genesis 1:16, Exodus 13:21, Psalm 111:27 God brings light into darkness
Exodus 25:36, Numbers 8:2 The Menorah
Leviticus 19:1-2, 20:7-8, Joshua 24:19b, Psalm 99:5-9, Isaiah 12:6, 43:14, 55:5, 48:17 God is holy
1 Samuel 2:1-11 Hannah's prayer
Exodus 3, Psalm 78:54, 99:9, 2:6, Zechariah 8:3   Holy ground, holy mountain, holy land
Exodus 31:13, 33:13, Leviticus 21:8b, 20:26 Makes Israelites holy, holy life
Nehemiah 11:1, Isaiah 48:2, 52:2, Zechariah 8:3 Jerusalem the holy city
Psalm 48:2 Jerusalem, Mount Zion city of the Great King
Exodus 3:1, 17:6, Deuteronomy 5:2 Mount Horeb
Joshua 3:10, Psalm 42:3, Daniel 6:21,27, Hosea 1:10 The Living God

Essence

Jeremiah 17:9-10, 11:20,20:12, Psalm 7:9 God has insight
Ecclesiastes 12:14, Daniel 2:2 Reveals what's hidden in darkness, judgment
1 Chronicles 28:9 David to Solomon
Proverbs 9:10 Knowing God, unsearchable ways
Isaiah 40:12-14 God needs no counsel
Deuteronomy 29:5-6 Clothes and sandals
Genesis 1-3, Isaiah 55:8-11 God speaks, words and thoughts
Isaiah 29:16, 45:9-10, 64:8 Potter and pottery
Psalm 90:4, Isaiah 45:11,44:7, Jeremiah 33:2-3, Amos 3:7 Time, prophets, ask God about future
1 Samuel 15:29, Isaiah 45:21 God doesn't lie, He declares He is righteous
2 Samuel 23:2-4, Daniel 9:14a God is right, rules in righteousness
Malachi 3:18, Deuteronomy 6:25 Those who serve God are righteous
Genesis 6:9, Genesis 15:5-7, Job 37:23 Noah, Abraham, Job
Psalm 9:8, 33:5, 94:15 God loves righteousness, foundations of God's throne
Psalm 85:11, Isaiah 45:8 Righteousness looks, rains down from heaven
Isaiah 66 Serve God the way He wants
Psalm 90:3-6, Isaiah 57:1-2 God has power over life and death
Numbers 10:11-12, 13: 14, 16,17 Twelve spies, opposing God
Exodus 20:6, Deuteronomy 5:10, Psalm 86:5, 103:17-18 God is love
Leviticus 19:18b, 34 Love another like oneself
Psalm 73:1, 84:11, 86:5, 100:4b-5 Only God is good, no darkness in Him
1 Chronicles 19:13, Hosea 56 Good gifts
Psalm 11:7, 15:1-2, 24:3-6 Those pure of heart
Proverbs 8:13 Resist evil
Exodus 34:5-7, Deuteronomy 7:9, Psalm 86:15, 89:8, Isaiah 25:1, God's faithfulness
Psalm 85:10-11 Faithfulness and love go together
Genesis 6:3, 48:15, 1 Kings 8:25 Faithful believers
1 Chronicles 28:2, Psalm 99:5, 132:7, Isaiah 66:1 God's residence, place of worship
1 Samuel 17:26,36, 2 Samuel 22:24-26 David
2 Samuel 7:1 Rest from all his enemies
1 Kings 2:1-12, 1 Samuel 13:14 The man after God's own heart

PRESENCE

In the beginning God created the heavens and the earth. Now the earth was formless and empty, darkness was over the surface of the deep, and the Spirit of God was hovering over the waters.

Genesis 1:2

Since the beginning of creation, God has been making His presence known to mankind. At the time there were no seeds to sprout in the ground, no plants on the earth's surface, and there was no rain, but only mist to moisten the ground. He who created all things was already present. God formed man from the dust of the earth, and made him a living being when He breathed the breath of life into his nostrils.

God had planted the garden of Eden in the East, where He placed Adam, giving him the responsibility to take care of it. In the garden, God made all kinds of trees and a river, which separated into four streams, to water the garden. In all this, God set the boundaries to the garden, just as He would do in the future for His land, and gave the rule to Adam – from which tree he shouldn't eat.

God wanted to create a suitable helper for Adam. So out of the dust He formed livestock, wild animals on land and birds in the sky, that Adam would name. When no suitable partner was found amongst them, God brought Adam into a deep sleep, took one of his ribs, covered the place with his flesh, created a woman out of the rib and He brought her to him who accepted her as part of himself to be one flesh with her. The Lord God would walk through the garden of Eden as He spoke to them.

God blessed them and said to them, Be fruitful and increase in number; fill the earth and subdue it. Rule over the fish in the sea and the birds in the sky and over every living creature that moves on the ground.

Genesis 1:28

God always made His presence noticeable to human beings. He interacted with them from the beginning, showing His love for them, and setting boundaries for them. He continued to make His presence known to Adam and Eve, even after their disobedience and sin, and to so many others despite their sins and short comings, though He did send Adam and Eve out of His garden.

He made His presence known to their sons, Cain and Abel. To Abel, by accepting his offering of a lamb. To Cain, He showed kindness by giving him a mark, after He sent him out of His presence, so people would not kill him because he killed his brother.

Every time He encountered a person who pleased Him, who was very dedicated to Him, He made His presence known to that person. One such person, Enoch, who lived during the seventh generation including Adam on earth, walked faithfully with God. He had several children including Methuselah, his son who lived to be 962 years.

Enoch lived 365 years faithfully with God: *'Then he was no more, because God took him away'*.

According to the book of Enoch, he was taken away by the Lord after which he received revelations about past and future events concerning the Nephilim. Although they were called 'men of renown', they brought much wickedness to the human race in the world at that time.

Which time? The period that the wickedness on the earth was so great, that people's every thought was only evil all the time, and that the people and society was full of corruption and violence.

God said, with His heart deeply troubled: *'I will wipe from the face of the earth the human race I have created – and with them the animals, the birds and the creatures that move along the ground – for I regret that I have made them.'*

So, because of the sin and wickedness of mankind, and not out of environmental considerations, God destroyed the then existing world, the first world, by a flood. But sometimes, as in this case, God would choose people who are faithful to him to play a key role within His plans with mankind. One such person was Noah, not an activist, but a righteous man in his generation.

God was pleased with Noah because he walked faithfully with God, and he was blameless amongst the people of his time. God told Noah to build an ark that he, with his whole family, would use to survive the flood. In addition, God would send animals to Noah that he would also take in the ark.

Seven pairs of every kind of clean animal, male and female, and one pair of every kind of unclean animal, both male and female. He was also to take seven pairs of every kind of bird, male and female.

Seven days later, after God told him to do the latter, when Noah was six hundred years old, all the springs of the great deep beneath the ground burst open and the floodgates of heaven were opened, causing forty constant rainy days and nights.

Noah and all those with him were safe for more than two hundred days in the ark. When Noah could see the top of the mountains, he sent out a raven through a window, which flew back and forth. Later he would send a dove out three times, with a period of seven days in between. The first time it came back, the second time it brought back a freshly plucked olive leaf, and the third time the dove didn't return.

Once it was time to leave the ark, God spoke to Noah and told him to come out. Noah built an altar to the Lord and brought burnt offerings, which were pleasing to the Lord. He told them that as long as the earth endures, there will always be a time to plant and to harvest. Periods of cold and heat, winter and summer, day and light.

The Lord had more to say. He made a covenant with Noah regarding the entire world concerning the flood and the consumption of blood. He said He would never again bring a flood over the earth, and after making His decision known to Noah, He placed a rainbow in the sky as a sign of the covenant He made with Noah. He also made it clear that now they could eat meat, but they must not eat meat with blood still in it, because life is in the blood. As for murdering someone, to the Lord this was not acceptable. He would demand an accounting for a human life.

Intermezzo

Food

> *Everything that lives and moves about will be food for you.*
> *Just as I gave you the green plants, I now give you everything.*
> *But you must not eat meat that has its lifeblood still in it.*
>
> Genesis 9:3-4

This rule is one of the basic rules for kosher food. A God-given law to one man, Noah, with his family and all their descendants. Centuries later God would incorporate this rule in His Laws that He gave to the Israelites.

Just as He had given the circumcision to one man, Abraham, with his household and through him to all his descendants, this would later be part of His Laws given to the Israelites. He did the same regarding

His weekly feast and rest day of the Sabbath, and those concerning clean and unclean animals.

Not complying with this rule, not to eat the blood of any creature does have consequences. God would be against any Israelite or any foreigner residing among them who does this, and that the person would be cut off. This was the reason for King Saul's actions when he was confronted with soldiers within his army who didn't keep this rule.

After Saul and his army won the battle against the Philistines from Michmash to Aiyalon, they were exhausted. Someone told him that some of the soldiers were sinning against the Lord because they took sheep, cattle and calves of the plunder to supply themselves with food, but they ate them while there was still blood in the meat.

Saul, realizing they broke the faith, gave orders to ready a place at once, by rolling a large stone, where the men could slaughter the animals properly. He sent men out to tell the soldiers not to sin against the Lord by preparing meat with blood still in it, but to slaughter the animals properly at the place he had arranged. So, that night everyone did as they were told. Afterwards Saul built, for the first time, an altar to the Lord.

To God, life is in the blood, and God meant this rule not to eat it nor drink it, which also means not using it in other food products, to be applied by all the descendants of Noah.

Aren't all people descendants of Noah?!

> *I will set my face against any Israelite or any foreigner residing among them who eats blood, and I will cut them off from the people. For the life of a creature is in the blood, and I have given it to you to make atonement for yourselves on the altar; it is the blood that makes atonement for one's life. Therefore I say to the Israelites, None of you may eat blood, nor may any foreigner residing among you eat blood.*
> Leviticus 17:10-12

Much later God would make His presence known to Abraham, Isaac, Jacob, and their descendants, the Israelites. He spoke to one of the leaders of His choice, Moses, face to face, not in riddles, visions or dreams.

When the Israelites were on their journey through the desert to Canaan, the Promised Land, God made His presence known to the Israelites with a pillar of cloud and fire, that enabled them to travel night and day through a territory they didn't know. They only moved their camp of more than six hundred thousand people when the cloud moved, while following its direction. As soon as the Israelites set up the Tent of the Lord's Presence, the Tabernacle in their midst, God made His presence known through a pillar of cloud, from which He sometimes summoned Moses, at its entrance.

> *Moses and Aaron were His priests, and Samuel was one who prayed to Him; they called to the Lord, and He answered them. He spoke to them from the pillar of cloud; they obeyed the laws and commands that He gave them.*
>
> Psalm 99:6-7

Years later when the Tent of God's Presence was replaced by the Temple King Solomon built in Jerusalem the capital city of the Kingdom of Israel, God made His presence known there. The first time was when the Temple was inaugurated by King David's son, King Solomon with the priests and all the musicians while the Israelites were gathered in Jerusalem.

> *When the priests withdrew from the Holy Place, the cloud filled the temple of the Lord. And the priests could not perform their service because of the cloud, for the glory of the Lord filled His temple.*
>
> 1 Kings 8:10-11

Since Adam's time, God has continued to make His presence known to people also through visions, dreams and prophecies He gave to His prophets. He also spoke to those He had chosen to be leaders, one of whom was a leader of the Israelites at the time of Judges – Deborah, a prophetess and judge, who ruled the Israelites for forty years. She saw herself as a mother in Israel leading them under God's guidance to victory at that time.

When did God make His presence known to David?

David always had faith in the God of Israel. To him He was the Living God, the Lord Almighty, the God of the armies of Israel. He counted on Him to deliver him from lions and bears that he fought to protect the sheep of his father. When he confronted the giant Goliath, his God was his strength in defeating him.

Later on, when David became a soldier and one of the commanders in Israel's army, he counted on his God in battle, who rendered him victory over his enemies. David would always seek His counsel, as he did when he went to fight at Keilah and when he returned to Hebron in Judah.

It is when God approached David by sending the prophet Samuel to anoint one of the sons of Jesse to become king, that God Himself makes His choice and presence known to David. This becomes more clear when David goes to Saul to play the lyre for him. Every time Saul was tormented by an evil spirit, David would play and Saul would feel better because the evil spirit would leave him.

God's presence would never leave David, as it did King Saul.

> *So Samuel took the horn of oil and anointed him in the presence of his brothers, and from that day on, the Spirit of the Lord came powerfully upon David.*
>
> 1 Samuel 16:13a

God has made His presence known since Adam, to Noah, to the rest of mankind. His message to Adam and Eve, to increase in numbers and populate the earth, set a process that has been on going for centuries, despite the flood that God brought over the earth at the time of Noah.

Although it is the same message He gave Noah and his family, God does not, unlike people under the influence of wisdom-less evil and sin, go around in circles. God's plan with mankind has not changed. He continues to move forward, making His presence known not only to one person as he started out with Adam, but from then on to many, up to a multitude of people and ultimately to the whole human race.

There will be a time when God has His tent among all His people, that His presence will be known to all mankind, at all times.

> *No longer will the sun be your light by day*
> *Or the moon be your light by night;*
> *I, the Lord, will be your eternal light;*
> *The light of My glory will shine on you.*
> *Your days of grief will come to an end.*
> *I, the Lord, will be your eternal light,*
> *More lasting than the sun and moon.*
>
> Isaiah 60:19-20

Endnotes

Genesis 1-3
Genesis 2:8, 15-16, 18 Entrusted Adam with Eden
Genesis 3:8 God walking through the garden of Eden
Genesis 4 Cain and Abel
Genesis 5:18-24 Enoch
Genesis 6:4 The Nephilim
Genesis 5:28-32 Noah
Genesis 6:8-22, Noah, the flood, the covenant, the rainbow
Genesis 9, Leviticus 7:26-27 Blood, the rainbow
Exodus 13:21,14:19-25, Numbers 14:14 Pillar of fire, pillar of cloud
Exodus 33, 40:38, Deuteronomy 31:15, Numbers 12 Pillar of cloud, or fire, at the entrance of the Tent of the Lord's Presence
Exodus 40:35-37 Israelites only moved their camp when the cloud moved
1 Kings 8:10-11, 2 Chronicles 5, Ezekiel 10:1-5 God's presence in his Temple
Judges 5:7 Deborah a mother in Israel
Isaiah 60:19-20 God's presence
1 Samuel 16:13, 23 God's Spirit with David
1 Samuel 17:26 Living God
1 Samuel 17:34-37, 45-47 God already helped him
1 Samuel 23:1-13 David asks God whether he should go to Keilah
2 Samuel 2 David asks whether he should return to the cities of Judah
Ezekiel 28:17 Loss of wisdom
Isaiah 60:19-20 God's presence known to all mankind

Intermezzo Endnotes

Genesis 9, Leviticus 7:26-27, 17:10-15, 19:26, Deuteronomy 12:23, Ezekiel 33:25 Don't eat meat with blood still in it
Genesis 2:1-3, Exodus 20:8-11 Sabbath
Genesis 7:1-3 Clean and unclean animals
1 Samuel 14:31-35 King Saul and his soldiers

CREATOR

> *Lord, the God of Israel, enthroned between the cherubim, You alone are God over all the kingdoms of the earth. You have made heaven and earth.*
>
> 2 Kings 19:15

In the beginning, God created heaven and earth. By His word they came into being. He formed the earth out of water. Within the visible universe God, who is Spirit, created first the earth which He suspended over nothing, and on the fourth day, the sun, moon and stars. It took Him six days to create the whole universe, which would continue to develop through time. He created different beings including angels and human beings to be part of His creation. A human being can't become an angel and vice versa. He gave them all a place in which to live and the ability to interact with each other. He also gave His angels responsibilities regarding humankind. Human beings experience influences from both the spiritual, and visible world, as from the visible one that God created. God allocated the people over the earth by assigning land to form nations when He divided the human race, and established the boundaries of the people according to the number of angels in His heavenly court. God Almighty, who is One, has one Kingdom encompassing the heavens and the earth.

Metaphorically the Kingdom of God can be compared with a kingdom, country on earth.

A country has land mass, water, for example the sea, and air. Whether someone is, while being within the borders of the country, on the land, on or in the country's territorial waters or in its airspace, that someone is in that country. He is part of that nation, that kingdom. The country isn't referred to as being three countries or kingdoms, but one kingdom, even though a kingdom has different regions.

In the kingdom, each space of land, water and air, has its own beings living in them and interacting with each other.

Who belongs where? Who lives in heaven and, who on earth?

When it comes to God Almighty, His dwelling place, His abode is in heaven where all the heavenly beings, including His holy angels reside with Him. It's where His heavenly court, His throne and His Temple are located. It's from where He observes everyone on earth.

The Lord does make His presence known on His footstool, the earth He created. He even chose Himself a place to be worshipped – the city of Jerusalem in the Land of Israel; a land that is compared to God's Garden of Eden.

> *How lovely is Your dwelling place, Lord Almighty! My soul yearns, even faints, for the courts of the Lord; my heart and my flesh cry out for the living God.*
>
> Psalm 84

When it comes to God's holy angels and human beings, He designated their living space for them. God created humans in His image. But unlike them, He is Spirit and He doesn't die. People who do, are gathered with their forefathers. Later on in time they will be part of the resurrection of the dead, which will also include that of a person's body to receive judgment by God.

Angels are heavenly beings, with their residence in heaven, but they can manifest themselves, interact and be in the visible space, also on earth. They are Spirit, with a spiritual body and soul. Angels interact in the visible world, but they always go back because they are heaven-bound.

Human beings on the other hand are earthly beings, with their residence in the visible space, on earth, but they cannot manifest themselves, interact and be in heaven. They are human, with a human body, spirit and soul. So human beings born on this earth are earth-bound.

People, as well as angels, have been assigned their own living space by God, although people, when they are alive, are able to be in heaven by God's will. Angels, on the other hand, can manifest themselves and be present on earth in different ways.

It was an angel that prevented Daniel's friends from burning up in the blazing furnace where Nebuchadnezzar, king of Babylon, had them thrown, because they refused to worship his gods and the gold statue he had put up in his image. When the king saw God's power, he promoted the three friends to high positions in his kingdom.

Years later, an angel shut the mouth of the lions in the lions' den where Darius the Mede, who became king of the Babylonians, saddened by the prospects of doing so, had Daniel thrown in because of the false accusations by the scheming officials of the king to get rid of Daniel.

Daniel refused to stop praying three times a day by his window in the direction of Jerusalem. Darius issued a decree that all people in his kingdom should fear and revere the God of Daniel. By God's grace, Daniel continued to prosper in Babylon while those, who in this case, dug a hole for him, fell literally in it themselves with their families and perished.

It was also an angel who provided the prophet Elijah with food when he was on the run in fear for his life, wishing he was dead rather than be captured by Jezebel's people, who wanted to kill him because he had her priests killed on the Carmel.

Twice the angel told him to get up and eat, otherwise his journey would be too much for him. Elijah did as the angel told him, after which he travelled forty days and forty nights until he reached God's mountain of Horeb.

Angels may provide people with food, though they don't eat the food of human beings, as an angel once made it clear to the parents of Samson.

Angels call human beings 'son of man' as an angel once called the prophets Daniel, Ezekiel and the parents of Samson, opposite to the holy angels called 'sons of God'. But, there is an exception. God Himself called Israel His firstborn son.

Angels are not to be revered as gods, as they themselves sometimes make clear. An example is again the angel who spoke to the parents of Samson, which is also an example of how angels can assume a human form, while they don't become humans, to address a person, as happened in the case of the angel Gabriel when he spoke to the prophet Daniel about the visions he received concerning the End of Days.

There is a hierarchy amongst God's holy angels. Those He ordained in a higher position present themselves before the Lord on a regular basis. There are angels He appointed to be watcher, who received the task of 'watching' over the human beings on earth. Watchers interact with and intercede for humankind, the sons of man. They also received authority from God Almighty to be part of His decision-making concerning human beings.

Nebuchadnezzar, the Babylonian king at the time of Judah's exile, spoke once of a watcher, a holy angel acting as a messenger to him on God's behalf.

Nebuchadnezzar had a dream that terrified him and made him afraid. In his dream he saw an enormously high, large and strong tree in the middle of the land. It grew so much that it touched the sky and was visible to the ends of the earth with its beautiful leaves, abundant fruits providing food for all. Birds lived in its branches, which in turn provided enough shelter for wild animals under it. But, the tree was to be cut down. He saw in his dream, vision, a holy watcher coming down from heaven. In a loud voice, the watcher called and said that the tree should be cut down and its branches trimmed. It's to be stripped of its leaves, and its fruits scattered. The animals and birds would flee from under it and out of its branches. The tree was not to be uprooted. Its stump and roots were to be bound with iron and bronze while remaining in the grass of the field. He was to live amongst the animals, the plants and be saturated with dew for seven times, while having the mind of an animal. This decision was taken by the decree of the watchers, and the sentence by the word of the holy ones, so that the whole world would know that it's the Most High who is sovereign over the kingdoms of the world that He can give to whoever He wishes.

Nebuchadnezzar told all the magicians, enchanters, Chaldean astrologers and diviners of Babylon his dream and asked them in vain for its interpretation. So, he turned to Daniel. It was the second time the king consulted with Daniel to interpret a dream. Only this time he did tell Daniel his dream, he didn't as before expect him to know what he dreamed beforehand. Daniel gave him the interpretation of the dream – the decree that the Most High issued was against this Babylonian king.

Why would God the Most High do this to Nebuchadnezzar? Because God wanted him to acknowledge that He is sovereign over all the kingdoms of the earth, and He has the power to give them, to anyone He wishes, even the lowliest of people.

Daniel's advice to Nebuchadnezzar, which still resonates:

> *Renounce your sins by doing what is right, and your wickedness by being kind to the oppressed. It may be that then your prosperity will continue.*

Twelve months after Nebuchadnezzar's meeting with Daniel, that which was revealed came to pass when his royal authority had been taken from him. He was walking on the roof terrace of his royal palace admiring the great Babylon that he had built by his own power for the glory of his own majesty, for which he praised himself. Suddenly he heard a voice from heaven. He heard what was decreed for him. His royal authority would be taken away, he would be driven from people to live with animals to eat grass like an ox, until seven times, years, had passed when he would acknowledge that God the Most High was sovereign over all kingdoms and could give them to whom He wants, even the most humble person.

The decree came immediately into effect. He was driven away, ate grass like an ox, his body was soaked with dew, his hair grew like feathers and his nails like a bird's claw. When his sanity was restored, he praised the Most High, honoured and glorified Him who lives for ever, saying: *'His dominion is an eternal dominion; His kingdom endures from generation to generation'*.

Angels are messengers, but also warriors. They offer each other mutual support in battle, as Gabriel did for Michael and vice versa at the time God sent Gabriel to Daniel during the Babylonian exile.

God positions His holy angels in His army to fight His battles. They obey God, to guard, to fight and do as He commands.

Of all His angels, He assigned Michael to His people, the Israelites. At the End of Days He will mobilise His army to battle.

> *Before them fire devours, behind them a flame blazes. Before them the land is like the garden of Eden, behind them, a desert waste nothing escapes them. Before them the earth shakes, the heavens tremble, the sun and moon are darkened, and the stars no longer shine. The Lord thunders at the head of His army; His forces are beyond number, and mighty is the army that obeys His command. The day of the Lord is great; it is dreadful. Who can endure it?*
>
> Joel 2

Intermezzo

The Fallen

Some of the holy angels did not keep their proper domain, their positions of authority, but left their dwelling place, their home. The first angel that sinned and left his abode was Satan. He fell at the time Adam and Eve were in God's Garden of Eden.

> *I will ascend above the tops of the clouds; I will make myself like the Most High.*
>
> Isaiah 14:11-14

Who was this angel that became evil? God gave him a position in Eden, God's garden. He was a covering cherub, full of wisdom and perfect in beauty. He was adorned with precious stones. God anointed him as a guardian cherub as He ordained him, and he was on God's holy mountain. He was blameless in his ways since God had created him. But wickedness, evil, was found in him. He wanted to be like God. On account of his beauty he became proud, and he corrupted his wisdom because of his splendour. He became full of violence, sinned, and fell, losing both his beauty and wisdom. God expelled him, drove him from His holy mountain, although he still attends the Lord's court to accuse people day and night. Ever since his degeneration process began, he has been known by his new true nature as the deceiver of the world, liar and the father of all lies, the accuser of the brothers and the prince of the world. Although he would never own the world, he became the sum of all evil. He was already placed by God in Eden. When he fell, he deceived Adam and Eve, leading to the first sin of man.

> *How you have fallen from heaven, morning star, son of the dawn! You have been cast down to the earth, you who once laid low the nations!*
>
> Isaiah 14:12

After Satan, meaning adversary, a group of angels also left their abode and became subjects of Satan. All these fallen ones were former holy angels, but they didn't have the full knowledge of God's plans, and His mysteries were not revealed to them. Whatever knowledge these heartless beings did have, they were worthless and harmful to human beings. They fell at the time of Jered, the father of Enoch, who lived nine hundred and sixty-two years. Their gathering place was Mount Hermon. The leaders of the fallen angels were notably Azazel and Samyaza with his seven associated angels.

Azazal is mentioned in connection with the Day of Atonement, Yom Kippur. On that day a goat was sent to him. Aaron, the high priest was to present two goats to the Lord. One for sacrifice for forgiveness of the sins of the Israelites, and the other one was to be sent into the desert carrying itself and the sins of the people. Azazel is often translated with scapegoat. These un-holy, impure angels instructed people in many sinful things including occultism, harmful technologies and warfare. They introduced the women to the practice of deception, and the use of damaging cosmetics. Their influence over the human race led to so much wickedness that the people were led astray and they became impure and corrupt in all their ways. The tendency of their thoughts was evil at all times.

These un-holy angels connected themselves with women and had children with them. They chose and imposed themselves on whichever woman they wanted. Their offspring were the giants also called Nephilim. Giants like those David with his heroes fought against to free the Land of Israel from their influence – a fight that had already started during the Israelites' journey to the Land of Israel, with them defeating Og, the king of Bashan.

By the grace of God they, unlike other people, successfully resisted these beings. Like Satan, these fallen angels have the ability to manifest themselves in a different form, for example in the form of a person, which was something the holy angels were also able to do, as the angel Gabriel did while talking with the prophet Daniel. Satan also took a different form to deceive the woman, Eve. Since there was only one man in those days, Satan couldn't have taken the appearance of a man. It would have raised questions by Eve, diverting attention from his primary goal.

Did these angels ask God for forgiveness for all the wickedness they brought in the world over humankind? They did have a petition made by Enoch requesting forgiveness and length of days. The petition didn't say anything about repentance, nor about them changing their ways. God, who is all-knowing, didn't accept their petition. It's up to God Almighty to rebuke. And He did.

Satan is still attending God's court to accuse those faithful to God, as he did with God's faithful servant Job, and before him the high priest Joshua when the second Temple was being rebuilt.

> *Then he showed me Joshua the high priest standing before the angel of the Lord, and Satan standing at His right side to accuse him. The Lord said to Satan, The Lord rebukes you, Satan! The Lord, who has chosen Jerusalem, rebukes you! Is not this man a burning stick snatched from the fire?*
> Zechariah 3:1-2

God's servant, Joshua son of Nun, who led the Israelites into the Promised Land, spoke about the gods of Egypt and about those at the other side of the Euphrates River. When the Lord led the Israelites out of Egypt, He said He would punish all the gods of Egypt. He did. Their punishment also came over those who worshipped them and lived by their pagan laws.

So would those who attached themselves to the fallen ones and the spirits of their offspring through occult practices, of which evil itself is the source, and the worship of idols. Ultimately all of the fallen ones will be punished at the time when the Messiah comes.

> *I said, You are 'gods'; you are all sons of the Most High. But you will die like mere mortals; you will fall like every other ruler.*
>
> Psalm 82

These fallen angels, their offspring and those connected to them, have been presenting themselves as gods to humanity in many different forms and ways. But, whoever, either angels or human beings, present themselves as gods, they are not God Almighty, the Creator of heaven and earth.

> *Do people make their own gods? Yes, but they are not gods!*
>
> Jeremiah 16:20

> *Then the word of the Lord came to Jeremiah: I am the Lord, the God of all mankind. Is anything too hard for Me?*
>
> Jeremiah 32

God brought angels into being when He created them to be part of His creation. God's Spirit can move people from place to place, as was the case of Enoch, the father of Methuselah. Enoch had more children, and Noah was one of his descendants. Enoch lived faithfully with God, and He was pleased with him. He lived in his community three hundred and sixty-five years, after which God took him away, something God's servant Obadiah also knew that God could do with his prophet Elijah. Ultimately He did.

The prophet Elisha witnessed how God took Elijah away on a chariot of fire. Unlike Elijah, Elisha would later die from an illness, but a dead man that was thrown in his grave would come back to life when he touched Elisha's bones. The Israelites who were burying him, were trying to avoid a confrontation with a band of Moabite raiders that they suddenly saw coming. This was one of the many miracles showing how the Lord exercises His might.

On one occasion during the fifth year that the people of Judah and Jerusalem were exiled to Babylonia, the son of Buzi called Ezekiel, who was the priest and prophet then, and had experienced God's Spirit, went near the Kebar River where the exiles lived. He stayed there for seven days.

The Lord sent Ezekiel to the Israelites in exile because He had made him a watchman to them, so he would warn them and speak His words to them. God doesn't take people from place to place by His Spirit to get them out of trouble, but to serve His purposes.

God can also choose to put His Spirit on people. When He does this, He can give a person strength, wisdom, understanding, knowledge, visions, dreams and prophesies, as well as the ability to speak different languages and other needed skills for a task.

God told Moses He filled Bezalel, son of Uri of the tribe of Judah, with His Spirit so he could do the necessary artistic designs for the Tabernacle, and He gave him, together with his helper Oholiab, son of Ahisamak of the tribe of Dan, the ability to teach others. God also provided the ability to make everything he had commanded to all skilled workers. God also put His Spirit on Moses and later on the seventy elders of Israel. At one time when Moses was troubled because he heard the Israelites at the entrance of their tents complaining about food, wanting to eat meat and God was already angry with them, he asked God for help. The support he had of the capable officials he appointed to serve as judges over simple cases of the Israelites on advice of his father-in-law Jethro were not enough. Moses chose these men, who had fear of God to be leaders of the people. They were trustworthy and hated dishonest gain. In addition Jethro, who brought Moses' wife and son to him, told him to teach the Israelites God's decrees, His instructions, the way to live and behave.

Moses followed Jethro's advice. But confronted again with complaints of the Israelites, Moses told the Lord he couldn't continue to carry the burden of the people. It was too heavy for him. The Lord told Moses to choose among Israel's elders seventy men whom he knew to be leaders and officials of the people. Moses was to bring them to the Tent of Meeting where God would speak to him and put some of the power of His Spirit he put on him, on them, so they would help him carry the burden of the people.

When Moses and the elders, except two who remained in the camp, were at the Tent of Meeting, God came down in the cloud and spoke to Moses. When the power of the Spirit rested on the elders, including the two in the camp, they all started to prophesy. Moses' aide, Joshua the son of Nun, told Moses that the two elders who remained in the camp also did, and that he should stop them. But Moses replied that he wished that all God's people were prophets and that God would put His Spirit on them, something which He will do with all his servants during the last days, so they will prophesy, have dreams and visions.

These elders were the seventy men with whom Moses went up Mount Sinai together with Aaron and his sons Nadab and Abihu. They stayed at a certain distance from God's cloud where they sat, ate, drank and saw the God of Israel with something under his feet, similar to a pavement of lapis lazuli which was as bright blue as the sky.

Moses and Joshua set out to meet with God. The cloud was six days on the mountain and the seventh day God called Moses from within it. He alone entered the cloud and stayed forty days and nights to receive God's instructions. To the Israelites, the glory of the Lord that settled on the mountain looked like a consuming fire on its top.

> *His splendour was like the sunrise; rays flashed from his hand, where his power was hidden.*
>
> Habakuk 3

God exercises His power and might over the whole universe He created, both in heaven as on earth.

He dominates the forces of nature, life, food supply, the coming and going of animals. The Lord has been doing miracles by His grace with wisdom.

At the time of the kings of Israel, the prophet from Gat Hepher, Jonah son of Amittai experienced God's power over the environment He created. After Jonah warned the inhabitants of Nineveh, he went outside the city to find himself a place to sit and watch what would happen to the city. He built himself a shelter, and God grew a leafy plant up over him for shade. Jonah was very happy with the plant. But at dawn God sent a worm to the plant that made it wither by the time the sun rose.

Centuries before, God provided plenty of bread, Manna from the sky, to the people of Israel when they were in the desert on their way to the Promised Land. The Manna was white, like coriander seed, looked like raisin and tasted like wafers made of honey. The Lord commanded Moses to keep an omer of Manna for generations to come. It was kept in a jar, placed before the Lord along with the Tablets of the Covenant Law.

The Lord quenched their thirst with water from a rock and with bitter water at Marah turned sweet by a piece of wood thrown in it by Moses on God's command.

With the wind He rained down meat for all of them, enough for them to eat for a month. Scattering quail around the camp as far as a day's walk and about ninety centimetres deep, supplying each one of the gatherers with nearly a ton.

The Lord made it possible for more than six hundred thousand people to journey through the desert for forty years with sandals and clothes on that wouldn't wear out.

The Lord's arm wasn't too short to provide again and again all what was needed.

Centuries later after the time of Moses when Israel was governed by kings, the Lord directed ravens to bring bread and meat in the morning and evening for the prophet Elijah, from Tishbe in Gilead, when he was hiding in the Kerith Ravine east of the Jordan River.

God's prophets would also do miracles to provide people with food, as did Elisha, son of Shaphat from Abel Meholah who was anointed by Elijah to be his successor.

Elisha was in Jericho when he threw a bowl of salt into a spring with bad water, which turned into pure water. God's word he spoke over it? *'I have healed this water. Never again will it cause death or make the land unproductive'*.

So it was healed. On another occasion, when Elisha had a meeting with the prophets in Gilgal, he wanted to serve them some stew. There was famine in that region and all they had was some herbs and gourds of a wild vine that they could gather in the fields. But when they started to eat the stew, they found out it was inedible. They told Elisha there was death in the pot. He put some flour in the pot and served the stew. There was nothing harmful in the pot.

One day Elisha told his reluctant servant to feed a hundred men, with nothing more than twenty loaves of barley bread and some heads of new grain. They ate and had some leftovers just as the Lord had told Elisha they would.

What did Elijah tell the widow living in Zarephath, whom God instructed to supply him with food, when she had to make bread with her last flour and oil at a time of famine in Israel?

The jar of flour will not be used up and the jug of oil will not run dry until the day the Lord sends rain on the land.

The Lord has the power to influence the body of human beings. He who gives life, also has the power to take life and give it back.

Moses had a radiant face after he came down from Mount Sinai with the Tablets of the Law. He spent forty days and nights on the mountain in the presence of the Lord, without eating or drinking. From that time, he covered his face with a veil and continued to do so each time he went before God's presence. When he spoke to God and to the people to give them His message, he would take the veil off.

When it comes to God giving people their life back, Elisha also prayed for the Shunamite's dead son on her request, so the boy would come back to life. By God's grace, he did. She knew Elisha, because every time he travelled to Shunem where she lived, he would stay at her house in a room she asked her husband to arrange for the 'holy man of God', as she called Elisha.

Later Elisha would also warn this well-to-do woman to leave Shunem with her family to live elsewhere because of the period of famine that God would bring over Israel. The famine lasted seven years, and it was so severe that some people ate each other's children. In the meantime, she lived in the territory of the Philistines. When she returned to Shunem she went to the king to appeal for her house and land. At that same moment Elisha's servant Gehazi, despite his skin disease, was talking to the king. He was telling him that Elisha restored a boy to life. As soon as he saw the woman with her son, he told the king that they were the people he was talking about, and so she told him. The king granted her request, assigned her case to one of his officials with the order to give everything back to her, including the income over her land during her absence.

> *The Lord is slow to anger but great in power; the Lord will not leave the guilty unpunished. His way is in the whirlwind and the storm, and clouds are the dust of his feet. He rebukes the sea and dries it up; He makes all the rivers run dry.*
> Nahum 1:3-4

The reason Elijah went into hiding at a creek in the Kerith Ravine had to do with his announcement by the word of God concerning a period of drought in Israel. God told him where to hide, to avoid Ahab, the king who did much evil in Israel in those days.

Ahab and his wife Jezebel, the daughter of the king of the Sidonians, didn't serve nor worship the Lord God. Instead they murdered God's prophets and had Elijah as number one on their wanted list.

Obadiah, a servant of God since his youth, at the risk of his own life, hid a hundred prophets in two caves while providing for them, to save their lives from Jezebel.

It was during Ahab's reign that the rebuilding of the city of Jericho took place by Hiel of Bethel, while he lost his eldest and youngest son as was prophesied by Joshua son of Nun after they destroyed the city.

When the creek dried up, the Lord sent Elijah to Zarephath in the region of Sidon. A widow who lived there would provide him with food, as God had directed her. She did, from her last flour and olive oil, after giving him some water to drink. Elijah assured her by the Lord's word spoken to him, that the jar of flour wouldn't get used up, nor would her jug of oil run dry. There was enough food for Elijah, her and her family every day. Later when the son of the widow died after a short illness, she got angry with Elijah. But he took his son, stretched himself three times over him, cried out to God, *'Lord my God, let this boy's life return to him'*!

God returned the boy's life to him, and Elijah gave him back to his mother. She told him that she believed he was truly a man of God, and that he speaks the truth.

During the third year without a drop of rain or dew in Israel, God commanded Elijah to present himself to Ahab. He encountered Obadiah who was afraid to go to Ahab on Elijah's behalf. Obadiah thought God's Spirit might take Elijah away from there, and if Ahab didn't find him, he would kill him. But, Elijah assured him he would meet with Ahab that day. He did, not only with him but also together with the whole of Israel and a total of eight hundred and fifty prophets, worshippers of Jezebel's two idols, on Mount Carmel. He put these idol worshippers to the test by challenging them and their idols. Whoever would answer with fire from the sky down on the altar they prepared would be the true God.

The Israelites, witnessing all this, would choose which God they would serve from then on. The idol worshippers prepared their altar with a bull on it, did not put it on fire, called the name of their idol, shouted at him, danced, prophesied deliriously, carved themselves with sword and spears as they were used to doing, from morning until noon.

Meanwhile Elijah, taunting them, told them to shout louder to get their idol to come with fire, because maybe he was sleeping, travelling, busy or just to deep in thought to listen to them. All their efforts had no effect, no one answered them, paid attention or gave any kind of response. They exhausted themselves and bled for nothing.

Then, when Elijah got the attention of all those present, he repaired the altar of the Lord that had been torn down with twelve stones representing each of the twelve tribes descending from Jacob, who received the word of God, saying, *'Your name shall be Israel'*.

Elijah dug a trench around the altar, arranged the wood on it, prepared the offering and had people pour water over the altar three times. The water ran down the altar and filled the trench. Then Elijah prayed to the Lord, the God of Abraham, Isaac and Jacob, asking Him to show that day that He is the God of Israel, and that His servant was acting on His command to show the Israelites that He is God, and that He would turn the hearts of the Israelites back to Him.

The Lord answered. Fire fell down from the sky, burned up the offering, wood, stones, and evaporated the water in the trench. The people of Israel fell down in reverence to God, saying that the Lord is God. Elijah commanded them to kill the prophets of Jezebel's idols, and they did.

To Ahab he said that he should go eat and drink, because there is a sound of heavy rain. Ahab did as he was told. Meanwhile Elijah climbed to the top of the Carmel, where he bent down to the ground with his face between his knees, and told his servant up to seven times to watch toward the sea for signs of rain clouds. When he told Elijah he saw a cloud the size of a human hand rising over the sea, Elijah told him to tell Ahab to hurry and go down to Jezreel before the rain stops him. God's power came over Elijah and he ran, with his cloak tucked under his belt, ahead of Ahab until they reached Jezreel. Heavy rain fell over the land in that third year of drought in Israel.

God doesn't only have the power over rainfall and fire from the sky, but also the power to influence winds and cause storms as He did at the time the prophet Jonah, who was reluctant to go to Nineveh and tried to flee from the Lord. He got him to the city of Nineveh anyway.

God brought a storm over the sea when Jonah was on a ship going to Tarshish. He was thrown overboard by the seamen, had a miraculous journey in the belly of a large fish that after Jonah showed repentance, spit him out the coast.

Once in Nineveh, it took Jonah three days to go through that large city of more than a hundred and twenty thousand inhabitants, while preaching against them and delivering God's message that Nineveh would be overthrown after forty days. The people believed Jonah's words. Ultimately Jonah's warning also reached the king, who issued a decree for fasting to all citizens, rich or poor, with their flocks and herds. The whole city repented and was saved. In the future, God would bless Assyria, where the city of Nineveh is situated, together with Egypt and Israel as He said, *'Blessed be Egypt my people, Assyria my handiwork, and Israel my inheritance'*.

He made the moon to mark the seasons, and the sun knows when to go down.

Psalm 104

With God's creation came His festivals and feasts. On the fourth day God created the lights to govern the day and the night. He marked and marks His festivals along with His feasts with the moon, not the sun. The Most High entrusted His set times for His festivals and feasts to His people, the Israelites. Set times He hasn't changed, unless by His own command.

Shabbat is the day of rest. It is a day that God made holy because on that day He rested from all His work of creation and He gave it to humanity to be a day of rest.

To the Israelites He made it clear how this day should be set and observed. It should be kept holy, without work and a sacred assembly ought to be held.

The Shabbat was followed centuries later by the other festivals of the Lord, appointed by Him and proclaimed as sacred assemblies. First was Pesach, also called the Festival of Unleavened Bread or Passover, which was held for the first time when the Israelites left Egypt. This festival lasts seven days.

Fifty days after the counting of the omer, which begins on the second day of Pesach, Shavuot, the Festival of Weeks, is celebrated, which is the harvest of the first fruits and when the Children of Israel received God's Laws (the Torah).

Months later, the Ten Days of Repentance (the first of Tishray) would start with the Festival of Trumpets also called Rosh Hashanah.

The Lord instructed the Israelites to make two trumpets of hammered silver for use on different occasions. If both were sounded, the whole assembly had to gather at the entrance of the Tent of Meeting, while if only one was sounded, only the heads of the clans, the leaders had to come. They were also used to signal the moment for the Israelite camp to break up and leave. The trumpets were also sounded on appointed festivals and feasts, as well as when the Israelites had to go to battle. Priests, the sons of Aaron, were the ones appointed to sound the trumpets.

Ten days later (the tenth of Tishray), the Day of Atonement or Yom Kippur was to be observed, which was a day of Sabbath rest, fasting and repentance.

A few days later (the fifteenth of Tishray) the holiday of Sukkot, the Festival of Tabernacles is to be observed. Sukkot, which also lasts seven days (but is followed on the eighth day with the holiday of Shmeni Atzeret) during which Israelites live in temporary shelters as a remembrance to the time the Israelites lived in booths while on their way to the Promised Land.

Three times a year during the annual festivals of Pesach, Shavuot and Sukkot the men were to appear before God at the appointed place, the Tabernacle and later the Temple. These three festivals became festivals of pilgrimage to Jerusalem. All who went up to Jerusalem to worship had to bring a gift and offerings in proportion to the way God had blessed them. In addition the Israelites commemorated the dedication of the Temple on the Festival of Dedication or Hanukkah, and as God commanded they celebrated the feast of the New Moon.

The new moon is the first visible light of the moon, which sets the first day of the month. It's on the second day of the feast of the New Moon at Saul's court that Jonathan found out without a doubt that his father, King Saul, wanted to kill David. After which he left the feast and went to warn David about Saul's intentions.

Some of these appointed times, with their corresponding festivals, will remain in God's New Kingdom during the age of the Jewish Messiah, the Messianic Age, such as the Shabbat, the Festival of Tabernacles which will become a universal festival, and the feast of the New Moon.

With God's Tabernacle and God's Laws came the objects used in the Tabernacle, which in turn became symbols to the people of Israel.

For example, the lamp stand, the Menorah symbolizing the seven eyes of God that range throughout the earth, and the Tablets of the Law or Tablets of Testimony with God's ground rules inscribed on them, the Olive Tree, which provided olive oil used in the Menorah, as well as for special anointment.

Then, there are the symbols that referred to the sons of Jacob that originated with the blessings that Patriarch Jacob gave each one of them. For example, to Joseph the vine and to Judah the lion. The Lord also gave the Israelites a memorial of the sons of Israel on the breastplate of decision that Aaron, the high priest, had to wear over his heart. It was a square breastplate with four rows, each of three precious stones. The names of the sons of Israel were engraved, each on one stone. The stones in the breastplate could have been in the first row a sardius or a red jasper, chrysolite and beryl, in the second, turquoise, lapis lazuli and emerald, on the third jacinth, agate and amethyst, and in the fourth row, topaz, onyx and jasper.

Creator

Although lapis lazuli is sometimes referred to as sapphire, this is incorrect because the gemstone sapphire became widely known during the era of the Roman Empire when they mined for it.

So many symbols have a deeper meaning to the Almighty Father and his people.

Centuries later at the time the Kingdom of Israel was divided for the second time into two kingdoms, that of Judah and Israel, the first king to rule over Israel, the Ephraimite Jeroboam, would introduce for personal and political reasons his pagan religion, together with a place of worship, idols and the symbols to go with it.

Of all the God-given symbols to the Israelites, which one was David's? David was of the tribe of Judah, for which the lion has always been used as a symbol. But, David also had a shield. Not his shield as a tool in battle, which was not the source of his strength. His strength was the one he considered to be his shield – The Living God Himself. As a shepherd, David already counted on the God of Israel to shield him.

> *But You, Lord, are the shield around me, my glory, the One who lifts my head high.*
>
> Psalm 3:3-4
>
> *The Lord is my strength and my shield; my heart trusts in Him, and He helps me. My heart leaps for joy, and with my song I praise Him.*
>
> Psalm 27:7
>
> *You make Your saving help my shield; Your help has made me great.*
>
> 2 Samuel 22:36

Except in the case of Uriah the Hittite, David kept all of God's commands, decrees, stipulations and laws for the Israelites. They were taught by Moses, and have been read every Sabbath for generations for all to hear and learn. David studied and taught God's Laws.

His attitude towards idols and their pagan ways? He didn't bow for, nor worship idols. Neither did David use their symbols including those of the heavenly bodies, the sun, the moon, or a star. After one of his victories over the Ammonites at Rabbah, David didn't bow for their idol. Instead, he took its crown, weighing about thirty-four kilograms of gold, together with a great quantity of plunder with him. Living by God's commands David was faithful to Him and God put his Spirit on David since the day he was anointed to be King of Israel by Samuel.

The earth is God's footstool. What is a person on it? Like a grain of sand? Yet, this Awesome God loves and cares for the people He created with earth's dust, and whom He placed on His planet.

God Almighty, the Creator of heaven and earth, David's Shield, remains who He is. He remains the same, He who is eternal. Still, and up to future generations God, the Great I AM who is truly the Great and Awesome One, a consuming fire, entrusted the Israelites with the ways He wanted to be worshipped. With reverence and awe in accordance to His set and appointed times as He commanded.

> *As the new heavens and the new earth that I make will endure before me, declares the Lord, so will your name and descendants endure. From one New Moon to another and from one Shabbat (Sabbath) to another, all mankind will come and bow down before Me, says the Lord.*
>
> Isaiah 66:22-23

Endnotes

Genesis 1 and 2, Psalm 104. Psalm 36:10, Psalm 104 God the source of all life and light, the Creator of heaven and earth
Genesis 2, Isaiah 53:3, Ezekiel 36:35 Garden of Eden
Genesis 2:7 Dust
Job 26:7, Job 37:1-12 Earth, weather
Jeremiah 10:10, 32:17, 26-27 Nothing impossible for God
Jeremiah 32:18b-19, 2 God's plans, hopeful future, patience
Psalm 11:4 Temple in heaven
Ezekiel 2-4, Daniel 8:17, Zechariah 2:12 Human beings 'son of man', precious
Deuteronomy 32:8 Human race, land
Deuteronomy 22:8, Psalm 8:5, 91:11, 103:20 Angels are spirits
Joel 2 God angels in God's army
Deuteronomy 6:4-5 God is one
Daniel 3:19-26 Daniel's friends in the burning oven with an angel
Daniel 6 Daniel in the lions' den
Daniel 10:4-8 The angel Gabriel talking with Daniel
2 Kings 6:15-17 Elisha with an army of angels
1 Kings 19:1-8 Angels came to serve Elijah
Enoch 15:6-7b, 10 Spirits of heaven, spirits of earth, their living place
Judges 13:3, 8-20 Angel spoke with parents of Samson
Daniel 8:15-17, 9:20-21, 10:1-10 Gabriel spoke with Daniel
Job 1-2 Angels present themselves before the Lord
Daniel 12:1 Michael assigned to Israel

Creator

Daniel 8:15-16 Angel in God's presence
Daniel 10:12-16, 20-21, 11:1 Angels warriors, mutual support
Enoch 15:2, 20: 1-8, Daniel 4:13,23a, 4:17 The messengers
Joshua 2:11, Joshua 10 Sun and moon stood still
Daniel 3:31-4:34 Nebuchadnezzar's dream and insanity
Exodus 4:21-23, Deuteronomy 32:6, 9-12 Israel God's firstborn son
Genesis 10, Deuteronomy 32:8 God gave the people living space
Ezekiel 3:14-15 God's Spirit took Ezekiel away
Genesis 4:18, 5:21-27, 1 Chronicles 1:3 Enoch, Methuselah, Noah
Exodus 24, 31:1-11, 35:30-35 Jethro, Bezalel, Oholiab
Numbers 11:10-16, 24-30 God's Spirit on people
Exodus 24 With seventy elders on Mount Sinai
Joel 2:18-32 (Joel 2:18-27 and 3:1-5) God's Spirit on his servants, end of days
Exodus 16, Numbers 11:4-35, Psalm 78:23-29 Bread and meat in the desert
2 Kings 4:8-37, 8 Shunamite's son, famine in Israel
Exodus 34:29-35 Moses' face
Leviticus 13:12-13 Skin disease over whole body
2 Kings 2:19-22, 4:38-44 Elisha, miracle water and bread
2 Kings 13:20-21 Man back to life
Jonah 4:5-11 God grows a tree
Exodus 15:21-26, 17:1-7, 16:14-36, Numbers 11:7 Water and Manna
Genesis 5:18-24, 1 Kings 18:12, 2 Kings 2:1-18 God's Spirit takes people away
1 Kings 17 Elijah, Widow of Zarethath
1 Kings 18:1-15 Rain
1 Kings 18:7-14 King Achab kills prophets, seeks Elijah, Obadiah
Jonah 1, 2 Kings 14:25 Jonah, Storm over the sea
Joshua 7:27, 1 Kings 16:34 Jericho rebuilt
Exodus 25, Numbers 8:1-4, Zechariah 4:1-5 and 10 Menorah
Zechariah 4 Olive tree
Exodus 24:9-12, Exodus 28, 29, Numbers 15:37-41 Colour blue
Exodus 31:18, 32:15-16, 34:27-29 Tablets of the Law
Exodus 28:15-30 The breastplate, gemstones
Genesis 1:14-19, Psalm 104:19 The moon as a mark to God's festivals
Genesis 2:1-3, Exodus 20:8-11, Isaiah 56:1-8, Jeremiah 17:19-27 Shabbat
Exodus 12, 23, Leviticus 23, Numbers 10:10, Deuteronomy 16:1-17 God's festivals
Daniel 7:25 Set times for festivals not to be changed by others
Numbers 10:1-10, 2 Chronicles 2:4, 8:13, 23:31 Trumpets and offerings
Ezekiel 46:3, Zechariah 14:16-19 Observance in God's Kingdom
Deuteronomy 4:24, Isaiah 66:1-4, 2 Kings 17:32-34 God's way to be worshipped
1 Samuel 20:18-42 David and Feast of New Moon

Who Is David?

1 Samuel 16:13 God's Spirit
Genesis 49:8-12 Symbol Judah, a lion
2 Samuel 12:26-31, 1 Chronicles 20:1-3 Idol's crown
Exodus 20:1-17, Deuteronomy 4:44-45, 5:30-33, 6:4-9, Psalm 51:13 God's Laws, God remains who He is: I AM
1 Samuel 15:29, Isaiah 43:10-13, Psalm 102:27-28 God doesn't change
Jeremiah 23:24-25 no one can hide from God, but He is good at hiding people

Intermezzo Endnotes

Exodus 12:12, Deuteronomy 5:7-10, Joshua 24:14-15 Punishment of Egypt's gods
Isaiah 19:16-25 God's mercy on Egypt and Assur
Job 1-2, Zachariah 3 The fallen angel that still attends God's court
Genesis 6:1-4, Ezekiel 28:6-17 The angels fell
Isaiah 14:12-14 Evil cast down
Genesis 3, Job 1-2, Zechariah 3:1-2 Evil's nature
Genesis 3:1-5, 1 Enoch 32:2b-6 First sin of man
Psalm 82 God Himself rebukes angels
Genesis 6:1-8, Enoch 6:1-2,6, 9: 8-10 The fallen went to the women, Nephilim
Genesis 5:15-16, 6-9:17, Enoch 10:1-4, 6a Jered, Noah and the flood
Genesis 3:1,14-15 Evil takes different forms
Enoch 14:4-7 God didn't accept the petition of the fallen
Daniel 12:1 Time of great distress
Enoch 10:1-14, 11b-12, 15:5, 16:4, 14:5, 19:1 Punishment of the fallen angels
Leviticus 16 Azazel
Enoch 15:7b, Enoch 15:10b Dwelling place spirits of heaven and earth
Daniel 4:13, 17, 23, Enoch 20:1 Watchers, messengers
Numbers 21, Deuteronomy 3:1-11 Og
Genesis 6-9, 2 The flood, destruction of civilisation
Enoch 56 The evil ones including their leaders will return
Isaiah 24, Isaiah 66:22, Daniel 12 Judgment and punishment, new earth, new heaven
The Book of Enoch
Genesis 9:18-24, Enoch 12:1-2 Enoch
The book of Enoch is generally considered to be a pseudepigrapha. It's about the acts of the fallen angels, their punishment by God with His holy angels, and the flood. It covers the period described in the first chapters of Genesis until the flood. The author is believed to be Enoch, who is mentioned in Genesis, and had received a special task concerning the fallen ones.
Daniel 2

WARRIOR

The Lord will march out like a champion, like a warrior He will stir up His zeal; with a shout He will raise the battle cry and will triumph over his enemies.

Isaiah 42:13

Once the prophet Elisha, the man of God who followed the prophet Elijah in serving the Lord, saw God's army ready for battle. This was at the time Aram's king went to war with Israel. Each time the king and his officers planned where to set up camp, Elisha warned the king of Israel and he would be careful and on his guard in those places. It made the king angry that each time Israel seemed to know what he was doing. He summoned his officers and asked them who was betraying him by giving information to his enemies. They told him that no one did such a thing, but that the prophet Elisha in Israel was to blame. So, the king sent a strong force of his men with horses and chariots to capture Elisha in Dothan, after receiving a report that he was there.

At night the men with their horses and chariots surrounded Dothan. Early in the morning Elisha's servant went out and saw the army. He became very afraid, and asked Elisha what they should do. Elisha, seeing the unseen, told him not to be afraid because those with them were more than those with the army he saw. Elisha prayed to the Lord and asked Him to open his servant's eyes so he would see. And the Lord did.

What did Elisha's servant see? He saw the hills full of horses and chariots with fire all around Elisha. Then, when the army came down toward him, he prayed and asked the Lord to strike all of them with blindness so they wouldn't recognise him. He told them that he would lead them to the man they were looking for, because they were on the wrong road and at the wrong city.

He led them to Samaria. Once there the Lord opened their eyes and they saw they were in Samaria. Israel's king asked Elisha whether he should kill them or not. He told him to prepare a great feast for them and to send them on their way when they finish. So he did. The army of Aram stopped raiding the territory of Israel for a while.

Who commands God's army? God's commander, as He showed His servant Joshua, Moses' aide and his successor, who died aged one hundred and twenty before the Israelites entered the Promised Land. Both Moses and his brother Aaron were not allowed to cross the Jordan River and enter the Promised Land because of their disobedience at the waters of Meribah Kadesh in the desert of Zin.

Aaron died aged one hundred and twenty-three on Mount Hor, and Moses on Mount Nebo in Moab across from the city of Jericho.

When the Israelites arrived at the Promised Land's borders they set up their camp at Shittim. Before the Israelites crossed the Jordan River, Joshua secretly sent two men to look the land over, especially the city of Jericho. They returned after a few days to the Israelite camp, before the Israelites crossed the Jordan River.

The spies told Joshua that the Lord had surely given the land in their hands because the people are very afraid of them. The whole nation of Israel left Shittim and set up camp at the Jordan River. While there, God told Joshua He will start to exalt him as He did with Moses, so the people would be in awe of him as they were with Moses.

They crossed the Jordan River after God dried it up for them, while the priests carrying the Ark stood in it. About forty thousand armed men ready for battle crossed up front. The nation of Israel went to Gilgal where they set up camp and all the men were circumcised on God's command.

When Joshua son of Nun, who was the first judge in the Land of Israel, was near Jericho, he saw a man standing in front of him. He had a drawn sword in his hand. Joshua wanted to know whether he was for the Israelites or for their enemies. He told him neither. In addition he told him he was the commander of the army of the Lord, and that he had come. In reverence, Joshua fell face down and asked him what the Lord's message was. He told him to take off his sandals because he was standing on holy ground. Joshua did as he was told. The message was that the Lord had delivered Jericho, its king and soldiers into Joshua's hand. He had to march with his army, the Ark and seven priests carrying trumpets of ram's horns for seven days around Jericho. On the seventh day they had to march seven times around, and at the sound of the trumpets, the wall would collapse. They charged straight in and took the city.

Jericho fell to the hands of the Israelites who destroyed the city. They spared the lives of Rahab the prostitute who lived on the city wall of Jericho and her entire family, as Joshua's two spies promised her. She was the one who told the two spies, sent by Joshua to do a reconnaissance of Canaan, that the people of Jericho were terrified of them because of the God of Israel. She hid them from the soldiers and helped them escape over the wall.

Why?

She told them: *'The Lord your God is God in heaven above and on the earth below'.*

They put her and her family in a place outside their camp, and they continued their lives among the Israelites. These episodes give a glimpse of God's heavenly army with His commander who would only execute orders given by Him.

God seeks peace, but He isn't a pacifist. He is a warrior and defender of His people, and so are His angels.

Daniel, the prophet and government official in the Babylonian court during the period of exile of Judah, spoke of God assigning his angel Michael specifically to the Israelites. The angel Gabriel, who had to fight along the way to get to Daniel to explain revelations God gave him about the end of days, called Michael one of the chief princes. He is the great prince that God entrusted with the protection of Daniel's people, the Israelites. Especially during the period of the end of days when a time of great distress such as has never been before would come over the nations of the earth.

Ever since God formed the Israelites to be His people and brought them up out of Egypt to the Promised Land, as He did with the Patriarch Abraham more than four centuries earlier, He has been fighting battles for them. But God's army consists not only of angels, but also of human beings, sons of man. He fights His battles together with His people, the Israelites. He expects them to do their part of the fighting, to protect, defend and conquer His land, the Promised Land.

To lead His people through the process of becoming a nation, God has been choosing leaders, both men and women, as rulers and warriors. Starting with His servant Moses, who led them through the desert to the Promised Land, to the judges and kings of Israel. At the time of Judges, they were governed by warriors. Joshua, Deborah, Gideon, Jephthah, Samson, and several others, up to the last judge, the prophet Samuel.

Even those before them knew how to defend themselves and protect others. This didn't exclude their Patriarchs. Abraham, in the days he was called Abram the Hebrew, went out to retrieve his nephew Lot who lived in Sodom, where he was taken captive with his family and all his possessions.

At that time five kings, including that of Sodom, rebelled against the king that ruled that region. As a consequence the ruling king with his three allies went to war with them. But, the king of Sodom and that of Gomorrah lost the battle, and as they fled to the hills, some of the men fell into the tar pits of the Valley of Siddim, the Dead Sea Valley. Those who won the battle took all the food, people's possessions, and prisoners with them.

One man escaped and went to Abraham who lived near the great trees of Mamre the Amorite. He told him about what happened to Lot. Abraham immediately gathered three hundred and eighteen trained men born in his household. He went in pursuit of them together with his allies, Mamre and his brothers Eshkol and Aner. Once he caught up with them, he then divided his men in groups and attacked them during the night. He brought back Lot with all his possessions, the women, the other captives, and he recovered all the goods.

After Abraham's return, two kings came out to great him in the Valley of Shaveh, the King's Valley. Melchizedek the King of Salem, brought bread and wine with him. He was a priest of God Most High, and he blessed Abraham (Abram) by saying: *'Blessed be Abram by God Most High, Creator of heaven and earth. And praise be to God Most High, who delivered your enemies into your hand'.*

Abraham gave him a tenth of everything. The other king was that of Sodom, who told Abraham to keep the goods he brought with him but to give the people to him. Abraham told him he didn't want anything for himself, but only what his men had eaten and the share for his allies Mamre, Eshkol and Aner who went with him.

His reason?

Abraham had sworn with his raised hand an oath to the Lord, God Most High, Creator of heaven and earth, that he wouldn't accept anything belonging to this king, so that he would never be able to say that he made Abraham rich. That is what he told the king.

The Lord has been doing great miracles to support His people in battle. At the time the Israelites left Egypt, they left ready for battle. Initially the Lord didn't guide them through the shortest route, which was in the territory of the Philistines, to avoid a confrontation which could have made the Israelites decide to return to Egypt.

God went in front of them to guide them. He was with them by day in a pillar of cloud and a pillar of fire by night, so they could travel day and night. This multitude of people walked out of Egypt on sandals that, during their long journey through the desert, did not wear out. They went to Sukkoth. They didn't stay there for long. Later they encamped at Etham on the edges of the desert. After which the Israelites encamped by the sea near Pi Hahirot directly opposite to Baal Zephon, as the Lord had instructed them.

Why? To give Pharaoh the impression that the Israelites were lost in the desert, so he would come after them. He did, with his army of horses, chariots and troops. When the Israelites saw them coming, they became terrified, and they reproached Moses for bringing them into the desert to die there. But Moses told them that they only needed to be still, because the Lord would fight for them that day.

The Lord asked Moses why he was crying out to Him. He instructed him to tell the Israelites to move on. In addition He told him to raise his staff and stretch out his hand over the sea, so the waters of the sea would divide and the Israelites could cross the sea on dry land. Then the angel of God went in front of them and the pillar of cloud moved from the front to the rear of the Israelite's camp, standing between the armies of Egypt and Israel. It brought darkness on the side of the Egyptians and to that of the Israelites, light all night long, so they couldn't come near each other.

Meanwhile, Moses, as instructed, raised his staff and kept his hand over the sea, and throughout the night the Lord brought a strong east wind that drove the sea back, turning it into dry ground and divided the waters. The Israelites moved on through the sea on dry land with a wall of water on both their left and right side.

A total of 603,550 men, twenty years old or more, together with women and children crossed the sea. The Egyptians, with their chariots and horses, pursued them into the sea. During the last watch of the night, the Lord acted again. He watched down from the pillar of fire and cloud, brought the Pharaoh and his troops into confusion by jamming the wheels of their chariots.

Realizing they were no match for the God of Israel who was fighting against them, they decided to get out of there. To late. Moses, at the other side with all the Israelites, stretched out his hand over the sea as the Lord commanded him to do, and at daybreak the waters went back to their place. The Egyptians tried to flee, but they got swept away by the sea. The Israelites saw their bodies lying on the shore. Not one survived. That day God saved Israel, they feared the Lord and they put their trust in God and His servant Moses. The Lord gained glory by showing His power over Pharaoh to Egypt and all nations.

Does the Lord want lions or mice in his army? Gideon and his men demonstrate that God wants lions. Gideon son of Joash, of the tribe

Who Is David?

Menasseh, was once one of the Judges in the Land of Israel. He was greeted by an angel of the Lord who said to him: *'The Lord is with you, mighty warrior'*.

When the Lord sent Gideon out to fight the Midianites and the Amalekites, he took thirty-two thousand soldiers with him. The Lord told him he had too many men for the task. He told him to send everyone who was afraid away. Ten thousand remained. Still too many. So the Lord told Gideon to let the men drink water and only those who lapped water like a dog instead of kneeling to drink should go with him. The three hundred. Gideon set out with them to the enemy camp.

The Midianite camp in the valley was full with soldiers of the eastern people and their camels. Once there, the Lord told Gideon he already gave the enemy into his hand, but if he was afraid of attacking them, he and his servant Purah should go down to the outposts of their camp and listen to what they were saying. Afterwards he surely would be encouraged to attack them.

So they did, and just as they arrived, they heard two friends talking about a dream one of them had. He dreamed that a round loaf of barley came down on the tent in the Midianite camp with such force, causing the tent to collapse. The friend interpreted the dream, and said that it's the sword of Gideon son of Joash the Israelite that went down on the camp, and that God gave the Midianite camp into his hands. When he heard this, Gideon bowed down in worship. He returned to his men, told them God would give them victory, divided the men into three groups, armed them with trumpets and empty jars with torches inside, turning the groups into three military companies, gave them their orders and set out to reach the edges of the enemy camp. Once they reached the camp, they shouted, a sword for the Lord and for Gideon, while they blew their trumpets, making a lot of noise. Each group held its position around the camp. At the sound of the trumpets, the Lord caused the soldiers to turn on each other, and the entire army fled. Gideon and his men went in pursuit and sent messengers ahead with word to the tribes of Asher, Naphtali, Menasseh and Ephraim to come out to attack the Midianite army as they fled. They did, and killed two of their leaders in the process, whose heads they brought to Gideon.

What did Balaam say about the Israelites while on their way to the Promised Land? On two occasions he couldn't curse, but had to bless them by God's command.

Warrior

> *It will now be said of Jacob and of Israel, See what God has done! The people rise like a lioness; they rouse themselves like a lion that does not rest until it devours its prey and drinks the blood of its victims.*
>
> *Like a lion they crouch and lie down, like a lioness – who dares to rouse them? May those who bless you be blessed and those who curse you be cursed!*
>
> Numbers 23, 24

The day the sun and the moon stood still was by God's grace a day of victory for Israel. Joshua marched with his entire army from Gilgal to Gibeon. The Gibeonites, Hivites living in Gibeon, who were non-Israelites, requested his help when the king of Jerusalem Adoni-Zedek went to war with them.

Adoni-Zedek's reason? He and his people became concerned about their safety when they heard that Joshua destroyed both Jericho and Ai with their Amorite kings, but not Gibeon. This was an important city, larger than those destroyed, and all the Gibeonite men were good fighters. This city became an ally of the Israelites. How did they manage to do that? They sent a delegation to put a request to Joshua for a peace treaty between their people. What they didn't tell Joshua was that they were their neighbours, whom Joshua wouldn't want to make his ally. Instead, they told him they were his servants who came from a distant country, sent by their elders and people.

The reason they came to him was because of the fame of the God of Israel. They heard reports of what He did to Egypt and how the Israelites fought the Amorites, won the battles against the kings of Heshbon and Bashan. They also heard of the destruction of Jericho and Ai. The Gibeonites, using a different name, wearing worn out clothes and sandals told them of their long journey. On their donkeys they had old, cracked and mended sacks of wine and all the bread in their provisions was mouldy and dry.

The Israelites checked their food supply and decided, without consulting the Lord, to make a treaty with them by an oath ratified by the leaders of the assembly. Three days later, they found out about the Gibeonites' deception. The Israelites set out for Gibeon and their other cities. Once there, despite the grumbling of the assembly against the leaders, they didn't attack them because of the oath they made to them, sworn by the God of Israel. Instead the assembly asked for them to be woodcutters and water carriers in service of the whole assembly. Joshua told the Gibeonites about the work, to provide for the altar at the house of his God, which they accepted. On his question why they used a ruse on them, the answer was because they feared them. They were told that their God told Moses to give the whole land to the Israelites and to wipe out all its inhabitants.

The Gibeonites, having a peace treaty with the Israelites and them being their servants, Joshua and his army set out for Gibeon when he received a message from the Gibeonites about the attack of the joint forces of the Amorite kings on Gibeon.

After Joshua and his troops marched all night long, they reached Gibeon and took the Amorites by surprise. Joshua prayed for all to hear: *'Sun, stand still over Gibeon, and you, moon, over the Valley of Aiyalon'*.

God granted Joshua his request, so the sun stood still in the middle of the sky and the moon stopped. The sun didn't go down for about a full day. The Lord also threw the Amorites into confusion. The Israelites fought, defeated them, and went in pursuit of the fleeing Amorite army. They went down the road from Beth Horon and Azekah, where the Lord hurled large hailstones on them. The Amorite soldiers either died by the sword or by hailstones.

As the Lord told Joshua when he left for Gideon: *'Do not be afraid of them; I have given them into your hand. Not one of them will be able to withstand you'*.

Except for these Gibeonites, Joshua didn't have a peace treaty with any other city in the land. Joshua went on to be a great servant of the Lord for his people. He died at age one hundred and ten.

> *One of you routs a thousand, because the Lord your God fights for you, just as He promised.*
>
> Joshua 23:10

Intermezzo

Rules of Engagement

The descendants of Jacob, Israel, had an army as early as the time when they left Egypt. At the age of twenty a man was allowed to enlist in the Israeli army. It's the same age by which Moses counted the male Israelites when they left Egypt. God commanded Moses to hold a census under the Israelites two years after they left Egypt. They were in the Sinai Desert. All who were twenty years or older and were able to serve in the army were listed by name. The men were from all the tribes of Israel: Ruben, Simeon, Gad, Judah, Issachar, Zebulon, Ephraim, Menasseh, Benjamin, Dan, Asher and Naphtali. However, God commanded Moses not to include the tribe of Levi in the census. These men and those aged one month and older were to be appointed by Moses as assistants to the priests, Aaron and his sons. Their responsibility would be the Tabernacle; its furnishings, its equipment and all that belonged to it. They were to set it up, to break it up and carry it wherever the Israelites would go during their journey through the desert and later in the Promised Land. They were also the ones to encamp in the immediate vicinity around it.

Moses and his brother Aaron, of the tribe of Levi, with Aaron's sons also received a designated area to set up their tents, at the east side toward the sunrise in front of the tent of meeting, where the entrance of the Tabernacle was. They were responsible for the care of the sanctuary. Earlier God assigned Aaron and his sons to be His priests. The rest of the Israelite tribes would encamp and break up camp in an orderly manner as God appointed to Moses, by their divisions around the Levite's camp. Three tribes would set up their tents under their standard holding the banners of their families on each of the four sides of the Tabernacle and at some distance from it, thus with the Tabernacle in the middle of the Israelite camp.

Judah encamped under their own standard on the east side, the same side as Moses and Aaron, with Issachar and Zebulon encamped alongside Judah. The Levites were also responsible for preventing trespassers to approach the Tabernacle. Anyone who did would be punishable by death. God Himself excluded the Levites from military service, and gave them a specific unique task regarding His Tabernacle.

Israel's army was meant to defend, to protect them from their enemies and later to conquer the Promised Land. To do so, the Lord commanded them not to enter into any peace treaty with the people living in the land. God gave Moses specific rules of engagement that the Israelites had to follow. Which rules of engagement the Israeli troops should follow depended on which city they would attack. One within the Promised Land or outside its borders. If it's a city outside its borders, they should first offer the people peace. If accepted, all those people would have to work for the Israelites or do forced labour. If not, and go to battle with them, then they should besiege that city. If the siege takes a long time, they shouldn't cut the fruit trees down, because they could eat their fruit. However they could cut trees of which they know it doesn't give fruits to build works for the siege for as long as needed. When the battle is won, they should kill all the men of that city. The women, children, livestock and everything else they should take as plunder for themselves.

But if the city belonged to the nations living in the land God had promised them, they shouldn't offer a peace treaty. They should engage in battle with them – the Amorites, Canaanites, Hittites, Hivites, Jebusites and Perizzites. Later they would also fight the Philistines. Besides the men, all those living in that city, including the livestock, should be killed. They should destroy them. Otherwise they would lead them astray into sin against God.

Before Israel's army set out for battle, both the priest and the officers have to address the troops, after which the officers appoint commanders over the soldiers.

The priest would say: *'Hear, Israel: Today you are going into battle against your enemies. Do not be faint-hearted or afraid; do not panic or be terrified by them. For the Lord your God is the One who goes with you to fight for you against your enemies to give you victory'*.

The officers would ask if anyone just planted a vineyard or just got engaged to be married. If so, they should return home. The same as those who are afraid or faint-hearted should do.

Why didn't the Lord want the Israelites to have peace treaties with the people living in the land He promised to them? Because He gave the Israelites the land as their inheritance. He also didn't want them to engage in practices of these people related to their worship of idols and gods. It was up to the leaders of the Israelites to set up an example of faithfulness to the Lord, regardless of their conduct.

> *Now fear the Lord and serve Him with all faithfulness. Throw away the gods your ancestors worshipped beyond the Euphrates River and in Egypt, and serve the Lord. But if serving the Lord seems undesirable to you, then choose for yourselves this day whom you will serve, whether the gods your ancestors served beyond the Euphrates, or the gods of the Amorites, in whose land you are living. But as for me and my household, we will serve the Lord.*
>
> *Then the people answered, Far be it from us to forsake the Lord to serve other gods!*
>
> Joshua 24

Centuries later, when the Israelites returned out of the Babylonian exile, God sent Nehemiah, as He sent Ezra before him with the approval of the king who ruled over the territory of Israel at that time. When he and the people of Judah started work at Jerusalem's city walls and gates, they encountered resistance from certain non-Israelite officials living in the Land of Israel.

Nehemiah's answer to them was his faith in the God of heaven, which motivated him to mobilise the workers. Half of the men who came with him was equipped for battle while the other half worked. The people of Judah, the builders, worked with their sword at their side. Some worked with their weapon in one hand, and their tools or working materials in the other. They stayed in Jerusalem so they could do shifts doing the work and as guards. So all these people, military or not, were ready to defend and protect themselves and others to get the job done.

At the time of Esther, would there have been an Israeli people left, if they wouldn't have fought to defend and protect themselves?

God had Samuel anoint David to be king over Israel. He would be the second king of Israel after King Saul. The Lord Himself also recruited David to be a soldier and commander when he was a young man, a teenager that wasn't enlisted in the king's army yet. He insured David would have enough training by fighting lion and bear while protecting his father's flock. With faith and confidence, he would be able to confront his future enemies.

> *Who is this uncircumcised Philistine that he should defy the armies of the living God?*
> 1 Samuel 17:26b

These were David's words when Israel was confronted by the giant Goliath.

Israel's army was part of God's army. God fought many battles together with David, who always consulted Him on his battle strategy. He wanted His anointed king to also be a warrior, a commander of his army here on earth. The phrase, 'those who live by the sword will die by the sword' did not apply to David.

Why? God gave David that sword as warrior and king, while he obeyed all God's Laws, except in the case of Uriah, for which God forgave him when he remorsefully repented. By the time David was thirty, he was anointed again as the king of Judah, and about seven and a half years later he was anointed king over the whole of Israel, making him the only king in Israel's history to be anointed three times for this position. God's efforts united the people of Israel to one kingdom. The

Lord still fights and will fight in the future for and with the Israelites, as He made clear through his servants the prophets.

> *On that day the Lord will shield those who live in Jerusalem, so that the feeblest among them will be like David, and the house of David will be like God, like the angel of the Lord going before them.*
>
> *Then the Lord will go out and fight against those nations, as He fights on a day of battle.*
>
> Zechariah 12,14

Should anyone deprive God of His warriors here on earth? Or leave His servant David without troops to command?

Endnotes

2 Kings 6:8-23 God's heavenly army
Joshua 5:13-15, 6 Commander of God's army
Daniel 10:13, 10:21, 12 Angel Michael assigned to Israel
Exodus 14:14, 14:25, 15:3, Deuteronomy 1:30, 3:21-22, 20:4, Joshua 23:3, 2 Chronicles 20:29 The Lord fights for Israel
Exodus 38:26 Number of Israelites who left Egypt
Exodus 13:18, Judges 2:1 God brought the Israelites up out of Egypt to Israel
Numbers 20:12, 27:14, Deuteronomy 32:51-52 Moses and Aaron will not go into the Promised Land
Joshua 2-6 The spies, Rehab
Joshua 3:7, 4:14 God exalted Joshua
Joshua 11:19 Peace treaty
Judges 2 Joshua and judges
Genesis 14 Abraham rescued Lot
Exodus 13:18, Joshua 5:6 Israel's army
Joshua 5:13-16, Joshua 6 Commander of God's army, Jericho walls fall
Joshua 9, 10:1-15 Sun and moon stood still
Nehemiah 4 Armed workers
1 Samuel 17:47 David against Goliath, it's God's battle
2 Samuel 5:4 David, thirty years old, became king of Judah

Intermezzo Endnotes

Exodus 38:26, Numbers 1-3, 2 Chronicles 25:5 Census, age twenty, enlist in the army of Israel
Exodus 28:1-3 Aaron and his sons, priests
Deuteronomy 20 Rules on going to war
Exodus 34:11-16, Deuteronomy 4:1-3, 23:6 No peace treaty

FORGIVING FATHER

Then say to Pharaoh, This is what the Lord says: Israel is my firstborn son, and I told you, Let my son go, so he may worship Me.

Exodus 4:22-24

God the Creator, the Immortal God with His divine nature, eternal power, limitless understanding and wisdom, made the earth and suspended it in the universe. There is no possible image that mortal men can make to define Him. When He allocated land to nations, He had chosen for Himself the ones whose descendants He would call His son. God formed Himself a people out of the descendants of Noah's son Shem. Through His people He would make His presence known, starting with those who later would be named the patriarchs of His people, Abraham, Isaac and Jacob.

The Lord upheld the descendants of Jacob, Israel, since their birth and carried them since they were born. From then on He would carry, sustain and rescue them. Much later He made His presence known to their descendants. To Joseph by dreams, to Moses and through him to those he called the Israelites. Then by great miracles to all the Israelites, the nation of Egypt, and the neighbouring countries in that area all the way to Canaan, the Promised Land.

On the Israelites' journey through the desert, Moses went up Mount Sinai, taking with him the leaders of the Israelites, where they sat. Through the Israelites the Lord revealed Himself to the neighbouring nations of the land He had promised them and further in time to the whole world. To do that, He designated a city and a place for Him to be worshipped. He made it known to King David, His servant and king whose royal household, his royal line would endure for ever. He entrusted them with His chosen place for Him to be worshipped, the city of Jerusalem, Shalem, the Bride, from where Jerusalem's king and priest came out to greet Abraham with wine and bread, blessed him and to whom Abraham gave one tenth of the plunder he had with him from saving his nephew Lot.

However, the Lord your God would not listen to Balaam but turned the curse into a blessing for you, because the Lord your God loves you.

Deuteronomy 23:5

God the Father shows His love for His firstborn through His blessings. He set the Israelites apart from other people. The firstborn has the right to a double portion of his father's inheritance, because that son is the first sign of his father's strength. The Lord doesn't call the whole humankind His son, although He does love each human being He created. He made this clear to His servant Abraham when He told him that through his offspring all nations on earth would be blessed.

Why through him? Because he had obeyed the Lord. God blessed both Abraham and Sarah. God would make Abraham the father of nations and kings would come from him. The descendants of Abraham himself would surely become a great and powerful nation. The Lord had also chosen Sarah to be the mother of nations. He told Abraham that He would bless him and her with a son to be named Isaac. In addition the Lord told him, He would make Sarah the mother of nations and that kings of people would come from her.

To the descendants of Abraham and Sarah, their son Isaac and grandson Jacob, the Israelites, God entrusted with His own Words, Laws, decrees, stipulations, rules and regulations, together with His worship, calendar, feasts, festivals, the tabernacle and the Temple, along with all His covenants, promises, His way of life, His inheritance and His Land, the only land on earth to which He put boundaries just as He did with the garden of Eden, with the city of His choice Jerusalem where He was to be worshipped.

The Lord also gave the Israelites His Messiah to be born and educated among them. In addition the Lord gave the Israelites a double-edged sword to deal with nations, their people, kings and nobles. Ultimately God's Messiah would be in charge of Israel using them as his sword. His vision for Israel has always been for Israel to be at the top, not the bottom, and for His people to go upfront, being the head not the tail. They would be His most precious and treasured possession, a kingdom of priests, a holy nation.

God Almighty chose Israel to be His servant, and He had not rejected them. Each one of the Israelites was and is God's servant. The Lord would be with them to strengthen them, help them and uphold them with His righteous right hand. The Lord gave all these to no other nation or people, but only to the nation of Israel. To the Israelites, the descendants of Jacob.

Why? Because of His love for Abraham and Sarah, their descendants and out of love for the whole humanity. God Almighty had chosen Abraham to be His friend. He told Abraham that he himself should walk before Him faithfully and blameless. Then the Lord would make His covenant between Him and Abraham and He would greatly increase his numbers.

God gave Abraham, and through him his descendants, the task to *'Direct his children and his household after him to keep the way of the Lord by doing what is right and just, so that the Lord will bring about for Abraham what He has promised him'.*

This would also be part of God's blessing to the people and all the nations on earth. The problem is, that people in turn either don't love God or they do but not to the extent of keeping His commands or worshipping Him the way He wants. Despite this, the Lord himself did make it clear to His people, through His servant the prophet Isaiah, that He would gather others to the Israelites.

Who? Those who proclaim God's glory to all nations, to bring in the Israelites from all nations to their land, and choose to bind themselves to the Lord by keeping the Shabbat and His regulations. They would be in-grafted branches in God's cultivated olive tree, Israel. God's Temple in Jerusalem would be called a house of prayer to all nations, as it had been in the past and will be up to the future days to come.

> *These commandments that I give you today are to be on your hearts. Impress them on your children. Talk about them when you sit at home and when you walk along the road, when you lie down and when you get up.*
>
> Deuteronomy 6:4-9

Fatherhood is to God of the utmost importance. Learning and teaching His commandments has always been an essential part of His children's and their children's upbringing, for them to live by them, as He made it clear to Abraham and Sarah, and later to all their descendants. But, the Lord didn't only ask the Israelites to keep and teach His commands, but also to use them as symbols besides all the other symbols, such as the Menorah, that He had given them also for practical use. They were to wrap His commands as symbols on their hands and bind them on their foreheads. He commanded them to write them on the door frames of their houses and gates.

Job was a father who had seven sons and three daughters. He was a wealthy man with a large number of servants, and he owned seven thousand sheep, three thousand camels, five hundred yoke of oxen along with five hundred donkeys. He lived in Uz. He was upright, blameless, feared God and avoided evil. On his sons birthdays they would organise feasts and invite their sisters to come and celebrate with them.

Job had a regular custom after such a feast was held. He would always make arrangements for his children to be purified, just in case his children would do or even think of anything that would be sinful and offend the Lord. He would sacrifice a burnt offering for each of his children early in the morning. Contrary to Job, Eli wasn't a father that cared for his children's well being in accordance to God's commands. Eli's sons, Hophni and Phinehas, were priests of the Lord at Shiloh at the time of Samuel, who was in Eli's care while ministering before the Lord. Samuel would later become a prophet and Israel's last judge, while Eli and his sons would be punished for their sins.

As priests, Hophni and Phinehas did have the right to have part of the meat of the offerings brought in by the Israelites, but only in accordance to certain rules as the Lord commanded through his servant Moses. Rules which Hophni, Phinehas and their servants sent to take the meat ignored, while threatening to use force if they didn't get what they wanted. In addition, Eli's sons engaged in acts of prostitution by sleeping with some of the women who did services at the entrance of the Tent of Meeting. Not only Eli but all of Israel knew of these sins.

Eli rebuked his sons about these deeds, but they didn't listen to him. Eli didn't take any further action on this. Eli himself had his own transgressions. He honoured his sons more than God, he failed to restrain his sons concerning their sins well known to him and he took part in the meals of the chosen parts of the meat offerings provided by his sons.

To God these priests' wicked acts were sinful and they were showing much contempt for Him. It's through a man of God and through the young boy Samuel that the Lord revealed His punishment for these priests including Eli. God would cut short Eli's strength, so his children and descendants wouldn't live a long life. They would die in the prime of their life. He would also cut the strength of Eli's priestly house leaving them without a priestly service in the Lord's dwelling. He declared, *'Far be it from me! Those who honour me I will honour, but those who despise me will be disdained'*.

The Lord would raise himself a faithful priest that would minister before His anointed one in accordance to what is in God's heart and mind. Eli's descendants would bow before him in the future asking for a position in God's service. That priest would be Zadok son of Ahitub who would replace Abiathar son of Ahimelek by King Solomon's orders. Because? Abiathar would conspire with King David's son Adoniah who would try to ascend to David's throne which was meant by God's grace for his son Solomon. As for Eli's sons Hophni and Phinehas, they would both die on the same day. As happened on the battlefield where Israel lost thirty foot soldiers. That would also be the day that the ark of the covenant was lost to the Philistines for a period of time. It's on that battlefield that Hophni and Phinehas both died. On receiving the breaking news that his sons were dead and of the capture of God's ark, Eli, who was an old man and nearly blind, fell backward off his chair, broke his neck and died.

God the Father provides for His children, as He provided for the Israelites in the desert and later in the good land He had promised them. A fertile land with brooks, streams, deep springs, and wells already dug. With wheat and barley, vines and fig trees, pomegranates, olive oil, honey, and fruit trees in abundance. A land for which God cares and that drinks its clear water from heaven each time it rains down on its mountains and valleys. The Israelites were well-nourished. The Lord also insured they knew how to handle the land. Within His Laws He gave instructions to leave the land unused every seventh year. The Shabbat year for the land. The poor among the Israelites were to get food from it, and then the animals were to eat what was left.

God provided for His children by listening to their prayers. All those who would seek to receive from Him, as their Father, He would grant them that which would be needed. Which parent wouldn't do that, despite the shortcomings of their child?

> *My son, do not despise the Lord's discipline, and do not resent His rebuke, because the Lord disciplines those He loves, as a father the son he delights in.*
>
> Proverbs 3:11-12

But, when it's necessary He would also chasten everyone He accepts as His child and educates them through wise lessons in life. He disciplines them for their own good to give them a chance to participate in His holiness. For God is Holy. The Lord's discipline would in time produce a harvest of righteousness and peace for those who have been trained by it.

He disciplined the Israelites in the past, because they turned away from Him to live a sinful life. By worshipping idols, gods and practicing the occult, pursuing evil, undermining justice by sinful acts, they defiled the land that much needed to have its Shabbat years. The land became cursed and a desolated waste. They became disobedient and they rebelled against the Lord, the One who in His great goodness provided for them. They turned their backs to God's Laws, killed His prophets who tried to warn them to turn back to the Lord and they committed awful blasphemies, disrespecting the Lord, causing Him much grief. The nation that was meant to be holy became a rebellious sinful nation that burdened the Lord Almighty with their sins while bringing Him unacceptable offerings.

So, when He couldn't endure their wickedness, He left them to their sins and delivered them into the hands of their enemies, who in time by themselves, would choose to curse and oppress them. He had them driven out of the Land of Israel by foreign nations, leaving the land and Jerusalem to become desolate with only a small group of Israelites living there, compared to the way it used to be, while foreigners moved in. The Lord scattered them under the nations. But, when they would choose to repent, He would listen to their prayers and out of compassion, He would send them deliverers. He would deliver them through His justice and righteousness.

The Lord made it clear through His servants the prophets, as He did through the prophet Jeremiah, that He would not destroy the Israelites. He would discipline them, but only in due measure, while He wouldn't let them go entirely unpunished.

At the time that He sent Judah into exile to Babylon, He encouraged them through Jeremiah to settle down in that land, to increase in numbers, and to pray for the places they would live, in the foreign nations. He knew the plans He had for them as He said to Jeremiah, *'Plans to prosper you and not to harm you, plans to give you hope and a future'*.

God promised that after seventy years, He would gather them back to the Land of Israel. So, He did. But, His prophecies also spoke of a time even further away in the future.

God Almighty, who is very jealous of Zion and Jerusalem, also declared that one day He would gather all the Israelites back to the Land of Israel leaving not one of them behind.

The aim of His punishment was to discipline His son for them to return to Him with their whole heart, so He would reveal Himself again to them in their land, and have them be part of the new covenant He would make with them.

The Lord would comfort Jerusalem. As for the nations where He scattered them, those who went too far, oppressing and killing the Israelites who were supposed to increase in numbers while living in those nations, He would destroy them. Those who cursed His people would also be cursed.

> *But now listen, Jacob, my servant, Israel, whom I have chosen, this is what the Lord says, He who made you, who formed you in the womb, and who will help you. Do not be afraid, Jacob, my servant, Jeshurun, whom I have chosen.*
>
> *I will pour water on the thirsty land, and streams on the dry ground; I will pour out My Spirit on your offspring, and My blessing on your descendants. They will spring up like grass in a meadow, like poplar trees by flowing streams.*
>
> *Some will say, I belong to the Lord; others will call themselves by the name of Jacob; still others will write on their hand, The Lord's, and will take the name Israel.*
>
> Isaiah 44

Intermezzo

Discipline

> *If someone has a stubborn and rebellious son who does not obey his father and mother and will not listen to them when they discipline him, his father and mother shall take hold of him and bring him to the elders at the gate of his town. They shall say to the elders, This son of ours is stubborn and rebellious. He will not obey us. He is a glutton and a drunkard. Then all the men of his town are to stone him to death. You must purge the evil from among you. All Israel will hear of it and be afraid.*
>
> Deuteronomy 21:18-21

When a son remains disobedient, rebellious and stubborn, despite the parents' discipline, he would be punishable by stoning to death; a punishment that is also used when children curse their parents.

To God, as He stated in His Ten Commandments, children should show respect to their parents. Another last resort to avoid stoning would be to send the disobedient son, or daughter, away. In that case the parents could send him away while giving him his part of the inheritance or a means to support himself. There are other reasons to do the latter. It could be that the sons for some reason would not inherit with the eldest son, as was the case of Abraham when it came to Isaac's inheritance and his other sons whom he gave gifts and sent them away. Otherwise Abraham's other sons could have rebelled against him or Isaac.

Another reason to send children away could be for the protection of that son as happened to Isaac's youngest son Jacob, who later the Lord renamed Israel. A son could return to his parents, but in that case he should show his utmost willingness to be obedient to his parents.

Basically this is what God did with His eldest son, the Israelites. He sent them away out of His land, off His property. The land was defiled by them and when they left, it received the rest it needed while being desolate, which was necessary because they were reluctant to celebrate the Shabbat years of the land. But, the Lord would keep His promise of gathering the Israelites back to their land when they chose to repent and show their willingness to obey Him.

> *No one calls on Your name or strives to lay hold of You, for You have hidden Your face from us and have given us over to our sins.*
>
> Isaiah 64:7

When God's teachings and His discipline along with punishment, if necessary, doesn't bring about the right conduct from His children, because they are reluctant to obey Him to put a stop to a sinful way of life, He decides to stop listening to them. Those who, instead of avoiding evil, persist in wickedness, evil acts and the worship of that which is created instead of worshipping the Creator, could not count on God's pity or mercy. He would leave them to their way of life, give them over to their sins. Because when He called through His prophets, no one answered, and no one listened when He spoke His words through His servants. When this happens, God's righteous judgment follows. His judgment reaches all the living beings in His creation who are accountable for their acts. Everyone who does wrong would be repaid for their wrongdoings.

> *He has shown you, O mortal, what is good. And what does the Lord require of you? To act justly and to love mercy and to walk humbly with your God.*
>
> Mica 6:8

> *But your iniquities have separated you from your God; your sins have hidden His face from you, so that He will not hear.*
>
> Isaiah 59:2

The Satan, the source of all evil and wickedness, brought Adam and Eve to be disobedient to God and they sinned. Through them the whole of humanity came under the burden of sin, leading to death.

God, who doesn't tempt people into sin, has been merciful to humanity ever since. But, still, evil and people's own wrong desires have been luring them into sinful acts, which separates them from God, who is Holy.

To avoid evil, and doing good, someone ought to do what would prevent him from being sinful. But, prayers fuelled by wrong motives, ends in disappointment, even quarrels and wickedness. And when sin gets its way, full-grown sin would give birth to death.

> *But you, Lord, are a compassionate and gracious God, slow to anger, abounding in love and faithfulness.*
> Psalm 86:15

God shows His love to those who love and fear Him – those who keep His commandments, His covenants and obey His teaching. He is good and forgiving showing His love to all who call to Him.

God's righteousness and drive to do good leads Him to be quick to forgive, slow to anger, abounded in love and faithfulness. The Lord forgives people's wickedness, rebellion and sinful acts.

Confessing sins, while being remorseful, leads to God being merciful. The Lord would redeem those who come to Him, and would no longer hide His face from them. He would sweep away their sins as clouds and mist, making their scarlet like sins whiter than snow.

God's forgiveness however, doesn't necessarily have to lead to an absence of punishment for wrongdoings. The Lord forgave the Israelites for not obeying Him, concerning conquering Canaan the first time they arrived at its border the second year after leaving Egypt. Still He punished them, except His servants Caleb and Joshua, by having them remain forty years in the desert so they wouldn't enter the Promised Land at all. During that time He continued to care for them. But, since they didn't want to enter Canaan anyway, the entire generation who disobeyed Him died in the desert. Their children did obey the Lord and entered the Promised Land under Joshua's leadership.

He forgave David, but He also punished him and Bathsheba. They lost their first child to an illness, despite David's remorseful repentance and his prayers.

Because of God's capacity to forgive, He can continue to move forward despite people's sins and mistakes. So would those who learn to forgive.

To be forgiving is therefore part of God's upbringing for all. As forgiving as He is, He wants his children and humankind to learn to be forgiving. The Lord always blesses those who seek His forgiveness and those who themselves choose to forgive and even pray for their wrongdoers.

One day God's angels attended God's court, and Satan was also amongst them. On God's question where he had been, he answered he came from wandering throughout the world. The Lord asked him whether he noticed Job, who was blameless and upright, and who feared God and shunned evil. He replied that that's the way he was because God cared for him and blessed him. But, he would change if all his possessions would be taken away. Later he would tell God that if Job's health would also be taken away, he would surely curse God. But, when God gave Job in Satan's hands, He didn't allow him to take Job's life. Job's days of troubles started with him receiving four terrible messages in one day.

Four messengers who survived what happened told him, the Sabeans attacked and took his oxen and donkeys, fire of God fell and killed all the sheep, raiding parties of the Chaldeans took all his camels and heavy winds caused the house of his eldest son to collapse, killing all his children who were feasting with him. All the servants present at the locations where tragedy struck were also killed. In one day Job lost his children, most of his servants and all his wealth. Job tore his robe, shaved his head and then he fell to the ground saying, *'Naked I came from my mother's womb, and naked I will depart. The Lord gave and the Lord has taken away; may the name of the Lord be praised'*.

Despite all his trouble and grieving, Job didn't sin by accusing God with wrongdoing. From then on, Job was submerged in intense grief. He lost everything including his health when he was afflicted with painful sores from the crown of his head to the soles of his feet. His wife, who encouraged him to curse God, was no support for him.

Three of Job's friends, who came to see him, to comfort and sympathize with him, weren't support either. They were Eliphaz the Temanite, Bildad the Shuhite, and Zophar the Naamathite. When his three friends saw him sitting on the ground in suffering, they could barely recognise him. They wept aloud, tore their robes, sprinkled dust on their heads and sat seven days and nights with him, without saying a word to him, because of his great suffering.

Later, Elihu son of Barakel the Buzite would also join them. After seven days, Job started to speak. Ultimately during their conversations with Job, his friends believed and told him that he must have done something sinful, while Job insisted he did not.

God told his friends to go to Job, prepare a burnt offering and ask Job to pray for them. God would only listen to Job's prayer. The Lord was angry with them because they didn't speak the truth about Him, as Job did. They did as they were told, and so did Job.

In order for Job to pray for his friends, he had to forgive them. Otherwise, how would he have been able to stand blameless before the Lord, for Him to even want to listen to his prayers?

After Job prayed for his friends, the Lord restored Job's health, his family and wealth. He made him more wealthier than before by giving him twice as much as he had before. All his brothers, sisters and those who knew him came to his house, ate with him and gave him gifts while comforting him for all his troubles.

Job had children again, because the Lord blessed him with seven sons and three daughters. His daughters were very beautiful, and when he granted his children their inheritance, he also granted this to his daughters, which was unusual because normally this would have been only possible if he didn't have sons, as happened to the daughters of Zelophehad, in the time of Moses. Job lived to be one hundred and forty years. God proved evil wrong.

Joseph was the eldest son of Jacob, that is Israel, and his second wife Rachel, who was the daughter of Jacob's uncle, Laban. Joseph was Jacob's favourite son, because he was born to him in his old age.

Because Jacob (Israel) loved his son more than all his other sons, the brothers hated Joseph and were unkind to him. At this time, Jacob lived with his family in Canaan. Once, when Joseph was tending his father's flocks, he brought a bad report about his brothers to Israel.

When Joseph was seventeen years old, his father made a robe for him. Sometimes Joseph would have dreams, and he told them to his brothers. They hated him even more. He told them two dreams.

In one dream he and his brothers were binding sheaves of grain out in the field when all of a sudden, his sheaf rose and stood upright, while his brothers sheaves gathered around his and bowed down to it. They asked him whether he would actually intend to reign over them one day.

Joseph's other dream was about the sun, the moon and eleven stars bowing down to him. He told his father and brothers about this second dream. His father rebuked him and said, *'What is this dream you had? Will your mother and I and your brothers actually come and bow down to the ground before you'?*

Joseph didn't have an answer to Israel's questions. At the time, neither his father nor his brothers realised that this was exactly what would happen in the future. But Israel kept his son's dreams in mind.

One day Israel sent Joseph to his brothers who were grazing the flocks near Shechem. He was to see how they were doing and bring word to Israel. He found his brothers near Dothan. They saw him coming in the distance, plotted to kill him, and agreed on telling the story that a ferocious animal killed him. Except Ruben, Israel's eldest son with Leah, his uncle Laban's eldest daughter, didn't agree on this. Instead he wanted to save Joseph and take him back to their father. So he told them to only throw Joseph in a pit, which was empty, and leave him behind. They agreed, took Joseph and threw him into the pit.

Later, when Ruben went to get Joseph out, he wasn't there. Without him knowing, his brothers sold Joseph to the Ishmaelites for twenty shekels, about eight ounces, of silver. It was Judah's idea to sell him to these merchants ,who would take Joseph to Egypt to be somebody's slave.

Ruben went back to his brothers. They decided to slaughter a goat and use its blood on Joseph's robe. They took the bloody robe to their father as evidence that a savage animal killed Joseph. Israel recognised the robe as belonging to Joseph, and was filled with grief. He wept and mourned for him many days, while all his children came to comfort him. But he refused to be comforted.

God was with Joseph in Egypt and He insured Joseph would prosper. Potiphar, the captain of Pharaoh's guard, bought Joseph. He lived in the house of his master, where he was in charge of his household.

But, the devious acts of Potiphar's wife got Joseph imprisoned. What happened? Joseph refused her advances, and didn't even want to be with her. Joseph told her that such an act would be wicked and a sin against his God.

While in prison, where the king's prisoners were confined, God didn't leave Joseph. Instead God showed him kindness, and gave him success at whatever he did. The prison warden put Joseph in charge of all the prisoners, and he was responsible for everything there. One day, both the chief cup bearer and the chief baker of the king, who were also were confined in the prison, had dreams. They needed someone to interpret their dreams for them.

Joseph said to them, '*Do not interpretations belong to God*'?

They told Joseph their dreams.

First the cup bearer, and Joseph gave him the favourable interpretation, that Pharaoh would restore him to his position within three days. Joseph asked him to remember him and to show him kindness when that time comes because he was carried out of the Hebrew's land against his will and even in Egypt he didn't do anything wrong to deserve being in a dungeon.

The interpretation for the baker wasn't favourable. He would be killed within three days. His king would have him be beheaded and his body impaled on a pole where the birds would eat his flesh. Both came to pass.

The cup bearer forgot Joseph.

After two full years, on the king's orders, Joseph was taken out of the dungeon. He shaved and changed his clothes to appear before the king. Pharaoh had dreams that troubled his mind, and no magician or the wise men in Egypt could explain them for him. After the cup bearer told him about Joseph, the king sent for him.

Joseph said that he himself couldn't interpret his dreams, but God could give him the answer. Pharaoh told Joseph his dreams. He dreamed of seven fat and sleek cows that came out of the Nile River to graze among the reeds. After them came seven scrawny, very ugly and lean cows, and they ate the seven fat ones. But afterwards, they were as ugly as before.

After this dream the king woke up, but he fell asleep and he dreamt again. The king's second dream was about seven full and good heads of grain growing on a single stalk. Then seven other heads sprouted. They were withered, thin and scorched by the east wind. These last heads of grain swallowed the first good ones.

Joseph told the king that both dreams mean the same. God had revealed to Pharaoh what He is planning to do. There would be seven years of abundance in Egypt, followed by seven years of famine, so severe that it would ravage the land and the people would forget all about the good years. Pharaoh received the dream in two forms because the matter had been firmly decided by God and He would execute His plan soon. Then Joseph told the king a plan to deal with this situation that the king and all his officials agreed on it to be a good plan.

The king wanted a discerning and wise man to execute this plan, which was to store up one fifth of Egypt's grain harvest during the period of abundance, to be a reserve for the country during the time of famine. The management of this operation in the whole of Egypt, was to be under the authority of the Pharaoh. The king put Joseph in charge of his palace and Egypt, since God had made all known through him. All of his officials had to submit to Joseph's orders. He positioned Joseph in such a way that only in respect to the throne would Pharaoh himself be greater than him.

During the years that Joseph performed his task, he married an Egyptian woman called Asenath. She was the daughter of Potiphera, priest of On. Before the years of famine, they had two children, Menasseh and Ephraim. It was during the period of famine that he would see his family again. First, all his brothers, except Benjamin, when they came to buy grain because there was famine also in Canaan where they lived.

Contrary to them, he did recognised his brothers. Later, after Joseph tricked them, on their second journey to Egypt also with Benjamin, in a private and emotional meeting at his home, he revealed himself to them as being their brother. Pharaoh and his officials were pleased to hear that Joseph's brothers had come. He told Joseph to tell his brothers to return to Egypt with their father, families and all their animals. They were to take carts with them. He would give them the best of the land of Egypt. So they did.

Israel sent Judah ahead of him to ask Joseph for the directions to Goshen. Once Israel met with Joseph, he embraced his father and wept for a long time. Israel was one hundred and thirty years old when he and his entire family, including Joseph and his family, seventy people in all, moved to Egypt. Joseph presented his father Israel and five of his brothers to Pharaoh. He instructed them to tell the king that they were shepherds. He allowed them, being shepherds with flocks and herds, to live in the best part of Egypt, Goshen.

Israel blessed Pharaoh before leaving his presence. Joseph provided his family with all they needed. Before Israel died, he blessed all his sons, and his grandchildren he adopted to be his sons, Menasseh and Ephraim.

After Israel's death all his brothers became afraid Joseph might take revenge on them. God's Law is very clear on the matter of kidnapping. The kidnapper of a fellow Israelite that threatens to sell him as a slave or treats him as such, is punishable by death. So, his brothers sent word to Joseph telling him that their father asks of him to forgive his brothers sins and the wrongs they had done to him.

When he received the message, Joseph wept. Joseph forgave his brothers telling them, *'Don't be afraid. Am I in the place of God? You intended to harm me, but God intended it for good to accomplish what is now being done, the saving of many lives. So then, don't be afraid. I will provide for you and your children'.*

With these words he reassured his brothers he didn't hold revengeful feelings towards them. On Joseph's forgiveness, God saved all of them and continued to form himself a people with the descendants of Israel. Joseph lived to be one hundred and ten. On his request he was embalmed and put in a coffin, awaiting the day his descendants would bury him in the Promised Land. Approximately four hundred years later when Israel's descendants, the Israelites, a people of more than six hundred thousand men, women and children left Egypt taking up the journey to the Promised Land, they took Joseph's remains with them.

Being forgiving enabled these men to endure hardships and still be able to continue living by God's will, fulfilling the plans He had for their personal life and others. Just as learning to read and write, which is an indispensable tool in society, continues every day at school, despite a pupil's personal problems, the same way forgiveness is so indispensable in God's society that it has to be learned no matter what. God is a forgiving Father. His redeemer would come from and to Zion, and ultimately to the whole world. And when people forgive one another, God can bless and do great things.

> *The Redeemer will come to Zion, to those in Jacob who repent of their sins, declares the Lord.*
>
> Isaiah 59:20

David was also forgiven and disciplined by God, while David himself counted on God's forgiveness and blessings when he forgave Shimei son of Gera. He was family of the same clan as Saul's family.

Once David promised King Saul he would not eradicate his family. At the time King David fled Jerusalem because his own son Absalom, together with his most trusted adviser Ahitophel orchestrated a coup against him. Shimei awaited him on his way out. Shimei was cursing him, calling him a murderer and threw stones to him. David's men were with him and they wanted to deal with Shimei. Abishai son of Zeruiah asked David why that dead dog should curse his lord the king, and offered to go to Shimei to cut off his head. But what did David choose to do instead? He asked God to turn the curses into blessings for him when he prayed and said to all his officials, *'Let him curse, for the Lord has told him to. It may be that the Lord will look upon my misery and restore to me his covenant blessing instead of his curse today'.*

David must have known that God had done this before. For example, at the time of Moses when God made Balaam say blessings instead of curses over the Israelites. In doing this he left justice concerning Shimei to the Almighty Father, who rendered it at his time.

Did the Lord bless David? Yes, his son Absalom could not take David's throne. So all the curses were turned into blessings for David. Later David had to swear to Shimei at the Jordan River, when he was on his way back to Jerusalem, that he wouldn't hurt him. But when it came to the reign of his son King Solomon, David did tell him to deal with Shimei because of what he had done to him, realizing Shimei might as well be a threat to Solomon's new reign. After David's death Shimei died by Solomon's orders when he refused to comply with his arrangement with him to stay in the city of Jerusalem.

David kept all God's Laws and decrees, except in the case Uriah the Hittite. He upheld God's Laws in the Kingdom of Israel. David not only kept God's Laws but he also thought to keep them. Surely he would have insured that his children, who had a good education, would have learned God's Laws and decrees too, even though as adults they would make their own decisions and execute their own plans.

David loved his children and blessed them. In days of trouble he showed much grief and sorrow because of them, like when he lost his sons Amnon and Absalom, to whom he also showed forgiveness. He was furious concerning the rape of his daughter Tamar. As a father and king, David followed the path of the Lord by choosing which of his sons would be his successor. All David's other sons were in agreement with his God-given choice of Solomon to be his successor on the throne. Ultimately all of them gave their support and allegiance to Solomon, together with all the officers, David's heroes and warriors.

Of all the children David had with several wives and his concubines, only two of his sons showed sibling rivalry concerning his throne, while one of them, Absalom, would resort to murder as a tool of vengeance instead of seeking justice. It was Absalom and Adonijah, his third and fourth son, who went to great lengths to acquire the throne of their father. With David's first son Amnon murdered, the second son Chileab for whatever reason didn't seek nor participate in attempts to take over his father's throne. Each one of David's four

Forgiving Father

eldest sons determined as adults their own path in life. Absalom and Adonijah allowed themselves to be led by their ambition with, unlike their father David, disregard for God's will and His Laws. David always counted on the Living God to bless him at all times.

> *While they curse, may you bless; may those who attack me be put to shame, but may your servant rejoice.*
> Psalm 109:28

Endnotes

Genesis 10 Table of nations
Job 26:7 The earth
Deuteronomy 8:1-8, 11:10-12, Nehemiah 9:25 The land
Proverbs 3:11-12 Disciplines his children
Exodus 4:23, Hosea 11:1, Isaiah 56:1-8 God's children
Psalm 89:25-29, Malachi 2:3a Father
Exodus 15:16-18, Isaiah 45:11, 46:3-4 God made his children
Genesis 12:1-9 God chose Abraham
Genesis 12:3, Numbers 24:9b Those who bless or curse Abraham and the Israelites
Genesis 17:1-2 God commands Abraham to walk faithfully and blameless before Him
Psalm 41:8 Abraham God's friend
Genesis 17:5-7 God's blessings for Abraham
Genesis 17:15-17 God's blessings for Sarah
Genesis 18:18, 22:18 Nations blessed through Abraham
Isaiah 56:6-8, 66:18-21 God joins others to Israel, in-grafted branches
Genesis 18:19 God's task for Abraham and through him for his descendants the Israelites
Isaiah 59:21, Jeremiah 31:31-37 Theirs are the covenants
Psalm 149:6-9, Isaiah 66:14-16 Israel a double-edged sword
Deuteronomy 28:13 Israel at the top not the bottom
Isaiah 41:8-10 Israel, Jacob and his descendants, Israel God's servant
Isaiah 59:20 The deliverer and Zion
Exodus 19:5-6 Israel kingdom of priests and holy nation
Psalm 147:19-20 Israelites entrusted with God's Words
Deuteronomy 21:15-17 Double portion of the inheritance
Isaiah 44: 2 Jeshurun means, 'the upright one'
Exodus 23:10-12 Shabbat year for the land
Jeremiah 29:4-14 God planned for Israel to prosper
Jeremiah 44:21-23 Israel's sinful acts
Nehemiah 9:26-27, Isaiah 1, Ezekiel 36:16-21, Micah 6 Israelites defiled the Land of Israel
Jeremiah 40 Those who remained in Judah during the Babylonian exile

Who Is David?

Isaiah 66:3-4, Jeremiah 30:11, Zechariah 1:12-17 God disciplines Israel and destroys nations
Isaiah 59:19-21, Jeremiah 31, Ezekiel 36:22-38, 37, 38 God gathers them in the Land of Israel
Genesis 12:1-4 Those who curse Israel will be cursed
Job 1:1-5, 42:12-17 Job an upright man
Numbers 27:1-9, 36 Daughters of Zelophehad
Exodus 29:27-28, Leviticus 7:28-38, Numbers 18:18-19, Deuteronomy 18:3-8 The priests' rights concerning the meat of the offerings
1 Samuel 2:12-36, 3:13-18, 4:13-18, 2 Samuel 8:17, Eli and his sons' wickedness
1 Samuel 2:22 Eli's sons prostitution
1 Samuel 2:24-25 Consequences of Eli and his sons' sins
1 Samuel 2:29, 3:13 Eli's own transgressions
1 Samuel 14:3, 22:20-23, 2 Samuel 8:17, 1 Kings 2:26-27,35 Eli's descendants
Exodus 20:6, Deuteronomy 5:10, Psalm 86:5, 103:17-18 God is love
Leviticus 19:18b, 34, Love others as oneself
Psalm 86:5 God is good
Numbers 22-24, Deuteronomy 23:4-6 God made Balaam bless Israel
Psalm 109:17-20 Those who curse instead of giving blessings
Psalm 109:26-29 Blessings instead of curse
Isaiah 59 Sinfulness, justice
Genesis 3 Adam and Eve sinned
Ezekiel 28:15-16 Cause of sin, temptation and desires
Isaiah 44:22, Proverbs 28:13 Confession, mercy
Isaiah 59:2, Ezekiel 39:24 God hides His face
Isaiah 27:9 God takes away Jacob's sins
Job 42, Genesis 50:15-2 The Lord blesses, forgives those who forgive
Deuteronomy 24:7 Kidnappers are punishable by death
Genesis 37 to 50 Joseph
Genesis 50:15-21 Joseph forgives his brothers
Exodus 34:6, Numbers 14:18, Nehemiah 9:17, Psalm 103:8, 145:8, Joel 2:13, Jonah 4:2, Nahum 1:3, Psalm 86:15 God slow to anger, forgiving
Exodus 34:6-7, Isaiah 43:24-25 God's forgiveness
Numbers 14:17-38 God forgave the Israelites, but they were punished
1 Chronicles 29:24 David's sons support Solomon
2 Samuel 16:5-14, 1 Kings 2:8-9, 36-46 David and forgiveness, Shimei
1 Samuel 24:20-23 David swears to Saul he would not destroy his family
Numbers 22-24 Balaam and the Israelites
2 Samuel 16 to 19 Absalom's coup and death
2 Samuel 12 God forgave David, but He also punished him
1 Kings 11:33, 15:5 David kept all God's Laws and decrees
Psalms 51:15, 122 David upheld the Law in his kingdom
Deuteronomy 6:1-9 God's Kingdom

2 Samuel 6:18-20a David blesses the people of Israel, and his household
2 Samuel 12, 13-14, 19:1-9 Amnon, Tamar, Absalom

Intermezzo Endnotes

Exodus 21:17, Deuteronomy 21:18-21 Rebellious son
Ezra 7:26 Banishment
Exodus 20:12, Deuteronomy 5:16 Honour father and mother
Exodus 21:15,17, Leviticus 19:3, 20:9 Punishment for cursing, dishonouring parents
Isaiah 66:4 No one listens to nor answers God
Exodus 20 The Law

KING OF KINGS

But HaShem God is the true God, He is the living God, and the everlasting King;

Jeremiah 10:10

God Almighty Whose splendour is like the rising sun, is such an awesome Divine Being that no image made by human design or skill can ever depict Him. He Whose Divine Presence hovered upon the surface of the waters at the time of creation, He Who gives life and nurture to all, isn't in need of anything that those living on His footstool should show any arrogance towards Him. To Him belongs the heavens and the earth with everything within them. He alone is God over all the kingdoms on earth. God Almighty has His throne in heaven where He sits enthroned between His holy angels, the cherubim and the seraphim, where He is seated high and exalted above all on His throne with the train of His robe filling the space of His, which at the calling of His holy angels glorifying Him fills with smoke. From His heavenly throne, within His court of holiness and splendour, the Lord looks down to the earth, His footstool.

He Who handles the forces of nature and the power of nations as tools with His mighty hand to move His plan with creation forward is truly the Most High God, who made out of one man, Adam, nations to inhabit the earth. Out of one man, Abraham, he brought forth His eldest son, the Israelites, and with them He formed His very own nation, the Kingdom of Israel. To realise His plan the Lord had carefully chosen the Patriarchs Abraham, Isaac and Jacob, as He did with His choice of the Matriarchs – Sarah mother of Isaac, Rebecca mother of Jacob, Rachel mother of Joseph and Leah the mother of Judah. Jacob, renamed Israel, had twelve sons, the twelve tribes of Israel.

As a Father the Lord always wanted to educate His children and all those who attach themselves to Him. Just as a man who becomes a father would discipline his son, God would discipline His children. He always expected them to observe all His commandments, to love Him, to be obedient to Him, to praise and serve Him, and to hold fast to Him. He wants His children to circumcise their heart to receive more of His love. But, besides being the Father of the Israelites, He is also the King of the nation of Israel.

The Lord gave the Israelites His Law, the Torah, in all His code of conduct, way of life, through Moses the man of God to prepare them for their new life in the Land that He had promised on oath to their ancestors and which under His guidance they would have to govern and care for. The Promised Land to which God Himself had been holding all rights, the Land He had brought the Israelites to inhabit while driving the nations in it, out.

Why did the Lord do this? He drove them out because as He told Abraham centuries before, it was the time that the sin of its inhabitants would reach its full measure. These people were dispossessed by God because they listened to those among them who practised sorcery or divination, interpreted omens, engaged in witchcraft, cast spells, or who were mediums, spiritists consulting the dead. In addition, there was much evil and lawlessness among these people, who brought much wickedness within their societies and whom also sacrificed their sons and daughters into the fire to their idols and gods. More than four centuries later since His promise to Abraham, including the period they spent living in Egypt, the Lord planted the Israelites in His Land.

They were not chosen because of their righteousness or their uprightness, as Moses told them that they were a stubborn, stiff-necked people who had to cut away the barrier from their heart. The only reason the Lord allowed the Israelites, the descendants of Jacob whom He had chosen, to take possession of the Land and live there was because of His love for their ancestors whom He cherished, and His promise to Abraham. The Lord had been showing His love and faithfulness to Abraham and his descendants ever since. For God, to whom a thousand years is like a day that has just gone by or like a watch in the night, it was just a few days ago He made that promise to Abraham. One day He will want to show him the ultimate result of his descendants living in the Land. On that day God will destroy death and Abraham with others asleep in the dusty earth will awake for everlasting life.

God chose the descendants of Israel's sons above all other people and made them from the seventy people that belonged to Jacob's household who went down to Egypt, into a people more numerous than the stars in the sky. Once there they joined Joseph, whom He had already sent up front only to provide later for his helpless father and brothers. Generations later the Lord brought them out of Egypt, while leaving no one behind, through the desert to His Land and made a nation out of them. The journey took forty years as a result of their disobedience, but during that time the Lord formed the Israelites as His people, ultimately making Judah his sanctuary, Israel his dominion, distinguishing them, who recognised Him as their God by living in accordance to His ways, as His most treasured people. They experienced His greatness, majesty, strong hand, outstretched arm and His fatherly discipline. To humble them He let them hunger only to give them Manna in the desert while teaching them that a human being does not live on bread alone but on every word that comes from the mouth of the Lord. In order to find out what was in their heart, He tested them revealing whether they would truly keep His commands and live by His code of conduct. All of this to ensure that in the end things would go well for them. For His Name's sake the Lord meant His people to be a supreme nation over all that He had made, for His praise, renown, and splendour. To be a holy people to Him.

Through Moses God gave the Israelites His Word, His Laws, statutes, commandments, stipulations and decrees. For what purpose? So that they might always prosper and live. With His Torah, the Lord gave them a moral and spiritual standard, both personal, as for their social life, the basis for their justice system, necessary rules to be implemented daily in a practical way within their society, their unique religious identity, their national feasts in keeping with God's feasts, and a glimpse into their future as individuals, together as a nation and as such their position within the world community.

Together with all this the Lord provided with His Torah the structure for their institutions which He formed with them, such as their army, their legislative and governmental entity, their basis for medical practice. The Lord appointed their political, social and spiritual leaders, assigned to them their task and provided them with His support. The Lord Himself did all these through which, with everything His people went and would go through, He moulded them into having the identity He had designed for them.

To obey God's Laws, live by His Torah as He commanded would be the Israelites' righteousness. Just as their ancestor Abraham, they had been meant to walk blameless before their Lord God. Through Moses He had told them to choose life with the blessings He gives, and not curses which would result in death. The Lord didn't want them to be rebellious, causing grief to Him, and ultimately to themselves. Therefore He already warned the Israelites on their way to the Promised Land not to engage in the worship of idols and false gods of the people living in the land, just as neither did He want them to do this regarding the gods of Egypt nor those beyond the Euphrates River where Terah, the father of Abraham, originally lived. Instead, consider these people, those living in the Promised Land, as enemies whom He would deliver into their hands together with their kings. The Lord Himself would go before them to conquer the Land He promised them, though the process of taking over the Land would be a slow one to protect the Israelites from being overcome by the wild animals living there. But, the Lord would give them the ability and the strength to be prosperous once they settle in the Land, as He gave to their ancestors Abraham, Isaac and Jacob. He would also give rain so the Land would produce. The Lord who is a faithful God would fulfil all the promises He had made to Moses by giving His people every place of the Land where they would set foot and give them rest within its borders. When the Lord made the descendants of Jacob a nation, He made it visible to the entire world that He was in the process of establishing His Eternal Kingdom on earth to be a blessing to all.

Foreseeing that one day the Israelites while living in the Land would want to have a king to rule over their nation like all the nations around them had, the Lord already addressed this matter when they were on their way to the Promised Land. Which person should they choose to be their king, how much wealth should he possess and which moral values should he have? These were determined by the Lord who provided rules for His king to be through his servant Moses. He had to be a man chosen by the Lord from amongst the Israelites. Not a foreigner, but someone born and raised in the Land. He wasn't to have many horses nor a great amount of silver and gold for himself. To prevent his heart from going astray following false gods, he wasn't to have too many wives. The king should have two copies of God's Law in a book, the Book of Law, approved by the Kohanim Levites to be read to him his entire life. By living this way the king of Israel would learn to fear the Lord, to observe His commands which would prevent him from being proud with a heart full of disdain towards his subjects, the people of Israel. All this would prolong the years of the king's reign, and of his sons' through hereditary succession over the Kingdom of Israel. God Almighty Himself would establish Israel's monarchy starting with King Saul. But before that time, the Lord as the King of Israel would choose judges to govern the Israelites in the Land, starting with Joshua and ending with Samuel. These judges of Israel also received God's command through Moses and Joshua, to keep the Book of Law always on their lips, to meditate on it day and night and to carefully do everything written in it. So, the Lord expected Israel's leaders, both judges and kings, to be faithful to Him, to live by His Law, and do what was right in His eyes in the Land, so He would continue to bless the nation of Israel. The choice of the national leader by succession instead of being directly chosen by the Lord however could go well or wrong. The kings could be either righteous, being models of spiritual greatness as well as of political leadership to the nation, as were notable the kings David, Hezekiah and Josiah. Or they could be wicked as were amongst others the kings Jeroboam, Ahab and Menasseh. Another possibility could be that they could start out in obedience to God and go astray later during their reign, as would happen to, for example, the kings Saul and Solomon. Governing in obedience to the Lord would meet with His blessing. Repentance from a sinful way of life and governance would bring about God's forgiveness and grace. Otherwise these leaders would cause the nation's downfall leading to catastrophe, destruction, and ultimately to exile.

> *I will open rivers on the high hills, and fountains in the midst of the valleys; I will make the wilderness a pool of water, and the dry land springs of water.*
>
> Isaiah 41:18

On their way to the Promised Land, the Lord would offer the Israelites rest through His presence amongst them. God, whose words endure for ever, spoke to them through Moses. The Lord's words do not return empty to Him, instead they always accomplish as He desires and achieve the purpose for which He had sent them, just as the rain and the snow do, coming down from heaven watering and moistening the earth to bring forth its fruits in abundance and all needed to nourish life, before returning to heaven.

It was God's Spirit that came over Balaam when he prophesied about the Israelites. He spoke about their king and blessed them when they were encamped in the plains of Moab along the Jordan River across from Jericho. Balaam son of Beor was not one of God's prophets, instead he practised sorcery, magic and divination. He was summoned by the king of Moab, Balak son of Zippor, who was terrified of the Israelites. They were numerous, they defeated other people such as the Amorites, and more importantly they had a mighty God. Balak chose Balaam, who wanted to be handsomely paid for his services, because he was convinced that whoever Balaam blesses would be blessed and whoever he curses would be cursed. He sent officials with a message and a divination fee to Balaam who lived in

Pethor near the Euphrates River. The officials told Balaam that their king wanted him to go with them to Moab to put a curse on a people that came out of Egypt and had settled next to his territory. They were too powerful for him, but if Balaam would put a curse on them, then maybe he could defeat them and drive them away. Balaam told the officials to stay the night and he would tell them the next morning what the Lord's response would be concerning their request. When he inquired of the Lord what he should do, God came to Balaam and asked him who those people were. Balaam told Him who they were and about their request. The Lord told him he shouldn't go with them, and that he shouldn't put a curse on the Israelites because they were a blessed people. The next morning Balaam told the officials to return to their country without him because God didn't allow him to go with them.

Back in Moab, Balak refused to accept Balaam's decision and sent another more distinguished and numerous group of officials with an even more substantial fee to Balaam with the message not to let anything keep him from coming to him, that he would repay him most handsomely and that he would do whatever he said. But Balaam answered them, that even if Balak would give him all his silver and gold, he couldn't possibly do anything that goes beyond God's command. Again he asked Balak's officials to stay the night, while he consulted with the Lord. That night when God spoke to Balaam, He told him to go with the king's officials, but he would have to do what He tells him to do.

In the morning Balaam saddled his donkey and with his two servants he set out of his native land for Moab. But the Lord became angry with Balaam because he was hastily going on a road to oppose Him. The Lord must have seen into Balaam's heart that his motives and intentions were not pure. He sent one of His angels to stand on the road to impede Balaam from passing through. Balaam's donkey reacted to the angel she saw standing there with his sword drawn by turning of the road into the field. Balaam who did not see the angel beat the donkey to get her back on the road. When they were going through a narrow path of a vineyard with walls on both sides, the donkey pressed herself against one of the walls while crushing Balaam's foot, because she saw the Lord's angel standing in a narrow place of the path through the vineyards. Balaam, for whom the angel remained unseen, beat his donkey again. Then the angel moved ahead and stood in a narrow place where it wasn't possible for the donkey to turn away, preventing Balaam to continue his journey. This time the donkey realizing she can't go pass the angel, crouched beneath Balaam who became so angry that he struck his donkey with his staff. All this time Balaam was unable to see the Lord's angel. Then the Lord gave the donkey the ability to speak and to reason with Balaam. She asked Balaam what she had done to him that he had beaten her three times already. Balaam answered that she had made a fool out of him, and that if he had a sword he would kill her. The donkey replied with a rhetorical question regarding her being his own donkey that he had been riding for years until that day. Then she asked Balaam whether she had ever treated him in the manner she did that day. On Balaam's answer with no, the Lord uncovered Balaam's eyes for him to see His angel standing there. Balaam bowed down low and he fell face down. The angel asked Balaam why he had beaten his donkey three times, because if it wasn't for his donkey he would have killed him already, but he would have spared her. The angel clearly stated to Balaam that he was there to oppose him. Balaam told him he had sinned, that he had not seen him on the road, and that if the Lord didn't want him to go to Moab, he would go back. The angel of the Lord replied that he should go with Balak's officials, but that he should only speak of what the Lord told him. So he did.

Balak went out to meet Balaam, who without Balak's knowledge, was already forced by the Lord to bless and not curse the Israelites. He met with him at Arnon, the border of his territory in a Moabite town. Balak asked Balaam why he didn't come immediately, whether he had doubts concerning his fee. Then Balaam told him that he couldn't speak whatever he pleased, but that he would only speak of what God put in his mouth. Balak held a feast and sacrificed cattle and sheep, but he didn't invite Balaam as a king would with an honoured guest, instead he sent the food to Balaam. Starting the next morning Balak took Balaam to a total of three high places where they could overlook the outskirts of the Israelites' vast campsite. At each site Balaam told Balak to build seven altars and sacrifice on each a bull and a ram. Balak prepared the sacrifices as Balaam requested and he stayed at that place with his officials. Then in the meantime Balaam went to a barren height to seek God's counsel hoping He would meet with him and speak to him on the matter concerning Balak's request, because as he told Balak he would only do and speak in accordance to God's revelation to him. Balak took him first to Bamoth Baal, afterwards to the fields of Zophim on the top of Pisgah and finally to the top of Peor which overlooked the wasteland. Twice the Lord met with Balaam and put a word in his mouth for him to tell Balak concerning the Israelites themselves, and the last time God's Spirit came on Balaam and he spoke a prophecy about them. Each time instead of cursing the Israelites Balaam blessed them. The second time Balak made it clear to Balaam, that if he doesn't curse the Israelites neither should he bless them at all. But as the Lord told Balaam before, the Israelites were a blessed people, so despite whatever Balak said or did, Balaam couldn't curse them. Balak ended up being displeased with Balaam.

The messages and blessings over the Israelites spoke of God's work, the future of the Israelites, the defeat of their enemies, their king, their dwelling place and of them being a blessed people. He spoke the first time of a people who were not cursed nor denounced by God. A nation that was set apart, them being the dust of Jacob that couldn't be counted. The second time Balaam mentioned God as being not a human being that He should lie nor change His mind. He acts upon what He has spoken and fulfils as He has promised. His blessings can't be changed and His command to bless should be followed.

Balaam spoke of God's presence among the Israelites, and friendship of the King. No divination or sorcery was found in Israel, nor were those needed because God Himself brought the descendants of Jacob out of Egypt by His might. These people rose like a lion's cub, a lion or lioness that wouldn't rest until he devoured his prey. When Balaam went to the third height, he prophesied about the beauty of the Israelites' dwelling place which spread out like valleys, like gardens beside a river. They would be planted by the Lord like cedars alongside waters. Their seed would have abundant water, which would flow from their wells. Their kingdom would be exalted, and their king would be greater than Agag, referring to the kings of the Amalekites. The Israelites would devour hostile nations. He spoke of them being like a lion, a lioness that crouches and lies down. Who would dare to arouse them? Balaam finished with the words, *'may those who bless them be blessed, and those who curse them be cursed'*. Afterwards Balaam spoke to Balak about how the Israelites would defeat their enemies, including the Moabites.

Balak had Balaam leave without his fee because after all he didn't fulfil his assignment to curse the Israelites.

Instead, while Balaam looked over the Israelites' campsite in the desert, the Lord gave him a prophecy, which included God's blessings that spoke of both their king and their water-rich dwelling place, the Land that one day they would inhabit. Through this prophecy Jacob's sons, the brothers Judah and Joseph, were united again as they themselves were once in Egypt by God's wisdom and forgiveness. The promise of leadership, of kingship, was already given years before to Judah through the blessing his father Jacob had given him. So the tribe of Judah already carried within it David's royal line, waiting to be revealed to the nation of Israel and to the world.

To his son Joseph, Jacob gave the blessings of the heaven above, of the springs deep below, of the breasts and womb, blessings given specifically to Joseph, not to Ephraim and Menasseh who already received their blessing from Jacob and who, contrary to Joseph's other children, would inherit with Jacob's sons because he had adopted them. Centuries later, Moses would bless each tribe of the Israelites.

Of Judah he said that the Lord would be a Helper against Judah's enemies, and of Joseph who was separated, exiled from his brothers, he said that the Lord would give blessings of heavenly abundance of dew and deep waters below, bounty of crops, bounty of the land and its fullness. God Almighty as the King of the Israelites, would on their own request provide a king to govern them in the Promised Land, while He would care for the Land by providing the necessary water for the produce of food and to be used for all that which is necessary to sustain their people. In both cases the Lord connected these essentials for a prosperous and fruitful nation to the people themselves, to the tribes, to the children and descendants of Judah and Joseph. Why did God Almighty turn the curses Balaam would have otherwise spoken over the Israelites into blessings? Because He loved them!

> *And unto his son will I give one tribe, that David My servant may have a lamp always before Me in Jerusalem, the city which I have chosen to put My name.*
>
> 1 Kings 11:36

Even though Bethlehem, Ephrathah, in Judah was a small place, this town brought a forth a great ruler whose offspring, his royal household, would govern over God's chosen people and ultimately over the earth. David! After the Lord provided for judges to lead the Israelites to conquer Canaan and make the Land their own, He established the Israelite monarchy with the Benjaminite Saul. Due to his disobedience, God put him aside and introduced a royal line to the Israelite monarchy that would eventually also bring forth a ruler just as David for His Eternal Kingdom on earth. With David,

Judah's descendant, whose family had been living in Bethlehem for generations, the Lord found the right man to fulfil His will. The Lord laid the foundation for His Kingdom on earth with His choice of the Patriarchs and Matriarchs, and by making a nation out of their descendants, the Israelites. It's for that purpose He had chosen Jacob's sons and their descendants. The Lord made a covenant with Jacob's grandfather Abraham and sealed it by way of circumcision. He was the first person to whom the Lord gave His promise of the Land, and David was chosen by Him to govern the nation of Israel, God's vineyard. God's Spirit, that rests on those He would choose for certain tasks, passed from Saul over to David from the day that David was anointed to be king of Israel by His prophet and judge Samuel. Later he would be anointed a second and third time, first to rule over Judah and then over the whole of Israel.

David was a man that would be and remain faithful to the Lord. He would keep His Law, govern the Land by doing what is right in His eyes, and he would hold fast to his God in a close heartfelt relation with Him. David was devoted to his Living God. He didn't disappoint God in any way with only one exception, being the matter of his sin.

Why did God choose David to be His king and warrior? He chose him because He expected David would keep His commands, hate evil and that he would do everything He would want him to do. The Lord also wanted a warrior together with whom He would fight His battles against Israel's enemies. David turned out to be as the Lord expected him to be. He wasn't arrogant, did not rebel against the Lord nor reject His Word and Law. David took heed, paid attention to God's guidance, wishes and obeyed Him in everything. He understood that rebellion and arrogance was like the sin of divination and the evil of idolatry, and that for him to be obedient and to take heed was a delight to the Lord, qualities that Israel's former king lacked. David kept God's Law within his heart. He was careful to lead a blameless life and he set out to conduct the affairs of his house with a blameless heart. He kept his eye on those who were faithful in the Land and sought those who walked blamelessly to minister to him. Instead of trusting his own wealth, he trusted in God's unfailing love, His faithfulness to him and to Israel. David made the Lord his stronghold, his shield. In turn David's shield made him secure during his entire life. He rather spoke the truth and loved good, instead of falsehood, deceit and wickedness. David sought God's grace, and he had shown to be grateful to Him all his days. God in turn shaped David through His Law, His Word,

Who Is David?

David's own personal life experiences, His closeness to him day by day, and having His Spirit rest on David since his youth when He chose him to be king of Israel.

Through hardships in his life, the Lord nurtured David so his spiritual potential would grow, mature and become visible both to himself as well as to those around him. The Lord made him a bearer of His code of conduct, an example to be followed, a source of inspiration. He made him His blueprint, His standard, the man whose kingship would set an example for kings, leaders through generations. Even when David sinned, he set an example for others in the way he humbled himself, while the Lord showed him mercy. He saw his sin in the first place as one against the Lord, a sin for which he repented, showed honest remorse and accepted God's judgment over him when He settled the matter with him during his life.

David showed exemplary wise leadership and governance over the Kingdom of Israel while he accepted the Lord's guidance, which was given not only through his advisers but also the Lord's prophets. The Lord who sees all which is in a person's heart, knew well all about David's heart. This was the man after His own heart, as He Himself testified about David through His servant Samuel. At the time of the division within the Kingdom of Israel, the Lord was not willing to destroy Judah, nor the House of David because He wanted to maintain a lamp for David His anointed king, whose crown would shine upon him and on his descendants in Jerusalem for ever, while his enemies would be clothed with shame. Again and again God protected the king that He had chosen to reign righteously over the nation of Israel. The Lord established David as the standard, the blueprint of both God's moral code of conduct and His required leadership to govern His nation. Even after the division of Israel in a northern and southern kingdom, to both nations King David was still meant to be the norm to all kings in the Land of Israel.

David who said he was like a green, ever-fresh olive tree in the House of God, is the only one to whom God said He would build a house set to endure for ever for him, referring to David's Royal House that would never fail to have one of his descendants to sit on his throne. There hasn't been a king, a ruler of a nation like King David, although there have been kings of Israel who followed David's example. However, only to David did the Lord give the promise of a royal household that He would keep because King David served him faithfully, a royal dynasty that would endure. The Almighty God has given His people King David to last!

Intermezzo

The Division

> *I will make them one nation in the land, upon the mountains of Israel, and one king shall be king to them all; and they shall be no more two nations, neither shall they be divided into two kingdoms anymore.*
>
> Ezekiel 37:22

At the time Samuel was judge over Israel, the Israelites wanted to have a king just as other people had. Despite the Lord's and Samuel's initial disappointment at the Israelites' request, He told him to anoint the Benjaminite Saul son of Kish, who was a man of standing, to be the first king of the Israelites. Before King Saul's reign, God Himself appointed judges to rule over the Israelites. But from then on, succession would determine who would be the next king. Saul ruled over the Kingdom of Israel until the Lord put him aside because of his disobedience. Then during his reign, He had Samuel anoint David to be the king of Israel. After Saul's death, the Kingdom of Israel was divided into the southern Kingdom of Judah, and the northern Kingdom of Israel. The tribes of Judah and Benjamin were mainly the inhabitants of the Kingdom of Judah, while the Kingdom of Israel was inhabited by the other ten tribes of Israel.

Judah supported David and had him anointed as their king, where he reigned for about seven and a half years from the city of Hebron. Meanwhile during those years, the Kingdom of Israel was ruled by Saul's son Ishboshet who became king for two years, a period during which there was much warfare between the two kingdoms. The diplomacy of King David and Israel's army commander Abner son of Ner ultimately led, in part, to the northern Kingdom of Israel choosing King David to be their king after both Abner and Ishboshet were assassinated. David became king at the age of thirty, first over Judah, then over the whole of Israel. God established King David's Royal House firmly to rule over a united Kingdom of Israel for a period of forty years.

Before David's death, he had his son Solomon anointed to be king after him. Solomon reigned forty years over the Kingdom of Israel after David's death. Solomon was the Lord's choice to succeed his father, and He told him that he should follow David's example. During his reign Solomon built and inaugurated the Temple of the Lord, fortified cities, expanded the nation and accumulated wealth. But in his old age, he went astray following the false gods and idols of his many foreign wives, and by building temples on high places for them in Israel, causing the whole of Israel to sin. God's punishment for Solomon's unfaithfulness was the division of the nation of Israel into once more the Kingdom of Judah, ruled by the descendants of David beginning with Solomon's son Rehoboam, and the Kingdom of Israel ruled by initially the Ephraimite Jeroboam son of Nebat. The new Kingdom of Judah was ruled from Jerusalem, and the Kingdom of Israel was ruled first from Shechem and ultimately from Samaria.

> *My mercy shall not depart from him, David, as I took it from Saul, whom I put away before you.*
>
> 2 Samuel 7:16a

One day after the Lord had raised up adversaries against Solomon, the Edomite Hadad and Rezon whose master was the king of Zoab, He caused Jeroboam who was an Ephraimite from Zeredah to rebel against him. The Lord sent the prophet Ahijah from Shiloh to speak to him.

Who was this Jeroboam? He was one of Solomon's officials, a man of standing whom Solomon noticed did his work for him well. At that time Solomon was doing building work in Jerusalem and he put Jeroboam in charge of the whole labour force of the tribes of Joseph. The day Jeroboam was going out of Jerusalem, Ahijah met him along the way in the countryside and spoke with him alone. Ahijah was wearing a new cloak that he tore in twelve pieces. He told Jeroboam to take ten of the pieces for himself. He said to him that God would tear the kingdom out of Solomon's hand and give him ten tribes over which He would make him king. He would also build for him a royal dynasty. Ahijah also told him God's reason to do all this. It was because Solomon had followed the false gods, the idols of his many wives and concubines. He didn't continue to walk in obedience to the Lord. So the Lord decided, just as He told Solomon earlier, that He would give the ten tribes to one of his subordinates after his death. Not during his lifetime because He had made him the ruler of Israel to reign his whole life for the sake of David who served Him faithfully. Furthermore, Ahijah told Jeroboam that the Lord would give Judah only one tribe, which was to be the tribe of Benjamin. In the past, centuries ago, it was Judah who assumed full responsibility for Joseph's brother Benjamin, Jacob's cherished youngest son, when they went to buy grain in Egypt. Years before, it was Judah who thought up the idea of selling their brother Joseph to merchants and therefore he was mainly responsible for this act. The Lord's reason to give Judah a tribe was again for the sake of His servant David to whom He made a promise and for the sake of Jerusalem where He had chosen to put His Name. But, Ahijah made it clear to Jeroboam that God would be with him, only if he would keep God's Laws, His commands and follow the example of David during his reign. He told him that the Lord would humble the descendants of David, but not for ever. After this, Jeroboam fled for his life to Egypt as Solomon was trying to kill him. He stayed there until Solomon's death after which he returned and became king of the northern tribes.

How did the separation within the Kingdom of Israel come about? Solomon died after a forty-year reign and his son Rehoboam succeeded him. Jeroboam returned to Israel as soon as he heard that Rehoboam was made king by the people of Israel in Shechem. He went together with the whole assembly of Israel, on their request, to speak with Rehoboam about lifting the heavy burden his father had put on them. If he would lighten the hard labour and heavy yoke, they would serve him.

Rehoboam consulted with the elders who had served his father, and they advised him to give them a favourable answer. But, contrary to them, the young men who grew up with Rehoboam advised him to make their burdens even harsher. He followed the advice of his friends. Jeroboam and the Israelites rebelled saying they had no share in David, no part in the son of Jesse, and that David should look after his own house. They went home where the Israelites living in the north of the kingdom made Jeroboam their king. When Rehoboam heard this, he assembled the men of Judah and Benjamin, one hundred and eighty thousand, to march out to battle the Israelites of the northern kingdom to regain the kingdom for Rehoboam. But then the Lord sent the prophet Shemaiah with His message telling them not to wage war against their brothers, because the division was His doing. They listened and obeyed the words of the Lord. From then on Rehoboam would only rule over Judah who remained loyal to the House of David, Benjamin and the Israelites of the northern Kingdom of Israel that continued to live in the towns of Judah. By God's grace Jerusalem remained the city from where the kings of Judah were given dominion for the sake of King David, who governed Israel in accordance to what was proper in the eyes of the Lord.

Jeroboam ruled over the northern kingdom from Shechem in Ephraim, which he had fortified. To insure the people he governed would not switch allegiance from him to Rehoboam, Jeroboam created his own religion with its gods, idols, religious rites and feasts, replacing God's feasts so the people wouldn't go up to the Temple of the Lord in Jerusalem. Listening to the counsel of his advisers, he had two golden calves made which he set up, one in Bethel and the other in Dan. He told the people it would be too much for them to go up to Jerusalem, and told them the idols he had made were their gods who brought them out of Egypt. Furthermore, he built shrines and altars on high places, appointed all sorts of people as priests, instituted a festival on the fifteenth day of the eighth month replacing the God-given seventh month festival of Sukkot. With all this Jeroboam altered the calender to God's feasts for the people residing in the Kingdom of Israel. He didn't only institute his own festival for the inhabitants of his territory, but he also went before them to the altars to bring sacrifices.

By institutionalizing his religion which was based on pagan religions, Jeroboam put a foundation of evil in the northern Kingdom of Israel that would bring the people to sin not only by worshipping false gods and idols, but also by leading the way for them in forsaking God Almighty's own festivals which were put in place by Him. Certain God-given festivals and feasts including the festival of Sukkot were given by the Lord to last and some, especially the Shabbat, to remain days of celebration and worship even in His Eternal Kingdom, insuring that He would be worshipped in the way and on the days in accordance with His calendar that He had created and in the manner as He had chosen. But all those who would follow Jeroboam's example, would be following a lie and they wouldn't learn nor teach God's ways concerning His feasts. Therefore they would be unable to do that which is right in His eyes.

How is it possible to be part of the new Jerusalem in God's Eternal Kingdom while holding fast to a lie, a religion, religious ways and days of worship that are sinful to God Most High? Isn't it out of Jerusalem, the city of the Great King, that the Lord sends forth His Law, truth and deliverance? Evil, deceit and untruthfulness would not have a place in the New Jerusalem, nor would people who connect themselves to evil and wickedness. The way that Jeroboam had forsaken the Lord was so deeply sinful to God. The Lord would destroy Jeroboam's royal household as He foretold through His prophet from Judah who prophesied against Jeroboam's altar and through the prophet Ahijah.

For David's sake, the Kingdom of Judah remained, with Jerusalem as its capital city and Bethlehem as one of its fortified towns. Even though God divided the Kingdom of Israel, He also gave the promise through His prophets that one day He would unify the Kingdom of Israel to be ruled by one king, a descendant of King David. The Lord would remain faithful to His servant David by keeping His promise to him!

King Hezekiah

Thus said HaShem, the King of Israel, and his Redeemer HaShem of hosts: I am the first, and I am the last, and besides Me there is no God.

Isaiah 44:6

Unlike King David's son Solomon, whose sin brought about the rupture within the Kingdom of Israel, King Hezekiah followed David's example in everything he did, making him in God's eyes one of the most fruitful kings of the Kingdom of Judah. He was the son of Ahaz king of Judah and Abi daughter of Zechariah. He became king when he was twenty-five years old, and reigned in Jerusalem for twenty-nine years. It was at the time of Hezekiah's reign that Samaria, the Kingdom of Israel, ruled by Hoshea fell to Shalmaneser the king of Assyria by the end of a three-year siege, in the fourth year of Hezekiah's reign. He captured and deported the Israelites, the ten tribes of Israel, living in the northern kingdom to Assyria where they settled in Assyrian towns. The kings of the northern Kingdom of Israel, with Jeroboam being the first, never listened to God's commands nor did they carried them out.

Hezekiah kept the Lord's commands given to Moses. He held fast to the Lord and he never stopped following Him. During his reign from Jerusalem, he did away with the idols, removed the high places, cut down the poles dedicated to gods and smashed the sacred stones just as his forefather David had done. He also cut to pieces the snake idol to which the Israelites had been burning incense. Moses had made it and put it on a pole, only for the purpose that God had commanded. That was so the Israelites who were bitten by the snakes God sent because of their sinful behaviour, would live by God's grace when they looked up to it. It was not meant to be an object of worship. Hezekiah made it clear to the people of Judah that they should worship and bring offerings only before one altar, that of God Almighty whose place to be worshipped was at the Lord's Temple. The Lord was with Hezekiah and He granted him success in whatever he undertook. He defeated the Philistines as far as Gaza, he rebelled against the king of Assyria whom he didn't serve. The Lord delivered Hezekiah from his enemies.

In the first month of the first year of Hezekiah's reign, he opened and repaired the doors of the Temple of the Lord which were closed by his father Ahaz who reigned sixteen years from Jerusalem. Ahaz, unlike his son, didn't follow in the footsteps of King David. During his reign, he asked the king of Assyria to help him fight against the Moabites and the Philistines. But Assyria's king didn't give him his support. Instead he demanded payment from Ahaz who took whatever he could find in the Temple of the Lord, in the royal palace and from his officials to present to him. Ultimately Ahaz took the furnishings of the Temple, cut them to pieces and closed the door of the Temple. Unfaithful to the Lord as he was, he set up altars for idols at every street corner in Jerusalem. The more he got troubled, the more he turned away from the Lord and got himself as well as the people of Judah entangled with idols from Damascus to which he did sacrifices thinking they would be able to solve his troubles concerning Judah's enemies.

Compared to Ahaz, Hezekiah's actions concerning the Temple of the Lord were initially rather the opposite. He restored the Temple and the Temple Service. He gathered the priests and the Levites whom the Lord had chosen to serve Him, to minister for him and to present offerings at his sanctuary. Hezekiah told the priests and the Levites to consecrate themselves, after which they were to purify and consecrate the Temple, the Lord's dwelling place. Hezekiah was determined to make a covenant with the God of Israel hoping to turn away His anger from Judah, after it was ignited by the sins of some former kings and the people of Judah who followed them in their sinful acts. Hezekiah restored the priests and Levites, whose right it was to serve God, by having them perform their duties regarding the Temple of the Lord and the Temple Service. They were again responsible for the Temple Service, for carrying the Ark of the Covenant, and pray God's blessing over the people. Some of them were also responsible in matters concerning God's Laws as judges. People were encouraged by law not to take matters into their own hands to settle disputes, but to abide by the ruling of the judges. The Levite priests were also consulted in medical matters. Hezekiah also followed King David's instructions, which he had received from the prophets Gad and Nathan, when he stationed the Levites with David's instruments to bring praise to the Lord in the Temple. Together with his officials, the priests, all those who ministered for the Lord, and the assembly they brought offerings and worshipped God. Later on they celebrated Pesach with the people of Ephraim and Menasseh whom Hezekiah had officially invited. He sent couriers out through Judah and Israel with a message to the people, to return to the God of Abraham, Isaac and Jacob. For seven days they celebrated Pesach and agreed to celebrate for seven more days. As soon as the celebration ended, the Israelites went out to the towns throughout Judah, Benjamin, Ephraim and Menasseh where they destroyed the objects used for the worship of idols. After all this Hezekiah restored the practice of bringing contributions to the Temple by commanding the people of Israel to bring in their contributions as was stipulated in the Law. This would enable the priests and Levites to devote themselves to the study and implementation of God's Laws, and to their duties. The Lord blessed the Israelites greatly, so they could give generously. Hezekiah was obedient to the Lord and His commands. He sought the Lord sincerely, did what was right throughout Judah, and so he prospered.

Years later, Hezekiah became seriously ill and the prophet Isaiah son of Amoz, who went to see him, told him to get his house in order because he was going to die. After Isaiah left his room leaving him alone, Hezekiah who was on his sickbed, turned his face to the wall and wept bitterly in prayer to the Lord asking Him to remember how he walked before Him faithfully and with sincere devotion doing what was right in His eyes. God's word reached Isaiah before he left the middle court of Hezekiah's palace telling him to go back to Hezekiah, the ruler of His people, to tell him that He had heard his prayer and seen his tears, that He would heal him and add fifteen years to his life during which He wouldn't allow Jerusalem to fall into the hands of the king of Assyria for the sake of His servant David. Hezekiah was to go up to the Temple of the Lord the third day from his recovery.

Isaiah prepared and boiled a poultice, a dressing of figs for Hezekiah, who asked him what God's sign to his recovery would be so he could go to the Temple. Isaiah replied by asking him whether the shadow on the stairway of Ahaz, which was a sundial used in those days as a tool to show the time of day, should go ten steps forward or backward. Hezekiah chose the latter, which would be the most difficult one to do. The Lord God who sometimes can give a sign to people when they didn't ask for it, answered Isaiah's call concerning the sign Hezekiah did ask for, by making the shadow go back ten steps on the sundial. This reassured Hezekiah that he would recover.

When the king of Babylon heard of Hezekiah's illness, he sent envoys with a gift to him. Hezekiah received them and showed them all his treasures and all he had in his storehouses. Concerning this Isaiah prophesied to Hezekiah that one day all his treasures would be carried off to Babylon where some of his own descendants would serve the Babylonian king as Eunuchs in his palace. Hezekiah had peace of mind over this prophecy, as he taught that these events wouldn't take place during his lifetime. Indeed they would take place after his lifetime.

Sometime after Hezekiah's illness, during the fourteenth year of Hezekiah's reign, Sennacherib, king of Assyria invaded Judah, attacked all its fortified cities and captured them. When he was laying siege to Lachish, he sent his officers with a message to Jerusalem. He threatened to conquer Jerusalem. Hezekiah, trying to prevent this from happening, sent a message back to the Assyrian king telling him that it was wrong of him to rebel, and that he would pay whatever the king demanded if he withdrew from Judah. Hezekiah gave him all the silver in the treasury of the royal palace and in the Temple. He added the demanded gold, by stripping the gilded doors of the Temple, thus acting, concerning the Temple doors, in a similar way as his father had done. But when Hezekiah realised that Sennacherib wanted to wage war against Jerusalem, he took measures to fortify Jerusalem to improve their chances of survival. After consulting with his officials and military staff, he decided to block all the water springs and streams outside the city so the Assyrian army wouldn't find water when they came to Jerusalem.

To be able to supply Jerusalem with water while under siege, Hezekiah made a pool and a tunnel to bring water within the city walls. In addition he fortified the city wall by repairing the sections of the wall that were broken, built towers on it and another wall outside the city wall, and he reinforced the terraces of the City of David. He also had large numbers of weapons and shields made. Finally he assembled the people over whom he appointed military officers. In the square at the city gate Hezekiah spoke words of encouragement to them. He told them not to be afraid or discourage and that he trusted in the Lord his God to help them fight their battle. The people gained confidence from Hezekiah's speech.

> *The fear of HaShem is to hate evil; pride, and arrogancy, and the evil way, and the froward mouth, do I hate.*
> Proverbs 8:13

Later the king of Assyria sent his supreme commander, chief officer and his field commander with a large army from Lachish to Jerusalem. Hezekiah sent out three of his officials to talk to the field commander who called out to Hezekiah when he and his men stopped at the Upper Pool's aqueduct on the road to Washerman's field. The field commander spoke with Hezekiah's officials against the Lord, Hezekiah and the military of Judah. He also spoke to the people of Judah on Jerusalem's wall in Hebrew instead of in Aramaic ignoring Hezekiah's officials request. Aramaic was a language Hezekiah and his officials would understand but not the people on Jerusalem's walls. The field commander replied that he was sent to speak with them too, because just like Hezekiah they would have to eat their own excrement and drink their own urine if their king waged war with Assyria. In his arrogance the field commander continued to insult and ridicule the Living God and Hezekiah. He told the people as well not to listen to Hezekiah. He even implied that Assyria marched to conquer Jerusalem and Judah on the Lord's command. He told the people to choose life, which would be in Assyria, not death. He continued by saying to them that they shouldn't listen to their king because he was misleading them into believing that his God would save them. But the people remained silent on Hezekiah's order not to answer the Assyrian officials. Hezekiah's officials, with their clothes torn as a sign of grief, reported to Hezekiah what the Assyrian field commander said. When Hezekiah heard the report of his officials he tore his clothes and put on a sackcloth. He sent his officials and the leading priests in sackcloth to speak with the prophet Isaiah. They gave him Hezekiah's message and told him how the Assyrian field commander ridiculed the Living God. They asked Isaiah for prayers, hoping that maybe God who heard the commander's words would rebuke the Assyrians. Isaiah told them to tell their king not to be afraid because of the words that the subordinates of the Assyrian king spoke to blaspheme the Lord. God would make the king of Assyria want to return to his own country when he hears of a certain report. There in his own land the Lord would have him cut down by the sword. The Assyrian king left Lachish to fight Libnah, a town in Judah that once revolted against one of the kings of Judah. As soon as the field commander heard about this he too withdrew from Jerusalem. But when Sennacherib heard that the king of Cush was marching out to fight him, he sent a letter for Hezekiah and all the people of Judah in Jerusalem in which he made it clear that the people of Judah shouldn't believe Hezekiah when he said that their God would save them. Just as the gods of other nations didn't save them from him either. He boasted that he destroyed both the nations and their gods.

Hezekiah went to the Temple to consult with God. In prayer he laid the letter he received open before Him. He asked Him, the One Who is God over all the kingdoms of the earth, to see, hear and listen to the insolent words the Assyrian king and his underlings spoke and wrote to ridicule Him, the Living God. Hezekiah asked his God Who is not fashioned by human hands as those of the nations laid to waste, to deliver them from the king of Assyria so all the kingdoms of the earth would know that He alone is God. The Lord sent word to the prophet Isaiah that He had heard Hezekiah's prayer and that He had spoken against the king of Assyria. Isaiah in turn sent a message to Hezekiah in which he foretold the demise of the Assyrian king and his army. Because of their insolence and rage against the Lord the Holy one of Israel, He would make the Assyrian king return to his own land, while the virgin daughter of Zion, the daughter of Jerusalem tosses, shakes her head as he flees. Isaiah also spoke of the sign the Lord gave to Hezekiah. That year Hezekiah and his people would eat what grows by itself, the next year what would spring from that, but the third year they would saw, harvest and eat the fruits, including those of the vineyards they had planted. The zeal, eagerness of God Almighty Himself would accomplish that out of Jerusalem will come a remnant and out of Mount Zion a band of survivors. The Lord declared that the king of Assyria would not attack nor enter the city of Jerusalem. He would go back to his land the way he came.

Hezekiah trusted the Lord God, Who defended, protected and delivered Jerusalem. Why would the Lord do this? Because of His own honour! Because of His enduring kindness promised to his servant David, whom He had appointed as a witness over the people, a ruler and commander to regimes. David, by God's grace, was the father of kings. That night the Lord sent an angel to the camp of the Assyrian king where he annihilated the army. A hundred and eighty-five thousand fighting men, their commanders and their officers were found dead in the morning, which brought disgrace to the Assyrian king and resulted in the withdrawal of the king to his own land. Once in Nineveh, on the day he went to the temple of his god, two of his sons killed him by the sword. Afterwards they escaped to the land of Ararat. As for Hezekiah, all nations and people held him highly in regard bringing him many valuable gifts and offerings to Jerusalem.

Other kings of Judah that followed David's example were King Asa and King Josiah. Asa became king of Judah long before the time of Hezekiah, and he reigned forty-one years. He was the third king to rule from Jerusalem over the Kingdom of Judah after King Solomon's death when the division took place within the Kingdom of Israel. There was constant warfare between the Kingdom of Judah and the Kingdom of Israel during his reign.

Unlike his own father, Asa did what was right in the eyes of the Lord just as King David, his forefather did. King Asa expelled the shrine prostitutes from the Land, he got rid of all the idols his ancestors had made, and he even destroyed a detestable pole or tree made by his grandmother Maacah, that she dedicated to her idol. He cut it down, chopped it, burned it in the Kidron Valley, and he deposed his grandmother from her position as queen mother.

The Lord had set artefacts of idolatry apart for destruction and whoever brought those in their house, would likewise be set apart for destruction. Whenever God set out to punish the gods, the fallen angels and their offspring to whom people attach themselves through their worship of idols and gods, these people would receive punishment along side with them, as happened in Egypt when the Lord took His people out to journey to the Land He promised their ancestors. The Lord never wanted His people to be initiated in pagan ways and rituals. Nor did He ever wanted to be worshipped in the same manner as these people did to their idols and gods. Because of the things they did, even sacrificing their sons and daughters to their gods by burning them in the fire. Neither did He want their poles, pillars, tree and sacred stones erected beside His altar or in His Temple. The people however continued to use the high places to burn incense and sacrifices, but Asa's heart was completely committed to the Lord his entire life. He brought silver, gold and artefacts he and his father had consecrated into the Temple of the Lord.

King Josiah reigned over Judah long after Hezekiah, who was followed first by Menasseh. He reigned fifty-five years and was followed by Amon who ruled only two years. Both kings were very unfaithful to the Lord. Contrary to them, Josiah was faithful to the Lord. He was eight when he became king, and he reigned for thirty-one years. It's during his reign that the Israelites found the Book of

Law, a Scroll of the Torah, which was brought to the king to renew the covenant with the Lord.

Josiah who was faithful to the Lord did what was proper in His eyes and he followed the example of King David. One day during the eighteenth reign of Josiah, he sent his secretary Shaphan with instructions for Hilkia the High Priest, the Kohen Gadol, to the Temple of the Lord. The priest was to ready the money brought into the Temple of the Lord by the doorkeepers and he was to give the money to the supervisors of the work on the Temple for them to pay the workers and purchase the necessary building materials to continue the repairs on the Temple. Hilkia told the king's secretary that he had found the Book of Law in the Temple. Shaphan reported to Josiah that Hilkia would make the necessary arrangements concerning the king's instructions and that he brought with him the Book of Law that the priest had found. He read from it for the king. Realizing that God's anger was burning against him, the people of Judah and their descendants because those before them didn't listen nor live by the words of the Book of Law, Josiah tore his clothes and wept. He sent Shaphan to Hilkia with two of his officials to inquire of the Lord about what was written in the book. They went to the prophetess Huldah, who lived in the New Quarter of Jerusalem. When they returned to Josiah they reported to him what the Lord had to say. Because the people of Judah had forsaken Him by worshipping gods and idols, His unquenchable anger burned against that place to which He would bring about disaster. But, because Josiah's heart was responsive to the words of the Book of Law and he humbled himself before the Lord, He would gather Josiah to his ancestors in peace, so he would not see the disaster that He would bring over the Kingdom of Judah. With the memory of Menasseh's faithless reign and foreseeing the reign of Judah's unfaithful kings after Josiah, the Lord would make Jerusalem, the Kingdom of Judah and its inhabitants a desolation and a curse because they angered Him with their handiwork and unfaithfulness.

Knowing this, King Josiah set out to eradicate all that which his ancestors and former kings of both Judah and Israel had done to anger the Lord igniting His wrath against the Kingdom of Judah. But before that, he gathered the elders of Jerusalem and Judah, and they went up to the Temple of the Lord together with all the Kohanim, the prophets, men of Judah and its inhabitants. In their presence Josiah read the words of the Book of the Covenant. The blessings for obedience to the Lord God Almighty but also the curses that would be the result of disobedience. This way Josiah sealed a covenant before God and the people, which the entire population accepted. They were to revere the honoured awesome Name of the Lord God, fear Him, while obeying His Law with all their heart and soul. After this Josiah started with the removal and destruction of high places, altars, erected stones, pillars, poles and trees dedicated to pagan idols, gods and goddesses. He did away with pagan rituals as well. He instructed Hilkia, the Kohanim, and the gate keeper to remove all artefacts dedicated to gods, goddesses, and to the hosts of the heaven from the Temple of the Lord to be burned in the plains of Kidron. The ashes were to be scattered away in Bethel on the site of Jeroboam's temple, which was an unclean, unholy place.

Josiah dismissed all the priests that burnt offerings to idols, the sun, the moon, the constellations and all the heavenly hosts. These were priests appointed in the past by some of the kings of Judah to bring offerings to those at the high places. He had the idols of a certain god and goddess removed from the Temple of the Lord. He burned and grounded them to dust in the Kidron Valley outside Jerusalem to be scattered over the graves of their worshippers. He had the quarters in the Temple where the women weaved curtains for their goddess demolished. Josiah brought the Kohanim from the cities of Judah. These were priests who sinned by performing services to idols. But, they didn't have permission to ascend to the Altar of the Lord to participate in the Temple Service. They were only allowed to receive food from the offerings that in accordance to the Law was distributed amongst the priests.

Josiah defiled and smashed the high places at the gates, including the one at the gate of the governor of the city of Jerusalem. The place in the Valley of Ben Hinnom where the people passed their sons and daughters through fire, was likewise destroyed. He abolished the horses, and burned the chariots, which were all used for the worship of the sun. The kings of Judah had designated these to race from the entrance of the Temple out towards the east in the outlying area of the city. They were meant to greet the sun as it came up. He also smashed and destroyed altars set up by the kings of Judah on the upper story of a building built by Ahaz and those placed by Menasseh in the courtyard of the Temple of the Lord. He threw their dust in the Kidron Valley.

Then Josiah did what no king before him had done since the time the Kingdom of Israel was divided by the Lord. Solomon's sinful acts concerning the worship of the gods and idols of his many wives caused the rupture of the Kingdom of Israel. Josiah defiled all the high places that Solomon had built dedicated to the idols of the Sidonians, the Moabites and the Amonites during his reign. They were placed facing Jerusalem, south of the Mount of Olives. Josiah shattered the pillars and cut down the tree they had dedicated to their goddess. Furthermore, Josiah dealt with what Jeroboam had created and institutionalised after Solomon. This was a new religion with pagan roots that brought much evil to the people that inhabited the kingdom of the northern tribes causing them to sin and later to the kings who would follow his example. Josiah went to the altar Jeroboam had built in Bethel for his idols, demolished its altar, burned the high places and ground them to dust, and burned the pole dedicated to their goddess. To show his disdain, Josiah had the bones, which belonged to Jeroboam's ordained priests, removed from the graves around on the hillside and burned them on the altar defiling it. But the grave of the man of God from Judah, who foretold that these things would take place on this altar by the hands of a son named Josiah who would be born to the House of David, remained undisturbed as Josiah was told whose grave it was by the people of the city. Thus, the prophesy against Jeroboam's altar came to pass. Both kings, Solomon and Jeroboam, were extremely unfaithful to the Lord God. Through King Josiah the Lord dealt with their pagan heritage.

The same as Josiah did to the altar and high places in Bethel, he did to all the high places in the cities of Samaria which were built by the kings of Israel to anger the Lord. He removed all their pagan temples as well. Then the king went back to Jerusalem and issued an order to all people to celebrate Pesach in accordance to all the instructions as given in the Book of the Covenant. Even more, to fulfil all the requirements of the Law written in the Book of Law that Hilkiah gave him, he got rid of all the household gods and idols. He also removed the people who practised spiritism and those who consulted the dead. Because Josiah humbled himself and wept in God's presence, and because of all the deeds he had done, the Lord didn't bring disaster in accordance to the Book of Law upon him and Judah during his reign. King Josiah died when he marched out to confront Pharaoh Necho who wasn't at war with Judah, but on his way to help the king of Assyria. Necho told Josiah that God had sent him to Assyria and not to wage war against Israel. Despite Necho's warning Josiah didn't listen, and Necho killed him. King Josiah's servants buried him in his own tomb in Jerusalem. There had not been a king like Josiah before or after him, who returned to the Lord the way he did, with all his heart, soul, strength and resources in accordance to the Laws of Moses.

And HaShem shall be King over all the earth; in that day shall HaShem be One, and His name one.
                                              Zechariah 14:9

God doesn't only put rulers in place to govern His Land, but also for other nations. He influences foreign kings and rulers by giving them dreams, interpretation of dreams, blessings, warnings but also when He finds it necessary by bringing punishment over them and their nation. The Lord warned Abimelech the king of Gera, a city-state of the Philistines, in a dream concerning Abraham's wife Sarah. In Moses' time He brought punishment on the Pharaoh and Egypt because he refused to let His people go. Sometimes the Lord would have kings act in a favourable way on behalf of His people. At one time He gave the Pharaoh of Egypt dreams having Joseph interpret them, which resulted in Joseph and his whole family being saved from hunger by moving to Egypt where they became a numerous people.

At the time of Ezra, the priest during Judah's exile, Cyrus the king of Persia granted the exiles permission to leave Babylon to return to Judah, with instructions to restore the Temple of the Lord in Jerusalem and the Temple Service. Later Artaxerxes the king of Babylon sent Nehemiah with his approval to Jerusalem where he and the people of Judah restored the walls of Jerusalem.

The Lord can also give power to his servants concerning kingdoms, as He once did with his prophet Jeremiah whom He appointed over nations and kingdoms, to uproot and to smash, to destroy and to overthrow, to build and to plant by God-given words that he would prophecy, while being under His protection against kings, leaders, priests and the people of the Land who would fight him but not overcome him because the Lord would be with him to rescue him. The words the Lord gave Jeremiah to prophesy reached the people during his lifetime and far further into the future where part of his prophesies were still set to be fulfilled.

God's choice for David to rule over His nation would also have far-reaching consequences from then on through future events, to eternity for Israel and ultimately the entire world. David always humbled himself before God and to whom his Living God wasn't far away. During his life he had an intense close and personal relationship with the Lord. He kept Him close, in prayers while seeking to do His will. He lived by His Laws and commands, keeping them within his heart. David was a man who counted on God's blessing in all matters and circumstances, including when he was being cursed. Once, as he was being cursed, he prayed to the Lord and asked Him to turn the curse into a blessing. The Lord answered his prayer. He had faith in his Living God, he trusted completely His unfailing love, confided in Him, sought His counsel and he fought his enemies together with Him. He was convinced that his Living God would always receive him and would never forsake him.

David shared his emotions with his God. His pain, grief, fears, sadness, sorrows, remorse, hopes, victories, joys, dreams and everything else. David was never shy to show his love for his God, and his gratefulness towards him with his deeds, in his prayers, songs, music and poems. He even danced with all his might before the Lord in Jerusalem. God entrusted David with His inspiration which he put to music, to writing lyrics and poems. As a musician and singer David tuned in, into people's hearts, bringing with his music and words peace and tranquillity to people's soul, as he did to King Saul, or have them rejoice because of God's unfailing love and justice. There is no higher source of inspiration than His, and no purer harmony than the Lord's.

David longed to be even closer to his Living God, to seek His face, to bring praises for Him, to learn His ways even more, to dwell and be rooted in the House of the Lord for all his days. To David there just wasn't anything more desirable than that. The Lord was his salvation, He strengthened his heart. To serve his Living God in closeness to Him was a delight for David. This was a sincere and heartfelt relationship, one through which the Lord God would do wonders for David but also for the nation He had formed out of the sons of Jacob. David, the father of Judah's kings and of His king to be. In all this there hasn't been a king or person in Israel like him. He was truly both in his heart and by his deeds a man to God's heart. Through David the Lord connected Israel's past, present and future to eternity.

God Almighty, the God of David, the Eternal King Who has the power to build and uproot kingdoms is the only Ruler, the God of gods, the Lord of lords and as the Great King, the King of kings. God created humanity with Adam and Eve. With Noah, He conserved humanity so one day He would establish His Eternal Kingdom on earth. With the Israelites the Lord made Himself a nation to live in His Promised Land by His Law, regulations and the richness of His Word. With David He set a standard of leadership for all rulers and unveiled the character, talents and spiritual strength of His king to be, to rule from the New Jerusalem, the city of the Great King. The Lord God established David's Royal House and the Davidic Throne to remain!

Your house and your kingdom shall be made sure for ever before you; your throne shall be established for ever. Your house and your kingdom will endure for ever before Me; your throne will be established for ever.

2 Samuel 7:16b

Endnotes

Deuteronomy 10:17, Psalm 136:3 God of gods, Lord of lords
Psalm 24 God is King
1 Samuel 4:4, 2 Kings 18:15 God enthroned between cherubim
Psalm 2:2, Isaiah 6:1-4, 63:15, 66:1 God's throne in heaven
Genesis 32:28, 35:16, 46:2-8 Jacob renamed Israel
Isaiah 40:6-8, 55:10-11 God's words
Isaiah 63:10-14 God's Holy Spirit
Deuteronomy 8:5-6, 10:15-16, 10:17-22, 11:22, 30:19-20 hold fast to the God in obedience
Deuteronomy 8:3-4, 8:2, 16 Manna, forty years in the desert
Deuteronomy 5:1-32, 6:1-9, 11:17-22 keep God's commands, rain in the Land
Deuteronomy 6:20-25 purpose of God's Laws
Genesis 24:1, 26:24, 28:13-15 and 32:10-13, Deuteronomy 8:17-18 prosperity
Psalm 105:37,44-45 God took them out of Egypt, no one left behind
2 Chronicles 2:1-2 sons of Israel, Jacob
Psalm 105:17-24 He sent Joseph up front
Psalm 114:1-2, Deuteronomy 26:16-19 God's people His treasured possession
Genesis 15:16, Deuteronomy 9:4-6, Psalm 105 reason Promised Land given to Israelites
Deuteronomy 18:9-14 sins of the inhabitants of Canaan
Isaiah 25:8, Daniel 12:1-3 The day of awakening, resurrection
Psalm 90:4 thousand years like a day
Deuteronomy 10:14-22 reason God's choice for the Israelites
Genesis 17:1, Deuteronomy 18:13 Israelites ought to be blameless before God
Deuteronomy 11:2 experience God
2 Chronicles 30:16 Moses the man of God
Psalm 98:3 God's love and faithfulness to Israel
Amos 9:15 God plants Israel in His Land
Psalm 115:1 God's Name's sake
Deuteronomy 7:16, 7:23-26 Israelite attitude towards their enemies and their gods
Leviticus 18:1-5, Joshua 24:14-15 no worship of gods from Egypt, Canaan, the Euphrates River

Who Is David?

Joshua 24:2 Abraham's father Terah came originally from beyond the Euphrates River
Deuteronomy 7:22, 9:3 take over the land, wild animals
Joshua 1:3-4, 1 Kings 8:56 God fulfils His promises to Moses and gives rest
Exodus 15:18 God eternal king
Judges 1:7-9 judges had to keep God's Laws
1 Chronicles 28:6, 29:23 Israel, kingdom of the Lord
Jeremiah 1:9-19 God builds and uproot kingdoms
Numbers 23:21-24, 24:7-9 God spoke of a king for the Israelites
Numbers 22-24 Balaam
Genesis 49 blessing Jacob's sons
Deuteronomy 33:7, 13-17 Moses' blessings for Judah and Joseph
Isaiah 41:18, 49:10 rivers and springs of water in the Land
Deuteronomy 11:11-12 God's rainfall
Deuteronomy 23:5-6 God loves the Israelites
1 Samuel 2:10b The Lord gives strength to His anointed king
Genesis 20 Abimelech of city state Philistine
2 Chronicles 35:20-24 Necho of Egypt
Daniel 1-4 Nebuchadnezzar
Ezra 1, 7 Cyrus king of Persia
Nehemiah 1-2 Artaxerxes king of Babylonia
Psalm 114:1-2 out of Egypt
Deuteronomy 17:14-20 rules for God's King
Judges 17, Ruth 1:22, 4:17-22, 1 Samuel :12, 58, 20:6, 2 Chronicles 11:5-12, Micah 5:1-2 David from Bethlehem Ephrathah in Judah
Isaiah 5:7 The nation of Israel is God's vineyard
1 Samuel 16:13 David anointed king
1 Kings 11:36, 2 Kings 8:19 Judah and House of David spared for the sake of David
Psalm 101 David's attitude as king
1 Samuel 15:22-23, Psalm 40:7-8, Hosea 6:6 reason God chose David
1 Samuel 16:7 God looks into the human heart
1 Samuel 13:14 David, a man after God's heart
Psalm 109:28 David counted on God to bless him despite people's curses
Deuteronomy 13:5, Psalm 27, 31:16, 52, 101 David's attitude to God, as a king
Psalm 51, 32 David repents
2 Samuel 22, Proverbs 2:7, Psalm 3:4, 28:7, 91:4 David called God his Shield
Psalm 132:17-18 a lamp for David
Psalm 52:8 or 10 David as an olive tree
Psalm 1:2-3, Jeremiah 17:7-8 trees planted by a stream of water
Psalm 40:7-8 God's Law within David's heart
Psalm 109:28 David counted on God's blessings

Psalm 27:10 God would always receive David
2 Kings 14:3, 18:3, 22:2, Isaiah 7:13 David, the father of kings
2 Kings 18:3 Hezekiah followed in King David's way
1 Kings 15:1-5 despite the sins of David's successors, God kept David's Royal Line for David's sake
1 Kings 15:5 The matter of Uriah the Hittite
2 Samuel 7:11-17, Daniel 2:43-45 David's kingship for ever
2 Kings 18-20, 2 Chronicles 29-32 King Hezekiah of the Kingdom of Judah
2 Kings 18:3-4, 2 Chronicles 29:2 he followed King David's example
Deuteronomy 7:25-26 idols should be destroyed
Numbers 21:4-9, 2 Kings 18:4, 2 Chronicles 31:1 destruction of the snake idol, poles, high places
Deuteronomy 10:8-9 duties of the Levites
Deuteronomy 16:18-20, 17:8-13, 18, 21:1-9 Levites also judges
Leviticus 13 priests also consulted in medical matters
2 Chronicles 28:21-24 King Ahaz closed the Temple
2 Chronicles 28 Ahaz' downfall
2 Chronicles 29 Hezekiah restored the Temple Service
Isaiah 7:13 God gives signs people didn't ask for
2 Kings 19: 9-19 The siege of Jerusalem by Assyria
Isaiah 22:9-11 Isaiah's comment on Hezekiah's pool to supply Jerusalem with water
2 Kings 19: 14-15 The open letter
2 Kings 19:34, 20:6c, Isaiah 37: 35, 55:3-5 God's reason to save Jerusalem
1 Kings 15:9-15, 12:29-32, 16:21-22 King Asa followed in King David's footsteps
Deuteronomy 7:16, idols and their worshippers set apart for destruction
2 Kings 22:2, 23:25, 2 Chronicles 34:1-2 Josiah followed in King David's footsteps
2 Kings 22-23, 2 Chronicles 34-35 King Josiah
2 Kings 22:8-10, 2 Chronicles 17:7-9 The Book of Law found, King Josiah
2 Kings 22:14-20 prophetess Huldah, lived in Jerusalem in the New Quarter
Deuteronomy 27:9-26, Deuteronomy 28, 31:9-13, 19-26 Book of the Covenant, of Law, Moses song
Deuteronomy 30:11-14 God's Laws not distant nor hidden
Deuteronomy 29:13-20 consequences also for the descendants of the Israelites
1 Kings 11:4-8, 2 Kings 23:13 destruction of Solomon's high places he dedicated to idols
1 Kings 13:1-10, 1 Kings 13:31-34 prophesy against Jeroboam and his altar
1 Kings 13:23-31, 2 Kings 23:16-18 The grave of the prophet who gave prophesy against Jeroboam
2 Kings 23:29-30 Josiah died in battle against Necho king of Egypt

Who Is David?

Isaiah 38:5 The God of David, father of kings
Isaiah 9:6 David's throne remains for ever

Intermezzo Endnotes

1 Kings 9:4-5 The Lord asked Solomon to follow David's example
1 Kings 11 Solomon's unfaithfulness and punishment
1 Kings 11 Jeroboam chosen to be king of northern tribes of Israel
1 Kings 11:38 God told Jeroboam to follow example David
1 Kings 12:1-24, 2 Chronicles 10:1-11:4 divided Israel
Genesis 44:17-34, 50:15-21 Judah and Joseph
1 Kings 12:25-33 Jeroboam's new religion
Exodus 32, 1 Kings 13:25-33 Jeroboam's unfaithfulness, the calves
Isaiah 56:1-2 and 6-8, Isaiah 66:23, Zechariah 14:16 certain feasts of God will remain
Psalm 101:7-8 Jerusalem free of evil, deceit
Daniel 2 God's Eternal Kingdom
1 Kings 15:4-5 Jerusalem remained capital of Judah
2 Chronicles 11:5-12 Bethlehem remained a town, fortified, in Judah

JUDGE OF CREATION

Shall any teach God knowledge? Seeing it is He that judges those that are high.

Job 21:22

God Almighty is the Living God, the Most High God, is the only One true God. The Lord is not some force, source, energy, or merely formless visible light. Nor is He, a god of the sea, plains, heights or a lifeless idol made of earthly materials. He is an awesome Creator of all. He has no equal! His creation, He created to give Him joy, gladness and to serve Him, depends on Him for their existence. The Lord is pure in His holiness and can't tolerate unholiness. Those who are not holy can't be completely connected with Him unless they are purified. Therefore He is always willing to forgive people's transgressions and sins. He provides His teachings and moral code through, first of all His Word, which in essence is truth. It contains His Laws, commandments, regulations and life experiences of those either faithful or unfaithful to Him. He gave these first to Israel, making each and every Israelite a carrier of His moral values. In doing so, He made Abraham, Isaac, Israel and Israel's descendants, the Children of Israel an example to those around them and the nations of the world. The Lord who sanctifies Israel, His servant, will show His splendour and He'll be glorified in them. The Lord has been providing the necessary guidance to the Israelites and through them to humanity for their own good while restraining evilness. He asks for people to be faithful to Him through these and to love Him above all. To love Him, is to hate evil and evilness. The Lord is good, He guards the life of His faithful ones, and delivers them from the hand of the wicked granting them passage to His everlasting life. His goodness always includes His righteousness, which He wants people to sow for themselves in during their lifetime, and with which He in turn wants to shower them.

Thus said HaShem: Keep justice, and do righteousness, for My salvation is near to come, and My favour to be revealed. Happy is the man that does this, and the son of man that holds fast by it: that keeps the Sabbath from desecrating it, and keeps his hand from doing any evil.

Isaiah 56:1-2

The Lord God, Who doesn't share His honour, is far greater than all other gods. He doesn't change, remaining the God of Abraham, Isaac, and Israel. The Living God of David, His servant. The Eternal One has an eternal lifecycle that enables Him to oversee millennia for ever, while man can't have merely less than a century to live a fragile life as an active part of society. God scans the whole earth, while He masters time, events and makes plans that are far above people's understanding. As the Creator, the Lord is law-maker, law-giver and judge! His Laws are not hidden nor distant. Even though He has been allowing people to participate in the processes of both, law-giving and judging in society, He Himself remains at the centre, the heart of law-making and justice. The Lord God Himself is the norm! His Laws are just, and in His infinite wisdom, He can turn wrongdoings into goodness, something He also did for David, who put his trust on God's merciful love. He loves righteousness and justice, and He would render justice to all. His judgment is divine, and is not based on simply a need for revenge but on His righteousness. Therefore even His revenge is divine. Since everything belongs to Him, it's His right to avenge and repay every being of creation. He judges the creation He created, and repays each and everyone by their deeds. The Eternal One's love endures for ever. He delights in those who fear Him, acknowledging that He is Most High while putting their hope in His unfailing love.

> *As for God, His way is perfect; The word of HaShem is tried; He is a Shield unto all of them that take refuge in Him. For who is God, save HaShem? And who is a Rock, save our God?*
> 2 Samuel 22:31

The Lord is the only being that has a complete and pure insight in the heart of a human being. So He is able to accurately assess the extent of the goodness or wickedness in a person's heart and mind. He can see the goodness He Himself had created in them, but He also sees the evilness and wickedness, brought to them by the fallen angels, which they in turn lived by ever since Adam and Eve. Moreover, the Lord has the deeds of each and every person recorded in the Books that one day will be opened showing without any doubt the state of being of each human being's soul. To keep God's Laws, commandments and teachings is to live in accordance to His way of life, His moral code, and a way to show personal love for Him. He is the Creator, the source and nourisher of life, the origin of goodness and truth.

Evil, the fallen angels and their offspring, on the other hand are pure evil, and therefore the source of evilness, wickedness, sinfulness and degeneration brought about through lies, deception and temptation. The question is, to which should a person choose to be connected with? Whose way of life should a person follow?

Evil people have a deep-rooted hate for God's righteousness, His moral values and Laws. They can't tolerate the people who uphold God's values. They are always out to destroy and annihilate these people, for whom they have a pure deep-seated hate and contempt, in an attempt to eradicate the Lord's moral code on earth to completely disconnect humanity from God. Evil brings about degeneration, violence, robbery, decay and ultimately lifelessness. Finally, wouldn't humanity be extinct?!

Who are these people that evil hates so much? In the first place those through whom the Lord has been showing and providing His moral values and Laws to humanity, the Children of Israel. Furthermore all those who accepted the blessings He has been giving through them, and have chosen to be His servant.

The battlefield is on earth. The bounty is humanity and their living space on earth. For those whose choice is to serve the Lord, He will show His mercy leading to a life in closeness to God Almighty and without the intrusion of evilness. For those who choose to live by evil ways await punishment. In the end, reward or not, payment will be given to all by done deeds.

> *Consider, you brute among the people; And you fools, when will you understand? He that planted the ear, shall He not hear? He that formed the eye, shall He not see? He that instructs nations, shall He not correct? Even He that teaches man knowledge? HaShem knows the thoughts of man, that they are vanity. Happy is the man who You instruct, O HaShem, and teach out of Your Law; That You may give him rest from the days of evil, until the pit be dough for the wicked.*
> Psalm 94:8-13

The Lord is the God of mercy and deliverance. He always offers a way out. The way of remorse for done deeds, of repentance for wrongdoings. Made known to Him through honest prayers, as King David had done twice and God showed him His mercy. The Lord doesn't impose harsh justice indiscriminately. He awaits with patience people's repentance. But, where evilness in people's heart comes to full growth through their deeds, punishment is inevitable. For sin causes separation from the Lord God.

Ever since Adam and Eve sinned, humanity has been subjected to sinfulness and degeneration which ultimately would lead to death. God's punishment is meant to reverse this process which is only possible when those involved would show honest repentance. Ahab, one of Israel's kings, experienced this concerning the designated time the Lord would bring disaster over his household. The inhabitants of the city of Nineveh were saved when they showed repentance after listening to prophet Jonah's message. But, once the fullness of wickedness within a person or nation is reached, God's divine vengeance will be triggered and finalised.

The destruction of both the cities Sodom and Gomorrah shows the ultimate result of an irreversible process of God's punishment, brought about by the people's sinful choices. At that time, Lot with his family was an example of those the Lord saved from the disaster which He brought over these cities. The Lord also gives people a period of time for them to change their way of life. The people of Noah's generation had one hundred and twenty years of time. Still they did not show remorse, repent and change their ways. But with Noah, who was righteous in God's eyes, He made a covenant binding for the whole earth. The inhabitants of Canaan had four hundred years since the Lord had chosen Abraham to change their sinful ways. They did not, as the Lord forsaw, so the Israelites conquered them. But Rehab with her family and later the inhabitants of the city of Gideon were spared. All this reflects God's mercy shown to mankind again and again. It also shows what happens when the Lord God ultimately may have to retract His mighty hand from people, nations and even the whole world as happened in Noah's days.

Without God's protection, individuals and nations are left defenceless. As a result, in Noah's days, the flood destroyed the people, their societies and nations. The Lord could also choose to lay His mighty hand on nations imposing acts of judgment to achieve His goals, as He did when He brought the Children of Israel out of Egypt. Since the time of Abraham, the Lord has granted His protection to His people, like He did at the time of Jehoshaphat's reign over the Kingdom of Judah. By the Lord's mighty hand, His wisdom, His understanding and sometimes with great terror He subdues nations, kingdoms and kings.

God's wisdom is at the core of His decision-making, for He is of a higher order than man's, with His untainted knowledge of both heaven and earth. Human beings on the other hand, while having a lack of insight, rely on incomplete and stained knowledge.

Hence the Lord said, *'Let not the wise man glory in his wisdom, neither let the mighty man glory in his might, let not the rich man glory in his riches; but let him that glories glory in this, that he understands, and knows Me, that I am HaShem who exercise mercy, justice, and righteousness, in the earth; for in these things I delight'.*

The nations that allied themselves with evil will also be judged. That's the reason evil should be avoided, as well as seeking comfort from idols through idolatry. God Almighty is a righteous God. If not, how else could evilness and wickedness be overcome?

There will be a time of judgment and punishment for all these nations and their gods. Divine punishment awaits nations during the lifetime of a generation appointed by the Lord, especially the nations who ill-treated God's people when in exile and as a nation. The Lord will avenge the blood of His people.

> *For thus said HaShem of hosts Who sent me after glory to the nations which plundered you: Surely, he that touches you touches the apple of His eye ... For behold, I will shake My hand over them, and they shall be a plundered to those that served them.*
>
> Zechariah 2:12-13

The Lord passes His judgment over those He wants to be judged during their lifetime or at the end of their life. His judgment came over Balaam, who was out for a profit by cursing the Israelites on Balak's request. Balaam, loving the earnings that his wicked practice would bring him, was ready to be of service to the king of Moab. Nevertheless the Lord made sure Balaam would bless the Israelites again and again. He even prophesied about their future king. Later when the Israelites were staying in Shittim, Moab's women followed Balaam's advice to lure the Israelites into becoming unfaithful to the Lord by mingling with their men. They invited them to the sacrifices they held for their idols, where the men bowed for the women's idols, ate their sacrificial food and committed sexual immorality. This aroused God's anger and He told Moses that all the leaders involved in such practices should be exposed and put to death. Moses in turn spoke to the judges and they carried out as they were told. This plague under the Israelites did not stop until Phinehas, the son of Aaron's son Eleazar, took a spear and killed Zimri son of Salu who was leader of a Simeonite family and the Midianite woman, daughter of a tribal chief of a Midianite family, who was with him at that moment in the Israelite encampment.

Moses, Phinehas and the rest of the assembly, who were weeping at the entrance of the Tent of Meeting because of the plague, saw Zimri take her into his tent. For Phinehas' act, with which he made atonement for the Israelites and restored God's honour, the Lord made a covenant of peace and a covenant of lasting priesthood with him and his descendants. Twenty-four thousand men were killed by the plague. Because of this Peor incident, the Lord told Moses to treat the Midianites as enemies as they had treated them as such when they deceived them with their women. When the Israelites were encamped on the plains of Moab, by the Jordan River across Jericho, they went to war with the Midianites. Among those killed were the five kings of Midian, Balaam and the Midianite women, except those who did not have sexual relations. The Lord told Moses to take vengeance on the Midianites for the Israelites before he would be gathered to his ancestors.

Centuries later, the Lord God would pass His judgment over the kings of the Kingdom of Israel and much later after the division into two kingdoms – the Kingdom of Judah and the northern Kingdom of Israel. He sometimes reveals His judgment in a personal manner through His servants the prophets, who would also speak of the consequences following people's actions. He then sends His prophets out to bring His message to the person in question, as he did to some of the kings of Israel and Judah. When the kings were personally punished, all the people who joined their king's sinful actions would be punished with him. The kings Saul, Solomon and even King David experienced this. So did kings during the reign of Asa, the third king of the Kingdom of Judah and the fifth king of the House of David. He succeeded his father Abijam son of Rehoboam, and ruled since the twentieth year of Jeroboam's Kingdom of Israel. During Asa's reign, several kings came and went to rule over the Kingdom of Israel. Asa ruled for forty-one years, with his son Jehoshaphat as co-regent the last two years of his reign. After his death Jehoshaphat succeeded him as king over Judah, while Ahab was in the fourth year of his reign over Israel. In the seventeenth year of Jehosaphat's reign, Ahaziah would succeed his father Ahab as king over Israel. Unlike Ahab and his descendants, Asa and his household were faithful to the Lord, although they didn't destroy the high places for idol worship in Judah.

God raised Jeroboam up from among the people and appointed him ruler over His people in Israel. But, the same prophet Ahijah who told Jeroboam he would be king, would later also prophesy against him and his house. God's judgment over Jeroboam and his house would come to pass at the hand of Baasha. After Solomon's death, Jeroboam became king of the northern Kingdom of Israel and wanted to insure that his subjects wouldn't rebel against him and join the Kingdom of Judah. He was sure that he could realise this by preventing the people from going to Jerusalem to celebrate the feasts of the Lord. So, he devised his own religion with its calendar, feasts, priesthood, altars and shrines on high places. He presented two calves as the god that brought the Israelites out of Egypt and placed one with its altar in Bethel and the other one in Dan. He consecrated anyone who wanted to be a priest, as priests for the high places. He himself brought offerings at the altar in Bethel. These sins would lead to the destruction of Jeroboam's household, the discontinuation of his royal line and finally to the expulsion of the Israelites out of the Land.

One day when Jeroboam stood at the altar in Bethel to bring his offerings, a man from God came from Judah. By God's word, he spoke against the altar saying, '*altar, altar, thus says HaShem: Behold, a son shall be born to the house of David, Josiah by name; and upon you shall he sacrifice the priests of the high places that offer upon you, and men's bones shall they burn upon you*'.

He also gave a sign saying, '*This is the sign which HaShem has spoken: Behold, the altar shall be split, and the ashes that are upon it shall be poured out*'. When Jeroboam heard this, he stretched out his hand and ordered his guards to seize the man. He became aware of the fact that he couldn't pull back his hand that became shrivelled, dried-up. The altar split and poured out its ashes. Then the king asked the man to intercede with God on his behalf concerning his hand. He did, and the king's hand was fine. Subsequently the man turned down an invitation of the king for a meal and a gift. The Lord commanded him not to eat bread, drink water, nor return by the same way he travelled to Bethel. Later on, two men who also witnessed what happened told their father, an old prophet in Bethel, the story and everything the man from Judah had said. Immediately he told his sons to saddle his donkey and he set out to meet the man of God. He found him sitting under an oak tree and after he inquired whether he was the one he was looking for, he asked him to come to his house for a meal. The man didn't want to go with him, and he told him the reason. But the old prophet insisted by telling him that an angel of the Lord had come to him and told him to bring the man back to his house in the city so he could eat bread and drink water. So they went to his house, where they sat down and had a meal. During the meal the Lord's word came to the old prophet and he said, *'Thus says HaShem: For as much as you have rebelled against the word of HaShem, and have not kept the commandment which HaShem your God commanded you, but came back, and have eaten bread and drunk water in the place of which He said to you: Eat no bread, and drink no water; your carcass shall not come to the sepulchre of your fathers'.*

As it happened, what the old prophet told him about the angel of the Lord, was a lie. After the meal the man left on his donkey. But along the way, a lion attacked him and left him dead on the road. Some people who passed by on that road saw the body with the lion and the donkey next to it. They reported about it in the city. As soon as the old prophet heard about this, he knew he had to be the man from Judah. Thinking his body was mutilated by then, he went on his donkey to him. But, the lion had not eaten the body nor cleaved the donkey. Both of them, lion and donkey, stood beside the man's body. He picked him up, brought him to his city where they mourned over him and buried him in his own grave. Afterwards he told his sons that when he dies they have to bury him in the same grave with the man from Judah. He also said that the word spoken against the altar at Bethel, the shrines and high places would certainly come to pass. His death and burial was also a sign that what he prophesied against Jeroboam's altar would certainly come through. It would, many years later at the hand of Josiah, a king of Judah. But despite the word of the Lord and the events at Bethel, Jeroboam didn't change his ways. He continued to consecrate whoever wanted to be priest as such for the high places he created, and to lead the inhabitants of his kingdom to a sinful path.

Years later, Jeroboam sent his wife, in disguise so he would not recognise her as being his wife, to speak to the prophet. She was to speak with Ahijah on the matter of his son Abijah who fell ill. Before she arrived the Lord spoke to Ahijah, who because of his age didn't have good eyesight, about Jeroboam's wife coming to see him while pretending to be someone else, and told him what to answer her. So, as soon as he heard her footsteps, he invited Jeroboam's wife in and told her immediately that the Lord had sent him with bad news. He told her to give Jeroboam the Lord's message. That because he didn't act like his servant David who kept God's commands and followed Him with all his heart, doing only what was right in His eyes, He would bring disaster over Jeroboam and his house. Jeroboam did more evil than all those before him. He had made for himself other gods, set up poles and shrines for them, made idols of metal, and turned his back on the Lord arousing His anger. Because of Jeroboam's sins and the sins he had caused Israel to commit, the Lord would cut off the family of Jeroboam and eliminate all his male descendants. He would annihilate Jeroboam's house. In time He would also give Israel up, by uprooting the Israelites and then scatter them beyond the Euphrates River. This would happen years later at the time Jehu would be king of Israel. But, Jeroboam's son Abijah would be the only one of Jeroboam's house that would be buried, because he is the only one in whom the Lord had found some good. All the others who would die in the city, would be eaten by dogs, and those who die outside the city would be food for the birds. Jeroboam's wife left and went to Tirzah. Abijah died of his illness as soon as his mother set foot in the city, just as Ahijah had prophesied. After Jeroboam died, he was succeeded by his son Nadab, who reigned two years over Israel. He and all Jeroboam's family was killed by Baasha in accordance to the word given by Ahijah.

God lifted Baasha, of the tribe of Issachar, up and appointed him ruler over His people. He reigned twenty-four years, but wasn't faithful to the Lord. Because he followed the ways of Jeroboam, prophesy was spoken against him by Jehu the son of Hanani, *'For as much as I exalted you out of the dust, and made you prince over My people Israel; and you have walked in the way of Jeroboam, and have made My people Israel to sin, to provoke Me with their sins; behold, I will utterly sweep away Baasha and his house; and I will make your house like the house of Jeroboam the son of Nebat. He that dies of Baasha in the city shall the dogs eat; and he that dies in the field shall the fowls of the air eat'.*

After Baasha's death, Elah his son succeeded him and ruled for two years. Elah would be followed by Zimri, who would only rule for seven days. He was one of Elah's officials, commander over half of his chariots. Zimri kept away from the army and their proclaimed king, Omri. They had chosen him instead of Zimri. Omri laid siege to Tirzah after they found out about Zimri's plot against Elah. While Elah was getting drunk in the house of the palace administrator at Tirzah, Zimri assassinated him, and declared himself king. Then he killed Baasha's entire family, leaving no male relatives or friends, as was prophesied would happen. Zimri killed himself by setting fire to the citadel of the royal palace in Tirzah where he was in hiding from Omri.

So, Zimri died in the flames and was followed by Omri the commander of Israel's army, who fought about four years to defeat his rival Tibni son of Ginath. Tibni died, and Omri became king over Israel and ruled six years from Tirzah, just as his predecessors, and six years from Samaria where he bought a plot of land and built a city. From then on, Israel would be ruled from Samaria. The tribal origin of both Zimri and Omri wasn't mentioned, nor any reference to their relatives. If they were not Israelites this would have been in contradiction to the Lord's regulation that only an Israelite should be king over the Israelites. All these events happened during the reign of Asa the king of Judah. Omri's son Ahab succeeded him and he reigned for twenty-two years. He was the seventh king of Israel.

> *See now that I, even I, am He, and there is no god with Me; I kill, and I make alive; I have wounded, and I heal; and there is none that can deliver out of My hand.*
>
> Deuteronomy 32:39

During Ahab's reign, the prophet Elijah fled after he received a message from Ahab's wife Jezebel. By her gods, she threatened Elijah with death, because he had her priests killed on Mount Carmel. Then Elijah, knowing his life was again in danger, travelled with his servant to Beersheba in Judah where he left him, and went a day's journey into the desert.

Ready to die, he sat under a broom bush and prayed to the Lord to take his life because he had enough, and he added that he was no better than his ancestors. He fell asleep under the bush. But, immediately an angel of the Lord came, touched him and told him to get up and eat. When Elijah looked around he found by his head some bread baked over hot coals and a jar of water. He ate, drank and fell asleep. The angel returned, woke Elijah up and told him to eat because otherwise his journey would be too much for him. Elijah then, strengthened by the food, travelled forty days and nights to the mountain of God, Mount Horeb, where Moses once met the Lord at the burning bush on holy ground. Once there Elijah hid himself in a cave to spend the night. But, the Lord saw him and His word came to him asking him what he was doing there. Elijah, convinced he was the only prophet left in Israel, replied that he was very zealous for Him, but that the Israelites had rejected His covenant, torn down His altars, killed His prophets and were seeking to kill him too.

Elijah was told to go out and stand on the mountain for the Lord God was about to pass by. A great wind came, followed by an earthquake, and then a fire. The Lord wasn't in these, but in a gentle whisper, a still sound. As soon as Elijah heard it, he put his cloak over his face, went out and remained standing at the entrance of the cave. Then a voice asked him what he was doing there. He gave the same answer as before. The Lord gave him an assignment despite everything Elijah had said. He was to travel to the wilderness of Damascus, where he had to anoint Hazael to be king of Aram. He also had to anoint Jehu son of Nimshi to be king over Israel and Elisha son of Shaphat from Abel Meholah to succeed him as prophet. The Lord also told Elijah that Jehu would kill all who escapes Hazael's sword, and Elisha would put to death anyone who escapes the sword of Jehu.

Elijah left Mount Horeb. Later on he found Elisha who left family and land behind to follow and serve Elijah. Sometime later Elijah ascended in a chariot with horses of fire leaving Elisha behind. As his successor, Elisha would prophecy to Hazael, a servant of Ben-Hadad the Aramean king, that he would become king of Aram and do much harm to the Israelites. Elisha would also send a prophet to anoint Jehu to be king over Israel.

The king of Aram, Ben-Hadad laid siege to Samaria and demanded Ahab's gold, silver and the best of his wives and children. After Ahab agreed to his demands, he consulted with his officials about a second message sent by Ben-Hadad. His officials, the elders and the people told him to refuse Ben Hadad's demand to let his officials search Ahab's palace and the houses of his officials the next day, and take everything of value with them. By his gods Ben-Hadad and the thirty-one allied kings with their horses and chariots went to war with Ahab. While Ben-Hadad's and his allies' army were preparing for an attack on Samaria, he and his thirty-two allied kings were in their tents getting drunk.

Meanwhile a prophet came to speak with Ahab. He assured Ahab that the Lord would give him the victory. On Ahab's questions regarding this victory, the prophet answered that he himself would start the battle and that his junior officers under the provincial commanders with their men would defeat the enemy. Ahab sent out his two hundred and thirty-two junior officers and seven thousand Israelites. They inflicted heavy casualties on the vast army of the Arameans. The prophet of the Lord told Ahab that Ben-Hadad would attack him again next Spring. So he was to strengthen his position. As prophesied the king of Aram returned the next spring to fight the

Israelites. He believed his officials who advised him to attack Israel again on the plains. They told him that the gods of the Israelites were gods of the hills, unlike their own gods who were of the plains. If they would attack Israel on the plains then they would win the battle.

Ben-Hadad went with his large army, compared with that of Israel, to Aphek. The man of God went to Ahab with the message that God would deliver Ben-Hadad's vast army in his hands, so he would know that He is the Lord. He also told him about the Arameans' belief concerning gods of the heights and plains. The two armies were encamped six days opposite each other and the seventh day the battle started. The Israelites were greatly outnumbered by the Arameans, but they inflicted one hundred thousand casualties on the Arameans, while another twenty-seven thousand that escaped to the city of Aphek, died when its wall collapsed. Ben-Hadad and his officials hid themselves in an inner room in the city. His officials convinced him to surrender to the king of Israel. He did, but instead of having Ben-Hadad killed, Ahab pardoned him. He even made a treaty with him, which would grant Israel the return of the places conquered from the Israelites by Ben-Hadad's father. This was a pact that Ben-Hadad wouldn't keep concerning Ramoth Gilead, and which would cause a new war between Aram and Israel three years later. The outcome of the war caused the Lord to send a prophet of the company of prophets to Ahab. The prophet told Ahab that because he disobeyed the Lord in taking the complete victory over Aram by killing its king in battle, it would be Ahab's life for Ben-Hadad's life, and Ahab's people for his people. Angry and glumly Ahab returned to his palace in Samaria. One day he would die in battle, but not before more prophecies would be spoken against him.

Sometime later in Samaria, Ahab showed an interest in acquiring some land. He inquired from Naboth the Jezreelite about the purchase of his vineyard which was close to his palace. He offered Naboth to pay what it was worth, or pay with another plot of land. But Naboth refused because of the emotional value the land had for him as he had inherited it from his ancestors. After he heard this, the king returned sullen and angry to his palace, where he laid sulking on his bed, refusing to eat. Jezebel came to see her husband and asked him why he was so moody. He told her about Naboth's vineyard and his refusal to sell it to him. Jezebel asked him whether that was the right way to act as king of Israel. She told him to get up, cheer up and eat. She would take care of it. She wrote letters in Ahab's name, placed his seal on them and sent them to all the elders and nobles who lived in the city with the king. The men followed the instructions she gave in the letters. They were to proclaim a day of fasting, seat Naboth on a prominent place among the people and have two scoundrels sit opposite to him to act as two witnesses that would falsely accuse him of cursing God and the king, a transgression for which he would be stoned. After the stoning took place, word was sent to Jezebel that Naboth was dead. Even though Jezebel used her husband's authority to conspire to have Naboth killed, it was known that she herself was behind this conspiracy, for word of Naboth's death was sent to her and not to Ahab. At once Jezebel told the king that Naboth was dead and that he should go to the vineyard to inherit it. Meanwhile word of the Lord came to Elijah telling him to go down to Naboth's vineyard where he would find the king who was there to take possession of it. Once there, Ahab said to Elijah that he, his enemy, had found him. Indeed Elijah had found him, and told him that he had sold himself to do what is evil in the eyes of the Lord. He had murdered a man to seize his property. Therefore at the same place where dogs licked up Naboth's blood, dogs would lick up Ahab's blood. Elijah continued his prophesy in telling Ahab that the Lord would bring disaster on him and his household. He would wipe out his descendants, every last male, slave or free. He would make his house as that of Jeroboam and Baasha because he had aroused His anger and had caused Israel to sin. Those belonging to him who would die in the city would be eaten by dogs, and birds would feed on those who would die outside the city. Furthermore, his wife Jezebel who engaged in occult practices, idol worship and had urged others including her husband to do so, would die a very violent death. She would be devoured by dogs on a plot of land at Jezreel. After hearing all Elijah had to tell him, unlike Jezebel, Ahab showed remorse. He tore his clothes, put on a sackcloth, fasted and he walked around meekly. The Lord noticed him. His word came to Elijah asking him whether he noticed how Ahab humbled himself before Him, and telling him that because Ahab did this, the disaster that He would bring over his household would happen after his death.

Intermezzo

The Rejection

Behold, HaShem's hand is not too short, that it cannot save, neither His ear heavy, that it cannot hear; But your iniquities

> *have separated between you and your God, and your sins have hid His face from you, that He will not hear. Therefore is justice far from us, neither does righteousness overtake us; we look for light, but behold darkness, for brightness, but we walk in gloom.*
>
> Isaiah 59

Since the division of the Kingdom of Israel into the Kingdom of Judah in the south and the Kingdom of Israel in the north, the two kingdoms were often at war with each other, although sometimes they would form alliances to fight their mutual enemies. Regardless of the division, the Lord still expected the inhabitants of both kingdoms to live by His Laws, commandments and regulations. The Lord also wanted their kings to follow King David's example. Neglecting to do these would result in punishment. Moses already foretold centuries ago what would happen to them if they wouldn't listen. The Lord would bring calamity, plague, war, wild beasts over their nation, and ultimately He would scatter them under the nations. But, He would not erase their name from human memory. It was His choice not to destroy them, because for one, the Lord dreaded the taunt of the enemy. Moses once spoke to the Lord about the taunt of the Egyptians if He was to destroy the Israelites in the desert – something He decided He wouldn't have. Secondly, He did make promises to the Israelites' ancestors and to David.

Actually it was the Israelites who rejected the Lord, their God by not keeping up with the moral code, way of life and standards He gave them. Since their deeds already estranged them from the Lord to such degree that He hid His face and would not listen to them anymore. He disciplined the Israelites by exercising measured punishment to that generation living in Israel and more than a century later to the inhabitants of Judah.

> *For My people have committed two evils: they have forsaken Me, the fountain of living waters, and hewed themselves out cisterns, broken cisterns, that can hold no water.*
>
> Jeremiah 2:13

During the reign of Hoshea son of Elah in Samaria, Shalmaneser king of Assyria seized Hoshea, who refused to continue to pay him tribute and conspired against him, and put him into jail. Afterwards he invaded the whole Kingdom of Israel and besieged Samaria three years. He captured Samaria in the ninth year of Hoshea's reign, after which he deported the Israelites to Assyria and had other people live in Israel. The Assyrians also invaded Judah and laid siege to Jerusalem. But, Hezekiah son of Ahaz, who began his reign over Judah in the third year of Hoshea, was faithful to the Lord and sought His help. The Lord intervened on their behalf, and the Assyrian army did not conquer Judah. It would be more than a century after Israel was exiled, during Zedekiah's reign, that God's judgment would come over the Kingdom of Judah.

The two kings, Menasseh and Amon, who were unfaithful to the Lord ruled over Judah after Hezekieah. Because of their wicked and sinful reign the Lord would bring His judgment over Judah. Unlike them, Josiah who reigned after Amon, ruled in accordance to God's will. Nevertheless, despite all King Josiah's efforts in accordance to the Book of Law that the High Priest had found in the Temple of the Lord, the Lord's decision regarding punishment upon the Kingdom of Judah remained because of the seriousness of Menasseh's sins. The Lord must have also foreseen that the kings who would follow after Josiah would also lead the people of Judah astray. Except for the remnant He would keep to Himself, the Lord would remove Judah from His presence as he did with Israel. He would reject Jerusalem, the city He had chosen for His Name to be. Judah would be conquered by the Babylonian king Nebuchadnezzar. He would have the elite, including the prophet Daniel, deported leaving part of the population behind to work the land under a governor appointed by him.

> *For a small moment I have forsaken you; but with great compassion I will gather you. In a little wrath I hid My face from you for a moment; but with everlasting kindness I will have compassion on you, says HaShem your Redeemer. For this is as the waters of Noah to Me; for as I have sworn that the waters of Noah should no more go over the earth, so I have sworn that I would not be wrathful with you, nor rebuke you. For the mountains may depart, and the hills be removed; but My kindness shall not depart from you, neither shall My covenant of peace be removed, says HaShem that has compassion on you.*
>
> Isaiah 54:7-10

Why did the Lord bring such judgment that ultimately led to their rejection upon the Israelites? Because their relation and connection with their God was ruined by their sinful ways, as once happened to Adam and Eve, and subsequently to all mankind. Their sins separated them from the Lord God who cherished them and cared for them, despite the fact that the Lord fulfilled all His promises He made to Israel through Moses. This was something his aide and successor Joshua, a warrior who was constantly present in the Tent of Meeting, also mentioned to the Israelites after they conquered the Land. Centuries later Solomon would confirm his words.

The Israelites ignored the Lord's warnings and calls for repentance brought through His servants the prophets. As a result, the inhabitants of the kingdoms of Judah and Israel of a certain generation, determined by the Lord, were expelled from the Land.

It wasn't the first time the Lord passed judgment over the Israelites. He did over the first generation He took out of Egypt before they conquered Canaan. He did not allow them, but their descendants with Joshua and Caleb, to enter the Promised Land. They would not experience the life He wanted to give them in the Land. But, the Lord showed mercy by allowing them to live as long as for forty years despite their sins and transgressions. He showed His compassion for them in taking care of them while they were wandering in the wilderness. That generation, who experienced crossing the Sea of Reeds, would not enter the Promised Land.

> *For HaShem will not cast off His people, neither will He forsake His inheritance.*
>
> Psalm 94:14

This time while the children the Lord Himself had brought up were living in the Land, they rebelled against Him. Israel didn't know their Lord, while even the ox knew his master and the donkey its owner's manger. So, with His eyes on this sinful kingdom, He said through the prophet Amos, *'I will destroy it from off the face of the earth; saving that I will not utterly destroy the House of Jacob'*, says HaShem, *'For I will command, and I will sift the House of Israel among all the nations, like as corn is sifted in a sieve, yet shall not the least grain fall upon the earth'*.

The Lord evicted them from the Land, leaving a few behind as He intended from the start. But as before, He would punish them for a time set by Himself. The Lord has always been a forgiving God to His people. Through His prophets He made it clear that this would not be for ever, because one day He Himself would return them from all over the world to the Land. Just as He had chosen by Himself to bring Abraham and centuries later his descendants to His Land, He would do this again, but then on a much larger and grand scale. Again, He would plant them in their own Land and nourish them with all they need. At that time the Israelites would have already began their process of showing their repentance from their actions and that of their ancestors. As the prophet Daniel would one day show and start to pray while in exile. They would as well have already begun to be and become even more faithful to the Lord. The same prophets who spoke about God's rejection also prophesied about His reconciliation with Jerusalem and with the Children of Israel, their return out of captivity to the Land, and the unification of the Kingdom of Judah and Israel to one nation governed by one ruler!

> *And the word of HaShem came to Jeremiah, saying: Have you not considered what this people have spoken, saying: The two families which HaShem did choose, He has cast them off? and they despise My people, that they should be no more a nation before them. Thus says HaShem: If My covenant be not with day and night, if I have not appointed the ordinances of heaven and earth; then will I also cast away the seed of Jacob, and of David My servant, so that I will not take of his seed to be rulers over the seed of Abraham, Isaac, and Jacob; for I will cause their captives to return, and will have compassion on them.*
>
> Jeremiah 33:23-26

> *Thus says the Lord God: When I shall have gathered the house of Israel from the people among whom they are scattered, and shall be sanctified in them in the sight of the nations, then shall they dwell in their own land which I gave to My servant Jacob.*
>
> Ezekiel 28:25

More War

Three years later after their last encounter, Ahab and Ben-Hadad were at war again. Ahab wanted the city of Ramoth Gilead, one of the cities Ben-Hadad neglected to return to Israel based on the treaty they agreed upon. This time Ahab allied himself with the king of Judah, Jehoshaphat the son of Asa. Ahab ignored the warning of the one prophet, summoned on Jehoshaphat's request, who truthfully spoke concerning Ahab's military campaign.

Micaiah, incarcerated afterwards by Ahab and put on a ration of bread and water, told Ahab that he saw all of Israel scattered on the hills like sheep without a shepherd. The Lord said that they had no master and therefore each should go home in peace. As for Ahab, he would not return home safely despite the fact that he went to battle in disguise, while Jehoshaphat wore his royal robe.

Meanwhile Ben-Hadad had ordered his thirty-two chariot commanders to only fight the king of Israel and no one else. He wanted to be sure that Ahab would be killed. During the battle they first started to pursue Jehoshaphat thinking, because of his clothes, that he was the king of Israel. As soon as they realised he was not Ahab they stopped chasing him. Suddenly someone fired a bow at random, which hit the king between the sections of his armour inflicting a fatal wound. The army commander Naaman was the one who fired the lethal arrow. This placed him in high regarded with his king. Sometime later Naaman went to see the prophet Elisha to find a cure for his skin disease. One of his wife's servants, a girl taken during a raid in Israel, told her about Elisha. Naaman went to see Elisha bearing gifts. Urged by his servants he followed Elisha's instructions given to him through Elisha's servant Gehazi, to wash himself seven times in the Jordan River for him to be cured. Elisha did not accept any of the gifts Naaman had brought for him, contrary to Gehazi who disobeyed Elisha. The Lord uncovered this to Elisha, and He punished him by giving him the skin disease that Naaman had. Elisha made it clear to Gehazi that it just wasn't the time for him to make money and acquire earthly wealth. Naaman returned cured to his country. Ahab, now severely wounded, ordered his chariot officer to take him out of the fighting. But, the battle fired up and raged all day long. So Ahab was forced to face his enemy. He was propped up in his chariot, while the blood of his wound ran down on the chariot until sunset, when a cry went through his army saying that every man should go to his town, to his land. Ahab died that evening, and was taken to Samaria where he was buried. At the pool where they washed his blood of his chariot, dogs licked up his blood, as was prophesied.

Ahab's ally Jehoshaphat returned to his palace in Jerusalem where he was confronted by the seer Jehu son of Hanani, who went out to meet him. He asked him whether he should have helped the wicked and make alliances with those who hate the Lord. However, he also told him there was some good in him because he had rid the Land of poles used for idol worship and he had set his heart on seeking God. Before the war campaign with Ahab, Jehoshaphat did what was good in the eyes of the Lord in Judah by following in the ways of his father David. His heart was devoted to God, while he sought God and followed His commands, rather than the practices of Israel's idol worshippers. He fortified cities and the Ephraimite towns that his father Asa had captured from Israel. He removed the high places and the poles. The Lord established the Kingdom of Judah firmly under his control. He gave him great honour and wealth while all Judah brought him gifts.

During the third year of his reign, Jehoshaphat sent his officials, some Levites and the priests Elishama and Jehoram to teach the people in all the towns of Judah. For that purpose they took the Lord's Book of Law with them. Moses commanded that at the end of every seventh year, the year of cancelling debts and setting Israelite slaves free, the Book of Law should be read during the Festival of Tabernacles.

The fear of the Lord fell on all the surrounding kingdoms, who didn't want to go to war against him. Instead they, the Philistines and Arabs, brought him gifts, silver and flocks. Jehoshaphat's power grew. He built fortresses and store cities in Judah, while he kept large supplies in Judah's towns. He kept experienced armed commanders and soldiers in Jerusalem, and also soldiers in Judah's fortified cities. After his military campaign with Ahab, Jehoshaphat went through Judah and the hill country of Ephraim, and appointed judges. He told them they would be judging for the Lord, and encouraged them to judge carefully. For Him injustice, partiality or bribery was not acceptable. In Jerusalem he also set up an administration of appointed Levites, priests and heads of families to administer the Law of the Lord and settle disputes. He told them to be faithful, to wholeheartedly be in fear of the Lord, and to warn people not to sin against Him. He appointed the chief Kohen, priest, over the officials, Levites, regarding the matters of the Lord, and the leader of Judah's tribe in matters concerning the king.

Sometime after the war with the Arameans, the Moabites, Ammonites and men from Mount Seir marched out to wage war against Judah. They were already at En Gedi, and Jehoshaphat, realizing that this combined army was to vast to be faced by Judah alone, proclaimed a fast for all Judah and inquired of the Lord what he should do. The people of Judah, men with their wives and children, came out of every town to stand before the Lord and seek His help. There in front of the new courtyard accessing the temple complex of the Lord's Temple on Mount Moriah in Jerusalem, Jehoshaphat stood up in the assembly of Judah and Jerusalem, and prayed, *'O HaShem, the God of our fathers, are You not alone God in heaven? And are You not ruler over all the kingdoms of the nations? And in Your hand is power and might, so that none is able to withstand You. Did not You, O our God, drive out the inhabitants of this land before Your people Israel, and gave it to the seed of Abraham Your friend for ever? And they dwelt there, and have built You a sanctuary there for Your name, saying: If evil come upon us, the sword, judgment, or pestilence, or famine, we will stand before this house, and before You – for Your name is in this house – and cry unto You in our affliction, and You will hear and save. And now, behold, the children of Ammon and Moab and mount Seir, whom You would not let Israel invade, when they came out of the land of Egypt, but they turned aside from them, and destroyed them not; behold, they render unto us evil, to come to cast us out of Your possession, which You has given us to inherit. O our God, will You not execute judgment on them? For we have no might against this great multitude that comes against us; neither know we what to do; but our eyes are upon You'.*

The Lord heard the king's prayer and His Spirit came on Jahaziel, a descendant of Asaph a Levite.

He said to the king and all who lived in Judah and Jerusalem to listen to what the Lord had to say to them, *'Fear not you, neither be dismayed by reason of this great multitude; for the battle is not yours, but God's. Tomorrow you go down against them; behold, they come up by the ascent of Ziz; and you shall find them at the end of the valley, before the wilderness of Jeruel. You shall not need to fight in this battle; set yourselves, you stand still, and see the salvation of HaShem with you, O Judah and Jerusalem; fear not, nor be dismayed; tomorrow go out against them; for HaShem is with you'.*

Jehoshaphat bowed down in worship to the Lord, and so did all the people present. Afterwards some Levites of the Kohathites and Korahites stood up and praised the Lord of Israel. The next morning before they left for the desert of Tekoa, the king told them, *'Listen to me, Judah and people of Jerusalem! Have faith in the Lord your God and you will be upheld; have faith in his prophets and you will be successful'.*

As the army set out, men appointed by the king, after consulting with the people, went upfront singing praise to the Lord for His splendour and holiness, giving thanks for His love that endures for ever. Once they arrived at the place that overlooks the desert where the vast army of their enemies were, they saw only dead bodies lying around with among them a great amount of equipment and objects of value. How could this be? The moment they started singing, the Lord caused the Ammonites and Moabites to attack and annihilate the men from Mount Seir. There they fought and destroyed each other. No one escaped. It took Judah three days to collect all the plunder. The fourth day they assembled and praised the Lord in the Valley of Berakah. Then under Jehoshaphat's leadership they returned joyful to Jerusalem, where they went to the Temple of the Lord with harps, lyres and trumpets.

The surrounding kingdoms were in great fear after they heard how the Lord fought for the Israelites. The Lord gave peace at every side of the Land during Jehoshaphat's further reign. Later the king would make an alliance with Ahaziah, Ahab's son and successor. His ways were wicked and he was unfaithful to the Lord. The king agreed with Ahaziah, to build a fleet of trading ships at Ezion Geber. Although Jehoshaphat refused to allow the ships to be partly manned by Ahaziah's men, Eliezer son of Dodavahu of Mareshah, prophesied against Jehoshaphat. He told him that because he had made an alliance with Ahaziah, the Lord would destroy the fleet. The ships were shipwrecked in port and had never set sail to Tarshish for trade. Jehoshaphat reigned twenty-five years, and his son Jehoram succeeded him.

Ahab's enemy Ben-Hadad lived to put Samaria under siege more than two years later, at the time Joram, Ahab's son, was king of Israel. After Ahaziah's death, Joram succeeded his brother who reigned only two years. He died of a serious illness caused by an injury suffered when he fell, leaving no children to succeed him. Joram became king in the second year that Jehoram, son of Jehoshaphat was king of Judah. Ben-Hadad at war with only Israel, would confer with his officers on where he would set up his military camp. One day the king of Aram was so enraged that he summoned his officers demanding from them to tell him which one of them was on the side of the Israelites. One of his officers replied that Elisha the prophet who is in Israel was the one hindering them by revealing their plans to the king of Israel, telling him the very words their king speaks in his bedroom. As it happened each time Ben-Hadad and his officers agreed on a place to set up camp, the man of God would send word to Joram telling him to beware of the Arameans being in such and such place. Joram would then send out his men to check out these locations.

After Ben-Hadad received his men's report about Elisha's whereabouts, he ordered a strong army force with horses and chariots to go to Dothan to capture Elisha. But, by divine intervention they didn't seize Elisha. So for a while the Arameans stopped their raids of Israel. But not for long. After sometime Ben-Hadad mobilised his entire army, laid siege to Samaria, having the inhabitants go through much suffering. The great famine in the city caused people to resort to cannibalism to survive. One time as the king walked by on the wall, a woman cried to him asking him for help. The king replied that if the Lord could not help her, from where should he get help for her, and subsequently asked her what the matter was with her. As it turned out, the woman had agreed with another woman that they would eat each other's son, one on that day, the other the following day. Having cooked and eaten the son of the woman who cried to the king first, the next day the other woman hid her son and refused to have her child eaten by them. The king tore his robe after he heard that horrific story, and everyone could see he had a sackcloth underneath it. The king swore by God about beheading Elisha on that same day, and he sent a messenger ahead to Elisha's house.

In the meantime Elisha, sitting at home with the elders, asked them whether they could see that the king, a murderer, is sending a man to cut off his head. He told them to shut the door for the man, while he spoke of the sound of the messenger's master's footsteps being behind him. But while he was talking to them, the messenger already arrived and approached him. So did the king soon after him. The king told Elisha that the unfolding disaster in Samaria was from the Lord, and he asked why he should wait for the Lord any longer. Then Elisha prophesied that by that time tomorrow there would be plenty of the finest floor and barley for sale at the gate of Samaria. The officer on whose arm the king was leaning could not believe it, and he said that even if God would open the floodgates of heaven, this prophesy just couldn't be possible. Elisha replied telling him, he would see it with his own eyes, but he would not eat any of it. The king was reluctant to have Elisha beheaded when he heard the prophesy. This was the second time the Lord saved Elisha's life, as He did sometime before, when Ben-Hadad sent a well-armed troop of his men to kill him.

Meanwhile four men with leprosy were at the entrance of Samaria's city gate. They had to decide amongst themselves what to do. Should they go inside the city and die of famine, or should they go to the Aramean camp and surrender whether they live or die? At dusk they went on their way. When they arrived at the edge of the camp, they found it to be deserted. Since no one was there, they entered one of the tents, ate, drank, took silver, gold and cloths, and went off to hide them somewhere. Afterwards they went to another tent, took some things and hid these too. But why was the Aramean camp empty? Because at nightfall the Arameans fled from their camp in such a hurry leaving everything untouched behind, while abandoning even their horses and donkeys. They were terrified of the great Egyptian and Hittite army with their chariots and horses attacking them. They were certain they were hired by the king of Israel to help him fight and defeat them. But, there was no army. They only heard the sound of a great army. A sound caused by the Lord. The four men, realizing that keeping the good news of the army's departure wasn't right and could bring about punishment for them, went to report it to the royal palace. At the city gate they called to the gatekeepers and told them the news. They in turn shouted the news to others that reported it to the royal palace. The king got up at night and said about the news that it was a trap of the Arameans to get into the city, for as soon as they would open the gate and go out, the Arameans would come from the countryside where they were in hiding and enter the city. But one of his officers said to let some men go out to find out what happened to the Arameans. If not, they would die anyway in the city. They sent some men with two chariots and horses. They chased the Arameans, following all the clothes and equipment that they left along their escape route, which led them to the Jordan River. They returned and reported to the king. The people of the city went out and plundered the camp. They were selling flour and barley as Elisha had prophesied, and his prophecy concerning the man on whose arm the king was leaning also came to pass. The king put him in charge of the gate, where he died when he was trampled by the people going through the gate. One day, long after this war, Samaria would come under siege of the Assyrians. That war would result in the expulsion of the Israelites out of the Kingdom of Israel.

Sometime later after Ben-Hadad besieged Samaria, he fell ill. When he heard that Elisha was in Damascus, he sent Hazael with a gift of forty camel-loads of Damascus' finest goods to Elisha, to inquire about his recovery. As soon as he asked the question to Elisha, he answered him to tell the king that he would certainly recover. Nevertheless Ben-Hadad would die, as the Lord also revealed to Elisha. Then to Hazael's embarrassment Elisha stared at him with a fixed gaze, as he started to weep. Hazael asked him why he was weeping. He replied, because he saw how much harm he would cause to the Israelites. He would burn their fortified places, kill their young men by the sword, dash their children to the ground and their pregnant women he would rip open.

Hazael asked him, how a mere dog like him could ever accomplish such deeds. Because, Elisha told him, he would become king of Aram. Hazael returned to Ben-Hadad and gave him the good news that he would recover. The next day he visited him again. He took a thick cloth, soaked it in water, put it on the king's face, and smothered Ben-Hadad to death. Hazael took over his throne.

Jehoram son of Jehoshaphat was king of Judah for eight years, after which his son Ahaziah son of Athaliah, who was a granddaughter of Omri the father of Ahab, ascended to the throne. Jehoram didn't follow in King David's footsteps and neither did his son Ahaziah who followed the ways of Ahab's house to which he was related in marriage. But for the sake of David, the Lord was not willing to destroy Judah, as he had promised to keep a lamp for David's descendants for ever. Ahaziah became king of Judah in the twelfth year of Joram's reign in Samaria. Ahaziah went together with Joram to war against Hazael, king of Aram. At Ramoth Gilead. Joram was forced to retreat to Jezreel where he could recover from a wound caused during battle.

In the meantime Elisha arranged to carry out the word spoken by the Lord to Elijah. That is, to anoint Jehu son of Jehosaphat, son of Nimshi, to be king of Israel. He sent a young prophet of the prophets' company to Jehu. He gave him specific instructions. As soon as he got there he was to look for Jehu, take him away from his companions into an inner room, pour the oil out of the flask on his head and declare, 'Thus says HaShem: I have anointed you king over Israel'.

As soon as he was finished, he was to run away from there to be safe. The prophet went to Ramoth Gilead and found Israel's army commander Jehu with his officers. With Joram absent, they were defending Ramoth Gilead against Hazael. He told them he had a message for the commander. Jehu got up and went into the house followed by the young prophet. He poured the oil over Jehu's head and declared, *'Thus says HaShem, the God of Israel: I have anointed you king over the people of HaShem, even over Israel. And you shall smite the house of Ahab your master, that I may avenge the blood of*

My servants the prophets, and the blood of all the servants of HaShem, at the hand of Jezebel. For the whole house of Ahab shall perish; and I will cut off from Ahab every man-child, and him that is shut up and him that is left at large in Israel. And I will make the house of Ahab like the house of Jeroboam the son of Nebat, and like the house of Baasha the son of Ahijah. And the dogs shall eat Jezebel in the portion of Jezreel, and there shall be none to bury her'.

Then without delay he opened the door and ran. Jehu returned outside to his fellow officers. Curious, one of them asked him why that maniac, referring to the prophet, came to see him. He replied that they knew the man and the sort of things he would have to say. They said that that wasn't true and insisted that he should tell them. Then, keeping the rest of the message to himself, he told them that the prophet anointed him king of Israel. Quickly they took their robes and spread them on the bare steps under him, and enthusiastically they blew the trumpet and shouted, *'Jehu is king'*.

Jehu conspired with the army officers against Joram, and told them that if they wished him to be king, they shouldn't let anyone leave the city to go and tell the news in Jezreel, where Joram was resting and his relative Ahaziah the king of Judah went to visit him.

Sometime later in Jezreel, the lookout on the tower shouted he saw some troops approaching. Joram ordered a horseman to ask whether they came in peace. Once the man reached the troops he didn't go back, instead he joined the flanks as ordered. So a second horseman was sent. The lookout reported that he too wasn't returning with news. He also said that the driver of the chariot drove like a maniac, so it had to be Jehu. Joram ordered for his chariot to be readied. Joram and Ahaziah, each one in his own chariot, rode out to meet Jehu. They met with each other at the plot of Naboth the Jezreelite, and as soon as Joram saw Jehu he asked him whether he came in peace. He replied, how could there be peace as long as the witchcraft and idolatry of his mother Jezebel was still going on. Joram immediately turned around, calling out treachery to Ahaziah to warn him. Jehu shot Joram with his bow. The arrow penetrated between his shoulders, pierced his heart, and he slumped down in his chariot. Jehu ordered his chariot officer to pick Joram up and throw his body on Nabot's plot of land. As Jehu remembered him of the prophecy spoken against Ahab, Joram's father, when they were riding behind him. *'Surely I have seen yesterday the blood of Naboth, and the blood of his sons, says HaShem; and I will requite you in this plot, says HaShem'.*

Then Jehu and his men chased Ahaziah. Jehu gave the order that they should kill him too. They wounded Ahaziah in his chariot on the way to Gur near Ibleam. But he managed to escape. He reached Megiddo where he died. His servants took him by chariot to Jerusalem where he was buried in his tomb in the City of David. There is where the other kings of Judah, including David, were also put to rest. Athaliah, Ahaziah's mother, seized his throne by murdering off Ahaziah's royal family, her own relatives, except for one. Ultimately she would be dethroned in the seventh year of her reign.

After the chase, Jehu went to Jezreel where Jezebel was staying. Jezebel already knew about what happened. She put on some makeup and arranged her hair. She looked out of the window as Jehu entered the gate of Jezreel. She looked down on him, asking him whether he came in peace. Jehu looked up at the window and shouted asking who was on his side. Two or three of Jezebel's eunuchs looked down at Jehu. He told them to throw her down. So they did. As the horses trampled over Jezebel, some of her blood spattered against the wall. Jehu went in the city, he ate, drank and told some people to take care of that cursed woman and bury her, after all she was a king's daughter. When they went out, they couldn't find her. They only found her skull, hands and feet. They went back and told Jehu, who replied, *'This is the word of HaShem, which He spoke by His servant Elijah the Tishbite, saying: In the portion of Jezreel shall the dogs eat the flesh of Jezebel; and the carcass of Jezebel shall be as dung upon the face of the field in the portion of Jezreel; so that they shall not say: This is Jezebel'*.

Jehu, still in Jezreel, planned to destroy Ahab's whole royal house. He wrote letters to Samaria, for the officials at Jezreel, the elders and guardians of Ahab's seventy sons, telling them to choose one of them as their king. At their fortified city with horses, chariots and their king they should fight for their master's house. This way he warned them that he was coming and at the same time gave them the chance to fight. But, they were so terrified saying amongst themselves that if two kings couldn't resist Jehu, how could they? So they wrote a letter back, telling him that they would not do such a thing, and that he, Jehu, should do whatever he thought was best. Jehu then replied with a second letter in which he gave them instructions concerning the princes. They were to behead them and have their heads brought to him in baskets the next day. The royal princes were with the leading men of the city who were rearing them, when the letter arrived. These men slaughtered all Ahab's sons and sent their heads in baskets to Jehu.

He ordered to put them at the entrance of the city gate until morning. The next morning Jehu stood before all the people telling them they were all innocent because he was the one who conspired against the king. But he also asked them, who killed all these? Referring to the princes of Ahab's house. He added, *'Know now that there shall fall unto the earth nothing of the word of HaShem, which HaShem spoke concerning the house of Ahab; for HaShem has done that which He spoke by His servant Elijah'.*

Jehu killed everyone of Ahab's house who remained in Jezreel, as well as all his chiefs, close friends and priests. He left no survivors.

Later on, he left in his chariot to go towards Samaria. When he arrived at Beth Eked of the Shepherds, he met with some people. They happened to be relatives of Ahaziah, the late king of Judah. Ignorant of the events of the last few days, these forty-two men were on their way to greet the king and his mother. He ordered his men to take them alive. They slaughtered them at the well of Beth Eked. Again Jehu left no survivors. Meanwhile Jehonadab son of Rekab, forefather of the Rekabites clan, was on his way to meet with Jehu. The Rekabites lived as nomads, tent-dwellers, amongst the Israelites. They were Kenites, foreigners who identified themselves with the God of Israel. They journeyed with the Israelites in the past, and entered the Land with them. They had been kind and loyal to the Israelites ever since. As soon as they met on the way to Samaria, Jehu greeted Jehonadab and asked him whether he was in agreement with him, as he himself was with him. He answered that he was, and Jehu helped him into his chariot, telling him to ride along with him and witness his zeal for the Lord. Once they were in Samaria, Jehu killed and destroyed all those who were left of Ahab's family.

After this Jehu devised a way to destroy Ahab and Jezebel's idol worship. Deceptively he said to the people that he would serve Ahab and Jezebel's gods even more than they did. He decided to invite all these gods' worshippers to a great sacrifice in honour of them and summoned all their prophets, servants and priests. Anyone who would not come, would no longer live. They all came, no one was missing. Then he said to call an assembly in the name of their gods. So they proclaimed it and Jehu sent word throughout Israel. All the worshippers came, no one stayed away. They crowded into their temple. They all received robes from the robe keeper, as Jehu ordered. Before Jehu and Jehonadab went into the temple, Jehu posted eighty of his men outside the temple with the order not to let anyone he would place in their hands escape. Otherwise it would be that man's life for their own. Once inside, Jehu told the people there to look around and be certain that not one servant of the Lord was amongst them. Thus insuring that they wouldn't be killed. As soon as Jehu had made his burnt offering, he went outside and ordered his guards and officers to go in and kill every single one of those inside. They killed them all by the sword, threw their bodies out, and went into the inner shrine of the temple to find their sacred stone. They brought it out, burned it, demolished it and tore down the temple leaving the ruin to be used as a latrine.

So, Ahab's wife Jezebel, her son Jehoram who was king at the time, and all Ahab's relatives and friends died at the hand of Jehu. He left no survivors. Jehu became the tenth king of Israel since the division of the Kingdom of Israel into a northern and southern kingdom. Jehu also killed Ahaziah son of Jehoram, the king of Judah at the time, because he was related to Ahab on his mother's side and a friend of Joram.

The word the Lord spoken to Elijah came to pass. Jehu would put to death Ahab's relatives who would escape the sword of Hazael, and Elisha would put to death anyone who escaped the sword of Jehu. However the Lord would reserve to Himself seven thousand men in Israel, those who had not bowed down or kissed their king's idol.

God rewarded Jehu for avenging the blood of all His servants and prophets murdered by Ahab's house. His descendants would rule Israel to the fourth generation. Jehu destroyed Ahab's and Jezebel's idol worship in Israel, but he was not completely faithful to the Lord. He did not keep the Law of the Lord with all his heart. Instead, in part he followed the path of the sins of Jeroboam by not destroying the two golden calves made by Jeroboam which he had placed at Bethel and Dan.

Judgment also came over Israel at the time of King David. He was incited against the Israelites causing him to order Joab, the commander of Israel's army, and his commanders to perform a census of all able-bodied men who could handle a sword in Israel's army. Joab respectfully disagreed with David, but David's word however overruled his and the commanders' word. It took Joab and his commanders nine months to do the census. When Joab brought his report to David, he didn't mention that he left the Levites and the fighting men from Benjamin out of it. Afterwards, David became conscious of his sin in counting the men. Why was this census sinful? Could it have been because the people, each person counted, failed to pay the ransom due to the Lord? As the Lord had said to Moses, *'When you take the sum of the children of Israel, according to their number, then shall they give every man a ransom for his soul unto HaShem, when you number them; that there be no plague among them, when you number them. ... Every one that passes among them that are numbered, from twenty years old and upward, shall give the offering of HaShem'*.

David prayed and begged the Lord for His forgiveness. The next morning the Lord had given the prophet Gad, David's seer, a word for him. Gad went to see David and told him that the Lord would give him three options of punishment to choose from. Three years of famine in Israel, three months fleeing while being persecuted by his enemies or three days of plague in the Land. David chose the latter, as he said to his seer, *'I am in a great strait; let us fall now into the hand of HaShem; for His mercies are great; and let me not fall into the hand of man'*.

In the designated three days seventy thousand people died of the plague in the Land. But, when the angel of the Lord that brought the affliction over the Israelites stretched his hand out to destroy Jerusalem, the Lord showed His mercy as David hoped for. He relented and told the angel to withdraw his hand. Then He sent His word to Gad for David who was in sackcloth still in prayer with the elders, that he should go up build an altar and bring offerings to the Lord. Obedient to the Lord, David went up Mount Moriah, built an altar to the Lord and brought burnt offerings. The Lord answered his prayer on behalf of Israel and the plague over Israel stopped.

Did this event come about in a similar way as it would regarding Job years later, with Satan presenting himself at God's heavenly court? Satan himself rose against Israel, and David was incited to do the census. In the case of Job, he was a righteous man in the eyes of the Lord, therefore the Lord wasn't angry with him. Still when Satan sought to bring Job to sinfulness through affliction, the Lord allowed this to happen, while keeping Job's bones healthy and expecting Job to remain faithful to Him. He even asked him to pray for forgiveness of his friends' sins, whom He sent to Job despite their accusations against him. David was to God, a man to His own heart. Initially the Lord wasn't angry with David. He was angry with the Israelites. One of the differences between David and Job was, that David himself didn't get ill while his subjects in Israel, except in Jerusalem, did. In his case it was himself and the inhabitants of Jerusalem that the

Lord kept healthy. And David unlike Job did sin by having the census carried out. The Lord punished David's subjects which brought grief to David. But He was also willing to forgive, while just as with Job, He expected David to intercede for others. In David's case for His nation, for which as king he was solely responsible. David asked the Lord for forgiveness, while fully taking the blame on himself. As a consequence of all this, the Lord showed David where His Temple was to be built in the future. This way the Lord turned wrongdoings into something good. Unlike other kings before and after David, that because of their wickedness and unfaithfulness to the Lord, they were destined by Him not to have any descendants to continue their royal line, the Lord had chosen a different path for his servant David and his descendants.

> *If they profane My statutes, and not keep My commandments; Then I will visit their transgression with the rod, and their iniquity with strokes. But My mercy I will not break off from him, nor will I be false to My faithfulness. My covenant I will not profane, nor alter that which is gone out of My lips. Once I have sworn by My holiness: Surely I will not be false unto David; His seed shall endure for ever, and his throne as the sun before Me. It shall be established for ever as the moon; and be steadfast as the witness in the sky.*
>
> Psalm 89

To God Almighty living in the Land goes with living by His Laws, moral code and way of life that He had provided to and through His eldest son, the Children of Israel. Through centuries the Lord has been making it clear to the nation of Israel and to the nations of the world that those living in the Land should abide by these. Since His chosen people, the shoot He Himself had planted in the Promised Land, were no exemption to this, He once evicted them from the Land when they discontinued living up to His standard. The Israelites' sinful ways caused their expulsion from the Land. The Lord scattered them amongst the nations, while leaving some of the people of Judah to remain.

If the Lord evicted even the Israelites, what would He do to those of other nations living in the Land who still wouldn't live up to God's moral code? Worse. He would uproot them, never to be planted again in the Land, just as He did with the people living in the Land, in Canaan, prior to the arrival of the tribes of Israel. They took ownership as the

Lord God Almighty had promised centuries earlier to their ancestors Abraham, Isaac and Jacob. Contrary to those people, the Lord would plant the Israelites again in the Land.

The Lord God as the Judge of creation will bring judgment upon humanity when the wickedness of the people and the nations reaches its fullness. When the Lord rises to shake the heavens and the earth, He who is good and a refuge in times of trouble will care for those who trust in Him.

Ultimately He and all those with Him will judge each and everyone when He raises up the righteous from the peacefulness of their grave to everlasting eternal life.

> *HaShem kills, and makes alive; He brings down to the grave, and brings up. He will thunder in heaven; HaShem will judge the ends of the earth.*
> 1 Samuel 2:6,10

Endnotes

Isaiah 26:11, Isaiah 27:11-13 God's zeal for His people, their creator
Isaiah 44:6 God the only one, Israel's redeemer
Nahum 1:7, Psalm 106 God is good, gives
Habakkuk 12 God is eternal, immortal
Psalm 52:8, 99:8-9 merciful, forgiving, holy, God
Psalm 100 God alone is God
Psalm 103:17-18 God's love endures for ever
Psalm 104:7 The whole creation depends on God
Psalm 104:31 Creation created to give God joy, gladness and serve God
Psalm 93:4,5,7, Psalm 119:160 Essence of God's Word
Isaiah 49:3 the Lord glorified in Israel
Psalm 97 God is righteous, hate evil
Hosea 10:12 Shower of righteousness
Daniel 7:10 Books at the tribunal
Psalm 33:4-5 The Lord loves righteousness and justice
Deuteronomy 30:11-14 God's Laws not distant nor hidden
Deuteronomy 10:11-13 Reason given Laws
Jeremiah 32:26-27 God is the Lord of and over all people.
Deuteronomy 32:35 Vengeance is the Lord's
Job 41:11 Everything belongs to God
Psalm 97:7,9 Most High God
Psalm 90:2,4, Psalm 95:3, 97:7-9 God greater and more powerful than gods
Psalm 135:14-18, 115:4-8 Idols, false gods
Psalm 94:1-7, 20-21,28, God, Judge of the world
Exodus 3:19, 6:1, 7:4, Jeremiah 32:21 God's mighty hand

Who Is David?

Jeremiah 9:22-24 God's wisdom
Genesis 50:19-20 The Lord turns evil deeds into good
Isaiah 56:2 Avoid evil
Deuteronomy 4:1-2, 6-8 God's Law is just
Isaiah 5:16 The Lord is righteous
Exodus 18:11 The Lord greater than all other gods
Isaiah 41:1 God brings gods for judgment
Isaiah 42:8 God doesn't share His honour
Malachi 3:6a The Lord doesn't change
Proverbs 5:21-23, Zechariah 4:10 God scans the earth
Psalm 103:14-16 A man's fragile life
Exodus 20:6, Psalm 103:17-18 God is for ever and so is His love
Isaiah 41:2b and 4 The Lord masters events
Isaiah 28:29 The Lord's plans
Psalm 147:10-11 The Lord's delight
Psalm 94:8-13 the nations should realise God is Judge
Psalm 90:5-6,8, Psalm 97:8, Psalm 110:6a, Jeremiah 9:24-25 God judges the people, the nations
Genesis 6:3 Time for people of Noah's generation
Genesis 6:18, 8:15-9:17 God's covenant with Noah
Genesis 15:13-16 Fullness of wickedness of the Amorites in Canaan
Psalm 82 gods will be judged
Isaiah 41:5, Ezekiel 20:39 people seek comfort with their idols
Deuteronomy 23:4-5, Joshua 24:9-1 God did not curse but blessed the Israelites
Numbers 31:8, Joshua 13:22 Balaam killed
Exodus 35:15-16, Numbers 25, 31:13-19 Balaam's advice, Moabite and Midianite women, Phinehas
1 Kings 15:8-14 Asa became king of Judah
1 Kings 15:16 war between Asa and Baasha
1 Kings 22:41-45 Jehoshaphat king of Judah in Ahab's fourth year
1 Kings 12:26-30 Jeroboam's installation of the two calve idols
1 Kings 13:1-10, 13:31-34 prophesy against Jeroboam and his altar
1 Kings 13:23-31, 2 Kings 23:16-18 prophet's grave, prophesied against Jeroboam
Exodus 32:4,8, 1 Kings 12:28, Nehemiah 16:18 calve idols as gods
1 Kings 12: 25-33 Jeroboam's religion
1 Kings 13:1-6 prophesy against Jeroboam's altar
1 Kings 13:33-34, 14:10, 15:25-16:7 punishment Jeroboam
1 Kings 14:1-20 Abijah's illness and death, and Ahijah's prophesy against Jeroboam
1 Kings 15:25-31 Baasha killed Nadab and all Jeroboam's family
1 Kings 15:33-34, 16:5-6 Baasha king of Israel
1 Kings 16:1-7 prophet Jehu son of Hanani brought the word about Baasha's punishment

Judge of Creation

1 Kings 16 Kings Baasha, Zimri, Omri, Ahab of Israel
1 Kings 19 Elijah on Mount Horeb
1 Kings 19:15-18 the Lord tells Elijah to anoint three men
2 Kings 2 Elijah's ascent
1 Kings 15:18 Ben-Hadad king of Aram, son of Tabrimmon, son of Hezion
1 Kings 20:29-34,42 Ahab's war and treaty with Ben-Hadad king of Aram,
1 Kings 20:35-43 prophecy against Ahab because he allowed Ben-Hadad to live
1 Kings 21:19-29 Nabot's land
1 Kings 21 Elijah's prophecy concerning Ahab and his wife
1 Kings 22:1-28 Micaiah's prophecies against Ahab
2 Kings 9:22 Jezebel practices idol worship and witchcraft
2 Kings 9:25-26 prophecy against Ahab
1 Kings 22:29-40, 2 Chronicles 18:28-33 alliance, Ahab's death in battle
2 Kings 5, 22:34 Naaman
2 Chronicles 17:1-19 good governance Jehoshaphat king of Judah
2 Chronicles 18:1-3 Jehoshaphat and the prophet Jehu
2 Chronicles 19: 4-11 Jehoshaphat positions judges in Judah
Deuteronomy 27:9-26, 28, 31:9-13 the Book of Law
2 Chronicles 20:1-30 Jehoshaphat's victory over the Moabites and Amorites
1 Kings 22:49-50, 2 Chronicles 20:35-37 Jehoshaphat's fleet
2 Chronicles 21:7 always a descendant of David on his throne
1 Kings 22:52-54 Ahaziah son of Ahab two years king of Israel
2 Kings 1:17 Joram succeeded his brother Ahaziah as king of Israel
2 Kings 8:25, 9:27 Ahaziah, son of Jehoram the successor of Jehosaphath, king of Judah
2 Kings 6:8-33, 7:1-20 Aramean siege of Samaria by Ben-Hadad
2 Kings 6:24-7:20, 7:1-2 Elisha's prophecy during Aramean siege
2 Kings 8:11-13 Elisha's prophecy about Hazael to be king of Aram
2 Kings 13:3, 24, 2 Chronicles 16 Hazael king of Aram and his son Ben-Hadad who succeeded him
1 Kings 23:23, 2 Kings 9:30-37 Jezebel's death
2 Kings 8:19 a lamp for David's descendants for ever
2 Kings 8:16 Joram son of Ahab king of Israel
2 Kings 9:1-4 Elisha sends a young prophet to anoint Jehu
2 Kings 9:5-6 Jehu anointed to be king of Israel
2 Kings 9:7-10 annihilation of Ahab's house by Jehu to avenge the prophets killed by Jezebel
2 Kings 9:11-13 Jehu becomes king of Israel
2 Chronicles 22 the Aramean Hazael, wounded Joram king of Israel
2 Kings 9:14-29 death of Joram and Ahaziah king of Judah
2 Kings 11:1-3 Athaliah killed Ahaziah's children and house hold
2 Kings 8:25-29 Ahaziah king of Judah was Achab's family
2 Kings 9:30-37 Jehu had Jezebel killed

2 Kings 10:1-17 All Ahab's house and those connected to him killed
2 Kings 10:15-17, Jeremiah 35:7-8 Jehonadab, the Rekabites
2 Kings 10:18-35 Jehu killed Ahab's priests, servants, and destroyed temples
2 Kings 10:30 the Lord's reward for Jehu
2 Kings 10:31-33 Jehu was not completely faithful to the Lord
2 Kings 10:29 Jehu didn't destroy Jeroboam's golden calves
2 Kings 10:30 prophesy against Jehu
2 Kings 10:32-33 God reduced Israel's territory at the east of the Jordan River
1 Kings 19:16-17 the Lord's word to Elijah
2 Samuel 24:1-19, 1 Chronicles 21:1-19 David's census of Israel and Judah
2 Samuel 24:1, 1 Chronicles 21:1 God's anger, Satan against Israel
Exodus 30:11-16 ransom to God for the Israelites
Job 1:6-22, 2:1-10 Job
Isaiah 60:21 the shoot planted by the Lord
Isaiah 2:21 the Lord shakes the earth
Nahum 1:7, Joel 3:16 the Lord a refuge, stronghold
Deuteronomy 32:40-43 the Lord will avenge the blood of His people
Isaiah 57:2, Daniel 12:2 peacefulness of the grave, resurrection of the dead

Intermezzo Endnotes

Deuteronomy 30, 32, Joshua 23:15 prophecy by Moses, Joshua
Isaiah 58 The Lord's requirements
Exodus 32 Moses about the taunt of the Egyptians
Joshua 21:45, 23:14, 1 Kings 8:56-57 God kept all His promises to Israel
Exodus 33:4 Joshua in the Tent of Meeting
Exodus 17:8-16 Joshua a warrior, fought the Amalekites
2 Kings 17:13, Isaiah 59:21,12, Ezekiel 18:30 warnings, call for repentance
2 Kings 17 Hoshea captured, Samaria's fall
2 Kings 23:26-27 Judah removed from God's presence
Nehemiah 9:16-21, Joshua 5:6 The Lord's compassion with the Israelites
Psalm 95:8-11 God's rest
Deuteronomy 29:13-20 consequences for the descendants of the Israelites
Deuteronomy 31:19-22, 24-26 Moses' song
Isaiah 1:2-3, Jeremiah 2:13 the ox and donkey, two sins
Amos 9:7-10 sinful kingdom, among the nations
Amos 9:15 plant them in the Land, their own
Jeremiah 30:11 Israelites disciplined, measured punishment
Exodus 13:17-18, Isaiah 64: 12-14 God gave them rest to cross the Sea of Reeds
Obadiah 17 Zion safe again
Nahum 1:12b God won't afflict Judah anymore

Part III
DAVID'S QUEEN

King David had several wives and concubines, with whom he had many children. David's first six sons were born in Hebron. The rest of his children, including Solomon, the son of Bathsheba, were born in Jerusalem. Only one of his daughters was mentioned by name, Tamar.

His first six sons were Amnon the son of his second wife Ahinoam, Chilieab his second son with his third wife Abigail, Absalom with his fourth wife Maacah, followed by his fourth son Adonijah whose mother was Haggith, Shephatia son of his wife Abital and Itbream son of Eglah who was his last son born in Hebron. David's sons were princes whose education laid in the capable hands of David's uncle, Jonathan, who was a scholar and a skilful adviser. King David's sons held high positions at the King's court and some of them, not mentioned by name, were priests. But three of his sons would cause difficulties and bring much grief to David during his life.

Among King David's wives were most notable his first wife princess Michal, King Saul's daughter. Ahinoam from Jezreel, Abigail, Nabal's widow from Carmel, Bathsheba the wife of Uriah the Hittite, and his last wife, Abishag from Shunem.

David's wives and concubines played an important, if not interesting, role in his life. Besides ensuring offspring for his royal family line, they also played a role in saving his life, preventing him from doing harsh things and taking care of him all the way in his old age until his death. David, on his part, took good care of every single one of them. But, which one of these women was King David's queen?

My heart exults in HaShem,
my horn is exalted in HaShem;
my mouth is enlarged over my enemies;
because I rejoice in Your salvation.

There is none holy as HaShem,
for there is none beside You;
neither is there any rock like our God.

At your right hand is the royal bride in gold of Ophir.
Listen, daughter, and pay careful attention:
Forget your people and your father's house.

Let the king be enthralled by your beauty;
honour him, for he is your lord.

The city of Tyre will come with a gift,
people of wealth will seek your favour.

All glorious is the princess within her chamber;
her gown is interwoven with gold.

In embroidered garments she is led to the king;
her virgin companions follow her –
those brought to be with her.

Led in with joy and gladness,
they enter the palace of the king.

Your sons will take the place of your fathers;
you will make them princes throughout the land.

Psalm 45

MICHAL

David's Princess

Michal was David's first wife. Her name could mean, 'What is God like'? She was the youngest daughter of King Saul from the tribe of Benjamin. Saul was king over Israel for forty-two years. After which, his son-in-law David became king of Judah, and his son Ishboshet became king of Israel. But, ultimately David became king over all of Israel. David married Michal before he became king.

How did David and Michal's relationship start, and how did it develop over the years?

Marriage

Michal was in love with David but she wasn't the one chosen by her father to marry him. King Saul had other plans and David marrying his eldest daughter Merab would fit these. The only thing he required from David was that he would be loyal to him, and serve him in the military fighting the Lord's battles. By this time David had already proven how successful he could be in battle, and he was liked both by the people and Saul's high officials – so much so that Saul was jealous of him.

What was this plan Saul had?

He wanted David dead. And this was something that would be easily achieved during the many wars that Saul fought against Israel's enemies at the time. But, there was one major problem. David said no. He didn't see himself as being worthy to marry the daughter of the king. He regarded himself and his family as part of an elite that would position him as the right man to marry a princess. When the time came for Merab to get married, Saul gave his daughter in marriage to Adriel from Meholah.

Before Saul had a change of plans, he heard that his youngest daughter Michal was in love with David. To him this was a perfect opportunity to put his plan in action.

So, for the second time Saul asked David to be his son-in-law. He offered him Michal's hand in marriage, hoping he would accept it. Again David said no, but this time Saul ordered his officials to have a

Who Is David?

talk with David in private telling him how pleased the king was with him, that his officials liked him and that it was a good time for him to marry the king's daughter.

Still David regarded himself as too insignificant to have the honour of marrying the king's daughter. But, this time Saul didn't give up his attempt to get David to marry his daughter. When his officials told him about David's answer, he again ordered them to speak to David but this time about the payment he would expect from David. The payment for Michal to be his bride would be the foreskins of one hundred dead Philistines as revenge on Saul's enemies. What Saul really hoped for was that David would die in battle at his attempt to acquire the foreskins of the Philistines.

There is a promise Saul must have forgotten or conveniently didn't care to speak of concerning giving his daughter away to be married. What was the reward Saul had in store for the one who would defeat Goliath?

> *Now the Israelites had been saying, Do you see how this man keeps coming out? He comes out to defy Israel. The king will give great wealth to the man who kills him. He will also give him his daughter in marriage and will exempt his family from taxes in Israel.*
>
> 1 Samuel 17:25

David was, in fact, already entitled to marry one of King Saul's daughters. But David agreed to meet with Saul's requirement for payment and was delighted with the thought of becoming King Saul's son-in-law. Meanwhile Michal, in love with David, was unaware of her father's planning the death of her husband-to-be. David and his men set out to fight and kill two hundred Philistines before the day set for the wedding. Let's leave the door closed on imagining how David got the foreskins of the dead Philistines. He brought the foreskins to Saul and counted all of them out for him. And that is how Princess Michal became David's first lawful wife.

Saul realised that God was with David and that his daughter loved him, which made Saul even more afraid of David. And he considered him to be his enemy. Michal, on the contrary, loved David so much that later she would prove that her loyalty to him was far more greater than to her father the king.

Intermezzo

Circumcision

The first man God wanted to be circumcised was Abraham, a descendant of Shem, the eldest son of Noah. Abraham's family originally came from Ur of the Chaldea, a city in the proximity of the Euphrates River in Babylonia, Mesopotamia. His father Terah took Abraham, his wife and his grandson Lot out of Ur to travel to Canaan, but on their way to this country they settled in Haran.

Abraham was seventy-five years old and living in Haran, where Terah died aged 205, when God asked him to leave Haran to go to a land that he was going to show him. God promised Abraham He would give him many descendants, they would become a great nation, he would bless him and bless those who bless him, whoever would curse him, He would curse, and all the people of the earth would be blessed through him.

Abraham took his wife, servants and all his possessions and left. His nephew Lot went with him. It wasn't until they arrived in Canaan that God gave him the promise of the land. He travelled through the land of Canaan and reached Shechem, where God appeared to him and said, *'to your offspring I will give this land'*. This was a message God repeated to him throughout his life, and to his son Isaac.

Much later God appeared also to Abraham's grandson, Isaac's youngest son of the twins his wife Rebecca gave him, Jacob. His brother Esau, after exchanging his firstborn right for a bowl of soup and missing out on Isaac's blessing, would ultimately receive another blessing from Isaac.

There he built an altar and worshipped God. From there he moved to the southern part of Canaan. Later, after separating from Lot, who moved to the east to live among the cities including Sodom in the Jordan Valley, Abraham settled in Hebron.

Why did God choose Abraham? *'Abram believed the Lord, and He credited it to him as righteousness'*. Abraham already showed his faith and trust in God by leaving Haran to go to a land that God would show him. After Abraham was blessed by Melchizedek, the king and priest of the most high God of Jerusalem, God gave him a vision in which he again assured Abraham of the promise He made to him regarding his descendants, who would be more than the stars in the sky. God would shield him from danger and give him a great reward. God made it clear that it wouldn't be his servant Eliezer from Damascus that would inherit his property. For God, a thousand years is as one day. So, it is less than a week that God made Abraham his friend.

> *But you, Israel, my servant, Jacob, whom I have chosen, you, descendants of Abraham my friend. I took you from the ends of the earth, from its farthest corners I called you. I said, You are my servant; I have chosen you and have not rejected you.*
>
> Isaiah 41

Twenty-four years later when Abraham was 99 years old, the Lord appeared to him. The Lord told him: *'I am God Almighty; walk before Me faithfully and be blameless. Then I will make My covenant between Me and you and will greatly increase your numbers'.*

Abraham fell face down to the ground. The Lord continued to tell Abraham His plans with him and his descendants.

The Lord would make His covenant with him and his descendants. Abraham would be the father of many nations. He promised Abraham that he and his descendants would inherit the whole land of Canaan, the Promised Land, where he lived at that time as a foreigner, to be an everlasting possession. The Lord would be their God. The Lord changed Abram's name, meaning 'exalted father', into Abraham, probably meaning 'father of many'.

The Lord also changed Abraham's wife's name from Sarai into Sarah. The Lord promised Abraham that He would bless her and she would give him a son. She would be the mother of nations, kings of people would come from her.

Again Abraham fell face down, this time laughing saying to himself whether a ninety-year-old woman and a hundred-year-old man could have a child.

He asked if Ishmael, his son with Hagar, Sarah's servant, should receive these blessings. But the Lord assured him that Sarah would give him a son to be called Isaac, which means 'he laughs', and His covenant to inherit the land would be with Isaac and his descendants after him, indicating that it is God's decision that not all descendants of Abraham who would be circumcised would inherit the land.

After generations it would become clear that the descendants of Abraham's grandson Jacob, the son of Isaac, would inherit the Promised Land. But, God also told Abraham he would honour his request and bless Ishmael with many children, twelve princes and make a great nation of his descendants. It is during this conversation that God gave Abraham, after His promises to him, the sign of the covenant, the circumcision. After God spoke with him, He went up away from him.

The Lord told Abraham he should circumcise his whole household, and for generations to come his descendants should do the same. The covenant he had to keep: *'Every male among you shall be circumcised. You are to undergo circumcision, and it will be the sign of the covenant between Me and you. For the generations to come, every male among you who is eight days old must be circumcised, including those born in your household or bought with money from a foreigner – those who are not your offspring'.*

God provided also for foreigners in Abraham's household, although this will cost him money, and the foreigners don't have a say on this transaction. In this way, being a member of Abraham's household is granted to them, with them being under the rules and laws of his household. The covenant in Abraham's and his descendants' flesh is to be an everlasting one.

Those who are uncircumcised would be cut off from their people because they have broken the covenant. That same day Abraham and his son Ishmael, and every male in his household were circumcised as God told him. The circumcision of the foreskin, or in the flesh, would be the sign of God's covenant with Abraham.

About a year later, Abraham was one hundred years old and he had his son Isaac circumcised when he was eight days old.

Generations later, more than 400 years as God foretold Abraham, his descendants through his grandson Jacob, also renamed Israel, God's eldest son, arrived at Gilgal in Canaan.

More than six hundred thousand Israelites with their families and the foreigners who joined them, left Egypt under the leadership of Moses, with his brother Aaron and sister Miriam. During their journey God gave them His Law, which also included those of circumcision, His feasts and the Tabernacle service.

Under the leadership of Joshua, assisted by Caleb, they crossed the Jordan River while God stopped the river from flowing, causing much fear under the Canaanites and other people in the region. The Israelites who died in the desert, except Joshua of the tribe of Ephraim and Caleb of the tribe of Judah, were circumcised. God told Joshua that all the men who were born during their decades long journey through the desert had to be circumcised.

Centuries later God Almighty made another promise to the descendants of Jacob, the Israelites, that of the circumcision of the heart, writing His Law on people's heart.

> *The new covenant that I will make with the people of Israel will be this: I will put My law within them and write it on their hearts. I will be their God, and they will be My people. None of them will have to teach a neighbour to know the Lord, because all will know Me, from the least to the greatest. I will forgive their sins and I will no longer remember their wrongs. I, the Lord, have spoken.*
>
> Jeremiah 31:33-34

God also provided for foreigners, non-Israelites, non-Jews, to share in the blessings God gives His people, and they are invited to come to Him. Those who bless Abraham's descendants, Israelites, will be blessed by God. People bought by Jacob's descendants with their own money to be part of their household. The nations that will be blessed by God through his people. Those who would go to God's Temple for prayer. Examples of people blessed through the Israelites are Rehab and Ruth.

> *And foreigners who bind themselves to the Lord to minister to him, to love the name of the Lord, and to be his servants, all who keep the Sabbath without desecrating it and who hold fast to My covenant – these I will bring to My holy mountain and give them joy in My house of prayer.*
> *Their burnt offerings and sacrifices will be accepted on My altar; for My house will be called a house of prayer for all nations. The Sovereign Lord declares – he who gathers the exiles of Israel, I will gather still others to them besides those already gathered.*
>
> Isaiah 56:6-8

After all, God shows mercy with whoever He wants as He told Moses:

> *I will make all My splendour pass before you and in your presence I will pronounce My sacred name. I am the Lord, and I show compassion and pity on those I choose.*
>
> Exodus 33:19

Loyalty

Not long after David and Michal's marriage, Saul told his officials that he planned to kill David. But Jonathan, who was very fond of David, spoke to his father on David's behalf, trying to change Saul's mind about him. Meanwhile, David, on Jonathan's request, went into hiding and awaited the result of Jonathan's intervention. Saul was convinced by him to let David continue to serve him, and so he did as he had before.

When war broke out, David fought the Philistines and defeated them, and they fled from the Israelites.

So, all ends well? No.

One day Saul, while at home and in the grip of an evil spirit, took his spear and tried to kill David. But David dodged the spear, leaving it to pierce the wall instead of him, and then escaped and ran away, all the way to his own home.

Saul sent men to watch David's house with his orders to kill David the next morning. But Michal found out about her father's orders and prepared a plan of her own for David to escape. First she warned David that if he didn't run away that same night, the next morning he would be dead. The only safe way out was the window, through which she let David down so he could run away to Samuel, escaping certain death. Then she made up the bed in such a way that it seemed that David was laying there, though David already left. When the men came to the door, she told them that David was ill. Believing her lie, they returned to Saul.

Saul wasn't at all satisfied with the result of their visit to David's house and sent them back with new orders. They were to carry David in his bed to Saul where Saul himself would kill him. But once at the house they discovered they were deceived by Michal. It wasn't David laying in that bed, and when Saul was informed about it, he felt betrayed by his own daughter, whom he asked why she tricked him and let his enemy escape.

Michal was a woman in love, a smart one, who chose the side of her husband, to remain loyal to him. Michal replied with a lie, probably fearing for her own life, that David said he would kill her if she didn't help him escape. It would take years before Michal, David's lawful wedded wife, would be reunited with David, who in the meantime married other women and ultimately became king of Judah in Hebron.

> *And David also sent messengers to Ishboshet to say, Give me back my wife Michal. I paid a hundred Philistine foreskins to marry her.*
>
> 2 Samuel 3:14

King David, in a message to Saul's son King Ishboshet of Israel, demanded that his wife be returned to him, a condition David agreed on before he would continue negotiating a peace agreement between Judah and Israel with Abner, the commander of the military troops of the ten tribes of Israel. After nearly seven years of war between the two kingdoms, there was a chance that King David could get his wife back. But there was a problem. Saul gave Michal away to another man that didn't want to let her go.

Problem solved by King Ishboshet who took Michal away from her then current husband, Paltiel son of Laish. When Michal was brought to Abner so he could take her to David, Paltiel followed her the whole way crying as he went. But when Abner saw Paltiel, he told him to go home. He did, leaving Michal behind, never to be with her again, because she was on her way to her first husband David, once a military man, now the king of Israel and married to other women.

Dancing

When the Ark of the Covenant was brought to Jerusalem, King David was dancing to honour his God. He was also very happy to bring the Ark of the Covenant to Jerusalem after what they had experienced with it earlier. It was not the first time there was a celebration to bring the Ark of the Covenant to Jerusalem. They took it from Abinadab's home in Baalah Judah and placed it in a new cart pulled by oxen and was guided by Abinadab's two sons. David gathered 30,000 of his best soldiers in Israel and the people of Israel went along with them. That time David was dancing and singing, people were playing harps, lyres, drums, rattles, and cymbals to honour God. But, when the oxen stumbled, Uzzah reached out and touched the Ark of the Covenant. He died on the spot.

God gave strict rules about how to handle the sacred objects of the Tabernacle, such as the Ark of the Covenant. If someone who wasn't allowed to touch these objects did so, that person would die. This is a rule that should have been known by David and those in charge of the sacred objects. David was at first angry with God, but his anger soon changed into fear of God. David didn't dare take the Ark of the Covenant to Jerusalem.

What to do? David decided to take it to Obed Edom in the city of Gath and leave it there.

Three months later, when David heard that because of the Ark of the Covenant, Obed Edom's family and all that belonged to him was blessed by God, he decided to retrieve it and bring it to Jerusalem, amidst a great celebration, offering a sacrifice to God and dancing with all his might to honour God.

He had nothing but a linen cloth around his waist. But, the book of Chronicles also mentions that he was wearing a robe of fine linen, just like the musicians and the Levites carrying the Ark were wearing, and a linen ephod. Meanwhile his wife, Michal, was watching him from a window. She saw him dancing, leaping with joy, and jumping around, and she despised him in her heart.

They came into Jerusalem with celebrations and they put the Ark of the Covenant in the Tent that David had set up for it. King David offered burnt sacrifices to God and afterwards he blessed the people in the name of God Almighty. King David gave to every man and woman in Israel a loaf of bread, a cake of dates and a cake of raisins before everyone went home. King David himself also went home to bless his household.

He was met by his wife, Michal, who expressed her disgust with him because of the way he was dancing at the celebrations, half-naked in full view of the slave girls of his servants as any vulgar fellow would do. With her comments on David's behaviour being indecent, Michal did sound like a jealous wife who thought her husband was putting up a performance to attract the attention of the women present. To David, he was celebrating before the Lord, the One who chose him above Saul to be king over the whole of Israel and to whom he was grateful. David himself wasn't ashamed of his dancing and would continue to do so to honour the Lord as he told Michal.

How could Michal have missed this?

Faithfulness

Could it be because of the difference in faith of her and her husband David? They did not serve the same God. Michal had a different attitude when it came to the use of idols than David. She had a household idol. At the time she helped David escape through the window of their house, she made up the bed to look as if David was sleeping to substantiate her lie that he was ill. She took the idol and laid it on the bed, covered it with a garment, and put a pillow of goat's hair at the head.

It is not said which idol. Perhaps one of Egypt, or of the people living in Canaan, or an idol of their ancestors living beyond the Euphrates River. But, the presence of such an idol in the house meant that at least one of them must have revered it.

The reason it couldn't be David is clear because of his faithfulness to God Almighty throughout his life, and his attitude towards idols. After the Philistines fled when David and his men attacked them, he took the idols they left behind and ordered for them to be burned. He must have been aware of God's commandments prohibiting the use of idols, and His warnings not to get involved with occult practices.

> *If a prophet, or one who foretells by dreams, appears among you and announces to you a sign or wonder, and if the sign or wonder spoken of takes place, and the prophet says, Let us follow other gods (gods you have not known) and let us worship them, you must not listen to the words of that prophet or dreamer. The Lord your God is testing you to find out whether you love Him with all your heart and with all your soul. It is the Lord your God you must follow, and Him you must revere. Keep His commands and obey Him; serve Him and hold fast to Him.*
>
> Deuteronomy 13

David was dancing for His God, that he loved regardless of what whoever else thought of him, and not for people or their idols. While Michal preferred her idols, she went from love and loyalty, sadly to disgust. She remained childless for the rest of her days. David as Joshua, the first judge of the Israelites in the Promised Land, chose to serve the Lord faithfully.

> *Now fear the Lord and serve Him with all faithfulness. Throw away the gods your ancestors worshipped beyond the Euphrates River and in Egypt, and serve the Lord. But if serving the Lord seems undesirable to you, then choose for yourselves this day whom you will serve, whether the gods your ancestors served beyond the Euphrates, or the gods of the Amorites, in whose land you are living. But as for me and my household, we will serve the Lord.*
>
> Joshua 24:14-15

Endnotes

1 Samuel 17-19 Michal
1 Samuel 14:49 Saul's daughters
Genesis 17:9-14 Circumcision
1 Samuel 19:9-17 Michal protects David
1 Samuel 19:16 Household idol
1 Samuel 25:44 Saul punishes Michal
2 Samuel 3:12-21 David tries to get Michal back
2 Samuel 6:14-23, 1 Chronicles 15:25-29 Michal disgusted
1 Samuel 19:13, 1 Chronicles 14:12 Idols
2 Samuel 6 The Ark of the Covenant
1 Chronicles 13:1-14, 15 and 16 The Ark of the Covenant
1 Chronicles 29:26-30 David's years as king
Numbers 4 Rules about caring for the sacred objects of the Tabernacle
Joshua 24:14-15 Idols or God
Deuteronomy 13 Other gods
2 Samuel 3:2-5, 5:13-16, 13:1, I Kings 1:3 Wives and children
1 Chronicles 27:32-34 Education, sons
2 Samuel 8:18 Priests
2 Samuel 20:23-26, 1 Chronicles 18:14-17 High officials

Intermezzo Endnotes

Genesis 12:1-3 Promise of many descendants and blessings
Genesis 12:4 Abraham 75 years
Genesis 12:7, 13:14-18 Promise of land
Genesis 15:13-16 God foretold Abraham about the future of his descendants
Genesis 15:6 Abraham's righteous
Isaiah 41:8-9 Abraham, friend of God
Genesis 17:1 Abraham, 99 years old
Genesis 17:1-14, 23-27 God appears to Abraham, first circumcisions: Abraham's household
Genesis 17:15-22 God promises Abraham a son to be called Isaac
Genesis 21:1-7 Birth and circumcision of Isaac the 8th day, Abraham 100 years
Genesis 22:18 All nations blessed through Abraham's descendants
Deuteronomy 12:31, 18:10, Isaiah 57:5, Jeremiah 19:5 God doesn't require human sacrifices
Genesis 25:7-11 Abraham died 175 years, buried beside Sarah by Isaac and Ishmael
Genesis 26:24-25 God's promise of the land to Isaac
Genesis 28:10-22, 35:1-15 God's promise of the land and many descendants to Jacob

Who Is David?

Genesis 27:39-40 Isaac's blessing to Esau
Exodus 4:22, Hosea 11:1 God's eldest son
Exodus 12:40-41 Israelites lived 430 years in Egypt
Exodus 12:37-38 More than 600,000 male Israelites with their families, and foreigners left Egypt
Micah 6:4 Leadership Israelites, Moses, Aaron and Miriam
Joshua 3:1-17, 5:1 Israelites crossing of the Jordan
Joshua 5 Circumcision by Joshua of all the male Israelites on arrival in the Promised Land, Canaan
Leviticus 12:12 Circumcision baby boy
Psalm 90:4 For God a thousand years is like a day
Genesis 12:2-3, Isaiah 56:1-8, 1 Kings 8:41-43 God's blessings also for non-Jews, foreigners
Joshua 2 Rehab
Ruth 1:16-18 Ruth's choice for God
Exodus 33:19-20 God's mercy, Exodus

ABIGAIL

David's Guardian Angel

Abigail was David's third wife and mother of his second son Chileab, born in Hebron. The name Abigail means my father's joy.

The name she gave her son Chileab means perfection of the father, protected by the father, or like the father. In the book of Chronicles, it is recorded that his name is Daniel, but this is believed to be a mistake. What is certain, however, is that Abigail did have David's second son.

Faith

How did Abigail and David meet? After Samuel's death and his burial at his home in Ramah, David and his six hundred men went to the wilderness of Paran. David heard that Nabal of Caleb's clan from the town of Maon was shearing his sheep in Carmel. It's not mentioned whether this clan was the one of Caleb, of the tribe of Judah, who was sent by Moses with eleven others to spy on Canaan.

Nabal, a very rich man who owned land near the town of Carmel with 3,000 sheep and 1,000 goats, was shearing his sheep in Carmel. He was known as a mean and bad-tampered man. The meaning of his name is fool. But his wife Abigail was intelligent, beautiful and as it turned out, she was a wise woman who averted a disaster on David's account.

David sent his men on a feast day to Nabal. He ordered ten young men to find Nabal to give him his greetings, to inform him that they guarded over his herd and men so that nothing that belonged to him would be stolen as long as he was in Carmel. He also instructed them to request Nabal to give them what he could. What exactly? Food.

After they gave the message in David's name, they waited for Nabal's answer. But, his reaction was unkind and an insult, regardless of David's goodwill in protecting Nabal's herd and shepherds.

After asking David, Who is David?, he continued by saying that he never heard of him, that the country is full of runaway slaves and that he wasn't going to take the bread, water and meat he prepared for his shearers to give to them, to people from he doesn't know where.

David's men returned to him and told him what had happened.

Who Is David?

David ordered his men to ready their swords, and he took four hundred men with him, leaving two hundred behind with their supplies. Meanwhile one of Nabal's servants told Abigail what had happened and how David and his men had protected the shepherds out in the field. The servant's attitude towards Abigail showed that they expected she would know what to do.

Abigail didn't have to think anything over. Instead, realizing that this could lead to disaster for all of them, she acted in good faith. Abigail was aware of the difficult position in which her husband Nabal manoeuvred his household with his decision. They needed David's protection, and refusing to comply with David's request would insure disaster for them. She acted quickly by collecting food and went with the servants on her way to meet David, without saying a word to her husband. She sent her servants ahead with donkeys loaded with two hundred loaves of bread, two leather bags full of wine, five roasted sheep, seventeen kilograms of roasted grain, a hundred bunches of raisins, and two hundred cakes of dried figs. Meeting David wouldn't have been easy for her, because by that time he was a very angry man seeking deadly revenge.

As it turned out, she did know who David was, Israel's king to be, and the one who fights God's battles, as she would tell him later. As soon as she saw him coming towards her round a bend on a hillside, she dismounted her donkey, and threw herself at his feet.

For Abigail to know before whom she should bow meant that she not only had heard about David, but she also must have seen him before; maybe at one of the feasts held in honour of the king and his military men, including David.

David was a well-known figure at the time. After all, the women came from every town in Israel celebrating the defeat of Goliath by David, and of the Philistines, singing *'Saul has killed thousands, but David tens of thousands'*. Abigail could have easily been one of them.

After a short conversation in which Abigail acknowledged who David was, asked him for forgiveness for any wrongdoing on her part, and offered him the present she brought for him, she managed to convince David to abort his plan, to accept the supplies, and to secure David's honest friendship.

> *And when the Lord has blessed you, sir, please do not forget me.*
>
> 1 Samuel 25:31

Marriage

Back at home, Abigail, a faithful wife and courageous enough to take matters into her own hands, risking her own life to save her husband's household, had to inform her husband about everything that had happened. Just in case things would go wrong with Nabal and she would get into serious trouble, she ensured David's friendship.

Still Abigail had some explaining to do. But Nabal was in high spirit having a feast, a banquet fit for a king at his house. At the time of sheep shearing, great festivities were held due to the profitable wool trade. Because Nabal was drunk, Abigail decided to speak to him the morning after. Obviously Nabal had other things on his mind. It seems he didn't even notice that some of his supplies were taken nor that his wife and servants were away from home. By daybreak when Nabal sobered up, she told him all about what happened – her journey to meet David, the present she took with her for him and her reason to act the way she did. She told him everything that happened.

Nabal had an unexpected reaction – he didn't say a thing. He was like a stone completely paralysed, because he had a sudden stroke. God struck him after about ten days of his illness and he died.

David, still in the wilderness of Paran with his men, heard what happened to Nabal. He sent his servants to Carmel with a proposal for marriage to Abigail. They told her David wanted to marry her. She bowed down to the ground and accepted. Abigail quickly mounted her donkey and, accompanied by her five maids, made the journey with David's servants to David to be his second wife. Abigail and David had a son, Chileab, who was his second son. Chileab isn't mentioned as being troublesome or a source of grief to King David.

King Solomon once called Adonijah, David's fourth son, born in Hebron and whose mother was Haggit, his eldest brother.

As the eldest, Adonijah would have the right to become King David's successor unless the king decides differently, which he did.

Before that time, David's first and third son were already dead, but there is no mention of the death of Chileab.

Why wouldn't Solomon call Chileab his eldest brother? Maybe because he meant that Adonijah, his senior, was the only one challenging him for his father's throne. Chileab himself, just like the other sons of King David, would have had a high position at the king's court, or maybe he was a priest as scripture does mention sons of David being priests. It is certain that he wasn't involved in the two major plots to overthrow King David orchestrated by his two sons Absalom and Adonijah. Although he was most likely, just like the other princes, deceived to be present at their feast in their attempt to succeed King David as King of Israel.

There is another possible reason that Solomon didn't regard Chileab as his eldest brother. That is that Chileab, being the son of a widow, would carry the name of his mother's late husband and ultimately inherit from him together with his other brothers and not directly from David. Abigail did not have children with Nabal. Otherwise, how could she have left Nabal's household so quickly? Although David did take good care of Abigail and their son, and he is mentioned in David's family lineage, it seems Chileab didn't have a claim on David's throne. So, in this case Solomon would not regard Chileab as his eldest brother, when it comes to having a claim on King David's throne. Although Chileab, knowing about God's choice for Solomon to succeed their father David, could have had, contrary to Absalom and Adonijah, a different attitude all together from the start.

> *Solomon had a vineyard in Baal Hamon; he let out his vineyard to tenants. Each was to bring for its fruit a thousand shekels of silver. But my own vineyard is mine to give; the thousand shekels are for you, Solomon, and two hundred are for those who tend its fruit.*
>
> Song of Songs 8:11-12

Intermezzo

Widows and Orphans

Widows, orphans and foreigners belong to the group of people who are most vulnerable in society. God provided for them in His laws and guidelines He gave to His people, the Israelites. When it comes to widows, He wants members of her family to take care of her. The close family member, called in a legal term the guardian-redeemer or the kinsman-redeemer, is the one responsible for the well being of the widow. Young widows could, of course, get married again and have children, which also offers the possibility for continuation of the family name of their deceased husband.

In accordance with Jewish custom, the choice for a wife could be made in three ways:

1) The parents choose a woman, as happened with Isaac and Rebecca. 2) The man himself chooses his woman, just as Jacob chose Rachel. 3) Or in the case of a widow, she offers herself to a man, sleeps with him and then he decides whether he chooses her for a wife, a practice which isn't encouraged by the Rabbis. Tamar did this with Judah, but she did deceive him because of the ill-treatment he and one of his sons gave her. Boaz obviously didn't choose this last described path to acquire Ruth as his lawful, legitimate wife. Neither did David, who proposed to Abigail by sending his servants to her.

Older widows generally will not have the chance to remarry and therefore they have to rely on their family members, or if not, on help and charity of others within society. Poor widows also need to rely on whatever help they can get from their family or within their community. Those who have children may allow them to be slaves to pay off the debts of the late husband, as the widow whom Elisha helped with the miracle of the oil, so she could earn money by selling it to pay her debt.

Although Israelites who become slaves and are not redeemed in any way, they and their children will ultimately be set free in the year of Jubilee. Israelites who were bought to be servants however should serve six years and are set free the seventh year, without having to pay their masters any money – unless he would prefer to stay and remain part of his master's household.

When it comes to widows who own property, such as land and cattle their husband left behind, it's a must to keep the property within the family, the clan, of the husband – as in the case of Naomi and Ruth. Should the guardian-redeemer choose to redeem the widow in this case, he has to purchase the property, marry the widow, and the children he has with her, would be regarded as offspring of the deceased husband and would inherit from him. His own children with other wives, will not inherit the property. This poses for some guardian-redeemers the question whether they should invest in property that their children will not own, which could raise problems to their own estate, as happened with the closest relative to redeem Ruth and Naomi.

> *Do not take advantage of the widow or the fatherless. If you do and they cry out to me, I will certainly hear their cry. My anger will be aroused, and I will kill you with the sword; your wives will become widows and your children fatherless.*
> Exodus 22:20-26

The obligation to redeem a relative, a widow or orphan, is a serious matter to God and those involved.

> *Learn to do right; seek justice. Defend the oppressed. Take up the cause of the fatherless; plead the case of the widow.*
>
> Isaiah 1:17

Within God's Laws He also gave guidelines to care for orphans, the fatherless. When a father dies leaving only daughters, while having an inheritance, the daughters may inherit. When they get married, they should do so in such a way to keep the property within their clan, as was arranged by God through Moses for the daughters of Zelophehad. In this way their father would provide for them after his death and his name will not disappear from his clan. Even when there are sons to inherit, the father may decide that his daughters would inherit too, as Job did.

> *A father to the fatherless, a defender of widows, is God in His holy dwelling.*
>
> Psalm 68:5

> *The Lord watches over the foreigner and sustains the fatherless and the widow, but he frustrates the ways of the wicked.*
>
> Psalm 146:9

Providence

God provided for Abigail just as he did for other widows related to King David; one of them being Ruth. But Ruth had a double problem, because she was a widow and a foreigner, a Moabite.

The Israelites and Moabites regularly had difficulties with each other resulting in war, ever since the Israelites left Egypt and had to pass through Moab's territory, with their king Balak trying to get them cursed by Balaam.

Israelites were prohibited to marry Moabite women because of their pagan beliefs. The Moabites were the descendants of Lot and his eldest daughter. Lot was Abraham's nephew, the son of his brother Haran. They went together to Canaan where they separated after quarrels between their men who took care of their herd of animals. Abraham stayed in Canaan and moved to Hebron, while Lot left to the Jordan Valley to live among the cities, camping near Sodom. After

Abraham's prayers to God to spare the righteous or innocent people in the cities, Lot and his family were saved out of Sodom, with his wife turning into a pillar of salt on her way out, when this city and Gomorrah were destroyed by God.

Ruth became a widow after ten years of marriage to one of the sons of Naomi and Elimelech, a man from Bethlehem in Judah, who took his wife and their two sons, Mahlon and Chilion, to live in Moab because of the famine in Israel. Naomi's husband and other son also died, and she decided to return to Bethlehem. Unlike Naomi's other daughter-in-law, Orpah, who decided to stay in Moab, Ruth, led by her faith in the God of Naomi, the God of Israel, went with Naomi.

> *Where you go I will go, and where you stay I will stay. Your people will be my people and your God my God. Where you die I will die, and there I will be buried.*
> Ruth 1:16-17

Once in Bethlehem, where the harvest of barley had just begun, Ruth lived with her mother-in-law, while word about Naomi and her daughter-in-law went through Bethlehem.

Ruth went to work in the field of Boaz, who noticed her as he greeted the harvesters on his arrival to the field. He asked the overseer of his harvesters who she was and told the overseer to treat Ruth kindly by allowing her to pick as much barley as she wanted and even leave some from the bundle for her.

Boaz greeted Ruth and invited her to continue to work on his field. In addition to insure her safety, he asked the men not to lay a hand on her as he told her, and whenever she was thirsty she could get a drink from the water jars. On Ruth's question, why he was so kind to her, Boaz's reply was clear, for he already heard about her and wished her well. He replied that he knew about what she had done for her mother-in-law, by leaving her homeland to live in a land with people she didn't know.

> *May the Lord repay you for what you have done. May you be richly rewarded by the Lord, the God of Israel, under whose wings you have come to take refuge.*
> Ruth 2:12

At mealtime Boaz told her to sit with the harvesters and he passed some food to her. On Ruth's arrival at home, she told Naomi where she gathered so much barley. She was treated so well on Boaz's field that she continued to work there until the barley and wheat harvest was finished, as Boaz had requested. Naomi realised that Boaz was a close relative of theirs, *their* guardian-redeemer who is responsible for taking care of them. She told Ruth to stay on his field to be safe, because elsewhere she might be harmed.

Later, Naomi feeling responsible to find a home where Ruth would be well-provided for, and herself not having other sons she could marry, gave Ruth instructions to approach Boaz discretely. She told her to put on perfume, dress in her best clothes and go down to the threshing floor without being noticed by Boaz. There she should wait until he goes to sleep after his meal, uncover his feet and lie down at his feet. When Boaz notices her, he would tell her what to do.

Ruth followed Naomi's instructions. In the middle of the night something startled Boaz and he woke up, finding a woman at his feet. Ruth identified herself and told him that he was her guardian-redeemer. Boaz assured her that he would redeem her if another relative that was closer related to Naomi and her would not do so. Ruth had to lay down until morning and leave without being noticed, because no one should know that a woman came to the threshing floor. He gave her a bundle of barley, which on Ruth's return home, was much appreciated by Naomi who was sure that Boaz would resolve the matter of redeeming Ruth as soon as possible.

Why did Ruth go to meet Boaz on the threshing floor like that, instead of just speaking to Boaz when she went to work?

She followed Naomi's instructions, which meant this was one of the ways Ruth could make clear to Boaz that she would be prepared to marry him, one of the close relatives responsible to care for her. To Ruth, it was God Himself whom she held dear through her faith that provided for her.

Boaz did resolve the matter that very same day at the town gate where he gathered eleven of the town elders and the relative that could also redeem Naomi and Ruth. Boaz told the relative that Naomi was selling the land that belonged to her late husband Elimelech and that he had the first right to buy it. The relative was prepared to buy it, and in doing so redeem Naomi and Ruth, but when Boaz told him that he would also acquire the widow Ruth, he declined to redeem because this would endanger his own estate. He would not invest in a land that his own children would not inherit. If he would have children with Ruth, they would be considered as Elimelech's children who would inherit, ensuring that the land would stay in Elimelech's family.

The relative settled the matter with Boaz when he said 'buy it for yourself', and he drew off his shoe, as was the custom of the Israelites in those days.

Was Boaz in love with Ruth? It's possible he was, because once he noticed her, he was immediately interested enough to inquire about her, and knowing whom she was, he treated her kindly. To Boaz, Ruth was a woman of noble character, which didn't go unnoticed by the people of his town. He saw as an act of kindness that Ruth had chosen him over younger men, either poor or rich. More over, he married her, redeemed her despite the consequences this could have for his estate.

Abigail and Ruth had a similar story when it comes to their second marriage. They were both widows who married a man who was already married. Abigail and Ruth had a son with their new husband, after having a childless marriage. It's unknown how long Abigail was married to Nabal, but Ruth was married ten years and still she didn't have children with her husband. Their sons were not mentioned as people causing trouble to their family.

Both Abigail and Ruth are connected to King David, the one as his great grandmother on his paternal side, and the other as the mother of David's second son. But, contrary to Abigail's son, Obed the son Ruth, mentioned in Boaz's family line, did inherit. The difference between these two cases might be that unlike Boaz, David is mentioned as having several sons, while this is not the case with Boaz, whose first wife isn't mentioned as having children, sons. So, his son Obed would carry his name and inherit. The latter could be the exception on the rule concerning the children of widows that remarry. These two notable widows impressed the man they ultimately married, especially with their character. They were well treated and cared for.

Another widow in the family line of David was Tamar, who became a widow, twice, after marrying the sons of Judah.

Judah was Jacob's fourth son, and was blessed by him when he blessed his twelve sons just before he died. He blessed Judah with the royal sceptre and told him his descendants would always rule.

Judah ill treated Tamar, the widow of his eldest and second son. She ultimately deceived him into sleeping with her by disguising herself as a prostitute, a drastic measure she must have felt she had to resort to, to secure her future.

Judah nearly had her burned because of her misconduct, but Tamar could prove, with the objects Judah gave her as a pledge, that she was expecting his child. Judah then had to admit that he failed Tamar in his obligation to her by not allowing her to marry his youngest son,

Shelah, when he grew up. Instead he sent her to her father's house. He didn't allow her to marry his youngest son, because he was afraid he would also die, just as Er and Onan did. Although both died by God's will, Er because his conduct was evil, and Onan died because he mistreated Tamar. Onan prevented himself from having children with Tamar because he knew that the children that he had with her would not belong to him. Judah never slept with Tamar again.

Judah and Tamar were the parents of the twins Peretz and Zerach. Peretz, the eldest, is from whom King David descends. Though the story of both Ruth and Abigail was more positive than that of Tamar, these three widows ended with male offspring in Judah's and therefore David's family line. It seems after all that, Tamar, Ruth and Abigail were God's choice to be part of Judah's, David's family line.

Revenge

It is mine to avenge; I will repay. In due time their foot will slip; their day of disaster is near and their doom rushes upon them.

Deuteronomy 32

As soon as David heard from his men what Nabal had to say, he was ready for revenge. He was angry, armed and dangerous, with a small army of six hundred men ready to fight and get what they perceived to be what they earned for watching over Nabal's herd of goats and sheep, and the shepherds too.

Was this only because Nabal insulted David while he treated him well? It was unlikely that Nabal didn't know who David was, and he could have easily granted David's request. The problem was that David was the leader of his men – men who fought many battles with him and trusted him with their lives as he did with his to them.

Being a soldier is also a job, and they should receive their pay for their work to care for their families. David would be in serious trouble if he didn't provide for these men, just as he would be at another occasion when his men were ready to stone him because their families, including their sons, were taken captive by the Amorites who attacked their village in their absence. As a leader, David had to act to avoid such trouble with his men. It's about getting the food. Nabal didn't only insult David, he also embarrassed him in front of his men. David was angry and sought revenge. Doing a raid on Nabal would provide him with both supplies for his men and the opportunity to avenge himself.

If it wasn't for Abigail's action, all of Nabal's men would have been dead by morning.

When David heard about Nabal's death he didn't shed a tear, but saw this as God taking revenge on his enemy for him. Could this experience have such an influence on him at the time of dealing with Joab when he murdered Abner, the commander of King Saul's army, in the future?

God does make clear that it's not up to people to take revenge on others. Even when forgiveness is difficult, it's not up to people to take revenge. They shouldn't let the sun go down on them while being angry, because anger could easily lead to sin. Instead they should be quick to listen, slow to speak and slow in becoming angry. The reason? Human anger doesn't produce the righteousness that God desires. However, people should realise that whoever digs a pit will fall into it, and if someone rolls a stone, it will roll back on them. The required attitude should be quite different.

> *If your enemy is hungry, give him food to eat; if he is thirsty, give him water to drink. In doing this, you will heap burning coals on his head, and the Lord will reward you.*
>
> Proverbs 25:21-22
>
> *Do not seek revenge or bear a grudge against anyone among your people, but love your neighbour as yourself. I am the Lord.*
>
> Leviticus 19:18
>
> *It is mine to avenge; I will repay. In due time their foot will slip; their day of disaster is near and their doom rushes upon them.*
>
> Deuteronomy 32:35

Whether David was initially in love with Abigail or not, he was impressed by her for him to abandon his plan concerning Nabal. He treated her with respect when asking her to marry him.

To David, Abigail was his guardian angel. She guarded him from taking revenge on Nabal so that he did not kill him and his men.

> *David said to Abigail, Praise be to the Lord, the God of Israel, who has sent you today to meet me. May you be blessed for your good judgment and for keeping me from bloodshed this day and from avenging myself with my own hands. Otherwise, as surely as the Lord, the God of Israel, lives, who*

Who Is David?

> *has kept me from harming you, if you had not come quickly to meet me, not one male belonging to Nabal would have been left alive by daybreak.*
>
> 1 Samuel 25

Endnotes

1 Samuel 25 David meets and marries Abigail
1 Samuel 25:34 Nabal's sons
1 Samuel 18:6-7 Feast
Deuteronomy 32:35, Proverbs 25:21-22 Revenge
1 Samuel 27:3 Lived in Gat
1 Samuel 30:1-31 The Amalekites
2 Samuel 2:2 Hebron
2 Samuel 3:3, 1 Chronicles 3:1 Chileab's name
1 Kings 2:22 Eldest brother
1 Kings 1:25 Feast
1 Kings 2:15 Expected successor
Ruth 4:18-22 David's family line
Ruth 2:20 Kinsman-redeemer
Leviticus 25:25-55 Rules on Israelites redeeming family member
Numbers 13:6 Caleb belongs to the tribe of Judah
Genesis 24:1-7 Isaac and Rebecca
Genesis 29:15-20, 27-30 Jacob and Rachel
Genesis 38:1-30 Judah and Tamar
Genesis 49 Judah blessed with royal sceptre
Genesis 13,14,18 and 19 Lot, origin Moabites
Numbers 22,23,24 and 25 Moabites, Balak and Balaam
1 Samuel 30:6 Threat to stone David
Proverbs 26:23-27 Deut. 32:35, Leviticus 19:18, Proverbs 25:21-22 revenge

Intermezzo Endnotes

Exodus 22:20-26, Deuteronomy 14:28-29 God's loyalty to widows
Exodus 21:1-11 Rules concerning Hebrew servants
Leviticus 25:25-55 Redeem rules, the year of Jubilee
2 Kings 4:1-7 Elisha and the poor widow
Numbers 27, 36 Zelophehad's daughters
Job 42 Job's daughters
Psalm 82:3, Isaiah 1:17, concerning widows
Isaiah 10:1-3, Jeremiah 7:5-7 the treatment of widows and the needy

AHINOAM

David's Courage and Grief

Ahinoam from Jezreel, David's second wife, whom David married while he was on the run from King Saul. Ahinoam means 'brother of pleasantness', thus 'pleasant'. She was the mother of David's eldest son, Amnon, born in Hebron. Amnon means 'faithful'. Ultimately he would not do honour to his name.

Courage

David's wives, Ahinoam and Abigail, both lived with David in the country town of Ziklag in the land of the Philistines, where the six hundred men who joined him also lived with their families, including their children.

David and his men just returned to Ziklag after their two-day journey from Aphek, where the Philistine kings gathered their men to fight the Israelites camping at the spring of Jezreel. They arrived the third day at Ziklag and found the town burned to the ground and deserted. Their wives, sons and daughters were all taken captive, along with everything of value that belonged to them. David and his men wept aloud until they didn't have any strength left, because they lost their family. The men became so bitter for losing those they loved that they were threatening to stone David.

> *David was greatly distressed because the men were talking of stoning him; each one was bitter in spirit because of his sons and daughters. But David found strength in the Lord his God.*
>
> 1 Samuel 30

After Abiathar the priest, son of Ahimalek, brought the ephod on David's request, David asked the Lord whether he should pursue the Amalekites who raided and destroyed Ziklag, to rescue their families.

The Lord's answer was clear: '*Pursue them. You will certainly overtake them and succeed in the rescue*'.

So David and his men pursued the Amalekites, who couldn't be too far away because of the burden of the great amount of plunder and the captives they took. They reached Besor Valley, where two

Who Is David?

hundred men, too exhausted to cross the valley, stayed behind with the supplies. David continued the pursuit with his four hundred men.

In a field in the countryside they found an Egyptian man who would give them valuable information. They brought him to David. The man was exhausted, because he had not eaten or had anything to drink in three days. They gave him water and food, cakes of raisin and pressed figs. David started to question him, *'Who do you belong to? Where do you come from'*? It soon became clear that he was an Egyptian slave of one of the Amalekites taking part in their raids. His master abandoned him after he became ill three days earlier. He told David they raided other town besides Ziklag. First the Negev of the Kerethites, then some territory belonging to Judah, and the Negev territory of Caleb. David asked him to lead them to the raiders. After asking David to promise him not to kill him or hand him over to his master, he led David and his men down to the raiders.

David and his men caught up with the Amalekites, scattered over the whole countryside, celebrating, eating and drinking. They had a great amount of loot taken from the land of the Philistines, including Ziklag, and from Judah. David and his men attacked them from dusk and fought them until dawn the next day. Not one of them escaped, except for four hundred young men that fled on camels.

David rescued his wives, Ahinoam and Abigail. And all those taken captive from Ziklag by the Amalekites were freed by David and his men. No one was harmed or missing. They brought everything their enemy had taken back to Ziklag.

On their way home, David's men drove the flocks and herds ahead of the other livestock saying, *'This is David's plunder'*.

Back in Basor, the men David left behind with the supplies because they were too exhausted to continue the pursuit with him, came out to meet him and he greeted them asking them how they were doing. Some of the men who went with him started to cause trouble because they didn't want to share the loot with them, and were only prepared to let them have their wives and children. David didn't agree with this. He was fair to all the men.

> David replied, 'No, my brothers, you must not do that with what the Lord has given us. He has protected us and delivered into our hands the raiding party that came against us. Who will listen to what you say? The share of the man who stayed with the supplies is to be the same as that of him who went

> *down to the battle. All will share alike'. David made this a statute and ordinance for Israel from that day to this.*
>
> 1 Samuel 30

David also sent part of the loot as a gift to the elders of Judah, and to those everywhere else he and his men had roamed.

> *When David reached Ziklag, he sent some of the plunder to the elders of Judah, who were his friends, saying, 'Here is a gift for you from the plunder of the Lord's enemies'.*
>
> 1 Samuel 30

Grief

Years later when David became king over all Israel and was living in Jerusalem, Ahinoam's son caused David great grief. Amnon made himself ill because he was very much in love and obsessed with his half sister Tamar, Absalom's beautiful unmarried sister. She was a virgin and it was impossible for him to meet her in private. His adviser Jonadab, son of David's brother Shimeah, asked Amnon what the matter was with him that he was so sad every day. He told him about his feelings for Tamar, and Jonadab, being a shrewd man, made up a plan. He told him to pretend he is really sick, and when his father David would visit him, he should ask him to allow Tamar to come to prepare food for him. Amnon, speaking to his father, did exactly as Jonadab told him, and David, unaware of Amnon's intentions, sent word to the palace for Tamar.

Tamar came to Amnon's house where he was lying down in his bedroom, prepared the bread, and served it to Amnon. But, he refused to eat, sent everyone out of his house and told Tamar she should bring the food to his bedroom. Once there, he grabbed her and told her to go to bed with him. She resisted him, and told him he should not force her, such a wicked thing should not be done in Israel, but to speak with the king, who would certainly allow her to marry him – something both she and Amnon knew David would not allow because he upheld God's Laws in Israel.

Amnon didn't want to listen, him being stronger than her, forced her and violated her. Afterwards he hated her with such an intense hatred that he rejected her, but Tamar didn't want to leave because of the shame Amnon brought on her. Amnon refused to listen to her, so he had his personal servant throw her out of his house and lock the door. Tamar put ashes on her head, tore the robe she was wearing, put her hands on her head and left crying.

Who Is David?

David was furious when he heard that Amnon violated his half sister Tamar. But, what was he to do?

David's hands were tied because Tamar didn't bring an accusation against Amnon at his court, which also would have made the matter more public. If she had, then her father could seek justice according to Israel's law and have Amnon banished from Israel.

Why didn't Tamar bring in charges against Amnon?

She was ashamed of what happened and more importantly she didn't have her brother's support. So she preferred to listen to what her brother Absalom told her to do. That is, not to say anything. Absalom himself didn't say anything either for his own reasons, which to him seemed to weigh more than the honour of his sister. It wasn't that he didn't love his sister, he just loved his own ambitions regarding Israel's kingship more. Absalom took his sister in to live at his house. She had a sad and lonely life, while Absalom remained revengeful.

> *Do not hate a fellow Israelite in your heart. Rebuke your neighbour frankly so you will not share in their guilt. Do not seek revenge or bear a grudge against anyone among your people, but love your neighbour as yourself. I am the Lord.*
>
> Leviticus 19:17-18

In another case of a young woman being violated by a man, Shechem, a Canaanite prince, had in certain respects a different outcome. Jacob returned to Canaan after he left his father-in-law Laban in Padam Aram. Back in Canaan he met first with his brother Esau. Then he travelled and set up camp near the city of Shechem, on land he bought from the sons of Hamor, the founder of the city. There he built an altar and called it, *El Elohe Israel*, which could mean, 'mighty is the God of Israel'.

One day Dinah, Jacob and Leah's daughter, went out to visit some of the Canaanite women. Shechem, son of Hamor, the ruler of that area, saw her, took her and he violated her. Afterwards, he fell in love with her and wanted to win her over to be his wife. He asked his father Hamor to acquire her to be his lawful wife. When Jacob heard that Dinah had been violated, he didn't do anything because all his sons, including Dinah's six brothers, were in the field with his cattle.

Shechem kept Dinah at his house while he and Hamor went to speak with Jacob on the matter of marriage to Dinah. Meanwhile Jacob's sons returned from the field as soon as they heard what happened.

> *They were shocked and furious, because Shechem had done an outrageous thing against Israel by sleeping with Jacob's daughter – a thing that should not be done.*

They joined their father in speaking to Hamor and Shechem. Hamor made no apologies for the behaviour of his son. Instead he was asking Jacob to please allow his daughter Dinah to marry his son. Hamor also told them that they could settle amongst his people in the area, they could trade, buy property and their people could intermarry. Shechem told them he would be prepared to pay whichever price they wanted for the bride and present them with a gift as great as they would like to receive. He would do whatever they ask as long as he could marry Dinah.

Jacob must have remembered that his parents, Isaac and Rebecca, urged him not to marry a woman from Canaan. For that reason they sent him to his mother's relatives, to Laban the father of Jacob's wives Leah and Rachel.

Would he want to do to their grandchildren what they didn't want for him?

But before Jacob had the chance to agree or not with the marriage proposal, his sons had a proposition of their own for Hamor and Shechem. *'We cannot do such a thing; we cannot give our sister to a man who is not circumcised. That would be a disgrace to us. We will enter into an agreement with you on one condition only: that you become like us by circumcising all your males'.*

They told them that, and only then they could settle amongst them, intermarry and become one people with them. If they didn't agree to be circumcised, they would take their sister and leave. Shechem, the most honoured member of Hamor's family, was delighted with the thought of marrying Jacob's daughter and wanted to arrange everything as soon as possible. Both Hamor and Shechem agreed with their proposal, and they went to their city gate to discuss it with the men of their city.

Hamor convinced the men of his city by pointing out the advantages of having Jacob, who at that time was a wealthy man, living amongst them. He brought it as a business opportunity. Jacob's livestock, property and all their other animals would belong to them. Their people could intermarry and trade in the land that provided plenty of room for all of them. The only condition Hamor told them, was that all males in their city should be circumcised, just like Jacob and his household were. They all agreed and were circumcised.

Three days later, when all the men were still recovering from their circumcision, Dinah's brothers, Simeon and Levi, took their sword, went to the city and killed every male. They also killed Hamor and Shechem while taking Dinah from their house. Then the sons of Jacob went and looted the city because their sister had been defiled. They seized everything that belonged to them, both in the city and the field. Their herds, flocks, donkeys, all their wealth, their women and children. Back home, Jacob was angry with his sons because of the anger they demonstrated by the way they attacked the city. He didn't approve of the bloodshed they caused in the city. He told Simeon and Levi they made the Canaanites and Perizzites hate him. If they would join forces and attack him, his whole household was at risk of being destroyed.

The brothers replied: *'Should he have treated our sister like a prostitute'?*

Jacob was in deep trouble because of what his sons had done. God Almighty who cared for and protected Jacob wherever he went, since the time he was fleeing from his brother Esau, told him what to do. Jacob had to go to Bethel where God revealed Himself in a dream to him the first time. It was the place Abraham went to when he arrived in Canaan, where God revealed himself to Abraham and promised him that land.

Jacob told his household and all with them to get rid of their foreign gods, purify themselves and change their clothes. Jacob then buried all the idols and the earrings under an oak at Shechem. When they left, no one of the towns around followed them, because God's terror fell on all of them.

Years later when Jacob blesses his children, he promises Shechem to Joseph. When Jacob speaks of Shechem, he speaks of it as a place he himself, his sons did of course being part of his household, conquered. When the tribes of Israel conquered Canaan much later, Shechem becomes part of the territory of Joseph's eldest son Ephraim. Joseph was buried there.

As for Jacob's blessing to Simeon and Levi: *'Simeon and Levi are brothers – their swords are weapons of violence. Let me not enter their council, let me not join their assembly, for they have killed men in their anger and hamstrung oxen as they pleased. Cursed be their anger, so fierce, and their fury, so cruel! I will scatter them in Jacob and disperse them in Israel'.*

Contrary to Tamar, Dinah wasn't rejected afterwards, but her brothers Simeon and Levi chose revenge above any other solution to this matter. It is possible that she did get pregnant from Shechem, and had a son called Shaul. A son is mentioned with the children of Simeon as the son of a Canaanite woman, Canaanite referring to the father being a Canaanite having Dinah in his house to be his wife. Shaul's descendants became one of the clans of Simeon. Dinah's name means 'judged, vindicated'.

Intermezzo

Unlawful Relations and Murder

God gave His Laws to the Israelites through Moses for their communities to keep so He could bless them. God's reason to give these laws to the Israelites was besides His wish to bless them, also His own holiness.

You are to be holy to Me because I, the Lord, am holy, and I have set you apart from the nations to be My own.
Leviticus 20:26

On the subject of an unlawful relation of a man with his sister, as Amnon did to his half sister Tamar when he violated her, God was clear: '*Do not have sexual relations with your sister, either your father's daughter or your mother's daughter, whether she was born in the same home or elsewhere*'.

And He was equally clear on the punishment for such transgression: '*Everyone who does any of these detestable things – such persons must be cut off from their people. Keep My requirements and do not follow any of the detestable customs that were practiced before you came and do not defile yourselves with them. I am the Lord your God*'.

When a woman is violated, like what happened in the case of Dinah, the man that violated her is not put to death. But, he must marry her and he would never be allowed to divorce her: '*If a man happens to meet a virgin who is not pledged to be married and rapes her and they are discovered, he shall pay her father fifty shekels of silver. He must marry the young woman, for he has violated her. He can never divorce her as long as he lives*'.

As for murdering an individual deliberately as Absalom did to Amnon, and as happened to the concubine of the Levite: '*Anyone who strikes a person with a fatal blow is to be put to death. However, if it is not done intentionally, but God lets it happen, they are to flee to a place I will designate. But if anyone schemes and kills someone deliberately, that person is to be taken from My altar and put to death'.*

Justice

At the time of Judges, when the Israelites already received God's Laws from Moses and lived in the Land of Israel, there was a Levite that had a problem with his concubine. He was from a remote area in Ephraim. His concubine, from Bethlehem, Judah, was unfaithful to him, left him, and went to live in her parents' house.

After four months, the Levite saddled his two donkeys and went with his servant to Bethlehem, in an attempt to convince his concubine to return home. His concubine's father took him in his home and he stayed five days to please him, because every time he wanted to leave his father-in-law would persuade him to stay. But the fifth day the Levite left with his concubine, servant and two donkeys.

It was late in the day because he wasn't willing to spend another night in the house of his father-in-law. On their way he told his servant he didn't want to go to Jebus, Jerusalem, a non-Israelite city in those days, to spend the night. He wanted to go to Ramah or Gibeah. By the time they reached Gibeah in the territory of Benjamin, the sun had set. They sat in the city square, but no one took them in. But, that evening an old man from Ephraim who lived in Gibeah came home from his work in the field and offered them to stay at his home. They went with him, and he provided them with everything they needed for themselves and his donkeys.

Suddenly there were wicked men from the city at the door asking the old man to send his visitor, the Levite, to them so that they could have sex with him – just as it happened at the door of Lot's home in Sodom. Sodom and Gomorrah were ultimately destroyed by God.

The old man refused and told them he would send his virgin daughter and the Levite's concubine to them. They insisted they wanted the man, but the Levite sent his concubine. They took her and left. The men violated and abused her the whole night, let her go by dawn, and at daybreak she reached the house of the old man. She dropped on the ground at the door and remained there.

In the morning, when the Levite opened the door to be on his way, he found her there laying with her hands on the threshold. She was dead. He put her on one of his donkeys and went home. Once at home, he cut up his concubine's body, limb by limb into twelve parts and sent the pieces to all the areas of Israel. He got everyone's attention.

Everyone who saw it was saying to one another, Such a thing has never been seen or done, not since the day the Israelites came up out of Egypt. Just imagine! We must do something! So speak up!

Judges 19

The men of the tribes of Israel gathered before the Lord at Mizpah, about twelve kilometres north of Jerusalem, to find out what had happened and to resolve the matter. The Benjaminites heard about the gathering. The leaders of all the tribes of Israel were present at the assembly of God's people, four hundred thousand armed men strong. The Levite was also present and told them on their request what had happened to him. The leaders decided, as one, to ask their brothers the Benjaminites to turn over the wicked men who violated and killed the woman to them so they could punish them by putting them to death. They sent messengers throughout Benjamin with this message. But the Benjaminites refused to comply with their request. So the assembly decided, as one, that they would go up against the city of Gibeah.

They had four hundred thousand swordsmen ready for battle against the more than twenty-six thousand men strong army of Benjamin. The army of Israel, except the tribe of Benjamin, went to Bethel where the Ark of the Covenant was with Phinehas, Aaron's grandson as priest, to seek God's guidance. He made it clear to them that they should go up against the Benjaminites and that the army of Judah should strike first.

The battlefield was near the city of Gibeah. The tribe of Judah suffered defeat at the hands of the Benjaminites, which caused great grief amongst the men. The second and third time an army with soldiers, all the tribes, went to battle. As the Israelites were suffering heavy casualties they consulted the Lord again.

They asked, Shall we go up again to fight against the Benjaminites, our fellow Israelites, or not? The Lord responded, Go, for tomorrow I will give them into your hands. Ultimately the Israelites won the third day they went out for battle. The war was at a great cost of tens of thousand lives lost on the battlefield on both sides. The Israelites also attacked and burned Gibeah and the towns on their path in the territory of Benjamin, killing men, women and cattle. This civil war in Israel nearly resulted in the tribe of Benjamin being cut off from Israel. The Israelites grieved heavily because of Benjamin's tribe. Also because the Benjaminites were left without women to marry due to the oath the tribes of Israel took not to allow their daughters to marry Benjaminites.

In those days Israel had no king. So they took measures to ensure the men of Benjamin would get or take young women for marriage. Seeking justice because of the violation and death of a woman came at a high price for Israel, because of the stubbornness of those who preferred to protect the wrongdoers.

Judges 20:23

Vengeance

Two years after the violation of his sister Tamar by Amnon, Absalom set his plan in motion. His day of vengeance came during a carefully planned feast with Absalom's guests, including all the princes of Israel, present. His sheep shearers were at Baal Hazor near the border of Ephraim. He invited all the king's sons to attend his feast there. He also asked his father to attend with all his officials, but he declined. Then Absalom asked him to allow his son Amnon and his other sons to attend. David did ask why Amnon should go, but Absalom insisted and David let them go with Absalom.

Before the feast started, Absalom had already given orders to his men to kill Amnon. He made it clear to them that they shouldn't be afraid, nor hesitate because he had given them an order. He himself would assume the responsibility for this act. While the king's sons were celebrating and Amnon was in a festive mood drinking wine, Absalom's men killed him. Immediately all the rest of the princes stood up, mounted their mules and fled.

While they were on their way, word already came to David that all his sons were killed. Thinking all his sons were dead, David stood up, tore his clothes as a sign of mourning and lay down on the floor.

Jonadab, who was also the adviser of Amnon, told David that it was Absalom's intention to kill only Amnon, because his mind was made up to do so, ever since the day Amnon violated his sister. He should not be concerned that all the other princes were murdered. Meanwhile the man standing watch saw many people coming down the road towards them. They were the princes, they came in crying loudly, and David and all his officials cried bitterly with them. David mourned a long time every day for his son Amnon. He didn't take action against Absalom.

Was this only because of his grief, or also because he remembered Nathan's prophecy concerning the punishment he was to receive because of the case of Uriah?

Absalom fled to Talmaid the son of Ammihud, the king of Geshur, where he stayed three years. More than nine years later Absalom would commit the same act as Amnon, but then to ten concubines of his father David. His motive? King David's throne.

Endnotes

1 Samuel 25:43, 27:3, 30:5, 2 Samuel 2:2, 3:2, 13, 1 Chronicles 3:1, 4:20 Ahimoam from Jezreel
1 Samuel 27 Ziklag, David's two wives and his men's family captured by the Amalekites
2 Samuel 13, 1 Chronicles 3:1 Amnon, Tamar, Absalom
Genesis 34, 35 Dinah
Genesis 33:18-20 Jacob in Shechem
Genesis 35:23, 46:15 Leah's sons and daughter with Jacob
Genesis 27: 46-28:1-2 Jacob not to marry a Canaanite woman
Genesis 32:14-17 Jacob's wealth: example gift to Esau
Genesis 12:1-9 Bethel: the first place in Canaan that God appeared to Abraham
Genesis 28:10-22 Bethel: God appeared the first time to Jacob
Genesis 48:21-22 Jacob promises Shechem to Joseph not his brothers
Genesis 46:10 Exodus 6:15 Shaul, son of a Canaanite woman
Genesis 49:5-7 Jacob's blessing for Simeon and Levi
Joshua 16:5-17:13 Shechem Ephraim's territory
Joshua 24:32 Joseph buried at Shechem
Judges 19,20, 21 Rape of a Levite's concubine, Israel at war with Benjamin
2 Samuel 13:38, 14:28, 15:7 Absalom three years in Geshur and six years in Jerusalem
2 Samuel 15:16-17, 16:20-22 David's ten concubines
Leviticus 19:17-18 No vengeance
Psalm 62:12, Proverbs 24:12, God repays

Intermezzo Endnotes
Leviticus 18, 20:10-23, Deuteronomy 27:15-26 Unlawful sexual relations
Leviticus 20:26 Be holy, God is holy
Deuteronomy 28:1-14 Blessings
Exodus 21:12-14 Murder
Deuteronomy 22:13-30 Violation of women

BATHSHEBA
David's Sin and Repentance

Bathsheba was a beautiful woman. Her name means 'daughter of the oath'. She was the daughter of Eliam, one of David's officers who fought with him, belonging to the group of soldiers called 'The Thirty'. Eliam was the son of Ahitophel from Gilo, a city in Judah. Ahitophel was one of David's chief advisers, who would betray him later. Thus Bathsheba came from the tribe of Judah, and she was Ahitophel's granddaughter. She was married to one of David's loyal officers, Uriah the Hittite, and they lived in Jerusalem. Later on, married to David, Bathsheba gave birth to her second son with David.

The Case of Uriah

The spring following the defeat of the Syrians by Israel, David sent Joab with his officers and troops of Israel's army to fight the Ammonites. They defeated them and brought their capital city Rabbah under siege. David himself remained in Jerusalem, a decision that would be disastrous for him, his household and Israel.

One day David went to his palace roof after he had a nap. It was late in the afternoon. While taking a walk on the roof he saw a beautiful woman bathing at her house. David, curious to know who she was, sent a messenger to find out. She was Bathsheba, daughter of Eliam and the wife of Uriah the Hittite. David wanted to see her and sent messengers to bring her. Once at his palace, he slept with her and sent her home. Soon after, Bathsheba sent a message to David telling him that she was pregnant with his child. Just before Bathsheba met David, she had just finished her ritual of purification because of her monthly period. So, she certainly wasn't pregnant at the time David met her. David thought of a plan to deal with this situation. If he could just have Uriah sleep with his wife, then the child would be believed to be Uriah's and not his. But, Uriah, being one of David's loyal officers, was out on a campaign to fight the Ammonites.

What did David do? He sent a message to Joab telling him to send Uriah the Hittite to him. When he arrived in Jerusalem, he went to see David, who asked him about Joab, the troops, and the progress of the war effort at Rabbah. Then he sent Uriah home to rest, and he had a present delivered for him at his home.

The next day, David heard that Uriah didn't go home, but that he had slept at the palace gate with the king's guards. David sent for him and asked him why he didn't go home after such a long absence.

Uriah replied: *'The men of Israel and Judah are away in battle, and the Covenant Box is with them; my commander Joab and his officers are camping out in the open. How could I go home, eat and drink, and sleep with my wife? By all that's sacred, I swear that I could never do such a thing'!*

David's plan failed. The man was too loyal to David and Israel's cause. David decided to invite him for supper at the palace, and the next day he would send him on his way to join Israel's army on the battlefield. During supper David deliberately got Uriah drunk, hoping he would go home to his wife. Uriah didn't. Even drunk, the man held to his principles. So, he slept on his blanket in the palace's guard room. Again David's plan failed.

The next morning David sent Uriah on his way with a message for Joab, written by David saying: *'Put Uriah in the front line, where the fighting is heaviest, then retreat and let him be killed'.*

So David had the man carry his own death sentence. Joab followed his orders. While they besieged the city of Rabbah, he sent him to a place where the enemy was strong which led to heavy casualties. Some of David's officers died that day, including Uriah. Joab sent a messenger with word about what happened, and knowing David's strategies in battle, he prepared the messenger well in dealing with David's reaction concerning the heavy casualties. He gave him specific instructions in case David would get angry about the strategy used for battle that day.

While fighting, Joab and his men drove the Amonites back to their city gate, getting too close to the city wall where the Amonites shot arrows at them, which was deadly to many of them. Close to a wall is a position the Israelites would rather not take, ever since Abimelech, son of Gideon, while standing close to the wall of a tower was seriously injured and ultimately died, a story well known by Joab and David.

The messenger did as Joab ordered, and he was clear about saying: *'Your officer Uriah was also killed'.*

David gave a message for Joab to the messenger: *'Encourage Joab and tell him not to be upset, since you never can tell who will die in battle. Tell him to launch a stronger attack on the city and capture it'.*

Who Is David?

Bathsheba, now a widow, mourned for her husband. In keeping with the traditions, seven days of mourning would have to be observed, with the day of the funeral counted as the first day of mourning. And for a period of thirty days, including the initial seven days of mourning, Bathsheba would not be allowed to get married again.

Possibly after these days, David had Bathsheba brought to the palace and he married her. This way David could still hide what he had done: Getting Bathsheba pregnant while she was married, and killing her husband to keep her and her child. Soon after their son was born.

But the Lord was not pleased with what David had done.
2 Samuel 11

Judgment

Abimelech was a son of Gideon, and his mother was Gideon's concubine from Shechem. But Gideon also had many wives with whom he had seventy sons. He was the son of Joash from the Menasseh tribe.

Joash once said, to protect Gideon, that if an idol is actually a god, surely he would be able to defend himself when someone breaks down his altar. One day God sent his angel to Gideon, which means 'mighty warrior', to recruit him to save Israel out of the hands of their enemy the Midianites.

It took God a lot of convincing to get Gideon to fight the Midianites. Once that happened, he destroyed the altar of an idol and built one for God. He took, as God told him, only 300 men, instead of the 20,000 who set camp with him, and defeated the enemy. He became the successor of Deborah of Ephraim in ruling over Israel as judge for forty years, during which there was peace in Israel.

After Gideon's death, the Israelites again turned away from God and they didn't show any loyalty towards Gideon's family.

Abimelech, unlike his brothers, wanted to be king and went to Shechem to seek the support of his mother's clan. He succeeded in convincing her brothers and the citizens of Shechem to support him, being their relative, as their leader, instead of the seventy sons of Gideon. They provided him with seventy shekels of silver from the temple of their idol, which Abimelech used to hire some men who became his followers. He went with them to his father's home in Ophrah, where he murdered all of his seventy brothers on one stone. But, Gideon's youngest son, Jotham, hid himself and escaped.

Then all the citizens of Shechem and the whole house of Millo gathered by the plain of the pillar, a stone that was set up in the past by

Joshua, the first Judge in the Land of Israel.

For what reason? It is where Joshua gathered the Israelites, made a covenant for the people, reaffirmed decrees and laws for them, recorded these in the book of Law of God and there under the oak tree he erected a stone as witness against the people if they would be untrue to God. This was the place where Jacob buried the idols of the people under the oak, before leaving Shechem to go to Bethel. It is also there that they crowned Abimelech their king.

When Jotham heard what had happened, he climbed on top of Mount Gerizim and shouted a parable, the earliest in Israel's history, for all to hear: *"One day the trees went out to anoint a king for themselves. They said to the olive tree, 'Be our king'. But the olive tree answered, 'Should I give up my oil, by which both gods and humans are honoured, to hold sway over the trees'?*

"Next, the trees said to the fig tree, 'Come and be our king'. But the fig tree replied, 'Should I give up my fruit, so good and sweet, to hold sway over the trees'?

"Then the trees said to the vine, 'Come and be our king'. But the vine answered, 'Should I give up my wine, which cheers both gods and humans, to hold sway over the trees'?

"Finally all the trees said to the thorn bush, 'Come and be our king'. The thorn bush said to the trees, 'If you really want to anoint me king over you, come and take refuge in my shade; but if not, then let fire come out of the thorn bush and consume the cedars of Lebanon'!"

After these words, Jotham continued by asking those present whether they acted honourably and in good faith towards Gideon, who did so much for them by rescuing them out of the hands of the Medianites, and his family by making Abimelech their king, while they financed him in murdering Gideon's sons.

Jotham finished by saying: *'If you have, may Abimelech be your joy, and may you be his, too! But if you have not, let fire come out from Abimelech and consume you, the citizens of Shechem and the house of Millo, and let fire come out from you, the citizens of Shechem and the house of Millo, and consume Abimelech! After this, Jotham fled to Be'er, and stayed there because he was afraid of his brother Abimelech who ruled over Israel'.*

After three years, God stirred animosity between the citizens of Shechem and Abimelech. They started to act treacherously against Abimelech, which resulted in a civil war between them, spreading out to other places in the region. Ultimately Abimelech and his men went to the tower in the city of Thebez to burn it down, just as they did in Shechem, killing more than a thousand people. A woman threw a millstone down. It fell on Abimelech, who was fighting close to the wall, and fractured his skull. Badly injured, he asked his armour-bearer to draw his sword and kill him, because he didn't want people to say that a woman killed him. His servant did as ordered.

Abimelech's death and that of the people of Shechem came about by animosity amongst themselves. The words spoken by Gideon's youngest son turned out to be prophetic. Unlike Uriah's death, the death of Abimelech and his supporters was a punishment imposed by God because they killed Gideon's children.

Repentance

It was not the first time David became interested in a married woman that he later on would marry. This was also the case with Abigail. David had met her only once, the day she went to speak to him to prevent him and his men from attacking her husband, Nabal, and she succeeded in her attempt. But in her case, it is after her husband died that David made it clear he was interested in her, and he sent his messengers to ask her to be his wife.

If David was patient concerning Bathsheba the same way he was with Abigail, would the same have happened? It is possible, for Uriah, being an officer in David's army, had many battles to fight. God, who rules supreme and has the sole power over life and death, is the one with the wisdom to deal with a matter like this.

Suppose things would have gone with Bathsheba as with Abigail, then David would have married a widow and their son would still be loved by God. But, David had chosen to act otherwise and in doing so, followed a sinful path. His sinful acts would have serious consequences, reaching far into his own and Israel's future. He showed contempt to God, who was prepared to give him everything.

> *I anointed you king over Israel, and I delivered you from the hand of Saul. I gave your master's house to you, and your master's wives into your arms. I gave you all Israel and Judah. And if all this had been too little, I would have given you even more.*
>
> 2 Samuel 12:7-13

One day, God sent Nathan to confront David. As soon as he arrived, he told David a little story about a poor and a rich man living in the same town.

The rich man had a lot of sheep and cattle, while the poor man only possessed an ewe lamb that he had bought. The poor man took care of the lamb like he did his own children. He shared his food and drink with it. The lamb was like a daughter to him, and he even let it fall asleep in his arms.

One day a traveller came to town and went to visit the rich man. Hospitable as he was, he wanted to prepare a meal for his guest. But this man, for whatever reason, didn't want to use one of his own sheep for the meal. Instead he took the ewe lamb of the poor man and prepared it for his guest.

David's reaction? Burning with anger he said: *'As surely as the Lord lives, the man who did this must die! He must pay for that lamb four times over, because he did such a thing and had no pity'*.

But then Nathan replied: *'You are the man'!* He continued to tell David what God had to say to him. After Nathan told David about everything God had given him and that He would have been prepared to give him even more, he asked David: *'Why did you despise the word of the Lord by doing what is evil in His eyes? You struck down Uriah the Hittite with the sword and took his wife to be your own. You killed him with the sword of the Ammonites. Now, therefore, the sword will never depart from your house, because you despised Me and took the wife of Uriah the Hittite to be your own'*.

And Nathan, still intervening on God's behalf, continued by saying: *This is what the Lord says: 'Out of your own household I am going to bring calamity on you. Before your very eyes I will take your wives and give them to one who is close to you, and he will sleep with your wives in broad daylight. You did it in secret, but I will do this thing in broad daylight before all Israel'*.

David's response to Nathan's rebuke: *'I have sinned against the Lord'*. And David realised that what he did could lead to his death. As David himself already made clear that he deserved to die, like he said the rich man in Nathan's story should. In fact, David did to Uriah what King Saul tried to do to him when he gave his daughter Michal away to marry him.

Where Saul was unsuccessful, David was. But God's mercy decided otherwise concerning David's fate. Nathan replied: *'The Lord has taken away your sin. You are not going to die'*.

The last matter Nathan had to settle? He said: *'But because by doing this you have shown utter contempt for the Lord, the son born to you will die'*.

David showed much of his remorse and repentance in his prayers.

> *Have mercy on me, O God, according to Your unfailing love; according to Your great compassion blot out my transgressions. Wash away all my iniquity and cleanse me from my sin. For I know my transgressions, and my sin is always before me. Against You, You only, have I sinned and done what is evil in Your sight; so You are right in Your verdict and justified when You judge.*
>
> *Create in me a pure heart, O God, and renew a steadfast spirit within me. Do not cast me from Your presence or take your Holy Spirit from me. Restore to me the joy of Your salvation and grant me a willing spirit, to sustain me.*
>
> Psalm 51

Intermezzo
Adultery and Murder

David broke two, and Bathsheba one of the laws of the Ten Commandments.

> *You shall not murder.*
> *You shall not commit adultery.*
> Exodus 20

God's commandments were well known by David, who kept all of them, except when it came to what he had done to Uriah.

> *For David had done what was right in the eyes of the Lord and had not failed to keep any of the Lord's commands all the days of his life – except in the case of Uriah the Hittite.*
> 1 Kings 15:5

Which punishment did God's Law stipulate concerning adultery?

> *If a man commits adultery with another man's wife – with the wife of his neighbour – both the adulterer and the adulteress are to be put to death.*
> Leviticus 20:10

In the case of murder, what would be the punishment? The person would have to go to trial and if found guilty he would receive the death penalty. When it was done intentionally, regardless whether the murder was done with an iron, stone or wooden object, the verdict would be the death penalty.

> *If anyone strikes someone a fatal blow with an iron object, that person is a murderer; the murderer is to be put to death.*
> Numbers 35:6-34

Even though David himself didn't kill Uriah, he did give the order. In fact, he used the weapons of the Ammonites as his murder weapon. As Nathan told him: '*You struck down Uriah the Hittite with the sword and took his wife to be your own. You killed him with the sword of the Ammonites*'.

Both David and Bathsheba could have died because of what they had done, but on David's remorse and repentance, God was merciful to forgive and decided otherwise without ignoring his own Law.

Punishment

After Nathan left, the child became ill. David wanted his son to get well, so he prayed daily to God. He wept, laid on the floor in his room, refused to eat any food, didn't wash himself or have a change of clothes. He fasted every day so severely that the elders of his household started to get worried about him. But he wouldn't listen to them when they tried to get him off the floor to get him to eat.

The seventh day, David noticed that his attendants were keeping something from him, because they were whispering amongst themselves. In fact, they were afraid to tell him what happened that day – afraid he might do something desperate when they tell him the news of his son's death. But David realised what had happened, and asked his attendants whether the child died. They replied that he had died.

Immediately David got up from the floor, washed up, had a change of clothes and some lotion. He went to the House of the Lord and worshipped. Afterwards, he returned to his home and he ate the food he had served to him.

David's attendants were astonished at how he was behaving. So, they asked him why, after all the fasting, weeping and praying when his child was alive, now that he is dead, his behaviour changed. It seemed to indicate he was in good spirit.

David gave a down-to-earth explanation. When he was alive he did everything possible to try to sway God in being gracious to him and let the child live. But now that he was dead, there was no point in doing all that, because there was no way he could bring him back.

On the contrary, while his son couldn't come to him, one day he would go to his son. And that was it.

Losing the child was painful, but so was the unjust way David treated Uriah, who was betrayed and lost his life in the process. God is righteous and wise when He intervenes where man-made problems are caused.

> *Can anyone teach knowledge to God, since He judges even the highest?*
>
> Job 21:22

There are other babies in much different circumstances for whom God provided for them to live. At the time the Israelites lived in Egypt, under a Pharaoh that didn't know Jacob's son Joseph. Jacob's descendants were becoming a numerous people. The Pharaoh was afraid that one day when Egypt's enemies attacked them, the Hebrews might join them in the fight, and ultimately leave the country. So, he put slave masters over them to oppress them into doing forced labour, either in the fields or construction work. They treated them harshly, worked them ruthlessly and made their lives hard and bitter. But, the more they were oppressed, the more numerous they became.

So, the Pharaoh took the drastic decision that all Hebrew baby boys should be killed at birth. He gave strict instructions to the midwives Shiphrah and Puah, that attended the Israeli women at delivery. They were to let the baby girls live, but kill the baby boys as soon as they were born. Once at work, the midwives didn't do as instructed because they feared God. Pharaoh summoned them to ask them why they let the boys live.

Shiphrah and Puah answered: *'Hebrew women are not like Egyptian women; they are vigorous and give birth before the midwives arrive'.*

Because they feared God, He was kind to them and gave them a family of their own, while the number of the Hebrew people increased even more.

Meanwhile the Pharaoh had to find another way to make sure the number of the Hebrew people would be contained, since his first attempt through his idea of birth control didn't work out as planned. He issued an order to all the people in the land of Egypt: *'Every Hebrew boy that is born you must throw into the Nile, but let every girl live'.*

The Hebrew families had to keep their new-born boys hidden to save their lives. So did one of the Levite families. Amram of the tribe of Levi married a Levite woman called Jochebed. They had three children.

When the youngest was born, the Pharaoh's order was in place, and his parents had to hide him. After three months this was no longer possible. His mother thought up a plan to save his life and with the help of his elder sister Miriam, she succeeded in her attempt. She got a papyrus basket or ark, coated it with tar and pitch, put baby Moses in it and put it among the reeds along the bank of the Nile River.

His sister, curious to see what would happen or in an attempt to protect her baby brother, stood at a distance watching over him. She saw the Pharaoh's daughter and her attendants walking along the riverbank. Then Pharaoh's daughter, who saw the basket, told her slave to get it. He brought it to her, and once she opened it, she saw a baby crying. She felt sorry for him and said to her attendants that he was one of the Hebrew babies. Then Miriam saw her chance, came forward and asked the Pharaoh's daughter whether she should bring a Hebrew woman to care for the baby for her. She agreed, so Miriam went home and got her mother to come with her.

Pharaoh's daughter told her that she would pay her to nurse the baby. But, she had to bring the child back to her as soon as he grew older. Later, she raised the boy that became her son and she named him Moses, because she said that she drew him out of the water. Moses, meaning 'the one who was drawn out', grew up to become a humble man, a leader, a prophet and lawgiver of God.

Under God's guidance, with him performing numerous miracles, Moses together with his siblings, Aaron and Miriam, led the Hebrew people out of Egypt to the Promised Land – land God had promised more than four hundred years before to Abraham.

In another case with completely different circumstances, a baby was saved by David's son Solomon. Two prostitutes came to see the King of Israel. The matter of dispute was a baby boy. Both women said the boy was their son. One of them told the story to the king. Their babies were born three days apart, while they were the only ones in the house. The morning after the second baby was born, the mother of the first baby got up to nurse her baby. She found him dead, while the one of the other mother was alive. She realised that the other woman had switched her dead baby for hers during the night. The other woman's baby was dead after she laid on him while sleeping.

But, the other woman insisted this wasn't true. So, they both continued to argue about the baby and wanted to keep him. The king sent for a sword, and then ordered for the baby to be cut in two pieces. Half for each woman. The mother of the baby, horrified at the thought of her baby dying, pleaded with Solomon to let the baby live, and to give him to the other woman. While the other wanted him to be killed, in that way no one would have him. Solomon, convinced who the real mother was, ordered the baby to be given to the first mother who, out of love, pleaded for his life. All Israel was in awe when they heard of this verdict. They realised God had given Solomon much wisdom to settle difficult disputes in a fair way.

David's sinful deeds against Uriah would have more consequences. Sadly, in this way he himself contributed to what was set to happen to him, his family and Israel in the future. In every generation the sword would not depart from his family, and someone from his own family would cause much trouble and grief to him.

> *I swear to you that I will cause someone from your own family to bring trouble on you. You will see it when I take your wives from you and give them to another man; and he will have intercourse with them in broad daylight. You sinned in secret, but I will make this happen in broad daylight for all Israel to see.*
>
> 2 Samuel 12:11-12

Who would this someone be? Would it be David's eldest son, Amnon, who in the future would commit a terrible act in David's household? Or Adonijah, who one day will be feasting thinking he is king, while he is actually missing out on it. None of the above. Not Amnon nor Adonihjah, but only Absalom.

> *So they set up a tent for Absalom on the palace roof, and in the sight of everyone, Absalom went in and had intercourse with his father's concubines.*
>
> 2 Samuel 16:15-23

Just as God would punish Ham for his wrongful act against his father Noah through one of his sons, Canaan, so would he David through one of his sons, Absalom. In both cases God made it clear they would be punished by one of their sons, but in the case of Ham, he mentioned the name of the son, while in David's, he only gave a clue to identify him in the future.

> *Can anyone teach knowledge to God, since He judges even the highest?*
>
> Job 21:22

Comfort

After his son's death, David comforted Bathsheba. She got pregnant and gave him a son. They named him Solomon, meaning 'peace'.

Nathan, one of the Lord's prophets, on God's behalf also called him Jedidiah, meaning 'beloved of the Lord'. The son out of the sinful relationship died, so he couldn't be heir to David's throne. The one out of his marital relationship with Bathsheba would. The mother of both Solomon and his elder brother Chileab, son of Abigail, were widows. But, for Solomon since he was God's choice to be the successor of David, who was in agreement with his God's wishes, this would not be an impediment.

Meanwhile Joab was still at Rabbah fighting the Ammonites. He sent word to David that he had captured the water supply of the city. He suggested to David that he come to Rabbah with the rest of the Israelite army to take the city. Otherwise Joab himself would take it, and the city would carry his name.

David decided to join the battle at Rabbah and he took the rest of Israel's troops with him. He attacked the city, captured it, and brought a great quantity of plunder out of the city, including a golden crown the Ammonites put on the head of their idol. David took the jewel in it and put it in his own crown. He put the people he brought out of the city, and those of the Ammonite towns, to work, after which he and his army went back to Jerusalem. David went out to fight his enemies and again returned victorious. This was sign that after all he had done to Uriah, his God didn't depart from him in battle, as He had done from Saul in the past.

Despite the case of Uriah and all the grief David would be going through from that point forward, David himself would be comforted by God through his son Solomon.

One day in his old age, when his officials congratulate him with his son Solomon becoming king, David will bow down in worship on his bed to say:

> *Praise be to the Lord, the God of Israel, who has allowed my eyes to see a successor on my throne today.*
>
> 1 Kings 1:48

Who is a God like you, who pardons sin and forgives the transgression of the remnant of His inheritance? You do not stay angry for ever, but delight to show mercy.

Micah 7:18

Endnotes

2 Samuel 11, 12:1-25 Bathsheba
2 Samuel 11:3, 15:12, 23:24-29 Eliam Bathsheba's father, son of Ahitophel
2 Samuel 12:26-31, 1 Chronicles 20:1-3 David conquers Rabba
2 Samuel 12:10-11a David's sin, reason troubles within his family
1 Samuel 25 Abigail David's third wife after Michal and Ahinoam
2 Samuel 23:34, 1 Chronicles 3:5 Eliam, one of David's soldiers of the group of thirty
2 Samuel 15:12 Ahitophel, David's adviser
Genesis 9: 18-29 Punishment of Ham through his son Canaan
Leviticus 15 Rules concerning uncleanness of men and women, woman's monthly period
Judges 6-9 Gideon and Abimelech
Genesis 35:1-4, Joshua 24:25-27 The place where Jacob left Shechem, the stone set up by Joshua
Exodus 1-2, 6:20, Numbers 12:3, 26:59 Moses, Aaron, Miriam, their mother Jochebed
Genesis 15 God's promises to Abraham concerning his descendants and the Promised Land
1 Kings 3:16-28 Solomon and the baby
1 Kings 1, 2 Solomon becomes king

Intermezzo Endnotes

Deuteronomy 5 Ten Commandments
Proverbs 6:22 Adultery
2 Samuel 12:9 David's murder weapon
Exodus 21:12-14, Leviticus 20:10 Death penalty for those who commit murder, adultery

ABISHAG

David's Companion

Abishag, a very beautiful young woman from the small village of Shunem in the territory of the tribe of Issachar, became David's wife. David didn't have intimate relations with her, so they didn't have children.

Companionship

Abishag, a virgin, was brought to David by his officials to be his companion in his old age. She was found after a search over all Israel. She took care of David, God's chosen king, and attended to his guests. She would also sleep close beside David to keep him warm, because although his servants covered him with blankets he could not keep himself warm.

> *Also, if two lie down together, they will keep warm. But how can one keep warm alone?*
>
> Ecclesiastes 4:11

By this time David didn't go out with his men on battles. Sometime earlier when he went out with them to fight the Philistines, David got exhausted. One of the Philistine soldiers, a giant and a descendant of Rapha in Gath, armed with spear and sword pinned his attention on David and went up to fight and kill him. But Abishai son of Zerujah quickly came to David's rescue and killed the giant. That day: *'David's men swore to him, saying, Never again will you go out with us to battle, so that the lamp of Israel will not be extinguished'*.

Abishag kept David company, showed him kindness and was present when he received visitors in his room. While she was taking care of David, she also witnessed the conversations between David and his visitors.

One day both Bathsheba, Solomon's mother, and the prophet Nathan came to see David to discuss the succession to his throne, because one of his sons had put himself forward to be his successor and organised a feast to celebrate this. But David already knew that God had chosen his son Solomon, and not Adonijah, the handsome son of his wife Haggit, to succeed him as king of Israel.

> *Of all my sons – and the Lord has given me many – He has chosen my son Solomon to sit on the throne of the kingdom of the Lord over Israel. He said to me: Solomon your son is the one who will build My house and My courts, for I have chosen him to be My son, and I will be his father.*
>
> 1 Chronicles 28:5-6

This must have been known by David's household, including Adonijah. Otherwise, why didn't he invite Solomon to his feast? And why did he choose this moment for his move to seize David's throne? Because he viewed David as old and weak? Perhaps isolated, having no allies of weight at his side to prevent him, Adonijah, from achieving his goal.

As Adonijah, revealing his state of mind at that time would say later: *'The kingdom was mine. All Israel looked to me as their king'*.

David did notice Adonijah's preparations. He got himself chariots with horses and fifty men to run in front of him. David's mind was made up, so he didn't have any reason to rebuke him.

What David wasn't aware of was what had been going on in Israel that same day when Bathsheba and Nathan came to see him. As happened before, God intervened through Nathan who arranged this meeting to inform David. That day without David's knowledge, his son Adonijah had already proclaimed himself king in the presence of all his guests attending a great feast he organised at the stone of Zoheleth, the serpent-stone, near the fountain of En Rogel. To Nathan, as far as Adonijah was concerned, those he didn't invite, including and especially Solomon, were already on his death list. That was also one of the reasons Nathan advised Bathsheba to speak with David on the matter of the succession to his throne.

Kindness

In the far future, Elisha the prophet would go to Abishag's village of Shunem. Once there he was invited to stay for a meal by a well-to-do Shunammite woman. Whenever Elisha went to Shunem, she would invite him over. She even asked her husband to build a small room on the roof of their home for Elisha. They put a bed in it, a table, a chair and a lamp for Elisha. As she said to her husband: *'I know that this man who often comes our way is a holy man of God'*.

Every time Elisha went to Shunem he would stay in the room at her house. One time when Elisha and his servant Gehazi were staying there, he wanted to know what he could do for her after all her trouble for him. He asked Gehazi to call her so he could ask. The Shunammite came in the room and stood before Elisha. He asked her what he could do for her. Maybe he could speak to the king of Israel or the commander of Israel's army in her behalf? She replied she had a home among her own people. So, she was happy with that. But after she left, Elisha was still wondering what could be done for her. Then Gehazi informed him of the fact that she didn't have a son.

Elisha told Gehazi to call her back in, so he did. She came and stood in the doorway. He told her: *'About this time next year, you will hold a son in your arms'*.

She objected to what he said and told Elisha not to mislead her. She didn't want her hopes raised. But, she became pregnant and had a son around the time Elisha said. The child grew up and when his father was with the reapers in the field, he went out to him.

Later on, he told his servant to carry the child to his mother because he cried that his head hurts. Once inside with his mother, the boy stayed on her lap until noon and she noticed that he had died.

What can she do about this?

She carried him up to Elisha's room and laid him down on his bed and shut the door. Then she called her husband and asked him for a servant and a donkey so she could quickly go to see the man of God, and return. She didn't tell her husband the reason. But, her husband replied by asking why she should go to him that day, because it wasn't New Moon or Shabbat. They were not having a feast. Still she wanted to go, and he provided her with what she asked for. She saddled the donkey, told her servant to lead on, and not to slow down unless she said so.

Elisha was at Mount Carmel. He saw her in a distance coming and told his servant Gehazi to run out to meet her and ask her whether she, her husband and son were all right. She said they were all right, but when she reached Elisha she bowed down and took hold of his feet. Gehazi wanted to push her away from Elisha, but he stopped him and told him she was obviously in great distress. The Lord hadn't revealed the reason to him yet. But, then she made it clear to him when she spoke about her son, that she didn't ask him for one, and that she told him not to raise her hopes to have a son.

Elisha immediately understood something was very wrong with her son. He told Gehazi to take his staff, run to the Shunammite's house and put it on the boy's face. To be as fast as he could, Elisha told Gehazi he was not to greet anyone he meets on his way or answer anyone who greets him. Gehazi did as he was told. The boy didn't react.

Meanwhile the boy's mother told Elisha that she would not leave. So, he decided to go with her to her house to attend to her son. On their way, they met up with Gehazi on his way back to tell Elisha the bad news, that the boy didn't wake up. When Elisha arrived at her house, he went to the room where the boy was dead on the bed, shut the door, prayed to the Lord, laid himself on the boy. As he stretched himself, he felt that his body was getting warm. Then he got up and walked back and forth in the room. Once more he laid himself on the boy as before, mouth to mouth, eyes to eyes, hand to hand and he stretched himself. The boy sneezed seven times, after which he opened up his eyes. Elisha called Gehazi to the room and told him to bring the boy's mother. Elisha told her to take her son. She fell at his feet, bowed down to the ground, got up and took her son with her. She was grateful her son was alive.

This Shunammite woman was also married to a man who was old, but unlike Abishag, she did have a son with her husband.

Strength

That day, Bathsheba came into David's room, bowed down, stood before the king, and he asked her what she wanted. She said to David that he once solemnly promised her, by the Lord his God, that her son Solomon would become king after him. But now Adonijah has proclaimed himself king, celebrating with all his guests, while sacrificing a great number of cattle, fattened calves and sheep. He had invited all the princes, Abiathar the priest, Joab the army commander, but not Solomon. Bathsheba told David that the eyes of all Israel are on him, expecting him to give clarity about Israel's next king after him. She also expressed her concern regarding her safety and that of her son after the king's death. She expected they would be treated as traitors. Punishable by death.

Meanwhile, Nathan came to the palace and David was notified of his arrival. Bathsheba left the room, Nathan came in, bowed with his face to the ground, and asked David if he declared Adonijah as his successor without his knowledge. Because that same day Adonijah was having a great feast with all the king's sons, the commanders and Abiathar, drinking with him saying, '*long live King Adonijah*'! Nathan continued and told David that Solomon, the priest Zadok, Benaiah son of Jehoiada and Nathan himself were not invited.

As often happened to David during the course of his life, it's when, to his enemies he seemed to be weak, that he finds strength with his God to be strong enough to follow His lead in doing His will.

After listening to what Nathan had to tell him, King David had Bathsheba called back in the room. She came, bowed down for the king and stood before him. David wanted her to be present while he took an oath saying: *'As surely as the Lord lives, who has delivered me out of every trouble, I will surely carry out this very day what I swore to you by the Lord, the God of Israel: Solomon your son shall be king after me, and he will sit on my throne in my place'*.

Bathsheba bowed down with her face to the ground before King David while wishing the king to live for ever.

Then David had the following people called to come to his room. Nathan, the priest Zadok and Benaiah son of Jehoiada. King David had a plan and he was in a hurry to execute it. Those who remained loyal to him would follow his orders. He ordered them to take Solomon his son to the Gihon Spring, the main water source of the City of David. David wanted Solomon to go mounted on his own mule, which was a sign of honour to Solomon. Once at the spring, Zadok and Nathan had to anoint Solomon King of Israel, blow the trumpet, shout 'long live King Solomon'! and then go up with him to sit on his throne.

Benaiah's answer to King David: *'Amen! May the Lord, the God of my lord the king, so declare it. As the Lord was with my lord the king, so may He be with Solomon to make his throne even greater than the throne of my lord King David'!*

So, they went down with David's personal guards, the Kerethites and Perethites. They escorted Solomon on David's mule to the Gihon Spring where Zadok, who took the horn of oil from the sacred tent with him, anointed Solomon King of Israel. Afterwards they proceeded as planned. Along the way up people joined in shouting, *'long live King Solomon'*, rejoicing greatly with singing and making music. They were so loud that the ground shook.

The city rejoiced and the royal officials went to congratulate David saying: *'May your God make Solomon's name more famous than yours and his throne greater than yours'!* *And the king bowed in worship on his bed and said, 'Praise be to the Lord, the God of Israel, who has allowed my eyes to see a successor on my throne today'.*

Meanwhile Adonijah and his guests were finishing their feast and were wondering about the sound of the trumpet and the loud noise coming from the city. At that moment Jonathan, son of the priest Abiathar, arrived and Adonijah was delighted with his presence, expecting him to bring him good news. But, news that Kind David had appointed Solomon King of Israel, had him anointed as such and sit on his royal throne, was far from good news for Adonijah.

Immediately everyone left, and Adonijah, fearing for his life, had no other place to go than to the Tabernacle, where seeking refuge, he took hold of the horns of the altar. Word came to Solomon about Adonijah's fear and his request that Solomon would swear that he wouldn't have him killed by the sword.

> *Solomon replied, If he shows himself to be worthy, not a hair of his head will fall to the ground; but if evil is found in him, he will die. Solomon sent men to bring Adonijah to his court. Once there, he bowed down to King Solomon, and he sent him home. Later Solomon would thank God for his kindness showed to his father David.*
>
> *You have shown great kindness to your servant, my father David, because he was faithful to you and righteous and upright in heart. You have continued this great kindness to him and have given him a son to sit on his throne this very day.*
>
> 1 Kings 3:6

Intermezzo

A Father's Wife

Adonijah tried to marry Abishag, his father's wife, but Solomon didn't allow this. Before him, Absalom violated ten of his father's concubines for Israel to see. God has been very clear in His Laws that a man should not have sexual relations with his father's wife because this act would dishonour his father.

> *No one is to approach any close relative to have sexual relations. I am the Lord. Do not have sexual relations with your father's wife; that would dishonour your father.*
>
> Leviticus 18:6,8
>
> *If a man has sexual relations with his father's wife, he has dishonoured his father. Both the man and the woman are to be put to death; their blood will be on their own heads.*
>
> Leviticus 20:11

But, even before God gave His Laws through Moses to the Israelites, this act was considered to be wrong and had serious consequences. Reuben, the son of Jacob for instance, slept with his father's concubine Bilha, and Israel heard of it.

Later when Jacob blessed his sons, he made it perfectly clear to Reuben, his eldest son, that because of his act, he would not be considered the most important one within his father's household.

> *Reuben, you are my firstborn, my might, the first sign of my strength, excelling in honour, excelling in power. Turbulent as the waters, you will no longer excel, for you went up onto your father's bed, onto my couch and defiled it.*
>
> Genesis 49:3-4

Punishment

Now evil was found in Adonijah. As soon as his father David died, Adonijah had one request. So, he went to Bathsheba. She didn't trust him, and asked him immediately whether he came peacefully. He replied that he came peacefully and had a request to make, adding that all Israel was expecting him to be king, but that the throne went to Solomon by God's choice. He asked Bathsheba not to refuse him in asking King Solomon to allow Abishag the Shunammite to marry him. Bathsheba agreed she would speak to the king, and so she did.

She went to see her son, King Solomon. He stood up from his throne to meet her, bowed for her and had her sit on a throne he had his servants bring in for her, at his right hand. Then she asked Solomon not to refuse her on the matter she wanted to present to him. Solomon told her he wouldn't refuse her. Then Bathsheba told him to let Abishag marry his brother Adonijah.

Solomon's reaction? *'Why do you request Abishag the Shunammite for Adonijah? You might as well request the kingdom for him – after all, he is my older brother – yes, for him and for Abiathar the priest and Joab son of Zeruiah'!*

Solomon saw in Adonijah's request that he still had aspirations to become king. He wanted to do a similar act as Absalom did in the past by sleeping with David's concubines. King Solomon swore by the Lord that Adonijah would be put to death that same day. He gave the order to Benaiah son of Jehoiada, and it was done.

Then Solomon showed leniency towards Abiathar the priest by not sentencing him to death, as he did with the two other conspirators to overthrow his father. Instead he removed him from the priesthood of the Lord and sent him home to Anathoth.

Even though, according to Solomon, he deserved to die, he did carry the Ark of the Lord in front of his father David and he did share in all his father's hardships. Solomon's decision was a fulfilment of the prophecy given to the priest Eli against his house, to which Abiathar belonged. That prophecy made it clear that Eli's house wouldn't continue to minister as priests to the Lord.

> *I will honour those who honour me, and I will treat with contempt those who despise me.*
>
> 1 Samuel 2:27-36

When word about what happened came to Joab who was part of Adonijah's conspiracy to take over King David's throne, he fled to the Tent of the Lord, the Tabernacle, and took hold of the horns of the altar. Solomon was informed about this, and he sent Benaiah with specific orders to kill Joab. Once there, Benaiah told Joab to come out of the Tent of the Lord. Joab refused and told him he would die there.

Back at Solomon's court Benaiah reported Joab's answer. Solomon told him to do as Joab said and bury him. Benaiah returned, entered the Tent of the Lord, carried out his orders and buried Joab at his home in the country. Solomon replaced Joab with Benaiah as commander of Israel's army and he installed the priest Zadok instead of Abiathar.

Adonijah failed at both attempts to become king, and ultimately he was killed by the orders of King Solomon.

David was thirty years old when he became king, first of Judah where he reigned seven years, after which he became king over all of Israel. David reigned forty years in total.

To David, Abishag was his companion, showing him kindness at a difficult period in his life, the time he survived a second coup d'etat and secured his succession to the throne. Sometime after he made Solomon king, King David who was more than seventy years old, died a natural death and was buried in the City of David, leaving the legacy of the Kingdom of Israel.

Through his life he showed his love and faithfulness to the God of his ancestors, the Almighty God, the God of Israel.

> *Love and faithfulness keep a king safe; through love his throne is made secure.*
>
> Proverbs 20:28

Endnotes

1 Kings 1:1-4,15 Abishag takes care of David
Joshua 19:17-19 Shunem territory of Issachar
1 Kings 1, 2 Abishag, Adonijah
2 Samuel 21:15-22 David and his men fighting descendant of Rapha
2 Samuel 12:24-25, 1 Chronicles 28:5-6 Solomon, God's choice for succession of David
1 Kings 2:17, 21 Adonijah wants to marry Abishag
2 Kings 4:8-37 Shunammite woman takes care of Elisha, he revives her dead son
Exodus 21:12-14 Refuge at God's altar
1 Samuel 2:27-36 Prophecy against the house of the priest Eli
2 Samuel 5:4-5, 1 Kings 2:10-12, 1 Chronicles 29:26-28 David's age and the time he reigned

Intermezzo Endnotes

Exodus 20:1-21 The Ten Commandments
Leviticus 18, 20:10-23, Deuteronomy 27:15-26 Unlawful sexual relations
Deuteronomy 28:1-14 Blessings
Genesis 35:22, 48:5 Reuben slept with his father's concubine, Bilha

THE LIONESS
David's Queen

The image of lions has been used as a symbol for many through generations. One of the oldest references of a lion used symbolically referring to a person, and later his descendants, is recorded in Genesis.

> *Judah, your brothers will praise you; your hand will be on the neck of your enemies; your father's sons will bow down to you. You are a lion's cub, Judah; you return from the prey, my son. Like a lion he crouches and lies down, like a lioness who dares to rouse him?*
>
> *The sceptre will not depart from Judah, nor the ruler's staff from between his feet, until he to whom it belongs shall come and the obedience of the nations shall be his.*
>
> Genesis 49

Judah was Jacob's fourth son with his first wife Leah, whose descendants became the Israelite tribe of Judah. The most renowned descendant of Judah, meaning literally 'thanksgiving' or 'praise', is David. The image of lions may be used as a symbol, but they are wild animals from which people sometimes have to protect themselves.

At a young age, David, himself strengthened by his faith, fought and killed lions, to protect his father's sheep. So did other Israelites. A person for whom an animal's image is used as a symbol, is more than that animal. He is a conscious being with whom God may have a relationship and to be friends.

The Nazirite and the Lion

> *Out of the eater, something to eat; out of the strong, something sweet.*
>
> Judges 14

The son of Manoah, of the tribe of Dan, from the town Zorah, gave this riddle to the people of his new wife. She was a Philistine woman he saw in the town of Timnah.

When he told his parents he wanted to marry the Philistine

woman, and asked his father to arrange the marriage, they were not overwhelmed with joy. They asked him whether there wasn't a suitable woman for him amongst their own people. But he insisted she was the right woman for him, so his parents went along with the wedding. They didn't realise that his decision had to do with God's plans for their son's life. This marriage would lead to a situation that would cause God to confront the Philistines.

They went to Timnah where he went to have a talk with the woman he saw, and he liked her. Sometime later, he returned to Timnah to marry her. His father went to talk with the woman.

As was customary for a young man, when he was married, he had a feast, and the people who saw him had chosen thirty Philistine men to be his companions at the feast. It's to these he told the riddle and asked them to solve it within the seven days of the wedding feast. He laid a wager with them for thirty linen garments and thirty sets of clothes.

As days went by and the men didn't have the answer to the riddle, they became angry, and demanded from the woman to get her husband to tell them the solution, otherwise they would burn her and her father's household. They asked her whether she invited them to the feast so they could get robbed.

She cried while asking her husband to tell her what the riddle meant. But, he told her he didn't even tell his parents, so why should he tell her. Finally he told her, and in fear for her life she told the men the significance of the riddle.

On the seventh day before sunset, the men of the town told him the answer.

> *What is sweeter than honey? What is stronger than a lion?*
> Judges 14

Was it the right answer? This riddle came to be on the way to Timnah. When he went with his parents to speak with the woman, a young lion came roaring towards him when they approached the vineyards of the town. The Spirit of the Lord came powerfully over him. He fought the lion, tore it apart with his bare hands, and killed it. Then he rejoined his parents, but he didn't tell them what had happened.

Later, when they returned to the town for him to get married, they passed through the same route. He stepped aside to take a look at the lion's carcass, without his parents noticing him, and found a swarm of bees and some honey in it. He scooped the honey with his hands, ate some of it and gave some to his parents to eat. But, he didn't tell them where he found the honey.

Yes, it was the right answer. It made him furious, because he realised that the only way these men could have known was through his wife. Again the Spirit of the Lord came powerfully over him. He went down to Ashkelon, struck thirty of their men, took their clothes and gave them to the men to whom he lost the bet. Still burning with anger, he returned home, but his wife was given to one of his companions at the feast.

Who was this man? A nazirite. He was dedicated as such to God from his mother's womb. His mother received a message from God twice. God sent one of His angels to his mother, telling her that she would be pregnant and have a son. Until then she wasn't able to have children.

The angel who appeared to her also told her: *'Now see to it that you drink no wine or other fermented drink and that you do not eat anything unclean. You will become pregnant and have a son whose head is never to be touched by a razor because the boy is to be a nazirite, dedicated to God from the womb. He will take the lead in delivering Israel from the hands of the Philistines'*.

Both men and women could choose to make the nazirite oath to be a nazirite for a certain period of time. But this child had to be one even before he was born. His strength would be in God. The woman went to her husband and told him what had happened. Her husband in turn prayed and asked God to send the angel again. The angel came for a second time and gave them the same message to answer Manoah's question about the rule that would govern their son's life and work.

When Manoah asked the angel his name so he could honour him, just as Jacob asked the one he fought in the past, he didn't give him one. Instead he told Manoah to honour the Lord when he did a burnt offering. Neither did the angel want to eat with them, while he did make clear that he would detain him.

During Manoah's burnt offering, the angel of the Lord ascended to heaven. It was only then that Manoah realised that he was speaking to an angel. He and his wife fell to the ground with their faces down and he told his wife that they were going to die because they have seen the Lord.

But his wife wisely said to him: *'If the Lord had meant to kill us, he would not have accepted a burnt offering and grain offering from our hands, nor shown us all these things or now told us this'*.

Later Manoah's wife became pregnant and gave birth to their son, whom they named Samson, meaning 'man of the sun'. He grew while the Lord blessed him. He would fight the Philistines, who at that time ruled over the Israelites. So he did, after what happened during his wedding feast in Timnah.

At the time of the wheat harvest Samson was at the door of his father-in-law's house. He wanted to see his wife, and brought a young goat with him. But, her father refused to let him in, and told him he gave her to one of his companions. He thought Samson hated his daughter, but he had a solution to the problem.

If Samson wanted, he could have his younger more attractive daughter instead. Samson wasn't interested, it's his wife he liked and wanted to be with.

He told them that this time he did have the right to harm the Philistines for what they had done to him. He left, took the time to catch three hundred foxes, tied them up in pairs at their tails, fastened a torch to every pair, lit them up, and let the foxes loose in the standing grain of the Philistines, burning down the vineyards and the olive groves together with the grain.

On the Philistine question, who did this to them, the answer was clear. Samson the Timnite's son-in-law, because the father-in-law gave Samson's wife to a companion. The Philistines did to his wife as they told her earlier. They burned her and her father to death.

Samson's reaction? Seeking revenge for the death of his wife, he attacked the Philistines viciously, killed many of them and retreated to a cave in the rock of Etam.

A small army of Philistines, determined to get Samson, camped in Judah near Lehi. The people of Judah asked them why they came to fight them. Their answer was, that they didn't. They only wanted to take Samson prisoner. So, three thousand men of the tribe of Judah went to the cave to take Samson prisoner and hand him over to the Philistines.

At the cave they asked Samson why he had caused problems with the Philistines, who ruled over them. Samson said he was only doing to them as they had done to him.

After the men of Judah assured him they wouldn't kill him, but would only bring him to the Philistines, Samson allowed them to capture him and deliver him to the Philistine army.

Once approaching Lehi, the Spirit of the Lord came upon him. He set himself free and fought their entire army, while picking up a fresh jawbone of a donkey he used as a weapon killing about a thousand men.

After saying that he killed a thousand men with the jawbone, he threw it away and went to Lehi. There he prayed to the Lord: '*You have given Your servant this great victory. Must I now die of thirst and fall into the hands of the uncircumcised*'?

The Lord gave him water from a spring he had opened for him, En Hakoreh which means 'caller's spring'. He drank and he was strengthened.

Later in his life, Samson would be betrayed by Delilah, meaning 'weakened', a woman he falls in love with at the Brook of Sorek. Her betrayal would lead to his death. She was paid by each of Samson's enemies, the Philistine kings, five in total, a hundred pieces of silver.

First when he was with her and she started asking him about his strength, he teased her. Each time she had Philistines in her other room waiting on her signal to tie Samson up in his sleep, and take him captive.

Twice it didn't work out because he didn't tell her the truth. But she persisted in asking him what the source of his strength was, until he finally told her: '*No razor has ever been used on my head, he said, because I have been a Nazirite dedicated to God from my mother's womb. If my head were shaved, my strength would leave me, and I would become as weak as any other man*'.

Delilah sent word to the rulers of the Philistines to have their people come back, because now Samson had told her everything. So they did.

She cut his seven long locks of hair, breaking the nazirite oath, and God left him. Then he was captured by the Philistines. They blinded his eyes and took him to Gaza. This was the same city where they once tried to kill him when he visited a prostitute, but failed. Samson took out the city gates with their post and brought them to one of the hills overlooking Hebron.

In Gaza, they put bronze shackles on him and let him grind grain in prison. Meanwhile his hair was growing again.

Samson became victorious over the five Philistine kings, while destroying their pagan temple in Gaza, dedicated to their idol to whom they attributed their victory over him. His victory came during a feast and sacrifice in honour of their idol that all five Philistine kings and their guests attended.

It is possible that Delilah, who played an important part in the capture of Samson, was also present, invited as an honourary guest.

All of them in high spirits, they asked that Samson be brought in to entertain them. But, Samson could only think of how to defeat the Philistines. He asked the servant that was taking him out of the prison to take him to the pillars that supported the temple so he could lean against them.

Once there he prayed: *'Sovereign Lord, remember me. Please, God, strengthen me just once more, and let me with one blow get revenge on the Philistines for my two eyes. Let me die with the Philistines'!*

With his hands on the pillars, he pushed them and brought the whole temple down, killing himself, the five Philistine kings and about three thousand people who were present.

The Israelite Judge Samson ruled Israel, despite the Philistines for twenty years. He got married once to a Philistine woman he liked, and fell in love once more later in his life. But, both women betrayed him to the Philistines. At his death, he killed more Philistines, including their five kings, than during his life. God did raise him as a nazirite from his mother's womb to bring down the Philistines.

> *I also raised up prophets from among your children and nazirites from among your youths.*
>
> Amos 2:11a

The Prophet and the Lion

> *Daniel, servant of the living God, has your God, whom you serve continually, been able to rescue you from the lions?*
>
> Daniel 6:20

What was Daniel doing in a lions' den? How did he get there?

After the Persians conquered Babylonia, their king Darius the Mede appointed one hundred and twenty satraps, governors, to hold office across his empire. He also appointed three administrators over them, to whom these men would be accountable. One of the administrators was Daniel, whose name means 'God is my Judge'.

How did Daniel end up working for a Persian king? Years before, at the time of the Babylonian king Nebuchadnezzar, Daniel with his three friends, together with thousands of Israelites, were taken into captivity to Babylonia after the conquest of Judah. Daniel and his friends were exiles of Jewish nobility, who received further education and training to be advisers to the king.

Now, Daniel got noticed by Darius who saw his exceptional

qualities while executing his work concerning government affairs. He was trustworthy, free of corruption and not negligent towards his work in any way. The king planned to let him oversee his whole kingdom. But, the satraps and two other administrators, not in agreement with the king, were trying to find something to bring charges against him. Finally they realised that they would only accomplish their goal if they press charges against Daniel about something concerning his faith instead of his work.

> *Whoever leads the upright along an evil path will fall into their own trap, but the blameless will receive a good inheritance.*
>
> Proverbs 28:10

The two administrators and the satraps appeared before the king as a group with a proposition for an edict to enforce a new decree that says that during thirty days anyone who prays to any god or a human being, except to the king, would be thrown into the lions' den. They insisted that this decree should be issued in writing in accordance to the law of the Medes and Persians, which can't be changed or repealed.

The king did as they asked, not realizing they were setting up a trap for Daniel, whom he valued greatly. When Daniel learned about the decree which was published, he went to his upstairs room, opened his window in the direction of Jerusalem, got to his knees and prayed, asking God for help. He had always prayed to his God in this manner three times a day.

The same group that went to the king came to Daniel's home and confronted him with the new decree. Then they went to the king, and informed him of Daniel's conduct. The king, now in great distress at what was about to happen to Daniel, tried everything possible to save him. But, despite his determination, he wasn't successful at his attempt.

At sundown, Daniel had to be taken to the lions' den on the king's order. The king spoke to Daniel and said: '*May your God, whom you serve continually, rescue you*'!

A heavy stone was placed over the opening of the den, and the king with his nobles sealed it with their ring, so Daniel's situation couldn't be changed in any way. Then the king returned to his palace to have a sleepless night, after not having a meal or any entertainment.

In the morning, at the first light of dawn, Darius hurried to the lions' den to find out what had happened, hoping that Daniel's God might have saved him somehow. He was overjoyed when he heard Daniel's voice. Answering his question after formally greeting him, he said: *'My God sent His angel, and He shut the mouths of the lions. They have not hurt me, because I was found innocent in His sight. Nor have I ever done any wrong before you, Your Majesty'.*

The king immediately gave orders to lift Daniel out of the den, and found out that he wasn't harmed at all because he had trusted in his God. The rest of the orders the king gave that morning concerned those who falsely accused Daniel. They, along with their families, were to be thrown into the den. Before they could reach the ground the hungry lions grabbed them, broke all their bones and killed them.

The king wrote a decree to nations and people:

I issue a decree that in every part of my kingdom people must fear and revere the God of Daniel. For He is the living God and He endures for ever; His kingdom will not be destroyed, His dominion will never end. He rescues and He saves; He performs signs and wonders in the heavens and on the earth. He has rescued Daniel from the power of the lions.
Daniel 6:26-27

Daniel lived on to tell more of God's prophecies, including those regarding a far future, the end of days.

Intermezzo

The Lion's Pride

Lions, often referred to as the king of the jungle, are keystone species. They have a large effect on their environment, playing a key role in an ecological community, while having affecting other species within an ecosystem. Lions, being at the apex, are at the top of their food chain. Of the biological family of the cats, lions are the second largest after the tiger, and they are the most socially inclined cat, being the only ones that live in groups. Lions have the loudest roar of any other cat, which is audible over a distance of more than eight kilometres.

They will follow the Lord; He will roar like a lion. When He roars, His children will come trembling from the west. They will come from Egypt, trembling like sparrows, from Assyria,

> *fluttering like doves. I will settle them in their homes, declares the Lord.*
>
> Hosea 10-11

Historically the lion's habitat reached from the southern parts of Eurasia from Greece to the Far East in India, and the continent of Africa. Lions were eradicated from the Middle East, including Israel, during the Middle Ages, 5th to 15th century.

Today, lions are a vulnerable species, only to be found living in the wild in sub-Saharan Africa and in India's Gir Forest. Although it's not yet completely clear why lions are threatened and likely to become endangered. Possible reasons for the major decline in their population are habitat loss and conflicts with people.

Lions are predator carnivores, meaning their diet consists mainly of meat. They are nocturnal animals that sometimes may be active during twilight, that is at dawn and dusk. In the daytime, lions mainly sleep, rest and wait. But contrary to general belief, they are not lazy. Lions are profoundly patient animals. As ambush predators, they lay in wait for their hunting opportunities, while not giving away their positions. Should that happen, their prey would avoid that area. Lions wait up to three to four days between meals. After dark, hungry lions do go out to search for prey to hunt.

Male lions get their beautiful mane as a mature adult lion. The darker, fuller and longer the mane, the healthier the lion and the more the lionesses favour them. The more rare white lions, like white tigers, are not albinos. They are completely white and don't have a darker mane.

Lions assume certain roles in their social behaviour. The males patrol their territory and stay with the cubs when the lionesses are away. They would fight intruding lions to keep their relationship with the lionesses. The lionesses are the most sociable, especially when it comes to raising their cubs together, and they mostly hunt together for their pride. Although both male and female lions hunt, physically lionesses are more suitable to hunt than the male. In turn he is more suitably built to attack and defend the pride from intruders. The male lions mark their territory with urine, they warn intruders by roaring menacingly and chase intruders out of their area. When they are nomadic they hunt for themselves. They also steal prey from other animals like the hyenas or wild dogs. Lions growl to warn other lions or animals, including when they have their prey.

The Lioness

> *As a lion growls, a great lion over its prey and though a whole band of shepherds is called together against it, it is not frightened by their shouts or disturbed by their clamour so the Lord Almighty will come down to do battle on Mount Zion and on its heights.*
>
> *Like birds hovering overhead, the Lord Almighty will shield Jerusalem; He will shield it and deliver it. He will pass over it and will rescue it.*
>
> Isaiah 31

Lions live mostly in a pride, with one to a maximum of four lions, and a group of about a dozen related lionesses with their young. Lionesses in a pride don't tolerate external females. This family unit can have a maximum of about thirty lions. Their lives in a pride is complex and not fully understood yet. Lions also live as nomads for a certain period of time. The males are always nomadic after they reach maturity, about two or three years old. They are excluded from their mother's pride. Related males often live in pairs. They leave to set up their own pride by taking over another pride from a resident male. Resident male lions may also become nomadic, living singular, or vice versa during their adult lives due to other reasons. He can get evicted by another stronger lion that would take over the pride, just the same as the sub-adult male and female lions are forced to leave. The latter can also happen when the pride tends to get too large. A female lion is always by herself the first weeks of her motherhood, hunting alone while caring for her cubs. But they can also become nomadic later on in life if she for whatever reason gets ousted from the pride. For these lionesses to join a pride is much difficult because she wouldn't be related to the lionesses of another pride. A nomadic lioness with cubs rarely succeeds in raising them due to lack of the protection she would otherwise have within a pride.

Lionesses give birth to one to four cubs. The cubs are born blind and they can't walk. It takes a week for their eyes to open, and about three weeks to learn to walk. After about six to eight weeks of caring alone for their cubs, the lionesses integrate themselves and their cubs back into the pride they belong to. Once in the pride the lionesses nurse their cubs together, the cubs can nurse from any of the mothers. The cubs mostly play amongst themselves. Tolerant male lions can sometimes be playful with cubs, otherwise they growl at them to keep them away. Young lions join the hunt when they are about one year, but they are at the bottom of the pecking order. About eighty percent of the cubs die before the age of two, either by starvation, killed by predators or by a new male in the pride that would kill all the existing cubs. A possible reason for this is that the lion wants to have the attention of the females, because they don't become fertile until their cubs either mature or die. A lioness tends to defend her cubs, but isn't strong enough to deal with the male lion unless she is aided by the rest of the females.

Lions communicate in many ways. Their peaceful gestures include head rubbing, and they have many other ways to socialise with each other such as visual gestures, body postures and facial expressions. Today the male lion's face is the most widely recognised animal symbol in human culture.

> *The wolf will live with the lamb, the leopard will lie down with the goat, the calf and the lion and the yearling together; and a little child will lead them.*
>
> *The cow will feed with the bear, their young will lie down together, and the lion will eat straw like the ox. The infant will play near the cobra's den, and the young child will put its hand into the viper's nest.*
>
> *They will neither harm nor destroy on all my holy mountain, for the earth will be filled with the knowledge of the Lord as the waters cover the sea.*
>
> Isaiah 11

The Lioness

In a song of lamentation regarding the princes of Israel mentioned by the prophet Ezekiel, Israel is personified by a vine, while Judah is especially personified by a lioness instead of a lion.

> *What a lioness was your mother among the lions! She lay down among them and reared her cubs.*
>
> Ezekiel 19:2

The lioness raised her cubs to be mature lions, thus her princes to be kings. But things don't end well for the kings in this lamentation. Both get caught by their enemies from the surrounding nations. One of these could have been Zedekiah, the last king of Judah who ruled eleven years. Jerusalem fell at the hands of Nebuchadnezzar, the king of Babylon when Zedekiah rebelled against him. He killed Zedekiah's sons and Judah's nobles before his eyes after which he took out Zedekiah's eyes before taking him as a prisoner. He put him in prison until the day he died. All this marked the start of the period of exile to Babylon for the people of Judah, including Daniel and his friends, except for those who were allowed to stay in Judah under a governor, one of their own people, appointed by the king. The Lord did announce through His prophets, including Jeremiah, that these events would happen.

But, in the song of Lamentations, the lioness herself didn't die, nor did she get caught. What if this is a reference to the future? To a real woman representing Israel? This woman could not be the Bride, because it's the city of Jerusalem, the city of God's choice, that is the Bride. Neither would she refer to the queen of nations as in the prophet Isaiah's prophecy concerning the judgment of Babylon.

Who is this that appears like the dawn, fair as the moon, bright as the sun, majestic as the stars in procession?
Song of Songs 6:10

Israel did have a few women leaders in its history. Esther of the tribe of Benjamin. Deborah, her name meaning 'bee', suggested by where she lived to be of the tribe of Ephraim. And Miriam of the tribe of Levi. Miriam's name has different meanings like, 'bitter' or 'wished-for child'. Deborah and Miriam had in common that they were both God's prophetesses.

Miriam

Miriam played a leading role during the journey of the Israelites through the desert to reach Canaan, the land God had promised their ancestors. As a little girl she watched over her little brother Moses, only three months old in an ark, a basket among the reeds along the banks of the river Nile. Miriam together with the Israelites and the foreigners who joined them left Egypt, while being chased by Pharaoh's army, because he changed his mind in letting them go. After the Lord drove the sea back with a strong wind, the Israelites crossed the Red Sea on dry ground.

Pharaoh's army, in their pursuit, drowned when the Lord covered them with the water of the sea. After Moses and the Israelites sang a song for the Lord, Miriam picked up her tambourine and started to sing a poetic song for them. All the women followed, dancing and playing their tambourines.

Sometime later during their journey, the Israelites set up camp at Hazeroth. Miriam, with Aaron, criticised Moses because of his wife, and they said that the Lord also spoke to them, not only to Moses. The Lord heard them and told the three of them to go to the tent of His presence. There He appeared in a cloud before the entrance. He was angry at them, and made it clear that with Moses, whom He put in charge of His people, He spoke to him in a different way. Not through visions, dreams and riddles, as He did with other prophets, but face-to-face. He even allowed him to see His form.

The Lord asked them: *'How dare you speak against my servant Moses'*?

Then He left, leaving Miriam behind with a skin disease making her white all over her body. This wouldn't have made her ritually unclean, leading to her being quarantined, unless she later would have had open sores on her skin. But when Aaron saw what happened to his sister, he pleaded with Moses to ask God to heal her. Moses did, and the Lord told him that she should be shut out of the camp for seven days, after which she could return.

When Miriam returned, she was healed. The Lord treated her as a father would treat a daughter in whose face he had spit, and who should carry her disgrace for seven days. If Aaron would have received this punishment, he wouldn't have been able to continue his priestly duties for the Lord. Other than this, Miriam didn't cause any other trouble with Moses during their journey through the desert. When the Israelites were camping at Kadesh in the wilderness of Zen, Miriam died and they buried her there.

> *I brought you up out of Egypt and redeemed you from the land of slavery. I sent Moses to lead you, also Aaron and Miriam.*
>
> Micha 6:4

Esther

Esther, daughter of Abihail, a young beautiful woman, who contrary to Miriam, became a queen when she married the Persian king Xerxes, also known as Ahasuerus, who ruled over his vast territory of 127 provinces, including Israel. She was an Israelite orphan named Hadassah, meaning 'myrtle', which is a flowery plant. She was raised by her uncle Mordechai, who told her to keep her family ancestry and nationality a secret.

While she was queen, Mordechai kept in contact with her. At one time Mordechai gave her a message to warn Xerxes that two of his officers guarding the king's doorway were planning to kill him.

Mordechai heard them plotting against the king when he was sitting at the king's gate. The matter was investigated and the result was that these two officers were indeed planning to assassinate the king. They were both impaled on poles.

All these events, including credit to Mordechai, were recorded in the books at the king's court. Much later when the highest official of the king, Haman son of Hammedatha the Agagite, planned to destroy all the Israelites in Xerxus's empire by means of a decree issued by the king on Haman's request concerning people who didn't keep the king's laws, Esther would intervene on Mordechai's persistent request on behalf of the Israelites. Haman's reasons? He just couldn't stand that one of them, being Mordechai, didn't bow before him nor paid him honour.

Killing just Mordechai wouldn't have been enough. He became more determined to execute his plan when he felt humiliated when he had to honour Mordechai, as the king ordered him. As he himself suggested to the king, not knowing that it was Mordechai that had to receive the king's honour, he had to walk in front of the king's horse with Mordechai dressed in one of the king's robes, proclaiming that this is what the king does to someone he wants to honour. This was a gesture of the king to Mordechai who earlier had saved his life by revealing the conspiracy to assassinate him, as the king found out when his attendant read the chronicles of his reign to him during a sleepless night.

Esther was at first reluctant to help, because she would risk her own life if she tried to speak to the king without being invited by him. It was against the law to do so. But, when Mordechai made it clear that her life would be in danger also, she decided to work out a plan of her own. She sent a message to Mordechai, telling him to gather all the Israelites in Susa to pray and fast for her. She would be doing the same, after which she would go to the king.

Would Esther live or die?

The third day, the king was sitting in the royal room on his throne facing the entrance, when he saw Esther standing in her royal robe, in the inner court of the palace. He was pleased to see her, and invited her in by holding out his golden sceptre to her. She approached, touched the tip of the sceptre and the king asked her: *'What is it, Queen Esther? What is your request? Even up to half the kingdom, it will be given you'.*

Then Esther invited the king, and Haman, to a banquet she prepared for him. The king was pleased to go. At the banquet the king again asked her what her petition and request was. But, Esther replied with a new invitation to a banquet the next day. Haman was so happy, just thrilled to be at the queen's table with the king, that he went home in high spirits. But, he became filled with rage when he went out of the gate, seeing Mordechai there who didn't honour him or fear him as he walked by.

Once at home Haman called his wife and all his friends to tell them about the banquet and the invitation for the next day. Talking about Mordechai, his wife suggested to him the idea to set up a pole for him and to ask the king next day to impale Mordechai. In that way nothing could disturb him from enjoying the banquet.

The following day, instead of Mordechai being impaled on the pole he set up for him, on the king's orders, Haman had to honour Mordechai in the streets. When he was back home telling his wife and friends what had happened, they told him he wouldn't be able to win from the Israelite Mordechai. At the banquet, matters got even worse for Haman. Esther's answer to the king's question was that her people and she wouldn't be annihilated.

On the king's question, who would do such a thing? Esther answered, 'Haman'.

The king was enraged and went to the palace garden. When he returned, he found Haman on Esther's couch, begging her for his life.

To the king, Haman was molesting his queen.

After the king rebuked Haman for this, one of his attendants told the king about the pole Haman had set up at his home, which he meant for Mordechai. The king ordered for Haman to be impaled on it.

The plan Haman had so cunningly devised backfired on him. His estate was given to Esther, who appointed her uncle over it. Mordechai now was appointed as a high official by the king, who handed over his signet ring to Mordechai, which the king had taken back from Haman.

Queen Esther already told the king about her people and her uncle. She wept and pleaded with the king for the lives of her people. Xerxes couldn't change the decree concerning the Israelites in his empire to save them, because these being according to the law of Media and Persia, couldn't be revoked.

So Xerxes issued a new decree which granted the Israelites the right to assemble and defend themselves. He ordered Mordechai, whom he promoted to be second in rank after himself, to write his orders, seal them with the king's signet ring and send mounted couriers out with the dispatches.

In every province and city where the edict came, the Israelites rejoiced and held celebrations. Fear of the Israelites came over the people of other nationalities, who decided to become Israelites. When the time came, the Israelites defended themselves against their enemy and killed thousands of people who attacked them.

In the citadel of Susa, the ten sons of Haman were impaled on poles as ordered by the king, granting a request Esther made to him. But the Israelites didn't touch the plunder. Esther, along with Mordechai, in her capacity as queen confirmed by decree the feast of Purim that the Israelites wished to be celebrated in remembrance of how the Israelites defended themselves in those days.

Deborah

Deborah, the wife of Lappidoth, was the fourth judge of the Israelites, and the only woman who was actually a legitimate direct ruler over the tribes of Israel. At that time, Jabin the king of Canaan who reigned in Hazor oppressed the Israelites. His army commander Sisera, based in Harosheth Haggoyim, had nine hundred iron chariots at his disposal.

Deborah used to sit under a palm tree between Ramah and Bethel in the territory of Ephraim. There people would come to her to settle any dispute that they may have had. When she received a prophesy from God concerning a battle against Jabin's army, she sent for the army commander, Barak son of Abinoam from Kedesh in Naphtali. She told him he should take ten thousand men from the tribes of Naphtali and Zebulon, lead them up to Mount Tabor to fight Jabin's army. God Himself would bring Sisera and his troops with his nine hundred chariots to the Kishon River below. God would give Barak victory over Sisera and his troops.

Barak told Deborah he would only go if she would go with him. She agreed but also told him that a woman would take credit for the death of Sisera. They went to Kedesh where Barak assembled an army of ten thousand men, who went under his command, with Deborah to Mount Tabor. When Sisera received word about Barak and his troops, he gathered his complete army with all his chariots and went down to the Kishon River.

Meanwhile, Heber the Kenite went with his wife to Zaananim near Kedesh, because he left the other Kenites who were descendants of Hobab, Moses' brother-in-law. There he pitched his tent near the great tree. His wife received an unexpected guest in her tent. It was Sisera who felt safe with her, because her husband's family had an alliance with Jabin.

Where was Sisera's army? Defeated by Barak and his men who went down off the mount to fight Sisera's army.

Deborah had said to Barak: *'Go! This is the day the Lord has given Sisera into your hands. Has not the Lord gone ahead of you'*?

When Barak advanced with his men, God made Sisera's men panic and, while they were fleeing, Barak's army chased all of them and killed them. There was no one left alive, except Sisera who got down from his chariot, ran away as fast as he could, and found a safe place to hide in Heber's wife's tent.

Or, so he thought. She went out and invited him in, gave him some milk to slake his thirst and offered him a place to sleep where she covered him up. He told her to stand in the doorway of the tent, and to say *'no'* to whoever asked whether someone was in her tent. Exhausted, he fell sound asleep.

Instead of standing in the doorway, she picked up a tent peg and a hammer, went quietly to Sisera and hammered the peg through his temple into the ground. He died.

Just when Barak came by her tent in pursuit of Sisera, Heber's wife, Jael, went out and took him into his tent to show him the man he was looking for, lying there, dead. Deborah's prophecy was then completely fulfilled.

Just like Abimelech, Sisera died, to them a degrading death, by the hand of a woman. The Israelites continued to fight Jabin the king of Canaan until they ultimately destroyed him.

Deborah could be the first woman ruler ever recorded in history as a warrior. She and Barak sang a poetic hymn of victory over a battle won not only by men, but also by two women, although they did owe their victory to God in the first place.

They sang their song of victory in God's honour, ending with the final verse: *'But may all who love You be like the sun when it rises in its strength'*.

Deborah ruled forty years, and the Land of Israel had peace.

There may not have been many female leaders in Israel, but those who were did a good job as God's prophetesses and servants at crucial times in Israel's history. But, none of the most notable women leaders in the past, before the time of the prophet Ezekiel, were of the tribe of Judah.

> *The Lord will create a new thing on earth. A woman will surround a man.*
>
> Jeremiah 31:22b

What could be the point in having such a lady in place in the future? Perhaps the unification of the two kingdoms, that of Judah and Israel, to one united kingdom as at the time of King David, which could happen by unifying Judah and Joseph.

> *Say to them, This is what the Sovereign Lord says: I am going to take the stick of Joseph and of the Israelite tribes associated with him, and join it to Judah's stick. I will make them into a single stick of wood, and they will become one in My hand.*
>
> *Hold before their eyes the sticks you have written on and say to them, This is what the Sovereign Lord says: I will take the Israelites out of the nations where they have gone. I will gather them from all around and bring them back into their own land. I will make them one nation in the land, on the mountains of Israel. There will be one king over all of them and they will never again be two nations or be divided into two kingdoms.*
>
> Ezekiel 37

David's Kingship

Who was David's queen? He didn't have one. He was married to several women and he had concubines. In fact David didn't position any of his wives or his mother as a queen, or a representative of Israel next to him. He didn't build a palace specifically for a queen, as his son Solomon would, but for his own personal use. Instead, 'After David had constructed buildings for himself in the City of David, he prepared a place for the ark of God and pitched a tent for it'.

David was God's servant, anointed three times to be king. God decided by Himself that David's kingship would remain for ever.

> *Once I have sworn by My holiness and I will not lie to David that his line will continue for ever and his throne endure before Me like the sun; it will be established for ever like the moon, the faithful witness in the sky.*
>
> Psalm 89:35-37

David didn't have a queen in his days, nor has there been a queen from the tribe of Judah yet. The lioness in Ezekiel's song of lament suggests that Israel may one day have one; a woman positioned as a representative, a queen of Israel. Only by God's will could this be possible, not otherwise.

> *The lion has roared – who will not fear? The Sovereign Lord has spoken – who can but prophesy?*
>
> Amos 3

Endnotes

1 Samuel 17:34-37 David fought and killed lions and bears
Judges 13-16 Samson
Numbers 6, Judges 13:4 Nazirite
Genesis 32:29 Jacob also asked the name of the one he fought
Daniel 6 In the lion's pit
Daniel 2, 3:31-4:34, 5:13-30 Daniel explaining dreams and signs
Daniel 9:1-20 Daniel fasting and praying for the sins of his people
Daniel 7,8,9:21-12:13 Daniel's prophecies about the end of days
Genesis 49:9, Ezekiel 19:1-9 The lioness
Genesis 49:22, Ezekiel 19:10-14 The vine
Jeremiah 39, 52 Zedekiah last king of Judah
Ezekiel 19:1-9 A woman as representative of Israel
Isaiah 54, Zechariah 1:17 Jerusalem the city of God's choice, the Bride
Isaiah 47, judgment of Babylon
Exodus 2:4-8, 15:1, 15:20-22, Numbers 12, 20:1 Miriam, prophetess and leader
Leviticus 13:1-46 Treatment of skin diseases
Leviticus 13:12-17 Treatment of skin disease all over the body
Leviticus 21:1-24 Laws for priests, also concerning physical illness
Book of Esther Jewish Queen Esther
Judges 4,5 Deborah, judge and prophetess
Numbers 10:29-32 Moses' brother-in-law
1 Chronicles 15:1 David constructed buildings for himself, not palaces for others

Intermezzo Endnotes

Snapshot Serengeti, Wikipedia, National Geographic

Part IV
DAVID'S ZION
The Apple Of God's Eye

Behold, I am HaShem, the God of all flesh; is there anything too hard for Me?

Jeremiah 32:27

For the portion of HaShem is His people, Jacob the lot of His inheritance. He found him in a desert land, and in the waste, a howling wilderness; He compassed him about, He cared for him, He kept him as the apple of His eye.

As an eagle that stirs up her nest, hovers over her young, spreads abroad her wings, takes them, bears them on her pinions – HaShem alone did lead him, and there was no strange god with Him.

Deuteronomy 32:9-11

In those days, and in that time, says HaShem, the children of Israel shall come, they and the children of Judah together; they shall go on their way weeping, and shall seek HaShem their God. They shall inquire concerning Zion with their faces toward it saying, Come and join ourselves to HaShem in an everlasting covenant that shall not be forgotten.

Jeremiah 50:4-5

And HaShem shall roar from Zion, and utter His voice from Jerusalem, and the heavens and the earth shall shake; but HaShem will be a refuge unto His people, and a stronghold to the children of Israel. So shall you know that I am HaShem your God, dwelling in Zion My holy mountain; then shall Jerusalem be holy, and there shall no strangers pass through her any more. And it shall come to pass in that day, that the mountains shall drop down sweet wine, and the hills shall flow with milk, and all the brooks of Judah shall flow with waters; and a fountain shall come forth of the House of HaShem, and shall water the valley of Shittim. ... But Judah shall be inhabited for ever, and Jerusalem from generation to generation. And I will hold as innocent their blood that I have not held as innocent; and HaShem dwells in Zion.

Joel 3:16-21

THE LAND

This land, from the Wadi of Egypt to the great river, the Euphrates...

Genesis 15

The Promised Land went from being the land where Canaan was situated to be the Land of Israel, followed by the Kingdom of Israel and ultimately in our time to be the State of Israel. The Land of Israel was and is currently situated at the eastern shore of the Mediterranean Sea in the territory of the ancient Near East, the modern-day Middle East. Through the millennia this region has been the center stage for kingdoms and empires.

But, what makes the region of the Middle East so special? Through the centuries, kingdoms and empires rose and fell in this region, and conquerors came and went fighting to overpower the city-states and nations of this region. So what made this territory worth forging all these wars for?

This region has been of major importance to ancient civilisations up to the modern-age because of its natural resources, such as bronze, gold and iron. Of equal or even more importance is its fossil fuel, crude oil, and its location for trade both by land and sea between the West and the Far East.

The Fertile Crescent

The region, often called the cradle of civilisation, is also referred to as the Fertile Crescent Mesopotamia, eastern shore of the Mediterranean Sea (Levant) and Egypt – which is a crescent-shaped region containing moist and fertile land, in comparison with the arid and semi-arid land of Western Asia and the Nile Delta and Valley of north-east Africa. The fertile regions were possible due to the rivers at the Euphrates and Tigris, Jordan and the Nile. The supplies and agricultural resources available in this region were of use to many of the first human civilisations, including western civilisations during their earliest development. Some of the technological inventions attributed to this region include writing, glass, the wheel and the use of irrigation.

The Fertile Crescent was the first region where the emergence of metallurgy occurred, giving way to the Bronze Age in the 4th millennium BCE after the Copper Age in the Middle East and the Caucasus is the 5th millennium BCE, which lasted for about a millennium. There was also an independent invention of copper and bronze smelting techniques by the people of the Andes civilisation in South America, passing it by sea trade to West Mexico. The European transition from the Copper Age to the Bronze Age occurred around the same time, between the late 5th and the late 3rd millennium BCE.

Bronze and Iron Age

The Middle East had been of extreme importance for the development of metallurgy in ancient history, both as a source for certain raw materials needed to make metal alloys and as a provider of the necessary routes for trade between the people at that time.

The beginning of written history, about the 4th millennium BCE, marked the start of the Bronze Age. This period was preceded by the Stone Age, which ended between 6000-2000 BCE, and followed by the Iron Age, 1200 BCE-700 CE. This is the three-part system for the chronological classification of prehistoric artefacts, divided into the Stone, Bronze, and Iron ages proposed by the Danish antiquarian Christian Jürgensen Thomsen in modern times for classification and study of ancient societies.

The Copper Age is considered part of the Bronze Age and not of the Stone Age because of the use of metals instead of stone. The Bronze Age started in the Middle East, from 3600 to 1200 BCE, until the beginning of the Iron Age, 2000-1000 BCE. In Southern Europe the Bronze Age started around 3200 BCE, in Northern Europe centuries later about 2500 BCE and lasted until the beginning of the Iron Age in Northern Europe 600 BCE. This period was characterised by the use of copper, its alloy bronze and the emerging of proto-writing – early writing system in the 3rd millennium BCE – in Eurasia, the continental land mass of Europe and Asia. It is also the period of other features of urban civilisation.

Bronze is an alloy of primarily copper and usually with tin as an additive. It made it possible for people to make objects that were harder and more durable, such as armour and various building materials, than those made in the previous ages of stone and copper. Brass – copper with zinc additive – is a copper alloy that is believed to have been known to the Greeks and came more in use by the Romans. Initially arsenic bronze was made out of copper and arsenic, a toxic raw material in the Middle East, or directly from naturally or artificially mixed ores of those. It is only later about 4000 years after the discovery of copper smelting that tin bronze, which was stronger and easier cast than arsenic bronze, was made by adding tin, not a toxic material, to copper during a more easily to control alloying process. Ores of copper and tin are rarely found together, so producing bronze always involved trade. Sources and trade of these materials had a major influence on developing cultures in ancient times in the Eastern Mediterranean, the Middle East and Europe.

An example of the usage of bronze was the gates of the Temple of Jerusalem for which Corinthian bronze made by depletion gilding – surface enrichment – was used. Depletion gilding was most used in Alexandria, Egypt, where alchemy is thought to have begun. Other practical uses for bronze were in holistic medical science in ancient India, for surgical instruments and other medical equipment. The Egyptians also used it for medical applications and to sterilise water.

The Iron Age

The Iron Age (c. 1200 BCE-700 CE) was marked by iron as the substance mainly used in society for many different purposes. The Iron Age distinguished itself from the preceding ages by the introduction of alphabetical characters and the consequent development of written languages.

The Bronze Age gave way to the Iron Age because Iron was easier to find and to process into poor grade metal and with more effort into higher grades, though Bronze was still used during the Iron Age. As iron-working improved, iron became cheaper and gradually people learned how to make steel, which was stronger than bronze and could maintain a sharper edge longer.

Crude Oil

Crude oil, just like natural gas and coal, is a fossil fuel. According to the Greek historians Herodotus and Diodorus Siculus, asphalt was used in Babylon for the construction of its towers. There were oil pits near Babylon and great quantities of oil were found on the banks of one of the tributaries of the Euphrates River.

Ancient Persian tablets mention the use of petroleum in their upper levels of society for medicinal and lighting purposes. By 347 CE bamboo-drilled wells were in use for oil production in China. Today about 80% of the world's readily accessible reserves are located in the Middle East. Russia, Saudi Arabia and the United States are the top three oil-producing countries. The Middle East has also been of significant importance for trade between people which added greatly to the development of early civilisations to become the modern-day nations.

Trade Routes

Several routes – a network of a series of pathways and stoppages either by land or sea used for transportation of goods and people connecting markets and nations – for trade went over the Mediterranean Sea through Mediterranean ports inland as far as the Far East and North Africa. One of the many goods traded over ancient trade routes was lapis lazuli. It is obtained from a deep blue coloured semi-precious stone acquired through mining in Afghanistan as early as the 7th millennium BCE. Afghanistan was the source of lapis lazuli for the ancient Egyptians, the civilisations of ancient Mesopotamia, and later for the Greeks and Romans. It was used to obtain different shades of blue in the ancient world, including ancient Mesopotamia. This blue was not that of sapphire. Because scholars agree that sapphires were not known before the Roman Empire, that imported sapphires from Sri Lanka – maintained close ties to European civilisations, including the Romans – to be used in their jewellery.

Lapis Lazuli has been exported to the Mediterranean people and South Asia, and was used in, for instance, ancient Canaan, in Egypt as eye-shadow, for ornaments and jewellery. In Mesopotamia the Akkadians, Assyrians and Babylonians used it for seals and jewellery, and in our current era at the end of the Middle Ages, it began to be exported to Europe where it was made into the most finest and expensive ultramarine pigment. Today mines in north-east Afghanistan are still a major source of lapis lazuli. This colour – symbol of divinity to Jews – is mentioned in biblical scripture, for instance Ezekiel 28:12-14 and Exodus 24:9-11.

> *Moses and Aaron, Nadab and Abihu, and the seventy elders of Israel went up and saw the God of Israel. Under his feet was something like a pavement made of lapis lazuli, as bright blue as the sky. But God did not raise His hand against these*

> leaders of the Israelites; they saw God, and they ate and drank. The Lord said to Moses, Come up to Me on the mountain and stay here, and I will give you the tablets of stone with the law and commandments I have written for their instruction.

Mediterranean Sea

The Mediterranean Sea which is surrounded by the Mediterranean region and connects to the Atlantic Ocean was an important central route of transport for travellers and merchants in ancient times, allowing trade and cultural exchange between the people of the region which contributed to the development of many ancient civilisations into the modern societies of today. The trade encompassed three continents, being Southern Europe, North Africa with Egypt playing an important role and Western Asia from the Near East to the Middle East to the Far East.

One of the notable ancient people who were known for their excellent sea fare were the people of Northern Canaan, also called by others, the Phoenicians. They had an extended commercial network over the Mediterranean Sea having their base on the east shore of the Mediterranean Sea in Sidon, Byblos and Tyre. In ancient times west-east canals were built to facilitate travel through the Nile in Egypt to the Red Sea. Much later the Suez Canal – a man-made 10-year project that opened in 1869 – connects the Mediterranean Sea with the Red Sea, providing a short-cut route enabling sea fare to Asia. There were several well-travelled trade routes in the Middle East, which shows the importance of this region for trade in the past. For instance the ancient Via Maris as early as the Bronze Age, Silk Road and the incense route between the 7th century BCE to the 2nd century CE.

Via Maris

Via Maris, Latin for 'The way of the sea', is the modern name for an ancient major trade route that linked Egypt with the northern empires of Syria, Anatolia – in modern-day Turkey – and Mesopotamia. The route dates from the early Bronze Age, from 3600 to 1200 BCE in the Middle East. It was crossed by other trading routes, in such a way that it was possible to travel from Africa to Europe or from Asia to Africa. It was also in use by the Romans and the Crusaders. The state in control of the route was in the position to insure safe passage for its own citizens and to impose tolls on outsiders using the route for either commercial trade or non-commercial travellers. Its name in ancient times was the Way of the Philistines, with a passageway through the Philistine Plain – modern-day Israel – branching out to the Mediterranean coast and to an inland route through Megiddo, the Jezreel Valley, the Sea of Galilee, from where the road continued through Hazor, Dan and further to cross the Jordan River, to go over the Golan Heights and continue its way north-east into Damascus. Travellers could continue over other routes to the Euphrates River or proceed northward into Anatolia. The name Via Maris seems to be based on a biblical passage in Isaiah 9:1 – *'For is there no gloom to her that was steadfast? Now the former has lightly afflicted the land of Zebulun and the land of Naphtali, but the latter has dealt a more grievous blow by the way of the sea (Via Maris), beyond the Jordan, in the district of the nations'.*

Silk Road

The Silk Road was a trade route of the ancient world that extended about 6,437 kilometres, which linked the West and the East by land and sea. It got its name from the lucrative Chinese silk trade (206 BCE-220 CE) – during the Iron Age – that began during the Han Dynasty. And besides silk, many other goods were traded, such as precious gems – Egypt was also a source of gems – incense, lapis lazuli and much more. There was also an exchange of various technologies – such as the art of Chinese paper-making – religions and philosophies amongst the people along this route. But, merchants also took diseases along with them on the Silk Road, the most devastating one was the bubonic plague or Black Death that was transferred from the East to the West, which caused the deaths of fifty million people worldwide including one-third of the European population at that time.

Incense Route

The ancient incense route was a major land and sea trading route linking the Mediterranean world with Eastern and Southern lands that provided luxury goods. The incense route stretched from the Mediterranean ports across the Land of Israel and Egypt through north-eastern Africa and Arabia to India and beyond.

Traded goods were spices, incense, precious stones, pearls, ebony, silk and fine textiles, frankincense and myrrh. From the Horn of Africa – modern-day Eritrea, Djibouti, Ethiopia and Somalia – rare woods, feathers, animal skins and gold were traded. Saudi Arabia's incense land trade flourished between the 7th century BCE to the 2nd century CE. Many travellers and merchants went through these routes, one of which was the Jewish Radhanites.

Radhanite Trade Routes

Jewish merchants known as the Radhanites also traded through the Silk Road between the Christian and Islamic worlds during the Early Middle Ages from 500 to 1000 CE. Historically most trade between Europe and East Asia had been conducted via Persian and Central Asian intermediaries travelling over the trade routes.

The Radhanites were among the first to establish a trade network stretching from Western Europe to Eastern Asia while themselves engaging in trade. They functioned as neutral merchants between Christian Europe, the Middle East and North Africa, who often banned each other's merchants from entering their ports and raided each other's shipping.

The Jewish merchants enjoyed significant privileges in France and throughout the Muslim world as a result of the revenues they brought in. The Radhanites are mentioned in the Book of Roads and Kingdoms, written by Abu'l Qasim Ubaid Allah ibn Khordadbeh around 870 CE. He was Director of Posts and Police for the Jibal province under the Abbasid Caliph al-Mu'tamid (ruled 869-885 CE). He described the Radhanites as being sophisticated in multilingual trading over four main trade routes, all starting in the Rhone Valley in southern France and ending on China's east coast. They traded in several goods, such as spices, perfumes, jewellery, silk oils, incense, steel weapons, furs and slaves.

Today trade routes such as the Silk Road still exist, though more for the purpose of tourism. Nation-states have other routes and means to trade their goods nowadays.

The extreme importance of this region made it a place worth fighting for. Israel's long history actually began in the prehistoric time, from which it went through various ages in history up to the modern age of today. From the Stone Age through the Bronze Age and the Iron Age, to the early Israeli period that witnessed the destruction of the first Temple in Jerusalem and later through the Hellenistic and Roman period, during which the Jewish-Roman Great Wars were fought and the second Temple was destroyed. The periods that followed were

Christianity, the Byzantine, the Persians, to the Islamic period with the Umayyad, Ayubid, Faimid, the Christian Crusader period. The next periods were the Mamluke, the Ottoman, and in more recent time the rise of Zionism, the British Mandate and ultimately to the State of Israel today.

GOING UP

> *The Lord had said to Abram, Go from your country, your people and your father's household to the land I will show you. I will make you into a great nation, and I will bless you; I will make your name great, and you will be a blessing. I will bless those who bless you, and whoever curses you I will curse; and all people on earth will be blessed through you. So Abram went, as the Lord had told him.*
>
> Genesis 12

Israel's history began with the *Aliyah* of the Hebrew people out of Mesopotamia to the Promised Land, which later became the Kingdom of Israel, the Jewish homeland. Through the ages holiday services on Pesach and Yom Kippur, traditionally conclude with Jewish people saying, 'Next year in Jerusalem', expressing their longing and/or wish to return to the Land of Israel. This overview doesn't cover all the countries from which Jewish people have been making Aliyah to their homeland, the Land of Israel. It only gives an impression of this massive move, ancient biblical prophecies foretold of Jewish people to the Promised Land, their homeland, the Land of Israel, Eretz Yisrael.

What is Aliyah? Aliyah is the immigration of Jewish people to the Land of Israel, Eretz Yisrael, from the diaspora. The word Aliyah means 'ascent' – the opposite would be *Yerida* which means 'descent', travelling from Israel – and within this context since ancient times it means travelling to Eretz Yisrael, an ascent to Israel. Visiting Jerusalem from the surrounding area and countries would also mean an ascent to Jerusalem, being built on a hill, and from there again an ascent to the Temple on the Temple Mount to worship the God of Abraham, Isaac and Jacob, and receive His blessing. In other words Aliyah is 'to go up'.

> *This is what Cyrus king of Persia says: The Lord, the God of heaven, has given me all the kingdoms of the earth and he has appointed me to build a temple for Him at Jerusalem in Judah. Any of His people among you may go up, and may the Lord their God be with them.*
>
> 2 Chronicles 36:23

Aliyah, immigration to the Land of Israel, has both a secular and a religious significance. Today Jewish people can attain Israeli citizenship through Rabbinical Law and through Jewish ancestry. Aliyah for people of Jewish descent is anchored in Israel's Law of Return, which grants them the right of returning to live in Israel. The law was proposed by the Knesset, Israel's Parliament, in July 1950 and it was extended in 1970, giving the right of entry and settlement to people of Jewish ancestry and their spouses.

Aliyah in Ancient Times

The Hebrew Abram put his trust in God, left his native land of Mesopotamia to ascended to the Promised Land, the land of Canaan – Genesis 12:1-4 – and to the kingdom of Jerusalem – Genesis 14:18-20 – with his family and followers circa 1800 BCE. There is where God changed his name – Genesis 17:5-6 – into Abraham. This could be considered as the first Aliyah within the context of ascending to the Promised Land which later would be named Israel and to its future capital city of Jerusalem that happened in the History of the Jewish people.

Jewish history started with the Aliyah of its first Patriarch Abraham. Abraham's grandson Isaac lived in that land and Isaac's son Jacob who left made Aliyah himself – Genesis 35 – by returning to this land. He is the one whose name God changed into Yisrael, Israel – Genesis 32:29 – the future name of a nation, while on his way to the Promised Land. Around 1300 BCE the descendants of Jacob's twelve sons left Egypt – Exodus 19:4 – where Joseph initially took care of them four centuries earlier when they arrived there because of famine in the land, under the leadership of Moses, assisted by Aaron, Miriam, Joshua and Caleb to make Aliyah – prophesied to Abram, Genesis 15:13-16 – to the Promised Land, the land of Canaan, to ultimately establish the Kingdom of Israel.

Between 538 and 459 BCE, Israelites returned to the Kingdom of Israel out of the Babylonian exile after the fall of the Kingdom of Judah. First a group of 50,000 Israelites returned and their main objective was to rebuild the Second Temple in Jerusalem. Years later the priestly scribe Ezra followed with a group of Israelites including Levites, musicians, priests, temple servants and watchers. His main goal was to study the Law, practice it and teach it to the people of Israel. Much later Nehemiah arrived with a group in Jerusalem, and they reinforced the walls of Jerusalem. All these people made Aliyah to Israel and Jerusalem with official permission of the kings under whose authority they lived during the Babylonian exile. The books of Ezra and Nehemiah tells their story. There has been a constant presence of Israelites in Israel ever since the Aliya of the Israelites out of Egypt to their homeland, the land of their forefathers, even at the time of the Babylonian exile – Jeremiah 40 – when they left Israelites behind to manage the land. And since the first Aliya of Abram to the Promised Land, Hebrews, Israelites and Jewish people have been making Aliyah to that same land that once more as ancient prophecies make clear – Daniel 2, Ezekiel 37 – they will build up to be the Kingdom of Israel.

Aliyah – Antiquity to 1882

During the period of 200 to 500 CE, many Jews living in the Babylonian territory moved to the Land of Israel. The territory where the Kingdom of Israel was situated fell from time to time under the government of several empires in the past. The region was under the power of the Roman Empire, the Byzantine Empire, and the Ottoman Empire. The Roman Empire was in power with its system of dual rule with the Latin West (27 BCE-476 CE) with Latin as the official language and the Greek East (330-1453 CE) with Greek as the lingua franca. After the collapse of the central government of Rome in the West, the Eastern part of the Roman Empire continued as the Byzantine Empire (500-153 CE) with Constantinople, modern day Istanbul, as its capital city. Kingdoms and Empires came and went in the region, with the Land of Israel including the city of Jerusalem being under their power and experiencing their influence. Ultimately the Ottomans came to power and put an end to the Byzantine Empire when they conquered Constantinople in 1453. The Ottoman Empire (1299-1922 CE) ruled over Turkey, the New Balkans and the region where the Land of Israel was situated was called Palestine by the Romans. The Ottoman Empire came to an end by the First World War (July 1914 to November 1918).

With the fall of the Ottoman Empire the region known today as the Middle-East came under the control of Western countries, namely the European countries, the British Empire and the French Empire. The British Mandate over Palestine, which included the Land of Israel, was put into place by the League of Nations – today the United Nations – from 1922 until mid-1948. After which the State of Israel was established. The rise and fall of these empires and the control by European countries over the region including the Land of Israel didn't deter determined Jews from continuing their return to their Jewish homeland, the Land of Israel. On the contrary, Aliyah increased and became more organised, and effective through the years. In the period from the 10th to the 11th century, Jews living under Persian rule also established themselves in their homeland. Between the 13th to the 19th century a significant number of Jews immigrated to the Land of Israel. At the time there was also the belief in the imminent coming of the Messiah, the ingathering of the exiles and the establishment of the Kingdom of Israel. The Messiah would be the leader that redeems the Land of Israel from Gentile rule, returns the Jews worldwide out of exile, and unites them in the Kingdom of Israel under a theocracy, based on Jewish religious law. The cause was a decline in the status of Jews and an increased religious persecution of the Jewish community in Europe. Jews were expelled from England in 1290, France in 1391, Austria in 1421, Spain in 1492, and from Portugal in 1498. Some made Aliyah, others returned to those countries or went to other countries.

Old and New

The Old Yishuv were Orthodox Jews who made Aliyah to the Land of Israel and established communities there at the time of Ottoman Southern Syria during the period of the Ottoman Empire. They were mainly ultra Orthodox Jews. They depended on Halukka, that is charity and external donations for their living and they didn't have land ownership. They mainly resided in the four Holy Cities of Judaism, being Jerusalem, Hebron, Safed and Tiberias, although some of them also lived in smaller communities like Jaffa, Acre and Haifa. The Old Yishuv was divided into two independent communities the Sephardim, including Mesta, Arabim – Arabic speaking Jews, mostly Mizrahi and Magrebi Jews who lived in the Middle East and North Africa before the arrival of Sephardi Jews – and the Ashkenazi Jews. The Sephardi Jews spoke Ladino – a Judeo-Spanish language – and they arrived in the Land of Israel in the 15th century after their expulsion out of Portugal and Spain in 1492. The Ashkenazi Jews who spoke Yiddish, made Aliyah since the 18th century. In 1860, the first new Jewish residential settlement was built outside the old walled city of Jerusalem. Sir Moses Montefiore used funds provided by Judah Touro to finance this settlement.

In 1878, the first Jewish farm settlement of Petah Tikva, east of Tel Aviv, was established predominantly by the Old Yishuv. In 1883, the settlement became permanent with the financial help of Baron Edmond de Rothschild. Today Petah Tikva has a population of more than 200,000 people. The Old Yishuv did get support of the New Yishuv, who called earlier settlers Old Yishuv to distinguish themselves from them. They came to the Land of Israel since the First Aliyah of 1882. They emphasised labour and self-sufficiency, with their ideology based more on socialism and secularism. They did have land ownership, financed by Jewish philanthropists, and they practised agriculture to sustain themselves and prevent themselves from being economically dependant as the Old Yishuv was. The first settlement in the Land of Israel of the new arrivals was Rishon LeZion established by Hovevei Zion in 1882 – regarded as the first Zionist settlement in the Land of Israel – which marked the beginning of the New Yishuv. Today this settlement also has more than 200,000 residents.

Aliyah and the Hebrew language

With Aliyah came also the revival of the Hebrew language as the everyday language in the Land of Israel that started with Eliezer Ben Yehuda (1858-1922), which ultimately led to the modern Hebrew spoken today in Israel. He joined the Jewish national movement and made Aliyah with his family to Israel in 1881 and dedicated himself to this task. Hebrew is historically regarded as the language of the Israelites and their ancestors. But, Jews living in many countries in the world used the language of the particular country where they lived and they developed dialects amongst themselves, such as Ladino a Judeo-Spanish dialect and Yiddish a Judeo-Germanic dialect.

Eliezer Ben Yehuda initiated the revival of the Hebrew language, which ceased to be an everyday language around 200 CE, by developing it from a language used in the Jewish liturgy and Rabbinic literature to standard Hebrew for daily usage. Later the standard Hebrew continued to be developed and evolved into modern Hebrew. Today the Academy of the Hebrew Language of the Hebrew University in Jerusalem and the Knesset, the Israeli parliament, have the important task to watch over the preservation of the Hebrew language, the proper use of it in daily life in general and by the Israeli governmental officials.

Aliyah, the immigration of the Jewish people out of the diaspora to the Land of Israel has been an ongoing process since ancient times. A new chapter would be added to the Jewish history of Aliyah with the Zionist movement in the late nineteenth century and the established of the Zionist Organization in 1897.

19th Century Onwards

In the first decades of the 19th century Jews from Persia, Morocco, Yemen and Russia immigrated to their Jewish homeland, the Land of Israel. But Aliyah continued in the late 19th and the 20th century. The immigration of Jewish people to the Land of Israel from 1882 to 1948 is also referred to as the period of the First to the Fifth Aliyah when mass immigration to the Jewish homeland was organised. The Jewish national movement, out of which organizations like Hovevei Zion, Bilu and subsequently the Zionist Movement came forth, played a key role at this time. At that time the Ottoman Empire (1299-1922) was in power, the territory where the Land of Israel was situated was referred to as Ottoman Palestine. The empire came to an end at the end of First World War, after which the region known today as the Middle-East came under the control of Western countries. The League of Nations rectified the British Mandate over Palestine (1922-1948) which also would make possible the establishment of the Jewish homeland in this region as was agreed with the British in the Balfour Declaration of 1917.

1882-1903 First Aliyah

In this period about 35,000 Jews moved to the Land of Israel, at that time southeastern Syria, a province of the Ottoman Empire. The majority belonged to the movement of Hovevei Zion and Bilu from the Russian Empire (1721-1917). A smaller group from Yemen also emigrated. Many established agricultural communities. Pogroms in the Russian Empire were carried out in 1821, 1859, 1871, 1881 and 1905 which affected the Jewish community. Combined with the implementation of the anti-Semitic May Laws introduced by Tsar Alexander III in 1882 resulted in about two million Jews fleeing this abuse between 1880 and 1920, the majority going to the United States and some to their Jewish homeland, the Land of Israel. The Hovevei Zion – also known as Hibbat Zion, 'lovers of Zion' – who promoted Jewish immigration to the Land of Israel were not involved with politics. They received funding for their projects initially from Jewish philanthropists. In 1882 a group of Ukrainian Jewish immigrants with Hovevei Zion founded the first Zionist settlement and second Jewish farm settlement, an agricultural cooperative, in the Land of Israel, named Rishon LeZion. Later the members of Bilu joined them. In 1884 Hovevei Zion set up their organisation in Katowitz Germany, today Katowice Poland. Their elected president was Rabbi Samuel Mohilever (1824-1898), a pioneer of Religious Zionism, and with Leon Pinsker (1821-1891), a physician, as their chairman. Both were regarded as the founders of Hovevei Zion. They were dedicated to practical aspects of establishing Jewish agricultural settlements in the Land of Israel.

But, Hovevei Zion and the Russian government officials who by now supported the immigration of Jews to the biblical Land of Israel, also needed a Jewish organisation within the Russian Empire with which the Russians could negotiate and which would make the arrangements for the emigration of the Jewish people out of Russia. Hovevei Zion established the pre-Zionist charitable organisation Odessa Comity – officially Society for the Support of Jewish Farmers and Artisans in Syria and Palestine – in Odessa in 1890. Odessa, in today's Ukraine, was a Russian free port from 1819 to 1859, which contributed to this city having an extremely diverse population including Jews. A large Jewish community lived in Odessa during the 19th century and by 1897 an estimate of 37% of the population was Jewish.

Bilu was another organisation that played a significant role when it comes to Aliyah. Its goal was to realise agricultural settlements in the Land of Israel. Their ultimate goal was the establishment of the State of Israel in Eretz Yisrael. Bilu is an acronym based on Isaiah 2:5, *Beit Ya'akov Lekhu Venelkha,* translated, 'House of Jacob let us go up'. The members of Bilu were called Bilu'im. The first group of Bilu pioneers arrived July 1882 in the Land of Israel; fourteen university students, idealists led by Israel Belkin (1861-1929), who later became a prominent writer and historian. In 1884 they established Gedera. Both Rishon LeZion and Gedera were established on land purchased from Arab villages with funds acquired from the philanthropists Edmund James de Rothschild (1845-1924) a French member of the Jewish Rothschild banking family who strongly supported Zionism and a German Jew, Maurice de Hirsch (1831-1896).

Hovevei Zion was responsible for the creation of thirty new Jewish settlements, particularly agricultural settlements, between 1870 and 1897. The Odessa Committee closed in 1913. These people were considered the forerunners and foundation builders of modern Zionism, while Bilu was the forerunner of the kibbutz movement.

1904-1914 Second Aliyah

About 40,000 Jews immigrated to the Land of Israel in this period. Some again from Syria, and others from Russia due to the pogroms held there. Greatly influenced by socialist ideals, they set up Degania Alef in 1909, Israel's first kibbutz – meaning gathering, clustering, a community that was traditionally based on agriculture – of the many kibbutzim to follow. They also formed a self-defence organisation to protect them from increasing Arab hostilities. During this period the Hebrew language was revived as the national language, and political parties as well as workers organizations were established.

1919-1923 Third Aliyah

The Land of Israel – now under the British Mandate over Palestine, who established immigration quotas for the Jews – experienced in this period the arrival of about 40,000 Jews. These immigrants were known as halutzim, that is pioneers, who were trained in agriculture, and capable of establishing self-sustaining economies. They came mainly from the Russian Empire. Additional national institutions were put in place including the Haganah, the forerunner of the Israel Defence Forces. The population of Jews grew despite of the British-imposed quotas.

1924-1929 Fourth Aliyah

Anti-Semitism in Poland and Hungary resulted in the arrival of 82,000 Jews in the Jewish Home. The United States issued immigration quotas to keep Jews out. A group of many middle-class families moved to the growing towns, while establishing light industries and small businesses. Later about 23,000 of these Jews left the country.

1929-1939 Fifth Aliyah

In the pre-Second World War period a group of about 250,000 immigrants arrived in the Jewish homeland. After the first group of about 174,000 arrived, the British increased the restrictions to Jewish immigration to the Land of Israel. Most arriving Jews were from Eastern Europe as well as professionals from Germany. Doctors, lawyers, professors and refugee artists who introduced Bauhaus (literally house of construction) – a school in Germany (1919-1933) that combined craft and fine art and that was famous for its different approach to design – to Tel Aviv, that has the largest Bauhaus buildings in the world. They also founded the Palestine Philharmonic Orchestra.

During this period significant industry was added to a predominantly agricultural economy when the port of Haifa and its oil refineries were completed. The Jewish population in this region grew to 450,000. Meanwhile tensions between Arabs and Jews grew, leading to several violent and deadly riots.

In 1929 Arab riots against the Jews depopulated the Jewish community of Hebron. After the Great Uprising from 1936 to 1939, the British issued the White Paper of 1939 – a policy paper issued by the British government – that restricted the Jewish immigration to the Jewish homeland to 75,000 over the five-year period of 1940 to 1944, years that were initially relatively calm in the Land of Israel, but with the rise of the Nazi regime in Germany in late 1930s, it was the period in which the Shoah, the Holocaust, took place in Europe. In 1935, groups of Jewish pioneers who made Aliyah to the Land of Israel from Europe, established the Religious Kibbutz Movement. They established three settlements with three blocs of kibbutzim each in Judah and Samaria during the period 1937 to 1948. After the State of Israel was established in 1948, a fourth bloc was added to the existing three clusters of kibbutzim. The reason for settlement in blocs, clusters, was the need for religious schooling, mutual assistance by veteran settlers to new arrivals and to counter effect the influence of the secular environment to defend community's religious and social principals.

Religious Jews believe that God promised Eretz Yisrael to the Israelites by promising it to their patriarch Abraham, his son Isaac and grandson Jacob. Furthermore, to them the right of the Jews to the Land of Israel is permanent and irrevocable. And they believe in the return to Eretz Yisrael as God foretold in biblical prophecies. Those who did support Zionism advocated that the natural way would be the way forward for the Jewish people, and they even considered it part of a divine plan for the return of the Jewish Messiah, hence Religious Zionism. Their ideology combines the Jewish religious faith with Zionism. They organised themselves in the Mizrahi organisation established at a world conference for Religious Zionists in Vilnius the capital of Lithuania in the Balkans. They founded the Bnei Akiva youth movement in 1929, and also organized a network of religious schools that still exists today. Shortly after the Nazis came to power in Germany, the Jewish Agency – served since 1929 as the Jewish non-profit organisation responsible for the immigration and absorption of Jewish immigrants into the Israeli communities – negotiated that 50,000 German Jews and their assets worth 100 million US dollars would be transferred to the Jewish homeland, the so-called *Ha'avara*, transfer agreement.

1933-1948 Aliyah Bet

Aliyah became illegal and clandestine because of the restricted quotas the British issued. Still, many Jews made the journey to the Land of Israel, which was organised by *Mossad Le'aliyah Bet* – a branch of the Haganah, and by the Irgun, an offshoot of the Haganah. This period of aliyah became known as *Aliyah Bet*, (*Ha'apalah*) meaning the illegal clandestine immigration to the Land of Israel, secondary immigration.

The immigration took place mainly by sea and sometimes over land through Iraq and Syria. During the Second World War until the establishment of the State of Israel in 1948, Aliyah Bet was the main form of immigration for Jewish people to their homeland. The reason?

The reason was that while the Nazis were systematically murdering the Jews either by death squads known as Einsatzgruppen or in concentration camps, the British maintained their quotas. To enforce their policy the British built their own internment camps or used existing camps as such to confine the Jews who fled to Israel. They detained 53,510 Jews in a total of twelve camps, nine of which were on Cyprus (1946-1949), the others on Mauritius – an island off the southeast coast of the African continent – and in the Jewish homeland itself. Thousands were interned at the Atlit detainee camp – a National Heritage site in Israel since 1987 – was in use by the British for this purpose.

Despite all this, and even though Jewish immigration exceeded the British quotas, many who survived the Holocaust still made their way to their homeland.

Endnote

www.thegreenolivetree.nl; Article: Aliyah an overview

THE PROMISE

On that day the Lord made a covenant with Abram and said, To your descendants I give this land, from the Wadi of Egypt to the great river, the Euphrates – the land of the Kenites, Kenizzites, Kadmonites, Hittites, Perizzites, Rephaites, Amorites, Canaanites, Girgashites and Jebusites.

Genesis 15

King David's ancestor, Abraham, moved to live in the land of Canaan, which would ultimately become the Land of Israel. At that time there was already a society of city-states in Canaan. The emergence of Canaan as a society occurred during ancient history.

Ancient History

Ancient history is the history of past events from the beginning of recorded human history to the Early Middle Ages – also referred to as the Post Classical Era – covering roughly 5,000 years, with the discovery of the earliest form of coherent writing – the Sumerian Cuneiform script – around the 30th century BCE. Prior to 3500 BCE (prehistory to Stone Age), hunter-gatherer societies slowly gave way to farming and herding societies, and early metal-working in the last thousand years. By the time it was Early Bronze Age (3500-2000 BCE) writing was invented, and city-states were emerging during the Middle Bronze Age (2000-1550 BCE), followed by the Late Bronze Age (1550-1200 BCE) in which Egyptian hegemony was realised. In the Iron Age divided into I and II, village societies of Iron Age I gave way to kingdoms in Iron Age II. After the Iron Age the periods would be named after the various empires that ruled the region, Assyrian, Babylonian, Persian, Greek (Hellenistic) and Roman.

The pre-Israeli Era

The period before the emergence of the Israeli people establishing their society of Israel in Canaan could be indicated as the pre-Israeli era. Where did the ancestors of those who conquered Canaan and made it their home, the Land of Israel, actually come from? The world after the flood was according to the biblical narrative in the book of Genesis given to Noah's sons, to Sham, Ham and Japhet. Noah and his three sons were blessed by God. Shem also received a blessing from Noah after an incident Ham had with Noah. Contrary to Shem and his sons, Ham's son Canaan was cursed by Noah.

> *Then God blessed Noah and his sons, saying to them, Be fruitful and increase in number and fill the earth.*
>
> Genesis 9:1

The Semitic Middle people are believed to be descendants of Noah's eldest son Shem. Shem's name means 'name', 'renown', 'prosperity'. He was the ancestor of all Hebrews. Shem's sons were Elam, Asshur, Arpachshad, Lud and Aram. Asher is associated with Assyriah. Arpachshad, he or his descendants are regarded as the founders of Ur of the Chaldees usually identified with the Ur in Mesopotamia. The Hametic Southern people are believed to be descendants of Ham, whose name means 'warm', and his sons were Cush, Egypt, Libya and Canaan. The people of Canaan initially populated the eastern shore of the Mediterranean sea, today Israel, Lebanon and Syria.

Noah's youngest son Japhet is the ancestor of the Japhetic Northern people. His name means 'open'. The sons of Japhet were Gomer, Magog, Madal, Javan, Tubal, Meshech and Tiras. These were the allocation of the descendants of Noah's sons Shem, Ham and Japhet according to the first century Jewish-Roman historian Flavius Josephus in *Antiquities of the Jews*. He was one of the first historians who tried to apply known ethnicities to the list of names in Genesis chapter ten, the Table of Nations or Table of Sons of Noah. Later authors used his work as a basis in their own work. Magog, Meshech and Tubal, sons of Japhet, are all mentioned in biblical scripture in connection with future wars with Israel. Notice that Magog, Meshech and Tubal are placed in modern-day Turkey and its northern neighbouring countries, although there is still debate on this subject. Ultimately the Hebrew Patriarch Abraham, a descendant of Shem, would establish himself in Canaan after moving out of Ur of Chaldea situated in Mesopotamia. Considering the borders mentioned in Genesis chapter fifteen, Canaan was situated in God's Promised Land to Abraham.

Modern History – 1917

The 1917 Balfour Declaration, a letter issued by the British Foreign

Office, was a result of affords made by Chaim Weizmann and Nahum Sokolow, Zionist leaders based in London. The letter, which fell short of what the Zionist Movement wanted, was meant for transmission to the Zionist Federation of Great Britain and Ireland. The letter, signed by Arthur Balfour, Foreign Secretary, reflected the position of the British Cabinet at the time, that the British government was in favour of the establishment of a national home for the Jewish people in Palestine.

This declaration was the result of a specific change made by the British government in the original declaration. Instead of 'that Palestine' it was changed into 'in Palestine'. This was done to avoid having to arrange that all the territory of Palestine would be assigned as a Jewish Homeland. This was confirmed by Winston Churchill's 'White Paper' in 1922. So the territory assigned to become the national homeland for the Jews was in the region called Palestine, on the eastern shore of the Mediterranean Sea, in the Middle-East. The name Palestine was given to the region by the Romans.

This declaration was included in the British Mandate for Palestine, a legal commission for the temporary administration of Palestine by the United Kingdom. The draft was formally confirmed in 1922 by The League of Nations and came into effect in 1923. The United Kingdom divided the Mandate territory into the administrative areas Palestine west of the Jordan River – modern-day State of Israel – under direct rule of the British, and autonomous Transjordan – modern day Jordan – to the east of the river. Transjordan came under the rule of a Jordanian monarchy – a dynasty of a family with origins in Saudi Arabia – that the British helped to set up in 1921. The latter was done to accommodate the agreements as a result of their McMahon-Hussein Correspondence in 1915 with the Arab leaders for their support in defeating the Ottoman Empire. The United Kingdom would later impose rules to bring the influx of Jews to Palestine to a minimum. This continued during and after the Second World War.

1948

Arrangements for a Jewish homeland in the territory west of the Jordan River had to be realised during the British Mandate, which came into effect in 1923 and would last until the 15th of May, 1948. Long before the Second World War during which the Holocaust would occur, nations in power at that time already agreed to having a Jewish homeland in the territory that at that time was called Palestine. In November 1947, the United Nations (UN) approved a Partition Plan for Palestine, that is the territory west of the Jordan River because of the tensions and hostilities between the Arabs living in the area, who after 1967 began to call themselves Palestinian, and the Jewish people.

There was an Arab Revolt in Palestine from 1936 to 1939. They were against the influx of Jewish people who continued to immigrate by means of Aliyah to Palestine. This revolt was one of the reasons the British issued the 1939 White Paper in November 1938 on the eve of Kristallnacht, the pogrom on Jewish people in Nazi Germany and Austria. The British government made it clear they would eventually stop the influx of Jews into Palestine. This in turn caused the rejection of thousands of Jewish people fleeing Nazi Germany, by the surrounding countries of Palestine and elsewhere.

The 1947 UN Partition Plan provided for two States in Palestine, one Jewish and one Arab, while Jerusalem would be an international city. The Jewish Community at that time accepted the plan, but the Arab League and the Arab High Committee rejected it after which the Committee declared a three-day strike in Palestine. This resulted in Arabs targeting the Jewish people and ultimately these hostilities resulted in the collapse of the Arab-Palestinian economy.

On the 14th of May 1948, the day before the expiration of the British Mandate, David Ben-Gurion, at the time the executive head of the World Zionist Organization and president of the Jewish Agency for Palestine, declared 'the establishment of a Jewish state in Eretz Israel, to be known as the State of Israel'.

Eretz Israel was the only term referring to the borders of the newly established state. The State of Israel would be independent upon the termination of the British Mandate for Palestine, the 15th of May 1948. The State of Israel was quickly recognised by the Soviet Union and the United States. Many other nations followed. The day following the declaration of the State of Israel, when the British would leave Israel, armies of the Arab countries attacked Israel. Egypt, Lebanon, Iraq and Saudi Arabia all sent a military contingent to fight under Egyptian command. Yemen also declared war on Israel, but didn't come into action. After a year of fighting a cease fire was agreed. In accordance with the 1949 Armistice Agreement temporary demarcation lines were agreed which became known as the Green Line. Transjordan annexed occupied East Jerusalem and parts of Samaria and Judah, which they called the West Bank. Meanwhile Egypt took control of the Gaza

Strip. About 700,000 Arabs fled the country or were expelled. Some of them or their descendants are nowadays still in so-called 'refugee camps' in the region.

In 1949, on the 11th of May, Israel was accepted as a member of the United Nations by a majority vote. With the establishment of the State of Israel, the Land of Israel became independent. Meanwhile Aliyah, which was at some point illegal under the restrictions of the British Mandate, continued. The Israeli government mandated the Jewish Agency for Israel to handle Aliyah of Jewish people out of the diaspora to the State of Israel. This non-profit organisation held office in Jaffa since 1908 – the Land of Israel was under Ottoman control – as an operational branch of the Zionist Organization. Since 1929 it has been serving as the primary organisation responsible for Jewish immigration to the Land of Israel. The State of Israel issued the Law of Return for Jews in 1950, and extended it in 1970, which made it possible for people who are not Jewish under Rabbinical Law to immigrate to Israel. These are people of Jewish descent with non-Jewish spouses. They all would have the right to live in Israel and to gain Israeli citizenship. Over half a million Jews made Aliyah to Israel between 1948 and 1950.

> *The Lord had said to Abram, Go from your country, your people and your father's household to the land I will show you. I will make you into a great nation, and I will bless you; I will make your name great, and you will be a blessing. I will bless those who bless you, and whoever curses you I will curse; and all people on earth will be blessed through you. So Abram went, as the Lord had told him.*
>
> Genesis 12:1-9

The process of Aliyah started with patriarch Abraham and his sons, whose offspring would be the people of Israel as well as other people. God sent one man, Abram, to Canaan with the promise He would make him a great nation. He would bless him and he would be a blessing to all the people on earth. The Lord brought Abraham out of Ur of the Chaldeans to entrust him with the land of Canaan. He and his offspring would take it into their possession. The Lord spoke to Abraham in a vision about his offspring.

> *Do not be afraid, Abram. I am your shield, your very great reward ... Look up at the sky and count the stars – if indeed*

you can count them ... So shall your offspring be. Abram believed the Lord, and he credited it to him as righteousness.
                                                         Genesis 15:1-7

At the same time the Lord made it clear to Abraham that his descendants would be treated as slaves for a long period of time. They would live about four hundred years in a foreign country where they would be enslaved and mistreated. Afterwards God would punish that nation and take His people, in the fourth generation of Abraham's descendants, out to take possession of the land He promised him. By that time, when the sin of the Amorites living in Canaan would have reached its full measure, Abraham himself would have already been gathered to his ancestors.

Sarah's Son, Isaac

At the time there was a famine in the land, Isaac went with his household to Gerar where Abimelech was king of the Philistines. Isaac was Abraham and Sarah's son. God appeared to Isaac and told him not to go to Egypt, but to remain in the land that God would tell him to stay. The Lord also promised him, He would fulfil the oath He gave Abraham to him.

Sojourn in this land, and I will be with you, and will bless you; for to you and to your descendants I will give all these lands, and I will fulfil the oath which I swore to Abraham your father. I will multiply your descendants as the stars of heaven, and will give to your descendants all these lands; and by your descendants all the nations of the earth shall bless themselves, because Abraham obeyed M voice and kept My charge, My commandments, My statutes, and My laws.
                                                         Genesis 26:1-5

Once there, in the land of the Philistines, Isaac presented his beautiful wife Rebecca as his sister, thinking that the men there might otherwise kill him because of her, something that his father Abraham also did in the past when he took his household to Gerar for the same reason as Isaac did. He told the people there that his wife Sarah was his sister. He thought that the people living in Gerar didn't have fear for his God. King Abimelech was interested in Sarah and even sent for her. But, before he would approach her to sleep with her, God appeared to Abimelech in a dream. He told him that he was as good as dead because he took a married woman. Abimelech told the Lord that Abraham said she was his sister, and that he acted with a clear conscious and clean hands. He also asked the Lord whether He would destroy a nation over this. The Lord was in agreement with him and told him that this was the reason He prevented him from sinning against him. He told him to return the man's wife to him, and Abraham who is a prophet would pray for him so he might live. Otherwise he and all who belonged to him would die. Abimelech did exactly what the Lord told him to do. His officials whom he told about what happened became very afraid. When Abimelech spoke to Abraham, he told him why he was afraid and that Sarah was actually his half sister, being the daughter of another mother than his own. Abimelech returned Sarah, and brought sheep, cattle, slaves both male and female slaves for Abraham and offered him to live where he wanted in his land. He also gave a thousand shekels of silver to cover the offence and told Sarah before everyone present that she was completely vindicated. Abraham then prayed to God for Abimelech. This was necessary because the Lord had kept all the females in Abimelech's household from conceiving. On Abraham's prayer, God healed him, his wife and female slaves so they could have children again. Later Abimelech would go to Abraham to make a treaty with him, and Abraham would give him gifts. Abraham would also settle a dispute about a well that he had dug. He would call that place Beersheba, where he lived for a long time in the land of the Philistines. Isaac went to live in the same region where his father Abraham had lived in the past and where he had dug wells.

In the case of Isaac, Abimelech didn't send for Rebecca because he noticed that she was his wife. One day when Abimelech looked down from a window, he saw Isaac with his wife. He was caressing her. So, Abimelech summoned Isaac and spoke to him about his lie. Isaac had the same fear as his father Abraham had. Abimelech gave orders that no one was to harm Isaac or his wife. Anyone who did would be punishable by death. It's while Isaac was living in this land that God blessed him and made him a wealthy man. The crops he planted yielded a hundredfold the same year. He had many flocks and herds. Also many servants. The Philistines envied him, and some filled all Abraham's wells that were in use by Isaac with earth. Abimelech told Isaac that he became too powerful for them and that he should move away from there. Isaac moved with his entire household and belongings to the valley of Gerar where he settled. But he had to move on again after the Philistines quarrelled with him about the water of the wells Abraham once dug there. Ultimately Isaac went to live in Beersheba where God appeared to him one night saying, *'I am the God of your father Abraham. Do not be afraid, for I am with you; I will bless you and will increase the number of your descendants for the sake of my servant Abraham'*. Isaac built an altar there. One day Abimelech went to visit Isaac, with his personal adviser and the commander of his forces. Abimelech told Isaac that it was clear that God was with him, and he wanted to enter an agreement with him. Abimelech made a treaty with Isaac that he wouldn't harm him and his people. Isaac made a feast for them after which he sent them away peacefully.

Abraham's Other Sons

Hagar's son Ishmael was Abraham's eldest son. Hagar was an Egyptian woman, Sarah's slave, to whom God spoke twice on behalf of Abraham concerning their son Ishmael. God cared for Abraham's eldest son Ishmael, whom He gave another inheritance although Abraham had to send him away. God told Abraham once, that it's through Isaac's descendants that Abraham's name would be reckoned. For this reason the Lord also told him to listen to his wife Sarah who told him to send Ishmael and his mother away. Ishmael had to leave at the age of fourteen to live in the desert of Paran east of Egypt. Later he married an Egyptian woman and he remained friendly with his brother Isaac as he was since Isaac was born. They buried their father together. God answered Abraham's request concerning Ishmael with the promise that Ishmael's descendants would become a nation and he would be the father of twelve rulers. Much later God made clear that Ishmael's descendants, being also of Egyptian descent, would be welcome to Israel's religious gatherings because the Israelites had resided in their land. Abraham's other sons, he remarried after Sarah's death and had concubines, would only receive gifts and they would be sent away to the east.

Abraham left everything he owned to Isaac.
Genesis 25:5

Abraham's Grandsons

Isaac married Rebecca the daughter of Betuel the Aramean. Isaac and Rebecca's youngest son Jacob was obedient to his father and mother. After deceiving Isaac, and in fear of Esau, because he took his blessing, Jacob went to the family of his mother in Paddan Aram. Rebecca's brother Laban lived there. Jacob was to choose one of Laban's daughters to marry, as his father commanded him to marry a non-Canaanite woman. Rebecca was in complete agreement with her husband on this matter.

Jacob married Laban's eldest daughter Leah after being deceived by Laban that he was marrying Rachel. Afterwards, Laban gave Jacob Rachel in marriage. Jacob had to work fourteen years for Laban for his two wives. Jacob deceived his father Isaac into blessing him with the blessing meant for his firstborn, *'May God give you heaven's dew and earth's richness – an abundance of grain and new wine. May nations serve you and people bow down to you. Be lord over your brothers, and may the sons of your mother bow down to you. May those who curse you be cursed and those who bless you be blessed'*.

His brother Esau was furious about this and sought to harm him. Before Jacob left, Isaac blessed him again, *'May God Almighty bless you and make you fruitful and increase your numbers until you become a community of people. May he give you and your descendants the blessing given to Abraham, so that you may take possession of the land where you now reside as a foreigner, the land God gave to Abraham'*.

On a few occasions God Himself appeared to Jacob and blessed him. One of those times was when he was on his way to his mother's family. He left Beersheba and was on his way to Harran. The Lord spoke to him in a dream, saying, *'I am the Lord, the God of your father Abraham and the God of Isaac. I will give you and your descendants the land on which you are lying. Your descendants will be like the dust of the earth, and you will spread out to the west and to the east, to the north and to the south. All people on earth will be blessed through you and your offspring. I am with you and will watch over you wherever you go, and I will bring you back to this land. I will not leave you until I have done what I have promised you'*.

Another occasion was after Jacob returned from Paddan Aram, a wealthy man with his entire household, God appeared to him again, blessed him and changed his name into Israel.

> *God said to him, Your name is Jacob, but you will no longer be called Jacob; your name will be Israel ... I am God Almighty; be fruitful and increase in number. A nation and a*

community of nations will come from you, and kings will be among your descendants.

Genesis 35:10-11

Isaac and Rebecca's eldest son, Esau, relinquished his firstborn rights to Jacob for some red lentil stew. That's why Esau was called Edom, meaning red. Esau sold his birthright to his brother Jacob by swearing an oath. He despised the birthright which in his eyes was no good to him anyway. Therefore Esau gave Jacob the right to receive Isaac's blessing. Esau's animosity with Jacob was solved during their lifetime, when they reconciled on Jacob's return from Paddan Aram. Esau was already married to two women from Canaan when he married one of Ishmael's daughters. Isaac did give Esau a blessing. When he wept aloud while asking Isaac to give him a blessing too. Isaac blessed Esau by saying, *'Your dwelling will be away from the earth's richness, away from the dew of heaven above. You will live by the sword and you will serve your brother. But when you grow restless, you will throw his yoke from off your neck'*.

The Edomites, Esau's descendants, would be just as the Egyptians, welcome unlike other people who were excluded because they were mortal enemies of the Israelites.

All three Jewish patriarchs, Abraham, Isaac and Jacob, lived in the Promised Land. All of Abraham's inheritance including the land God promised him went to Isaac, later to Israel and through Israel's sons to all their descendants, including King David, permanently.

My servant David will be king over them, and they will all have one shepherd. They will follow my laws and be careful to keep my decrees. They will live in the land I gave to my servant Jacob, the land where your ancestors lived. They and their children and their children's children will live there for ever, and David my servant will be their prince for ever. I will make a covenant of peace with them; it will be an everlasting covenant. I will establish them and increase their numbers, and I will put my sanctuary among them for ever. My dwelling place will be with them; I will be their God, and they will be my people.

Ezekiel 37:24-27

Endnotes

Genesis 11:10-32, 21:1-7, 25:19-26, 38:27-30, 46, Ruth 4:18-22 King David's ancestors
Genesis 6- 9 Noah's sons
Genesis 9:18-29 Ham's son Canaan cursed by Noah
Genesis 10 table of nations
Genesis 9:18-29 incident Ham
Ezekiel 38, 39, future wars
Genesis 12:1-4, 17 Sarah's son Isaac
Genesis 21:12 Abraham's name reckoned through Isaac
Genesis 20 Abraham and Sarah in Gerar
Genesis 21:22-34 Abimelech's treaty with Abraham
Genesis 21:8-9 Isaac's birth, Ishmael friendly
Genesis 24 Isaac and Rebecca
Genesis 26 Isaac in Gerar
Genesis 26:1-5, God's promise to Isaac
Genesis 28:6-7 Jacob obedient to his father and mother
Genesis 27:27-29 Isaac's blessing for Jacob
Genesis 28:10-15 God's promise to Jacob
Genesis 25:27-34 Esau gave firstborn right to Jacob
Genesis 28:10-15 God appeared in a dream to Jacob and blessed him
Genesis 32:28, 35:9-10 God changed Jacob's name to Israel, and blessed him
Genesis 25:27-34 Esau sold his birthright to Jacob
Genesis 27:38-40 Isaac's blessing to Esau
Genesis 28:9 Esau married one of the daughters of Ishmael
Genesis 33 Esau and Jacob's reconciliation
Genesis 16:7-16, Genesis 21:14-21 Ishmael's inheritance
Genesis 21:10-12 Ishmael left with his mother
Genesis 21:20-21 Ishmael married an Egyptian
Genesis 17:20, 21:11-13, 25:12-18 Ishmael's, a nation and twelve rulers
Genesis 25:6 Abraham sent other sons away
Genesis 25:8-9 Ishmael and Isaac buried Abraham
Deuteronomy 23:2-8 Egyptians and Edomites welcome to Israel's gatherings
Genesis 25:6 Abraham's sons sent away with gifts
Genesis 25:5, Genesis 17:15-19, 21 Abraham's inheritance to Isaac
Genesis 28:1-15, Inheritance to Jacob and his descendants

Source: www.thegreenolivetree.nl
Articles:
Balfour Declaration 1917
Israel: Arab-Israeli War 1948 and 1967
Aliyah an overview Part 2 and 4

CONTEMPT

For a small moment have I forsaken you; but with great compassion will I gather you. In a little wrath I hid My face from you for a moment; but with everlasting kindness will I have compassion on you ... For this is as the waters of Noah unto Me; for as I have sworn that the waters of Noah should no more go over the earth, so have I sworn that I would not be wroth with you, nor rebuke you. For the mountains may depart, and the hills be removed; but My kindness shall not depart from you, neither shall My covenant of peace be removed, says HaShem that has compassion on you.
Isaiah 54:7-10

For an instant in eternity God Almighty, Who watches over the entire world, would abandon His people. Because of their sinfulness and disobedience He would bring divine judgment over them. The Lord God had granted the Children of Israel a special place amongst the nations by making them His people while giving them His Land as their inheritance. They were to abide by His Law and Commandments, love Him above all else, with all their heart and all their soul and all their strength. They were not to hate a fellow Israelite in their heart, but to love their neighbour as themselves. Instead of holding a grudge against anyone while seeking revenge, they were to rebuke their neighbour frankly so they wouldn't share in their guilt, and leave disputes to be solved by those who uphold the Law in righteousness. Taking up God's moral code also meant they were not to take up Egyptian nor Canaanite pagan traditions in their way of life. This would prevent them and the Land from becoming unclean. If they would do otherwise, the Land would vomit them out as it did the former inhabitants. In doing these they would enjoy the riches of the Land and the Lord's protection. Despite all their shortcomings, only HaShem had a delight in your fathers to love them, and He chose their seed after them, *'even you, above all people, as it is this day. Circumcise therefore the foreskin of your heart, and be no more stiff-necked'*.*

From the start the Lord wanted the Israelites to circumcise the foreskin of their heart so they could receive more of His love, His care, and develop more understanding of Him. In turn they would show their love for Him by being faithful and obedient to Him. But they, except those who remained faithful to the Lord, did otherwise and so the Lord turned against them as He warned them ages ago that He would, if they wouldn't listen to Him anymore. The Lord was about to remove His protection as He had given to their Patriarchs, and their ancestors ever since He took them out of Egypt, led by the prophet Moses. These were the people with whom the Lord made a covenant, a written agreement at Mount Sinai. In doing this, the Lord Himself kept His promises made to their forefather Abraham, Isaac and Israel. This covenant was renewed by Joshua when they finally entered the Promised Land. Later Judah's kings would confirm the Lord's covenant, His contract with the inhabitants of Jerusalem and Judah as for example King Asa did during his reign. More than a century later King Josiah did this as well. But the Lord expected His kings to remain faithful to Him during their reign. The Lord wanted them to commit their heart fully to Him and to rely only on him so He would strengthen them. If not, this would lead to a period of war instead of peace in their nation, as happened to King Asa when in the later days of his reign he made the mistake of relying on his allies instead of the Lord. This led to a period of constant war after the nation had enjoyed a time of peace in Judah.

> *Hearken unto My voice, and I will be your God, and you shall be My people; and walk you in all the ways that I command you, that it may be well with you.*
>
> Jeremiah 7:23

The Lord Himself also spoke to the leaders He had appointed, or He would send either His prophets or angels to them. Sometimes the Lord Himself approached His appointed leader and He had them stand on holy ground, for example Moses at Mount Horeb when the Lord gave him His message concerning His plan of deliverance for the Children of Israel out of Egypt's slavery to lead them to the Promised Land. Joshua stood on holy ground with the commander of God's army who afterwards would support him during battle defeating Jericho. Centuries later the Lord entrusted them with the city He wanted His Name to be placed for ever. The Temple of the Lord would stand on holy ground in Jerusalem, the city of which David had the knowledge of how to conquer it. The Lord's word by Jeremiah to the House of David during Judah's last ruler Zedekiah's would be, "*O House of David, thus says HaShem: 'Execute justice in the morning, and deliver the spoiled out of the hand of the oppressor, lest My fury go forth like fire, and burn that none can quench it, because of the evil of your doings'."*

The Israelites living in Judah believed that they wouldn't be conquered because the Lord's Temple had been in Jerusalem for generations. The Temple of which the Lord had said to David and to Solomon, *'In this house, and in Jerusalem, which I have chosen out of all the tribes of Israel, will I put My name for ever; neither will I cause the feet of Israel to wander any more out of the land which I gave their fathers; if only they will observe to do according to all that I have commanded them, and according to all the Law that My servant Moses commanded them'.*

But these people and their leaders didn't live carefully by everything the Lord had commanded them to do. They themselves didn't take the graveness of their sinfulness seriously enough to seek repentance, while the Lord did know their wrongdoings and wickedness, even those hidden.

> *For I have no pleasure in the death of him that dies ... therefore turn yourselves, and live!*
>
> Ezekiel 18:32

The Almighty God chose the Children of Israel to be His people, His son. He took both intentional and unintentional sins of His people into account when He gave them His Laws and Commandments, showing them, with these, the way to Him through obedience and repentance. When it came to sinfulness, every person would carry responsibility for their own sins. Although sinful acts might also have consequences throughout generations. So much so, that children might be punished for the sins of their ancestors. But for those who would repent, there would always be the possibility for them to pray for forgiveness of their own sins, and even for those of their ancestors, something the prophet Daniel would once do for himself and his people the Israelites, and the Lord would answer his remorseful and truthful prayers.

Sinfulness and wickedness angers the Lord, even though He didn't expect the Children of Israel to be sinless, nor perfect. They were to be faithful to the Lord, maintain justice, do that which is upright and keep doing righteous deeds instead of evil acts. Those, including foreigners residing amongst the Israelites, who hold fast to this and keep the Sabbath without desecrating it, would be blessed by the Lord. He, Who wouldn't change and would always see everything the Children of Israel did, wanted them to return to Him so He could return to them. To the Lord sincere repentance with honest offerings were of importance when it came to Him listening to His people. He didn't want them to die a senseless death as a result of sinfulness. He wanted them to listen to Him and to respond to His discipline. People who intentionally sinned by blaspheming the Lord, showing much contempt for Him, despising His Word, Laws, and Commands, and insisting in doing these would ultimately be exiled from His Land. He Himself would be in charge of this process.

> *And justice is turned away backward, and righteousness stands afar off; for truth has stumbled in the broad place, and uprightness cannot enter. And truth is lacking, and he that departs from evil makes himself a prey. And HaShem saw it, and it displeased Him that there was no justice.*
>
> Isaiah 59:14-15

Despite the Lord's way out through repentance, His teachings and warnings through His servants the prophets, the nation of Israel and eventually that of Judah became unfaithful to the Lord. Several prophets of the Lord prophesied about the fall of both Israel and Judah years before the fact and during the period these events would take place. Several of them were ill-treated and some even lost their life while carrying out their God-given task. But, their message was rejected again and again. So, the Lord decided on the measure of their punishment and carried it out. They would be punished in accordance to their own sinful ways. The reason was their reluctance to listen to the Lord, their sinful way of life they wanted to hold on to, promote and support in the nation. First for Israel and more than a century later for Judah. This time the Lord wouldn't spare Jerusalem from destruction as He did for instance at the time of Hezekiah's reign. The Lord's honour and His promise to David wouldn't prevent this from happening, but it would be the basis for His guarantee to Jerusalem's restoration in the future.

> *Thus says HaShem: If you will not hearken to Me, to walk in My law, which I have set before you, to hearken to the words of My servants the prophets, whom I send unto you, even sending them be times and often, but you have not hearkened; then will I make this house like Shiloh, and will make this city a curse to all the nations of the earth.*
>
> Jeremiah 26:4-6

Corrupt Leaders

Although Judah initially, after the division of the Kingdom of Israel into the two nations Judah and Israel, remained loyal to the Lord and kept the Temple Service, they did not let go of a sinful way of life, which generations later would ultimately lead to their expulsion from the Land.

> *I, even I, know Ephraim, and Israel is not hid from Me; for now, O Ephraim, thou hast committed harlotry, Israel is defiled. Their doings will not suffer them to return unto their God; for the spirit of harlotry is within them, and they know not HaShem. But the pride of Israel shall testify to His face; and Israel and Ephraim shall stumble in their iniquity, Judah also shall stumble with them.*
>
> Hosea 4:3-5

In the period before Judah fell the leaders and inhabitants of Judah, including Jerusalem, showed much contempt for the Lord. Judah was subject to bad and wicked leadership. The Lord warned the leaders, as Jeremiah proclaimed in the palace to the king of Judah, "*Thus says HaShem: 'Go down to the house of the king of Judah, and speak there this word, and say: Hear the word of HaShem, O king of Judah, that sits upon the throne of David, you, and your servants, and your people that enter in by these gates. Thus says HaShem: Execute you justice and righteousness, and deliver the spoiled out of the hand of the oppressor; and do no wrong, do no violence, to the stranger, the fatherless, nor the widow, neither shed innocent blood in this place. For if you do this thing indeed, then shall there enter in by the gates of this house kings sitting upon the throne of David, riding in chariots and on horses, he, and his servants, and his people. But if you will not hear these words, I swear by Myself, says HaShem, 'that this house shall become a desolation'.*"*

But, they didn't listen, and as a consequence Judah's government and society became corrupt. To Hosea the Lord said, '*Therefore, HaShem has also a controversy with Judah, and will punish Jacob according to his ways, according to his doings will He recompense him*'.*

Judah's dishonest and poor governance with kings unfaithful to the Lord with appointed judges and officials passing unfair judgment and a dysfunctional sinful priesthood led the people and the nation of Judah astray. The king, princes, nobles, elders, leaders, and watchmen were busy with their sinful acts while missing on the Lord's wonders that He would have performed as He had done in the past. Those who were supposed to guide the people in righteousness, led them away from the Lord God. To the Lord those who were wise shouldn't boast of their wisdom, strength nor riches but of their understanding to know Him, the One Who exercises kindness, justice and righteousness on earth. These were the things that pleased the Lord. Instead Judah's leaders were unfaithful, they set up kings without the Lord's consent, and they chose princes without His approval.

> *Therefore My people are gone into captivity, for want of knowledge; and their honourable men are famished, and their multitude are parched with thirst. Therefore the netherworld has enlarged her desire, and opened her mouth without measure; and down goes their glory, and their tumult, and their uproar, and he that rejoices among them. And man is bowed down, and man is humbled, and the eyes of the lofty are humbled.*
>
> Isaiah 5:13-15

Robbery

Judah's leaders just as those of Ephraim, more than a century before Judah would fall, became dedicated to enriching themselves, while they and Judah's people showed gross lack of care for the poor, the widows, the fatherless and foreigners.

> *His watchmen are all blind, without knowledge; they are all dumb dogs, they cannot bark; raving, lying down, loving to slumber. The dogs are greedy, they know not when they have enough; and these are shepherds that cannot understand; they all turn to their own way, each one to his gain, one and all. Come you, I will fetch wine, and we will fill ourselves with strong drink; and tomorrow shall be as this day, and much more abundant.*
>
> Isaiah 56:10-12

The tribe of Ephraim was full of arrogance, and they boasted, 'Surely I have become rich, I have found me wealth; in all my labours they shall find in me no iniquity that were sin'.*

But as the Lord said to Hosea making it clear that this wasn't the case, 'As for the trafficker, the balances of deceit are in his hand. He loves to oppress'.*

Didn't the people of the generation of Ephraim who were expelled from the Land and the generation of Judah who would fall realise that He that augments his substance by interest and increase, gathers it for him that is gracious to the poor?* And that He that gives unto the poor shall not lack; but he that hides his eyes shall have many a curse?* Didn't Judah learn anything of Ephraim's, the Kingdom of Israel's, mistakes?

> *As the partridge that broods over young which she has not brought forth, so is he that gets riches, and not by right; in the midst of his days he shall leave them, and at his end he shall be a fool.*
>
> Jeremiah 17:11

The Lord was clear that the justice system should be free of corruption and that no partiality should be shown to the poor in general. But contrary to God's regulations, the justice system was corrupt with people who instead of judging fairly, perverted justice, showing favouritism to the great to their convenience. Didn't they realise that to the Lord, He that turns away his ear from hearing the law, even his prayer is an abomination.*

These people, except those who remained faithful to the Lord, didn't honour the Lord by keeping His Shabbat a holy day as He had commanded their ancestors, by not doing any kind of work, and not carrying a load out of their houses nor through Jerusalem's city gates for business. But they didn't pay attention, listen, nor respond to discipline. God's words spoken by Jeremiah concerning the violation of the Shabbat, *'But if you will not hearken unto Me to hallow the Shabbat day, and not to bear a burden and enter in at the gates of Jerusalem on the Shabbat day; then will I kindle a fire in the gates thereof, and it shall devour the palaces of Jerusalem, and it shall not be quenched'.*

Instead, if they would have obeyed Him, then the kings who would sit on David's throne would come in their chariots and on horses through the city gates of Jerusalem, accompanied by their officials, the men of Judah and its inhabitants. People would come to Jerusalem bringing offerings, sacrifices and incense for the Lord. The city of Jerusalem would have remained inhabited for ever.

> *As a cage is full of birds, so are their houses full of deceit; therefore they become great, and waxen rich; They waxen*

> *fat, they become sleek; they overpass in deeds of wickedness; they plead not the cause, the cause of the fatherless, that they might make it to prosper; and the right of the needy do they not judge. Shall I not punish for these things? ... shall not My soul be avenged on such a nation as this?*
>
> Jeremiah 5:27-29
>
> *HaShem will enter into judgment with the elders of His people, and the princes thereof: It is you that have eaten up the vineyard; the spoil of the poor is in your houses. What mean you that you crush My people, and grind the face of the poor? says the Lord, the God of hosts.*
>
> Isaiah 3:14-15

There was much robbery in the Kingdom of Judah with people enriching themselves at the expense of the less fortunate. When it came to business and commerce the Lord commanded them, *'You shall do no unrighteousness in judgment, in mete yard, in weight, or in measure. Just balances, just weights, a just ephah, and a just hin, shall you have: I am HaShem your God, who brought you out of the land of Egypt. And you shall observe all My statutes, and all My ordinances, and do them: I am HaShem'.**

In case of wrongdoings, they were to show remorse and pay restitution regarding what they had taken from others. Even so, these people continued to steal, even from the Lord God Himself, as He said to His prophet Malachi, *"Will a man, a mere mortal, rob God? Yet you rob Me. But you say: 'Wherein have we robbed You'? In tithes and heave-offerings. You are cursed with the curse, yet you rob Me, even this whole nation."**

If instead they would bring in all the tithes in the Lord's storehouse so there would be food in His House and do all the offerings properly, the Lord would have blessed them abundantly. If they did, as He said to Malachi, wouldn't He, *'open the windows of heaven, and pour you out a blessing, that there shall be more than sufficiency. And I will rebuke the devourer for your good, and he shall not destroy the fruits of your land; neither shall your vine cast its fruit before the time in the field, says HaShem of hosts'.**

The Land would be so fruitful, that it would provide enough produce, and even more than enough produce for the seventh year when the Israelites would give it its Shabbat year of rest. A year in which by God's command they were not to plant nor harvest crops. The Land's produce in the sixth year would cover all they needed for their nation up to the next harvest in the ninth year, which would have been planted the eighth year. The Lord would have made their Land a delightful place, that all nations would call blessed.

> *Behold, the eyes of the Lord God are upon the sinful kingdom, and I will destroy it from off the face of the earth; saving that I will not utterly destroy the house of Jacob, says HaShem.*
>
> Amos 9:8

Idol Worship

Through idolatry the Israelites expressed much contempt to the Lord God. What did the whole of Judah and Israel have with idols and lifeless gods? *'Of their silver and their gold have they made themselves idols, that they may be cut off'*,* as the Lord told Hosea.

Didn't they realise they were making these to their own destruction? The Lord God just doesn't accept any god or idol next to Him, and there is none with Him whom He would have to consult in any way. The only one who could ever say this about himself, could only be the One, true, genuine Living God, the Almighty Creator of heaven and earth. Because only He could actually live by these words, *'See now that I, even I, am He, and there is no god with Me'*.*

> *At that time, says HaShem, they shall bring out the bones of the kings of Judah, and the bones of his princes, and the bones of the priests, and the bones of the prophets, and the bones of the inhabitants of Jerusalem, out of their graves; and they shall spread them before the sun, and the moon, and all the host of heaven, whom they have loved, and whom they have served, and after whom they have walked, and whom they have sought, and whom they have worshipped; they shall not be gathered, nor be buried, they shall be for dung upon the face of the earth. And death shall be chosen rather than life by all the residue that remain of this evil family, that remain in all the places whither I have driven them, said HaShem of hosts.*
>
> Jeremiah 8:1-3

Against God's commands they even burned their sons and daughters in the fire when making sacrifices to demons. Idol worship continued even when part of Judah's remnant went to live in Egypt after the Babylonians conquered Judah. The Lord spoke to His servant

Jeremiah about His people provoking Him with the pagan customs and traditions they adopted saying, *'See you not what they do in the cities of Judah and in the streets of Jerusalem? The children gather wood, and the fathers kindle the fire, and the women knead the dough, to make cakes to the queen of heaven, and to pour out drink-offerings unto other gods, that they may provoke Me. Do they provoke Me'?* says HaShem; *'Do they not provoke themselves, to the confusion of their own faces'? Therefore thus says the Lord God: 'Behold, My anger and My fury shall be poured out upon this place, upon man, and upon beast, and upon the trees of the field, and upon the fruit of the land; and it shall burn, and shall not be quenched'.**

Their multitude of gods were not only self-made idols, but also objects made to revere the sun, moon, stars and all the objects of the heavenly array. They worshipped, bowed down and served hand-made gods that were not gods. Didn't they know there is no salvation for those who hold onto the lie of the idols they worshipped? That *"He strives after ashes, a deceived heart has turned him aside, that he cannot deliver his soul, nor say: 'Is there not a lie in my right hand'?"**

Why couldn't they know and understand how worthless these self-made, man-made objects really were? *'They know not, neither do they understand; for their eyes are bedaubed, that they cannot see, and their hearts, that they cannot understand'.** Their idol worship was not an exception for the Israelites though, for their ancestors also engaged in these, as it happened at the time they were wandering in the desert when Moses went up Mount Sinai, and during Jeroboam's reign when he made idols to be worshipped by the people of the Kingdom of Israel. Only the people who remained truly faithful to the Lord abstained of such practices.

> *You shall not plant yourselves an Asherah of any kind of tree beside the altar of HaShem your God, which you shall make yourselves. Neither shall you set yourselves up a pillar, which HaShem your God hates.*
>
> Deuteronomy 16:21-22

Sinful Priests

The Lord repeatedly sent His warnings to Judah's priests so that His covenant with Levi might continue. The Lord's covenant with Levi was one of life and peace, which He gave to Levi causing him to be in awe with the Lord while serving Him faithfully. Unlike the priests who showed contempt for the Lord, Levi acted differently in the past, as the Lord said about him, *'The law of truth was in his mouth, and unrighteousness was not found in his lips; he walked with Me in peace and uprightness, and did turn many away from iniquity. For the priest's lips should keep knowledge, and they should seek the law at his mouth; for he is the messenger of HaShem of hosts'.**

To the Lord both His Altar and Temple Service were to be kept holy, ever since He ordained the priests to serve in His Tabernacle. The Lord is holy and the holiness of the priesthood comes from Him. It's also up to the priests to keep themselves holy for the Lord. The descendants of the Levite priest Zadok, one of the officials of David, remained like Levi faithful to the Lord, despite all the sinful acts of the other priests. In the Lord's future Temple, He would allow Zadok's descendants to serve Him in His Temple.

Many priests of Judah didn't walk the same path as Levi did. They corrupted themselves, showing partiality in matters of God's Law. They neglected to uphold the Lord's name, and they didn't give proper instructions to the people. These were days of so much contempt for the Lord at the Lord's Temple because the priests were not interested in performing the Temple Service in accordance to what God commanded. They also put others in charge of the Lord's holy artefacts, disregarding their duties at the Temple of the Lord. Just as for instance at the time of Judges the Lord punished Eli, who honoured his sons Hophni and Phinehas more than the Lord while they showed much contempt for Him through their wrongful deeds, so would He deal with the sinful priesthood in Judah.

> *You have caused many to stumble in the law; you have corrupted the covenant of Levi, says HaShem of hosts. Therefore have I also made you contemptible and base before all the people, as you have not kept My ways.*
>
> Malachi 2:8-9

The Lord spoke to the prophet Malachi telling him that if the priests were able to respect their masters and honour their father, why didn't they honour and respect God, their Father? They showed contempt by offering defiled food on His altar. They said that the Lord's food is contemptible and His table is defiled. But, they were the ones offering and accepting blind, injured, lame and already diseased animals as sacrifices, while they would later sniff at the food contemptuously saying, 'what a burden'. They would never offer these animals to their governors, because they wouldn't accept them or be pleased with these people if they did. So, why should the Lord accept them? The Lord said that He wasn't pleased with these people and that someone should shut the door of His Temple so they wouldn't light useless fires on His altar anymore, nor would He accept offerings from their hands anymore. They have burdened the Lord, as He once said at the time of Hezekiah, to His prophet Isaiah, *'but you have burdened Me with your sins, you have wearied Me with your iniquities. I, even I, am He that blots out your transgressions for My own sake; and your sins I will not remember'.**

These people and those before them were actually burdening the Lord with their sinful acts. There were priests, such as Pashhur son of Immer, who prophesied lies to the people. Pashhur was the priest in charge of the Lord's Temple. He had the prophet Jeremiah beaten up and put in stocks at Benjamin's Upper Gate of the Temple of the Lord, because his prophecies didn't coincide with his own. The Lord was displeased with these priests and sent His word for Jeremiah to prophecy to Pashhur the next day when he had him released. Jeremiah spoke against him, telling him that the Lord would take away all his wealth, sending him with his friends into exile to Babylon where he would die.

> *Who is wise, let him understand these things, who is prudent, let him know them. For the ways of HaShem are right, and the just do walk in them; but transgressors do stumble therein.*
>
> Hosea 14:10

False Prophets

The Lord continuously sent His prophets to speak out His words to the people and their leaders. His prophets' task? The ruler was to build the wall. The prophets were to, if needed, go up to the breaches of the wall to repair it for the people of Israel, so on the day of the battle of the Lord it would stand firm ensuring protection. In this case the breaches were made in the first place by Judah's own leadership through wickedness causing the people to go astray. They preferred to listen to false prophets, who followed their own spirit while they had seen nothing, prophesying out of their own imagination, bringing out false divinations and lies when they said that the Lord declared, while He had not spoken. For some reason they did expect the Lord to fulfil their lies. They spoke even of visions they had seen, but were not given by the Lord. As the Lord said, *"Have you not seen a vain vision, and have you not spoken a lying divination, whereas you say: 'HaShem says, albeit I have not spoken'?"**

Didn't these false prophets realise that one day the Lord would hold them accountable for their deeds, as He said to Hosea, *'And the sword shall fall upon his cities, and shall consume his bars, and devour them, because of their own counsels'.**

One of those false prophets was Hananiah son of Azzur, who at the time of the fourth year of Judah's last king, Zedekiah, dared to speak in the presence of one of the Lord's faithful prophets, Jeremiah, challenging the Lord. But the Lord would silence him, as He had Jeremiah speak against Hananiah saying, *"Hear now, Hananiah; HaShem has not sent you; but you make this people to trust in a lie. Therefore thus says HaShem: 'Behold, I will send you away from off the face of the earth; this year you shall die, because you have spoken perversion against HaShem'."**

In that same year, Hananiah died in the seventh month. Meanwhile the leaders content with the messages of the false prophets telling them what they wanted to hear, deceiving lies agreeable with their views, were mistreating the Nazirites by telling them to drink wine, which was against their vows. They had orders for the Lord's prophets too. They were forbidden to speak the Lord's truthful Word. For the truth was inconvenient to the leadership. Israel's kings in the past, such as Ahab, but also Judah's kings, such as Jehoiakim, went so far as having the Lord's prophets killed. The Lord would avenge those killings. His Hand was against those who see false visions and utter lying divinations misleading His people, telling them of visions of peace for Jerusalem while there was no peace. They also spoke of Judah's exiles returning in two years, while the Lord made it clear through His faithful and loyal prophets that it would take decades before they would return.

> *Your words have been all too strong against Me, says HaShem. Yet you say: Wherein have we spoken against you? You have said: It is vain to serve God; and what profit is it that we have kept His charge, and that we have walked mournfully because of HaShem of hosts?*
>
> Malachi 3:13-14

Rejection

In their arrogance the unfaithful people of Judah and Jerusalem, both men and women, concluded by themselves that it was senseless to listen to the Lord or His prophets. These people and their society didn't become corrupted by chance, but by choice. Concerning the women the Lord once said to Isaiah, *'Moreover HaShem says: because the daughters of Zion are haughty, and walk with stretched-forth necks and wanton eyes, walking and mincing as they go, and making a tinkling with their feet; Therefore the Lord will smite with a scab the crown of the head of the daughters of Zion, and HaShem will lay bare their secret parts'.*

But as Isaiah also prophesied, *'one day, it shall come to pass, that he that is left in Zion, and he that remains in Jerusalem, shall be called holy, even everyone that is written unto life in Jerusalem; when the Lord shall have washed away the filth of the daughters of Zion, and shall have purged the blood of Jerusalem from the midst thereof, by the spirit of judgment, and by the spirit of destruction'.*

These people lost all interest in serving the Lord. They were determined to follow their own ruthless wicked evil path. Eventually they didn't want to learn from God anymore. They remained stubborn in continuing their sinful way of life, while showing no remorse what so ever for their wicked deeds.

> *And I sought for a man among them, that should make up the hedge, and stand in the breach before Me for the land, that I should not destroy it; but I found none. Therefore have I poured out My indignation upon them; I have consumed them with the fire of My wrath; their own way have I brought upon their heads, says the Lord God.*
>
> Ezekiel 22:30-31

The word of God came to Jeremiah, and told him to go to the men of Judah and the inhabitants of Jerusalem to tell them, *'Will you not receive instruction to hearken to My words'? says HaShem.*

But, they turned their backs to God Almighty, the Source of Life and the God of gods. The One Who examines the mind and searches the heart, rewarding each and every person in accordance to their conduct, as their deeds show they deserve, and bringing divine judgment over mankind and all His creation. Ultimately they refused to know the Lord! As was said by Jeremiah, *'Your habitation is in the midst of deceit; through deceit they refuse to know Me', says HaShem.*

Due to their unfaithfulness, dishonesty, and persistent unwillingness to listen to the Lord, He would cease to listen to them.

> *He that turns away his ear from hearing the Law, even his prayer is an abomination.*
>
> Proverbs 28:9

The Lord had no alternative then to melt Judah as iron, leaving a remnant that one day would be completely faithful to Him. As Jeremiah spoke, "*Therefore thus says HaShem of hosts: 'behold, I will melt them, and try them; for how else should I do, because of the daughter of My people'?*"*

The Lord would make that generation, the generation of His anger. Because of all their sins and their remorseless acts of wickedness, the Lord rejected them, as He told Jeremiah, "*Therefore you pray not for this people, neither lift up cry nor pray for them, neither make intercession to Me; for I will not hear you. ... Therefore you shall say unto them: 'This is the nation that has not hearkened to the voice of HaShem their God, nor received correction; faithfulness is perished, and is cut off from their mouth. Cut off your hair, and cast it away, and take up a lamentation on the high hills; for HaShem has rejected and forsaken the generation of His wrath'.*"*

The Lord wouldn't even answer the prayers of his servant for these people anymore. He wouldn't speak to them any longer, not by dreams, visions or Urim, nor by His Word, He spoke to His faithful prophets.

> *Hear this, O you priests, and attend, you house of Israel, and give ear, O house of the king, for unto you pertain the judgment; for you have been a snare on Mizpah, and a net spread upon Tabor.*
>
> Hosea 5:1

Even the Lord's priests' were sinful and ignored Him, so much so that their acts would lead to them being cursed by the Lord, as He told His servant Malachi, '*But cursed be he that deals craftily, whereas he has in his flock a male, and vows, and sacrifices unto the Lord a blemished thing; for I am a great King, says HaShem of hosts, and My name is feared among the nations'.*

He added, "*And now, this commandment is for you, O you priests. 'If you will not hearken, and if you will not lay it to heart, to give glory unto My name,' says HaShem of hosts, 'then will I send the curse upon you, and I will curse your blessings; I curse them, because you do not lay it to heart'.**

Because of their deeds the Lord would smear dung from their festival sacrifices on their faces and have them carried off into exile with it, and He would rebuke their descendants.

> *For the mountains will I take up a weeping and wailing, and for the pastures of the wilderness a lamentation, because they are burned up, so that none pass through. And they hear not the voice of the cattle; both the fowl of the heavens and the beast are fled, and gone. And I will make Jerusalem heaps, a lair of jackals; and I will make the cities of Judah a desolation, without an inhabitant.*
>
> Jeremiah 9:10

Divine Visions

In the fifth year of Jehoiachin king of Judah's exile and Judah was under Zedekiah's rule, the thirty-year-old priest Ezekiel son of Buzi was among the exiles in Babylonia, where the Lord's Hand was upon him. One day when he was at the Kebar River, the heavens were opened showing Ezekiel visions of the Lord God. He saw the glory of the God of Israel. God spoke to Ezekiel telling him that He was sending him, a son of man, to speak to the rebellious and stubborn people of Israel, whether they would listen to him or not. The Lord called him to be His prophet and watchman over the people of Israel to bring them His warnings.

The Lord told him, *'And you, son of man, be not afraid of them, neither be afraid of their words, though defiers and despisers be with you, and you do dwell among scorpions; be not afraid of their words, nor be dismayed at their looks, for they are a rebellious house. And you shall speak My words unto them, whether they will hear, or whether they will forbear; for they are most rebellious'.**

The Lord also told Ezekiel not to rebel like them, and to eat the scroll which was written on both sides with words of lament, sorrow and suffering. Ezekiel saw the scroll in a hand stretched out to him, that unrolled it for him. He opened his mouth and the Lord gave him the scroll to eat. It tasted as sweet as honey. The Lord sent him to the exiles and He warned him, *'But the house of Israel will not consent to hearken unto you; for they consent not to hearken unto Me; for all the house of Israel are of a hard forehead and of a stiff heart. Behold, I have made your face hard against their faces, and your forehead hard against their foreheads'.**

After this event, Ezekiel came to the exiles near the Kebar River in Babylonia where he stayed for seven days, deeply distressed.

Later on the Lord would speak to Ezekiel about the time of the destruction of all idols and idol worshippers. That day would come over the whole Land, to all the hills, ravines and valleys. He gave Ezekiel divine visions of the hidden practices of seventy leaders of Judah at the Lord's Temple in Jerusalem. The Lord told him to prophesy about doom and disaster against Jerusalem and the mountains of the Land of Israel. Concerning Jerusalem, Ezekiel prophesied, *'Therefore thus says the Lord God: Behold, I, even I, am against you, and I will execute judgments in the midst of you in the sight of the nations. And I will do in you that which I have not done, and where unto I will not do any more the like, because of all your abominations. Therefore the fathers shall eat the sons in the midst of you, and the sons shall eat their fathers; and I will execute judgments in you, and the whole remnant of you will I scatter unto all the winds'.**

About a year later, when Ezekiel was sitting in his house and the elders of Judah came to speak to him, the Lord gave him divine visions of the sinful acts of Judah's leaders. God's Hand was upon him when he saw a figure like that of a man, who was from his waist down like fire and from there up like glowing metal, that stretched out his hand, took him by a lock of his hair and lifted him up between earth and heaven and took him in visions to Jerusalem to the entrance of the north gate to the inner court, there where the idol that provoked to jealousy stood. Then he saw the glory of the God of Israel in front of him, as he had seen before in a vision at the Kebar River. He spoke to him telling him to look towards the north. He looked and saw the idol of jealousy, the provocative image of provocation, standing at the entrance of the north gate to the altar, and the Lord said, *"And He said unto me: 'Son of man, you see what they do? Even the great abominations that the house of Israel do commit here, that I should go far off from My sanctuary'?"**

Afterwards the Lord would show him two more of the detestable things Judah's leaders were doing at the House of the Lord. He brought him to the entrance of the court and told him to tunnel through a hole in a wall where he found a doorway. Once inside, he saw a room with walls that were covered with carved depictions of all sorts of crawling things, unclean animals and all the idols of the House of Israel. There seventy elders of Israel, including Jaazaniah son of Shaphan, were standing in front of the idols with each a censer with fragrant incense in their hand. The Lord told him, 'Son of man, have you seen what the elders of the house of Israel do in the dark, every man in his chambers of imagery? for they say: HaShem sees us not, HaShem has forsaken the land'.*

At the entrance of the north gate of the House of the Lord, He showed him the women sitting there weeping in mourning for their god. Then he brought him to the inner court of the Lord's House where he saw between the portico and the altar, about twenty-five old men with their backs toward the Temple of the Lord and their faces facing the east, bowing down in adoration of their god, the sun. Then the Lord said to Ezekiel, 'Have you seen this, O son of man? Is it a light thing to the house of Judah that they commit the abominations which they commit here in that they fill the Land with violence, and provoke Me still more, and, look, they put the branch to their nose? Therefore will I also deal in fury; My eye shall not spare, neither will I have pity; and though they cry in My ears with a loud voice, yet will I not hear them'.*

After these Ezekiel heard the Lord call out with a loud voice, to bring out those who were appointed to execute divine judgment over the city of Jerusalem. Six men came forth through the upper gate which faced north. Five of them held a deadly weapon in his hand. The other man was clothed in linen and he had a scribe's slate, a writing kit, at his side. They all came in, and stood beside the bronze altar. The glory of the God of Israel moved from above the Cherubim angels to the threshold of the Temple, from where He called the man dressed in linen and gave him the task to, 'Go through the midst of the city, through the midst of Jerusalem, and set a mark upon the foreheads of the men that sigh and that cry for all the abominations that are done in the midst thereof'.*

These were the ones who by the time of Jerusalem's destruction were destined by the Lord to survive. Thousands of them were taken gradually through years into exile by Nebuchadnezzar to Babylon, while others survived in the Land. The Lord himself would care for His remnant. Then the Lord commanded the others, 'Go yourselves through the city after him, and smite; let not your eye spare, neither have you pity; lay utterly the old man, the young man and the maiden, and little children and women; but come not near any man upon whom is the mark; and begin at My sanctuary'.*

So, they went out and executed their task starting with the old men in front of the Temple. They didn't have to worry whether they would defile the Lord's Temple, because as the Lord showed Ezekiel it already was. While they were killing in the city, Ezekiel was left alone, and he fell face down crying to the Lord, asking Him whether He was going to destroy the entire remnant of Israel. On Ezekiel's question, the Lord answered, *'The iniquity of the house of Israel and Judah is exceedingly great, and the Land is full of blood, and the city full of wresting of judgment; for they say: HaShem has forsaken the Land, and HaShem sees not. And as for Me also, My eye shall not spare, neither will I have pity, but I will bring their way upon their head'.**

After showing Ezekiel all these, the Lord gave him more divine visions and prophecies concerning Jerusalem and Judah. Ezekiel also witnessed how the glory of the God of Israel departed from His Sanctuary at the east gate. But before He left, He gave Ezekiel one last message saying, *"Son of man, as for your brethren, even your brethren, the men of your kindred, and all the house of Israel, all of them, concerning whom the inhabitants of Jerusalem have said: 'Get you far from HaShem! Unto us is this Land given for a possession;' therefore say: Thus says the Lord God: 'Although I have removed them far off among the nations, and although I have scattered them among the countries, yet have I been to them as a little sanctuary in the countries where they are come;' therefore say: 'Thus says the Lord God: I will even gather you from the people, and assemble you out of the countries where you have been scattered, and I will give you the land of Israel. And they shall come thither, and they shall take away all the detestable things thereof and all the abominations thereof from thence. And I will give them one heart, and I will put a new spirit within you; and I will remove the stony heart out of their flesh, and will give them a heart of flesh; that they may walk in My statutes, and keep My ordinances, and do them; and they shall be My people, and I will be their God. But as for them whose heart walked after the heart of their detestable things and their abominations, I will bring their way upon their own heads,' says the Lord God."**

It would be only after the generation of the Lord's wrath receives its punishment, while the Lord sheltered the remnant who sought humility and His righteousness, that He would no longer rebuke His people. He would care for those He kept to Himself. Those who with His divine mark on their forehead survived, and their descendants.

> *HaShem your God is in the midst of you, a Mighty One who will save; He will rejoice over you with joy, He will be silent in His love, He will joy over you with singing.*
>
> Zephaniah 3:17

Endnotes

* Deuteronomy 10:15-16, Jeremiah 21:12, 2 Kings 21:7-8, Jeremiah 22:1-5, Hosea 12:2 (JPS: Hosea 12:3), Hosea 12:8 (JPS: Hosea 12:9), Hosea 12:7 (JPS: Hosea 12:8), Proverbs 28:8, Proverbs 28:27, Proverbs 28:9, Jeremiah 17:27, Leviticus 19:35-37, Malachi 3:8-9, Malachi 3:10-11, Hosea 8:4b, Deuteronomy 32:39, Jeremiah 7:17-20, Isaiah 44:20, Isaiah 44:18, Malachi 2:6-7, Isaiah 43:24-25, Ezekiel 13:7, Hosea 11:6, Jeremiah 28:15-16, Isaiah 3:16-17, Isaiah 4:3-4, Jeremiah 35:13, Jeremiah 9:6 (JPS: Jeremiah 9:5), Jeremiah 9:7 (JPS: Jeremiah 9:6), Jeremiah 7:15-16, 28-29, Malachi 1:14, Malachi 2:1-2, Ezekiel 2:6-7, Ezekiel 3:7-8, Ezekiel 5:8-10, Ezekiel 8:6, Ezekiel 8:12, Ezekiel 8:17-18, Ezekiel 9:4, Ezekiel 9:5-6, Ezekiel 9:9-10, Ezekiel 11:14-21.

2 Chronicles 16:9 the Lord watches over the entire world
Leviticus 20:22!-24,26 Israelites' special place amongst the nations
Deuteronomy 6:4-9, 11:13,18-20 love God above all else
Leviticus 19:17-18 to love each other
Leviticus 18:1-5, 18:24-25, 19:28 Egyptian or Canaanite traditions, prevent uncleanness
Leviticus 20:1-7, Leviticus 18:20 the Lord would turn against them
Genesis 13:14-17 God gave the Land to Abraham and his descendants
Joshua 24:19-20 consequence for forsaking the Lord
2 Chronicles 14:5, 15:9-15, 23:1-3 Kings Asa, Josiah renewed covenant
2 Chronicles 16:7-10 Asa's mistake
Deuteronomy 24:16, Ezekiel 18, Ezekiel 33:30-33, Jeremiah 32:18 responsible for sins, fathers' sins
Leviticus 4-5, Numbers 15:22-29, Number 15:30-31 sin and guilt offerings
Leviticus 6:4-5 restitution
Deuteronomy 29:18 root that produces the poison of occultism
Ezekiel 18:19-32 righteous deeds
Isaiah 56 salvation also for foreigners
Isaiah 59:14 honesty, justice
Ezekiel 19 the monarchy
Jeremiah 21:2 the Lord's wonders
Leviticus 19:15, Deuteronomy 16:18 judge fairly
Jeremiah 9:23-24 the wise
Malachi 3:6-8 withholding tithes
Hosea 8:4 choosing leaders without God's approval

Jeremiah 22:1-5 judgment over wicked kings
Jeremiah 7:30-31 burning children in fire
Leviticus 17:7 sacrifices to demons
Leviticus 19: 35-37 dishonest commerce
Leviticus 25:35-43 the poor
Jeremiah 17:19-27 keep the Shabbat a holy day
Malachi 3:8-12 Judah stole from the Lord
Deuteronomy 11:10-17, Leviticus 25:18-23 blessings for the Land
Exodus 32:1-35, 1 Kings 12:28-33 idols Israelites made
Exodus 20:4,23, Leviticus 26:1 do not make idols
Deuteronomy 32:39 no God beside Him
Jeremiah 30-32 false prophets
Ezekiel 13 God against false prophets, and magic
Ezekiel 13:4-5 repair breached wall
Jeremiah 28-29 confrontation Jeremiah with false prophets
Ezekiel 13:7 see false visions
Amos 2: 11-12 mistreatment Nazirites and killing prophets
1 Samuel 28:6 the Lord's means to answer
Deuteronomy 16:21-22 no idol objects next to the Lord's altar.
Leviticus 21:1-24, 22:32, Malachi 2:6-7 God's covenant with Levi, holiness priests
Ezekiel 44:7-14 sinful priests not allowed to serve in the Temple
2 Samuel 8:17, 1 Kings 1:8, 2:35, Ezekiel 44:15-16 faithful descendants of Zadok
Leviticus 22:21-25, Malachi 1:6-14, 2:1-9 priests' contempt for God and the Temple Service
Jeremiah 19-20 Jeremiah beaten up on a priest's orders
Jeremiah 17:13c, Psalm 51:1 God the source of life, God of gods
Jeremiah 17:10, 32:19 the Lord treats people by their deeds
Jeremiah 7:15-16, 7:28-29, 11:14, 14:11 No more prayers for Judah
Jeremiah 36:2 God spoke to Jeremiah since reign of King Josiah
2 Kings 22:13, 23:26-27, 21:10-16, Jeremiah 16:1-13 Jerusalem rejected
2 Kings 22:13, 23:26-27, 21:10-16 reason Jerusalem rejected
Jeremiah 44, 16: 10-13, Hosea 9:10-17 reason rejection, idolatry, idol worship
Jeremiah 1:16, 6-7, 8:8-17 Sins, reason rejection and judgment Judah
Isaiah 3-5, 5:20 judgment over Israel, Judah, Jerusalem
Ezekiel 1:1-3 Ezekiel was a priest of the Lord
Ezekiel 6-7 prophesy against the mountains of Israel
Ezekiel 21-22, Ezekiel 22:1-22 Jerusalem's unfaithfulness
Ezekiel 4, 9, 11:1-13 Jerusalem's punishment
Ezekiel 9:6 the mark
Ezekiel 8-11 visions of desecration of the Lord's Temple, the Lord departing, and other visions
Ezekiel 11:14-25 the Lord will bring the Israelites, the Jews back

THE FALL OF ISRAEL, SAMARIA

Thus says HaShem: For three transgressions of Israel, yea, for four, I will not reverse it: because they sell the righteous for silver, and the needy for a pair of shoes; That pant after the dust of the earth on the head of the poor, and turn aside the way of the humble; and a man and his father go unto the same maid, to profane My holy name; And they lay themselves down beside every altar upon clothes taken in pledge, and in the house of their God they drink the wine of them that have been fined.

Amos 2: 6-8

More than a century before Judah would fall, the Lord brought the Israelites in the northern Kingdom of Israel into exile at the time Hosea son of Elah ruled over the nation. He was an officer in Israel's army who became king after he attacked and assassinated Pekah son of Remaliah, who reigned over Israel for twenty years. Hosea seized power after Pekah had lost the war against Assyria, which resulted in the deportation of the inhabitants of Galilee and Gilead to Assyria.

Once the Lord told Isaiah whose wife, a prophetess, gave birth to their son, '*Call his name Maher-shalal-hashbaz. For before the child shall have knowledge to cry: My father, and My mother, the riches of Damascus and the spoil of Samaria shall be carried away before the king of Assyria*'."*

Indeed this would come to pass during Hosea's reign. He became a vassal of Shalmaneser, the next king of Assyria. As such he was forced to pay tribute to the Assyrian king. In those days, and even before then, Ephraim strived after wind, and followed after the east wind; all the day he multiplied lies and desolation.* Hosea decided to end his payment, which he had done every year to the Assyrian king. Instead he sent envoys to the Egyptian king seeking his help. Hosea clearly a traitor to Shamaneser, was seized and put into prison. Then the king marched out with his army and invaded the entire land, laying siege to Samaria for three years. During the ninth year of Hosea's reign the king captured Samaria, making Hosea the last king of the Kingdom of Israel.

> *Seek HaShem, and live, lest He break out like fire in the house of Joseph, and it devour, and there be none to quench it in Bethel.*
>
> Amos 5:6
>
> *When Ephraim spoke, there was trembling, he exalted himself in Israel; but when he became guilty through Baal, he died.*
>
> Hosea 13:1

The territory the Assyrian king conquered did not include Israel's territory at the east of the Jordan River. That part of Israel was already conquered earlier by the Arameans during Jehu's reign over Judah, when the Lord decided to reduce Israel's territory. The Assyrians also attempted to conquer Judah, as the prophet Isaiah prophesied they would, but by God's grace they were unsuccessful.

The Assyrians deported Israel's inhabitants to Assyria, settling them in towns of the Medes, in Halah and in Gozan on the Habor River. In turn they brought people from Babylon, Kuthah, Avva, Hamath and Sepharvaim to settle in the towns of Samaria replacing the former inhabitants. Initially the Lord sent lions to attack these people. The Assyrians believed this happened because the people didn't know how to serve the god of that region. On the report of these incidents the Assyrian king decided to send one of the priest he took captive to Bethel to teach them to serve the Lord. Ultimately the new inhabitants worshipped the Lord, but at the same time they worshipped their own idols and gods, which they placed in the shrines on the high places previously built by the Israelites. These people even sacrificed their own children in fire as burnt offerings to their gods, an utterly sinful practice to the Lord, that some inhabitants in Judah would also adopt years later.

> *When they were fed, they became full, they were filled, and their heart was exalted; therefore have they forgotten Me. Therefore am I become unto them as a lion; as a leopard will I watch by the way; I will meet them as a bear that is bereaved of her whelps, and will rend the enclosure of their heart; and there will I devour them like a lioness; the wild beast shall tear them.*
>
> Amos 2:6-8

Why did the Lord bring such disaster over the Kingdom of Israel? Because of Jeroboam's sins and the sins he caused the inhabitants of the nation to commit by the institutionalised religion that he had created, led by the false priesthood he had appointed. He led the Israelites astray into idol worship of the calves he had made while taking part in feasts and festivals in honour of these idols. The Israelites continued to be engaged in secret activities that were not in accordance with God's commands. They also built themselves high places for idol worship in every city and town. Set up sacred stones and poles on every hill, under every spreading tree for their gods and idols. They worshipped, served, bowed down for their idols and sacrificed to them. These people showed no intentions of changing their ways. They persisted in their sinful actions despite the Lord's constant warnings through His prophets. In all their arrogance they resolved by themselves not to listen to God Almighty anymore. They were stiff-necked as their ancestors who also forsook God's Law and commandments. With their wickedness, sinful deeds and disobedience they didn't uphold the statutes of the covenant, the contract the Lord had made with their ancestors and with them. Instead they ignored it and in doing so, turned their backs to the Lord.

> *Yet I am HaShem your God from the land of Egypt; and you know no God but Me, and beside Me there is no Saviour. I did know you in the wilderness, in the land of great drought. When they were fed, they became full, they were filled, and their heart was exalted; therefore have they forgotten Me.*
> Hosea 5:3-6

In the days of Jeroboam the Lord already spoke of the disaster that awaited the Kingdom of Israel in the future. The Lord took Amos from attending his flocks and sent him to prophesy to the people of Israel. Amaziah the priest Jeroboam appointed at Bethel didn't agree with Amos' messages, because according to him his prophesies were not good for the nation of Israel, that couldn't bear to hear the word he spoke. Amos said that, *'Jeroboam shall die by the sword, and Israel shall surely be led away captive out of his land'.*

Amaziah plotted against Amos by sending a message to the king telling him the very words Amos prophesied and that Amos was raising a conspiracy against him. Then he went to speak to the seer. He told Amos not to prophesy against Israel, to stop preaching against the sons of Isaac, to leave the country and go to Judah where he could earn a living with his prophesies. But Amos told him that he wasn't a prophet nor a son of a prophet. He was merely a shepherd and he also took care of some sycamore-fig trees. It was the Lord Who told him to go and speak to the king and Israel. Ending their conversation Amos told Amaziah, *'Your wife shall be a harlot in the city, and your sons and your daughters shall fall by the sword, and your land shall be divided by line; and you yourself shall die in an unclean land, and Israel shall surely be led away captive out of his land'.**

One day the Lord showed a basket of ripe fruit to Amos, asking him what he saw. On his answer, *'A basket of summer fruit, the Lord told the seer. The end has come upon My people Israel; I will not again pardon them anymore'.**

The Lord spoke to Amos of the Israelites' sinful acts saying, "*Hear this, O you that would swallow the needy, and destroy the poor of the land, Saying: 'When will the new moon be gone, that we may sell grain? and the Shabbat, that we may set forth corn? Making the ephah small, and the shekel great, and falsifying the balances of deceit; That we may buy the poor for silver, and the needy for a pair of shoes, and sell the refuse of the corn'?*"*

He also spoke to him of the disasters He would bring over Israel who through their pride and complacency had turned justice into gall, and the fruit of righteousness into wormwood.* During the reign of Hoshea son of Elah these practices did not end. So, the Lord removed Israel from His presence as He had spoken through His prophets.

> *God heard, and was wroth, and He greatly abhorred Israel; And He forsook the tabernacle of Shiloh, the tent which He had made to dwell among men; And delivered His strength into captivity, and His glory into the adversary's hand.*
> Psalm 78:59-61

When the Lord brought devastation to Israel, He didn't spare Shiloh in the hill country of Ephraim. It's the place where Joshua apportioned the Land to the Tribes of Israel, the first place in the Land where the Lord made a dwelling for His Name by placing the Tent of Meeting, the Tabernacle there. Samuel grew up there at the time the Aronite Eli and his sons, who were unfaithful to the Lord, were priests. Samuel became the Lord's prophet and the last judge to rule over Israel. It's where the Lord continued to appear and later would revealed Himself to Samuel through His Word. Other prophets also resided there, such as Ahijah who spoke to Jeroboam concerning the division of the nation of Israel and him becoming king of the northern Kingdom of Israel. He spoke to Jeroboam's wife as well, prophesying concerning the illness and death of their son Abijah. Once centuries earlier Jacob prophesied regarding his son Judah, his descendants and kingship that, *'The sceptre shall not depart from Judah, nor the ruler's staff from between his feet, as long as men come to Shiloh; and unto him shall the obedience of the people be'.**

Regardless of this blessing and prophecy, the Lord didn't prevent Shiloh's destruction by the Assyrians.

> *And now they sin more and more, and have made them molten images of their silver, according to their own understanding, even idols, all of them the work of the craftsmen; of them they say: They that sacrifice men kiss calves. Therefore they shall be as the morning cloud, and as the dew that early pass away, as the chaff that is driven with the wind out of the threshing-floor, and as the smoke out of the window.*
>
> Hosea 13:2-3

During the reign of the last kings of Judah, the Lord repeatedly sent His prophets, such as Uriah, to warn Judah's kings, leaders and inhabitants. The prophet Jeremiah did this as well. One day he would speak in the Temple of the Lord taking past events of Shiloh's destruction as a warning of the divine judgment that was to come over Jerusalem if they didn't repent. The Lord told them by Jeremiah, *'And I will cast you out of My sight, as I have cast out all your brethren, even the whole seed of Ephraim'.**

But, ultimately the inhabitants of Jerusalem and Judah would not learn from Israel's mistakes nor their own.

> *For go you now unto My place which was in Shiloh, where I caused My name to dwell at the first, and see what I did to it for the wickedness of My people Israel. And now, because you have done all these works, says HaShem, and I spoke unto you, speaking be times and often, but you heard not, and I called you, but you answered not; therefore will I do unto the house, whereupon My name is called, wherein you trust, and unto the place which I gave to you and to your fathers, as I have done to Shiloh.*
>
> Jeremiah 7:12,14

The Fall of Judah, Jerusalem

Thus says HaShem: For three transgressions of Judah, for four, I will not reverse it: because they have rejected the Law of HaShem, and have not kept His statutes, and their lies have caused them to err, after which their fathers did walk. So will I send a fire upon Judah, and it shall devour the palaces of Jerusalem.

Amos 2:4-5

More than a century after Samaria fell, Judah would also be conquered as was proclaimed by the Lord's prophets during King Josiah's eighteen-year reign. Josiah succeeded his father Amon whose reign came to an end after two years, when he was assassinated. Josiah ruled in accordance to God's commands, followed King David's example and rid the nation of much evil. Nevertheless, the Lord spoke of removing Judah from His presence because of the sinful ways of especially one of Josiah's predecessors, Amon's father Menasseh. He reigned fifty-five years in Jerusalem after he succeeded his father Hezekiah. The Lord wasn't willing to forgive all Menasseh's sins, which included the fact that he shed so much innocent blood in Jerusalem.

At the age of twelve Menasseh succeeded his father. He didn't follow in King David's footsteps nor did he follow his own father's example. In fact he was extremely unfaithful to the Lord and caused Judah to follow him on his sinful path. He reversed all the reforms his father Hezekiah had introduced and added much more worse acts of wickedness to the sinfulness of Judah than all his predecessors did, actions even worse than all the surrounding countries. He reinstituted pagan worship by rebuilding high places Hezekiah had destroyed and erecting altars and poles for his idols. He put the pole he himself had carved for his own idol in the Temple of the Lord. He also built altars in the Lord's Temple, and in its two courts to all the starry hosts for which he bowed down in worship. He practised divination and witchcraft, sought omens, consulted with mediums and spiritists. Furthermore, Menasseh sacrificed his own son and other children in the fire. This was something no other king of Judah had done. He led the whole of Judah astray committing sinful acts worse than those of the former people that the Lord had driven out of the Land. Moreover, Menasseh shed so much innocent blood that he could fill Jerusalem with it from end to end. The Lord would hold him accountable for each person's blood that he had shed. He spoke to His servants the prophets, who warned Menasseh and the people telling them, *"Because Menasseh king of Judah has done these abominations, and has done wickedly above all that the Amorites did, that were before him, and has made Judah also to sin with his idols; therefore thus says HaShem, the God of Israel: 'Behold, I bring such evil upon Jerusalem and Judah, that whosoever hears of it, both his ears shall tingle. And I will stretch over Jerusalem the line of Samaria, and the plummet of the house of Ahab; and I will wipe Jerusalem as a man wipes a dish, wiping it and turning it upside down. And I will cast off the remnant of My inheritance, and deliver them into the hand of their enemies; and they shall become a prey and a spoil to all their enemies; because they have done that which is evil in My sight, and have provoked Me, since the day their fathers came forth out of Egypt, even unto this day'."* *

But neither Menasseh nor the people of Judah were paying any attention to His words. So, the Lord sent his enemy, the army commanders of the Assyrians who took him prisoner. During his reign, Israel was already conquered by the Assyrians and much of its inhabitants deported. The Assyrians put a hook in Menasseh's nose, bound him with bronze shackles and took him to Babylon. While enduring so much distress, he humbled himself greatly before the God of his ancestors seeking the Lord's favour and help. The Lord was so moved by his request through prayer, that He listened to his plea. He brought him back to Jerusalem to rule Judah. Now Menasseh knowing that the Lord God is mighty, changed his ways. He rebuilt the outer wall of the City of David and made it much higher, and he stationed military commanders in all Judah's fortified cities. He removed all the foreign gods from Jerusalem, the pole in the Lord's Temple as well as the altars he had built there, and threw all of it outside the city. He restored the altar of the Lord, brought offerings on it and he told his people to serve the Lord, the God of Israel. The people did continue to bring offerings at the high places, though they did this for the Lord. After Menasseh's death, his son Amon succeeded him as king of Judah. Menasseh wasn't buried in the City of David amongst other kings of Judah, but in the garden of Uzza, the garden of his own house.

After Josiah, all the kings that ruled Judah were unfaithful to the Lord, and they ignored His warnings brought to them by His servants the prophets. The people of Judah made Josiah's son Jehoahaz king after his father was killed by Necho, the Pharaoh of Egypt. He reigned only three months. Necho captured him, and put him in chains in

Riblah in the land of Hamath. Later he took him to Egypt where he died. Necho made Eliakim, another son of Josiah, king of Judah and he changed his name into Jehoiakim. Jehoiakim taxed the land to be able to pay the Pharaoh the levy of silver and gold he demanded from Judah.

The prophet Jeremiah son of Hilkiah, who was one of the priests at Anathoth in Benjamin's territory spoke prophesies concerning the House of David, the kings of Judah as well as regarding the fall of Jerusalem and Judah. He wasn't married, as the Lord told him not to because of the disaster the Lord was about to bring to Judah. Jeremiah would witness these historical events he prophesied about. The Lord began to send His word to Jeremiah since the thirteenth reign of King Josiah son of Amon, saying, *"'Before I formed you in the belly I knew you, and before you came forth out of the womb I sanctified you; I have appointed you a prophet unto the nations'. Then said I: 'Ah, Lord God! Behold, I cannot speak; for I am a child'. But HaShem said unto me: 'say not: I am a child; for to whomsoever I shall send you, you shall go, and whatsoever I shall command you, you shall speak. Be not afraid of them; for I am with you to deliver you, says HaShem'."*

At the beginning of Jehoiakim's reign Jeremiah prophesied in the palace of the king of Judah against Jehoiakim and his son Jehoiachin concerning their reign and the consequences. The Lord would send destroyers against them, send Jehoiachin into exile where he would die, and Jehoiachin was to be *'childless, a man that shall not prosper in his days; for no man of his seed shall prosper, sitting upon the throne of David, and ruling any more in Judah'.*

The reason the Lord spoke against them was that Jehoiakim's rule over the nation was corrupt. He was not doing what was just and right in the Land. Rescuing those robbed from their oppressors, preventing wrong doings and violence against foreigners, orphans and widows, and restraining those who shed innocent people's blood in Judah. On the contrary he himself accumulated more and more wealth and shed innocent blood. Sometime later, Jeremiah told the people, in the courtyard of the Lord's House, that the Lord would make that place as Shiloh. That is, bring disaster to that place as He did with Shiloh in the Kingdom of Israel when He had them sent into exile years before. After this event, Jeremiah himself was seized and threatened with death. But after he spoke to these people of Hezekiah who in his days did not kill Micah of Moresheth who prophesied, *'Thus says HaShem of hosts: Zion shall be plowed as a field, and Jerusalem shall become heaps, and the mountain of the house as the high places of a forest'.**

And there was the guilt of shedding innocent blood that would come over them, the city and those living in it. So, they decided he shouldn't be put to death and they let him go. Unlike him, the prophet Uriah who was hiding in Egypt out of fear for his life, was brought out of Egypt and beheaded.

During Jehoiakim's reign the word of the Lord came to Jeremiah telling him to set an example of loyalty for His people. He was to invite the Rekabite family to come to one of the side rooms of the Lord's House, and offer them some wine to drink. So he went to get Jaazaniah son of Jeremiah, the son of Habazziniah with his sons, brothers and their whole family. At the House of the Lord he brought them to a room next of that of the officials, the room of the sons of Hanan son of the man of the Lord, Igdaliah. Once in the room Jeremiah put a bowl full of wine and some cups for the Rekabites. He told them to have a drink. But they refused to drink and told Jeremiah the reason for this. They still didn't drink wine since their forefather Jehonadab commanded them, more than a century ago, not to ever drink wine, to live as tent-dwellers, never to build houses, have fields or crops nor plant vineyards. Because then they would live a long life in the Land as nomads. They have always lived as their forefather had commanded them to do. The only reason they remained in Jerusalem was because they came there to escape the Babylonians. So, besides giving warnings to the Jews, Jeremiah also spoke of these foreigners as being a good example of fidelity.

On the Rekabites refusal to drink the wine, the Lord's word came to Jeremiah telling him to go to the people of Judah and Jerusalem, and speak of the Rekabites' loyalty towards their ancestor Jehonadab, which they showed by keeping his commands to that day. The Lord had spoken again and again to His people, but they did not listen. The Lord told Jeremiah to go and tell the people of Judah and Jerusalem who didn't want to learn from Him, *'Will you not receive instruction to hearken to My words'?**

And to tell them that, up to that day the Rekabites were still obedient to their forefather, carrying out his commandment not to drink wine, yet despite all the Lord spoke to His people, they were reluctant to listen to Him and obey Him. Repeatedly He spoke to them about turning away from their wicked way of life, about changing their actions and to stop following other gods, so they could continue to live in the Land. He called to them, but they didn't answer, and they were still reluctant to obey Him. So, He would bring down disaster over Judah and Jerusalem.

> *Who is wise, let him understand these things, who is prudent, let him know them. For the ways of HaShem are right, and the just do walk in them; but transgressors do stumble therein.*
> Hosea 14:10

Intermezzo

Foreigners

> *And if a stranger sojourn with you in your land, you shall not do him wrong. The stranger that sojourns with you shall be unto you as the home-born among you, and you shall love him as thyself; for you were strangers in the land of Egypt: I am HaShem your God.*
> Leviticus 19:33-34

Foreigners joined the Children of Israel when they left Egypt under the leadership of Moses and Aaron. The Lord always required from foreigners who resided amongst the Israelites, including the Kenites, that they would keep His Laws and decrees, while the Israelites were to treat them well.

David treated foreigners well, as he did for Ittai the Gittite who was also an exile from his homeland. They could also present a burnt offering or a gift to the Lord. No foreigner, uncircumcised in heart or flesh was allowed to enter God's Sanctuary, not even those living amongst the Israelites. The Lord expected that both the Israelites and the foreigners residing amongst them would abide by His Law and Commandments. If they would not, He would impose His divine judgment on them.

> *You therefore shall keep My statutes and My ordinances, and shall not do any of these abominations; neither the home-born, nor the stranger that sojourns among you.*
> Leviticus 18:26

This was also expected from Rahab and her family who joined the Israelites at the time Joshua led the Israelites into the Promised Land. Another much larger group of foreigners than Rahab's family was that of the Kenites, that consisted of several clans. The Rekabites who lived as foreigners amongst the Israelites, were a clan of the Kenites, who identified themselves with the God of Israel. Moses' father-in-law was a Kenite. The Rekabites were tent-dwellers, while other Kenites were city-dwellers. They were foreigners that accompanied the Israelites to the Promised Land, although they camped apart. At that time when the Israelites were wandering through the desert, Balaam who stood from a distance to bless the Children of Israel, saw the Kenites' tents encamped alongside the campsite of the Israelites in the wilderness. He spoke of their dwelling place being secure, but also of the Kenites being destroyed when Ashur would take them captive. The Rekabites were loyal in the manner they showed support and goodness to the Israelites on their way to the Promised Land. Later on they would live in the Land alongside the Israelites and continue to be loyal to them and the Lord.

At the time of Judge Deborah, Sisera the army commander of Jabin the king of Canaan, was killed by Jael who was married to the Kenite Heber. When King Saul was about to destroy the Amalekites at the city of Amalek all the way from Havilah to Shur near the eastern border of Egypt, he told the Kenites who were in the region to, *'Go, depart, get yourself down from among the Amalekites, lest I destroy you with them; for you showed kindness to all the children of Israel, when they came up out of Egypt'.* *

They listened to Saul, and moved away from the Amalekites. Later when David attacked the Amalekites to free his and his men's family they took captive when they raided Ziklag, they also took a great amount of plunder. David shared this plunder not only with his men, but also with many others including the Kenites to whom he sent gifts. Much later Jehu allied himself with Jehonadab son of Rekab when he was on his way to destroy Ahab's royal house with his wife Jezebel and their cult of idol worship. The Rekabites lived as nomads following the strict rules given to them by their forefather Jehonadab. The Lord rewarded the Rekabites because of their loyalty and their service to Him.

> *And unto the house of the Rekabites Jeremiah said: 'Thus says HaShem of hosts, the God of Israel: Because you have hearkened to the commandment of Jonadab (Jehonadab) your father, and kept all his precepts, and done according unto all that he commanded you; therefore thus says HaShem of hosts, the God of Israel: There shall not be cut off unto Jonadab the*

son of Rechab a man to stand before Me for ever.
Jeremiah 35:18-19

In the fourth year of Jehoiakim the Lord told Jeremiah, whom He gave the authority to uproot but also to build people, nations and kingdoms, to write all the words He had spoken to him concerning Israel, Judah and all other nations since he began speaking to him on a scroll. He was to read this scroll containing all the disasters the Lord planned to bring over Judah to the people and leaders of Judah. Because of their wickedness, these people had been moving backwards instead of forward, backsliding to catastrophic events in Judah. If, when hearing these words, each of them would repent, bring their petition before the Lord, turn away from their wicked ways, then the Lord would forgive them.

The Lord hoped and Jeremiah hoped with Him that the king of Judah with all his officials and attendants, and Judah's inhabitants would listen to him, preventing disaster from happening to Judah. It took Jeremiah more than a year to dictate all the Lord had spoken to the scribe Baruch son of Neriah who wrote everything down. Baruch realised the task given to him by Jeremiah would add sorrow to his life and could even be hazardous to him. He was already restless and worn out with groaning. But the Lord gave Jeremiah a message for him saying, *"Thus says HaShem: 'Behold, that which I have built will I break down, and that which I have planted I will pluck up; and this in the whole land. And seek you great things for thyself? Seek them not; for, behold, I will bring evil upon all flesh,' says HaShem; 'but your life will I give unto you for a prey in all places whither you go'."**

One day the Lord's word came to Jeremiah with a message to himself. By that time there were plots threatening his life, for which the Lord warned him, and he had difficulties doing God's task which weighed heavily on him. So heavy, one time he even wished he was never born. But the Lord wanted him to repent from this, to continue with his task. So, the Lord's message to Jeremiah was that, *"'If you return, and I bring you back, you shall stand before Me; and if you bring forth the precious out of the vile, you shall be as My mouth; let them return unto you, but you shall not return unto them. And I will make you unto this people a fortified brazen wall; and they shall fight against you, but they shall not prevail against you; for I am with you to save you and to deliver you', says HaShem. 'And I will deliver you out of the hand of the wicked, and I will redeem you out of the hand of the terrible'."**

Soon the Lord would start to uproot what He had planted, and Jeremiah with Baruch would be His servants during these events.

In the ninth month of the fifth year of Jehoiakim's reign, Jeremiah who was restricted from going to the Lord's Temple, sent Baruch to read all the words on the scroll to everyone at the Lord's Temple. He sent him on a day of fasting before the Lord, proclaimed for all the inhabitants of Jerusalem and those from the towns. Baruch went to one of the rooms in the upper courtyard at the entrance of the new gate of the Temple. That particular room was in use by Gemariah son of Shaphan the secretary. When Gemariah's son Micaiah heard the words of the scroll, he went down to the secretary's room in the royal palace where the officials were; his father Gemariah, the secretary Elishama, Shemaiah's son Delaiah, Akbor's son Elnathan, Hananiah's son Zedekiah, and all the other officials. When he told them everything he heard Baruch read, they sent Nethaniah's son Jehudi to Baruch asking him to come to them and take the scroll with him. Once he arrived, they asked him to sit down and read the scroll to them. He did as they asked. While they were listening, they looked at each other in fear realizing they had to report this to the king. They asked Baruch whether Jeremiah dictated these words to him. He replied he did and that he only wrote everything down in ink on the scroll. They told Baruch to tell Jeremiah to hide together with him and to let no one know where they were. In the meantime the officials went to the king in his courtyard. He was sitting in his winter apartment with a lit fire pot in front of him. They told him about the scroll and he sent Jehudi to fetch the scroll containing the words the Lord had spoken to Jeremiah where they left it in the secretary's room. Jehudi read the manuscript to the king with all his officials beside him. While listening, the king and all his attendants with him showed no fear, nor did they tear their clothes out of regret and grief.

> *Who is the wise man, that he may understand this? And who is he to whom the mouth of HaShem has spoken, that he may declare it? Wherefore has the land perished and laid waste like a wilderness, so that none pass through? And HaShem says: Because they have forsaken My law which I set before them, and have not hearkened to My voice, neither walked therein; But have walked after the stubbornness of their own heart, and after the Baalim, which their fathers taught them.*
> Jeremiah 9:11-13

Not listening to his officials, who told him not to destroy the scroll, the king cut part of the scroll with a scribe's knife each time Jehudi read three or four columns of it, and threw it bit by bit into the fire pot until it was completely consumed by fire. Then he ordered his son Jerahmeel and two other men to arrest Jeremiah and Baruch, and throw them in jail. But, they couldn't find them because the Lord who gave them their hazardous task had hidden them. After all this, the word of the Lord came to Jeremiah entrusting him with a new task. He was to record all God's words on a new scroll, just as he had done before and add a new message to it. So, Jeremiah again dictated the Lord's words to Baruch and addressing Jehoiakim added, *"Thus says HaShem: 'You have burned this scroll, saying: Why have you written therein, saying: The king of Babylon shall certainly come and destroy this land, and shall cause to cease from thence man and beast? ... He shall have none to sit upon the throne of David; and his dead body shall be cast out in the day to the heat, and in the night to the frost. And I will visit upon him and his seed and his servants their iniquity; and I will bring upon them, and upon the inhabitants of Jerusalem, and upon the men of Judah, all the evil that I have pronounced against them, but they hearkened not'."**

Jehoiakim would reign eleven years, and after his death, his eighteen-year-old son Jehoiachin succeeded him. But, the Lord said that Jehoiakim himself would not have a descendant to sit on David's throne. So, Jehoiachin would not remain on the throne.

> *Woe unto them that call evil good, and good evil; that change darkness into light, and light into darkness; that change bitter into sweet, and sweet into bitter!*
>
> *Woe unto them that are wise in their own eyes, and prudent in their own sight!*
>
> *Woe unto them that are mighty to drink wine, and men of strength to mingle strong drink;*
>
> *That justify the wicked for a reward, and take away the righteousness of the righteous from him!*
>
> *Therefore as the tongue of fire devours the stubble, and as the chaff is consumed in the flame, so their root shall be as rottenness, and their blossom shall go up as dust; because they have rejected the law of HaShem of hosts, and contemned the Word of the Holy One of Israel.*
>
> Isaiah 5:20-24

Who Is David?

The officers of Nebuchadnezzar the Babylonian king besieged Jerusalem. Nebuchadnezzar himself went up to Jerusalem where Jehoiachin with his family, officials and nobles all surrendered to him. He put an end to Jehoiachin's reign by taking him captive to Babylon where he imprisoned him. Jehoiachin would rule only for three months. He installed Jehoiakim's uncle, Mattaniah, whose name he changed into Zedekiah, to rule over Judah. As the prophet Isaiah foretold to King Hezekiah in the past, the Babylonian king removed all the treasures from the royal palace and the Temple of the Lord, including all the gold artefacts that King Salomon had made for the Temple. He had the artefacts cut up and he took them to Babyloina. He also took Jehoiachin's mother, wives and officials, prominent people of Judah, including the priest Ezekiel, all the officers and a force of seven thousand fighting men, skilled workers and artisans out of Jerusalem to Babylon, leaving only the poorest people behind.

After these events, the Lord showed Jeremiah two baskets of figs. One basket had very good figs, while the other had very bad inedible figs. Concerning the bad figs He said, *"And as the bad figs, which cannot be eaten, they are so bad; surely thus says HaShem: 'So will I make Zedekiah the king of Judah, and his princes, and the residue of Jerusalem, that remain in this land, and them that dwell in the land of Egypt; I will even make them a horror among all the kingdoms of the earth for evil; a reproach and a proverb, a taunt and a curse, in all places whither I shall drive them. And I will send the sword, the famine, and the pestilence, among them, until they be consumed from off the land that I gave unto them and to their fathers'."**

Sometime later Jeremiah would send a letter from Jerusalem to the surviving elders, priests, prophets and all the people taken into exile from Jerusalem to Babylon. He entrusted the letter to two officials of Zedekiah, Elasah son of Shaphan and Gemariah son of Hilkiah who the king sent to Nebuchadnezzar who was in Babylon. In the letter Jeremiah wrote about what the exiles should be doing in Babylon, how long the period of the exile would be, about their attitude towards the city or place they now lived, that they shouldn't let prophets and diviners amongst them deceive them, and about the citizens of Judah who didn't go into exile. He also wrote about prophecies concerning false prophets. Those in exile were to settle down, build houses, plant gardens and eat their produce. They should also get married and have children, find wives for their sons and give their daughters into marriage so their number would increase, not decrease. They were to pray for peace and prosperity for the places they lived, because if those places would prosper so would they. He warned them not to listen to false prophets nor encourage them to have dreams for them. The Israelites would be solitary for a long time, *'without king, and without prince, and without sacrifice, and without pillar, and without ephod or teraphim; afterward shall the children of Israel return, and seek HaShem their God, and David their king; and shall come trembling unto HaShem and to His goodness in the end of days'*.*

It would be a long stay in Babylonia until the years of Babylonia would be completed. Only then, the Lord would return them to the Land from where He exiled them. About the king that remained on David's throne in Judah and the citizens of Judah who didn't go into exile, Jeremiah wrote that the Lord would send to them and pursue them with plague, famine and the sword, making them bad inedible figs. They would become repulsive and detestable to all the kingdoms of the earth. The Lord would make them a curse, an object of horror, contempt, scorn and reproach. A disgrace, *"'because they have not hearkened to My words,' says HaShem, 'wherewith I sent unto them My servants the prophets, sending them be times and often; but you would not hear,' says HaShem"*.*

And he also wrote prophesies about the punishment that those in exile in Babylon who didn't listen to Him either, would receive. Regarding the false prophets Ahab son of Kolaiah and Zedekiah son of Maaseiah who as the Lord Himself witnessed did outrageous things in Israel, spoke lies in His name and committed adultery with their neighbours' wives, he wrote that the Lord would deliver them in the hands of Nebuchadnezzar who would have them put to death by burning them in fire.

Later Jeremiah would also send a message in response to Shemaiah the Nehelamite's who sent letters in their own name to the priest Zephaniah son of Maaseiah, to all the other priests and to all the people of Jerusalem. He told them once that they should put Jeremiah, a maniac who acts like a prophet, into stocks and neck-irons. But, Zephaniah who was priest instead of Jehoiada and in charge of the House of the Lord, read the letter to Jeremiah without Shemaiah's knowledge. The Lord was clear, *"Send to all them of the captivity, saying: 'Thus says HaShem concerning Shemaiah the Nehelamite: Because that Shemaiah has prophesied unto you, and I sent him not, and he has caused you to trust in a lie;' therefore thus says HaShem: 'Behold, I will punish Shemaiah the Nehelamite, and his seed; he shall* not have a man to dwell among this people, neither shall he behold the good that I will do unto My people', says HaShem; because he has spoken perversion against HaShem".*

To all those in exile who would remain faithful to the Lord, Jeremiah had a message of hope and comfort.

> *For thus says HaShem: After seventy years are accomplished for Babylon, I will remember you, and perform My good word toward you, in causing you to return to this place. For I know the thoughts that I think toward you, says HaShem, thoughts of peace, and not of evil, to give you a future and a hope.*
>
> Jeremiah 29:10-11

Zedekiah, who kept his position in Jerusalem for eleven years, was to rule over Judah while paying tribute to the Babylonian king. In the fourth year of Zedekiah's reign, although he, his officials and attendants and the inhabitants of Judah did not pay any attention to the Lord's words spoken to Jeremiah, he sent Shelemiah's son Jehukal and the priest Zephaniah son of Maaseiah to Jeremiah with a message asking him to pray to the Lord their God for them all, because the Babylonians were still besieging them. Meanwhile Pharaoh's army marched out to support Zedekiah, causing the Babylonians to retreat after they received the report. But, the word of God spoken to Jeremiah warned Zedekiah not to deceive himself in thinking the Babylonians would surely leave them alone. Pharaoh would return to his own land, the Babylonians who withdrew from him would return, capture Jerusalem and burn it down. Even if he was to defeat the Babylonian army leaving only wounded men, they would come out of their tents and burn Jerusalem. This message was to be delivered to the king.

As soon as the Babylonian army had withdrawn from Jerusalem because of the Egyptian army, Jeremiah planned on leaving the city to go to Benjamin's territory to do arrangements to get his share of the property among the people there. Since Jeremiah was not yet put in prison, he was free to come and go as he pleased. But, on his way out at the Benjamin Gate, he was arrested by the captain of the guard, Shelemiah's son Irijah who thought he was deserting Judah to go to the Babylonians as several others did while believing the Lord's words Jeremiah had spoken telling them, *"Thus says HaShem: 'Behold, I set before you the way of life and the way of death. He that abides in this city shall die by the sword, and by the famine, and by the pestilence; but he that goes out, and falls away to the Chaldeans that besiege you, he shall live, and his life shall be unto him for a prey. For I have set My face against this city for evil, and not for good,' says HaShem; 'it shall be given into the hand of the king of Babylon, and he shall burn it with fire'."* *

Despite the fact that Jeremiah denied the guard's allegations, he was taken to the officials who were angry with him. They had him beaten and imprisoned into the house of Jonathan, the secretary. They put him in a vaulted cell in the dungeon where he remained for some time.

One day Zedekiah sent for him and had him brought to the palace where he spoke to him privately, asking him whether there was any word from the Lord yet. His answer? *'You shall be delivered into the hand of the king of Babylon'.**

Jeremiah asked the king a few questions of his own. What crime did he commit against him, his officials or the people that he should be imprisoned? Where were the prophets that prophesied to him that the Babylonians would not attack him nor his land? Then Jeremiah brought his petition before the king, to not let him return to the place where he was imprisoned, because he would surely die there. The king gave the order to put Jeremiah in the courtyard of the guards and to give him a loaf of bread from the bakers' street every day, until there was no more bread in the city.

Shortly after, Jeremiah would be lowered down into a waterless muddy cistern in the courtyard. The cistern belonged to the king's son Malkijah. This was decided by four officials of the king being, Mattan's son Shephatiah, Pashhur's son Gedaliah, Shelemiah's son Jehukal, and Malkijah's son Pashhur. They were angry with Jeremiah because of everything they heard him say to everybody despite his imprisonment, telling people, *"Thus says HaShem: 'He that remains in this city shall die by the sword, by the famine, and by the pestilence; but he that goes forth to the Chaldeans shall live, and his life shall be unto him for a prey, and he shall live'. Thus says HaShem: 'This city shall surely be given into the hand of the army of the king of Babylon, and he shall take it'."**

So, they spoke to the king about Jeremiah discouraging the soldiers and the people of Jerusalem, resulting in the king giving Jeremiah into their hands to do with him as they wished. But, a Cushite Ebed-Melek one of the officials of the palace heard about how Jeremiah was treated and he went to the king requesting for his release before he starves to death in the cistern when there is no bread in the city.

Who Is David?

The king commanded him to take thirty men to help him lift Jeremiah out of the cistern. So they did, but Jeremiah remained imprisoned as before in the courtyard of the guard.

Sometime later the king met in secret with Jeremiah. He sent for Jeremiah to question him again privately, and they brought him to the third entrance of the Lord's Temple. The king told Jeremiah he was going to ask him a question and that he should give him a straight answer without hiding anything. Jeremiah replied by asking Zedekiah whether he wouldn't have him killed when he gave a direct answer. And he told him that if he was to counsel him, he wouldn't listen anyway. But the king swore a secret oath by the Lord to Jeremiah telling him that he would not kill him, neither would he hand him over to those who would want to kill him. Jeremiah told him, *"Thus says HaShem, the God of hosts, the God of Israel: 'If you will go forth unto the king of Babylon's princes, then your soul shall live, and this city shall not be burned with fire; and you shall live, you, and your house; but if you will not go forth to the king of Babylon's princes, then shall this city be given into the hand of the Chaldeans, and they shall burn it with fire, and you shall not escape out of their hand'."*

Zedekiah told him he feared that he would be captured and handed over to the Israelites that went over to the Babylonians. He expected they would mistreat him. Jeremiah replied that they would not hand him over. He should obey the Lord by doing what he told him and his life would be spared. He also added that if he wouldn't listen, all the women left in his palace would be handed over to the enemy, all his wives and children would be brought to Babylon, he himself wouldn't escape, and he would cause the city to be burned down. Then Zedekiah told Jeremiah not to tell anyone about the subject of their conversation, and in case his officials would ask, he was to tell them he was pleading to him not to be sent back to Jonathan's house to die there. None of the king's officials heard their conversation, so they questioned Jeremiah. In fear for his life, he did exactly as the king told him to do, and they left him alone. Jeremiah remained imprisoned. He was more then four years confined to the courtyard of the guard until Jerusalem's fall occurred.

In the ninth year of Zedekiah's reign, he rebelled against Nebuchadnezzar. By that time, the king of Egypt himself didn't march out on military campaigns anymore, because the Babylonians had conquered all his territory, from the Wadi of Egypt to the Euphrates River. Contrary to the Egyptian king, Nebuchadnezzar did fight wars.

So he marched out with his whole army and laid siege to Jerusalem. Encamped outside Jerusalem he built siege works all around it. His army wasn't only besieging Jerusalem, but it was also fighting other cities of Judah including the fortified cities of Lachish and Azekah that were still holding out. Meanwhile the Lord spoke to the prophet Jeremiah and told him to bring word to Zedekiah. He told him that the Lord is about to deliver Jerusalem in the hands of the Babylonian king that would burn it down. Zedekiah would not escape, but he wouldn't die by the sword either. He would see the king of Babylon with his own eyes, speak to him face to face, and be taken capture to Babylon. Jeremiah told him that he would die peacefully and that the Lord promised that people will mourn for him and that a fire would be lit in his honour.

Soon after, Zedekiah made a covenant with all the inhabitants of Jerusalem proclaiming freedom for the Hebrew slaves. So all the officials and people who entered this covenant agreed to set free their Hebrew slaves, the men and women of their own people. This was right in the sight of the Lord.

One of the commandments he gave the Israelites at the time He brought them out of the slavery of Egypt, was that they should release the Hebrew people, male and female, that sold themselves to them and became their slaves every seventh year. These were often people who fell into poverty, although the Lord once said that as far as He was concerned poverty shouldn't occur in the Land. But, He also stated that there would always be poor people in the country and through His Laws He provided for them and those with a weak position in society, such as widows, orphans and foreigners. The owners were not to enslave those they set free again. Instead they were to treat them well by supplying them from their flock, threshing floor and wine press. The Lord gave the Israelites this command in remembrance that He once redeemed them from slavery out of Egypt. The shame of them being used as slaves by the Egyptians was taken away by the Lord when the men of the whole nation were circumcised at their arrival in the Promised Land under Joshua's leadership. So, the Israelites were to treat slaves well, while abiding by the Lord's Laws and instructions, and set them free at the right time. But, later those who agreed on the covenant changed their minds, took those they had let free back and forced them to be their slaves again. By ignoring His command, they desecrated His name. The Lord sent word to Jeremiah for Zedekiah. Jeremiah prophesied that all those who didn't fulfil the terms of the contract they made before Him, He would deliver in the hands of their enemies. Zedekiah, Judah's leaders, court officials, priests and common people were part of this covenant. The Lord Himself would proclaim 'freedom' for these people, by the sword, famine and plague. He would give the order and Nebuchadnezzar's army that started to withdraw from Israel would return, fight them, take Jerusalem, burn it down, and lay the towns of Judah to waste so no one would live there. They would kill them leaving their bodies as food for the birds and wild animals.

During the time Jeremiah spent in the courtyard of the guard, Hanamel son of Shallum came to see him to sell a field at Anathoth. This would take place during the tenth year of Zedekiah's reign. Jeremiah bought it from a relative as God commanded him, making it clear to him that one day life would be as usual again in the Land. He was to keep the contracts in a clay jar so they would last a long time, *"For thus says HaShem of hosts, the God of Israel: 'Houses and fields and vineyards shall yet again be bought in this land'."**

Nebuchadnezzar's siege would remain at Jerusalem until the eleventh year of Zedekiah's reign. On the ninth day of the fourth month in that year, when the famine in the city of Jerusalem was so great that there was nothing to eat for its inhabitants, the Babylonians broke through the city wall. Then the chief officer, the high official and all the other officials of the king of Babylon took seats in the Middle Gate. When Zedekiah and all his soldiers saw them, they fled. Even though the Babylonians were surrounding the city, at night Zedekiah and his army managed to flee through the gate between the two walls near the king's garden. They fled towards Arabah in the Jordan valley. The Babylonian army went in pursuit and caught up with them in the plains of Jericho, where all Zedekiah's soldiers were separated from him and got scattered. Zedekiah was captured in the plains of Jericho, taken to the Babylonian king in Riblah where he was sentenced. All his sons were killed before his eyes, and all the nobles of Judah were also killed. Afterwards his eyes were put out, he was bound with bronze shackles, taken captive, and imprisoned in Babylon until his death.

> *Run you to and fro through the streets of Jerusalem, and see now, and know, and seek in the broad places thereof, if you can find a man, if there be any that does justly, that seeks truth; and I will pardon him.*
>
> Jeremiah 5:1

An official of the king and commander of his imperial guard Nebuzaradan set out with his guard in charge of the Babylonian army to plunder and destroy Jerusalem. At the Temple of the Lord they broke up the more than eight meters high bronze pillars with their removable stands and the bronze Sea, and took the bronze to Babylon. These were made by Solomon. They also took all the bronze artefacts used in the temple service, with the pots, shovels, wick trimmers and dishes. The censers, sprinkling bowl and everything made of pure silver and gold were also taken. After they plundered the Temple of the Lord, they set fire to it. They burned down the royal palace, the important buildings and the houses of Jerusalem. The commander of the guard took Seraiah the chief priest, Zephaniah the priest next in rank, three door keepers, the officer in charge of the fighting men, five royal advisers, the secretary in charge of the conscripts and sixty conscripts who were found in the city as prisoners to the king in Riblah Babylon. There the king had all of them executed. Next they took the inhabitants of Jerusalem and all who deserted to the Babylonian king into exile to Babylon leaving only some of the poorest people behind to work on the vineyards and fields. Nebuchadnezzar appointed Gedaliah son of Ahikam, son of Shaphan, as governor over the people he had left in Judah.

Nebuchadnezzar gave strict orders to Nebuzaradan concerning Jeremiah who was still in confinement. He was to take Jeremiah, look after him and he had to do whatever Jeremiah asked him. So, he sent his officers and officials to take Jeremiah out of the courtyard of the guard. They found him, bound in chains, among the captives they were taking into exile to Babylon. They freed him and brought him to Nebuzaradan. The commander spoke with Jeremiah telling him that everything he had prophesied occurred because of Judah's sins. That he was free to go with him to Babylon where he would take care of him or he could stay in Judah. In case he would choose the latter, he could go to Gedaliah who would take him back to his home. Nebuzaradan gave him provisions and a present. Jeremiah went to Gedaliah and remained among his own people in Judah.

When all the army officers had heard that Gedaliah was governor, they went to see him at Mizpah.

Nethaniah's son Ishmael, Johanan and Jonathan the sons of Kareah, Tanhumeth's son Seraiah, the sons of Ephai the Netopathite, and Maakathite's son Jaazaniah, and their men, all came to talk to Gedaliah. He took an oath and he assured them that they had nothing to fear from the Babylonian officials who were there with him. He told them to settle in Judah, serve the Babylonian king, and all would go well for them. All the Israelites in Moab, Ammon, Edom and other countries returned to Judah when they heard that the Babylonian king left a remnant in Judah with Gedaliah as their governor. Together they harvested an abundance of wine and summer fruit in Judah.

One day Kareah's son Johanan and all the army officers who were still staying in the open country, came to speak in private with Gedaliah. Johanan told him that Baalins, the king of the Ammonites sent Nethaniah's son Ishmael to kill him. He told Gedaliah to let him kill Ishamael, otherwise he would kill him and have all the Israelites gathered around him to be scattered and Judah's remnant to perish. But, Gedaliah didn't believe him, and he told him he shouldn't do such a thing. Less than two months later however, Gedaliah was dead. So were some men of Judah and the Chaldean officials. Assassinated by Ishmael son of Nethaniah, the son of Elishama, who was of royal blood and had been one of the king's officers. He took ten men with him to commit the murders. The day after, they also killed seventy of a group of eighty men, who came unaware of the murders, from Shechem, Shiloh and Samaria to bring offerings and incense at the Lord's Temple. They let ten men go because they gave them the wheat, barley, olive oil and honey that they kept hidden in a field. Ishmael hid the bodies of all the dead in a cistern, once made by Asa king of Judah. Afterwards he took all those in Mizpah, including the king's daughters captive and set out to cross over to the Ammonites. When Johanan and the army officers with him heard of Ishmael's crimes, they took their men and went out to fight him. The captives chose Johanan's side, while Ishmael and eight of his men escaped to the Ammonites.

Johanan with the army officers took all the people to Geruth Kimham. In fear for their lives, expecting the Babylonians to be enraged about Ishamael's actions and taking this out on them, they intended to go to Egypt to escape from them. But before they left, Johanan wanted to consult with the Lord. So they approached Jeremiah and asked him to hear their petition and to pray for their entire remnant that was left. They wanted him to tell them where the Lord wanted them to go. Jeremiah replied he would and told them he would hold nothing back from the Lord's message. Johanan and the army officers assured Jeremiah that they would do everything the Lord would tell them to do. Ten days later they would call him a liar and ignore the Lord's instructions.

Jeremiah told them, "Thus says HaShem, the God of Israel, unto whom you sent me to present your supplications before Him: 'If you will still abide in this land, then will I build you, and not pull you down, and I will plant you, and not pluck you up; for I repent Me of the evil that I have done unto you. Be not afraid of the king of Babylon, of whom you are afraid; be not afraid of him, says HaShem; for I am with you to save you, and to deliver you from his hand. And I will grant you compassion, that he may have compassion upon you, and cause you to return to your own land'."*

And Jeremiah added, "'But if you say: We will not abide in this land; so that you hearken not to the voice of HaShem your God; saying: 'No; but we will go into the land of Egypt, where we shall see no war, nor hear the sound of the horn, nor have hunger of bread; and there will we abide'. Now therefore hear you the word of HaShem, O remnant of Judah: Thus says HaShem of hosts, the God of Israel: 'If you wholly set your faces to enter into Egypt, and go to sojourn there; then it shall come to pass, that the sword, which you fear, shall overtake you there in the land of Egypt, and the famine, whereof you are afraid, shall follow hard after you there in Egypt; and there you shall die. So shall it be with all the men that set their faces to go into Egypt to sojourn there; they shall die by the sword, by the famine, and by the pestilence; and none of them shall remain or escape from the evil that I will bring upon them'. For thus says HaShem of hosts, the God of Israel: 'As My anger and My fury has been poured forth upon the inhabitants of Jerusalem, so shall My fury be poured forth upon you, when you shall enter into Egypt; and you shall be an execration, and an astonishment, and a curse, and a reproach; and you shall see this place no more'."*

Then Jeremiah told the remnant of Judah again not to go to Egypt, but to stay in the Land. As soon as Jeremiah finished talking the men in their arrogance told him he was lying and that Baruch was inciting him into tricking them to stay in Judah so they would either be killed or be carried out into exile to Babylon. They left Judah as they intended before and took Jeremiah and Baruch with them to Egypt as far as Tahpanhes. There the Lord's word came to Jeremiah. The Lord told him to take some large stones and bury them in clay on the brick pavement at the entrance of Pharaoh's palace in Tahpanhes. He was to do this while all the Israelites were watching and then he had to tell them what the Lord had to say. The Lord would send His servant Nebuchadnezzar king of Babylon to attack Egypt, bringing death, captivity and the sword to all those destined for these, to burn down the temples of the gods of Egypt, to take their gods captive, to pick Egypt clean and depart. Nebuchadnezzar would put his royal seat above the stones Jeremiah had buried and spread his canopy above it. Jeremiah also received God's word concerning all the Israelites who settled in upper and lower Egypt remembering them about the disaster He brought about over Jerusalem and Judah's towns making them desolated places, all because of their wickedness, idolatry, reluctance to listen to the Lord's warnings, brought to them by His servants the prophets, and their disobedience, asking them why they cut off the people from the Land leaving Judah without a remnant and why did they continue to burn incense to other gods in Egypt. They were ruining themselves and making themselves an object of reproach amongst the nations. Until then they had not humbled themselves, nor had they shown any reverence, while ignoring the laws and decrees given to them through their ancestors.

> *And many nations shall pass by this city, and they shall say every man to his neighbour: Wherefore has HaShem done thus unto this great city? Then they shall answer: Because they forsook the covenant of HaShem their God, and worshipped other gods, and served them.*
>
> Jeremiah 22:8-9

Jeremiah told them about the Lord's determination to bring disaster over them there in Egypt. They would die by the sword, famine and plague. None of the remnant of Judah who settled in Egypt would escape, except a few fugitives who would return to Judah. But the people didn't listen, instead they told Jeremiah they would not listen to the messages he brought them in the name of the Lord, and they would continue to burn incense and bring offerings to their idols as they did in Jerusalem and Judah. The women had their husband consent to engage in their idol worship. Jeremiah made it clear to them that just as the Lord handled Jerusalem and Judah because He could no longer endure the wickedness of the inhabitants of Judah, He told them what He would do to them: "*'Behold, I have sworn by My great name,' says HaShem, 'that My name shall no more be named in the mouth of any man of Judah in all the land of Egypt saying: ' As the Lord God lives'. Behold, I watch over them for evil, and not for good; and all the men of Judah that are in the land of Egypt shall be consumed by the sword and by the famine, until there be an end of them. And they that escape* *the sword shall return out of the land of Egypt into the land of Judah, few in number; and all the remnant of Judah, that are gone into the land of Egypt to sojourn there, shall know whose word shall stand, Mine, or theirs'."**

Jeremiah also gave them a sign to all that would happen to them. That the Lord would deliver Pharaoh Hophra in the hands of his enemy Nebuchadnezzar, just as He did Zedekiah. Nebuchadnezzar did defeat the Pharaoh's army, keeping him from engaging in new military campaigns.

The Israelites that Nebuchadnezzar gradually took into exile were three thousand and twenty-three during his seventh year of reign, eight hundred and thirty-two in his eighteenth year, and seven hundred and forty-five Israelites in his twenty-third year. Years later in the thirty-seventh year of his exile, Jehoiachin king of Judah would be released from prison by Awel-Marduk a new king of Babylon. He was kind to him and gave him a seat of honour, higher than those of the other kings with him in Babylon. For the rest of his life he regularly received an allowance from the king, and he ate at the king's table.

> *Yet in spite of this, when they are in the land of their enemies, I will not reject them or abhor them so as to destroy them completely, breaking my covenant with them. I am the Lord their God. But for their sake I will remember the covenant with their ancestors who I brought out of Egypt in the sight of the nations to be their God. I am the Lord.*
>
> Leviticus 26:44-45

Replanted

Within that generation, the Lord had burned and broken the branches of His thriving olive tree, Judah and Israel, that He Himself had planted in the Land. The Children of Israel were God's chosen family, of all the families on earth, to be His own. As their Father He had imposed harsh punishment on them after they constantly refused to learn from His discipline. Ultimately, people of both Israel and Judah together with the those of the towns that Asa king of Judah had captured from Ephraim including people from Ephraim, Menasseh and Simeon that had joined and settled in Judah, went into exile away from the Land.

> *And you will I scatter among the nations, and I will draw out the sword after you; and your land shall be a desolation,*

> *and your cities shall be a waste. Then shall the land be paid her Shabbats, as long as it lies desolate, and you are in your enemies' land; even then shall the land rest, and repay her Shabbat. As long as it lies desolate it shall have rest; even the rest which it had not in your Shabbats, when you dwelt upon it.*
>
> Leviticus 26:33-35

The Lord always wanted His king to be a bearer of His moral code, and for him to rule by example.

When the kings failed, so would their subjects, led astray by their leaders. The Lord repeatedly through generations warned His people including their leaders, set examples for them, and gave them opportunities to prevent disaster. Still they didn't listen to Him, nor did they obey Him. Even when He gave their remnant a chance to survive, their disobedience reduced their group of people to a much smaller one than the Lord had intended. So, He scattered the inhabitants of the nation of Israel and Judah, making His City and His Land desolated so it could have the Shabbat years and rest it needed.

> *I will heal their backsliding, I will love them freely; for My anger is turned away from him. I will be as the dew unto Israel; he shall blossom as the lily, and cast forth his roots as Lebanon. His branches shall spread, and his beauty shall be as the olive tree, and his fragrance as Lebanon. They that dwell under his shadow shall again make corn to grow, and shall blossom as the vine; the scent thereof shall be as the wine of Lebanon.*
>
> Hosea 14:5-8

But the time would come that the Lord would not afflict nor uproot His people anymore. He would turn His anger away from them and love them freely. With compassion He would bring them back, plant them, root them in the Land, and rebuild the House of David. Just as the Lord, like a father, disciplined King David and He told David that He later would do to his son Solomon, and didn't let go of Solomon nor David's Royal House, as he previously did with Saul, the same way He would discipline His nation, scattering the people of Judah and Israel only to return them to the Land, after a period of seventy years of absence.

I, Daniel, meditated in the books, over the number of the years, whereof the word of HaShem came to Jeremiah the prophet, that He would accomplish for the desolations of Jerusalem seventy years. And I set my face unto the Lord God, to seek by prayer and supplications, with fasting, and sackcloth, and ashes.

And I prayed unto HaShem my God, and made confession, and said: O Lord, the great and awesome God, who keeps covenant and mercy with them that love You and keep Your commandments, we have sinned, and have dealt iniquitously, and have done wickedly, and have rebelled, and have turned aside from Your commandments and from Your ordinances; neither have we hearkened unto Your servants the prophets, that spoke in Your name to our kings, our princes, and our fathers, and to all the people of the land.

Now therefore, O our God, hearken unto the prayer of Your servant, and to his supplications, and cause Your face to shine upon Your sanctuary that is desolate, for the Lord's sake.

O my God, incline Your ear, and hear; open Your eyes, and behold our desolations, and the city upon which Your name is called; for we do not present our supplications before You because of our righteousness, but because of Your great compassion. O Lord, hear, O Lord, forgive, O Lord, attend and do, defer not; for Your own sake, O my God, because Your name is called upon Your city and Your people.

Daniel 9:2-19

Years later, one of the exiles, the prophet Daniel, showed repentance and asked the Lord God for forgiveness for himself and all the people of Israel, those under the leadership of the tribe of Judah as well as those who were led by Ephraim; those of the past and present, the dead and the living. He did the only righteous deed the living could do for the dead. Daniel was sincere with the Lord, honestly seeking His forgiveness and His truth. Believing every single word the Lord's prophets had spoken on his behalf, Daniel sought to understand these. The Lord would let Daniel find Him and He would answer his prayers. He would even send His angel to speak to Daniel about things to come, all which at that time was already written in the Lord's Book of Truth. Didn't the Lord himself tell Jeremiah as well about things to come regarding those He considered to be the good figs in the basket.

> *And the word of HaShem came unto me, saying: Thus says HaShem, the God of Israel: Like these good figs, so will I regard the captives of Judah, whom I have sent out of this place into the land of the Chaldeans, for good.*
>
> *And I will set My eyes upon them for good, and I will bring them back to this land; and I will build them, and not pull them down; and I will plant them, and not pluck them up.*
>
> *And I will give them a heart to know Me, that I am HaShem; and they shall be My people, and I will be their God; for they shall return unto Me with their whole heart.*
>
> Jeremiah 24:6-7

Endnotes

* Isaiah 8:3-4, Hosea 12: 1, Amos 7:11, Amos 7:17, Amos 8:2, Amos 8:4-6, Amos 6:12, Genesis 49:10, Jeremiah 7:15, 2 Kings 21:11-15, Jeremiah 1:5-8, Jeremiah 22:30, Jeremiah 26:18, Jeremiah 35:13, 1 Samuel 15:6, Jeremiah 45:4-5, Jeremiah 15:19-21, Jeremiah 36:29-31, Jeremiah 24:8-10, Hosea 3:4-5, Jeremiah 29:19, Jeremiah 29:31-32, Jeremiah 21:8-10, Jeremiah 37:17, Jeremiah 38:2-3, Jeremiah 38:17-18, Jeremiah 32:15, Jeremiah 42:9-12, Jeremiah 42:13-18, Jeremiah 44:26-28.

2 Kings 15:29-30 Hosea seized power
2 Kings 17 the fall of Israel to the Assyrians
Isaiah 8:5-8 Isaiah's prophesy about Assyria and Judah
2 Kings 17:1-23 reason rejection northern Kingdom of Israel
Hosea 11:8 God's love for Ephraim
Jeremiah 2, 3:4-5, Hosea 12 to 14 Israel's sins
1 Kings 13:1-10, 1 Kings 13:31-34 prophesy against Jeroboam and his altar
1 Kings 13:23-31, 2 Kings 23:16-18 the grave of the prophet who prophesied against Jeroboam
2 Kings 18:9-12 Israel rejected by God
2 Kings 24-41 new inhabitants of Israel
2 Kings 14:14-16 rejection of Israel because of Jeroboam
2 Kings 10:32-33 God reduced Israel's territory east of the Jordan River
Amos 7 Amaziah's plot against Amos
Amos 8 basket of ripe fruit
Amos 9:8-10 the sieve
Amos 6 Israel became complacent and proud
Joshua 18:1, Jeremiah 7:12 Tent of Meeting placed the first time in the Promised Land in Shiloh
Judges 18:31, 1 Samuel 1:3, 2:27-36, 3:21, 4 the House of God, priests Eli and his sons

The Fall

1 Kings 14:2 Ahijah lived in Shiloh
Jeremiah 26:6,9 the Lord would make the Temple and Jerusalem as desolated as Shiloh
1 Samuel 3:21 Samuel
Ezekiel 6 destruction of idols, altars and idol worshippers
2 Kings 21:1-17, 2 Chronicles 32:33-33:1-20, Jeremiah 15:4 Menasseh king of Judah
2 Kings 21:17-18 Menasseh's burial place
Genesis 9:5 people are accountable for someone's death
2 Chronicles 33, 2 Kings 21 King Menasseh
Jeremiah 19:5-6 child sacrifices
Jeremiah 22:13-15, 17-19, Jeremiah 26 prophecy against Jehoiakim's corruption
Jeremiah 11:18-21 plot against Jeremiah
Jeremiah 16:1-2 Jeremiah should not marry and have children
Jeremiah 26:1-19 Jeremiah's prophesy concerning the Temple, death threats
Jeremiah 35 the Rekabites
Jeremiah 1:10 Jeremiah's God-given authority
Jeremiah 36 the scroll burned by Jehoiakim
Jeremiah 26:20-24 Jehoiakim kills prophet Uriah
Jeremiah 22:24-30, 24:1 prophecy against Jehoiachin, exile and childless
Jeremiah 24: the basket of fruits
Jeremiah 29 letters from Jeremiah and false prophet Shemaiah to the exiles
Jeremiah 25:10-14, 29:4-14 prophesy Jeremiah concerning Judah's exile
Jeremiah 11:1-17 punishment for Judah, Jacob
Jeremiah 23 false prophets
Jeremiah 28 confrontation false prophet with Jeremiah
Jeremiah 37:13-14 Jeremiah arrested by Irijah
Jeremiah 32:1,6-15 Jeremiah bought land to help a family member
2 Kings 23:30-25:30, Jeremiah 8, 34 to 45 and 52 the fall of Judah
2 Kings 25:26 people of Judah fled to Egypt
Exodus 21:1-11, Jeremiah 34:14, Deuteronomy 15:12-15 free slaves every seventh year
Deuteronomy 15:1-11 poverty
Joshua 5:8-9 shame of slavery taken away by the Lord
Jeremiah 34:21 Babylonian army withdrew
Jeremiah 52:11 Zedekiah died in prison
1 Kings 15:20, 2 Chronicles 15:8,17:2 towns of Ephraim captured by Asa king of Judah
Psalm 95:8-11 God's judgment over Israelites in the desert
Deuteronomy 27:9-26, Deuteronomy 28 Book of the Covenant
Deuteronomy 30:11-14 God's Laws not distant nor hidden
Deuteronomy 29:13-20 consequences also for the descendants of the Israelites

Deuteronomy 31:9-13 the Book of Law
Deuteronomy 31:19-22, 24-26 Moses' song
Jeremiah 52:28-30 people of Judah into captivity
2 Chronicles 15:9, 11:16-17 some of Ephraim, Menasseh and Simeon joined Judah under Asa
Amos 3:1-2 God's chosen family
Leviticus 26:43 Shabbat years of the Land
Hosea 11:8-11, 14:4 the Lord's compassion and love
Amos 9:11-15, Nahum 1:12 no affliction, no uprooting, replant and rebuild House of David
2 Samuel 7:12-15 the Lord would discipline, not let go
Deuteronomy 30:1-5 God would return them to the Land
Daniel 10:20-21 the Book of Truth
Leviticus 26:40-42 Daniel asked forgiveness

Intermezzo Endnotes

Leviticus 22:17-18, Ezekiel 44:9 foreigners bring offerings, not to enter God's Sanctuary
2 Samuel 15:19-22 David and Ittai
2 Kings 10:15-17 Jehu and Jehonadab son of Rekab
Numbers 24:21-22 Balaam noticed the Rekabite tents
Judges 1:16 Moses was married to a Kenite
Judge 4: 11-21, 5:24 Heber the Kenite
1 Samuel 15:5-8, 30:23-30 Saul and David's kindness to the Rekabites, Kenites
1 Samuel 30:20 Rekabites way of life

Note: Babylonians are also referred to as Chaldeans

THE RECONCILIATION

Sing, O daughter of Zion, shout, O Israel; be glad and rejoice with all the heart, O daughter of Jerusalem. HaShem has taken away your judgments, He has cast out your enemy; ... HaShem your God is in the midst of you, a Mighty One who will save; He will rejoice over you with joy, He will be silent in His love, He will joy over you with singing. ... I will gather them that are far from the appointed season, who are of you, that has born the burden of reproach. ... At that time I will bring you in, and at that time I will gather you; for I will make you to be a name and a praise among all the people of the earth, when I turn your captivity before your eyes, says HaShem.
Zephaniah 3:14-20

God's servant Daniel must have had hope for a future in prosperity, prepared by the Lord God for His people when he humbled himself in prayer before the Lord. Despite his life in exile together with many Jews, Daniel still believed and trusted the Lord's every word that His faithful and truthful prophets had spoken concerning the future of Israel. He remained faithful to the Lord, true to His Law, and he didn't walk the way of the wicked. He must have been one of the faithful Jews the Lord had given a mark on his forehead signifying that he and his descendants, along with other Children of Jacob, would survive the time of exile, to be the ones to rebuild Jerusalem and the Land of Israel. Daniel was like a tree planted by a pond, remaining steadfast, firm in his faith everytime the heat came, surviving even threats against his own life.

Blessed is the one who trusts in the Lord, whose confidence is in Him. They will be like a tree planted by the water that sends out its roots by the stream. It does not fear when heat comes; its leaves are always green. It has no worries in a year of drought and never fails to bear fruit.
Jeremiah 17:5-8, Psalm 1:2-3

As David did in the past, Daniel came to the Lord with prayers of sincere repentance. He didn't pray for forgiveness only for himself, but also for the sins and iniquities of his forefathers and of all the Children of Jacob, the House of Judah and the House of Israel. Daniel did as Jeremiah once said, 'Remember HaShem from afar, and let Jerusalem come into your mind'.*

When did Daniel turn to God in prayer about this subject? When he understood the Lord's word given to Jeremiah concerning the people of Judah and the Land; that the country would be a desolated wasteland for seventy years, after which the Lord would come to the Children of Israel and fulfil His good promise to them. When this period of time was completed, Judah's time to return to the Land and Jerusalem, to be planted and remain had arrived.

> Neither have we hearkened to Your servants the prophets, that spoke in Your name to our kings, our princes, and our fathers, and to all the people of the land.
> Neither have we hearkened to the voice of HaShem our God, to walk in His ways, which He set before us by His servants the prophets.
>
> Daniel 9:6-10

While Daniel was in prayer, one of God's angels, the angel Gabriel who had spoken to him before, came to give him a message. Gabriel told him that as soon as he had started praying, a word of the Lord went out, about which he came to tell him to give him insight and understanding, because Daniel was highly esteemed by the Lord. Gabriel told him, 'Seventy sevens, weeks, are decreed for your people and your holy city to finish transgression, to put an end to sin, to atone for wickedness, to bring in everlasting righteousness, to seal up vision and prophecy and to anoint the Most Holy Place'.*

He continued his message by telling him about the period of time set by the Lord for Jerusalem to be rebuilt during times of trouble, the coming of a ruler, his death by a new ruler, afterwards war and desolation would follow while the ruler puts an end to sacrifice and offering, placing an abomination that causes desolation in the Temple. This ruler's time would come to an end at the appointed time. The word spoken by Gabriel confirmed that Jerusalem and the Temple of the Lord would be restored as the Lord made clear through the Scriptures up to Daniel's time, but it also made clear that one day another period of war, followed by desolation, would occur in Jerusalem's future after its restoration.

> *Come and let us return unto HaShem; for He has torn, and He will heal us. He has smitten, and He will bind us up. After two days will He revive us, on the third day He will raise us up, that we may live in His presence. And let us know, eagerly strive to know HaShem, His going forth is sure as the morning; and He shall come unto us as the rain, as the latter rain that waters the earth.*
>
> Hosea 6:1-3

The God of Israel, Who determines the number of the stars and is able to call each of them by name cared for the Children of Jacob, Israel. To Him Israel was a thriving olive tree with fruit beautiful in form.* Israel was His vineyard which He had the Assyrians and later the Babylonians trample on. But He would reconcile Himself with His people, and in days to come Jacob and therefore Israel ... will take root, Israel will bud and blossom and fill all the world with fruit.* Daniel and his descendants would witness that day and rejoice with all the Children of Jacob who would return home to inhabit the Land given by the Lord to their ancestors. They would rebuild the capital city of Jerusalem, the Temple of the Lord, and Jerusalem's walls with its gates.

> *In that day, Sing about a fruitful vineyard. I, the Lord, watch over it; I water it continually. I guard it day and night so that no one may harm it.*
>
> Isaiah 27:2-3

Like Daniel, the prophet Habakkuk lived at the time the Babylonian kings ruled and subjugated Israel and Jerusalem. To the Babylonians their power was their god. In those days, when false prophets gave false hopes and the Israelites, both the leaders and the masses neglected the covenant their ancestors made with the Lord God. Meanwhile they held onto their idols, about which the Lord said, *"Of what value is an idol carved by a craftsman? Or an image that teaches lies? For the one who makes it trusts in his own creation; he makes idols that cannot speak. Woe to him who says to wood, 'Come to life'! Or to lifeless stone, 'Wake up'! Can it give guidance? It is covered with gold and silver; there is no breath in it."*

Habakkuk instead trusted his God and Saviour, and he didn't refuse to stay faithful to the Lord and His Law. As a carrier of the Lord's moral code and therefore His way of life, he was deeply disturbed by the troubles and the injustice all around, and he prayed to the Lord,

"How long, Lord, must I call for help, but you do not listen? Or cry out to you, 'Violence'! but you do not save? Why do you make me look at injustice? Why do you tolerate wrongdoing? Destruction and violence are before me; there is strife, and conflict abounds. Therefore the law is paralyzed, and justice never prevails. The wicked hem in the righteous, so that justice is perverted".*

The Lord's answer to Habakkuk's prayers made him realise that a righteous person should live by his faith and that all would come in God's good time.

> *For the revelation awaits an appointed time; it speaks of the end and will not prove false. Though it lingers, wait for it; it will certainly come and will not delay.*
>
> Habakkuk 2:3

During those seventy years, Daniel himself lived in exile. He was one of the young men selected from among the Jewish exiles to serve the king of Babylonia. They were men from the royal families and the nobility of Judah. Only the men who complied to the king's wishes were selected. He ordered the chief of his court officials to choose young men who were physically healthy, handsome, intelligent, well informed, quick to understand and learn, and qualified to serve in his palace. They were to receive a three-year training, during which they learned the Babylonian language and literature. After their training they would enter the king's service. During that period the king provided them with food and wine from his table.

On Daniel's request, he and three other young men were provided with vegetables and water on the condition that after ten days they still had to be healthy and remain in good health. These men wanted to prevent themselves from becoming unclean by eating the food offered at the king's court. Daniel, Hananiah, Mishael and Azariah passed this test, after which they entered the king's court, where the Lord provided for them. But to the Babylonians, Daniel and others like him were slaves, bondsmen or bond servants. The Babylonian king owned their lives. They were not hired servants. As slaves they didn't have the right to buy themselves out of slavery, nor their family members or other fellow Jews. Neither did they have the right to go back to the Land and their homes where their possessions would be returned to them. They couldn't expect to be free in the year of general pardon, the year of Jubilee, as the Lord commanded the Children of Israel to do in their society.

> *And if your brother be waxen poor with you, and sell himself unto you, you shall not make him to serve as a bond servant. As a hired servant, and as a settler, he shall be with you; he shall serve with you unto the year of jubilee. Then shall he go out from you, he and his children with him, and shall return unto his own family, and unto the possession of his fathers shall he return. For they are My servants, who I brought forth out of the land of Egypt; they shall not be sold as bondsmen. You shall not rule over him with rigour; but shall fear your God. ... but over your brethren the children of Israel you shall not rule, one over another, with rigour.*
>
> Leviticus 25:39-46

So, Daniel hoped for God's mercy as was foretold by both Moses and later Jeremiah. Meanwhile, during the period they had to remain in exile, the Lord granted Daniel, Hananiah, Mishael and Azariah wisdom and understanding in every matter the king would question them, making the times better than any magician or enchanters the king would consult. In addition the Lord granted Daniel understanding of all sorts of visions and dreams, and He answered their prayers every time they sought His help, saving them out of hazardous situations.

> *And the remnant of Jacob shall be in the midst of many people, as dew from HaShem, as showers upon the grass, that are not looked for from man, nor awaited at the hands of the sons of men.*
>
> Micah 5:6

Daniel's friends, who didn't fall down to worship Nebuchadnezzar's image nor his idols, were brought into a blazing furnace. The Lord saved them, and no harm came to them. Later on during Darius de Mede's rule the Lord saved Daniel, who refused to cease his prayers to the Lord, out of a lions' den. These four men were among the prisoners that Nebuchadnezzar, the Chaldean Babylonian king, took into exile to Babylon after he besieged Jerusalem and captured King Jehoiakim during his third year of reign. By God's grace Daniel was placed at the Babylonian court in service to the kings of Babylonia, where the Lord inspired him to do His will. Daniel remained at the king's court until the first year of the reign of Cyrus the Persian.

> *In that day, says HaShem, I will assemble her that halted, and I will gather her that is driven away, and her that I have*

> *afflicted; And I will make her that halted a remnant, and her that was cast far off a mighty nation; and HaShem shall reign over them in Mount Zion from thence forth even for ever. And you, Migdal-eder**, the hill of the daughter of Zion, unto you shall it come; yes, the former dominion shall come, the kingdom of the daughter of Jerusalem.*
>
> Micah 4:6-8

Intermezzo

Chronology

At the conclusion of the seventy-year period mentioned by Daniel and foretold by the prophet Jeremiah, the Children of Judah and Benjamin would go up to Jerusalem, to the Land of Judah. Through time several kings came to power. They ruled over their empire which also included the region of Trans-Euphrates, where the Land of Israel was situated. The kings who ruled over Babylonia, since the time of Nebuchadnezzar, king of Babylonia, were his son Evil-merodach, succeeded by Nebuchadnezzar's son Belchazar. Nebuchadnezzar was of a Chaldean dynasty. The Babylonian Empire was later conquered by Darius the Mede and his son-in-law Cyrus the Persian, also known as Koresh and Cyrus the Great. They were succeeded by Ahasuerus, also identified with Xerxes I of Persia or Artaxerxes, and later by his son Darius the Persian. Artaxerxes was a generic name used for king in Persia, like the name Pharaoh was used in Egypt.

> *But the mercy of HaShem is from everlasting to everlasting upon them that fear Him, and His righteousness unto children's children; To such as keep His covenant, and to those that remember His precepts to do them.*
>
> Psalm 103:17-18

Ahasuerus was Queen Esther's husband. In the third year of his reign, he removed Vashti, his queen, from her position. He made Esther his queen in the seventh year of his reign. She was faithful to the Lord and her actions saved the life of the Children of Jacob living in exile in her husband's empire at the time. Ahasuerus ruled over 127 provinces that stretched from India to the upper Nile region, Cush. Darius the Persian was their son and his father's successor. Both Esther's husband and son were kings of Persia, and both of them would be approached by the opponents of the Children of Judah, through official letters meant to create troubles for them. Ahasuerus would receive a defamation letter against the Jews, but he wouldn't take any measures regarding them. Esther's son Darius the Persian though would react to the letter sent to him, but in an unexpected manner. One of these foreign rulers would be the king to grant the Jews the first permission to go up to Zion and rebuild the Temple of the Lord. That king would be chosen by the Lord Himself. He would be someone to serve the Lord in achieving His purpose with the remnant of the Children of Israel.

> *For the sake of Jacob My servant, and Israel My elect, I have called you by your name, I have surnamed you, though you have not known Me.*
>
> Isaiah 45:1-8
>
> *He is My shepherd, and shall perform all My pleasure; even saying of Jerusalem: She shall be built; and to the Temple: My foundation shall be laid.*
>
> Isaiah 44:28

During days to come, there would also be leaders among the Children of Judah to guide the Jews to Zion. First Zerubbabel would go up with a group of more than forty-two thousand Jews to build the Temple of the Lord. Under Nehemiah's leadership the wall would be rebuilt, and Ezra with a group of five thousand Jews would come to teach the Law given to Moses. Both Ezra and Nehemiah would arrive in Judah at the time Artaxerxes reigned over Persia. Ezra would leave Babylonia in the seventh year of Artaxerxes, while Nehemiah's arrival in Jerusalem would be in the twentieth year of Artaxerxes.

> *As you know not what is the way of the wind, nor how the bones do grow in the womb of her that is with child; even so you know not the work of God who does all things.*
>
> Ecclesiastes 11:5

However it's still an ongoing debate which of the two, Nehemiah or Ezra, arrived at first in Jerusalem because the kings who ruled at that time could have been two different kings called by the generic name of Artaxerxes. Artaxerxes I or II. There are two more common possibilities. If the events mentioned in Ezra 7:8 and Nehemiah 2:1-9 happened when Araxerxes I reigned, then Nehemiah arrived in Jerusalem before Ezra. The latter in 458 BCE and Nehemiah in 445

BCE. But, assuming it was during the reign of Artaxerxes II that five thousand men went with Ezra, of which Nehemiah had no knowledge of, and the prayer mentioned in Ezra 9:9* occurred, then Ezra arrived in Jerusalem before Nehemiah; Ezra in 398 BCE and Nehemiah after him in 445 BCE. It's also not clear whether Ezra the scholar of the book of Ezra was the same Ezra mentioned by Nehemiah.

Blessings

Wash you, make you clean, put away the evil of your doings from before My eyes, cease to do evil; Learn to do well; seek justice, relieve the oppressed, judge the fatherless, plead for the widow. Come now, and let us reason together, says HaShem; though your sins be as scarlet, they shall be as white as snow; though they be red like crimson, they shall be as wool. If you will be willing and obedient, you shall eat the good of the Land.

Isaiah 1:16-19

The Lord God, the Holy One of Israel, Who is great in purpose and deeds, watches over all mankind and sees their ways is the Highest Judge. He loves righteousness and hates theft. When He judges He shows no favouritism towards the great or the small, the rich or the poor. He rewards each person in accordance to their conduct, by their deeds as they deserve and He brings judgment or blessings over each and every person. No one and no nation could escape God's power to bring judgment, nor His grace to bring blessings through forgiveness. The Lord foresaw the unfaithfulness and disobedience of the Children of Jacob as He had told Moses ages earlier. Moses spoke, with heaven and earth as his witness, about their false gods. By God's command Moses wrote a song that he had to teach the Israelites and which they were to sing as a witness for the Lord against them. They forgot their God, who has been as a father to them and gave birth to them as a mother. The Lord also foretold the consequences through His prophets before He would send Israel and afterwards Judah into exile.

HaShem will bring you, and your king who you shall set over yourselves, unto a nation that you have not known, you nor your fathers; and there shall you serve other gods, wood and stone.

Deuteronomy 28:36

> *Hear this, you leaders of Jacob, you rulers of Israel, who despise justice and distort all that is right; who built Zion with bloodshed, and Jerusalem with wickedness. Her leaders judge for a bribe, her priests teach for a price, and her prophets tell fortunes for money. Yet they look for the Lord's support and say, Is not the Lord among us? No disaster will come upon us. Therefore because of you, Zion will be plowed like a field, Jerusalem will become a heap of rubble, the Temple Hill a mound overgrown with thickets.*
>
> Micah 3:9-12

The Lord's wish was to bless His people whom He taught to live in accordance to His Law and moral code. As His servant Samuel once said, *Does the Lord delight in burnt offerings and sacrifices as much as in obeying the Lord?*

To obey is better than sacrifice, and to heed is better than the fat of rams.* They were to obey every word of His Law and to command their children to do so as well, *'For it is no vain thing for you; because it is your life, and through this thing you shall prolong your days upon the Land, whither you go over the Jordan to possess it'.*

Their obedience to the Lord would be a sign of their love for Him, and would prolong their life while living in the Land. As the Lord's word spoken by Jeremiah, *"this thing I commanded them, saying: 'Hearken unto My voice, and I will be your God, and you shall be My people; and walk you in all the way that I command you, that it may be well with you'."*

It was the Lord's wish that they would learn of His teachings, and live by these without forsaking Him as their Rock. He who is pure and faithful, whose work is perfect and the One that brings justice in the Land and to all people.

> *Give ear, you heavens, and I will speak; and let the earth hear the words of my mouth. My doctrine shall drop as the rain, my speech shall distil as the dew; as the small rain upon the tender grass, and as the showers upon the herb. For I will proclaim the name of HaShem; ascribe you greatness unto our God. The Rock, His work is perfect; for all His ways are justice; a God of faithfulness and without iniquity, just and right is He.*
>
> Deuteronomy 32:1-4

The Children of Israel should have come to the Lord with truthful, sincere repentance, as King David once said in His prayers, *'My sacrifice, O God, is a broken spirit; a broken and remorseful heart, you, God, will not despise'.**

The Lord, to whom the ways of the Children of Jacob were not hidden nor their sinfulness concealed, would have listened to them. He saw all their wrongdoings, their rebellion and their sinful requests. All the sins of the priesthood. Especially the High Priest, with the priests, brought the heaviest burden and much guilt on the entire nation of Judah. There was much corruption among the priests, and some took part in prostitution as the sons of the High Priest Eli once did with the women serving at the entrance of the Tent of Meeting at the time of the Judges of Israel. The Lord's judgment over them was severe. Eli himself acknowledged the reason for this.

> *If one man sins against another, God shall judge him; but if a man sins against HaShem, who shall plead for him?"*
>
> 1 Samuel 2:25a

> *For the spirit of prostitution has caused them to err, and they have gone astray from under their God.*
>
> Hosea 4:12

They made God's Sanctuary impure, so the Lord rejected His altar and abandoned His Sanctuary; the one place about which the Lord said to Solomon, *'Now My eyes shall be open, and My ears attend, unto the prayer that is made in this place. For now have I chosen and hallowed this House, that My name may be there for ever; and My eyes and My heart shall be there perpetually'.**

They also brought sacrifices to demons at numerous places in the Land. But, the wicked also brought sacrifices to the Lord while they didn't live by God's righteousness and justice anymore, making their sacrifices detestable in His eyes.

> *To do righteousness and justice is more acceptable to HaShem than sacrifice.*
>
> Proverbs 21:3

By following other gods, idols and by living in accordance to their self made belief-systems and traditions they got themselves and their nation corrupted. They honoured each other above God, just as the High Priest Eli once did, by honouring his sons above the Lord. Their wicked deeds at the Temple of the Lord and the way they treated the

Lord's inheritance, the fertile Land that gave its fruits and its rich produce, made it impure and a detestable place in God's eyes. They themselves turned from being a vine of choice, over which the Lord watched and watered continually, into a corrupt wild vine.

> *Will you steal, murder, and commit adultery, and swear falsely, and offer unto Baal, and walk after other gods whom you have not known, and come and stand before Me in this House, whereupon My name is called, and say: We are delivered, that you may do all these abominations? Has this House, whereupon My name is called, become a den of robbers in your eyes? Behold, I, even I, have seen it, says HaShem.*
>
> Jeremiah 7:1-15,30

> *For these are rebellious people, deceitful children, children unwilling to listen to the Lord's instruction. They say to the seers, See no more visions, and to the prophets, Give us no more visions of what is right! Tell us pleasant things, prophesy illusions. Leave this way, get off this path, and stop confronting us with the Holy One of Israel!*
>
> Isaiah 30:9-11

Even though the Lord's arm wasn't too short to save them nor His ear to dull to hear them, their prayers at that time were not sincere, 'My Father, my friend from my youth, will you always be angry? Will your wrath continue for ever'?

'This is how you talk, but you do all the evil you can'.*

They continuously failed to live as the Lord commanded them. By following a sinful path, the Israelites individually and as a society let go of God's moral code, except for a remnant that the Lord kept, of which some would eventually also be unfaithful to Him. God's moral code and His life standard didn't have much meaning anymore to these people. The Lord was displeased with them, because there was so much evil and no justice anymore in the Land.

> *By mercy and truth iniquity is atoned; and by the fear of HaShem men depart from evil.*
>
> Proverbs 16:6

> *Thus says HaShem: Let not the wise man glory in his wisdom, neither let the mighty man glory in his might, let not the rich man glory in his riches; But let him that glories glory in this, that he understands, and knows Me, that I am HaShem*

> who exercise mercy, justice, and righteousness, in the earth; for in these things I delight, says HaShem.
>
> Jeremiah 9:22-23

The prophet Amos spoke of the judgment that the Lord brought over His people by saying, *'You only have I chosen of all the families of the earth; therefore I will punish you for all your sins'.**

The determination of these people and those before them, except those who remained faithful to the Lord, in being disobedient to the Lord led to their downfall, as the Lord told them centuries earlier, *'If you ever forget the Lord your God and follow other gods and worship and bow down to them, I testify against you today that you will surely be destroyed. Like the nations the Lord destroyed before you, so you will be destroyed for not obeying the Lord your God'.**

The Lord did not only speak of punishment in case of unfaithfulness towards Him, but He had also made the blessings to those who would remain faithful to Him known to the Children of Israel. He gave His promise to Moses that, despite their wrongdoings resulting in them being scattered amongst the nations, He would never reject the Children of Israel.

> And yet for all that, when they are in the land of their enemies, I will not reject them, neither will I abhor them, to destroy them utterly, and to break My covenant with them; for I am HaShem their God.
>
> Leviticus 26:44

> For I am with you, says HaShem, to save you; for I will make a full end of all the nations whither I have scattered you, but I will not make a full end of you; for I will correct you in measure, and will not utterly destroy you.
>
> Jeremiah 30:11

The Lord Who is great in counsel, and mighty in work; whose eyes are open upon all the ways of the sons of men, to give every one according to his ways, and according to the fruit of his doings,* would either reward or bring punishment to the Children of Jacob by their conduct and deeds. They had chosen not to return to the Holy One of Israel. The consequence was that the Lord decided to bring His judgment over them because, *'although you wash yourself with soap and use an abundance of cleansing powder, the stain of your guilt is still before me,' declares the Sovereign Lord.**

Their sinful ways caused their Land to become *'a Land that is not cleansed, nor rained upon in the day of indignation'.*

The Lord brought His punishment over both Samaria and Jerusalem. Jerusalem had to drink the same cup Samaria drank years before. Jerusalem killed the righteous, including God's prophets of whom the Lord said, *'Touch not My anointed ones, and do My prophets no harm'.*

Jerusalem kept listening to the wicked false prophets telling untrue visions about peace while there was none. They made up visions and prophecies by their own minds, enabling those who did evil deeds in Jerusalem and the Land.

> *Yes, her prophets find no vision from HaShem ... Your prophets have seen visions for you of vanity and delusion; and they have not uncovered your iniquity, to bring back your captivity; but have prophesied for your burdens of vanity and seduction.*
>
> Lamentations 2

> *Therefore it shall be night unto you, that you shall have no vision; and it shall be dark unto you, that you shall not divine; and the sun shall go down upon the prophets, and the day shall be black over them.*
>
> Micah 3:6

> *We see not Your signs; there is no more any prophet; neither is there among us any that knows how long.*
>
> Psalm 74:9

Jerusalem, virgin daughter of Zion, was the city that once was called the joy of the whole world and the perfection of beauty. To the Lord Jerusalem and its people had become like Sodom and Gomorrah. He compared Jerusalem with worthless wood of the vine, an unfaithful spouse and He said Jerusalem's daughters would be as unfaithful as Jerusalem was. Still, the Lord is always willing to show His mercy.

> *This is what the Sovereign Lord, the Holy One of Israel, says: In repentance and rest is your salvation, in quietness and trust is your strength.*
>
> Isaiah 30:9-11

> *Or else let him take hold of My strength, that he may make peace with Me; yes, let him make peace with Me.*
>
> Isaiah 27:5

> *I love them that love me, and those that seek me earnestly shall find me.*
>
> Proverbs 8:17

The Lord's judgment on His people would not endure for ever, and He would make amends for them. One day the Lord would take vengeance on his enemies and make atonement for His Land and people.* In the meantime He wanted their sincere repentance. As the Lord once told King Solomon, *'If My people, upon whom My name is called, shall humble themselves, and pray, and seek My face, and turn from their evil ways, then will I hear from heaven, and will forgive their sin, and will heal their Land'.*

Therefore by His prophets He told them again and again to return to Him.

> *Return, Israel, to the Lord your God. Your sins have been your downfall! Take words with you and return to the Lord. Say to him: Forgive all our sins and receive us graciously, that we may offer the fruit of our lips.*
>
> Hosea 14:1-2

> *I have blotted out, as a thick cloud, your transgressions, and, as a cloud, your sins; return unto Me, for I have redeemed you.*
>
> Isaiah 44:22

> *And a redeemer will come to Zion, and unto them that turn from transgression in Jacob, says HaShem.*
>
> Isaiah 59:20

Was the Lord too harsh on them? The Lord did teach them again and again to keep His Law, commandments and to live by His moral code. But they didn't want to listen or respond to the Lord's discipline. Despite knowing the consequences, they chose to follow their own path. The punishment He brought over the Children of Israel would gradually bring about remorse and repentance under His people regarding their wrongdoings, and a longing for Him and the Land.

The Lord would then remember them, His covenant with their ancestors and the Land itself, as He told His servant Moses centuries ago. Daniel understood this. He must have known God's word spoken by Moses to the people of Israel centuries earlier, as he prophesied to them about their future disobedience to their God, resulting in the Lord's attempts again and again to turn them away from their wickedness that would ultimately lead them to destruction. Failing to respond to the Lord's warnings and invitations to return to Him, led to their punishment with the hope of their future rehabilitation. In order to save the Children of Israel from their destructive sins, Moses showed them the way back to the Lord. The Almighty God required from them that they would follow the path of humble prayer, sincere repentance and obedience to Him.

> *And they shall confess their iniquity, and the iniquity of their fathers, in their treachery which they committed against Me, and also that they have walked contrary unto Me. I also will walk contrary unto them, and bring them into the land of their enemies; if then perchance their uncircumcised heart be humbled, and they then be paid the punishment of their iniquity; then will I remember My covenant with Jacob, and also My covenant with Isaac, and also My covenant with Abraham will I remember; and I will remember the land.*
> Leviticus 26:39-42

The result of their punishment would be honest remorse making their prayers sincere. The Children of Jacob would then turn their back to evil, abandon wickedness and seek the Lord God of Israel with a truthful, circumcised heart. They would put their trust in Him, hoping for His everlasting love and for Him to care for them with divine kindness.

> *A Song of Ascents.*
> *Out of the depths have I called You, O HaShem.*
> *Lord, hearken unto my voice; let Your ears be attentive to the voice of my supplications.*
> *If You, HaShem, should mark iniquities, O Lord, who could stand?*
> *For with You there is forgiveness, that You may be feared.*
> *I wait for HaShem, my soul does wait, and in His word do I hope.*
> *My soul waits for the Lord, more than watchmen for the morning; yes, more than watchmen for the morning.*
> *O Israel, hope in HaShem; for with HaShem there is mercy, and with Him is plenteous redemption.*
> *And He will redeem Israel from all his iniquities.*
> Psalm 130

As soon as Daniel's prayers of repentance for himself and his family, for the Children of Jacob and their ancestors had reached the Lord, the long process of reconciliation had been put in motion. Despite all their transgressions, the Lord God was willing to reconcile Himself with the Children of Jacob. God Almighty Who is the King and Redeemer of Israel, the One who is the first and the last, would be merciful to them.

> *For the Lord will not cast off for ever. For though He causes grief, yet will He have compassion according to the multitude of His mercies. For He does not afflict willingly, nor grieve the children of men.*
>
> Lamentations 3:31-33
>
> *This I recall to my mind, therefore have I hope. Surely HaShem's mercies are not consumed, surely His compassion fails not.*
>
> Lamentations 3:21-26
>
> *In those days, and in that time, says HaShem, the iniquity of Israel shall be sought for, and there shall be none, and the sins of Judah, and they shall not be found; for I will pardon them who I leave as a remnant.*
>
> Jeremiah 50:20
>
> *Sing, O you heavens, for HaShem has done it; shout, you lowest parts of the earth; break forth into singing, you mountains, O forest, and every tree therein; for HaShem has redeemed Jacob, and does glorify Himself in Israel.*
>
> Isaiah 44:23

The Almighty God that can change the course of bad things into good ones, would in the future bring a turn in Israel's fortunes. He Himself would take away the cup of His wrath from Jerusalem and Israel, as Isaiah prophesied, *"This is what your Sovereign Lord says, your God, who defends His people: 'See, I have taken out of your hand the cup that made you stagger; from that cup, the goblet of my wrath, you will never drink again'."**

So the time of judgment that came over that generation would one day come to an end while the Lord would reconcile Himself with the Children of Jacob as He foretold through His faithful and trustworthy prophets. He Himself would insure that a remnant of Jacob would remain amongst many people of the nations. From these would come forth the ones that would go up to Jerusalem, return to Zion and settle there to stay. God Almighty would gather the exiles of Israel to their homeland, the Land of Israel, and He would build up Jerusalem.

> *Consider you not what this people has spoken, saying: The two families which HaShem did choose, He has cast them off? And they contempt My people, that they should be no more a nation before them.*
>
> Jeremiah 33:24

> *And it shall come to pass that, as you were a curse among the nations, O house of Judah and house of Israel, so will I save you, and you shall be a blessing; fear not, but let your hands be strong.*
>
> Zechariah 8:13

> *And it shall come to pass in that day, that the remnant of Israel, and they that are escaped of the house of Jacob, shall no more again stay upon him that smote them; but shall stay upon HaShem, the Holy One of Israel, in truth. A remnant shall return, even the remnant of Jacob, unto God the Mighty. For though your people, O Israel, be as the sand of the sea, only a remnant of them shall return.*
>
> Isaiah 10:20-22a

It was God's mercy that He who created the Israelites to be their God didn't destroy them. Instead, after He brought judgment over them, He would free the Israelites from the curse which was upon them and they would return to Zion, the Land the Lord gave them as an inheritance. The Lord would take the cup of His wrath away from them, a cup that He later would give to the nations that had punished the Israelites too heavily. For the Lord only wanted to discipline the Children of Jacob, but not reject them. As Obadiah spoke, *'For as you have drunk upon My holy mountain, so shall all the nations drink continually, they shall drink, and swallow down, and shall be as though they had not been'.**

The Lord would take Israel's disgrace away, bring a turn in the Children of Israel's fortune, while offering Judah and Ephraim, Jerusalem and Samaria, the whole of Israel, a new everlasting covenant for their future. They once inhabited and ruled the Land of Israel, and so they would again. There in Jerusalem they would go up to worship the Almighty God.

Who Is David?

> *Behold, I will gather them out of all the countries, ... and I will bring them back unto this place, and I will cause them to dwell safely; and they shall be My people, and I will be their God; and I will give them one heart and one way, that they may fear Me for ever; for the good of them, and of their children after them; and I will make an everlasting covenant with them, that I will not turn away from them, to do them good; and I will put My fear in their hearts, that they shall not depart from Me. I will rejoice over them to do them good, and I will plant them in this Land in truth with My whole heart and with My whole soul. For thus says HaShem: Like as I have brought all this great evil upon this people, so will I bring upon them all the good that I have promised them.*
>
> Jeremiah 32:37-42

> *From afar HaShem appeared unto me. Yes, I have loved you with an everlasting love; therefore with affection have I drawn you. Again will I build you, and you shall be built, O virgin of Israel; again shall you be adorned with your timbrels, and shall go forth in the dances of them that make merry. Again shall you plant vineyards upon the mountains of Samaria; the planters shall plant, and shall have the use thereof. For there shall be a day that the watchmen shall call upon the Mount Ephraim: Arise you, and let us go up to Zion, unto HaShem our God.*
>
> Jeremiah 31:3-4

> *I will put my Spirit in you and you will live, and I will settle you in your own Land. Then you will know that I the Lord have spoken, and I have done it, declares the Lord. ... They will live in the Land I gave to my servant Jacob, the Land where your ancestors lived. They and their children and their children's children will live there for ever, and David my servant will be their prince for ever.*
>
> Ezekiel 37:14-25

After Saul, King David ruled over the unified Land of Israel, the southern Kingdom of Judah and the northern Kingdom of Israel, having Jerusalem as his capital city. The Lord would one day restore David's Zion and have one of David's descendants rule over the unified nation of Israel. That is why the Lord would establish the fallen tabernacle of David.

> *In that day will I raise up the tabernacle of David that has fallen, and close up the breaches thereof, and I will raise up his ruins, and I will build it as in the days of old.*
>
> Amos 9:11

As for the tents of Joseph, including Ephraim who wouldn't have kingship over Israel anymore, the Lord's love for them would remain.

> *Is Ephraim a darling son unto Me? Is he a child that is dandled? For as often as I speak of him, I do earnestly remember him still; therefore My heart yearns for him, I will surely have compassion upon him, says HaShem.*
>
> Jeremiah 31:20

The remnant of His people, the Children of Israel, would again be one nation, both the House of Judah and the House of Israel together, amongst the nations of the world. The Lord would continue to bless nations through the Children of Israel and their nation, Israel.

> *And the remnant of Jacob shall be among the nations, in the midst of many people, as a lion among the beasts of the forest, as a young lion among the flocks of sheep, who, if he goes through, treads down and tears to pieces, and there is none to deliver.*
>
> Micah 5:7

> *That they may possess the remnant of Edom, and all the nations, upon whom My name is called, says HaShem that does this.*
>
> Amos 9:12

The process of them returning to Zion would start with a remnant going up, and this would continue until the time would come for the Lord's Kingdom on earth. Until then, the Children of Israel would have a long period of time to return and restore to the Land of Israel with its capital city Jerusalem. Daniel did speak about God's Kingdom to come when he gave Nebuchadnezzar the meaning of his dream about a large statue made of pure gold, silver, brass, iron, with its feet made part of iron and part of clay. Daniel praised the Lord for revealing this dream and its meaning to him, which saved many lives including his own and that of his friends.

> *Blessed be the name of God from everlasting even unto everlasting; for wisdom and might are His; And He changes*

> the times and the seasons;
> He removes kings, and sets up kings; He gives wisdom unto the wise, and knowledge to them that know understanding.
> He reveals the deep and secret things; He knows what is in the darkness, and the light dwells with Him.
> I thank You, and praise You, O You God of my fathers, who has given me wisdom and might, and has now made known unto me what we desired of You; for You have made known unto us the king's matter.
>
> Daniel 2:20-23

When would the Lord begin His restoration of Jerusalem and His Land? After the Land had enjoyed the Shabbat (Sabbath) years it had missed. It was desolate without the Children of Israel to attend to it for seventy years.

> As long as it lies desolate it shall have rest; even the rest which it had not in your Sabbaths, when you dwelt upon it.
>
> Leviticus 26:35

> For thus says HaShem: After seventy years are accomplished for Babylon, I will remember you, and perform My good word toward you, in causing you to return to this place.
>
> Jeremiah 29:10

> Then the angel of the Lord said, Lord Almighty, how long will you withhold mercy from Jerusalem and from the towns of Judah, which You have been angry with these seventy years? ... I will return to Jerusalem with mercy, and there My house will be rebuilt. And the measuring line will be stretched out over Jerusalem, declares the Lord Almighty. Proclaim further: This is what the Lord Almighty says: My towns will again overflow with prosperity, and the Lord will again comfort Zion and choose Jerusalem.
>
> Zechariah 1:12-17

The Lord, who again and again made it clear to all the Children of Jacob, to both the House of Judah and the House of Israel, to be faithful to Him in living in obedience to His Law and stipulations, would bring the Children of Jacob out of exile. In exile they would have been like dew for the nations where they lived, while experiencing persecution and hardships, as Daniel clearly experienced, and many others as well.

Meanwhile the Lord would still care for them. When the time would come for them to be gathered out of exile, a remnant would go up to Jerusalem and return to the Land. Others would go out of exile, but not to return to the Land.

> *To everything there is a season, and a time to every purpose under the heaven.*
>
> Ecclesiastes 3:1

The Lord would lead them out of exile, to go into the desert of the nations, as their ancestors once went into the desert of Egypt, where the Lord, despite everything, cared for them during their journey, so their children could enter the Promised Land.

> *As I live, says the Lord God, surely with a mighty hand, and with an outstretched arm, and with fury poured out, will I be king over you; and I will bring you out from the people, and will gather you out of the countries wherein you are scattered, with a mighty hand, and with an outstretched arm, and with fury poured out; and I will bring you into the wilderness of the people, and there I will plead with you face to face. Like as I pleaded with your fathers in the wilderness of the land of Egypt, so will I plead with you, says the Lord God. And I will cause you to pass under the rod, and I will bring you into the bond of the covenant; and I will purge out from among you the rebels, and them that transgress against Me; I will bring them forth out of the land where they sojourn, but they shall not enter into the land of Israel; and you shall know that I am HaShem.*
>
> Ezekiel 20:33-38

As for those who would be part of the remnant, the Lord warned them, as He did to their ancestors since they were in the wilderness of Egypt, not to make the same mistakes their forefathers and parents made, but to live by His commandments and keep the Shabbat as a holy day, to remember that the Almighty God is the One that is their God. For those who would keep these, would live in prosperity. The Lord already knew all the plans He had in store for them.

> *Walk you not in the statutes of your fathers, neither observe their ordinances, nor defile yourselves with their idols; I am HaShem your God; walk in My statutes, and keep My ordinances, and do them; and hallow My Sabbaths, and they*

> *shall be a sign between Me and you, that you may know that I am HaShem your God.*
>
> Ezekiel 20:18-20
>
> *For I know the thoughts that I think toward you, says HaShem, thoughts of peace, and not of evil, to give you a future and a hope. And you shall call upon Me, and go, and pray unto Me, and I will hearken unto you. And you shall seek Me, and find Me, when you shall search for Me with all your heart. And I will be found of you, says HaShem.*
>
> Jeremiah 29:11-14

The Lord wouldn't only forgive them for their sins and return them to the Land of Israel, but He also promised that one day each and everyone would be held responsible for their own sins. The children would no longer be punished for the sins of their fathers.

> *And the word of HaShem came unto me, saying: What mean you, that you use this proverb in the land of Israel, saying: The fathers have eaten sour grapes, and the children's teeth are set on edge? As I live, says the Lord God, you shall not have occasion anymore to use this proverb in Israel. Behold, all souls are Mine; as the soul of the father, so also the soul of the son is Mine; the soul that sins, it shall die.*
>
> Ezekiel 18:1-4

The Lord Himself would stir up the spirit of one of the kings of Persia to allow the remnant of the Children of Judah to go up to Zion, with Zion referring to Jerusalem with its hills, as well as to the Land of Israel. All those living in exile would be allowed to go but only a fraction of them would actually return.

> *All the kingdoms of the earth has HaShem, the God of heaven, given me; and He has charged me to build Him a house in Jerusalem, which is in Judah. Whosoever there is among you of all His people – his God be with him – let him go up to Jerusalem, which is in Judah, and build the house of HaShem, the God of Israel. He is the God who is in Jerusalem. And whosoever is left, in any place where he sojourns, let the men of his place help him with silver, and with gold, and with goods, and with beasts, beside the freewill-offering for the house of God which is in Jerusalem.*

> *Then rose up the heads of the fathers' houses of Judah and Benjamin, and the priests, and the Levites, even all whose spirit God had stirred to go up to build the house of HaShem which is in Jerusalem.*
>
> Ezra 1:1-5

The return of the Children of Israel to the Land would be a process taking centuries to complete.

For some, going up would be peaceful, others would have to flee out of the country where they were residing. The Lord who also spoke of the Children of Israel as being Zion, He Himself called Zion to flee and return to Jerusalem and the Land, as His word spoken by Zechariah says, 'Ho, ho, flee then from the land of the north, says HaShem; for I have spread you abroad as the four winds of the heaven, says HaShem. Ho, Zion, escape, you that dwells with the daughter of Babylon'.*

And along the way the Lord God Himself would give the necessary strength and support to all those He gathers in the Land.

> *Have you not known? Have you not heard that the everlasting God, HaShem, the Creator of the ends of the earth, faints not, neither is weary? His understanding is past searching out. He gives power to the faint; and to him that has no might He increases strength. ... But they that wait for HaShem shall renew their strength; they shall mount up with wings as eagles; they shall run, and not be weary; they shall walk, and not faint.*
>
> Isaiah 40:28-31

The Almighty God created the Israelites through the Patriarchs Abraham, Isaac and Jacob, and the Matriarchs Sarah, Rebecca, Leah and Rachel to be His servant and witness. He would still bless them so that all the nations of the world would know about their salvation and would fear Him. In this manner He blesses the nations as well. He once assured the Children of Israel's existence through Joseph, later He set them free from slavery out of Egypt, and under the leadership of Moses He brought them to the Promised Land to plant them there. Joshua divided the Land among them as their inheritance. Then the Lord gave them David to fulfil His plans. One day the people that He had chosen would become a nation again in the Land that the Lord God Himself tends to.

> *Ask you of HaShem rain in the time of the latter rain, even of HaShem that makes lightnings; and He will give them showers of rain, to every one grass in the field.*
>
> Zechariah 10:1
>
> *Yet now hear, O Jacob My servant, and Israel, who I have chosen; Thus says HaShem that made you, and formed you from the womb, who will help you: Fear not, O Jacob My servant, and you, Jeshurun**, whom I have chosen. For I will pour water upon the thirsty land, and streams upon the dry ground; I will pour My spirit upon your seed, and My blessing upon your offspring; And they shall spring up among the grass, as willows by the watercourses.*
>
> Isaiah 44:1-4

The Lord would keep His new covenant with the Children of Israel through generations to come. He would never reject, but redeem His people who He had formed, because of His love for them and their ancestors. He wouldn't ever forsake His allotted inheritance, Jacob.

> *And as for Me, this is My covenant with them, says HaShem; My spirit that is upon you, and My words which I have put in your mouth, shall not depart out of your mouth, nor out of the mouth of your seed, nor out of the mouth of your seed's seed, says HaShem, from henceforth and for ever.*
>
> Isaiah 59:21
>
> *But now thus says HaShem that created you, O Jacob, and He that formed you, O Israel: Fear not, for I have redeemed you, I have called you by your name, you are Mine. When you pass through the waters, I will be with you, and through the rivers, they shall not overflow you; when you walk through the fire, you shall not be burned, neither shall the flame kindle upon you.*
>
> *For I am HaShem your God, The Holy One of Israel, your Saviour; I have given Egypt as your ransom, Ethiopia and Seba for you. Since you are precious in My sight, and honourable, and I have loved you; therefore will I give men for you, and people for your life.*
>
> Isaiah 43:1-4

As for David's capital city of Jerusalem, the city the Lord had chosen to put His name, He would choose it again, and He would dwell in the midst of it.

Thus says HaShem: Behold, I will turn the captivity of Jacob's tents, and have compassion on his dwelling-places; and the city shall be built upon her own mound, and the palace shall be inhabited upon its proper place.

Jeremiah 30:18

HaShem will be a refuge unto His people, and a stronghold to the children of Israel. So shall you know that I am HaShem your God, dwelling in Zion My holy mountain; then shall Jerusalem be holy, and there shall no strangers pass through her anymore.

Joel 3:16-17

O praise HaShem, all you nations; laud Him, all you people. For His mercy is great toward us; and the truth of HaShem endures for ever. Hallelujah.

Psalm 117

Endnotes

**Micah 4:8, Genesis 35:19-21 Migdal-eder, in Hebrew 'Tower of Eder', meaning 'Tower of the flock', located near present day Bethlehem, a city southeast of Jerusalem. The exact location isn't known. ** Isaiah 43:1-4 Jeshurun means 'the upright', and is Israel. Deuteronomy 32:15, 33:5a, 26.

* Jeremiah 51:50, Daniel 9:24, Jeremiah 11:16a, Isaiah 27:6, Habakkuk 2:18-19, Habakkuk 1:2-4, 1 Samuel 15:22, Deuteronomy 32:47, Jeremiah 7:23, Psalm 51:17, 2 Chronicles 7:15-16, Jeremiah 3:4-5, Amos 3:2, Deuteronomy 8:19-20, Jeremiah 2:22, Jeremiah 32:19, Ezekiel 22:23-24, Deuteronomy 32:43, Psalm 105:15, 2 Chronicles 7:14, Isaiah 51:22, Obadiah 16, Zechariah 2:10-11.

Daniel 1, 3, 6, Habakkuk 2:3-4 Daniel and his friends, the righteous lives by his faith

Psalm 147:4, Ezra 1:2, 7:13,21,23, 5:11 God of heaven and earth

Leviticus 25:38, 25:44-46a, 47-55, 48-49 rules to slavery

Leviticus 21:6-8, 22:9-16, 23:1-2, 26:43, 45 holiness priests, Shabbat years, remember the covenant

Isaiah 9:15, Jeremiah 23:14-16, 32:31-32, Ezekiel 13:16, Micah 3:11, Zephaniah 3:4 false prophets

Jeremiah 23:14-16, Lamentations 4:13 Jerusalem like Sodom and Gomorrah, kills the righteous

Who Is David?

Isaiah 59:1-15, Jeremiah 2:7, 2:21, 16:17, Hosea 5:1, 9:10 sinfulness, the Land defiled, the vine
Leviticus 17:1-9, 20:1-5, 2 Chronicles 11:15, Isaiah 34:14, 65:3, 66:3 offerings to demons
Exodus 38:8, 1 Samuel 2:22-36, 3:11-14, 4:1-22, Hosea 4:6-19 Eli, prostitution, priests' sinfulness
Leviticus 26:14-46, 2 Chronicles 24:20, Jeremiah 7:21-28, 34, Jeremiah 8:10 judgment
Ezekiel 15-16,22-24, 23:33-34, Isaiah 51 sinfulness Samaria and Jerusalem, the cup
Deuteronomy 32:43, Psalm 32, 51, Isaiah 1:16-20, 45:22-23, 65:1 amends, God's forgiveness
Isaiah 6:6-7, Micha 7:18-19, Lamentations 1:7, 3:40-42 God's forgiveness, repentance
Isaiah 61:8, Jeremiah 9:23-24, Jeremiah 32:19 God loves righteousness and hates theft, rewards
Deuteronomy 1:16-18, Judges 11:27 judges no favouritism, God the Highest Judge
Deuteronomy 31, 32 the Land as inheritance, Law and prophecy, Moses' song, Jacob as inheritance
Deuteronomy 32:29-42, Isaiah 44:6 no one escapes God's power, the first and last, the only God
Isaiah 30, 66, Hosea 14, Ezekiel 14:6 sinfulness, judgment and hope, repentance and blessings
Genesis 12:1-3, Psalm 67:2,7, Psalm 94:14 God's blessings for the Israelites and nations
Psalm 78:38-39, Isaiah 27:11, 43:1-7,15, not total destruction, He created the Israelites
Ezekiel 20:44, Isaiah 51, Zechariah 1:15 punishment less than deserved, cup to the nations
Deuteronomy 8:15-18, Isaiah 43:22-24, Hosea 6 God cares for His people, truthful repentance
Isaiah 25:8, Zechariah 8:13 Israel's disgrace taken away, the Israelites free from the curse
Psalm 147:2, Isaiah 43:18-21 God builds Jerusalem, He would make something new
Isaiah 43:1-4,9d-10, 13, 43:11-12,14 Israel's Saviour, Israel is God's witness, deliverance
2 Chronicles 36:11-20, 36:21, 22-23 Judah's disobedience, the Land had to rest, the king's edict
Leviticus 4:3, 10:8-11, Lamentations 2:7 high priest and priests, God rejected His altar
Exodus 20:9, 12, Leviticus 19:3-4, Zechariah 10:2 don't be misled by idols and false gods

The Reconciliation

Exodus 34:7, Deuteronomy 5:9, Jeremiah 31:29-30 punish children for the sins of their fathers

Isaiah 5:1-7, 27:2-6 , 27:7-9, Amos 9:8-10 Israel and Judah are God's vineyard, atonement, remnant

Exodus 20:13, Deuteronomy 26:12-15, Ezekiel 20:13, 20 obedience to God's regulations, prosperity

Genesis 45:7, 50:20, Zechariah 2:12 Joseph, God's goodness and choosing Jerusalem, inherit Judah

Intermezzo Endnotes

Ezra 1:1, 5:14 Cyrus king of Persia, Koresh

Ezra 4:6, 4:24, 5:6, Esther 1:1, 2:16-18 Ahasuerus Esther's husband, Darius the Persian Esther's son

Daniel 5:11, 6:1, 9:1, Nehemiah 2:1, Ezra 1:1, 4:3-7, 11, 23, 5:11 Babylonian and Persian kings

Ezra 7:1,7, Nehemiah 2:1 Ezra left in 7th year of Artaxerxes, Nehemiah in 20th

* Ezra 7:8, Nehemiah 2:1-9 Ezra and Nehemiah's arrival in Jerusalem

* Ezra 9:9 Ezra mentions the wall and the Temple

THE RETURN TO ZION

Depart you, depart you, go you out from there, touch no unclean thing; go you out of the midst of her; be you clean, you that bear the vessels of HaShem. For you shall not go out in haste, neither shall you go by flight; for HaShem will go before you, and the God of Israel will be your rear guard.

Isaiah 52:11-12

Nehemiah son of Hakaliah was in Susan (Susa), the capital city of Babylonia, where he inquired from his brother Hanani and the men from Judah about the Jews that lived in Jerusalem and Judah. Years earlier this group of Jews left the Babylonian captivity under the leadership of Sheshbazzar* to go up to Jerusalem, returning to the Land of their ancestors. At that time, in answer to Daniel's prayers, He aroused the spirit of Cyrus the king of Persia during his first year of reign. The king then, convinced that the Temple of the Lord of heaven should be rebuilt, issued an edict in all his kingdom proclaiming that the Children of Judah and Benjamin, the Jews, should go up to Jerusalem in Judah. This meant that all the Jews were allowed to return to their homeland, where they were to rebuild the Temple of the Lord on Mount Zion and settle in the Land of Judah. The Lord aroused the spirit of the Jews as well, and the leader of Judah, Sheshbazzar, acted on this by making arrangements together with the head of the families of Judah and Benjamin, the Kohanim and the Levites for the people to return. A remnant of Judah's and Benjamin's descendants were the first to ascend to Jerusalem. With them the return of the Jacob's Children out of exile to Zion had started. This process of return would continue until it would reach its completion in the far future, when the Jewish Messiah would come to the City of the King, Jerusalem, to rule. And so, the Lord's prophecy given to Jeremiah, seventy years earlier, came to pass.

The Jews ascended to Jerusalem with gifts of silver and gold, valuables, animals and cattle, some of which they also received from their neighbours as the king had ordered. They returned with the vessels of the Lord's Temple, which Nebuchadnezzar had taken from God's Sanctuary, and now were returned by Cyrus, along with contributions for the Temple. Also returned were the vessels which Nebuchadnezzar's son Belshazar, who was king at the time, had used to drink wine, an act for which the Lord removed him from power. The artefacts of the Temple included the Urim and the Tummim, which were used by the priests to determine God's will for Israel, something they also did for King David.

Among the exiles that ascended to Jerusalem were Sheshbazzar, the leader of Judah who the king made their governor, Mordechai (Bilshan)*, the children of the Governor of Moab*, along with the Kohanim and the Levites with their families. The Nethinim, descendants of the Gibeonites who were assigned to do work for the Temple of the Lord, also left with them. They did manual tasks such as water-drawing and woodcutting. Although they were allowed to live among the Jews by Joshua at the time the Israelites conquered Canaan to establish themselves in the Promised Land, intermarriages were not permitted. More than seven thousand male and female slaves also went with the Jews. Two hundred male and female singers returned with them while singing songs of praise, thanksgiving and joy. The entire congregation that went up to Zion numbered more than forty-two thousand people.

When they arrived in Jerusalem, the heads of the families went to the site of God's Sanctuary. They brought their contributions to the work fund for the re-establishment of God's Temple. The people settled in the cities of Judah. They, the Kohen Gadol Joshua, son of Jozadak, with the priests and Zerubbabel son of Shealtiel with his brothers, built the altar of the Temple of the Lord and from the first day of the seventh month they offered burnt offerings to the Lord in accordance to His commandments. From that day on, they continued to offer burnt offerings to the Lord in the mornings, the evenings, and during the sanctified festivals of the Lord. The first festival they observed was the Festival of Sukkoth, and they would also bring burnt offerings to the Lord during the feast of the New Moon. The foundations of the Temple of the Lord however had not been laid. It would not be until the second year of their arrival in Jerusalem that the construction work on the Temple would start. They paid the quarries and carpenters, and they also made arrangements with the Sidonians and Tyrians as well, paying them with food, drink and oil. They were the ones in charge of the transportation of the necessary cedar wood from Lebanon to the Sea of Jaffa as Cyrus, king of Persia had authorised. When the workers had finished laying the foundations of the Lord's Temple, they all praised the Lord with Psalms of David, the king of Israel. Those who were very happy shouted with a great shout, while some remembering the splendour of the first Temple built by Solomon, wept.

> *I will heal their backsliding, I will love them freely; for My anger is turned away from him. I will be as the dew unto Israel; he shall blossom as the lily, and cast forth his roots as Lebanon. His branches shall spread, and his beauty shall be as the olive tree, and his fragrance as Lebanon. They that dwell under his shadow shall again make corn to grow, and shall blossom as the vine; the scent thereof shall be as the wine of Lebanon.*
>
> Hosea 14:5-8

Leaders of the foreign tribes, non-Israelites living in Samaria, came to ask Zerubbabel and the heads of the families to work on the Temple of the Lord together with them for as they said, they too worshipped the God of Israel. These Samaritans were the descendants of the foreign tribes installed in Samaria by the Assyrians when Sennacherib deported the Israelites, the ten tribes of Israel, to other places at the time the Kingdom of Israel fell. The Jews answered that they had to build the Temple for the God of Israel by themselves as Cyrus, king of Persia had commanded. Moreover, these people didn't worship the Lord God as they should, as the Lord God commanded He wished to be worshipped, and with offerings brought in accordance to His stipulations. The Jews may have also suspected that these Samaritans were not as trustworthy as they pretended to be, in which case they could sabotage the construction work on the Temple. Soon the true intentions of these people became clear, when they took hostile actions against the Jewish people.

During the days of Cyrus, king of Persia, also called Cyrus the Persian, until the second year of the reign of Darius the Persian, these people would try to disrupt the plans of the Jews or frighten them from rebuilding God's Sanctuary. They even hired advisers against them and wrote official letters to the kings of Persia; letters that showed how much the Samaritans opposed their construction efforts out of fear for the Jews. Their correspondence was in Aramaic, the official language in those days.

One of the letters that the Jews' opponents wrote was to Artaxerxes* who was king of Persia. In this letter written by Rehum the counsellor, commanding officer, and Shimshai the scribe, secretary, who lived in Samaria, they told the king that the Jews were doing construction work in the city of Jerusalem where they were rebuilding the Lord's Sanctuary. They warned him that, should the Jews succeed, they would no longer pay levy, tax and duty to him causing damage to the royal revenue. They also requested the king to examine the book of records where he would find that Jerusalem was a rebellious city which was destroyed in the past, because of its insurrections since ancient days that brought damages to kings and their provinces. Therefore a restored city of Jerusalem would be a threat to the king and his dominion over the Trans-Euphrates region.

After research in the books of record by the king's officials, the king replied with a message to Rehum, Shimshai and the rest of the Trans-Euphrates region. In his letter the king informed them of the findings of his officials, which was a confirmation of their earlier message. He also wrote that mighty kings once reigned over Jerusalem. They had dominion over all of the Trans-Euphrates region that paid them levy, tax and duty. He instructed them to issue a decree to halt the work. Until a decree was issued by the king himself, the city would not be built. As soon as they heard this message, Rehum and Shimshai, and those with them went to Jerusalem and stopped the construction work of the Jews. Sometime later, the Jews' opponents would write more letters, of which one would have an unexpected outcome. But for now, as a result of the king's decision, the work on the Temple of the Lord was halted for a long time.

> *This is the word of HaShem unto Zerubbabel, saying: Not by might, nor by power, but by My Spirit, said HaShem of hosts. Who are you, O great mountain before Zerubbabel? You shall become a plain; and he shall bring forth the top stone with shoutings of Grace, grace, unto it. Moreover the word of HaShem came unto me, saying: The hands of Zerubbabel have laid the foundation of this house; his hands shall also finish it.*
> Zechariah 4:6-9

Eighteen years* later, during Darius the Persian's second year of reign, the prophets Haggai and Zechariah son of Iddo prophesied that the work on the Lord's Temple would be finished. They encouraged them to restart the construction work regardless of their enemies' efforts to obstruct it. At that time part of the walls of the Lord's Temple were built but the construction of it had not been completed. The prophets continued to support Zerubbabel and Joshua to inspire the people to continue with the work. Once they restarted, Tattenai who was the governor of the Trans-Euphrates region with Shethar-bozenai and their accomplices approached the Jews to ask them by whose authority they were building the Lord's Temple. But, they

Who Is David?

didn't halt the work. Instead they brought the matter before the king. They sent a message informing him that in the province of Judah the Temple of the Great God was rapidly being built of marble stone with wood reinforcing its walls.

They also wrote the Jews' reply to their question about their permission to build. They said, *'We are the servants of the God of heaven and earth, and build the house that was built these many years ago, which a great king of Israel built and finished. But because our fathers had provoked the God of heaven, He gave them into the hand of Nebuchadnezzar king of Babylon, the Chaldean, who destroyed this house, and carried the people away into Babylon. But in the first year of Cyrus king of Babylon, Cyrus the king made a decree to build this house of God. And the gold and silver vessels also of the house of God, which Nebuchadnezzar took out of the Temple that was in Jerusalem, and brought them into the temple of Babylon, those did Cyrus the king take out of the temple of Babylon, and they were delivered unto one whose name was Sheshbazzar, who he had made governor; and he said unto him: Take these vessels, go, put them in the Temple that is in Jerusalem, and let the house of God be built in its place. Then came the same Sheshbazzar, and laid the foundations of the house of God which is in Jerusalem; and since that time even until now had it been in building, and yet it is not completed'.**

The Jews didn't mention the king's decree that had halted the construction work.

Like those before them, these men requested the king to have his officials conduct a search in the royal archives in Babylon. By Darius' orders a search to find Cyrus' first decree concerning the Lord's Temple was done in the archives at the library in Babylonia. The king's reply to Tattenai stated that he should leave the construction of the Temple of God where it stood to the governor of the Jews and their elders, and distance himself from this place. He was to cooperate immediately with the elders of the Jews providing whatever they required and the expenses for these were to be paid from the taxes of the Trans-Euphrates' royal estate, thus enabling the work to continue until completion. In addition Tattenai was to supply whatever the Jews needed for the burnt-offerings dedicated to the God of heaven every day without failing, such as young bulls, sheep, rams, but also salt, wheat, olive oil and wine; all in accordance to the specifications of the Lord's priests there in Jerusalem. The king wanted to ensure that pleasing offerings would be brought to the God of heaven, and also prayers for his life and that of his children would be done. He also issued severe punishment for those who would refuse to implement his decree. A beam would be torn out of his house upon which he would be hanged and his house would be designated a dung area. As for those who would try to damage the Temple of God in Jerusalem, Darius wrote that, *'May the God that had caused His name to dwell there overthrow all kings and people, that shall put forth their hand to alter the same, to destroy this House of God which is at Jerusalem'.**

Tettenai acted speedily on all the king had stated in his decree.

By the decree of the God of Israel, and that of the Persian kings Cyrus, Darius and Artaxerxes, the Lord's Sanctuary was completed in the sixth year of Darius' reign on the third day of the month of Adar. The prophecies of Haggai and Zechariah regarding finishing the Lord's Temple came to pass. The inauguration of the Lord's Temple was a celebration by the Jews including those who stayed behind in the Land during the seventy years of exile. The Kohanim and the Levites also took part in this gathering. They brought sin-offerings corresponding with the number of tribes of Israel. The priests were established in their groups and so were the Levites in their divisions; all according to the regulations as written in the Book of Moses. From that day on, the Temple of the Lord continued to be of service to the Jews. Later on the fourteenth day of the first month they brought Pesach-offerings and celebrated the Festival of Matzos, unleavened bread, for seven days.

> *But now says HaShem that created you, O Jacob, and He that formed you, O Israel: Fear not, for I have redeemed you, I have called you by your name, you are Mine. When you pass through the waters, I will be with you, and through the rivers, they shall not overflow you; when you walk through the fire, you shall not be burned, neither shall the flame kindle upon you. For I am HaShem your God, The Holy One of Israel, your Saviour.*
>
> Isaiah 43:1-3a

Now, in the month of Kislev in the twentieth year of Artaxerxes'* reign, after the completion of the Second Temple of the Lord, which took fourteen years, Jerusalem's wall was still breached and its gates which had been burned down by Nebuchadnezzar were still not repaired, leaving Jerusalem a vulnerable city lacking protection for its inhabitants. The Jews lived in great misery and humiliation as Hanani, Nehemiah's brother, was very clear about this difficult situation of

Who Is David?

the Jews in Jerusalem and Judah. Nehemiah wept, grieved, fasted and prayed to the God of heavens for days because of what his brother Hanani and the men from Judah had told him. He prayed, *'I beseech You, O HaShem, the God of heaven, the great and awesome God, that kept covenant and mercy with them that love Him and keep His commandments; let Your ear now be attentive, and Your eyes open, that You may hearken unto the prayer of Your servant, which I pray before You at this time, day and night, for the children of Israel Your servants, while I confess the sins of the children of Israel, which we have sinned against You; yes, I and my father's house have sinned. We have dealt very corruptly against You, and have not kept the commandments, nor the statutes, nor the ordinances which You did command Your servant Moses. Remember, I beseech You, the word that You did command Your servant Moses, saying: If you deal treacherously, I will scatter you abroad among the people; but if you return unto Me, and keep My commandments and do them, though your dispersed were in the uttermost part of the heaven, yet will I gather them and will bring them unto the place that I have chosen to cause My name to dwell there. Now these are Your servants and Your people, who You have redeemed by Your great power, and by Your strong hand. O Lord, I beseech You, let now Your ear be attentive to the prayer of Your servant, and to the prayer of Your servants, who delight to fear Your name; and prosper, I pray You, Your servant this day, and grant him mercy in the sight of this man'.**

A few months later, in the month of Nissan, Nehemiah brought wine to the king, Darius the son of Queen Esther, who noticed he was downhearted, something Nehemiah had never done before. When the king inquired of him what the matter was, Nehemiah became very afraid. But still he told the king, and the queen who was sitting beside him, about his ancestor's city and that its wall and gates were in ruin. The king asked him what his request was. Then he prayed to the God of heaven and afterwards he answered by asking the king if he would send him to Judah to rebuild his ancestors' Jerusalem. The king granted him his request, and they agreed on the time of his return to Susan. Then the king gave him his leave, and as Nehemiah requested he also gave him letters for the governors of the Trans-Euphrates region and a letter for Asaph. The governors were to grant him safe passage until he reaches Judah, and Asaph, who was the keeper of the king's forest, had to supply him with timber for the construction work on Jerusalem's wall and gates, and for his new home there. The king also provided for an escort of army officers and horsemen to go with him. Nehemiah went up to Jerusalem seeking to contribute to the welfare of the Children of Israel in Jerusalem and Judah.

> *Do good in Your favour unto Zion; build Yourself the walls of Jerusalem.*
>
> Psalm 51:20

Three days after his arrival in Judah, Nehemiah went, accompanied by a few people, to inspect the wall. He went at night, but he didn't inform the nobles, aristocrats, priests and the construction workers about where he was going, nor about his intentions. He kept to himself what the Lord had conveyed to him to do for Jerusalem. It was after his inspection that he spoke of God's grace, granting him all which he needed for his task through the king. He encouraged them to build the wall and gates so they would no longer be subject to humiliation. They resolved to do the work for the city together. But their enemies Sanballat the Horonite, and Tobiah the Ammonite, who had been ridiculing the Jews, expressed their contempt towards them. These men were already extremely disturbed when they heard about Nehemiah and his plans. Geshem, an Arab slave, joined them in expressing contempt towards the Jews. Nehemiah's reaction, *'The God of heaven, He will prosper us; therefore we His servants will arise and build; but you have no portion, nor right, nor memorial, in Jerusalem'.**

The Jews started with restoring the stones they could use to build and reinforce the wall, and they worked to put its doors in place. Each group built at the section of the wall they were assigned to work on. They worked side by side to seal the breaches of the wall. Starting with Eliashib the High Priest who together with the priests rebuilt the Sheep Gate and made its doors after which they sanctified that part of the wall up to the towers of Hananel and the Hundred. The eastern, northern, western and the southern walls were also rebuilt. The Nethinim who stayed in the Ophel also did their assigned section of the work. So did Rephaiah son of Hur, who was the officer ruling over half of Jerusalem's district. They all worked dispersed along the wall. Sanballat became extremely angry and enraged when he heard of the Israelites' construction activities. He and Tobiah ridiculed them before his companions and the people living in Samaria. Nehemiah prayed, *'Hear, O our God; for we are despised; and turn back their reproach upon their own head, and give them up to spoiling in a land*

of captivity; and cover not their iniquity, and let not their sin be blotted out from before You; for they have vexed You before the builders'.*
The Jews continued their work. After they joined the wall half way, the people were happy with what they had accomplished.

As long as the work was progressing, the enemies of the Jews plotted against them. At times they would even succeed in halting the construction and restoration work for some years. Sanballat and Tobiah together with the Arabs, Ammonites and the Ashdodites tried to bring about confusion to disrupt the work and if possible halt it. Again and again Jews living in the area among the non-Jews warned Nehemiah and the builders about them. Some of the workers became afraid, but Nehemiah encouraged them to trust the Lord to fight for their land and family, and to continue with their work. After Nehemiah's prayers to the Lord, he came up with a plan to insure the safety of the workers so the work would not be halted. He took measures to protect them by posting guards beneath the site, on the cliffs and behind the wall to watch day and night over them. He put the workers in groups by family and armed them. Some had swords, others spears or bows to keep each other safe. They worked with one hand, and used the other to hold their weapon. Half of the able men stood guard and half built. Those who built did so with one hand holding a weapon while lifting and carrying burdens with the other. The builders had their swords girded to their side as they built. In case of an emergency, one man who stayed with Nehemiah would sound the shofar so they would know where they should gather. The officers and the House of Judah backed Nehemiah's effort. He told the leaders, the officials and the people that God would fight for them all. The work was so extensive that they built from dawn until after sunset under a sky full of stars. Nehemiah told the leaders and their helpers that they should remain in Jerusalem at night to guard the city. Nehemiah didn't take the time to take off his clothes nor did his companions, servants and guards, while they all kept their weapon with them.

One day a most urgent matter came to Nehemiah's attention, the outcry of those who were oppressed by the nobles and aristocrats. Some of these people had to buy grain for their numerous children to keep them alive for they didn't have enough themselves. Others had to borrow money to pay the king's tax while they gave their fields and vineyards as a guarantee. There were those whose children were pressed into slavery, or to become servants while they didn't have the means to redeem them because their vineyards and fields were held by others. Nehemiah was moved by all this and he was very angry with the nobles and aristocrats who, after some thought, gathered to confront them with these issues. He told them that they had ransomed their fellow Jews from the gentiles to whom they sold themselves out of necessity, and thus became their slaves, only for these Jews to sell themselves back to them? The nobles and aristocrats remained silent. He continued by saying that they should act in fear, awe of God because of the reproach of their enemies. He himself, with his brothers and servants, had lent people money and corn to help them. He said, *'Restore, I pray you, to them, even this day, their fields, their vineyards, their olive yards, and their houses, also the hundred pieces of silver, and the corn, the wine, and the oil, that you exact of them'.*

Then said they: *'We will restore them, and will require nothing of them; so will we do, even as you say. Then I called the priests, and took an oath of them, that they should do according to this promise'.**

Nehemiah also said, *'So God shake out every man from his house, and from his labour, that performs not this promise; even thus be he shaken out, and emptied'. And all the congregation said: 'Amen', and praised HaShem. And the people did according to this promise.**

Out of reverence for God, Nehemiah himself refused to accept the governor's food as long as he was the appointed governor of the Land of Judah since the twentieth year until the thirty-second year of Artaxerxes' reign. He didn't, as the previous governors did, impose burdens on the people, take their wine and breath, take payment in silver from them, nor did he have his servants predominate over them. Instead Nehemiah put all his resources and the manpower at his disposal, that would otherwise have to do farming or other work to provide for an income for him, to support the repair and restoration of the wall. By doing so, he didn't have to buy farmland, or a field from the people living there when he settled in Judah. It was clear that Nehemiah set an example for all of them.

By the time the breaches in the wall were rebuilt and only the doors had to be placed in the gateways, Judah's enemies tried to find ways to harm Nehemiah. Sanballat, Tobiah and Geshem received report of the progress made on Jerusalem's wall, and they sent an invitation to Nehemiah for a meeting in one of the villages in the valley of Ono. This invitation went out up to four times. But each time Nehemiah replied the same way, by sending messengers to tell them, *'I am doing a great work, so that I cannot come down; why should the work cease, whilst I leave it, and come down to you'?**

The fifth time Sanballat sent him an open letter in which he accused Nehemiah and the Jews of planning to rebel against the king, so Nehemiah could become their king. The accusations went further saying that Nehemiah had also arranged for prophets to proclaim that he was the king of Judah. Sanballat also threatened Nehemiah telling him that the king would hear about all this. To prevent this, it would be best for Nehemiah to meet with him to resolve this matter. Nehemiah replied that everything he said were lies and again he refused to meet with him. He did go to the house of Shemaiah son of Delaiah who was confined indoors. This man spoke to Nehemiah as if he was prophesying for him telling him to go with him into the Sanctuary of the Temple to save his life for there were people coming to kill him. But Nehemiah realised this man was telling him to disobey God's commands concerning His Sanctuary. Tobiah and Sanballat could have hired him to cause Nehemiah to sin, to give his enemies a reason for a scandal against him which would have caused much trouble hindering the construction work. Nehemiah's enemies themselves were doing exactly what they were accusing him of, by hiring false prophets and spreading lies. They continued to do so by hiring Noadiah the prophetess and others to speak out false prophecies against Nehemiah. They didn't stop their efforts to intimidate Nehemiah, and they had support of some of the Jewish aristocrats, who wrote letters to him. There were also some people living in Judah that allied themselves with Tobiah because of his association with and family ties to people of standing. They would even recite Tobiah's merits to Nehemiah, while Tobiah kept sending letters to discourage him. Nevertheless the wall was completed the twenty-fifth of Elul. After the wall was finished and its gates were put in place, tasks were designated to the gatekeepers, the singers and the other Levites. The Lord accomplished this work with the Jews under governor Nehemiah's leadership.

Jerusalem was a large city with wide open spaces and with houses still in ruins. There weren't many people living in the city to watch over it and to keep the infiltrations out. So Nehemiah also appointed his brother Hanani and Hananiah, a God-fearing and honest man who was officer of the palace, over Jerusalem. He gave them instructions concerning the security of Jerusalem and the inhabitants within its wall. Jerusalem's gates were to be opened by the gatekeepers only for a very short while during the heat of the day to let people pass through. People were also appointed as watchers. Each man was to keep watch opposite to his own home.

Nehemiah found the Book of Lineage of the Jews who went up to Zion the first time during Cyrus, the king of Persia's reign. He felt inspired by the Lord to assemble the nobles, aristocrats and the people to have them trace their lineage. In the book those who returned were registered by family and by city, including the Kohanim and Levites who ministered to the Lord's Temple, the Nethinim, and the descendants of Salomon's slaves. Those who went up but could not declare their descent, the families of their fathers, were also registered in the book. Three Kohanim families who couldn't find the genealogical record of their family were listed as well. There was also a record of the leaders' contributions for the work, to the treasury or to the work fund.

One day all the people gathered at the plaza before the Water Gate. They asked the scholar Ezra* to bring the Torah scroll. On Rosh Hashanah the first day of the seventh month of Tishray, Ezra stood on a wooden tower, which was made for this purpose, and he read from the scroll to the silent and attentive audience. Ezra read from the Torah scroll since early morning until midday. When he opened the scroll, he blessed the Great God and all present answered saying 'Amen, amen' with their hands raised up to heaven. Then they bowed down face to the ground. After this, Ezra read the Torah for all to hear until noon. Priests and Levites explained and translated the scripture to the people who only understood Aramaic, the language of Babylonia. When the people realised that they had been negligent of the Lord's commandments, they were sad and they wept. Nehemiah, Ezra, and the Levites encouraged them to rejoice in the Lord for that day was a sacred day to their God. Nehemiah told them, *'Go your way, eat the fat, and drink the sweet, and send portions unto him for whom nothing is prepared; for this day is holy unto our Lord; neither be you grieved; for the joy of HaShem is your strength'.**

They did as Nehemiah told them. The second day of Rosh Hashanah the heads of the families, the priests and the Levites went to Ezra to study the words of the Torah. They discovered that the Lord had commanded to Moses, that the Children of Israel should dwell in *succos* (hut shelters) during the festival in the seventh month, the Festival of Sukkot. They announced that a proclamation should go out to the people in all the towns, cities and Jerusalem, telling the people to go out to the mountains to find branches with olive leaves, myrtle leaves, palm leaves, leaves of the braided tree, and pine needles. They used these to build themselves shelters on the roof of their houses and in their courtyards, and in the Water Gate plaza as well as the Ephraim plaza. They celebrated the festival with great joy for seven days, and on the eighth day the assembly came together. Ezra read the Torah day by day.

After the festival of Sukkot the Jews separated themselves from other people living in the Land and they gathered together for a public penance. On this twenty-fourth day of the seventh month they fasted and wore sackcloth with earth upon themselves to show repentance for their transgressions. They confessed their sins and those of their ancestors. Part of that day they spent reading the Torah, after which they stood before their God and confessed their sins. The Levite Joshua with seven others stood up on the platform of the Levites and instructed all to rise up to bless the Lord their God. Then they said their prayers to the Lord, and they spoke of the history of the Children of Israel since Abraham to Moses. They followed with the conquest of Canaan and the rule of the Israelites over the Kingdom of Israel and Judah, which included part of the Trans-Euphrates region, to the time of their exile until their return to the Land, to Zion. They spoke of God's divine compassion, kindness and willingness to forgive them and their ancestors. Then they ended their prayers with a plea for God's mercy and by inscribing God's lasting covenant that was signed by their officers, the Levites and priests, the Kohanim. Nehemiah the Hattirshatha, a Persian title, also signed while the rest of the people gathered also accepted God's Torah, His Law given to Moses. The rest of the people understood and acknowledged the covenant, supported their leaders and they entered into a curse and took an oath to be faithful in following God's Torah given to Moses, to observe and fulfil all His commandments, decrees and His Laws. They also committed themselves to the following. They wouldn't allow mixed marriages that would result in people being led astray from the Lord God. They wouldn't do business on the Shabbat, nor on other holy days of the Lord, and in the seventh year they would relinquish the land they worked on and all loans. They also instituted the commandments concerning the Temple offerings that they would bring every year. They would bring the first fruits of their field and of all their fruits, the firstborn of their cattle and flock to the Temple of the Lord. They would also redeem their firstborn son, and the firstborn of their animals. They would pay a tithe of the tithe of the produce to the Levites, who in turn would bring a tithe of the tithe to the Temple. The Children of Israel and the Levites would also bring separated portions of oil, wine and grain to the Sanctuary of the Lord to the ministering Kohanim, the gatekeepers and the singers. All these and other measures, all in accordance with God' commands, were taken to prevent them from forsaking God's Temple.

At the time Jerusalem was underpopulated and therefore vulnerable. One tenth of the people, both Children of Judah and Benjamin, volunteered through the casting of lots to settle in Jerusalem together with the officers of the people, the heads of the provinces, and more than three hundred priests and Levites who were in charge of the Temple service. Everyone else who settled in the cities and towns of Judah did so on the property of their ancestors. Nehemiah went from being the cup bearer of the king, to becoming the governor of the Land of Judah, leading the people of Judah by example.

Intermezzo

One People

And say unto them: Thus said the Lord God: Behold, I will take the children of Israel from among the nations, whither they are gone, and will gather them on every side, and bring them into their own land; and I will make them one nation in the land, upon the mountains of Israel, and one king shall be king to them all; and they shall be no more two nations, neither shall they be divided into two kingdoms any more at all.

Ezekiel 37:21-22

The Kingdom of Israel in the Land was once one nation ruled by one king, King David who conquered Jerusalem and established it as his capital city. But because of his son Solomon's sins, the Lord divided the kingdom into two kingdoms. The Kingdom of Judah, the Land of Judah, in the southern part of the Promised Land and the Kingdom of Israel in the northern part of it. The latter was where the ten tribes, also referred to as Joseph or Ephraim, lived and the former was where mainly the descendants of Judah and Benjamin, the Jews, including those with them lived. In time all the descendants of the Israelites, the Children of Israel, that is Jacob, would be referred to as Jews, and they would no longer be regarded as two nations.

And the children of Judah and the children of Israel shall be gathered together, and they shall appoint themselves one

> *head, and shall go up out of the land; for great shall be the day of Jezreel.*
>
> Hosea 1:11 or 2:2

The Children of Judah and Benjamin were the first to return to Zion. They, and those who went with them, went up to rebuild the Temple of the Lord on Mount Zion, to settle in Jerusalem and in the Land of Judah. Even though the Lord started the homecoming of His people with the return of the Jews, who previously lived in the Southern part of the Land, in the Land of Judah, He had promised that all the Children of Jacob would one day return to the Land. The Lord would not destroy Ephraim. He would unify the Children of Israel to one people and one nation as they were under the leadership of King David. So, the House of Judah and the House of Joseph would no longer be each other's enemies. The Kingdom of Judah and the Kingdom of Israel would be one kingdom, a unified Nation of Israel, with one day David's descendant as their king.

> *And I will strengthen the house of Judah, and I will save the house of Joseph, and I will bring them back, for I have compassion upon them, and they shall be as though I had not cast them off; for I am HaShem their God, and I will hear them.*
>
> Zechariah 10:6

The Lord is the Holy One planting them firmly in the Land of their ancestors. As the Lord spoke to Jeremiah, *'Behold, I will gather them out of all the countries, whither I have driven them in My anger, and in My fury, and in great wrath; and I will bring them back unto this place, and I will cause them to dwell safely;and they shall be My people, and I will be their God'*.

The Lord God had already given the Land its seventy years to rest and the Children of Jacob had to atone for their sins, for those of Jerusalem and their nation. As they had been showing sincere repentance ever since, the Lord would never again uproot them to go into captivity.

> *The punishment of your iniquity is accomplished, O daughter of Zion, He will no more carry you away into captivity.*
>
> Lamentations 4:22a

The Children would lawfully retake possession of their inheritance to remain in the Land the Lord Himself had once promised them.

> *But on Mount Zion will be deliverance; it will be holy, and Jacob will possess his inheritance. Jacob will be a fire and Joseph a flame.*
>
> Obadiah verse 17-18a

Ezra and Nehemiah

After finishing the work on the wall of Jerusalem, the Jews dedicated the wall with a celebration bringing thanksgiving offerings. The musicians used instruments that were ordained by the Lord through his prophet Gad to King David. Nehemiah arranged two processions alongside the wall, having one pass upon the steps of the City of David ascending over the wall's stairs, going over the house of David. Both marches, one led by Ezra and the other by Nehemiah, ended at the Temple of God where they brought many sacrifices. That day men, women and children rejoiced in Jerusalem and they were heard from afar. That same day arrangements were made to provide the portions ordained by the Torah for the Kohanim, including the sons of Aaron, for the Levites who were stationed at the Temple to keep watch of purity and for their God, insuring that nothing impure or an impure person would enter the Temple ground. For the gatekeepers and the singers as well arrangements were made as was the custom in the days of King David and Asaph, and as King David had commanded to his son Solomon. As long as Nehemiah was in charge the people provided for them.

One day, when the Book of Moses was read for the people, they found out that Amonite and Moabite men were not allowed by the Lord to ever be part of the congregation of Israel. Unlike their women, who were allowed to be part in the same manner as David's great grandmother, once did. The reason? The Amonites and Moabites did not greet the Israelites with bread and water when they were on their way to the Promised Land. Instead, the king of Moab hired Balaam to curse the Israelites, a curse that the Lord God turned into a blessing for the Israelites because of His love for them.

Nehemiah returned to Babylonia in the thirty-second year of Artaxerxes. After a period of time he had spent in Babylonia, he requested his leave of the king and he returned to Jerusalem. During Nehemiah's absence in Jerusalem, Eliashib, one of the priests, and a relative of Tobiah arranged a large chamber for him in the courtyards of the Lord's Temple. When Nehemiah arrived in Jerusalem, he found out about Eliashib's arrangement with Tobiah. He was very distressed about this. Nehemiah threw all Tobiah's possessions out of the chamber, he gave the order to purify it, to return to it all the utensils of the Temple and everything else that was previously stored there. Also, Nehemiah distanced himself from a grandson of the Kohen Gadol, because he was a son-in-law of Sanballat the Honourite, an enemy of the Jews. Nehemiah became aware that the Temple of the Lord had been forsaken for a while leaving the Levites, the singers and those who carried out the Temple service without their portions, causing them to leave Jerusalem, each to his own field. Nehemiah argued with the nobles about this matter. Afterwards he gathered the Levites and he made sure they would resume their responsibilities for the Lord's Temple, each performing his designated task. As for their portions, Judah's inhabitants brought the much needed tithe of grain, wine and oil to the storehouses. Nehemiah also appointed trustworthy men, being a priest, a scholar and a Levite, as treasurers for the storehouses. After Nehemiah had passed reforms for Jerusalem, the Lord's Temple and Judah he prayed, as he did before, to the Lord to have compassion for him, and for Him to remember his deeds done for Him, His Temple and for the watchers.

There were two other problems that Nehemiah noticed in Judah. One was that the people of Judah did not keep the Shabbat in accordance with God's commandments. Instead of sanctifying it as a day for the Lord, they would work and do business on the Shabbat. People would work wine presses, they brought sheaves that they loaded to the donkeys, as well as wine and fruits. Nehemiah argued with the aristocrats and warned them about desecrating the Shabbat day. Tyrians would come to sell their merchandise, including fish, to the people of Judah and Jerusalem on the Shabbat. He remembered them of their past, their ancestors' and Jerusalem's punishment because of their disobedience and unfaithfulness to the Lord. Nehemiah gave orders to close Jerusalem's gates in the afternoon just before Shabbat begins and to open them after this day of rest. He also stationed some of his servants at the gates. No burden would be allowed in or out during Shabbat. Still the merchants kept coming to Jerusalem's gates even though they weren't allowed entrance. The second time they gathered at the city's gates, Nehemiah warned them to leave and not return on a Shabbat again, otherwise he would send his men against them. From that day onward, the merchants didn't come to Jerusalem's wall on Shabbat. Nehemiah told the Levites to regularly purify themselves and to come as guards at the gates, thus sanctifying the Shabbat day.

The other matter of concern to Nehemiah was the intermarriages with Ashdodite, Moabite and Amonite women. Half of their children didn't speak the language of the Jews. People with different backgrounds, including priests and Levites, married non-Jews and took up their pagan beliefs and customs which contradicts God's Laws. In fact leaders and officials were the main offenders. Nehemiah took Solomon as the example on why the Israelites should not be married to non-Israelites who hold on to their gods with their traditions and feasts. These would lead the Israelites astray from the Lord as indeed happened to Solomon, who because of this practice went astray from the Lord, ultimately resulting into the Kingdom of Israel falling apart into the southern Kingdom of Judah and the northern Kingdom of Israel.

Among the Children of Judah that once married Moabite women were the brothers Mahlon and Kilion. Even though these sons of Jewish parents acted against the Lord's teaching, He chose one of these Moabite women to be the mother of the royal house of His people, because of her faith and commitment towards the Lord. Widowed, she preferred to go to a foreign land and live a life in poverty to be with the people of whom she learned about the Lord God, than to remain in her own familiar environment with her family and remarry there. Unlike the women in Nehemiah's time, she held onto the Lord the One God she believed in. This was a choice the Lord Himself affirmed by guiding her to the one man that would care for her, and by granting her a baby boy to be her first child.

Ruth, David's great grandmother, set an example of a non-Jewish woman who chose the God of Israel as her God. As for these women who hold on to their beliefs in their gods and did not choose the Almighty God, Nehemiah contended with their husbands. He cursed them, beat some of the men and tore their hair out. But, he also prayed that the Lord would remember the priests for their desecration of the priesthood, of the covenant of the priesthood, and of the Levites. He prayed and he took action to clean the priesthood by establishing watchers over the priests and Levites. He scheduled times for wood offerings and for the first fruits offerings. Nehemiah's last prayer, *'Remember me, O my God, for good'.**

The Temple of the Lord and Jerusalem's wall were completed as commanded by the Lord, and ordered by Cyrus and Darius kings of Persia.

> *The law of truth was in his mouth, and unrighteousness was not found in his lips; he walked with Me in peace and uprightness, and did turn many away from iniquity. For the priest's lips should keep knowledge, and they should seek the law at his mouth; for he is the messenger of HaShem of hosts.*
> Malachi 2:6-7

Later, after the Lord's Temple was rebuilt by the first group that went up to Jerusalem, during a period that the condition of Jerusalem's wall wasn't mentioned, a scholar of the Torah ascended, by his own request, from Babylonia to Jerusalem during the seventh year of Artaxerxes, king of Persia. This was Ezra who the king referred to as Ezra the Kohen, scholar of the Law of the God of heaven and master of it. Ezra, son of the priest Seraiah, set his heart on teaching statute and Law of the Torah in the Land of Israel, hence shaping the moral standard and values of the Jews living in Jerusalem and Judah.

Ezra received a letter from the king regarding the Jews who would want to go up with Ezra to Jerusalem. The Kohanim, Nethenim, singers and gatekeepers also ascended with him. Ezra himself assembled the leaders of their community to ascend with him. He also received contributions for the Lord's Temple, donated by the king, his counsellors and officers, and by the Jews as well. Furthermore, by the orders of the king those who served the Temple of the Lord were exempt from payment of levy, tax and duty. These were the priests, Levites, Nethenim, the singers, the gatekeepers and whoever else who served the Lord's Temple. Vessels for the Temple service were also delivered to Ezra.

In his letter the king provided Ezra with the authority to appoint judges and magistrates. They would be trustworthy men who knew the Law of the Lord or taught people these, to judge over the people in the Land of Judah. Those who would not abide by the king's order or God's Law would be subject to punishment by death, uprooted, imprisoned or would lose property. Ezra gave thanks to the Lord God with praise For He showed His kindness through the king and his court.

Strengthened by all this, Ezra then assembled the leaders of Israel. Heads of families with Levites to minister for the Lord's Temple and the Nethinim to be of service for the Levites. He began making preparations to go up with them and all the people that were willing to go with them to Jerusalem. But first he proclaimed a collective fast at the River Ahava to pray for a safe passage to the Land for them, their young children and all their possessions. Ezra was embarrassed to put a request to the king for troops and horsemen to guard them along the way, for he told the king they could count on God's protection, for the Lord's benevolence would be with everyone who seek Him. The Lord would grant them what they requested, saving them from ambush and enemies during their journey.

Afterwards, on the twelfth of the first month, they left from the Ahava River for Jerusalem. They took with them the king's contribution for the Temple that he donated in silver, gold and golden-covered vessels. All of this he had weighed and gave for safe keeping to twelve chiefs of the priests, and which would be weighed again before the priests, the Levites and the family heads. Ultimately these contributions would be checked again and stored in the chambers of the Lord's Temple on the fourth day of their arrival. On that day they also brought burnt-offerings to the God of Israel. After this the royal decrees were given to the king's officials, the satraps, and the governors of the Trans-Euphrates region. From then on they were to respect the Jews and the Temple of the Lord.

After this matter was concluded, ranking Jewish officers informed Ezra on the matter of mixed marriages. There were priests and Levites who didn't keep themselves from the other people living in the Land. They had accepted intermarriages for themselves and their children. There were also officers and chiefs involved in this matter. When Ezra heard of this transgression, he tore his garment, tore hair from his head and his beard and sat down in grieving silence until the time of the afternoon offering. Meanwhile a large group of Jews who wanted to hear God's word about this case gathered around him at the Temple of the Lord. Ezra wept and said a prayer to the Lord God confessing their sins and seeking His forgiveness for all of them who had forsaken God's commandments. Although Ezra didn't commit this sin, for he wasn't mentioned on the list of one hundred and twelve men who had a foreign wife who didn't make the choice as David's great grandmother Ruth once did, he included himself in his prayer for forgiveness. The acts of these people added to the guilt Judah and Israel had before the Lord God, Who by His grace allowed a remnant to survive destruction and exile. So, the conduct of these men could have consequences for the entire community just as that of the rulers over Israel and Judah had in the past. They were afraid of the possible repercussions for the whole nation. Their sins and wrongdoings and the unholy pagan customs would make the Land impure. The Lord God Who is holy wants His Land and His people to be holy, to be pure. Their holiness derives from Him and depends on their willingness to be and remain faithful to Him, His Law and Commandments, and for them to be a bearer of these at all times.

Ezra as teacher of the Law, took the responsibility upon himself to pray for all of them while hoping his prayers, out of sincere grief, would bring about God's forgiveness for the whole nation. Then Shekaniah son of Jehiel, one of the sons of Elam, spoke to Ezra. He suggested, while accepting the fact of the wrongdoings against God, that they should seal a covenant with the Lord, promising to send away all the women and their children. He gave Ezra his support, and that of those with him, and encouraged him to be strong, and act in accordance with the Torah to have this matter carried out. Ezra stood up and administered an oath to which the leaders of the priests, the Levites and all of Israel swore. They would carry out this matter. After this, Ezra went to the chamber of Jehohanan son of Eliashib where he fasted and remained in mourning over the unfaithfulness shown to the Lord. By proclamation they gathered an assembly of the people of Judah and Benjamin in Jerusalem within three days. Those who refused to come would have all his property destroyed and themselves isolated from the congregation. This was determined by the counsel of the elders and the officers agreed because of the seriousness of the matter. So, at the beginning of the winter, on the twentieth of the month Kislev, all the people gathered in the plaza of the Temple of the Lord. The seriousness of this matter and the chill of the winter rains caused them to tremble, while Ezra stood before them and spoke to them. He told them they had been unfaithful to the Lord, adding to Israel's sins and therefore they should make a confession before the God of their fathers. They should separate themselves from the other people and from the women they married. The whole assembly called out and exclaim loudly, *'As you have said, so it is for us to do'*.*

Due to the difficulty for all to remain outdoors, because it was the cold rainy season, the assembly agreed to the following way of action as they themselves requested. The men who transgressed should appear before the elders and the judges at appointed times to resolve this matter. Only two men and two Levites who supported them were against this proposal which was accepted by all others. On the first day of the next month Ezra and the heads of families started the investigations and by the first month of the next year they resolved the matter. A list was written down of those who repented from their wrongdoings. To those who were sent away, the possibility of choosing to seek the Lord and be faithful to Him had always been available and would remain. As it once was for Ruth, who by her faith in the Lord God had chosen to stay and not to be sent away by her mother-in-law Naomi. The scribe Ezra continued his task by teaching the Jews to seek the Lord their God and to walk in His ways.

The return to Zion started after the seventy years of exile with the first group of Jews ascending to Jerusalem and the Land of Judah. They went up and many would follow them through ages until the time that David's descendant, the Jewish Messiah, would arrive in Jerusalem to rule over the unified Kingdom of Israel.

> *And it shall come to pass in that day, that HaShem will beat off His fruit from the flood of the River unto the Brook of Egypt, and you shall be gathered one by one, O you children of Israel.*
>
> *And it shall come to pass in that day, that a great horn shall be blown; and they shall come that were lost in the land of Assyria, and they that were dispersed in the land of Egypt; and they shall worship HaShem in the holy mountain at Jerusalem.*
>
> Isaiah 27:12-13

Endnotes

*Ezra 5:11-16, *Ezra 6: 12, *Nehemiah 1:5-11, *Nehemiah 2:20, *Nehemiah 3:36-37, *Nehemiah 5:11-12, *Nehemiah 5:13, *Nehemiah 6:3, *Nehemiah 8:10b, *Nehemiah 13:31, *Ezra 10:12

Commentary Tanach Artscroll: *Ezra 1:8 Sheshbazzar was Daniel or Zerubbabel. *Ezra 2:2 Mordechai. Bilshan was Mordechai of the book of Esther. *Ezra 2:5 The children of the Governor of Moab were David or Joab's descendants. *Ezra 4:7 Artaxerxes was a generic term for king, as for example Pharaoh in Egypt. *Ezra 4:24 Eighteen years halt of the work on the Temple of the Lord. *Nehemiah 1:1 Artaxerxes identified as Darius of Persia, who was the son of Queen Esther and her husband Ahasuerus king of Persia. Ahasuerus was also referred to as Xerxes I or Artaxerxes. *It's still a debate whether Ezra who read the scroll at the time of Nehemiah, is Ezra the scribe that went to Judah with the king's permission.

Ezra 7:1,7, Nehemiah 2:1 Ezra leaves in 7th year of Artaxerxes, Nehemiah in 20th year

Ezra 7:2-5 Ezra son of Seraiah descendant of Aaron

Nehemiah 1:11, 5:14-19, 8:9, 1 Samuel 12:3-4, 12:22-23 cup bearer, governor of Judah, allowance
Ezra 6:12 Jerusalem God's choice as the place for Him to be worshiped
Ezra 1:1, 5:14, 6:1-5 Cyrus king of Persia, Koresh, edict
Ezra 4:6 Ahasuerus king of Persia, Xerxes I, Esther's husband, defamation letter
Ezra 4:7,11, 23, 7:11-26 Artaxerxes king of Persia, Shimshai and Rehum letter
Ezra 4:24, 5:6-7 Darius king of Persia, Esther's son, Tattenai letter
Ezra 1-6, 3:1, 3:7-6:22 Sukkot, rebuilding and dedication of the Temple
Ezra 3:5, 3:6, 6:19-22 New Moon festival, start burned sacrifices, Pesach (Passover)
Nehemiah 1-6 rebuilding the wall of Jerusalem
Daniel 5:2-5 Belshazar
Ezra 2:43, 8:20, Joshua 9:21 the Nethinim, Gibeonite servants
Ezra 2:63, Nehemiah 7:65, Exodus 28-30, Deuteronomy 28:30, Numbers 27:21 Urim, Tummim
Ezra 2:61-62 priests' ancestry unclear
Ezra 2:2, Haggai 1:1,12 Zerubabel son of Shealtiel governor of Judah
Haggai 1:1-11, 2:1-23 messages Haggai for Zerubabel, Joshua and priests
Ezra 2:2, 3:2, 5:1, Zechariah 3:1-10, 6:9-15, Haggai 2:2 Joshua son of Jehozadak, priest, High Priest
Ezra 3:1-6, Numbers 28:1-8 built the Lord's altar, worship began, Festival of Sukkot (Shelters)
Ezra 4:1, 2 Kings 17:24-41 foreign people in Samaria
Zechariah 3:7, 4:6-10 the Lord hears their prayers, Zerubabel will finish the Temple
Ezra 4:24-5:17, Ezra 6:1-12 restart work in second year of Darius' reign, Cyrus and Darius orders
Ezra 3:2, Exodus 27:1-8 the Temple remained on the same place, the Law of Moses
Ezra 3:7, 1 Kings 5:15-32 contributions for the work, traded with Tyre and Sidon
Ezra 3:3-9, 4:1-24, 2 Kings 17:24-41, 5:6-7 opposition to the work, enemies of the Jews
Ezra 5:1-5, 6:14, Haggai 1:1,12, Zechariah 1:1, 4:6-9, Ezra 6:6-12 encouragement, Darius' orders
Nehemiah 2:7 Judah was part of the West Euphrates Province of Persia
Nehemiah 13:6-7 in the 32nd year Nehemiah returned to Babylonia to report to Artaxerxes
Ezra 9:8, Nehemiah 5:1-13, Deuteronomy 15:12-18 oppression of the poor, slavery
Nehemiah 10:31, Exodus 23:10-11, Leviticus 25:1-7, Deuteronomy 15:1-2, Isaiah 58:13-14 Shabbat

Nehemiah 5:19, 13:14, 22, 29, 31 Nehemiah prayed that the Lord would remember him

Nehemiah 13:1-3, Deuteronomy 4-6 intermarriages Moabite and Amonite men

Nehemiah 9:1-2, 10:28-30, 13:1-3, 23-29, Ruth 1:1-5, 4:13-14, Psalm 127:3 intermarriages women

Ezra 9:1-14, Exodus 34:11-17, Deuteronomy 7:1-5, Malachi 2:10-16 intermarriages, unfaithfulness

Nehemiah 9:38-10:1-27, 10:28-39, 13:31 Exodus 30:11-16 covenant renewed, agreement, tithes

Intermezzo Endnotes

*Jeremiah 32:37-38

Hosea 9:10-17, 11:8-11 despite Ephraim's sins, Ephraim would not be destroyed

Jeremiah 29:10, Daniel 9:24, Isaiah 27:7-9 replanted after seventy-year period, atonement

Who Is David?

> But you, Israel, My servant, Jacob whom I have chosen,
> the seed of Abraham My friend;
>
> You whom I have taken hold of from the ends of the earth,
> and called you from the uttermost parts thereof, and said unto you:
> You are My servant,
> I have chosen you and not cast you away;
>
> Fear you not, for I am with you,
> be not dismayed, for I am your God;
> I strengthen you, I help you;
> I uphold you with My victorious right hand.
>
> Behold, all they that were incensed against you shall be ashamed
> and confounded;
> they that strove with you shall be as nothing, and shall perish.
> You shall seek them, and shall not find them, even them that
> contended with you;
> they that warred against you shall be as nothing, and as a thing of
> naught.
>
> For I HaShem your God hold your right hand, who say unto you:
> Fear not, I help you.
> Fear not, you worm Jacob, and you men of Israel;
> I help you, says HaShem, and your Redeemer, the Holy One of
> Israel.
>
> Behold, I make you a new threshing-sledge having sharp teeth;
> you shall thresh the mountains, and beat them small, and shall
> make the hills as chaff.
> You shall fan them, and the wind shall carry them away, and the
> whirlwind shall scatter them;
> and you shall rejoice in HaShem, you shall glory in the Holy One
> of Israel.
>
> The poor and needy seek water and there is none,
> and their tongue fails for thirst;
> I HaShem will answer them,
> I the God of Israel will not forsake them.

I will open rivers on the high hills,
and fountains in the midst of the valleys;
I will make the wilderness a pool of water,
and the dry land springs of water.

I will plant in the wilderness the cedar, the acacia tree,
and the myrtle, and the oil tree;
I will set in the desert the cypress, the plane tree,
and the larch together;
That they may see, and know, and consider,
and understand together,
That the hand of HaShem has done this
and the Holy One of Israel has created it.

Isaiah 41:8-20

Pray for the peace (shalom) of Jerusalem;
may they prosper, those who love you.
Peace (Shalom) be within your walls,
and prosperity within your palaces.
For my brethren and companions' sakes, I will now say:
Peace (Shalom) be within you.
For the sake of the House of HaShem our God
I will seek your good.

A Song of Ascents,
of David. Psalm 122

I rejoiced when they said to me,
Let us go (up) to the House of HaShem

A Song of Ascents,
of David. Psalm 122

TIME TABLES

History of Israel: Prophets, Judges and Kings

And He said to him (Abram): I am HaShem that brought you out of Ur of the Chaldees, to give you this land to inherit it.
Genesis 15:7

The Eternal God gave Canaan to the Patriarch Abraham, to his son Isaac and to Abraham's grandson Jacob (later to be known as Israel). Abraham, Isaac, and Jacob were buried in Hebron. Their wives were also buried there, except Rachel who was buried along side the road to Ephrathah. Israel's children, and their descendants inherited the Promised Land. The God of Israel also gave many prophets, both men and women, to the twelve ancestral tribes of the Children of Israel, the first one being Moses.

Believe in HaShem your God, so shall you be established; believe His prophets, so shall you prosper.
2 Chronicles 20:20

For the Lord God will do nothing, but He reveals His counsel to His servants the prophets.
Amos 3:7

Prophets

Before Current Era (BCE) dates and notes

ca 1592/1571 – Moses. He led the Children of Israel out of Egypt to Canaan. They asked God for a prophet, Exodus 20:18-19.

ca 1107 – Deborah. She was a Judge, Judges 4:4-5.

ca before 1070-1012 – Samuel. He was the last Judge, 1 Samuel 7:15-17.

ca 1000-692 – Abigail. King David's third wife, 1 Samuel 25.

9th century – Hulda. She lived at the time of King Ahab of the northern kingdom, 2 Kings 22:14–20, 2 Chronicles 34:22.

9th century – Elijah. Lived at the time of King Ahab, in the northern kingdom.

9th century – Elisha. Successor of Elijah. He lived in Ephraim's territory during the period after the death of King Ahab, Kingdom of Israel.

He was a disciple of Elijah. He witnessed the siege of Samaria by Benhadad, king of Aram, at the time of King Joram, 2 Kings 6:22-7:20. He died of an illness, 2 Kings 13:14.

- **9th century** – Azariah. He lived at the time of King Asa, Kingdom of Judah, 2 Chronicles 15:1-7. He encouraged him in his efforts for the Lord and the nation.
- **8th century** – Isaiah. His books were possibly written in the periods between 740 BCE and c. 686 BCE. Active as prophet at the time of the kings of Judah, Uzziah or Azariah, Jotham, Ahaz, and Hezekiah, Isaiah 1:1. And maybe for some years during Manasseh's reign.

There were prophets who witnessed the Babylonian exile of the House of Judah, and who were themselves also among the exiled people of Judah.

- **7th-6th century** – Jeremiah. Born into a priestly family, Jeremiah 1:1. Active as A prophet from the 13th year of Judah's King Josiah, king of Judah, 626 BCE until the Babylonian exile. Judah had five kings in that period, starting with King Josiah, Jehoahaz, Jehoiakim, Jehoiachin, and ending with King Zedekiah.
- **ca 622-570** – Ezekiel. He was a priest, Ezekiel 1:1-2. Witnessed the Babylonian exile. King Jehoiakim deposed in 598 BCE. According to calculations he was fifty years old when he had his last vision. His prophecies occurred for about twenty-two years. His last words were dated 570 BCE.
- **7th-6th century** – Daniel. He was carried off to Babylonia with his three friends by Nebuchadnezzar, Daniel 1. Ezekiel mentioned Daniel, Ezekiel 4:14, 14:20, 28:3. Visions concerning the Jewish people, and the rise and fall of the Greek and Roman Empires.

Three of the prophets that prophesied at the time of the House of Judah's return out of Babylonian captivity, ca 520 BCE Haggai, Zechariah and Malachi.

- **6th century** – Haggai. Lived at the time of the return of the House of Judah out of Babylonian captivity. He prophesied to encourage the Jews to rebuild the Temple in Jerusalem, Ezra 5:1-2, Haggai 1 and 2.
- **6th century** – Zechariah. He also prophesied to encourage the continuation of rebuilding the Temple, Ezra 5:1-2, Zechariah 4:1-14.
- **5th century** – Malachi. He prophesied after Haggai and Zechariah, when the Temple was finished, Malachi 3:1, 3:10. Possibly about 420 BCE,

Who Is David?

after or before Nehemiah returned for the second time, Nehemiah 13:6. Comparing Nehemiah 13:15 with Malachi 2:8 or Nehemiah 13:23 with Malachi 2:10-16.

The Patriarchs Abraham, Isaac and Jacob all lived in Canaan. Jacob and his family left Canaan due to famine, and went to Egypt. After at least four centuries they returned to Canaan under the leadership of Moses, Aaron and Miriam. Jacob's, that is Israel's descendants, formed the twelve Tribes of Israel, and they conquered Canaan under Joshua's leadership. About 1273 BCE, the Israelites crossed the Jordan River into Canaan. They set up a tribal nation, which was first ruled by the Judges. The first one was Joshua.

Judges of the Nation of Israel

ca 1245 – Joshua or Hosea, of the Tribe of Ephraim, Numbers 13:8,16. Under his leadership the Israelites crossed the Jordan River into Canaan, Joshua 3. He is also considered a prophet. Death: natural causes, aged 110 years, Joshua 24:29-31.

ca 1228 – Othniel ben Kenaz of the Tribe of Judah, Numbers 13:6, Joshua 3:9. He was the second Judge, Judges 3:9-11. The nation of Israel had 40 years of peace, Judges 3:11. He became judge 8 years after Joshua's death. Death: natural causes.

ca 1188 – Ehud ben Gerah of the Tribe of Benjamin, Judges 3:15. The nation had 80 years of peace. He became judge 18 years after Otniel's death, Judges 3:14. Death: natural causes.

ca 1107 – Shamgar ben Anathof. Death: natural causes.

ca 1107 – Deborah of the Tribe of Ephraim, Judges 4:5. The nation had 40 years of peace. She became judge 20 years after Shamgar's death, Judges 4:3. She was also a prophet. At that time, Barak son of Abinoam was one of the commanders of the Israelite army, Judges 4:6. Death: natural causes.

ca 1067 – Gideon or Jerubaal[*a], Judges 6:32. He was of the Tribe of Manasseh, Judges 6:15. The nation had 40 years of peace. He became judge 7 years after Deborah, Judges 6:1. Death: natural causes, he was very old, Judges 8:32.

ca 1027 – Abimelech, son of Gideon, Tribe of Manasseh, Judges 9:1. He was judge 3 years, Judges 9:22. He killed his seventy brothers, sons of Gideon, except the youngest, Jotham, Judges 9:5, 56. Death: during battle a woman threw a millstone on his head and his weapon-bearer killed him with his sword on his request, Judges 9:53-54.

- **ca 1024** Tola, son of Pua, of the Tribe of Issachar, Judges 10:1. He was judge 23 years. He became judge after Abimelech's death. Death: natural causes.
- **ca 1003** – Jair, the Gileadite, Judges 10:3. He was Judge 22 years. He became judge after Tola's death. Gilead was in the Land to the east of the Jordan River, and in the territory of Manasseh, Reuben and Gad. Jair, with his thirty sons, also led thirty towns within the territory, Judges 10:4. Death: natural causes.
- **ca 982** – Jephtah (HaGil'adi) from Gilead, Judges 12:7. He was judge 6 years, Judges 12:7. His daughter was killed, Judges 11:34-40. Death: natural causes.
- **ca 975** – Ibzan from Bethlehem, Judges 12:8. He was Judge 7 years.
- **ca 969** – Elon (HaZevuloni) of the Tribe of Zebulun, Judges 12:11. He was judge 10 years, Judges 12:11. Death: natural causes.
- **ca 959** – Abdon ben Hillel of the Tribe of Ephraim, Judges 12:15. He was judge 8 years, Judges 12:14. Death: natural causes.
- **ca 951** – Samson or Bedan*[b] of the Tribe of Dan, Judges 13:2. He was a nazirite, Judges 13:5. He was judge 20 years, Judges 16:31. Death: he died while he brought down a building killing the Philistines with their kings, Judges 16:23-31.
- **ca 931** – Eli the Kohen, High Priest, of the Tribe of Levi. He was judge 40 years, 1 Samuel 4:18. He and his sons, who were corrupt, were ultimately punished because they didn't remain faithful to the Lord, 1 Samuel 2:27-36. Death: he broke his neck when he fell backward from his seat, Judges 4:18.
- **ca 890** – Samuel of the Tribe of Ephraim, 1 Samuel 1:1. He was a prophet and became judge after Eli's death. He served the nation of Israel as long as he lived, 1 Samuel 7:15. He anointed both Saul and David to be king of Israel. He was always faithful to the Lord, but his sons accepted gifts, 1 Samuel 8:1-3 Death: natural causes.

> *Moreover HaShem tells you (David) that HaShem will make you a house (House of David) ... I will set up your seed after you, that shall proceed out of your body, and I will establish his kingdom.*
>
> 2 Samuel 7:11-12
>
> *And HaShem shall inherit Judah as His portion in the holy land, and shall choose Jerusalem again.*
>
> Zechariah 2:16

The first kings of an undivided nation state of the Kingdom of Israel were King Saul, followed by King David and his son King Solomon.

Who Is David?

David was the first king over Judah, only one Israelite tribe. He was born about 1000 BCE. He was a shepherd, musician, artist, warrior and a prophet. He ruled from Hebron over the Kingdom of Judah for about seven years. After Saul and his son Ishboshet, who was king over the ten-tribe Kingdom of Israel, died, David became king of the Kingdom of Israel and Judah. King David made Jerusalem the capital city of the unified Kingdom of Israel. Jerusalem, the city which God had chosen for Him to be worshipped, over which He watches, and which He defends, 2 Chronicles 12:13, 2 Chronicles 7:15-16, 2 Kings 20:6. King David's successor was his son Solomon.

Kings of the Kingdom of Israel

Albright date[1]*, BCE Common name / Regnal Name and Notes*

The House of Saul

ca 1011-1010 Saul, Sha'ul – Ruled over Israel and Judah, unified Kingdom of Israel, for 40 years. Saul tried to kill himself with his spear during a battle with the Philistines on Mount Gilboa. He was ultimately killed by an Amalekite, 2 Samuel 1:5-10.

ca 1010-1008 Ishbosheth – He was also called Eshba'al or Ashba'al or Ishbaal. Ruled over the ten-tribe Kingdom of Israel for 2 years. Death: murdered in his bedroom by two of his officers, 2 Samuel 4:1-12.

The House of David

ca 1000-692 David, David ben Yeshai – Ruled over the unified Kingdom of Israel for 33 years from Jerusalem and about 7 years in Hebron. 2 Samuel 4:4-5, 1 Kings 2:11 Death: natural causes.

ca 962-922 Solomon, Shlomo ben David – Ruled over the unified Kingdom of Israel for 40 years from Jerusalem, 1 Kings 11:42-43. At the end of his reign, his actions caused the kingdom's division into two kingdoms, 1 Kings 11-12:24. Death: natural causes.

After King Solomon's death, the ten northern tribes revolted and established the Kingdom of Israel in the north. Their first king was Jeroboam I of the tribe of Ephraim, who were descendants of the Matriarch Rachel through her son Joseph. The other tribe of Joseph was Manasseh. All the kings of this kingdom followed the pagan religion, with its own feasts and priesthood, that King Jeroboam introduced. They ruled first from Shechem, then Tizrah and later on from Samaria.

The House of Jeroboam

ca 922-901 – Jeroboam 1, Yerav'am ben Nevat, Ruled over the ten-tribe Kingdom of Israel 22 years. His residence was in *Shechem*, 1 Kings 12:1. At war with King Rehoboam of Judah, 1 Kings 14:30. He introduced a pagan religion to the kingdom, 1 Kings 12:25-33, 13:33, 2 Kings 17:16-17. Death: natural causes.

ca 901-900 – Nadab, Nadav ben Yerav'am, Ruled over the ten-tribe Kingdom of Israel for 2 years. Death: Killed by Bassha, son of Ahijah of the house of Issachar, along with his whole family.

The House of Baasha

ca 900-877 – Baasha, Ba'asha ben Achiyah, Ruled over the ten-tribe Kingdom of Israel in Tizrah for 24 years. Death: natural causes.

ca 877-876 – Elah, Elah ben Ba'asha, Ruled over the ten-tribe Kingdom of Israel from *Tizrah* for 2 years. Death: One of his officials, Zimri, made him drunk and killed him at his house in Azra.

The House of Zimri

ca 876 – Zimri, Ruled over the ten-tribe Kingdom of Israel from Tizrah for 7 days. Death: Died when he set his palace on fire. Occurred when Omri, together with the Israelites who joined him withdrew from Gebbethon. They laid siege to Tizrah.

The House of Omri

ca 876-869 – Omri, Ruled over the ten-tribe Kingdom of Israel from the capital of Samaria for 12 years. Death: Natural causes.

ca 869-850 – Ahab, Ah'av ben Omri, Ruled over the ten-tribe Kingdom of Israel from *Samaria* for 22 years. Confrontation of the prophet Elijah and the priests of idols on the Carmel occurred, 1 Kings 18. He was married to Jezebel, who encouraged idol worship, 1 Kings 16:31-33, 21:25. She also persecuted the prophets of the Lord, 1 Kings 18:4. She had a violent death, 1 Kings 21:23, 2 Kings 9:7-10 and 9:30-37. Jericho was rebuilt by Hiel from Bethel, 1 Kings 17:34. Death: During the battle at Ramoth Gilead he was shot by an archer. He died upon his arrival in Samaria, 1 Kings 21:20-24, 2 Kings 22.

ca 850-849 – Ahaziah, Ahaziyahu ben Ah'av, Ruled over the ten-tribe Kingdom of Israel from *Samaria* for 2 years. Death: He was injured when he fell through the lattice of his upper room. The prophet Elijah told him that he would stay in his bed and die on it, 2 Kings 1.

ca 849-842 – Joram, Yehoram ben Ah'av, Ruled over the ten-tribe Kingdom of Israel from Samaria for 11 years. Joram was the brother of Ahaziah,

Who Is David?

who didn't have sons. Once wounded in battle, 2 Kings 8:28-29. Death: Jehu, future king of the Kingdom of Israel, killed him and his entire family, 2 Kings 9:14-26, 2 Kings 10.

The House of Jehu

ca 842-815 – Jehu, Yehu ben Nimshi, Ruled over the ten-tribe Kingdom of Israel from Samaria for 28 years, 2 Kings 10:32. Prophet Elisha anointed Jehu to be king of Israel, 2 Kings 9:1-6,12-13, and 10:29-31. He was against idol worship, 2 Kings 10:18-30, but did not completely remove Jeroboam's cult. The Kingdom lost territory to the east of the Jordan River, 2 Kings 10: 32-33. Death: natural causes.

ca 815-801 – Jehoahaz, Yeho'ahaz ben Yehu, Ruled over the ten-tribe Kingdom of Israel from Samaria for 17 years. Death: natural causes.

ca 801-786 – Jehoash, Yeho'ash ben Yeho'ahaz, Also called Joash. Ruled over the ten-tribe Kingdom of Israel from *Samaria* for 16 years. Death: natural causes.

ca 786-746 – Jeroboam II, Yerav'am ben Yeho'ash, Ruled over the ten-tribe Kingdom of Israel from *Samaria* for 41 years. Death: natural causes.

ca 746 – Zachariah, Zakharyah ben Yerav'am, Ruled over the ten-tribe Kingdom of Israel from *Samaria* for 6 months. Death: He was killed by Shallum son of Jabesh in front of the people. He succeeded him as king.

The House of Shallum

ca 745 – Shallum, Shallum ben Yavesh, Ruled over the ten-tribe Kingdom of Israel from *Samaria* for 1 month. Death: He was attacked and killed by Menahem son of Gadi. He succeeded him as king.

The House of Menahem

ca 745-738 – Menahem, Menahem ben Gadi, Ruled over the ten-tribe Kingdom of Israel from *Samaria* for 10 years. Death: natural causes.

ca 738-737 – Pekahiah, Pekahyah ben Menahem, Ruled over the ten-tribe Kingdom of Israel from *Samaria* for 2 years. Death: Assassinated in his palace at Samaria by Pekah son of Remaliah, one of his chief officers with 50 men, and he succeeded him as king.

The last House of Israel

ca 737-732 – Pekah, Pekah ben Remalyahu, Ruled over the ten-tribe Kingdom of Israel from *Samaria* for 20 years. Death: Killed by Hoshea son of Elah, who conspired against him to become king.

ca 732-722 – Hoshea, Hoshe'a ben Elah, Ruled over the ten-tribe Kingdom of Israel from Samaria for 9 years. Death: King Shalmanser attacked the Kingdom of Israel. He captured the capital Samaria. Hoshea was charged with treason and he was imprisoned, 2 Kings 17:1-4. The Israelites were exiled to Assyria, 2 Kings 17:1-6, 2 Kings 18:9-11. He let other people live in their Land, 2 Kings 17:24.

The ancestral tribes of Judah, descendants of Matriarch Leah, and Benjamin, descendants of Matriarch Rachel, remained loyal to the House of David, to Solomon's son Rehoboam. Also the tribe of Levi, descendants of Matriarch Leah remained. The priesthood of the Levites attended to the Temple and religious life in the kingdom. He ruled over the Kingdom of Judah in the south with Jerusalem as its capital city. The descendants of the House of David continued to rule over the Kingdom of Judah. They all reigned from Jerusalem.

Kings of the Kingdom of Judah

The House of David

ca 1000-692[*1] David, David ben Yeshai, Ruled over the Kingdom of Judah, only the tribe of Judah, from Hebron 7 or 7½ years, 2 Samuel 4:4-5, 1 Kings 2:11. Afterwards, he ruled over the unified Kingdom of Israel for 33 years in Jerusalem. He made Jerusalem the capital city of the nation of Israel. Reigned in total 40 years. Death: natural causes.

ca 928-911 – Rehoboam son of Solomon, Ruled 17 years, 1 Kings 14:21, 2 Chronicles 12:41, from Jerusalem over the Kingdom of Judah after the death of King Solomon. He kept the Temple Service. Priests and Levites all over the Land of Israel went to Judah because Jeroboam made it impossible for them to serve the Lord God, 2 Chronicles 11:13-15. Others also followed their example and went to Judah, 2 Chronicles 11:16-17. He was at war with Jeroboam, 1 Kings 14:30, 2 Chronicles 13:15. Death: natural causes.

ca 911-908 – Abijah/Abijam son of Rehoboam, Ruled 3 years, 1 Kings 15:2. He was not completely faithful to God, 1 Kings 15:3. The two Israelite kingdoms were still at war with each other, 1 Kings 16:6. Death: natural causes.

ca 908-867 – Asa son of Abijah, Ruled 41 years, 1 Kings 15:40. He was faithful to God, 1 Kings 15:11-15. Renewed covenant with the Lord, 2 Chronicles 15:12, 15:8-19. He removed his mother, queen mother Maacah, from her position because of her idolatry, 1 Kings 15:13, 2 Chronicles 15:16. He restored, built fortresses nation wide, 2 Chronicles 14. He was at war with Basa, king of Israel, 1 Kings 15:16. Israelites of Ephraim, Manasseh and Simeon went over to Judah's side to live in Judah, 2 Chronicles 15:9. Death: At the end of his reign, he had a severe foot disease and was crippled, 2 Chronicles 16:11-13.

ca 867-851 – Jehoshaphat son of Asa, Ruled 25 years. Was faithful to God. Death: natural causes.

ca 851-843 – Jehoram/Joram son of Jehoshaphat, Ruled 8 years, 2 Kings 8:16-18. Not faithful to God, but followed bad example of the House of Ahab. He was married to Ahab's daughter, 2 Kings 8:18. Death: natural causes.

ca 843-842 – Achaziah/Jehoahaz son of Jehoram, Ruled 1 year, 2 Kings 8:26. He wasn't faithful to God. Son of Athaliah, granddaughter of King Omri of the Kingdom of Israel, 2 Kings 8:25-27. Death: Killed by Jehu, the future king of the Kingdom of Israel, 2 Kings 9:27-29.

House of Omri

ca 842-836 – Athaliah granddaughter, Ruled 6 years, 2 Kings 11:3. She was anof King Omri.Illegitimate ruler. She was not a descendant of the House of David. She did a coup d'état. After her husband Ahaziah died, she murdered her own family, all the children of the royal family, except Joash, so she could become queen, 2 Kings 11:1-1. Death: Killed, so the legitimate heir, Joash, could become king, 2 Kings 11:4-20.

The House of David

ca 836-799 – Joash/Jehoash son of Ahaziah, Ruled 40 years, 2 Kings 12:1-2. Joash was 7 years old when he became king. He was saved from Athaliah by his aunt, Jehosheba. She hid him in the Temple, 2 Kings 11:2-3. He was faithful to God. The priest Jehoiada helped him, 2 Kings 11:4, 2 Kings 12:3. He wanted the Temple to be repaired. Death: He was murdered by officials who plotted against him, 2 Kings 12:21-22.

ca 799-786 – Amaziah son of Joash, Ruled 29 years, 2 Kings 14:1-2. He was faithful to God. He had the officials who killed his father killed, but not their children, 2 Kings 14:5-6. Death: Killed. There was a plot against him in Jerusalem. But, the people of Judah made his son king, 2 Kings 14:19-22.

ca 786-758 – Azarjah/Uzziah son of Amaziah, Ruled 52 years, 2 Kings 15:1-2. He was faithful to God. When he had an illness of his skin, his son Jotham became regent, 2 Kings 15:5. Death: natural causes.

ca 758-742 – Jotham son of Uzziah, Ruled 16 years, 2 Kings 15:33. He was faithful to God. He did some construction work on the Temple in Jerusalem, 2 Kings 15:35. Death: natural causes.

Time Tables

- **ca 742-726** – Ahaz son of Jotham, Ruled 16 years, 2 Kings 16:1-2. He was not faithful to God. He followed the practices of the kings of Israel. He let his son go through fire, 2 Kings 16:2-4. He made changes at the Temple, 2 Kings 16:10-18. Death: natural causes.
- **ca 726-697** – Hezekiah son of Ahaz, Ruled 29 years, 2 Kings 18:1-2, 2 Chronicles 29:1. He was faithful to God and followed David's example, 2 Kings 18:3, 5-7. He destroyed the pagan high places of idol worship and sacrifices, which until his reign were in use, 2 Kings 4. He repaired and purified the Temple, 2 Chronicles 29. And he reestablished the Feast of Pesach and Unleavened Bread, and restored the Jewish religious life, 2 Chronicles 30 and 31. Purified and restored the Temple, 2 Chronicles 29. Reestablished the Temple Service, 1 Kings 20:20. During his reign Samaria fell to the Assyrians, start of exile northern kingdom. Assyrians besieged cities of Judah and Jerusalem, but they didn't fall, 2 Kings 18:13-19:37. Hezekiah recovered from an illness, 2 Kings 20:1-11. He did waterworks regarding the Gihon Spring to bring water into the city, 2 Kings 20:20, 2 Chronicles 33:30. Death: natural causes.
- **ca 697-642** – Manasseh son of Hezekiah, Ruled 55 years, 2 Kings 21:1. He was not faithful to God. Worship of idols and stars increased in Judah and he placed idol objects in the Temple and its courtyard, 2 Kings 21:2-9, 2 Chronicles 33:1-9.. He was taken captive by the Assyrians, repented and returned to Jerusalem, 2 Chronicles 33:10-13. Death: natural causes.
- **ca 642-640** – Amon son of Manasseh, Ruled 2 years, 2 Kings 21:19. He was not faithful to God. Death: His officials plotted against him and murdered him, 2 Kings 21:23. The people of Judah made his son king, 2 Kings 21:24.
- **ca 640-609** – Josiah son of Amon, Ruled 31 years, 2 Kings 22:1. He was faithful to God. An important scroll of the Torah was found, 2 Kings 22:8-10. He introduced reforms in Jerusalem and Judah, 2 Kings 23. He made a covenant together with the people, with Lord to obey Him, 2 Chronicles 35:29-33, 2 Kings 23:1-20. Celebrates Pesach, 2 Chronicles 35:1-19. Death: wounded by Egyptian arrows in battle against Pharaoh Neco. He died in Jerusalem, 2 Chronicles 35:23-24. The people of Judah made his son king. After King Josiah's death, Egypt gained influence over the Kingdom of Judah. Later on Babylonia besieged and captured Jerusalem, and brought Judah into exile.
- **ca 609-608** – Jehoahaz son of Josiah, Ruled 3 months. He wasn't faithful to God. Death: Died in Egyptian captivity, Pharaoh Neco, 2 Kings 23:34.
- **ca 608-597** – Jehoiakim/Eliakim son of Jehoahaz, Ruled 11 years. He wasn't faithful to God. Appointed king by Pharaoh Neco, 2 Kings 23:36. Death: natural causes.

ca 597 – Jehoiachin son of Jehoiakim, Ruled 3 months, 2 Kings 24:8. He was captured and taken to Babylonia, with other important men, and he lived in captivity at the king's court in Babylonia, 2 Kings 24:15-17, 27-30. Death: natural causes.

ca 597-587 – Zedekiah uncle of Jehoiachin, Ruled 11 years, 2 Kings 24:18. He was appointed by Nebuchadnezzar, 2 Kings 24:17. He wasn't faithful to God. He rebelled against Nebuchadnezzar. He and his family were taken into captivity, 2 Kings 24:20-25:7. His sons were killed before his eyes and he was made blind. Judah taken into captivity to Babylonia by Nebuchadnezzar II (ca 634-562 BCE), king of Babylon, who ruled from 605 to 562 BCE. He appointed Gedaliah as gouvernor, 2 Kings 25:21-26, Jeremiah 40:5-41:3. Gedaliah was murdered by Ishmael, of royal descent, and the group they fled to Egypt, 2 Kings 25:25-26, Jeremiah 40:13-18

> *For thus says HaShem: After <u>seventy years</u> are accomplished for Babylon, I will remember you, and perform My good word toward you, in causing you to return to this place.*
>
> Jeremiah 29:10
>
> *Thus says HaShem: Behold, I will turn the captivity of Jacob's tents, and have compassion on his dwelling-places; and the city (Jerusalem) shall be built upon her own hill, and the palace shall be inhabited upon its usual place.*
>
> Jeremiah 30:18

After seventy years of exile, King Cyrus (r. 559-530 BCE) of Persia issued a decree allowing the Jews to return to *Jerusalem*, to *Judah*. They would return to their ancestral Land, joining the Jewish inhabitants that were still living there. They rebuilt the Temple of the Lord and the walls of Jerusalem under the leadership of Ezra and Nehemiah.

Second Temple Period 516 BCE-70 CE

ca 10th century - 587 BCE – First Temple Period

ca 740 or ca 733 – Assyrian Exile. Kingdom of Israel.

586 BCE – Destruction of the First Temple by the Babylonians.

597-538 BCE – Babylonian Exile. Kingdom of Judah. The Jews remained seventy years in captivity. Jerusalem in ruins. Jeremiah 29:10, Daniel 9:1-2.

559-530 BCE – Cyrus the Great (ca 600-530 BCE) king of Persia issued a decree that allowed the Jewish people to go out of the Babylonian exile, return to Jerusalem, Judah and rebuild the Temple. 2 Chronicles 36:23, Ezra 1:1-2, Isaiah 44:28, 45:1,13. Jewish leaders were Zerubbabel, Joshua and Ezra, Ezra 2:1-2, 3:2 and Ezra 7:1-6.

538-332 BCE – Period rebuilding the Temple, after the Babylonian exile. Temple finished ca 516 BCE, Ezra 6:15. During the reign of Darius the Great of Darius I (ca 550-486 BCE), Artaxerxus I (ca 465-424 BCE), Ezra 6:14.

5th century BCE – Rebuilding the walls of Jerusalem under Nehemiah's leadership, at the time of Artaxerxus I (ca 465-424 BCE) reign.

516 BCE - 70 CE – Second Temple Period

336-64 BCE – Greek period, started with Alexander the Great (336-323 BCE). Region including the Land of Israel under Ptolomaic rule 301-200 BCE, under Seleucid rule 200-135/63 BCE.

The Maccabian/Hasmonean Kingdom of Judah (167 BCE-4 CE) was established during the 2nd century before current era. Jerusalem was its capital city. It was ruled by Jewish kings, and encompassed a great part of the territory of the former two Israelite kingdoms, the two-tribe Kingdom of Judah and the ten-tribe Kingdom of Israel.

64 BCE – Romans defeat Seleucid Kingdom.

167 BCE-4 CE – Period of Jewish kings ruled over the Land of Israel, the Kingdom of Judah. Maccabean and Hasmonean period. Followed by Herod the Great.

167 BCE – Maccabee revolt, against the Seleucid's imposed Hellenization and oppression. Beginning of the revolt of the priestly family of the Maccabees from the village of Modein. Maccabee, the hammer, was actually a nickname for one of the leaders, Judas.

164 BCE – Re-dedication of the Second Temple

161 BCE – Judas Maccabee made a treaty of friendship with Rome, at the time the Roman Republic 509-27 BCE, classical Roman period. Roman Empire 27 BCE-395 CE. Western Roman Empire 395-476 CE. Eastern Roman Empire, Byzantine Empire, 395-1453 CE.

The Hasmonean Kingdom of Judah. Encompassed great part of the territory of the unified, of the twelve tribes, Kingdom of Israel. The Hasmoneans were descendants of the Maccabees.

The Herodian Kingdom of Judea was ruled by Herod the Great (r. 37/40-4 CE), starting in the 1st century before current era. He was appointed king by the Romans. He ruled over a great part of the territory of the former Hasmonean Kingdom of Judah, and had autonomy. After his death, his kingdom was divided between his three sons. Archelaus (r. 4 BCE-6 CE), Herod Antipas (r. 4 BCE-39 CE), Philip (4 BCE-33/34 CE).

37/40 BCE-4 CE – Herodian Kingdom of Judah. Herod the Great established the Herodian Dynasty (37/40 BCE-93 CE). He ruled over most part of the Hasmonean Kingdom of Judah, which encompassed a great part of the ancient unified Kingdom of Israel. He was a Jewish*[2] client king to the Romans.

4 BCE-33/34 CE – Herod the Great's sons succeeded him. Each ruled over a part of the territory of Herod's kingdom. Archelaus (r. 4 BCE-6 CE), Herod Antipas (r. 4 BCE-39 CE), Philip (4 BCE-33/34 CE).

4 BCE-66 CE – Period of Roman Prefects, followed by a period of Roman *Procurators*, which started 44 CE, appointed over Roman provinces. Also over regions within the Land of Israel. Territory of the Land of Israel, Judea became gradually part of the Roman province, after Agrippa I. After Agrippa II all the territory part of the Roman province came under complete control of the Roman Empire.

26-36 CE – Roman prefect Pontius Pilate

Later on Herod's grandson Agrippa I (r. 37-44 CE) ruled while having autonomy, over Herod's entire kingdom. After he died in ca 44 CE, his son Agrippa II (ca 50-92/93 CE) ruled over part of the territory of Herod's kingdom, while having a nominal autonomy. So, Jewish rulers of Herodian and Hasmonean descent continued to rule the territories of the Jewish people, while having autonomy for their territories, until the end of the 1st century current era. During this period, the First Jewish-Roman War (66-74 CE) took place, led by Jewish Zealot rebels. Jewish governance would return during the next century.

37 CE-92/93 CE – Herod the Great's grandsons, Agrippa I and Agrippa II. They were also of Hasmonean descent. Agrippa I (r. 37-44 CE) became, eventually, king over his grandfather's entire kingdom from 41 to 44 CE. He was king of Judea. His son Agrippa II (r. 50?-92/93 CE) succeeded him as king over a relatively small part of his father's territory. He was the 7th and last of the Herodian Dynasty.

70-135 CE – Period of Roman Legates. A governing high-ranking military officer. He was also capable of commanding a Roman legion. Only ca 124 a Prefect for about one year.

- **66-74 CE** – First Jewish-Roman War, and civil war within the city of Jerusalem from 68 to 69 CE.
- **70 CE** – Siege of Jerusalem led by future Roman Emperor Titus (r. 79-81). Destruction Second Temple, which Herod the Great had fully refurbished, in Jerusalem Conquest of Jerusalem by the Romans. Jewish rebels were sold into slavery or scattered.
- **73-74 CE** – Siege of Masada, the last Jewish stronghold. Led by Lucius Flavius Silva (born ca 43 CE). The Jewish historian Flavius Josephus (ca 37-100) chronicled what happened.
- **ca 74-429 CE** – Period of Rabbinical Patriarchate with reduced authority, with their seat outside of Jerusalem. Started with Gamaliel I (ca 10 BCE-70 CE), president of the Great Sanhedrin in Jerusalem. His father was Shimon ben Gamaliel (died ca 52 CE), who was a Sanhedrin leading authority. This period ended with Gamaliel VI, between 270 and 290 CE. He was leader of the Sanhedrin. They were leaders of the Jewish people and as such attended to the Jewish communities in the Land.

During the 2nd century current era the Jewish people would briefly have an autonomous government seated in Jerusalem, during the Bar Kochba Revolt (132-135). Jewish governance would return to their ancestral homeland during the 20th century, to both Jerusalem and a great part of the ancestral Land of Israel.

- **115–117 CE** – Kitos War was a Jewish revolt against the Romans that occurred in the Jewish Diaspora. Thus, outside the Land of Israel, but within the territories of the Roman Empire.
- **132-135 CE** – Bar Kochba Revolt. During this period Jerusalem was under Jewish rule. They minted their own coins. Jerusalem captured by the Romans. Jerusalem renamed Aelia Capitolina, and the Jewish ancestral Land was also renamed to Syria Palaestina by the Romans. Attempt to erase Jewish historical ties. Heavy Jewish casualties. Jewish captives of war were sold into slavery, and Jews barred from the city of Jerusalem.
- **284–305 CE** – Roman Emperor Diocletian (r. 284–305 CE). The region of Syria Palaestina was divided into the provinces:

    Palaestina Prima, territory: Judea, Samaria, Idumea, Peraea and the coastal plain, capital was Caesarea Maritima. Palaestina Secunda, territory: Galilee, Decapolis and Golan, capital was Beth-Shean.
    Palaestina Tertia, territory: the Negev desert, capital was Petra.

- **14th of May 1948 CE** – Founding modern-day State of Israel, governed by a Jewish government. In 1967, Jerusalem was unified to one city under Jewish rule. In 1980, Jerusalem was proclaimed the capital city

Who Is David?

of the State of Israel by the Knesset, parliament. In 2018, the United States recognized Jerusalem as the capital city of the State of Israel.

> *For I know the thoughts that I think toward you, says HaShem, thoughts of peace (shalom), and not of evil, to give you a future and a hope.*
>
> *And you shall call upon Me, and go, and pray to Me, and I will listen to you.*
>
> *And you shall seek Me, and find Me, when you shall search for Me with all your heart.*
>
> *And I will be found of you, says HaShem.*
>
> Jeremiah 29:11-14a
>
> *I will turn your captivity, and gather you from all the nations, and from all the places whither I have driven you, says HaShem; and I will bring you back to the place whence I caused you to be carried away captive.*
>
> Jeremiah 29:14
>
> *Thus says HaShem of hosts: I am jealous for <u>Jerusalem</u> and for <u>Zion</u> with a great jealousy ... Therefore thus says HaShem: I return to Jerusalem with compassion: My House shall be built in it, says HaShem of hosts, and a line shall be stretched forth over Jerusalem. Again, proclaim, saying: Thus says HaShem of hosts: <u>My cities</u> shall again overflow with prosperity; and HaShem shall yet <u>comfort Zion</u>, and shall yet <u>choose Jerusalem</u>.*
>
> Zachariah 1:14-17
>
> *Thus speaks HaShem of hosts, saying: Behold, a man whose name is <u>the Shoot</u>, and who shall shoot up out of his place, and build the temple of HaShem; even he shall build the temple of HaShem; and he shall bear the glory, and shall sit and rule upon his throne; and there shall be a priest before his throne; and the counsel of peace (shalom) shall be between them both.*
>
> Zachariah 6:12-13

Time Table Notes

This is not a complete list. Not all the prophets are mentioned. And it only gives some information about the history of the nations of the Kingdoms of Israel and Judah and certain leaders and events. Also, a few of the many prophesies concerning the Children of Israel and their ancestral home, the Land of Israel.

*ᵃ Jerubaal: – And HaShem sent Jerubbaal, and Bedan, and Jephthah, and Samuel, and delivered you out of the hand of your enemies on every side, and you dwelt in safety, 1 Samuel 12:11.- Artscroll Stone Edition Tanach, notes to 1 Samuel 12:11: Jerubaal was Gideon, Judges 6:9.

*ᵇ Bedan: – And HaShem sent Jerubbaal, and Bedan, and Jephthah, and Samuel, and delivered you out of the hand of your enemies on every side, and you dwelt in safety, 1 Samuel 12:11.- Artscroll Stone Edition Tanach, notes to 1 Samuel 12:11: Bedan was Samson. Bedan is the equivalent of ben dan which means, son of Dan. Samson was of the Tribe of Dan, a Danite, Judges 13:16 (Judges 13:2).- Wikipedia: Dedan, https://en.wikipedia.org/wiki/Bedan

*¹ Most historians follow chronologies established by William F. Albright, Edwin R. Thiele, or Gershon Galil. All these dates follow the William F. Albright chronology and are before current era (BCE).

*² Who is David? The Kingdom and the Bride Volume II
Part VI David's Ancestral Judah, The Kingdom of Judah II, Intermezzo: Herod the Great's Dynasty

Sources:

Biblical books: Genesis, Exodus, Joshua, Judges, 1 Samuel , 2 Samuel, 1 Kings, 2 Kings, 1 Chronicles, 2 Chronicles, Ezra, Nehemiah, Isaiah, Jeremiah, Ezekiel, Daniel, Haggai, Zechariah, Malachi.

The History of the Jews in the Greco-Roman World by Peter Schäfer
Harwood Academic Publishers, 1995 and Routledge, 2003

National Geographic, Het Romeinse Rijk (The Roman Empire)
Speciale Uitgave (Special Edition)

The New York Post, The history of Israel's contentious 'eternal capital'
By Yaron Steinbuch, December 7, 2017
https://nypost.com/2017/12/07/the-history-of-israels-contentious-eternal-capital

Chabad.org, Timeline of Jewish History by Mattis Kantor
https://www.chabad.org/library/article_cdo/aid/3915966/jewish/Timeline-of-Jewish-History.htm

Jewish Virtual Library, Timeline for the History of Judaism https://www.jewishvirtuallibrary.org/timeline-for-the-history-of-judaism
Jewish Virtual Library, Ancient Jewish History
https://www.jewishvirtuallibrary.org/ancient-jewish-history

Who Is David?

Jewish Virtual Library, Ancient Jewish History: The Temples (Beit HaMikdash)
https://www.jewishvirtuallibrary.org/the-jewish-temple-beit-hamikdash
Jewish Virtual Library. Ancient Jewish History: The Kings of Ancient Israel
https://www.jewishvirtuallibrary.org/the-kings-of-ancient-israel
Jewish Virtual Library, Ancient Jewish History: The Kings of Judah
https://www.jewishvirtuallibrary.org/the-kings-of-judah

Wikipedia: Ancient Jewish History: List of Jewish Prophets
https://www.jewishvirtuallibrary.org/list-of-jewish-prophets
Wikipedia: Prophets in Judaism, https://en.wikipedia.org/wiki/Prophets_in_Judaism
Wikipedia: Moses, https://en.wikipedia.org/wiki/Moses#Historicity
Wikipedia: Ezekiel, https://en.wikipedia.org/wiki/Ezekiel#cite_note-2
Wikipedia: Malachi, https://en.wikipedia.org/wiki/Malachi
Wikipedia: Timeline of Jewish History, https://en.wikipedia.org/wiki/Timeline_of_Jewish_history
Wikipedia: Jewish History, https://en.wikipedia.org/wiki/Jewish_history
Wikipedia: Judea (Roman province)
https://en.wikipedia.org/wiki/Judea_(Roman_province)#Judea_as_Roman_province(s)

Time Tables

Aliyah – Immigration to Israel

It shall come to pass that, instead of that which was said to them: You are not My people, it shall be said to them: You are the children of the living God.
And the children of Judah and the children of Israel shall be gathered together, and they shall appoint themselves one head, and shall go up out of the land.
                                                                    Hosea 2:1-2

Aliyah: the process of the immigration of Jews out of the diaspora to the Land of Israel. Also, making Aliyah, being the act of a Jewish person going up to Jerusalem.

I bore you on eagles' wings, and brought you to Myself.
They shall mount up with wings as eagles ...
                                                Exodus 19:4-Isaiah 40:31

Before Current Era (BCE) dates and notes

ca 1800 – Abram and his family left Ur of the Chaldeans in Mesopotamia, and went to Canaan. Genesis 11:31-32 and 12:1-9.

ca 1300 – The Israelites left Egypt and returned to Canaan after about a forty years journey through the wilderness. About four centuries earlier, Genesis 15:13, Jacob and his family left Canaan and went to Egypt. His son Joseph was already in Egypt.

ca 538 – King Cyrus' declaration that the Jews in his empire were allowed to return to Jerusalem and rebuild the Temple of the Lord. Ezra 1:1-11.

ca 538-459 – Jews returned out of the Babylonian Exile to Judah (Judea), where there were still Jewish inhabitants. Jeremiah 40:6-7 and 9-12, 44:28, 52:16 and 28-30. Book of Ezra and Nehemiah.

ca 516 BCE-70 CE – Second Temple era. During this period Jewish people continued to return to Jerusalem and Judah.

Current Era (CE) dates and notes

200 to **500** – People of Jewish communities living under Persian rule, continued to move to the Land of Israel joining those who were already living there. For instance the Karaite Jewish community.

Who Is David?

10th to 11th century – Jews under Persian rule moved to the Land of Israel.

13th to 19th century – Jews immigrated to the Land of Israel. During this period many Jews were expelled from European countries. From England in 1290, France in 1391, Austria in 1421, Spain in 1492, and from Portugal in 1498. Some immigrated to the Land of Israel, while others went to other countries.

1200-1882 – Old Yeshuv, Jewish communities in the Land of Israel, during the Ottoman rule, until the time of the New Yeshuv.

18th century – Ashkenazi Jews immigrated to the Land of Israel.

ca 1830s-1878 – Modern Zionism's precursors or proto-zionist, who promoted Zionist ideas before Theodor Herzl's (1860-1904) time. Philosopher Moses Hess (1812-1875), son of a rabbi, was the founder of Labour or Socialist Zionism. Sephardic rabbis Yehuda Aryeh Leion Bibas, or Yehudah Bibas, (ca 1789-1852) and Judah ben Solomon Chai Alkalai (1798-1878), or Judah Alkalai, and Orthodox German rabbi Zvi Hirsch Kalischer (1795-1874). The rabbis' Zionist activism to promote settlement of Jews in the Land of Israel, through their published work and promotional tours, was based on their religious beliefs. Their activism led to the Aliyah of groups of Jews to the Land of Israel.

1839-1840 – Rabbi Yehuda Bibas did a promotional tour to Jewish communities throughout Europe, where he encouraged Jewish people to make Aliyah to Palestine. Rabbi Judah Alkalai was one of his students. Bibas also cooperated with Sir Moses Haim Montefiore (1784-1885), a Jewish banker and financier, a philanthropist and an activist.

1852 – Rabbi Judah Alkalai established the Society of the Settlement of Eretz Yisrael in London. In 1851 to 1852, he toured Western Europe, including Great Britain, to speak about his views regarding Jewish settlement in the Land of Israel. Theodor Herzl was probably influenced by Judah Alkalai's work through his grandfather Simon Loeb Herzl. In 1857 he published 'Goral la-Adonai – A Lot for the Lord', in Vienna. In which he wrote about the Jews being restored to their ancestral homeland.

1862 – Rabbi Zvi Hirsch Kalischer published his book, 'Derishat Tzion', on the topic of Jewish settlement in the Land of Israel.

1862 – Moses Hess published his work, 'Rome and Jerusalem', which called for the establishment of a Jewish socialist community in Palestine.

1860 – First new Jewish residential settlement built in Jerusalem outside the Old City, by Sir Moses Montefiore.

1878 – Old Yishuv. First Jewish farm settlement. Settlement of Petah Tikva, east of Tel Aviv. Groups of Jews made Aliyah to the Land of Israel. They bought the land with donated money, as did those after them.

1881 – Eliezer Ben-Yehuda (1858-1922) immigrated to the Land of Israel.

Dedicated himself to the revival of the Hebrew language as a modern, daily language.

1882-1948 – New Yishuv. Period of the Zionist First Aliyah to the Fifth Aliyah. A period of mass immigration.

1881 – Hovevi Zion or Hibbat Zion began as an organization for different organizations, forerunners of modern Zionism. It became an official group in 1884 at a conference led by its founder and leader Leon Pinsker (1821-1891). He was a Russian Jewish physician, activist and Zionist pioneer.

1882 – Leon Pinsker published anonymously the pamphlet 'Auto-Emancipation', with the subtitle, Mahnruf an seine Stammgenossen, von einem russischen Juden, that is, Warning to His Fellow People, from a Russian Jew. It was a call for Jewish independence.

1882 – Beginning of the Zionist Aliyah. This new wave of immigrants to Israel were called the New Yishuv. Mass immigration with individual naming and numbering of immigrants for immigration permits beforehand. Start of the period of the First to the Fifth Aliyah and Aliyah Beth. First Zionist settlement was Rishon LeZion, established by Hovevi Zion.

1882-1903 – First Aliyah

1896 – Theodor Herzl published his book, Der Judenstaat, The State of the Jews, on the topic of the Jews moving to their homeland in Palestine.

1897 – Establishment of the Zionist Organization (ZO), todays World Zionist Organization (WZO), formed by Theodor Herzl (1860-1904) at the First World Zionist Congress in 1897 in Basel, Switzerland, to promote Jewish immigration to the Land of Israel. The beginning of modern political Zionism. He was a Jewish journalist, writer and political activist. Herzl is regarded as the spiritual father of the modern Jewish State. He is specifically and officially mentioned in Israel's Declaration of Independence.

1904-1914 – Second Aliyah

1908 – Jewish Agency for Israel. The Jewish Agency has been the organization responsible for handling Jewish immigration to Israel out of the diaspora to the State of Israel. This non-profit organization held office in Jaffa since 1908 – Palestine was under Ottoman control – as an operational branch of the Zionist Organization. In 1929 renamed The Jewish Agency for Palestine by the 16th Zionist Congress. In 1948 renamed Jewish Agency for Israel. Since 1929 it has been serving as the primary organization responsible for Jewish immigration to the Land of Israel. The organization assisted about three million Jewish people to immigrate to Israel. Today more than seven million Jews live in Israel.

1917-1921 – The Jewish Legion (1917-1921), five battalions of Jewish volunteers fought alongside the British against the Ottoman Empire during WWI (1914-1918). Ze'ev Jabotinsky (1880-1940) was co-founder with Joseph Vladimirovich Trumpeldor (1880-1920) of the legion. He was a Russian Jew, a soldier, author and a Revisionist Zionist. He established several Jewish organizations, including the paramilitary group Irgun (1931-1948), in Palestine. Later on he had a profound influence on politics in Israel. Former members defended the Jewish communities in Palestine during Arab riots. Israel's first Prime Minister David Ben-Gurion (1886-1973) was also a member of the legion.

1919-1923 – Third Aliyah

1922 – Collapse of the Ottoman Empire.

1922-1948 – British Mandate over Palestine given by League of Nations, later on became the United Nations.

1924-1929 – Fourth Aliyah

1929-1939 – Fifth Aliyah

1933-1948 – Aliyah Bet – A clandestine movement facilitated illegal immigration for Jews. A period of struggle against the British administrative power during the British Mandate over Palestine. Despite the atrocities of WWII (1940-1945) and the nearly non-existent migration possibilities for Jews, the British imposed a strict quota on the influx of Jews in Palestine under the British Mandate (1922-1948), partly because of riots and revolts of Arabs living in Palestine. Jews caught were held in British detention camps.

1939 – British White Paper 1939. The British introduced policies on the restriction of Jewish immigration to Palestine. Countries around the world refused to accept Jewish refugees fleeing Europe because of the Holocaust.

14th of May 1948 – Establishment of the State of Israel.

1948 – Beginning of the period of mass immigration, without the process of naming or numbering individual immigrants. The Jewish Agency for Israel mandated by the state with the organization of the immigration of Jewish people.

1948-1951 – Major Jewish immigration, mainly from post-Holocaust Eastern and Western Europe, and Jews who were expelled and fled from Arab (1948-1970) and Muslim countries.

1948-1960 – Mass immigration to the State of Israel of hundreds of thousands. Special operations were undertaken to evacuate entire Jewish communities out of countries in Europe, the Middle East, and Africa, also DP (displaced persons, i.e. Holocaust survivors) camps, and British detention camps.

Time Tables

1948-1970s – About 900,000 Jews from Arab countries came to Israel.

1948-1967 – The Soviet Union allowed minimum emigration. Elderly people, or for reunification of families. Very difficult procedure. Only 22,000 Jews emigrated. From 1960 to 1970 only 4,000 Jews were allowed to emigrate.

1949-1950 – Operation Magic Carpet/On Wings of Eagles, 49,000 Yemenite Jews were brought to Israel.

1950 – Law of Return for Jews issued by the Jewish State of Israel.

1951-1952 – Operation Ezra and Nehemiah, 120,000 Jews airlifted from Iraq to Israel.

1948-1953 – A total of at least 723,090 Jews from different countries immigrated to Israel.

1950-1956 – Polish Jews immigrated to Israel after Poland made Jewish emigration free. About 50,000 Jews came to the State of Israel. Gomulka Aliyah, named after one of the leader of communist Poland.

1952-1964 – Smaller wave of Jewish groups from North African Egypt, Morocco, Algeria and Tunisia. Others from Iran, Asia and Latin America.

1968 – Mass emigration of Jews out of the Soviet Union began. During the period of 1968 to 1973 almost all of them immigrated to Israel. They received official permission of the Soviet authorities to leave the Soviet Union and were transported by train to Austria where they were processed and airlifted to Israel.

1970 – The Jewish State extended the Law of Return for Jews to include people with one Jewish grandparent, and people who are married to a Jew.

1970-1980 – About 250,000 emigrated out of the Soviet Union. Some went to Israel, but a great part also went to western countries such as the United States.

1979 – After the Islamic Revolution of 1979, Iranian monarchs ousted, the country became anti-western. Iranian Jews, about 30,000, immigrated to Israel.

1970s-1991 – Ethiopian Jews immigrated to Israel. Operation Moses and Operation Solomon.

1984-1985 – Operation Moses, between 6,500 and 8,000 Ethiopian Jews airlifted from Sudanese refugee camps to Israel.

1989 – United States granted Soviet Jews unconditionally status of refugees. Mikhail Gorbachev lifted all restrictions on Jewish emigration. In 1991 the Soviet Union collapsed. About a million Jews immigrated to Israel.

1991 – Operation Solomon, 14,325 Ethiopian Jews brought from Addis

Ababa to Israel in one day by 34 airplanes. Currently over 100,000 Ethiopian Israelis live in Israel.

1999-2002 – About 4,400 Jews from Argentina immigrated to Israel. In 2000 an additional 10,000 Jews left Argentina. And about 20,000 Jews moved from Uruguay to Israel, due to economic crises those countries.

2000s – More than 10,000 Jews left Venezuela and immigrated to Israel.

21st century – The process of Aliyah is still ongoing. Due to anti-semitism, political, economic crises in the countries where Jews live or otherwise. Also Jews from countries such as India, and western countries, including the United States and European countries such as France. Organizations like Shavei Israel and Nefesh B'Nefesh or Jewish Souls United, have been assisting the immigrants to Israel.

Behold, I have graven you (Jerusalem) upon the palms of My hands; your walls are continually before Me.
Isaiah 49:15-17

For I, says HaShem, will be to her (Jerusalem) a wall of fire round about, and I will be the glory in the midst of her.
Zechariah 2:9

Whosoever there is among you of all His people, then HaShem his God be with him – let him go up.
Chronicles 36:23

Time Table Notes

This is not a complete list on Aliyah. It gives a summary of certain events regarding the immigration of the Jewish people to the Land of Israel. Also, it gives an impression of how massive Aliyah has been throughout history, since ancient times until today.

Sources:

Jewish Agency for Israel, www.jewishagency.org

Jewish Virtual Library, Time line for the History of Judaism https://www.jewishvirtuallibrary.org/timeline-for-the-history-of-judaism

Jewish Virtual Library, articles on: Zionism, https://www.jewishvirtuallibrary.org/zionism

Wikipedia: Aliyah, https://en.wikipedia.org/wiki/Aliyah

Wikipedia: Jewish Agency for Israel, https://en.wikipedia.org/wiki/Jewish_Agency_for_Israel#History

Wikipedia: Proto-Zionism, https://en.wikipedia.org/wiki/Proto-Zionism

Wikipedia: Yehuda Bibas, https://en.wikipedia.org/wiki/Yehuda_Bibas#Zionist_activism

Wikipedia: Judah Alkalai, https://en.wikipedia.org/wiki/Judah_Alkalai

Wikipedia: Zvi Hirsch Kalischer, https://en.wikipedia.org/wiki/Zvi_Hirsch_Kalischer

Wikipedia: Leon Pinsker, https://en.wikipedia.org/wiki/Leon_Pinsker

Wikipedia: Moses Hess, https://en.wikipedia.org/wiki/Moses_Hess

Wikipedia: Ze'ev Jabotinsky, https://en.wikipedia.org/wiki/Ze%27ev_Jabotinsky#Jewish_self-defense_in_Palestine

Time Tables

Establishment of the Modern-Day State of Israel

For HaShem will not forsake His people <u>for His great name's sake</u>; because it has pleased HaShem to make you a people to Himself.

1 Samuel 12:22

During the twentieth century two major events happened to the Jewish people which had a worldwide impact on their communities and on the nations; the Shoah or Holocaust, and the establishment of the Jewish State of Israel.

Thus says the Lord God: Behold, I will take the Children of Israel from among the nations, whither they are gone, and (I) will gather them on every side, and bring them into their own Land; and <u>I will make them one nation</u> in the Land, upon the mountains of Israel, and <u>one king shall be king</u> to them all; and they shall be no more two nations, neither shall they be divided into two kingdoms.

Ezekiel 37:21-22

In that day will <u>I raise up</u> the <u>tabernacle of David</u> that has fallen, and close up the breaches thereof, and <u>I will raise up his ruins</u>, <u>and I will build it as in the days of old</u>; And I will turn the captivity of My people Israel, and they shall build the waste cities, and inhabit them; and they shall plant vineyards, and drink the wine thereof; they shall also make gardens, and eat the fruit of them.

Amos 9:11,14

Dates in the Current Era and Notes

1916 Sykes-Picot Agreement – Secret treaty of the United Kingdom and France, with agreement of the Russian Empire and Italy, regarding partition of the Ottoman Empire (ca 1299-1922). They divided the territory in the Middle East under Ottoman rule, anticipating the Ottomans losing the war during WWI (1914-1918). Ratified January 1916. Negotiations began 23rd of November 1915.

1917 Balfour Declaration – The letter signed by Arthur James Balfour, British Foreign Secretary. This was the position of the British Cabinet concerning a Jewish Home in the territory called Palestine.

1922 White Paper – Churchill's White Paper – a policy document approved by the British government that confirmed the British position.

1922 League of Nations – Modern-day United Nations (UN) confirmed the legal draft for the British Mandate for Palestine. This was for the temporary administration of Palestine. It came into effect in 1923. The British divided the territory into the area to the west of the Jordan River and to the east of the river. The former became Israel, the latter Jordan (initially Transjordan), based on the British promises to the Arab leaders, the **1915** McMahon-Hussein Correspondence.

1922-1948 British Mandate – By creating the Mandate for Palestine, in 1919 to 1922, the British officially introduced the term 'Palestine' to refer to the territory of the Levant. The term 'Palestine' used, not officially, by the Greeks, referring to the coastal and inland areas of the Levant in the 5th century BCE, Hellenistic period (323-31 BCE). Romans renamed Jewish territory 'Syria Palaestina' in 135 CE, and Jerusalem Aelia Capitolina, after the Bar Kokhba Revolt (132-136 CE). This term became common in Early Modern English (ca 15th to 17th century). The ancient Egyptians and Assyrians used a term with some similarity to refer to a nation in this same region. But, prior to using the term 'Palestine' for a state in modern history, there has never been a Palestinian country or state.*[1]

1933 Arab riots – Beginning of Arab riots in Jaffa and in Jerusalem in protest to the British 'pro-Zionist' policies.

1933 Nazi boycotts – Adolf Hitler becomes Chancellor of Germany. Germany begins anti-Jewish policies boycotting Jewish people. The persecution of Jews by Hitler and his Nazi Party began in Nazi Germany (1933-1945) during the early 1930s.

1935 Nuremberg Laws – Jewish rights in Germany were revoked by the Nazis' Nuremberg laws.

1936-1939 Arab riots – Arab revolt in Palestine against the Jewish inhabitants. The Arabs were against the influx of more Jewish immigrants into the territory of British Mandate Palestine.

1938 White Paper – The 1939 White Paper, issued on the eve of Kristallnacht, the 9th of November.

1938 Kristallnacht – A pogrom on Jews living in Nazi Germany and Austria that took place on the night of 9th to 10th of November. Synagogues were burned, businesses of Jews vandalized, Jews attacked and imprisoned.

1939 Einsatzgruppen – On the 1st of September, Nazi Germany invaded Poland. The Second World War had begun in Europe. Einsatzgruppen, Nazi paramilitary death squads under the SS administration, were sent to Poland. They were responsible for mass murder of civilians, starting with the intelligentsia, in Nazi-occupied territories of Poland and the

Who Is David?

Soviet Union. Their operations were mostly done by shooting. By the end of WWII an estimate of 2 million people, of which 1.5 million were Jews, were murdered by the Einsatsgruppen.

1940-1945 WWII – Period of genocide, mass murder of civilians, including Jewish people. The Holocaust (also called the Shoah) on the Jewish people took place. It ended in the deaths of 6 million Jews, of which 1.5 million where children. The systematic discrimination, isolation and murder of the Jewish people had already started in the 1930s. In May 1945 an end came to World War II in Europe.

1947 UN Partition Plan. – Due to hostilities between Arab and Jewish inhabitants of Palestine, initiated by the Arab population, the United Nations approved a Partition Plan in November 1947. It provided for two states in Palestine, one Jewish and one Arab. And for Jerusalem to have a special status, that of an international city, under neither an Israeli nor an Arab sovereignty. The territory to the west of the Jordan River was referred to as Judea and Samaria.[*2] The Jewish leaders accepted it, but the Arab leaders rejected it unanimously.

> *For thus says HaShem: sing with gladness for Jacob, and shout at the head of the nations; announce you, praise you, and say: O HaShem, save Your people, the remnant of Israel.*
> Jeremiah 31:7
>
> *Peace, peace, (Shalom, shalom) to him that is far off and to him that is near, says HaShem that creates the fruit of the lips; and I will heal him.*
> Isaiah 57:17-19

14th of May 1948 – David Ben-Gurion, executive head of the World Zionist Organization and president of the Jewish Agency for Palestine, declared the establishment of the State of Israel. He also declared Jewish immigration to Israel to be unrestricted. The first country to recognized the newly established State Israel de facto was the United States, and the former Soviet Union was the first country to recognize the State of Israel de jure on the 17th of May 1948. Recognition de jure by the US was on the 31st of January 1949. The State of Israel's seat of power was in Tel Aviv. Against all odds the Jewish nation was lawfully established.

15th of May 1948 – Expiration date of the British Mandate over Palestine. The British left.

15th of May 1948 – Israel's War of Independence (May 1948 to July

1949), a defensive war had stared. Muslim countries in the Middle East, Arab leaders, declared war on Israel and invaded the country. Jordan occupied and annexed East Jerusalem including the Old City and the area to the west of the Jordan River, Judea and Samaria. Later on referred to as the West Bank. Egypt occupied Gaza.

1949 Armistice Agreement on temporary demarcation lines. The Green Line.

11th of May 1949 – The State of Israel accepted as a member of the United Nations. The acceptance was by majority vote.

13th of December 1949 – First Knesset, parliament of the Jewish government, voted to move the seat of government to Jerusalem.

1950 – The State of Israel issued the Law of Return for Jewish people and they extended it in 1970. Between 1948 and 1950, over half a million Jews moved to Israel.

1967 – Six Day War – Israel captures East Jerusalem from the Jordanians, who had occupied it since 1948, when they invaded, together with other neighbouring countries, the newly formed independent State of Israel.

1980 – The Knesset passed a law which declared that Jerusalem, 'complete and united', to be the capital city of the State of Israel.

2018 – United States President D. Trump recognizes Jerusalem as the capital city of the State of Israel.

2019 – United States President D. Trump recognizes the Golan Heights of strategic value to Israel's security, as territory of the State of Israel.

> *I will command, and I will sift the House of Israel among all the nations, like corn is sifted in a sieve, yet shall not the least grain fall upon the earth … And I will plant them upon their Land, and they shall no more be plucked up out of their Land which I have given them, says HaShem your God.*
>
> Amos 9:9,15

> *And they shall dwell in the Land that I have given unto Jacob My servant, wherein your fathers dwelt; and they shall dwell therein, they, and their children, and their children's children, for ever; and David My servant shall be their prince for ever. Moreover I will make a covenant of peace with them. It shall be an everlasting covenant with them; and I will establish them, and multiply them, and (I) will set My sanctuary in the midst of them for ever. My dwelling place also shall be over them; and I will be their God, and they shall be My people. And the nations shall know that I am HaShem that sanctifies*

Israel, when My Sanctuary shall be in the midst of them for ever.

Ezekiel 37:25-28

I will cause you (David) to rest from all your enemies ...

2 Samuel 7:11

The Spirit of HaShem caused them (the Children of Israel) to rest ...

Isaiah 63:14

Time Table Notes

This is not a complete list of the events that led to the establishment of the State of Israel in 1948. It merely gives some information, an impression, of some of the events that resulted in the establishment of this State.

Sources:

*[1] and *[2], Christenen Voor Israel, www.cvi.nl, Israel Aktueel nr. 321, May 2019

Column: Wie Zijn de Palestijnen? (Who Are the Palestinians), by Oscar Lohuis

The New York Post, The history of Israel's contentious 'eternal capital' By Yaron Steinbuch, December 7, 2017, https://nypost.com/2017/12/07/the-history-of-israels-contentious-eternal-capital

Jewish Virtual Library, Timeline for the History of Judaism https://www.jewishvirtuallibrary.org/timeline-for-the-history-of-judaism

Wikipedia: Timeline of the name "Palestine", https://en.wikipedia.org/wiki/Timeline_of_the_name_%22Palestine%22

Wikipedia: Sykes-Picot Agreement, https://en.wikipedia.org/wiki/Sykes%E2%80%93Picot_Agreement

Wikipedia: Mandate for Palestine, https://en.wikipedia.org/wiki/Mandate_for_Palestine

Wikipedia: Einsatzgruppen, https://en.wikipedia.org/wiki/Einsatzgruppen

Wikipedia, International recognition of Israel, https://en.wikipedia.org/wiki/International_recognition_of_Israel

BIBLIOGRAPHY

Bible / Tanach
JPS, 1917
Committee on Bible Translation (CBT), Howard Long, 2011
Tanach, the Stone Edition, MPL, 1996
Complete Jewish Bible, David H. Stern, MJP, 1998
Good News Bible, The Bible Societies/Collins, 2004
Groot Nieuws Bijbel, Nederlandse Bijbelgenootschap, Haarlem and Katholieke Bijbelstichting, 's-Hertogenbosch, 1998
www.breslov.com
www.biblegateway.com

Books
Flavius Josephus, The Complete Works, translated by William Whiston A.M. Thomas Nelson Publishers, 1998
The History of the Jews in the Greco-Roman World, by Peter Schäfer Harwood Academic Publishers, 1995 and Routledge, 2003
The Five Books of Maccabees in English, by Henry Cotton, D.C.L. Forgotten Books & c Ltd. 2015, www.forgottenbooks.com
The Book of Enoch, translated by R.H. Charles Printed in Scotts Valley, CA-USA, IAP 2009
Ancient Book of Jasher, by Ken Johnson, Th.D. Bible facts Ministries 2008
Discovering the City of David, by Ahron Horovitz, Megalim, City of David Institute for Jerusalem Studies 2010, www.cityofdavid.org.il
Jerusalem, Places and History, by Roberto Copello, Steimatzky LTD 2005
Elsevier, Special Edition Elsevier, Het Midden-Oosten (The Middle-East), RBI, Reed Business Information
Elsevier, Special Edition Elsevier, Jodendom (Judaism), RBI, Reed Business Information
Elsevier, Special Edition Elsevier, Jeruzalem (Jerusalem), RBI, Reed Business Information

Articles
National Geographic Magazine December 2010, Kings of Controversy, by Robert Draper, https://www.nationalgeographic.com/magazine/2010/12/david-and-solomon/
What Is Rosh Chodesh? The Jewish New Moon, by Menachem Posner https://www.chabad.org/library/article_cdo/aid/1928828/jewish/What-Is-Rosh-Chodesh.htm
The Jewish Month: How is it Calculated? https://www.chabad.org/

library/article_cdo/aid/2100146/jewish/The-Jewish-Month.htm

The 29th Day, https://www.chabad.org/parshah/article_cdo/aid/2764/jewish/The-29th-Day.htm

Why is Rosh Chodesh sometimes one day and sometimes two?, by Naftali Silberberg https://www.chabad.org/library/article_cdo/aid/526942/jewish/Why-is-Rosh-Chodesh-sometimes-one-day-and-sometimes-two.htm

The Laws of Rosh Chodesh, by Eliezer Wenger, https://www.chabad.org/library/article_cdo/aid/2100147/jewish/The-Laws-of-Rosh-Chodesh.htm

King David, by Angeline Leito, http://www.thegreenolivetree.nl/index.php/14-articles/king-david/36-king-david

Where is Israel's King David?, by Angeline Leito, http://www.thegreenolivetree.nl/index.php/14-articles/king-david/10-king-david-joseph

David and Jonathan: outstanding friendship!, by Angeline Leito, http://www.thegreenolivetree.nl/index.php/14-articles/king-david/95-astounding-friendshipjonathan-and-david

David and Saul: father and son reconciliation, by Angeline Leito, http://www.thegreenolivetree.nl/index.php/14-articles/king-david/108-david-and-saul-father-and-sons-reconciliation

David and Joab: wisdom and justice, by Angeline Leito, http://www.thegreenolivetree.nl/index.php/14-articles/king-david/113-david-and-joab-wisdom-and-justice

David and Absalom: from betrayal to victory by grace, by Angeline Leito http://www.thegreenolivetree.nl/index.php/14-articles/king-david/126-david-and-absalom-from-betrayal-to-victory

King David's Palace, Jerusalem's Palace?!, by Angeline Leito http://www.thegreenolivetree.nl/index.php/14-articles/king-david/128-king-davids-palace

David's Shield, not the "star of David"!, by Angeline Leito, http://www.thegreenolivetree.nl/index.php/14-articles/king-david/115-king-davids-shield

Christenen voor Israel (Christians for Israel), by Angeline Leito, www.cvi.nl / https://christenenvoorisrael.nl

Chabad-Lubavitch Media Center, www.chabad.org: Rosh Chodesh: The New Moon https://www.chabad.org/library/article_cdo/aid/2100138/jewish/Rosh-Chodesh-The-New-Moon.htm

The New York Post, The history of Israel's contentious 'eternal capital', by Yaron Steinbuch, December 7, 2017 https://nypost.com/2017/12/07/the-history-of-israels-contentious-eternal-capital/

Documentaries

Jerusalem, National Geographic, Source: https://youtu.be/JRBGKZBeaUg

Jewish History, Evidence of Ancient Israel / The Bible's Buried Secrets, KPBS, http://www.kpbs.org, Source: https://youtu.be/-Zw2TH7pWf4

Promises and Betrayals Middle East, History Channel Documentary, Source: https://youtu.be/9xbP6Eda6AA

The Birth of Israel, Source: https://youtu.be/vCC3BEwdS0M

Short videos (4-5 min.)

Prager University, www.pragerU.com:

Israel's Legal Founding, https://youtu.be/12KJa4a0d64

Is the UN fair to Israel? https://youtu.be/2tYdL-jiBQE

The Middle East Problem, https://youtu.be/8EDW88CBo-8

Purim Animated, March 3rd 2012, by aish.com, https://www.aish.com/h/pur/mm/Purim_Animated.html?s=rab

The Death of Stalin: The Untold Purim Story, March 11th 2019, by B. Gordon, https://www.aish.com/h/pur/mm/The-Death-of-Stalin-The-Untold-Purim-Story.html?s=rab

Short videos (10-15 min.)

The Truth on Israel Palestine Conflict, Joe Israel Productions, Source: https://youtu.be/Nc8EjQEpZ3s

What is Palestine? Who are Palestinians?, Historical and Investigative Research, www.hirhome.com, Source: https://youtu.be/W9ReF4UUa4E

Time Table

The History of the Jews in the Greco-Roman World by Peter Schäfer, Harwood Academic Publishers, 1995 and Routledge, 2003

Jewish Virtual Library, Timeline for the History of Judaism https://www.jewishvirtuallibrary.org/timeline-for-the-history-of-judaism

Jewish Virtual Library, Ancient Jewish History, https://www.jewishvirtuallibrary.org/ancient-jewish-history

Jewish Virtual Library. Ancient Jewish History: The Kings of Ancient Israel, https://www.jewishvirtuallibrary.org/the-kings-of-ancient-israel

Jewish Virtual Library, Ancient Jewish History: The Kings of Judah, https://www.jewishvirtuallibrary.org/the-kings-of-judah, Jewish Virtual Library, Ancient Jewish History: The Temples (Beit HaMikdash), https://www.jewishvirtuallibrary.org/the-jewish-temple-beit-hamikdash

Who Is David?

Chabad.org, Timeline of Jewish History by Mattis Kantor, https://www.chabad.org/library/article_cdo/aid/3915966/jewish/Timeline-of-Jewish-History.htm
Wikipedia, Timeline of Jewish History, https://en.wikipedia.org/wiki/Timeline_of_Jewish_history
Wikipedia, Jewish History, https://en.wikipedia.org/wiki/Jewish_history

Websites, sources for articles, information
The Green Olive Tree, by Angeline Leito, www.thegreenolivetree.nl
Jewish Learning Institute, http://www.myjli.com
Torah Café, http://www.torahcafe.com
Chabad-Lubavitch Media Center, Chabad.org, www.chabad.org
Jewish Virtual Library, www.jewishvirtuallibrary.org
City of David in Jerusalem, www.cityofdavid.org.il
Yad Vashem in Jerusalm, www.yadvashem.org
My Jewish Learning, www.myjewishlearning.com
Israel Today, http://www.israeltoday.co.il
Jerusalem Post, https://www.jpost.com/
Christenen Voor Israel, https://christenenvoorisrael.nl
Christians For Israel International, http://www.c4israel.org/c4i/ or www.whyisrael.org
Christians United For Israel, http://www.cufi.org/site/PageServer
Wikipedia, www.wikipedia.nl
Youtube, www.youtube.nl
Vemeo, www.vemeo.com

News TV-websites
TV7 Israel News, https://www.tv7israelnews.com
TV7 Israel News, Jerusalem Studio (JS), https://www.tv7israelnews.com
i24news, www.i24news.tv
i24news: programma: Ñews24 en Español, www.i24news.tv

But you, Israel, My servant, Jacob whom I have chosen, the seed of Abraham My friend; You whom I have taken hold of from the ends of the earth, and called you from the uttermost parts thereof, and said unto you: You are My servant, I have chosen you and not cast you away.

Fear you not, for I am with you, be not dismayed, for I am your God; I strengthen you, yea, I help you; yea, I uphold you with My victorious right hand.

Behold, all they that were incensed against you shall be ashamed and confounded; they that strove with you shall be as nothing, and shall perish. You shall seek them, and shall not find them, even them that contended with you; they that warred against you shall be as nothing, and as a thing of naught.

For I HaShem your God hold your right hand, who say unto you: Fear not, I help you. Fear not, you worm Jacob, and you men of Israel; I help you, says HaShem, and your Redeemer, the Holy One of Israel.

Behold, I make you a new threshing-sledge having sharp teeth; you shall thresh the mountains, and beat them small, and shall make the hills as chaff. You shall fan them, and the wind shall carry them away, and the whirlwind shall scatter them; and you shall rejoice in HaShem, you shall glory in the Holy One of Israel.

The poor and needy seek water and there is none, and their tongue fails for thirst; I HaShem will answer them, I the God of Israel will not forsake them.

I will open rivers on the high hills, and fountains in the midst of the valleys; I will make the wilderness a pool of water, and the dry land springs of water.

I will plant in the wilderness the cedar, the acacia tree, and the myrtle, and the oil tree; I will set in the desert the cypress, the plane tree, and the larch together; That they may see, and know, and consider, and understand together, that the hand of HaShem has done this.